COLLECTABL

HANDBOOK & PRICE GL

COLLECTABLES

HANDBOOK & PRICE GUIDE

Judith Miller
and Mark Hill

MILLER'S

Miller's Collectables Handbook & Price Guide 2016-2017

An Hachette UK Company
www.hachette.co.uk

First published in Great Britain in 2016 by Miller's,
a division of Octopus Publishing Group Ltd
Carmelite House
50 Victoria Embankment
London EC4Y 0DZ
www.octopusbooks.co.uk

While every care has been exercised in the compilation of this guide, neither
authors nor publishers accept any liability for any financial or other loss incurred
by reliance placed on the information contained in Miller's Collectables Price Guide
2016–2017.

ISBN 978 1 78472 077 3

A CIP catalogue record for this book is available from the British Library.

Printed and bound in China

10 9 8 7 6 5 4 3 2 1

Authors Judith Miller & Mark Hill
Editorial Co-ordinator Zenia Malmer
Proofreader John Wainwright
Indexer Hilary Bird
Design and Prepress Ali Scrivens, TJ Graphics
Senior Production Manager Peter Hunt

We would like to thank Mick Briggs for providing invaluable IT support to the
Miller's team over the years.

Photographs of Judith Miller and Mark Hill by Simon Upton,
Chris Terry and Graham Rae

CONTENTS

LIST OF CONSULTANTS

CERAMICS

Will Farmer
Fielding's Auctioneers,
Stourbridge

**Rita Hasdell &
Dorothy Tennant**
www.hornseapottery.co.uk

David Rago
Rago Arts, Lambertville.
New Jersey, USA

COINS

**Timothy Medhurst,
Duke's**
www.dukes-auctions.com

COMICS

Phil Shrimpton
phil-comics.com

COMMEMORATIVES
& POT LIDS

Andrew Hilton
Historical & Collectable,
Reading

DOLLS

Sue Brewer
britishdollshowcase.co.uk

GLASS

Will Farmer
Fielding's Auctioneers,
Stourbridge

Mike & Debby Moir
manddmoir.co.uk

INUIT

Duncan McLean
waddingtons.ca

MARINE &
NAUTICAL

Charles Miller
Charles Miller Ltd., London
charlesmillerltd.com

SCIENTIFIC
INSTRUMENTS

Charles Miller
Charles Miller Ltd., London
charlesmillerltd.com

SPORTING

Graham Budd
Graham Budd Auctions,
London
grahambuddauctions.co.uk

We'd also like to thank our
friends and colleagues who
have helped and supported us
in many ways with this book
including, Beth & Beverly Adams
of Alfies Antiques Market, Dr
Graham Cooley, Steven Moore
of Burleigh Pottery, Paul Roberts

of Lyon & Turnbull, Geoffrey
Robinson of Alfies Antiques
Market, Adam Schoon, Lee
Young of Lyon & Turnbull, Kathy
Plaskitt of Potteries Auctions,
Christa Ouimet of Waddington's,
Sarah Bailey of Tennants, Alison
Snowdon of Fieldings, Faridah
Younes and Nadine Becker of
Quittenbaum, Rachel Hough
and Rachel Morgan of Bellmans,
Nigel Dawson-Ellis of Ewbanks,
Tori Billington and Marissa
Billinge-Jones of Dreweatts &
Bloomsbury, Tim Brophy and
David Taws of W&H Peacock,
Claire Pitts of Dominic Winter,
Andy Stowe of East Bristol
Auctions, Louise Harker of
Vectis, Diane Baynes of Sworder,
Tamzin Corbett of Woolley &
Wallis, Thomas Plant of Special
Auction Services.

HOW TO USE THIS BOOK

Subcategory heading Indicates the
sub-category of the main heading.

Caption The description of the item
illustrated, including when relevant, the
period, the maker or factory, medium,
the year it was made, dimensions and
condition. Many captions have **footnotes**
which explain terminology or give
identification or valuation information.

Page tab This appears on every page
and identifies the main category
heading as identified in the Contents
List on pages 5-6.

Judith/Mark Picks Items chosen
specifically by Judith and Mark,
either becuase they are important or
interesting, or because our experts
believe that these pieces are good
investments.

The price guide These price ranges give
a ballpark figure for what you should
pay for a similar item. The great joy
of collectables is that there is not a
recommended retail price. The price
ranges in this book are based on actual
prices, either what a dealer will
take or the full auction price.

Quick reference Gives key
facts about the factory, maker
or style, along with stylistic
identification points, value tips
and advice on fakes.

Closer Look Does exactly that.
These are where we show
identifying aspects of a factory
or maker, point out rare colours
or shapes, and explain why a
particular piece is so desirable.

The object The collectables are
shown in full colour. This is a
vital aid to identification and
valuation. With many objects, a
slight colour variation can signify
a large price differential.

Source code Every item has
been specially photographed
at an auction house, a dealer,
an antiques market or a private
collection. These are credited by
code at the end of the caption,
and can be checked against the
Key to Illustrations.

INTRODUCTION

Welcome to the new edition of the Miller's Collectables Handbook and Price Guide. We're delighted to present over 4,000 completely new, specially selected collectables representing the international market from Carltonware to Comics, modern posters to metalware, and studio glass to scientific instruments. There really is something for everyone.

Every image is accompanied by a full caption and a price guide and, for many, you'll find specially written footnotes that highlight interesting details. In addition to this, you'll find a wealth of extra information in our 'Closer Look', 'Miller's Compares' and 'Mark Picks' and 'Judith Picks' features, as well as our regular 'Quick Reference' boxes, which give you a brief but useful introduction to an area, maker, designer or range. Interest in and prices being paid for many more traditional collecting areas have remained largely static. It's all about fashion, and pieces that are deemed passé by the majority of today's buyers have stagnated. One such area is scientific instruments. Although finely made feats of engineering excellence, their historical importance only appeal to a diminishing group of collectors. Few new buyers have come to the market, but canny collectors take note.

It's possible that this may change in the future, particularly if those who work in the ever-booming digital technology industry grow to appreciate what is, in effect, the work of their predecessors. Collecting is an intensely personal activity. Deeply revealing in this age of ridiculous consumerism and mass production, a collection is a

An early 20thC wood-cased 'Comptometer'. £30-50

An early 1980s Palitoy 'Star Wars, The Empire Strikes Back' Boba Fett figure. £22,000-28,000 VEC

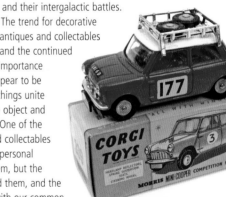

declaration. It says, "This is who I am, this is my story." Lying at the core of this is nostalgia, which has always been a strong driver behind collecting. As generations mature, and gain more disposable income or downsize, so what is collected changes. Prices paid for some pre-War Dinky toys have softened as those who remember them as children stop collecting. In return, prices for Corgi Toys from the 1950s-60s have risen, particularly gift sets, as more from the generation that loved them as children start collecting. However, the biggest material rises in price over the past five years have arguably been for Star Wars toys, some of which have regularly fetched over £10,000 in mint, 'carded' condition. This represents a rise of tens of times the price a piece may have fetched a decade ago. Unusually, this growth may continue for a long period as, unlike diecast toys or memorabilia from most rock or pop performers, many generations have lived with and loved the films, which have now been popular for and renewed across nearly forty years. With the recent purchase of the franchise by Disney, even more generations look set to be introduced to the Skywalker family and its associated droids and their intergalactic battles.

The trend for decorative antiques and collectables and the continued importance of nostalgia may appear to be disparate, but two things unite them: a love for the object and the story behind it. One of the joys of antiques and collectables is not just our own personal connection with them, but the wider stories behind them, and the way they connect with our common history and experience.

Enjoy!

A mid-late 1950s moulded plaster advertising display for 'Gentlemens Hairdressing'. £150-200 FLD

A Corgi Toys 'Mini Cooper S Monte Carlo 1967'. 1967-71 £150-200 W&W

A mid-19thC pocket compass sundial dial. £300 CM

QUICK REFERENCE - ADVERTISING AND PACKAGING

- Advertising and packaging offer a fascinating insight into period fashions, designs, social trends, and aspirations. Most pieces found on the market today date from the 20thC. Many items are fragile and were not made to last or to be kept.
- Collectors tend to focus on one type of material such as enamel signs, on specific product areas such as tobacco advertising, or on a particular character associated with a brand such as Coca Cola's Santa Claus. Larger brands that produced plenty of material over a long period of time, such as Guinness, Coca Cola, or Shell, tend to attract the most collectors. Prices can be higher due to competition. However, as much collecting is driven by nostalgia and an interest in brands of the past, appealing and indicative pieces will always have value. Look out for the work of major designers or artists, as that can increase values further.
- Always look for items that are in good condition that represent the brand, subject area, or period well. Items in the Art Nouveau style of the late 19thC and early 20thC are usually highly sought-after, as are those in the Art Deco style popular during the 1920s and 30s. Pieces made during the 1950s and 60s with a strong 'vintage' or 'retro' appeal have risen dramatically in value over the past decade, and look set to rise even higher as they appeal to many generations.
- Consider materials used, colours, and the style of any graphics and lettering, as this can help you date a piece. Examine corners and edges closely for marks which may help confirm this. Due to the popularity of these items in interiors, many reproductions and fakes exist, so consider wear and tear and grime. Both can be applied to make a piece look older, so they should be consistent with how old a piece is and how it may have been used. The way a piece was made can also help to date it and identify whether it is a reproduction or not.
- Also consider everyday items that would usually have been thrown away. Much packaging falls under this category, making surviving examples in mint condition scarce. The presence of the original contents does not necessarily add value in itself - it is more important that the package is unopened and may have its seals (such as those on tobacco packets) intact.

A 1960s 'SHELLMEX' glass petrol pump advertising globe, by Hailwood & Ackroyd, of shell form with relief-moulded lettering picked out in red, stamped 'Hailware British Made' and 'Property of Shell-Mex and B.P. Ltd. Returnable on demand'.

Shellmex was the commercial brand of oil giant Shell. 'Mex' was added after 1921, when Shell acquired the Bowring Petroleum Co Ltd, who used the 'Mex' brand.

17.25in (44cm) high

£300-500   FLD

A 1930s-60s 'SHELL DIESOLINE' glass petrol advertising globe, by Hailwood & Ackroyd, with rubber ring to the base, marked 'Hailware British Made' & 'Property of Shellmex & BP Ltd. Returnable on Demand'.

17in (43cm) high

£250-350   LAW

A 1950s 'FORD MUSTANG' illuminated glass advertising sign, by The Cinn. Adv. Products Co., marked 'CAPCOLITE No.216, REG. US. PAT. NO.1.933.866 THE CINN. ADV. PRODUCTS Co.'.

18in (45.5cm) high

£700-1,000   QU

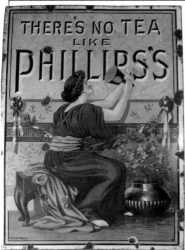

A 'THERE'S NO TEA LIKE PHILLIPS'S' tea large advertising sign, with some losses to enamel and rusting.

Although an unusual subject, the large size, detail, and high quality of the enamelling makes this as valuable as it is. Although it is damaged, the damage is mainly around the edges, with only a few spots on the main image.

48in (122cm) high

£1,500-2,000   HALL

A 'Brooke Bond dividend Tea' enamelled tin advertising sign, with some corrosion around screw holes.

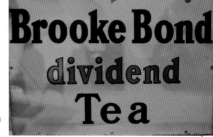

30in (76cm) wide

£60-90   TEN

ADVERTISING

A CLOSER LOOK AT AN ADVERTISING SIGN

Reverse-painted glass signs in good condition are rarer than enamelled metal signs due to their fragility and the fact that the painted or printed decoration often flakes away over time.

Tobacco advertising is highly collectable, particularly for cigars. There is a large following for cigar smoking advertisements, even if smoking in general is declining.

The graphics showing a Cuban tobacco field are appealing and representative.

Named after early American politician Henry Clay (1777-1852), the brand was launched in the 1840s by Julian Alvarez, a Cuban tobacco magnate. It still exists today.

A 'LA FLOR DE HENRY CLAY' 'HAVANA CIGARS AND CIGARETTES OF QUALITY' reverse-painted on glass advertising sign, with some flaking and chipping to the image, cigar label inserted into cut-out area, framed.

23.75in (60.5cm) wide

£800-1,200   **SWA**

A mid-late 20thC The Spastics' Society street collecting box, the box reading 'Please Help Your Local Spastics'.

Figural charity boxes such as this stood outside many British shops until theft and damage to them became a serious issue. This prompted charities to collect money in other ways. The Spastics' Society was founded in 1951 to help people with cerebral palsy. By the 1980s, the word 'spastic' had come to be used as an insult. Its use today is highly inappropriate and it is considered offensive and incorrect to describe someone suffering from cerebral palsy in that manner. The word is commonly held to be one of the worst insults to anyone who speaks English. The society was renamed Scope in 1994.

40in (102cm) high

£220-280   **TEN**

A mid-late 20thC butchers' shop display model cow, the body covered with genuine cow hide, modelled in a standing position, raised on hard wood base.

19.25in (49cm) wide

£80-120   **LOCK**

A 'The Golden Spirit' painted composition bar advertisement, showing an African American rolling a barrel.

Other examples have been found advertising Lemon Hart rum. Despite this being deemed politically incorrect today, part of the interest here comes from collectors of Black Americana.

10.25in (26cm) high

£150-200   **POOK**

A mid-20thC 'EXCLUSIV PIPE TOBACCOS' advertising standee figure of a Guardsman.

20in (51cm) high

£60-80   **FLD**

A 1950s Miss Twilfit shop counter corset advertising bust, finished in white.

27in (68cm) high

£100-150   **FLD**

A mid-late 1950s 'Gentlemens Hairdressing' moulded plaster advertising display, impressed 'R.H & S London' with registered number 869550 for 1953.

This sort of quirky advertising piece is now sought-after by interior decorators or collectors looking for something unusual and decorative.

19.25in (49cm) wide

£150-200   FLD

A CLOSER LOOK AT A COCA COLA FOUNTAIN

It was designed by Raymond Loewy (1893-1986), one of America's most influential modern industrial designers who has been referred to as 'The Man Who Shaped America' and 'The Father of Streamlining'.

He redesigned a number of items for Coca Cola, such as refrigerators and delivery trucks and king-size and family-size packages, although he wasn't responsible for their hallmark bottle shape.

It follows many of the themes behind streamlining, which is reflected in the curved and tapered shape. It is reminiscent of an outboard motor for a boat, suggesting speed and mechanisation.

Introduced in 1947, this fountain was not only a hit due to its looks, but it increased profits for the shop as it allowed servings to be made quicker.

A late 20thC 'Pepsi Cola' enamel sign, in the form of a bottle cap, made for the Italian market, with two hanging brackets on the back, marked 'Marchio Reg, Marque De Trademark'.

19.25in (49cm) diam

£150-200   LAW

A mid-20thC Dole 'Deluxe' Coca Cola fountain dispenser, designed by Raymond Loewy, of outboard motor shape, bearing 'Dole Valve Company Chicago' label numbered 73861, later mounted on a black wooden base.

The vendor worked for the Coca Cola Company between 1969 and 2003.

20.5in (52cm) deep

£800-1,200   FLD

A Progress Refrigerator Company 'things go better with Coke' Coca Cola twin-handled advertising chest cooler, the side of the chest further impressed 'Progress Refrigerator Co, Louisville, KY'.

The vendor of this item worked for the Coca Cola Company between 1969 and 2003.

17.75in (45cm) wide

£300-500   FLD

A late 20thC Beswick 'DUBONNET' ceramic advertising figural group, raised on a pale blue base with red lettering.

7.5in (19.5cm) wide

£120-180   LOCK

A 1970s Beswick 'LOTUS' cars ceramic ashtray, the top rim moulded and painted as a steering wheel, the base printed 'MADE FOR LES LESTON LIMITED BY BESWICK, ENGLAND, REGISTERED DESIGN NO.934440', with registered design number for 1969.

This is an early example - later examples have the 'LL' motor accessories logo on the steering wheel spokes.

7.5in (19cm) diam

£100-150   GBA

ADVERTISING

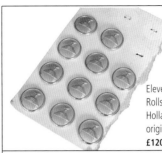

Eleven early-mid 20thC gilt-metal Rolls Royce advertising buttons, by Holland and Sherry, mounted on original card.

£120-180   FLD

A French 'F. BOCCINO' 'LEFÈVRE-UTILE' colour lithographed biscuits advertising card, printed by Chamenois, Paris.

As well as being a charming subject, the colour printing is extremely high quality, has plenty of detail, and is a large format.

c1896   *26.5in (67.5cm) wide*

£700-1,000   SWA

An 1880s 'THE DERBY' 'WE STRIVE TO EXCEL' colour lithographed tobacco label, framed.

10.75in (27.5cm)

£180-220   SWA

A French 'GAUFRETTES PRALINÉES LEFÈVRE-UTILE' biscuit tin paper label, designed by Alphonse Mucha.

9in (23cm) wide

£250-350   SWA

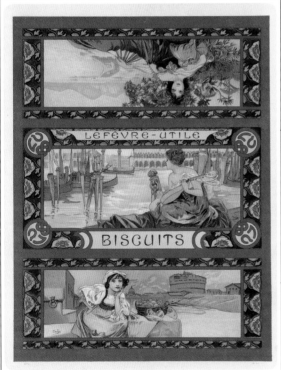

An early 1930s Huntley & Palmers farmhouse biscuit tin, with swivelling fence section and lift-off roof, lithographed with farming scenes.

Part of a set, these are hard to find in good condition as they were given to children to play with after the biscuits had been eaten.

6in (15cm) wide

£100-150   TEN

A 'LEFÈVRE-UTILE' 'BISCUITS' tin paper label, designed by Alphonse Mucha.

Czech artist and designer Alphone Mucha (1860-1939) was a celebrated Art Nouveau designer whose advertising work is highly collected. This is an excellent example of his work.

c1896   *11.25in (29cm) high*

£800-1,200   SWA

An early 20thC 'Black Cat CIGARETTES' silver-plated advertising vesta case, with a trick-opening cover, inset with an amusing celluloid plaque, unmarked.

1910-20   *2.4in (6cm) long*

£180-220   LAW

QUICK REFERENCE - CARLTON WARE REPRODUCTIONS & FAKES

● After Carlton Ware went into liquidation, the moulds for many items were used for reproductions. This was not always to deceive - licensed examples produced by the owner of the Carlton Ware name and brand are legitimate. They are typically marked differently to enable people to differentiate them from earlier production. However, some are direct fakes and there are a number of key points that can be used to identify them. Firstly, consider the colours used. Fakes tend to be brighter and in different colours to the originals. The glazes also tend to be less well applied. Secondly, look at the beaks. The orange to yellow should be graduated, not clearly delineated. Thirdly, look at the Carlton Ware mark, which is often raised and applied over the glaze on fakes.

A Carlton Ware Guinness 'DRAUGHT GUINNESS' penguin advertising figure.

3.75in (9.5cm) high

£30-50   FLD

A set of three graduated Carlton Ware for Guinness flying toucans, each with two pints of beer to their beaks, printed 'My GOODNESS' 'My GUINNESS', printed script mark to the reverse of each, impressed GA2259A, GA2259B and GA2259C.

£150-250 the set   FLD

A group of five Carlton Ware Guinness advertising figures, comprising the zoo keeper, a kangaroo, a tortoise, a seal, and a slightly damaged ostrich, all entitled 'My Goodness - My GUINNESS', the bases with black and red printed script marks.

£150-250 for five   FLD

A Carlton Ware for Guinness advertising money box, in the form of a London Transport double decker bus.

This is a comparatively scarce Carltonware for Guinness model. One of the most desirable and valuable models is also the seal balancing a blue globe-shaped lamp on his nose, which can easily fetch in excess of £300.

3.9in (10cm) high

£50-80   WHP

A 1950s 'GUINNESS TIME' 'GUINNESS IS GOOD FOR YOU' electrically operated Perspex advertising clock.

15.75in (40cm) high

£120-180   FLD

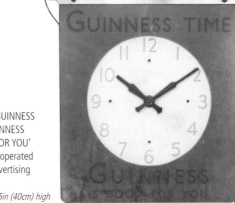

A flying scale model of a De Havilland Gipsy Moth, 'G-EBLV', the wood airframe covered with fine fabric, with a four-stroke petrol engine with silencer, with fully working flying control surfaces, dummy pilot and some cockpit detail.

60in (152cm) wingspan

£950-1,200   DN

A free-flight model of Albatros C1, No.C2014/15, the wood airframe covered with doped tissue, with a dummy Mercedes-Benz 160/150 h.p. engine, side radiators and rear cockpit machine gun, with natural linen for the wings, with national markings of the period.

25.5in (65cm) long

£300-350   DN

A trench art model of a German Taube aeroplane.

4.5in (11cm) long

£200-250   FLD

An Indian carved propellor boss, with a 1920-30s clock, stamped on the boss is 'GI520 N56-DH-9A-400 HP Liberty-22699RH-D 3050-P 2230', 'GL520' stamped on the reverse side.

The foliage carvings include an RAF logo and wings at 12:00 o'clock and 'Crashed at Ambala October 2nd 1919' below. This was the first 99 squadron fatality since World War One. The plane that crashed was flown by Lt J Clarke MC, of the Worcestershire regiment and Royal Flying Corp. The family of Lt Clarke owned the boss before the present owner of some 40 years.

1919

£300-350   LAW

An enamelled copper patch box, with an air balloon scene and attendant figures.

Memorabilia produced in the golden age of ballooning in the late 18thC is scarce and highly sought after by a comparatively small group of dedicated collectors. The type of balloon shown can indicate the aeronaut who developed and/or flew in it, and thus the date.

c1790   *2in (5cm) long*

£400-450   LAW

A rare original 1930s patent document, for 'Means of Adjusting Wings of Aircraft', awarded to Geoffrey Terence Roland Hill, of Yeovil, assignor to Petters Ltd of Yeovil, issued by the United States of America, document no.1868417, dated 19th July 1932, folio format A4 size.

Professor Geoffrey Terence Roland Hill, who died in 1955, was an aeronautical engineer of note working on tailless aircraft for Westland, barrage balloon cable cutters, and the experimental '®ro-isoclinic' wing for Short Brothers.

£60-80   DN

A Bewley Court silver trophy, in the form of a silver hot air balloon, with a silver plaque inscribed 'Bewley Court Cup 1999', the plaque and balloon both with hallmarks.

8in (20cm) high

£100-150   LAW

A chrome-plated 'Jet Plane' cruet, stamped 'Reg. no.876205' for 1955, with detachable pepper and salt.

c1950s   *4.5in (11.5cm) high*

£90-120   SWO

QUICK REFERENCE - ARCADE MACHINES

- Arcade machines and 'penny slots' (so named as they were operated by putting an old penny into a slot) became popular as visits to the seaside, tourist attractions or city centres became affordable and logistically possible to more people from the mid-19thC onwards. The Bank Holiday Act and holidays from work gave time off, and slowly increasing salaries gave people money to spend on enjoying themselves. A growing railway network gave them the ability to move around. Machines were located in places such as on piers at the seaside or, increasingly, from the 1920s onwards, in special buildings in cities.

- The first machines were mechanical, with many focusing on mysticism (particularly in the Victorian era), pre-cinema 'moving' images such as a Kinetoscope, and figural automata such as sailors. As such, the penny slot provided entertainment and amusement. Some also provided a challenge, or demanded skill, for example dropping a penny onto a pile with a moving slider at the right moment to cause more pennies to fall down into a collection tray, or operating a mechanical hand to grab a prize from a pile within a given time.

- Many machines remained in use for decades, until technology changed making them obsolete. The first major change was in the 1970s and 1980s when mechanical arcade machines began to be replaced with electronic machines such as Pong (introduced 1972), Pacman (introduced 1980) and Super Mario Bros (introduced 1985). As a result, many earlier arcade machines were scrapped, dismantled or left to fall apart, especially as many were in tired and worn condition.

- Collecting can be hard as a large amount of space is required, but many add one or two to a room as functionally entertaining decoration, much like a jukebox. Many newly-found machines are also in poor condition, meaning often expensive cosmetic and/or mechanical restoration is necessary. Some arcade machines are deemed gambling machines, so be aware of any regional or national legislation concerning the buying or selling of gambling equipment.

An Edwardian 'Palm Reader' arcade machine, by Marvin & Casler Co. NY, the oak cabinet with nickelplated and brass fitttings, small panel at front missing, converted to 20p coin.
Patented 1905   64in
                    (163cm) high
£1,800-2,200   AST

A late19thC or early 20thC 'The Burglar' arcade machine, by British Automatic Co. Ltd., the repainted wooded cabinet with panel reading 'Working Model', the interior with original safe-cracking burglar, frightened householder and policeman.
                    67in (170cm) high
£4,500-5,000   AST

A 'Novelty Merchantman' grab-type arcade machine, by Exhibit Supply Co. Ltd. Chicago, with stained-wood cabinet, bevelled-glass panels, mostly original, converted to 20p coin.
                66.5in (169cm) high
£1,200-1,600   AST

An 'Imperial' grab-type arcade machine, by the Exhibit Supply Co. Chicago, USA, in original walnut-veneered case with Art Deco chromed-metal design, converted to 20p coin.
                66.5in (169cm) high
£2,000-2,500   AST

A 'Pussy Shooter' arcade machine, by British American Novelty Co., London, rd no.750896, wooden construction with chromed-metal fittings, cabinet re-painted, converted to 20p, originally 1d.
c1930s   78.7in (200cm) high
£1,600-2,000   AST

A 1950s 'Laughing Sailor' coin-operated arcade automaton, possibly by Modern Enterprises, London, with mahogany and plywood case, with a moving and laughing sailor doll, with some restoration, converted to 20p coin operation.
                70in (177cm) high
£4,500-5,000   AST

A 1950s Allwin 'Flick Ball' machine, in oak cabinet, coin operation.

27.25in (69cm) high

£300-350   **FLD**

QUICK REFERENCE - MUTOSCOPES

- The Mutoscope was an early, pre-cinema 'moving picture' machine, developed by American inventor Winsor McCay and later patented by Herman Casler in 1894.
- It was similar to, but cheaper than, Thomas Edison's 'Kinetoscope' and contained 850 photographic cards mounted on a revolving cylinder - as the cylinder was revolved, the image 'moved' like a flip-book and told a story.
- It was most popular from the 1890s into the 1940s, and stories were usually titillating tales similar to 'What the butler saw', some of which were questioned as morally corrupting at the time.
- Examples were made in the US from 1895 until the 1920s by either the American Mutoscope and Biograph Co. or its licensee Marvin & Casler Co. but from the 1920s onwards, a license was granted to the company that made this example, the International Mutoscope Reel Company run by William Rabkin.

A 1920s-30s 'Balloon Tease' machine, by American International Mutoscope Reel Co. Inc., painted metal construction with brass fittings, on later wooden baseboard, converted to 20p operation (originally 1 cent).

74.8in (190cm) high

£1,800-2,200   **AST**

An early 20thC French table football game, with hand-painted figures on ebonised supports.

59in (150cm) wide

£750-850   **BELL**

A solo-ride 'The Galloper', by Bryan's of Kegworth Derby, UK, stamped '268', cast aluminium and wood construction, with settings - 'Hunt', 'Gallop' and 'Rock', 20p coin operation.

Always examine these sprayed plastic forms all over. Not only can the spray-painted effects be hard to repair, and even repaint, but the plastic can be damaged. Brightly coloured signs, machines and similar equipment from showgrounds, travelling fairs or circuses are currently extremely fashionable in interior design.

c1950s   *53in (135cm) high*

£850-950   **AST**

A mid-1980s 'Burger Time' coin-operated table-top gaming machine, by Bally Midway, in working order, with keys.

'Burger Time' was released in 1982. Many such cabinets are bought by young people to use as retro-style coffee tables, even though they certainly don't remember the games!

34.25in (87cm) wide

£250-300   **FLD**

A 'Sopranos'-themed pinball machine, by Stern Pinball, Inc., Melrose Park, Illinois, with autographs from cast members.

The autographs raise the value of this machine greatly. 'Sopranos' entertained an entire generation across many ages from 1999-2007. If it is remembered as a series, which seems likely, this game could prove to be a wise investment. Furthermore, it crosses two markets - arcade and pinball game collectors and collectors of 'Sopranos' memorabilia.

2005   *52in (132cm) high*

£4,500-5,000   **DRA**

QUICK REFERENCE - AUSTRIAN BRONZES

● From the late 19thC onward, miniature and tabletop bronze figures were created in Vienna, Austria. Around 50 manufacturers were present in Vienna at the time. Vienna bronzes were considered luxury pieces that quickly attracted the attention of collectors. They depicted life-like subjects including pets, farm, forest or exotic animals, and travel-inspired subjects that reflected aspects of the Orient.

● Vienna bronzes were made following labour-intensive methods that required a high level of craftsmanship. The casting moulds that were used to produce the bronzes were designed by artists who simply sold their work to bronze manufacturers and had no further influence on the production of the bronze figures. Sometimes, a bronze figure was cast in separate parts and then welded together. Cold-painting, one of the main elements of

Austrian bronzes, is a technique that involved applying several layers of lead-based paint to the bronze. The cold-painting determined to a significant extent the quality and desirability of the final piece.

● Franz Bergman was the most well-known maker of the day. He took over from his father and was the main instigator of the 'Vienna bronze boom'. His pieces are marked with a 'B' within an amphora-type vase. Most auction houses describe the presence of his mark as 'B within a vase'. Carl Kauba is another collectable bronze maker who is perhaps not as well-known as Bergman. His most impressive pieces depict Native Americans and cowboys.

● 'Geschützt' is German for protected and relates to patents. It is the mark that is most commonly found on Austrian bronzes.

An early 20thC Austrian cold-painted bronze cat, stamped 'GESCHÜTZT'.

6.75in (17cm) long

£500-550   WW

A late 19thC Austrian cold-painted bronze cat, stamped twice 'GESCHÜTZT' and 'E E'.

4.75in (12cm) long

£300-350   WW

An early 20thC Austrian cold-painted bronze bulldog, stamped 'GESCHÜTZT', previously mounted.

4.75in (12cm) wide

£250-300   WW

An Austrian cold-painted bronze spaniel with a pheasant.

5.25in (13.5cm) long

£250-300   WW

An early 20thC Austrian bronze puppy, stamped 'GESCHÜTZT'.

2.75in (7cm) high

£80-120   WW

An Austrian cold-painted bronze foxhound, stamped 'GESCHÜTZT'.

4.5in (11.5cm) high

£120-180   WW

Judith Picks

I'm afraid I have a tremendous soft spot for terriers - our last two dogs have been an Airedale called Fred and now we have an enormous Russian Black Terrier called Vladimir. So I have over the years bought some (quite a few!) of these Austrian cold-painted figures of terriers. In many cases the modelling is of extremely high quality and the artist captures the spirit of the dog perfectly. One word of warning, some of the figures have been over-painted and this reduces the value considerably. Better to have evidence of a life well-lived than modern paint.

An Austrian cold-painted bronze terrier.

4.25in (10.5cm) long

£250-300   WW

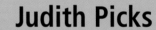

AUSTRIAN BRONZES

A late 19thC/early 20thC Austrian cold-painted bronze pug vesta case, with a hinged neck and a strike on its back, stamped 'GESCHÜTZT'.

2.5in (6cm) high

£280-320   WW

A late 19th/early 20thC Austrian cold-painted bronze dog, indistinctly stamped.

3.75in (9.5cm) long

£80-120   WW

A late 19thC Austrian cold-painted bronze seated dog, stamped 'GESCHÜTZT'.

4.5in (11.5cm) high

£180-220   WW

An early 20thC Austrian cold-painted bronze pig.

2in (5cm) long

£150-200   WW

An early 20thC Austrian cold-painted bronze partridge, with wings outspread and beak open.

The partridge and the cockerel (right) are more unusual, hence the higher prices. They are also in good condition.

6.8in (17.3cm) high

£350-400   BELL

A late 19th/early 20thC Austrian cold-painted bronze sheep and lamb.

2.5in (6.5cm) long

£120-150   WW

A late 19th/early 20thC Austrian cold-painted bronze cockerel.

5in (13cm) wide

£450-550   WW

A late 19th/early 20thC Austrian cold-painted bronze fox.

This is a very animated figure with a great sense of movement and is very naturalistically coloured.

8.5in (21.5cm) long

£1,500-2,000   WW

A late 19th/early 20thC Austrian cold-painted bronze fox.

5in (12cm) long

£120-150   WW

An early 20thC Austrian cold-painted bronze hare.

This has been unfortunately over-painted which is reflected in the price.

3.25in (8.5cm) long

£90-120   WW

A CLOSER LOOK AT A COLD-PAINTED BRONZE

This finely modelled fox has such a soulful expression. Its face has features that are naturalistic and appealing. One can imagine it sitting next to a lake in its natural habitat, completely undisturbed by the world around it. ___

Other cold-painted bronze foxes come with their own marble vide poche as well, but it is still quite an unusual feature. Meaning 'empty pocket' in French, the vide poche dish is meant to hold essential items like keys or loose change.

A lot of thought has gone into painting this piece. Shades of brown and auburn highlight the hind legs, head, chest, paws, and bushy tail. ___

An Austrian cold-painted bronze fox, seated atop a variegated marble vide poche.

fox 6in (15cm) high

£700-800   BELL

A late 19thC Austrian cold-painted bronze seated hare 'go to bed', with a small hole on its tail to hold a match and with ribbed 'striker' soles to its feet.

3.5in (8.5cm) high

£400-450   WW

An Austrian cold-painted bronze running hare, with Bergman stamp 'B in a vase'.

4.5in (11.5cm) long

£180-220   WW

A late 19th/early 20thC Austrian cold-painted bronze hare, stamped 'GESCHÜTZT'.

3.75in (9.5cm) long

£400-450   WW

A late 19thC large Austrian cold-painted bronze rabbit, by Franz Bergman, stamped '1273 DEPOSE GESCHÜTZT' and 'B in a vase'.

This rabbit is so well-modelled... you think you can almost feel his fur.

6.5in (16.5cm) long

£5,000-6,000   WW

AUSTRIAN BRONZES

An early 20thC Austrian cold-painted bronze kingfisher, stamped 'GESCHÜTZT'.

2.5in (6cm) high

£200-250   WW

An early 20thC Austrian cold-painted bronze kingfisher.

2.5in (6.5cm) high

£150-200   DN

An early 20thC Austrian cold-painted bronze pair of pigeons.

2.5in (6.5cm) long

£50-60   WW

Miller's Compares

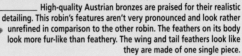

High-quality Austrian bronzes are praised for their realistic detailing. This robin's features aren't very pronounced and look rather unrefined in comparison to the other robin. The feathers on its body look more fur-like than feathery. The wing and tail feathers look like they are made of one single piece.

The painting around its eyes and on its beak looks almost cartoon-like. The red patch on its chest is quite striking, but looks rather overdone.

The claws of the robin point upwards, which means that the figurine can't rest properly on flat surfaces. They also look slightly grotesque and disproportionate.

This robin's features are very well executed. Individual feathers are not just perceptible on its chest and wings, but on its head as well.

Bronze is a metal that weighs a lot, but when such a well-modelled, life-like bird such as this is made, it looks like it could fly away. The value of it reflects that this is an exceptional piece.

A late 19th/early 20thC Austrian cold-painted bronze robin, by Franz Bergman, no.1835, stamped 'GESCHUTZT' and faintly a 'B in a vase'.

3.25in (8cm) long

£220-280   WW

A late 19th/early 20thC Austrian cold-painted bronze robin, stamped 'GESCHÜTZT'.

3.5in (8.5cm) high

£550-650   WW

A late 19th/early 20thC Austrian cold-painted bronze swallow.

2.25in (5.5cm) long

£180-220   WW

An Austrian cold-painted bronze blue tit, no.1295, stamped 'DEPOSE' and 'GESCHÜTZT'.

2.5in (6cm) long

£120-160   WW

A late 19thC Austrian cold-painted bronze wren, stamped 'GESCHÜTZT'.

1.5in (4cm) long

£150-200   WW

A late 19thC Austrian cold-painted bronze wren, stamped 'GESCHÜTZT'.

1.5in (4cm) long

£150-200   WW

A late 19th/early 20thC Austrian cold-painted bronze grouse.

3.5in (9cm) high

£350-400   **WW**

A late 19th/early 20thC Austrian cold-painted bronze grouse, in the manner of Bergman, no.7508, stamped 'GESCHÜTZT'.

6in (15.5cm) high

£550-650   **WW**

A late 19th/early 20thC Austrian cold-painted bronze hedgehog.

1.75in (4.5cm) long

£150-200   **WW**

A late 19th/early 20thC Austrian cold-painted bronze pheasant.

7.5in (19cm) long

£160-200   **WW**

A late 19th/early 20thC Austrian cold-painted bronze owl, no.478, stamped 'GESCHÜTZT' twice.

3.5in (8.5cm) high

£600-700   **WW**

A late 19thC/early 20thC Austrian cold-painted bronze stork, with her five chicks.

3.75in (9.5cm) high

£350-400   **WW**

A late 19th/early 20thC Austrian cold-painted bronze woodcock.

4.5in (11.5cm) long

£300-350   **WW**

AUSTRIAN BRONZES

An Austrian cold-painted bronze budgerigar, by Bergman, stamped 'AUS' and 'B in a vase'.

6.25in (15.5cm) long

£300-400   WW

An early 20thC Viennese cold-painted bronze African grey parrot, the underside stamped 'GESCHÜTZT'.

3.5in (9cm) high

£500-600   DN

An early 20thC Austrian cold-painted bronze parrot pin cushion, no.2837, stamped 'GESCHÜTZT' and 'B in a vase'.

4.25in (10.5cm) long

£400-500   WW

A CLOSER LOOK AT A COCKATOO INKSTAND

Who would not want this mischievous-looking cockatoo as a desk companion? This delightful bronze bird is both decorative and functional.

The head and neck are hinged and when opened reveal a circular aperture within where the ink was stored.

This bronze has cross-market appeal. It will certainly attract both bronze and inkstand collectors. This is already reflected in the high price.

The inset glass eyes add that extra bit of realism.

An early 20thC Austrian cold-painted bronze cockatoo inkstand.

11.5in (29.5cm) high

£900-1,000   DN

An early 20thC Austrian cold-painted bronze lizard, by Franz Bergman, stamped Amphora mark.

£200-300   L&T

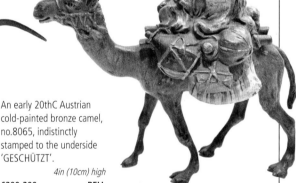

An early 20thC Austrian cold-painted bronze camel, no.8065, indistinctly stamped to the underside 'GESCHÜTZT'.

4in (10cm) high

£200-300   BELL

An Austrian cold-painted bronze of a young boy, lying on his front smoking a pipe, stamped 'B in a vase' for Bergman, 'GESCHÜTZT' and '4219'.

3.5in (8.5cm) long

£160-200   WW

A late 19th/early20thC Austrian cold-painted bronze snake attacking a young boy, stamped 'GESCHÜTZT'.

5.5in (14cm) long

£180-220   WW

An early 20thC Austrian cold-painted bronze of an Arab praying, in the manner of Bergman, no.9, kneeling on an oriental rug, stamped 'GESCHÜTZT'.

5.75in (14.5cm) wide

£600-700   WW

QUICK REFERENCE - BOOKS

● A true first edition is from the first print run of a hardback. Books from later print runs may be changed in some way, such as having errors corrected. Paperback first editions can also be collectable, but most are not yet as valuable as hardback first editions and do not have as many collectors.

● The quantity of true first editions is limited. The rule of supply and demand is important - as supply drops and demand rises, values rise exponentially. Iconic titles will always be sought-after, but a classic title published by an author at the height of his career will often be worth less than an earlier or less well-received work, mainly as fewer copies of the 'first' will have been printed.

● Learn how to recognise a first edition by looking for a number of features. Firstly, check that the publishing date and copyright date match. Also ensure that the original publishing date and publisher are correct, using a reliable source. Then look for a number '1' in the series of numbers on the inside copyright page. Some publishers state clearly that a book is a first edition, and some use a sequence of letters. There may also be other features such as errors or different content on dust jackets. In general, book club editions tend to be ignored by collectors.

● An author's signature will usually add greatly to the value, particularly if it is a limited or special edition. Personal dedications are less desirable, unless the recipient was or is somehow connected to the author or is famous in their own right. The work of some authors, such as Ian Fleming, is consistently popular and sought-after. Changing fashions or events, such as the release of a film or TV series based on a book, can also affect the value.

● Condition is important and collectors always aim to buy the best. To fetch the highest values, a first edition should be in undamaged condition and should come with its original dust jacket. Some damage, such as tears to a dust jacket can be repaired, but the value will still be affected detrimentally. Any first edition in mint condition will always fetch a premium.

'A Caribbean Mystery', by Agatha Christie, first edition, original cloth cover with dust jacket, some insect damage to spine.

This presentation copy was inscribed by Christie 'For Dr Mitchelmore, with thanks for advice (!), Agatha Christie, Wallingford, December 1964'. Dr. Gordon Mitchelmore was Agatha Christie's doctor and friend when she lived in Wallingford. They used to discuss poisons, medicines, and other related topics of mutual interest. One of the characters in this book, Major Palgrave, is poisoned, as Miss Marple discovers. There are other plots involving belladonna and Serenite, a drug for high blood pressure.
1964
£1,200-1,800   DW

'Hallowe'en Party', by Agatha Christie, first edition, with original cloth covers and dust jacket with a few short closed tears.

Presentation copy, inscribed by Christie 'To Dr Mitchelmore - from Agatha Christie, Nov 1969'.
1969
£1,000-1,500   DW

'Postern of Fate', by Agatha Christie, first edition, with original cloth covers and dust jacket with a tiny closed tear.

Presentation copy, inscribed by Christie 'To Doctor Mitchelmore, from Hannibal (alias Bingo), with best wishes from Agatha Christie, Nov. 1973'.
1973
£800-1,200   DW

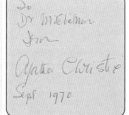

'Passenger to Frankfurt', by Agatha Christie, first edition, with original cloth covers and dust jacket.

Presentation copy, inscribed by Christie 'To Dr Mitchelmore - from Agatha Christie, Sept 1970'.
1970
£800-1,200   DW

BOOKS

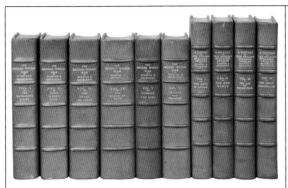

'The Second World War', by Winston S. Churchill, six volumes, first editions, with contemporary red half-calf covers by Zaehnsdorf, spines with raised letters slightly faded, together with 'A History of the English-Speaking Peoples', by the same author, four volumes, first editions, bound by Zaehnsdorf.

1948-56

£1,000-1,500 both sets   DW

'Portrait of a Model', by John Everard, first edition, published by George Routledge & Sons Ltd, London, with oatmeal cloth binding and original dust jacket, signed on the half title page by Everard.

1939

£70-100   WHP

'Dr No', by Ian Fleming, first edition, second impression, published by Cape, London, original cloth covers, price-clipped dust jacket, spine a little faded, one or two light spots.

Examples without the dancing girl on the hard covers are possibly rarer. The first print run was 20,000 copies.

1958

£600-800   DW

'For Your Eyes Only', first edition, published by Cape, London, original cloth covers and dust jacket, spine lettering faded to orange, light crease mark at foot.

The first print run was 21,712 copies.

1960

£400-600   DW

'Goldfinger', by Ian Fleming, first edition, published by Cape, London, with original cloth covers and dust jacket, spine slightly toned with stain at foot, a few minor stains to rear panel.

The first print run was 24,000 copies.

1959

£450-550   DW

'From Russia With Love', by Ian Fleming, first edition, published by Cape, London, original cloth covers, upper cover with gun design blocked in silver and red, price-clipped dust jacket, spine a little darkened and chipped at ends, one or two tears and nicks to folds.

The first edition was 15,000 copies. The very first printing was rejected by Cape as the sheets were not of suitable quality. Although they were sold off to a book club who later published them, the second printing was published before that by Cape, so is considered the first edition.

1957

£600-800   DW

'The Spy Who Loved Me', by Ian Fleming, first edition, published by Cape, London, with original cloth, upper cover slightly bowed, with dust jacket with light black mark to spine.

The first print run was 30,000 copies. Look closely at Fleming's surname on the title page. A spacer between the letters 'E' and 'M' worked itself loose in the printing machine when the first edition was being printed and left a quad mark. Examples with this quad mark are scarce and fetch a premium, which can top 25%, depending on the condition of the book.

1962

£500-700   DW

'Thunderball', by Ian Fleming, first edition, published by Cape, London, light spotting to top edge, original cloth covers and dust jacket with tiny crease mark at one fold.

The first print run was 50,938 copies.
1961
£400-600 DW

'Belshazzar', by Henry Rider Haggard, first American edition, Doubleday, Doran & Co., New York, ownership signature of Roger Allen in blue ballpoint pen to front pastedown, original cloth in pictorial dust jacket, a little rubbed and soiled with very minor edge wear.

This was Haggard's last novel, which was set in ancient Babylon. It was finished in late 1924, but not published until 1930, five years after his death.
1930
£150-250 DW

QUICK REFERENCE - H. RIDER HAGGARD

● Sir Henry Rider Haggard (1856-1925) was a Victorian novelist known for his adventure stories, often set in Africa. He is best known for 'King Solomon's Mines' (published in 1885) and the larger than life character, Allan Quatermain. By 1965, his serialised novel 'She' (1886-87) had sold over 83 million copies. Although they were 'lighter' than most Victorian novels, they are as popular and influential today as they were then. After spending time in South Africa from 1875-82, he wrote a book about the political situation there. This led to a series of successful novels. Roger Allen (1946-2014), from whose collection these books come from, was the founder and secretary of the Rider Haggard Society. He wrote and published extensively about Rider Haggard and his work.

'Heu-Heu, Or the Monster', by Henry Rider Haggard, first edition, published by Hutchinson & Co., illustrated publisher's catalogue at rear, ownership signature of Roger Allen in blue ballpoint pen to front pastedown, original red cloth lettered in black, pictorial 7/6 dust jacket, slightly rubbed and soiled with some edge wear and minor loss to spine ends.
1924
£500-700 DW

'Allan and the Ice-Gods', by Henry Rider Haggard, first American edition, published by Doubleday, Page & Co., New York, ownership signature of Roger Allen in blue ballpoint pen to front pastedown, original blue cloth in dust jacket, slightly rubbed and toned, a few short marginal closed tears and small nicks at head and foot of spine.
1927
£350-450 DW

'Marie', by Henry Rider Haggard, first edition, published by Cassell & Co. Ltd., 4 plates including colour frontispiece, after illustrations by A.C. Michael, occasional spotting, heaviest at front and rear, ownership signature of Roger Allen in blue ballpoint pen to front pastedown, original red cloth gilt in dust jacket with '6/-' to spine, a little chipped and soiled.
1912
£1,800-2,200 DW

'Marion Isle', by Henry Rider Haggard, first American edition, published by Doubleday, Doran & Co., New York, ownership signature of Roger Allen in blue ballpoint pen to front pastedown, original blue cloth lettered in white, pictorial dust jacket, a little spotted and toned with a few tears, relined with heavier paper, 'Price, net, $2.00' at head of inner flap.
1929
£200-300 DW

'Moon of Israel', by Henry Rider Haggard, first edition, published by John Murray, 4 leaves of undated publisher's adverts at rear, ownership signature of Roger Allen in blue ballpoint pen to front pastedown, some spotting at front and rear, inner hinges cracked, dust jacket a little chipped at extremities and lacking upper inner flap.
1918
£2,000-3,000 DW

BOOKS

'Master and Commander', by Patrick O'Brian, first edition, original cloth covers and dust jacket, slight toning to spine, one or two small nicks and closed tears.

This is the first 'Jack Aubrey' novel. Set in the Napoleonic Wars, it was published in the US in 1969. In 2003, it was turned into a film starring Russell Crowe as Jack Aubrey. Such events often increase the value of the first edition.

1970

£250-350   DW

'Quick Service', by P.G. Wodehouse, first edition, published by Herbert Jenkins, London, with four pages of advertisements, publisher's gilt-stamped burgundy cloth covers, dust jacket design by Fenwick, tape repairs on verso at corners and spine ends, scattered minor creasing, endpapers browned as usual.

1940

£900-1,200   SWA

A CLOSER LOOK AT A FIRST EDITION

Interest in the works of Eric Ravilious (1903-42) and his peers such as Edward Bawden, Edward Ardizzone, and Barnett Feedman has been growing since the early 2000s.

Only 2,000 copies of the first edition were printed, making surviving examples in good condition extremely rare. Illustrations from books in poor condition were often individually framed and sold.

The illustrations were finished in 1936. They provide a charming snapshot of high street shops, and reveal a time when retail and life in general was changing dramatically.

The first inspiration behind the book dates back to a drawing done with Bawden in 1924. Ravilious was also influenced by his father, a shopkeeper, by Russian books showing everyday life, and French books showing shop fronts.

The lithographic plates for the illustrations were destroyed in WW2 when the Curwen Press was bombed, making postwar reprints impossible.

'High Street', by J.M. Richards and Eric Ravilious, first edition, published by Country Life, twenty-four colour lithograph plates, light spotting, original pictorial boards, a little rubbed at edges, slight loss to foot of spine.

1938

£1,800-2,200   DW

Judith Picks

Charlotte Perkins Gilman (1860-1935) was a pioneering feminist, sociologist, and novelist at a time when such activities were unusual for women. This is her best-known work and was written on 6th and 7th June, 1890, in her home in Pasadena. It was published in the January 1892 edition of The New England Magazine. Concerning mental illness, confinement, and a woman's lack of independence and place in society, it was inspired by how she was treated by her first husband. This is an excellent surviving example of this very important early work of American feminist literature and is the first edition in book form.

'The Yellow Wall Paper', by Charlotte Perkins Stetson (Gilman), first edition in book form, published by Small, Maynard & Company, Boston.

1899

£2,500-3,500   SWA

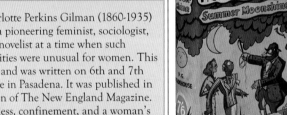

'Summer Moonshine', by P.G. Wodehouse, first British edition, published by Herbert Jenkins, London, with eight pages of advertisements, publisher's black-stamped red cloth covers and dust jacket, two 2-inch closed tears along folds, moderate rubbing and edgewear.

The American first edition was published by Doubleday the year before, in October 1937.

1938

£550-750   SWA

'The Years', by Virginia Woolf, first edition, published by Hogarth Press, London, contemporary presentation inscription to front endpaper, original cloth in dust jacket designed by Vanessa Bell, spotting and light browning to inner flaps and verso, a little nicked at head and foot of spine.

The painter and interior designer Vanessa Bell (1879-1961) was Virginia Woolf's sister. Both were leading members of the Bloomsbury Group of artists, writers, and thinkers.

1937

£300-500   DW

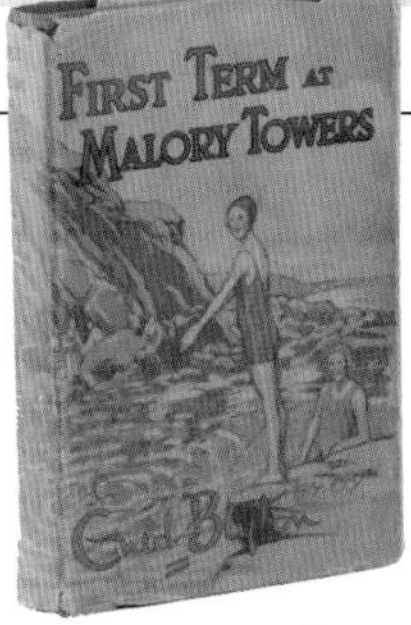

'First Term at Malory Towers', by Enid Blyton, fifth edition, published by Methuen & Co, with a signed slip by the author, pasted on the front end paper, clipped dust jacket.

Although not a first edition, the value is raised due to the slip that was signed by Blyton.

1950

£100-150 ECGW

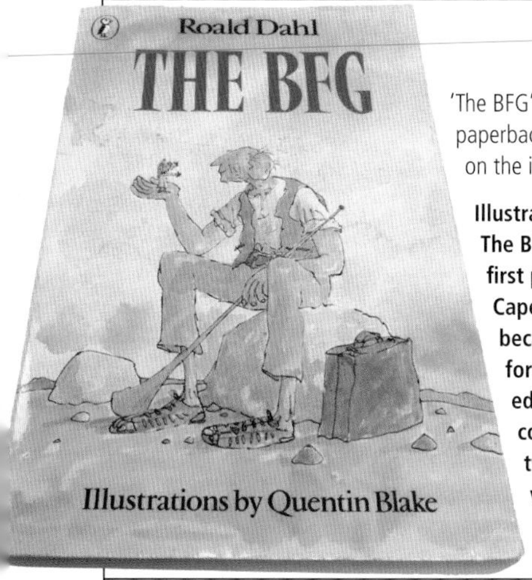

'The BFG', by Roald Dahl, paperback signed by the author on the inside front cover.

Illustrated by Quentin Blake, The Big Friendly Giant was first published by Jonathan Cape in 1982 and quickly became a modern classic for children. A signed first edition hardback in great condition may fetch two to three times this value, or more.

1985

£100-150 WHP

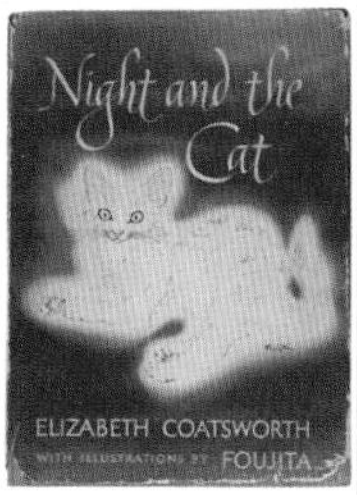

'Night and the Cat', with poems by Elizabeth Coatsworth and illustrations by Tsuguharu Foujita, first edition published by Macmillan, New York, with original cloth covers and price-clipped dust jacket stamped 'USD 3.00', a poem by Coatsworth in pencil in unknown hand on recto, some wear and a few tears.

1950

£180-220 SWA

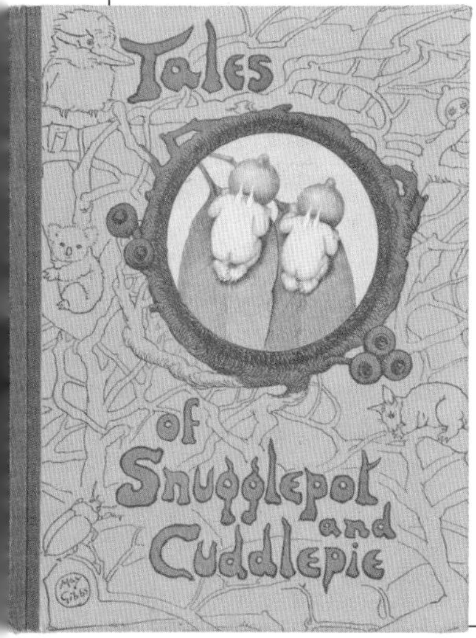

'Snugglepot and Cuddlepie - Their Adventures Wonderful', by May Gibbs, first Australian edition, published by Angus & Robertson, Sydney, pictorial endpapers, contemporary manuscript inscription on half-title, hinges stained due to previous strengthening with adhesive tape, with original cloth boards with illustration mounted on upper cover.

1918

£150-250 DW

A CLOSER LOOK AT GOODNIGHT MOON

This is an extremely rare first edition of Margaret Wise Brown's best-selling bedtime storybook about a little bunny saying goodnight to his surroundings.

Examples of this first edition, complete with its dust jacket, are extremely rare.

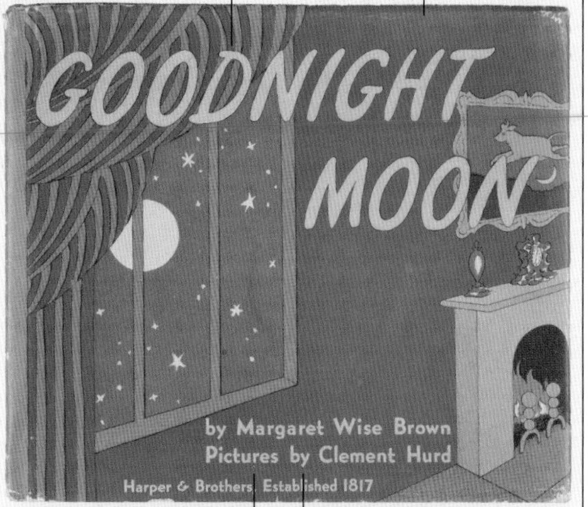

It has 'Little Fur Family' advertised on the rear flap and 'Other Books by Margaret Wise Brown' listed on the rear panel that include 'The Runaway Bunny', 'Little Chicken', and 'SHhh-BANG!'.

True first editions are also marked as being published by Harper & Brothers (later editions are by Harper & Row) and have a 30-60 code on the bottom flap of the dustjacket.

'Goodnight Moon', by Margaret Wise Brown, published by Harper & Brothers, USA, ownership ink stamp on front endpaper, green cloth-backed pictorial boards and price-clipped dustjacket, slightly rubbed and frayed to extremities, with 30-60 on front flap.

1947

£1,500-2,000 DW

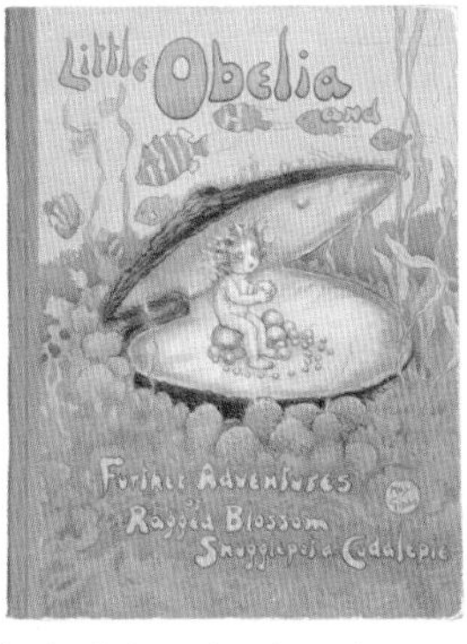

'Little Obelia and Further Adventures of Ragged Blossom Snugglepot & Cuddlepie', by May Gibbs, first Australian edition, published by Angus & Robertson, Sydney.

1921

£150-200 DW

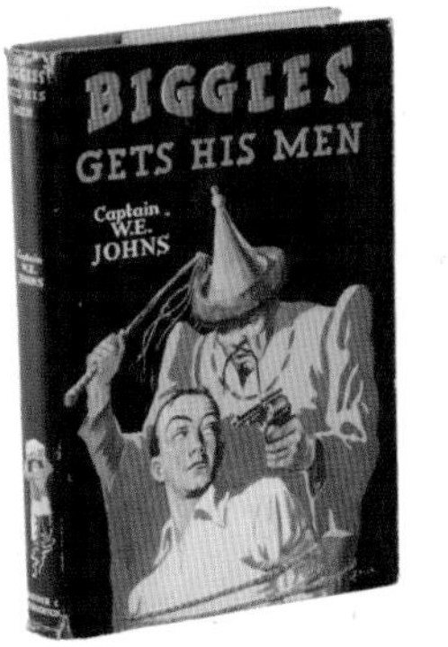

'Biggles Gets his Men', by William Earl Johns, first edition, published by Hodder & Stoughton, with dust wrapper showing '6/-net price', bound in blue cloth.

1950

£30-50 ECGW

BOOKS

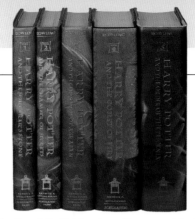

'Biggles Goes to School', by William Earl Johns, first edition, published by Hodder & Stoughton, with dust wrapper showing '6/-net' price, bound in red cloth.

1951

£30-50   ECGW

A group of five Harry Potter first American editions, comprising 'Harry Potter and the Sorcerer's Stone', 'Harry Potter and the Chamber of Secrets', 'Harry Potter and the Prisoner of Azkaban', 'Harry Potter and the Goblet of Fire', 'Harry Potter and the Order of the Phoenix', by J.K. Rowling, published by Scholastic, all with publisher's cloth boards and pictorial dust jackets.

These are early issues of the first editions. They bear Rowling's signatures that match, indicating they were signed at the same time.

1998-2003

£2,000-2,500 for the group   SWA

'Harry Potter and the Chamber of Secrets', by J.K. Rowling, first American edition, published by Scholastic, New York, with green cloth over patterned purple boards, silver lettering to spine, dust jacket with soft creasing to extreme upper edges.

This is the first printing of the first edition with the complete number line on the copyright page. Neither the book nor the jacket is marked with a 'Year 2' indication.

1999

£300-500   SWA

'Harry Potter and the Prisoner of Azkaban', by J.K. Rowling, first American edition, published by Scholastic Press, New York, with publisher's purple cloth over green patterned boards, with dust jacket and complete number line on the copyright page.

1999

£250-350   SWA

'How the Grinch Stole Christmas', by Theodor Geisel Seuss, first edition, published by Random House, New York, with original pictorial laminated boards with minimal rubbing, pictorial dust jacket, with bookplate on recto and verso of front flyleaf.

This is the first printing of the first edition, with fourteen titles by Seuss listed on the rear flap - Grinch being the last one listed. The printed price '250/250' is listed on the lower front flap.

1957

£1,000-1,500   SWA

'THE CAT IN THE HAT COMES BACK', by Theodor Giesel Seuss, first edition, first printing, published by Younger & Hirsch, 11, New York, with original colour pictorial laminated boards and first edition dust jacket with very light surface wear, contents clean with bookplates to prelims.

1958

£350-450   SWA

'The Adventures of Two Dutch Dolls', by Florence Kate Upton, illustrated, published by Longmans Green and Company.

Florence Kate Upton (1873-1922) is best known for her series of books about Gollies. This was the first to feature the character. The story revolves around two Dutch dolls who encounter the Golly and exclaim, 'To see a horrid sight! The blackest gnome'. Despite this being uncomfortable and obviously politically incorrect today, the character proved popular at the time.

1895

£60-80   FLD

QUICK REFERENCE - BOXES

- Despite the downturn in much traditional Georgian, Victorian, and Edwardian furniture that has been badly marketed as 'brown' furniture, desirability of and prices paid for their smaller counterparts in the form of boxes have remained largely steady. This is mainly due to their size and combination of decorative and practical use. A single box displayed on a surface is decorative enough, and will always be used, but a small collection can look highly appealing.

- Values depend on the type of box, its age, and the level of quality, both in terms of materials and craftsmanship. Tea caddies are amongst the most valuable and desirable types of boxes, and are widely collected. Most examples on the market today date from the mid-18thC onwards, but particularly from the late 18thC into the 19thC, when tea became more affordable and widely drunk. Many lock to prevent tea being stolen by servants, or to protect their contents from accidental spillage. Different materials abound and include ivory, exotic woods, and tortoiseshell, and shapes vary widely.

- Dressing boxes and large boxes containing games are also often found and the same rules apply as regards value. See the Quick Reference box on page 31 for more detailed information about dressing boxes. Always look for a decorative appeal in terms of the form and how that works with any pattern of applied materials. Carved, painted or applied components should be well-executed and ideally in the style of the period the piece was manufactured in, or representative of the box or place it was made.

- Check condition carefully. Replaced locks, tortoiseshell panels, key escutcheons or hinges can dramatically reduce the value, unless well done. Pay close attention to locks and any maker's name or label. Prestigious retailers or makers and high quality locks, such as those by Bramah, will often raise the value and could provide an interesting research project.

A George III blonde tortoiseshell tea caddy, with a silvered loop handle finial, escutcheon, monogrammed name plate and ball feet, internal cover, plaque engraved 'J.A.C.', cover with small chips, ball feet possibly replacements.

Even though the ball feet are possibly replacements, this is worth more than the others on this page as it is a more unusual shape, and the desirable blonde tortoiseshell is original, in excellent condition, and has a good natural pattern.

c1780   *4in (10cm) high*

£1,000-1,400   DN

A late George III tortoiseshell-veneered and ivory-banded tea caddy, the hinged cover with silver-plated metal ball finial, four silver-plated copper ball feet, the twin covers within also tortoiseshell-lined.

c1800   *6.5in (16.5cm) high*

£500-600   BLEA

A Regency tortoiseshell-veneered and ivory-banded and mounted tea caddy, tortoiseshell-veneered twin covers within, repair to cover, stains and damage to interior velvet, one of the lids with repair.

c1815   *7in (18cm) wide*

£550-650   DN

A George III tortoiseshell-veneered and ivory-strung tea caddy, the interior with twin covers with turned-bone handles, repairs to tortoiseshell, new covers, painted areas.

c1800   *6.75in (17cm) wide*

£550-650   BLEA

A Regency penwork tea caddy, the lid decorated with a country house scene, the body with classical ornament.

7in (18cm) wide

£500-600   BELL

BOXES

A CLOSER LOOK AT A TEA CADDY

Penwork, where the design was applied in black ink to a coloured varnished base using a quill pen, was commonly used from the late 18thC to the mid-19thC.

The Chinese-inspired design that also features almost Classical elements such as the columns would have been highly fashionable when it was made around 1815.

A 19thC Tunbridgeware tea caddy with concave sides, the top with a scene of Eton College from across the river.

Tunbridgeware is characterised by intricate, often geometric, inlays arranged in a mosaic to create a scene or pattern. It was produced primarily as souvenir ware in the Kent spa town of Tunbridge Wells, with most pieces found on the market today dating from the 19thC.

9in (23cm) wide

£400-450   BELL

A George III paperscroll-decorated pine tea caddy, of navette section, the cover with brass swing handle, the front with a printed roundel depicting a standing maiden, the interior with subsidiary cover, small area of rear edging missing.

Paperscroll decoration, sometimes known as scrollwork, is a low relief, three dimensional decoration made from thin tubes of rolled up paper. The tubes are then moistened and bent and manipulated into different forms and designs before being glued to the body of the piece. Designs can be highly intricate. Losses or damage to the surface can reduce value dramatically as it is so hard to repair.

7.25in (18.5cm) wide

£600-700   BLEA

A Russian papier mâché lacquer tea caddy, by Vishniakov, marked inside the cover, re-glued shallow chip rear cover, cover has craquelure, medal marks faded.

The sarcophagus form was derived from funeral caskets from Classical Antiquity. It was a popular form during the Neoclassical period of the late 18thC and early 19thC, particularly for wine cellars and tea caddies.

This example is richly decorated with a variety of designs and is in excellent condition, even though the feet are, curiously, coquilla nut replacements, which does reduce the value slightly.

A Regency penwork tea caddy, decorated in the Chinoiserie taste, raised on four coquilla nut feet, the interior with twin covers with further penworked scenes, minor rubbing and nibbles, feet are replacements.

c1815   *9in (23cm) wide*

£700-800   DN

For information on Vishniakov, please see page 35.

c1860   *6.25in (16cm) long*

£200-250   DN

A Victorian macassar ebony tea caddy, with a later bone escutcheon, the interior with twin-lidded compartments with turned-bone handles.

8in (20.5cm) wide

£80-120   WW

A George III mahogany and marquetry tea caddy, with a silver-plated handle, enclosing contrasting inlaid canisters with sliding covers.

8in (20cm) wide

£600-700   BELL

A 20thC reproduction Georgian-style apple-shaped tea caddy, carved from fruitwood, lined in silver paper, with an ivory escutcheon.

4in (10cm) high

£80-100   LOCK

QUICK REFERENCE - DRESSING BOXES

● Dressing boxes such as these were the preserve of the wealthy middle classes, aristocracy, and even royalty. Typically made from exotic woods, and often embellished with precious metals, the interiors were fitted with small compartments, each containing a useful bottle or vessel to contain scents or creams, or dressing accessories such as brushes or combs. Bottle lids are often made from silver, or sometimes washed in gold, and they often bear the monogram of the original owner. Look carefully as the hallmarks will indicate the year the piece was made in, provided they are original to the box. Some pieces are inlaid with tortoiseshell or embossed or engraved with intricate patterns. Effectively, the more lavish the materials, the more expensive it would have been. Always look for complete examples as finding matching replacements can be extremely hard. As well as being practical, these boxes acted as status symbols when the the owner was travelling. Lockable, they were also the secure, private domain of the owner, who could store letters and other precious items inside. It's incredible to think that many have survived as long as they have, particularly when complete examples like this are found. But, the question is, what do we do with them today apart from display them as examples of historic craftsmanship, wealth, and vanity? Times and habits have changed, and they certainly wouldn't pass through airport customs! That's the reason why they typically fetch such low values today. Sadly, this situation is unlikely to change. They are cumbersome, making them difficult to collect. There are exceptions to the rule, however, particularly for boxes with a provenance that connects them to a famous or well-known person.

A 19thC brass-mounted coromandel dressing box, by 'W Leuchars, 38 Piccadilly London', with 'Bramah' lock.

Leuchars was a prestigious London maker and retailer that was founded in 1794 and based in Piccadilly. In 1888, it was acquired by Asprey & Sons.

13in (33cm) wide

£500-600

BELL

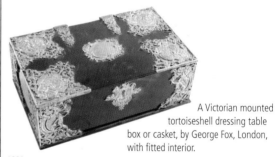

A 19thC French prisoner-of-war straw-work box, decorated with a river scene, the back, sides, and front with landscape vignettes, the interior with a mirror to the lid and a lift-out glazed lidded tray with compartments for pen and ink above further lidded compartments, pin cushions, and drawers.

14.75in (37.5cm) long

£400-500

WW

A Victorian mounted tortoiseshell dressing table box or casket, by George Fox, London, with fitted interior.

1888

7.6in (19.2cm) long

£350-400

LAW

A George IV rosewood dressing box, with brass stringing, with silver-plated topped jars and bottles with ivory-handled utensils with a lift-out tray, with sunken brass handles, with a leather letter pouch with a printed paper trade label inscribed 'E.ELVEY, POCKET BOOK, DRESSING CASE, & DESK MAKER. to the Royal Family the KING of PRUSSIA And His Serene Highness the Prince of Orange, 9 NEW BOND STREET LONDON'.

11.25in (28.5cm) wide

£220-280

WW

A late Victorian black leather-cased toilet set, with bottles and jars, a soap case, brushes, a glove stretcher, comb, scissors, and other utensils.

8.75in (22cm) long

£100-150

WW

A 19thC mahogany Tunbridgeware writing slope and box, inlaid with parquetry geometric panels and borders enclosing a replacement leatherette skiver and three small drawers.

18in (46cm) high

£90-120   MOR

A Victorian blue leather-cased writing box, the lid inset with a paper compartment and a lift-out tray with compartments for pen and ink, stamped 'EDWARDS & SONS, 161 & 159, REGENT ST. W. BY APPOINTMENT TO THE KING & QUEEN'.

14in (35.5cm) wide

£140-180   WW

A late 19thC Anglo-Indian horn and ivory jewellery box, with fret-carved panels and lac decoration, the lid with a central panel of a goddess, the interior with divisions and lidded compartments and a hinged clock aperture.

8.75in (22cm) long

£200-250   WW

A Victorian walnut stationery box, the cover inset with a porcelain plaque, the whole with gilt-metal mounts.

8.7in (22cm) wide

£150-200   LOC

A mahogany artist's box, by Windsor & Newton, with drawer to base and two lift-out trays, with watercolour paints and pallets, maker's label to underside of lid.

£350-400   TEN

A 19thC Biedermeier walnut jewellery box, with lift-top and secret compartments.

Biedermeier refers to a period of time, a group of similar styles applied to furniture and decorative objects, and a way of living that was fashionable in Central Europe from 1815-48.
Furniture is characterised by heavy forms that have simplified, often almost geometric lines and pared-down Neoclassical details and inspirations - as can be seen with this jewellery box.
The box is almost like a miniaturised Biedermeier chest of drawers, which is a desirable feature.
The walnut has beautiful figuring and a good colour. The box has additional secret compartment features.

22in (56cm) wide

£1,000-1,400   BELL

A 'Royal Cabinet of Games' with chess, draughts, cribbage, and a racing game, in a walnut box.

A games compendium, the pine box with a reversible games board inside the lid, and rule book by J W Spear & Sons.

The games inside this compendium include chess, draughts, dominoes, a horse racing game, and whist markers and cribbage board.

6.75in (17cm) high

£350-400   LAW

Unlike dressing boxes (see page 31), games compendia are very popular and desirable, simply because they are more practical. They also make popular gifts at Christmas. The value depends on the quality of the box and the quantity of games contained inside. High quality Victorian sets with features such as carved ivory pieces, an inlaid exotic wood box, and notable maker's or retailers' names will fetch the most.

13in (33cm) wide

£650-750   CHOR

A late Victorian mahogany games compendium, inlaid with brass escutcheon and key plate, with chess/draughts board, Bezique spinners, dominoes, draughts, cribbage board, shaker and instruction manuals.

13in (33.5cm) wide

£90-120   DW

A Victorian 'Staunton' pattern boxwood and ebony chess set, by Jaques, London, two rooks and two knights with crown marks, , the white king stamped 'JAQUES LONDON'.

Together with a carton-pierre 'Gothic' casket and 'The Chess-Player's Text-Book' by H. Staunton.

the king 3.25in (8.5cm) high

£600-800   WW

A late Victorian mahogany and brass-bound games compendium, the lid inset with a folding leather chequer, backgammon and horse racing games board, above a lift-out tray with a rosewood cribbage board and bone dominoes and eight dice, above another tray with two packs of playing cards and Whist and Bezique markers, the base with counters, a shaker and painted lead jockeys and horses, with a Staunton pattern boxwood and ebony chess set, marked with a red crown, with key.

13in (33.5cm) wide

£100-150   WW

A late Victorian pine games compendium, retailed by Benetfink & Co., with a folding leather chequer, backgammon and 'The Steeple Chase' board, to a lift-out tray with ebony and boxwood counters, cribbage board, dominoes and six dice, above painted lead horses, dice shaker, gavel, Bezique and whist markers and coloured counters, with two packs of playing cards, with an ebony and boxwood Staunton pattern chess set, with an inset ivorine plaque 'BENETFINK & Co., GAMES DEPT. CHEAPSIDE, LONDON, E.C.', with original guide book, with key.

13in (33.3cm) wide

£500-700   WW

A mid-18thC French fruitwood table box, the cover carved and pierced with couples, on a scroll ground with mirror backing, the sides with ranges of buildings, glued small crack to front.

5in (13cm) long

£250-300   DN

A late 19thC Anglo-Indian sandalwood and ivory cribbage box, with inlaid sadeli decoration, with a divided interior for cards and pegs, on bun feet.

Sadeli is a form of inlaid micro-mosaic of geometric patterns. Highly intricate, it is time-consuming and requires great skill to create. Practised since the 16thC in India and the Middle East, it saw a high point in the 19thC as exports of boxes, chess sets and similar objects increased. Bombay became a key centre, and many such boxes became known as 'Bombay boxes'.

10in (27.5cm) wide

£100-120   WW

A George III carved bone faced counter box, the fitted interior with four bone trays with sides pierced as basket weave, with bone playing counters.

c1800   *8.5in (21.5cm) wide*

£200-250   BLEA

A Victorian oak cigar box, with bi-fold top and two sprung drawers incorporating cigar cutter.

10.75in (27cm) wide

£350-400   BELL

A leather and brass-mounted case for a pair of shot guns, the lid inscribed 'Douglas Pennant', with a paper trade label inscribed 'WILKINSON AND SON, Gun & Sword Manufacturers TO HER MAJESTY, The War Department and the Council of India, NO. 27 PALL MALL, LONDON.'.

34in (86cm) long

£200-300   WW

A 19thC deception cube parquetry inlaid rosewood box.

9in (23cm) wide

£100-140   BELL

QUICK REFERENCE - VISHNIAKOV

- The Vishniakov workshop was founded in the Russian village of Ostashkovo during the 1780s by a freed serf called Osip Fillipovich Vishnyakov. It produced high-quality lacquered boxes, eggs, and similar items, and became a competitor of the leading workshop, the Korobov workshop, which was run by Piotr Lukutin. Scenes from both focus around traditional Russian characters, stories, and scenes, such as troika, and are hand-painted. Both flourished into the 19thC. Lukutin's and Vishnyakov's workshops closed in 1904 and 1910 respectively, when the artists moved to found a collective.

A late 18th/early 19thC Russian carved walrus bone casket, from Kholmogory, with polychrome decoration and fretwork panels, the hinged lid with a pin cushion to a vacant interior.

Kholmogory has been known for its bone carving since the 17thC, with the best workshops turning out highly complex, intricately worked objects such as boxes and small furniture. Until the revolution, the best masters were employed to fulfill orders from the Tsars, with the 'golden age' being during the reign of Peter The Great (1682-1725).

8.75in (22.5cm) long

£250-300   WW

A Russian papier mâché lacquer table box, by Vishniakov, the cover with a troika scene, marked inside cover with date 1896, suface with craquelure, hinge restored, chip around key hole.

5in (13cm) long

£200-250   DN

A mid-20thC silver-gilt and wood-lined box, set with turquoise and pearls, marked 'Foreign' and with import mark for London, 1961.

£250-300   BELL

An early 18thC Italian tortoiseshell and gilt metal oval snuff box, decorated with a piqué work and applied button cartouche, the interior inset with a late 18thC ivory portrait miniature after Angelica Kauffmann of the Queen of Naples Marie Caroline with her son.

The subject matter for the portrait miniature is probably taken from Angelica Kauffmann's monumental portrait 'Ferdinand IV, King of Naples and Sicily and His Family', which can be found in the Museo di Capodimonte, Napoli.

3.5in (8.9cm) wide

£400-600   WW

An early 19thC ivory box and cover, inset with the portrait miniature of a girl.

3.1in (8cm) diam

£150-200   LAW

A 19thC ivory box, the cover inset with a gilt-metal medallion, signed 'G.LOOS D.BERLIN'.

3.25in (8cm) diam

£150-180   LAW

An early 19thC French tortoiseshell snuff box, the hinged lid with a fixé-sous-verre shipping scene in the manner of Vernet, within a gilt metal frame.

3.5in (8.8cm) wide

£400-600   WW

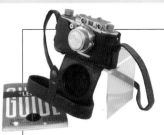

An Ernst Leitz Leica IIIB 35mm camera, serial no.326357, with a Summar lens f=5cm 1:2 no.481286, lens cap and black leather case, with the 1979 edition of 'Focal Press Leica Guide'.
camera 1939
£250-300   **DA&H**

An Ernst Leitz Leica IIIc camera, serial no.368965, with a Leitz Wetzlar Summar f2 50mm lens no.387857, with Leitz viewer.

A large part of the black fabric body covering is missing from one side of this camera. Condition is critical to the value of Leicas, particularly amongst serious collectors who prize those in mint condition. Had this been in pristine condition, it may have fetched up to twice this value.
1941
£150-200   **TEN**

A Leica IIIF camera, no.539322, black and chrome case with lens cap.
1950-51
£400-500   **FLD**

An Ernst Leitz Leica M2 camera, serial no.989449, with a Leitz Canada Tele-Elmarit f2.8, 90mm lens no.2658464 in maker's leather case, together with a Leitz Summicron f2, 50mm lens no.1143410, an early Leica leather case, a light meter, and a lens hood.
1960
£800-1,200   **TEN**

An Ernst Leitz Leica IID camera, serial no.218377, with a Leitz Elmar f=5cm 1:3,5 lens, with Leica guide, in a Leica case, with a German WW2 shoulder strap.

Paperwork sold with this camera indicated that this was owned by a German soldier. However, there is a major difference between a camera bought privately by a German soldier and one owned by a military organisation. Had the top plate had a special engraving such as those for the German airforce ('Luftwaffen-Eigentum'), the German army ('W.H.' for Wermacht Heer), or the British military (PATT followed by a number), then the value would have been three, five, or even over ten times as much as this, depending on the engraving and the exact model.

1936
£400-600   **LAW**

An Ernst Leitz Leica R5 camera, serial no.1697862, a Leitz Summicron R f2, 50mm lens no.3353569, a Leitz Elmarit R f2.8, 90mm lens no.3345917, both in leather cases in original boxes, a Leitz Elmarit R f2.8, 35mm lens, a carrying strap and copies of Leica Reflex Practice books.

Always consider the value of individual lenses as well as the camera as they also have financial value.
1986
£900-1,200   **TEN**

A Leica Minilux camera, no.2117556, with f2.4 40mm Summarit lens, with black case and instruction booklet.

1995
£200-300   **TEN**

A Coronet Midget mottled blue Bakelite miniature camera, in its original leatherette case.

Produced in different colours, these popular Art Deco cameras are highly desirable today. For more information, see p51 of the Miller's Collectables Price Guide 2014-2015.

1934-39   *3in (7cm) high*

£350-450   GYM

A Franke & Heidecke Rolleiflex TLR camera, no.1604240, with a Schneider-Kreuznack 1:2.8/80 lens, in fitted leather case.

£420-480   FLD

A Franke & Heidecke Rolleiflex model K8 T2 TLR camera, no.2162676, with a Carl Zeiss Tessar f3.5. 75mm lens, in manufacturer's leather case with magnifier/viewer.

£200-300   TEN

A Hasselblad 500EL/M camera, with Carl Zeiss Distagon T* f4, 50mm lens no.6366382 and 4 additional film backs, in carry bag, showing signs of use.

£300-500   TEN

A CLOSER LOOK AT A CAMERA

Distributed by Walter Kunik of Frankfurt and made by a couple of factories, the PETIE camera is a miniature camera that takes 16 exposures on a 17mm roll film with a 25mm f9 fixed lens.

As well as being sold on its own, it was also housed or mounted with certain objects including cigarette lighters, a music box and a compact. Hard to find, these are highly sought-after.

Introduced in 1956 and costing 31.55 Deutschmarks, the compact version is known as the 'PETIE Vanity' and it came in a variety of finishes, including black, red, green, blue, marbled enamel, leather, and snakeskin.

Enamel and skin-covered examples are the most desirable, and value depends on the colour and design, but condition is paramount. This is in excellent condition and retains its rare box.

A Japanese Mamiya 645 1000S camera, with Sekor 1:2.8 80mm lens, no.158942, spare Sekor lens 1:2.8 70mm, no.14852, together with a Sekor 1:4 210mm lens and a Nikkor-Q 1:28 35mm lens N264818, cased.

£250-350   FLD

A Palliard Bolex H16 Reflex cine camera, with Vario-Switar f2.5 18-86mm lens and trigger hand grip, with signs of light use.

£200-300   TEN

A late 1950s-60s Walter Kunik 'Petie Vanity' camera, with tan 'snakeskin' leather covering, compact with opening door, mirror, and lipstick holder, with instructions in original box.

£600-800   TEN

CANES

QUICK REFERENCE - CANES

- Decorated canes first became popular during the 16thC, but reached their 'golden age' in terms of variety and quality in the late 18thC and 19thC. Favoured by the upper classes and the bourgeoisie, they largely went out of fashion after World War One. As well as being of practical use, the material and quality of decoration acted as a status symbol, and a display of wealth and taste.
- The shaft is usually made from wood and the handle or pommel may be too, or may be made from ivory, bone, silver, gold or another type of wood, such as fruitwood. The tip of the stick or cane is typically tipped in metal to prevent it being worn - this is known as a ferrule. The variety of styles and types of decoration is huge.
- Most canes found today date from the Victorian or Edwardian period and can be divided into two types - decorative canes and 'gadget' canes. Decorative canes may be plain or carved or embellished somehow, and 'gadget' canes usually have another function, such as containing something useful like a small bottle or a telescope. Some canes cross into folk art and can attract large sums, particularly for rare and desirable American examples.
- In all instances, the quality of the decoration or objects inside, and of the material used, counts greatly towards value. Also consider the age and place of manufacture. Many sticks do not bear maker's marks, but may bear hallmarks if in a precious metal, or a retailer's mark such as Swaine & Adeney. Condition is also important - always examine carving all over to ensure parts are not missing.

A late 19thC fruitwood walking cane, carved with hounds and a single man on horseback chasing a fox, with a horse's head handle.

34.25in (86.5cm) long

£600-700   WW

An ebonised walking cane, the handle modelled as a dog with glass-inset eyes, silver collar, tapering shaft, marked 'Birmingham 1910'.

c1910   *36in (91cm) long*

£300-400   L&T

A Schtockschnitzler Simmons carved and painted walking stick, with a bird and hand grip retaining a vibrant polychrome surface.

Schtockschnitzler Simmons was an itinerant walking stick carver and seller who is now seen as an American folk art 'hero'. His first name is unknown, so 'Schtockschnitzler' is German for 'cane carver'. He travelled through Germany and other communities in Berks County, Pennsylvania, from around 1885-1910 and carved his canes from the root ends of dogwood saplings. Many were carved with birds or, more rarely, a horse's head, before being lacquered with shellac, and sometimes painted. Those that have their

original painted decoration are highly prized by top American folk art collectors, particularly if carved with an animal as this one is.

31in (78cm) long

£5,500-6,500   POOK

A 19thC carved mahogany walking cane, with a Mr. Punch handle, with glass eyes, the cane with a brass tip.

35.75in (90.5cm) long

£500-600   WW

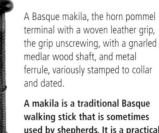

A Basque makila, the horn pommel terminal with a woven leather grip, the grip unscrewing, with a gnarled medlar wood shaft, and metal ferrule, variously stamped to collar and dated.

A makila is a traditional Basque walking stick that is sometimes used by shepherds. It is a practical tool, a cultural symbol of authority and strength, and can also be used as a weapon.

1929   *33in (84.5cm) long*

£130-180   SWO

A walking stick, the terminal carved with a bust of a man, the shaft entwined with a snake and inscribed 'Samuel Sampson, Martlesham, Suffolk February 1 18(0)13'.

c1813   *34in (87cm) long*

£500-600   SWO

Miller's Compares

This is much more realistically carved with a plethora of detail, from the row of leaves to the snake and fingernails.

Marine ivory is from walrus tusks, and is also sometimes known as morse ivory. It can be denser and harder than elephant ivory.

This also has a silver collar and a once-fashionable ebonised shaft. It would have been an expensive item in its day, rather than being made or bought by a sailor as a souvenir.

On sticks such as this, marine ivory is often cut into discs and combined with whalebone discs - this example is completely made from marine ivory.

A Victorian walking cane, the ivory pommel carved with a fist holding a snake and a stiff leaf carved band, a silver collar with an ebonised shaft.

35.75in (90.5cm)

£750-850 SWO

A Victorian carved marine ivory walking stick, the grip modelled as a clenched fist holding a snake, with brass ferrule.

33.75in (85.5cm) high

£350-450 DN

An ebonised walking cane, the ivory handle carved as a fist clenching a snake.

32in (81.5cm) long

£160-200 WW

A late 19thC Victorian carved ivory and white metal mounted malacca walking stick, the grip modelled as the head of a hound, the shaft with metal ferrule.

35in (88.5cm) long

£200-250 DN

A 19thC walking cane, the malacca shaft below presentation silver collar and carved ivory handle modelled as a dog's head with stone-set eyes.

35in (89cm) long

£250-300 FLD

A late 19thC Victorian carved ivory and brass-mounted stained hardwood walking stick, modelled as a hound's head, with inset-horn eyes, the shaft unscrewing at the midpoint, with brass ferrule.

36in (91cm) high long

£220-280 DN

A late 19thC Victorian carved marine ivory and brass mounted hardwood walking stick, the grip modelled as the head of a spaniel, with inset-horn eyes, the shaft unscrewing at the midpoint, with brass ferrule, the shaft is scuffed and knocked, the grip might be associated to the shaft.

36in (91.5cm) long

£300-350 DN

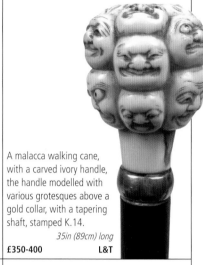

An ivory and malacca walking stick, the handle carved as a head of a man, with a yellow metal collar, with a horn ferrule, stamped 'Brigg, London'.

32in (82cm) long

£300-350   **SWO**

A malacca walking cane, with a carved ivory handle, the handle modelled with various grotesques above a gold collar, with a tapering shaft, stamped K.14.

35in (89cm) long

£350-400   **L&T**

A briar walking stick, the handle carved as an eagle's head with an ivory bill and glass eyes.

The wrinkles and other details make this characterful stick as valuable as it is.

34in (87cm) long

£550-650   **SWO**

A late 19thC carved ivory and brass-mounted stained hardwood walking stick, the grip modelled as a stylised human skull, with articulated jaw, the shaft unscrewing at the midpoint, with brass ferrule.

36.75in (93cm) long

£400-500   **DN**

An ivory and malacca walking stick, on a tapering malacca shaft, lacking collar, later copper ferrule, the terminal inscribed 'John Fowler of Yarmouth 1703', and initialled 'JS' to the central cap.

This stick is unusual and desirable as it is very early in date. It is also named and dated. All these features appeal greatly to collectors.

41.5in (105cm) long

£750-800   **SWO**

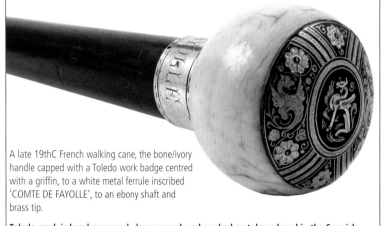

A late 19thC French walking cane, the bone/ivory handle capped with a Toledo work badge centred with a griffin, to a white metal ferrule inscribed 'COMTE DE FAYOLLE', to an ebony shaft and brass tip.

Toledo work is hand-engraved, damascened, and worked metal produced in the Spanish town of Toledo since 500BC. It is typically found on guns, armour, and other weaponry.

32in (81cm) long

£250-300   **WW**

A late 19thC ivory walking stick, the handle in the form of a pierced pennant, with a silver ring collar, and finely tapered shaft.

35in (89cm) long

£400-500   **SWO**

A George V malacca and Chinese white metal mounted walking stick, above scenes of figures amongst pavilions, the shaft with brass ferrule, the knob grip inscribed to the top 'H.H.A. FROM C.C. Dec 25th 1919'.

This was previously the property of Herbert Henry Asquith (1852-1928), a British politician and prime minister, who possibly received it as a Christmas present from Clementine Churchill. Later, it was owned by Roy Jenkins, Lord Jenkins of Hillhead.

A late 19thC
Victorian brass-
mounted bamboo
'system' walking
stick, the grip
unscrewing to a
hollow interior,
containing a cane
fishing rod in four
sections.

A late 19thC stingray tail cane, with silver-embossed terminal, marks worn, lacking ferrule.

32in (82cm) long

£300-350   SWO

1919   *37.25in (94.5cm) long*

£250-300   DN

37.5in (95cm) long

£500-550   DN

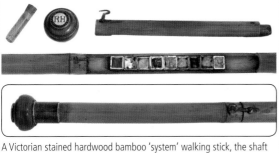

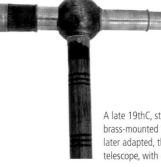

A Victorian stained hardwood bamboo 'system' walking stick, the shaft with a removable section opening to reveal nine porcelain pallette pots containing paint, the knob grip with enamelled roundel inscribed 'PALMA NON SINE PULVERE' (no reward without effort), monogram 'RH'.

c1900   *36.25in (92cm) high*

£500-550   DN

A late 19thC, stained hardwood and brass-mounted 'gadget' walking stick, later adapted, the spherical grip holding a telescope, with eyepiece and five sections.

The telescope was possibly added in the early 20thC.

40in (100.5cm) high

£500-550   DN

A bamboo walking cane, with integral aluminium horse measurer.

35.4in (90cm) long

£100-150   WHP

An exceptional Continental gold and bloodstone walking cane handle with concealed watch, the hinged cover opening with a mine-cut diamond button to reveal a watch, the key in a compartment below, the base of the pommel with enamelled band reading 'Avec Vous Dieu Toujours'.

The quantity of the precious materials and the quality of the workmanship make this as rare and valuable as it is. The watch inside is also an added feature. The French wording means 'With You, God Always', or effectively 'God is always with you'.

3in (8cm) high

£6,000-7,000   ROS

CERAMICS

ESSENTIAL REFERENCE - BESWICK

● The Beswick Pottery was founded in Loughton, Staffordshire, in 1894. It initially produced tableware and vases. The earliest animal figurines were produced from 1900. By 1930 they had become so successful they had become a major part of the factory's production. Many figurines were designed by Arthur Gredington, who worked from 1939-57. Other notable designers include Colin Melbourne, Graham Tongue, and Albert Hallam.

● Collectors tend to focus on one type of animal, whether it is dogs, farm animals, wild animals or horses. Rare bulls are currently very sought-after. Potteries Auctions sold a rare red strawberry roan Hereford bull for £5,500, but sometimes prices do fall when the main collectors have an example. Potteries Auctions sold a belted Galloway bull for £3,400 - they are now selling for around £1,000.

● Another collectable series is the Beatrix Potter figurines launched in 1946.

● Important areas to consider are colour, glaze and form as these will affect value. 'Roan' and 'Rocking Horse Grey' are typically more valuable than brown or white. Matt glazes tend to be more valuable than gloss. Differently positioned legs and tails can also affect value. Early pieces can be the most valuable but they can be hard to identify as the back stamp and shape numbers were only introduced in 1934. An extremely rare or prototype figurine can break all these rules.

● Condition is paramount to the value and desirability of all figurines, but collectors may make an exception with an extremely rare or unique figurine that is damaged.

● Limited editions, even from the 1990s can be valuable if the edition was small and you have all the documentation.

● The company was sold to Royal Doulton in 1969 but the Beswick name was used until 1989. After this the production of Beswick and Doulton animal figurines was merged under the Royal Doulton name. The Beswick name was used again from 1999 until the factory closed in 2002. Prices tended to rise after the closure. In the present climate prices for common figurines have fallen, whereas prices for rare figurines are very strong.

A Beswick pottery 'Galloway Bull', modelled by Arthur Gredington, belted, black and white, model no.1746B, printed marks.
1963-69   *4.5in (11.5cm) high*
£700-800   **HT**

A Beswick pottery 'Galloway Bull', modelled by Arthur Gredington, silver dunn, fawn and brown, model no.1746C, printed marks.
1962-69   *4.5in (11.5cm) high*
£600-700   **HT**

A Beswick 'Dairy Shorthorn Bull' 'CH Gwersylt Lord Oxford 74th', designed by Arthur Gredington, model no.1504.
1957-73   *5in (12.7cm)*
£300-400   **FLD**

A Beswick pottery 'Galloway Bull', modelled by Arthur Gredington, silver dunn, fawn and brown, model no.1746C, printed marks.
1962-69   *4.5in (11.5cm) high*
£600-700   **HT**

A Beswick 'Connoisseur Cattle' series 'Hereford Bull', designed by Graham Tongue, matt, model no.A2542A, on a plinth base.
1976-89   *7.3in (18.5cm) high*
£120-180   **WHP**

A Beswick 'Connoisseur' series 'Charolais Bull', model no.A2600, on a wooden oval plinth.
£80-120   **FLD**

A CLOSER LOOK AT A BESWICK SHIRE MARE FIGURINE

This is a rare model particularly in the piebald colourway and harnessed.

The harnessed second version was produced from 1974-83. There are very few piebald examples known. The more common are brown and grey gloss.

A black gloss shire mare was commissioned by the Beswick Collectors Circle in 1990. Approximately 135 of these were issued with a gold backstamp.

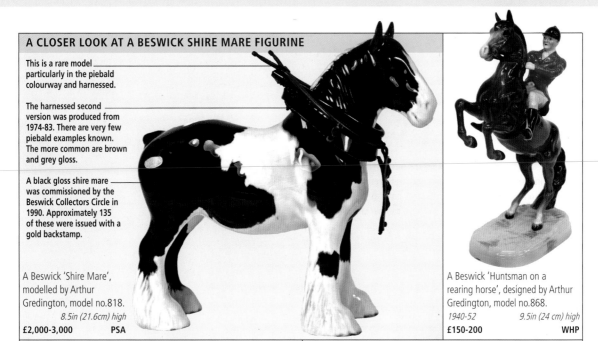

A Beswick 'Shire Mare', modelled by Arthur Gredington, model no.818.

8.5in (21.6cm) high

£2,000-3,000   **PSA**

A Beswick 'Huntsman on a rearing horse', designed by Arthur Gredington, model no.868.

1940-52   *9.5in (24 cm) high*

£150-200   **WHP**

A Beswick 'Foal', designed by Arthur Gredington, lying, palomino gloss-glazed, model no.915.

1961-89   3.25in (8.5cm) high

£10-20   **GAZE**

A small Beswick 'Shire Foal', designed by Arthur Gredington, rocking horse grey gloss-glazed, model no.1053.

This colourway is the rarest and most valuable version of this model.

c1947-62   5in (12.5cm) high

£500-600   **WHP**

A Beswick pottery 'Canadian Mountie', modelled by Arthur Gredlington, model no.1375.

1955-76   8.25in (21cm) high

£400-500   PSA

A Beswick 'Canadian Mounted Cowboy', designed by Mr Orwell, palomino gloss-glazed, model no.1377.

1955-73   7.5in (22cm) high

£600-800   PSA

A Beswick 'Indian on Skewbald Horse', modelled by Mr. Orwell, with unusual satin matt glaze and Indian dress, different colourway, model no.1391, restored leg.

8.5in (21.6cm) high

£250-350   PSA

CERAMICS

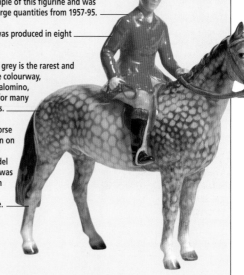

A Beswick 'Huntsman', designed by Arthur Gredington, upon a grey gloss horse, wearing a green jacket, model no.1501, restored.

1962-75   *8.25in (21cm) high*

£250-300   **FLD**

A Beswick 'Huntsman', designed by Arthur Gredington, on a brown horse, model no.1501.

1957-95   *8.25in (20.5cm) high*

£70-100

and a 'Foxhound', designed by Graham Tongue, second version, thin legs and tail, gloss, model no.2265.

1969-97   *2.75in (7cm) high*

£10-15   **WHP**

A CLOSER LOOK AT A BESWICK 'HUNTSMAN'

The gloss brown colourway (see the other example on the left) is the most common example of this figurine and was produced in large quantities from 1957-95.

The figurine was produced in eight colourways.

Rocking horse grey is the rarest and most desirable colourway, followed by palomino, which is true for many other figurines.

The rocking horse grey Huntsman on rearing horse, style one, model no.868 which was produced from c1940-52 is extremely rare.

A Beswick 'Huntswoman', modelled by Arthur Gredington, on a white horse, style two, model no.1730.

1960-71   *8.25in (22cm) high*

£100-150   **WHP**

A Beswick 'Huntsman', designed by Arthur Gredington, rocking-horse grey, gloss-glazed, standing, style two, model no.1501.

c1958-62   *8.25in (21cm) high*

£3,000-4,000   **TEN**

A Beswick 'Connoisseur Horses' series 'Bedouin Arab' on horseback, designed by Albert Hallam, chestnut matt-glazed, model no.2275.

1970-75   *11.5in (29cm) high*

£1,000-1,500   **CHT**

A Beswick 'Connoisseur' series 'Ann Moore on Psalm', model no.2535, with wooden plinth.

£250-350   **FLD**

A Beswick 'Spirit of Earth', designed by Graham Tongue, bay, matt, model no.2914, with wooden plinth.

1987-89   *8.5in (21.5cm) high*

£20-30   **WHP**

A Beswick 'Leghorn Cockerel', designed by
Arthur Gredington, model no.1892.

1963-83   *9.5in (24cm) high*
£120-180   **WHP**

A Beswick 'Sussex Cockerel', modelled by
Arthur Gredington, model no.1899, impressed
and printed mark.

1963-71   *7.25in (18.5cm) high*
£500-600   **HT**

A Beswick 'Gamecock', modelled by Arthur
Gredington, model no.2059.

1966-75   *9.5in (24cm) high*
£350-450   **HT**

A Beswick 'Pair of Pheasants', modelled by Arthur Gredington, model
no.2078, moulded mark.

1966-75   *6.75in (16.5cm) high*
£150-200   **HT**

A pair of Beswick boar and sow figures, (right) Wessex saddleback sow
'Merrywood Silver Wings 56th', designed by Colin Melbourne, model
no.1511.

1957-69   *6in (15cm) long,*
and (left) 'Champion Wall Boy 53rd', gloss, designed by Arthur
Gredington, model no.1453A, with original label.

1956-98   *7in (17.5cm) long*
£200-300   **DW**

A Beswick 'Hare', modelled
by Arthur Gredington,
seated, tan gloss, model
no.1025.

A Beswick 'Connoisseur' series 'Puma on a Rock', designed by Arthur
Gredington, in a matt finish, model no.1702.

1945-63   *7in (17.8cm) high*   *1970-73*   *8in (20cm) high*
£500-600   **PSA**   **£45-60**   **FLD**

CERAMICS

A Beswick Beatrix Potter 'Head Gardener', modelled by Shane Ridge, model no.BP11A, boxed.
2002
£110-150   **PSA**

A Beswick/Royal Albert Beatrix Potter 'Tom Kitten', designed by Arthur Gredington, first version in small size, second variation with light blue outfit, model no.1100.
c1980-99   *3.5in (9cm) high*
£25-40   **CHEF**

A Beswick Beatrix Potter 'Timmy Tiptoes' squirrel, designed by Arthur Gredington, brown-grey and red gloss-glazed, first variation with red jacket, backstamp 1a, model no.1101.
1948-c1980   *3.75in (9.5cm) high*
£90-110   **CHT**

A Beswick Beatrix Potter 'Mr Jeremy Fisher', modelled by Arthur Gredington, brown spots on head and legs, lilac coat, back stamp BP2, model no.1157, some restoration.
3in (7.6cm) high
£50-80   **PSA**

A rare Beswick Beatrix Potter 'Tommy Brock', modelled by Graham Orwell, with blue jacket, pink waistcoat, and yellow trousers, back stamp BP1, model no.1348, professionally restored handle.

Until c1972 the eye patches curved inward towards the centre of the forehead and had a feathery appearance.
1955-73   *3.5in (8.9cm) high*
£300-600   **PSA**

Judith Picks

This is a great example of an object whose unpopularity when it was released has led it to become extremely collectable now. 'The Duchess holding flowers' was designed by Graham Orwell in 1955. Most Beatrix Potter figures were painted in pale pastel shades and that is what the buyers expected. This rather 'clumpy' black gloss dog (or is it really a cat?) was produced for a short period and did not sell very well. With its odd stance, it was also prone to break. This rarity explains the high price.

A Beswick Beatrix Potter black gloss-glazed 'Duchess' dog, style one with flowers, model no.1355.
3.75in (9.5cm) high
£1,000-1,500   **CHT**

A Beswick Beatrix Potter 'Duchess' dog, with pie, designed by Graham Tongue, black, blue, and brown, model no.2601.

1979-82   *4in (10cm) high*
£150-200   **CHT**

A Beswick Beatrix Potter 'Anna Maria' mouse, designed by Albert Hallam, blue and white gloss-glazed, model no.1851.

1963-83   *3.5in (9cm) high*
£50-70   **PSA**

A Beswick/Royal Albert Beatrix Potter 'Little Pig Robinson Spying', designed by Ted Chawner, blue, white, and rose-pink gloss-glazed, model no.3031.

1987-93   *3.5in (9cm) high*
£35-45   **CHT**

A Beswick Beatrix Potter 'Peter Rabbit', designed by Martyn Alcock, second version in large size, first variation with yellow buttons, model no.3356.

1993-97   *7in (18cm) high*
£40-60   **TRI**

A Beswick 'Susie Jamaica', modelled by Mr. Orwell, gold script title to base, model no.1347, shield mark.

1954-75   *7in (18cm) high*
£100-150   **FLD**

A Beswick Kitty McBride 'Family Mouse', designed by Graham Tongue, brown, mauve, turquoise, light and dark-green gloss-glazed, model no.2526.

1975-83   *3.5in (9cm) high*
£15-25   **PSA**

A Beswick Thelwell 'An Angel on Horseback' horse, designed by Harry Sales, modelled by David Lyttleton, grey, brown, and yellow gloss-glazed, first variation with grey horse, model no.2704A.

1982-89   *4.5in (11.5cm) high*
£100-150   **PSA**

A Beswick 'Rupert and his Friends' 'Rupert Snowballing', designed by Harry Sales, red, yellow, and white gloss-glazed, model no.2779.

1982-86   *4.25in (11cm) high*
£120-180   **PSA**

CERAMICS

QUICK REFERENCE - BLUE & WHITE TRANSFER-PRINTED WARES

- The transfer-printed process was developed in the mid-18thC as an alternative to hand-painting decoration onto ceramics. It was quicker and cheaper as the design was engraved onto a copper plate which was covered in ink, which was then transferred to the ceramics body using paper. The design was then sealed under a clear glaze.
- An underglaze cobalt blue glaze was used because, at the time, it was the only one that could withstand the heat of the kiln. This, and the use of glazes containing lead oxide, gave the wares their characteristic deep colour.
- To tell whether a piece was decorated with transfer-printing or by hand, look closely at the design. If it was transfer-printed you will be able to see the cross-hatching or dots created by the engraving on the copper plate. The transfer-printed pattern will also lack the lines and slightly raised profile created by a pattern that has been painted with a brush. You may even be able to see a join where the edges of different transfer sheets failed to match.
- From the 19thC onwards, transfer-printing was used by many factories to create ceramics for the growing middle classes and for the wealthy to furnish their staff quarters.

Factories using the process included Worcester, Spode, Davenport, and Copeland & Garrett, but many are unknown.
- The pattern, shape, or a combination of the two determine the value of a piece. Common items that would have been bought in large quantities, such as dinner plates, tend to be less valuable, unless they are decorated with a rare pattern. Rare and desirable shapes include baby feeders and complete tureens on stands. The 'Willow' pattern is possibly the most common and although it is popular, prices tend to be low unless the shape is rare. Scarce – and therefore valuable – patterns include Spode's 'Indian Sporting' series and 'The Durham Ox'.
- If you are looking to start a collection of blue and white transfer-printed wares, now is a good time to buy. Prices for all but exceptionally rare pieces have remained low for the past 10 to 15 years. If collecting these pieces becomes fashionable again, prices will rise. Avoid damaged pieces (unless they are extremely rare and you can get a good price) and anything with a brown stain (which cannot be removed). Large items such as meat plates, which show patterns well, are a good buy if you want something with visual impact.

An early 19thC Rogers meat platter, printed with the 'Monopteros' pattern.

The Monopteros is the remains of an ancient building near Firoz Shah's Cotilla in Delhi. The pattern was based on Thomas Daniell's 'Oriental Scenery' aquatints. A similar version by the Swansea Pottery contains two oxen, mountains in the background, and a fruiting tree on the left.

21in (53cm) wide

£250-350   GORL

A Don Pottery meat dish, 'Named Italian Views' series, printed with the 'Cascade at Isola' pattern within the usual border of flowers and flying putti, unmarked, minor crazing at one end of well.

c1820-30   *17in (42.5cm) long*

£500-600   DN

A Minton meat dish, printed with a scene identified as Castle Gantully in Perthshire, 'English Scenery' series, printed series title mark.

This is a rare pattern. See Priestman 7.29 and 7.30 for a similar well-and-tree dish and the original source print.

c1825-35   *18.5in (47.5cm) long*

£800-900   DN

A Brameld well and tree meat dish, decorated with the 'Castle of Rochfort' pattern of figures in a European landscape, of slightly lobed ovoid shape, impressed no.20.

c1825   *20.5in (52cm) wide*

£100-150   MOR

A Spode rectangular dish or stand, 'Caramanian' series, printed with Caramanian Castle, of deeper than usual form, impressed lower-case mark.

8.5in (22cm) long

£600-700   DN

A Spode meat dish, 'Aesop's Fables' series, printed with the 'The Dog in the Manger' pattern, printed title mark with 'SPODE' and impressed upper-case mark, broken and glued.

18.5in (47cm) long

£80-120   DN

A pearlware plate, printed with the 'Beemaster' pattern, the rim panelled with animals alternating with flowers.

10in (25.5cm) diam

£300-350   PC

A Thomas Godwin plate, 'Indian Scenery' series, printed with 'Supseya Chart, Khanpore', printed title mark.

c1840-45   *10.25in (26cm) diam*

£80-120   PC

A Spode soup plate, 'Indian Sporting' series, printed with the 'Chase After A Wolf' pattern, with impressed and printed factory marks to reverse, with blue printed title.

c1820   *9in (24cm) diam*

£90-120   TOV

A Spode dinner plate, 'Indian Sporting' series, printed with the 'Death of the Bear' pattern, with impressed and printed factory marks to reverse, with blue-printed title.

c1820   *10in (25cm) diam*

£130-180   TOV

An early 19thC Spode vegetable tureen and cover, 'Indian Sporting' series, titled 'HOG-HUNTERS MEETING BY SURPRISE A TIGRESS & HER CUBS', printed and impressed marks.

9.5in (24cm) wide

£600-700   DN

CERAMICS

QUICK REFERENCE - DECORATION

- Initially, the decoration on 18thC blue and white transfer-printed wares was based on Chinese designs. However, the trade boom that followed the Napoleonic Wars in 1815 saw a new fashion for British, European, Indian, and US scenes. Most views were taken from popular books of topographical prints of Britain, Italy, India, and the US.

- From c1812 to 1860 the Staffordshire potteries exported more than 40 per cent of their blue and white transfer-printed wares to the US. Many of these pieces were made specifically for the American market. The majority of these used a very dark blue underglaze colour and many feature American views and patriotic subjects. The value of a piece will depend on its rarity and condition. Obscure subjects tend to be the most valuable. As with many collectables, views that were not particularly successful at the time can now command a premium.

A 19thC Staffordshire plate, printed with the 'Harvard College' pattern.

10in (25.5cm) diam

£150-200   **POOK**

A 19thC Staffordshire toddy plate, printed with the 'Church in the City of New York' pattern.

6.25in (16cm) diam

£250-300   **POOK**

A 19thC Staffordshire plate, printed with the 'Wright's Ferry on the Susquehanna' pattern.

9in (23cm) diam

£350-400   **POOK**

A 19thC Staffordshire plate, printed with a 'View on the Way to Lake George', impressed 'Stevenson'.

8.75in (22cm) diam

£450-500   **POOK**

A 19thC Staffordshire reticulated basket and undertray, 'Historical' series, printed with the 'Boston State House' pattern.

10.5in (26.7cm) wide

£400-450   **POOK**

A 19thC Staffordshire small platter, printed with the 'Arms of Massachusetts' pattern, impressed 'T. Mayer'.

9.5in (24cm) wide

£3,000-3,500   **POOK**

A 19thC Staffordshire relish dish, 'Historical' series, printed with the 'Boston State House' pattern.

6in (15.2cm) wide

£600-700   **POOK**

A 19thC rare Staffordshire coffee pot, 'Historical' series, printed with the 'Commodore MacDonnough's Victory' pattern.

11in (28cm) high

£500-600   **POOK**

A 19thC Staffordshire small bowl, 'Historical' series, printed with the 'City Hall, New York' pattern.

6.5in (16.5cm) wide

£250-300   **POOK**

A 19thC Staffordshire pitcher, 'Historical' series, printed with the 'Views of the Erie Canal' pattern, with a basin printed with the 'Erie Canal View of the Aqueduct Bridge at Little Falls', impressed 'Wood & Sons'.

basin 12.25in (31cm) diam

£500-600   **POOK**

A 19thC Staffordshire mustard jar, 'Historical' series, printed with the 'Catskill Mountains Hudson River/Castle Garden Battery New York' pattern.

Mustard jars are rare and this is a desirable print.

2.75in (7cm) high

£700-800   **POOK**

A 19thC Staffordshire handled cup, 'Historical' series, printed with the 'Catskill Mountains at The Hudson River' oattern.

£200-250   **POOK**

A 19thC Staffordshire sugar bowl, printed with the 'Boston State House' pattern, impressed 'Rogers'.

5in (12.5cm) high

£350-450   **POOK**

A 19thC Staffordshire leaf dish, 'Historical' series, printed with the 'Boston State House' pattern.

5.75in (14.6cm) wide

£250-300   **POOK**

A 19thC Staffordshire tureen ladle, 'Historical' series, printed with the 'Hoboken' pattern.

Tureen ladles are rare. Their fragile shape meant that many were broken. Always check for restoration as that reduces value considerably.

9.5in (24cm) long

£1,000-1,200   **POOK**

CERAMICS

QUICK REFERENCE - BOCH FRÈRES

- The Keramis pottery was founded by Boch Frères at La Louvière in Belgium in 1841. By the early 20thC it had become a well-established producer of domestic faïence (tin-glazed earthenware) and grès (stoneware). However, the pottery's focus shifted to artistic wares after Frenchman Charles Catteau (1880–1966) joined the firm in 1906 and became its artistic director in 1907 (a position he held for 42 years). His success brought greater success to the company. Catteau had been an apprentice at the Sèvres porcelain factory in France, and also worked for the Nymphenburg factory in Germany. His early Boch Frères designs were mostly vases decorated in the Art Nouveau style. However his greatest success was the Art Deco pieces he created from the early to mid-1920s until the later 1930s. These were sold by prestigious stores and galleries around the world and are highly sought-after today.

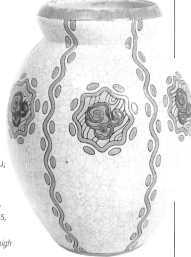

A Boch Frères Keramis vase, designed by Charles Catteau, pattern no.D.1208, painted with stylized crocus flowers on a crackled-white ground, printed and painted marks.

12.5in (31.5cm) high

£150-250   WW

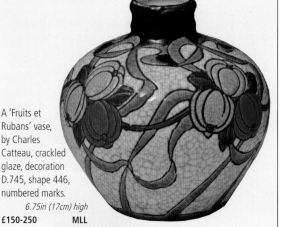

A 'Fruits et Rubans' vase, by Charles Catteau, crackled glaze, decoration D.745, shape 446, numbered marks.

6.75in (17cm) high

£150-250   MLL

A Boch Frères Keramis vase, designed by Charles Catteau, pattern no.D.750, painted with stylised flowerheads on a crackled-white ground, impressed and printed marks, facsimile signature.

13.75in (35cm) high

£400-500

A Boch Frères Keramis vase, the design attributed to Charles Catteau, pattern no.D.2854, shape no.909, painted with a band of birds amongst flowering foliage, printed and painted marks.

12.2in (31cm) high

£180-220   WW

A rare Boch Frères Keramis vase, designed by Charles Catteau, pattern no. D.2531, ovoid with collar rim, painted in enamels with exotic cranes, printed and painted marks.

9in (23cm) high

£1,200-1,500   WW

A Boch Frères Grès Keramis vase, designed by Charles Catteau, pattern no.D.771, painted with flowerhead roundels on a gun-metal grey ground, impressed, printed, and painted marks, facsimile signature.

10.75in (27cm) high

£150-250 **WW**

A Boch Frères Grès Keramis vase, designed by Charles Catteau, pattern no.D.914, decorated with panels of bell flowers on a crackled-white glaze, impressed, printed, and painted marks.

9.75in (24.5cm) high

£150-250 **WW**

A CLOSER LOOK AT A BOCH FRÈRES VASE

The hand-painted imagery depicts a stylized Classical imagery. Catteau's decoration was influenced by Cubism, modernism, abstract expressionism, and exotic pre-industrial cultures including Ancient Greek, African, and primitive Neolithic.

This example shows his confident use of colour with two bold shades juxtaposed against each other and outlined in gold. This contrasts with many other pieces where the hand-painted enamels are set strikingly against an off-white craquelure ground.

Most pieces are clearly marked, often with a she-wolf (louvière in French, the name of the town where the pottery was based). Many also have Catteau's signature impressed into the clay.

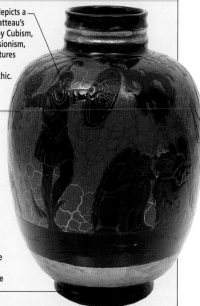

A Boch Frères Grès Keramis vase, designed by Charles Catteau, pattern no.E.2466, decorated with a chevron band in brown on a rust-coloured ground, impressed, printed, and painted marks, hand-painted signature.

8in (20cm) high

£100-150 **WW**

Many of Catteau's designs also display a pleasing symmetry.

A fine Boch Frères Keramis vase, 'Perseus and the Gorgons', designed by Charles Catteau, enamelled with warriors fighting the Gorgons, on a red-crackled glaze, highlighted in gilt, printed and painted marks.

14in (36cm) high

£900-1,200 **WW**

A large Boch Frères Keramis vase, designed by Charles Catteau, pattern no.D.2305, painted with a frieze of scrolling flowers and foliage, printed and painted marks, facsimile signature.

13.75in (35cm) high

£300-400 **WW**

A 1920s Charles Catteau Boch Frères Grès Keramis vase; decorated with grape clusters, marked 'Grès Keramis KERAMIS MADE IN BELGIUM 894/D642'.

8.75in (22cm) high

£800-1,000 **DRA**

A Boch Frères Grès Keramis stoneware vase, designed by Charles Catteau, pattern no.D.820, decorated with a band of scrolling foliage on a crackled-white ground, printed marks, 'Pomone' mark.

5in (13cm) high

£200-250 **WW**

CERAMICS

A limited edition Border Fine Arts figure, 'Having Ten', depicting a farmer resting with his dogs, B1079, number 22 of 950.

6.75in (17cm) high

£120-180   PSA

A limited edition Border Fine Arts figure, 'Out With The Dogs', depicting a farmer setting his dog on rabbits, A2648.

11in (30cm) high

£100-150   PSA

A Border Fine Arts figure, 'Large Sitting Great Dane', B1291.

10.25in (26cm) high

£40-50   PSA

A limited edition Border Fine Arts figure, 'Blackie Tup Ewe' on hilltop, B0354.

9in (23cm) high

£120-180   PSA

A limited edition Border Fine Arts figure, 'Loading Sheep Into a Car', 1850.

4.75in (12cm) high

£120-180   PSA

A limited edition Border Fine Arts figure, 'Warey', depicting a very large hare, B1298, number 62 of 150.

19.75in (50cm) high

£250-300   PSA

A Border Fine Arts figure, 'Three Otters On A Log'.

6in (15cm) high

£40-50   PSA

A Border Fine Arts figure, 'A Watchful Eye', depicting an owl and three chicks, S0C8.

6.25in (16cm) high

£20-50   PSA

A Border Fine Arts figure, 'Lunch At The Savoy', depicting chickens eating lettuce, B0441.

6in (15cm) high

£20-50   PSA

QUICK REFERENCE - CARLTON WARE

● Carlton Ware is a trade name used by the Wiltshaw & Robinson company (founded 1890) in Stoke from the mid-1890s. The pottery produced tablewares, earthenware, and crested souvenir-type wares. The company's output underwent a revolution in 1918 when Frederick Cuthbert Wiltshaw, the son of the founder, took over. Having seen the success of Wedgwood's lustre ware ranges, he launched a similar product. The Carlton Ware lustre range features flowers in more than twelve different colours, animals and birds, and Oriental and Egyptian motifs. The influence of the 1925 Paris Exhibition can been seen in geometric, stylized designs. Collectors look for larger pieces – especially wall plaques, chargers and vases – which display the patterns well. A simpler 'Handcraft' range was introduced in the late 1920s. Its matte glazes and floral designs were less time-consuming to produce. Another innovation was the first 'oven to table' ceramics introduced in 1929. Other popular ranges include the naturally coloured tablewares modelled on two-dimensional flowers and fruit and salad leaves and the 1950s 'Royal' lustre range. These are generally less valuable today. Carlton Ware's last popular success was the 'Walking Ware' range of tablewares in the 1960s. The company also used the 'Crown China' mark. The name became Carlton Ware Ltd in 1958 and various manufacturers now make limited edition pieces under license.

A 1930s Carlton Ware 'Fantasia' vase, decorated with a large exotic bird with its wings outstretched amid stylized foliage, all to a blue ground, printed script mark.

7in (18cm) high

£550-650   **FLD**

A Carlton Ware 'Forest Tree' vase, with flared neck decorated with stylizised trailing trees with orange foliage against a sponged-blue ground, printed script mark, restored.

11in (28cm) high

£150-200   **FLD**

A Carlton Ware 'Secretary Bird' ovoid vase, gilt line transfer and enamel-decorated with stylized exotic bird amidst stylized trailing trees and large flower heads, all to a ruby lustre ground, printed marks.

7.5in (19cm) high

£500-550   **FLD**

A Carlton Ware 'Fan' footed vase, decorated with enamel and gilt panels above stylized flower heads all to a red ground, printed script mark.

10in (25cm) high

£400-500   **FLD**

A 1930s Carlton Ware 'Fan' bomb-shape vase, decorated with enamel and gilt motifs against a deep-blue ground, printed script mark, restored.

This is a rare shape and highly desirable pattern, but it has been restored, which has reduced the value by over 50%.

10in (25cm) high

£150-200   **FLD**

CERAMICS

A 1930s Carlton Ware 'Mandarins Chatting' ginger jar base, decorated with enamel and gilt figures in conversation beneath a gilt trailing tree all to a black ground, printed script mark.

6in 915cm) high

£100-150   **FLD**

A 1930s Carlton Ware 'Nightingale' ginger jar and cover, decorated with an Art Deco enamel and gilt stylized bird amid stylized flowers, all to a blue ground, printed script mark.

6.25in (16cm) high

£250-300   **FLD**

A 1930s Carlton Ware 'Egyptian Fan' Art Deco single-handled flower jug, decorated with gilt and enamel fan motifs all to a red ground, printed marks.

7.5in (19cm) high

£500-700   **FLD**

A Carlton Ware 1930s 'Flower and Falling Leaf' Art Deco ginger jar and cover, decorated with gilt and enamel stylized flower heads and stems of lily of the valley against a mottled-green ground, printed script mark.

6.5in (17cm) high

£350-400   **FLD**

A 1930s Carlton Ware 'Needlepoint' Art Deco bowl, raised to three fin feet, the central well with enamel and gilt decoration against a sponged-blue ground, printed marks.

9in (23cm) diam

£300-350   **FLD**

A 1930s Carlton Ware 'Sketching Bird' Art Deco bowl, decorated to the interior with a gilt and enamel bird in flight against a stylized trailing tree and flower heads, all to a lemon-yellow ground, script mark.

9in (23cm) diam

£400-500   **FLD**

A Carlton Ware 'Sketching Bird' ginger jar and cover, decorated with a line transfer and enamel-decorated with a stylized bird in flight against trailing trees and foliage, all to a lemon-yellow ground, printed script mark.

6.5in (17cm) high

£200-300   **FLD**

A Carlton Ware vase, decorated with fish-moulded relief and sea plants with gilt and enamel fish.

5.2in (13cm)

£40-50   ECGW

A Carlton Ware vase, 'Sketching Bird' pattern.

6in (15.5cm) high

Est £80-100   LOC

A Carlton Ware dish, 'Anemone' pattern, with a green ground and gilt border.

10.4in (26.5cm) long

£40-50   LOC

A Carlton Ware 'Handcraft' dish, pattern no.4241, painted with geometric radiating designs, the rim gilt, printed and painted marks.

7in (18cm) diam

£180-220   WW

A Carlton Ware 'Melon' shape coffee set, 'Awakening', pattern no.3450, designed by Violet Elmer, with coffee pot and cover, milk-jug, sugar basin, six cups and saucers, printed script mark, painted marks.

c1931   *coffee pot 8.5in (21cm) high*

£2,000-3,000   PC

Judith Picks

We all love a baddie and Carlton Ware really captured that evil look. This 'Mephisto' figure is a striking design based on 'The Red Devil'. This motif was used on other highly popular Carlton Ware items such as chargers, mugs and vases from the 1930s onwards. He is most probably based on Mephistopheles – a character that originally appeared in the German legend of Faust, who often went by Mephisto as a nickname. The blue colourway is worth roughly the same. Still inexpensive, these might be a good investment.

A Carlton Ware 'Mephisto' character series figure, modelled by Andrew Moss, printed marks, numbered 311 of 500.

10in (25cm) high

£100-150   FLD

A Carlton Ware model of a policeman, designed by John Hassall, with articulated head, printed mark, facsimile signature, repaired damages.

5.7in (14.5cm) high

£100-150   WW

CERAMICS

ESSENTIAL REFERENCE - CLARICE CLIFF

- Clarice Cliff is one of Britain's most recognised and celebrated 20thC ceramics designers. Born in the heart of the Staffordshire potteries in 1899, she began her career as an apprentice enameller at the local Tunstall company of Linguard Webster & Co. in 1912. In 1916, she moved to the larger company of A.J. Wilkinson.
- She made great progress and drew the attention of the pottery's owner, Colley Shorter, who gave her her own studio in the recently acquired Newport Pottery in 1925. Showing her resourcefulness, she took defective blank wares and decorated them with handpainted, thickly applied bright colours in geometric and floral patterns, which hid the faults. The new range was given the name 'Bizarre' and was launched in 1928.
- The range proved extremely popular and was produced until 1935. 'Bizarre' does not indicate any one pattern or shape, but was applied to the whole range of designs as a general title. 'Fantasque', used as a title from 1928-34, is similar. Cliff trained a group of dedicated female decorators, who became known as The Bizarre Girls. As well as continuing to introduce new patterns, she also introduced a range of new, fashionable shapes from the mid-1920s onwards.
- Patterns included stylised floral designs, stylised landscapes, abstract shapes and geometric forms. Some are rarer or more desirable than others. Many patterns were produced in different colours and some are rarer than others. Orange is commonly found, with pastels and blue and purple being scarcer. The Bizarre Girls had some freedom to vary designs, and variations in terms of colour or pattern will usually be of great interest.

A Clarice Cliff vase, shape no.265.
c1929   *6in (15.5cm) high*
£150-200   **WW**

A Clarice Cliff bud vase, 'Orange Roof Cottage' pattern, shape no.186, hand-painted with a stylised cottage and bridge landscape between black, orange, and yellow banding, with 'Fantasque' and 'Bizarre' mark.

Cliff's landscape designs featuring trees and buildings are highly popular with collectors.
c1932   *6in (15cm) high*
£800-900   **FLD**

A Clarice Cliff vase, 'Blue Autumn' or 'Balloon trees' pattern, shape no.265, with printed 'Bizarre' marks.
c1930   *8in (20.5cm) high*
£400-500   **L&T**

A Clarice Cliff vase, 'Blue Chintz' pattern, shape no.265, painted in colours between green and blue bands, with printed 'Fantasque Bizarre' marks.
6.25in (15.5cm) high
£250-300   **WW**

A Clarice Cliff vase, 'Inspiration Caprice' pattern, shape no.265, in a Latona glaze, painted marks 'Inspiration Bizarre by Clarice Cliff, Newport Pottery, Burslem, England'.

'Caprice' was the most popular pattern in the 'Inspiration' glaze range. Due to the volatility of the matte glazes, a separate, small team of 'Bizarre Girl' decorators was created and trained by Cliff to specialise in this range. Look out for the 'Knight Errant' pattern, featuring a knight on horseback in front of a castle as this is unusual and rare.
c1930   *6.25in (15.5cm) high*
£1,200-1,500   **SWO**

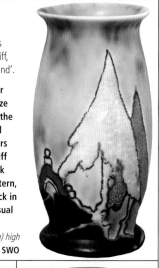

A Clarice Cliff 'Mei Ping' vase, 'Secrets' pattern, shape no.14, hand-painted with a stylised tree and cottage landscape between graduated green to brown banding, with 'Bizarre' mark, restored.

The Chinese inspired 'Mei Ping' shape was also produced as a lamp base.
c1933   *6in (15cm) high*
£400-500   **FLD**

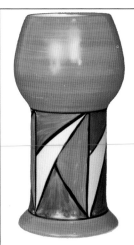

A CLOSER LOOK AT A CLARICE CLIFF VASE

The design of this vase is attributed to Clarice herself, and is one of the many new shapes she introduced from c1925-1939.

Art Deco in style, it was produced from c1928-c1933 in two sizes.

When it is 8in (20cm) high, it is shape no.268 and when it is 6in (15.5cm) high, it is shape no.269.

Produced from 1930, Autumn was produced in many colours - Red was the first produced and Blue and Pastel are two of the harder colours to find.

A Clarice Cliff vase, 'Double V' pattern, shape no.269, hand-painted with a band of stylised leaves and chevrons between black, orange, and green banding, with 'Bizarre' mark.
c1929   *6in (15cm) high*
£500-600   **FLD**

A Clarice Cliff vase, 'Green Autumn' pattern, shape no.269, hand-painted with a stylised tree and cottage landscape with black and blue banding, with printed 'Fantasque' and 'Bizarre' mark.
c1930   *6in (15cm) high*
£650-750   **FLD**

A Clarice Cliff vase, 'Secrets' or 'Seven Colourway' pattern, shape no.358, hand-painted with a stylised tree and cottage landscape between orange and black banding, with printed 'Fantasque' and 'Bizarre' marks.

In production from 1929-c1936, this vase was produced in one size only and was designed by Clarice. The ribbed neck and the bulbous base were inverted to produce shape no.362, in production for the same period.
c1933   *8in (20cm) high*
£850-950   **FLD**

A Clarice Cliff vase, 'Melon' or 'Picasso fruit' pattern, shape no.365, of facetted outline with inverted rim, with printed 'Fantasque' mark.

'Melon' was produced 1930-32 and orange is the most commonly found colourway.
8in (20.5cm) high
£600-700   **L&T**

A Clarice Cliff vase, 'Melon' or 'Picasso fruit' pattern, of lozenge outline with everted rim, with printed 'Fantasque' mark.
c1930   *8in (20cm) high*
£500-600   **L&T**

A Clarice Cliff vase, 'Pastel Autumn' pattern, painted in colours between pink, blue and green, with printed 'Bizarre Tolphin' factory marks.
10in (25cm) high
£1,000-1,500   **WW**

CERAMICS

ESSENTIAL REFERENCE - LOTUS JUGS

● The 'Lotus' jug is one of the most characteristic shapes associated with Clarice Cliff. Despite this, it was actually designed in 1919 by her predecessor at Wilkinson's, John Butler, as part of a jug and bowl wash stand set. The simple form was intended to suggest Antiquity, and it was produced with one or two handles, or no handles. Some examples are stamped 'LOTUS' or 'ISIS', the original name of the shape. Today collectors call examples with no handles the 'Isis' vase. At the time, examples with handles were classed as functional rather than decorative wares, so attracted a lower tax. Their popularity means fakes abound - the simplest way to identify one is to look at the inside edge of the handle. If a hole is found, it is a reproduction or fake. Values vary depending on the pattern and condition - this example is a scarce and desirable pattern.

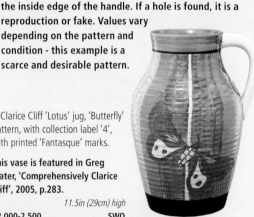

A Clarice Cliff 'Lotus' jug, 'Butterfly' pattern, with collection label '4', with printed 'Fantasque' marks.

This vase is featured in Greg Slater, 'Comprehensively Clarice Cliff', 2005, p.283.

11.5in (29cm) high

£2,000-2,500   SWO

A Clarice Cliff twin-handled 'Lotus' jug, 'Limberlost' pattern, hand-painted with a stylised garden landscape with tree and flowering bushes, with 'Bizarre' mark.

c1932   *11.5in (29cm) high*

£850-900   FLD

A Clarice Cliff vase, 'Forest Glen' pattern, shape no.702, with a 'Delecia' streaked glaze, with moulded mark.

c1936   *9in (22.5cm) high*

£280-340   SWO

A Clarice Cliff 'Archaic' vase, 'Sunburst' pattern, shape no.374, hand-painted with a radial sun burst motif in yellow, orange, and red between black and orange banding, with 'Bizarre' back stamp, small chip to the base.

c1930   *12in (30cm) high*

£1,800-2,200   FLD

A Clarice Cliff flower vase, 'Blue Autumn' or 'Balloon trees' pattern, shape no.187/1, of tapered form with bulbous base, printed 'Bizarre' marks.

c1930   *8.75in (22cm) high*

£450-550   L&T

A Clarice Cliff vase, 'Coral Firs' pattern, shape no.566, painted in colours between yellow and brown bands, with printed factory 'Bizarre' mark.

6.25in (16cm) high

£500-600   WW

A Clarice Cliff double 'Conical' bowl, 'Castellated Circle' pattern, shape no.380, hand-painted with a repeat band of stepped lines and circles with green, black, and orange banding, with 'Fantasque' mark, heavily restored.

Although this is a rarer pattern than the other example on this page, the damage and extensive restoration has reduced the value by over two thirds. This complex to make form is very desirable.

c1930   7in (18cm) high
£650-750   FLD

A Clarice Cliff double 'Conical' bowl, 'Oranges' pattern, shape no.380, hand-painted with panels of stylised fruit and foliage with orange banding, with 'Bizarre' mark, slight damage and chips.

c1931   6.75in (17cm) high
£1,400-1,800   FLD

Judith Picks

This vase combines so much of what is loved about Clarice and would make either an eye-catching stand-alone statement piece or a superb addition to a collection. The geometric Art Deco form is scarce, the bright orange is a hallmark colour for Clarice, and the presence of a curving tree made up of rounded forms is typical of her patterns. The form was produced from 1931-c1935 in one size and was designed by Clarice herself. Clarice's competitor Myott produced a similar vase, but it has less pronounced, curving buttresses terminating with a hole for flowers. 'Windbells', produced from 1933, is also always popular with collectors.

A Clarice Cliff 'Stamford' vase, 'Windbells' pattern, shape no.460, hand-painted with a stylised tree against wave-effect sky and orange banding, with 'Bizarre' mark.

c1933   6in (15cm) high
£750-850   FLD

A Clarice Cliff stepped cylinder vase, 'Delecia Citrus' pattern, hand-painted with stylised fruit and foliage over a dripped 'Delecia' ground, printed 'Delecia' and 'Bizarre' marks.

This form is reminiscent of the new skyscrapers that were being erected in cities like New York. They were a recurring theme within Art Deco. At the time, this more geometric style was known as 'Art Moderne'.

c1933   7in (17.5cm) high
£600-700   FLD

A Clarice Cliff 'Double D' vase with applied foot, unknown pattern, shape no.465, hand-painted in an unknown abstract floral below 'Patina' ground, printed 'Patina' and 'Bizarre' mark.

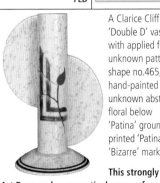

This strongly Art Deco and comparatively scarce form was produced from 1931-c1934 in one size. Always examine the edges carefully for damage.

c1932   8in (20cm) high
£850-950   FLD

A Clarice Cliff flower bowl, 'Secrets' pattern, shape no.515, of footed square section with fin handles, hand-painted with a stylised tree and cottage landscape with matched banding, with 'Bizarre' mark.

c1933   5in (12.5cm) high
£550-650   FLD

CERAMICS

A Clarice Cliff vase, 'Double V' pattern, with printed 'Bizarre' marks, worn.

3in (7.5cm) high

£200-250   **SWO**

A Clarice Cliff vase, 'Picasso' pattern, with printed 'Bizarre' marks and impressed '3'.

2.75in (7cm) high

£250-300   **SWO**

A Clarice Cliff fern pot, 'Chester' pattern, with printed 'Original Bizarre' marks.

3.5in (9cm) high

£120-150   **SWO**

A Clarice Cliff sugar bowl, 'Sunrise' pattern, with printed 'Fantasque' marks.

2in (4.5cm) high

£120-150   **SWO**

A Clarice Cliff large octagonal fruit bowl, 'Windbells' pattern, hand-painted with a stylised tree landscape with tonal orange to green banding, printed 'Fantasque' and 'Bizarre' marks.

8.25in (21cm) wide

c1933

£200-250   **FLD**

A Clarice Cliff fruit bowl, 'Idyll' pattern, with printed 'Bizarre' marks.

8in (20.5cm) wide

£100-150   **SWO**

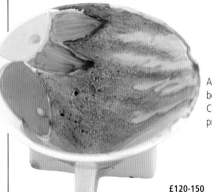

A Clarice Cliff sugar bowl, 'Delecia Citrus' pattern, with printed marks.

1.5in (4cm) high

£120-150   **SWO**

A Clarice Cliff 'Conical' bowl with decorated 'penny' feet, 'Green Erin' pattern, shape no.383, hand-painted with a stylised flowering tree with graduated green banding, with 'Bizarre' mark, restored.

With its disc feet, this is a very scarce and strongly Art Deco form. It is part of the highly desirable 'Conical' range, designed by Clarice Cliff, which also includes a coffee set with the coffee pot and cups having angular handles that reflect the angular form of the bowl.

c1933

9.25in (23.5cm) wide

£600-700   **FLD**

Mark Picks

Focusing on plates can be one of the most rewarding ways of collecting Clarice Cliff. They are often affordable as more of them were made and have survived than other shapes. This is because original buyers would have bought more plates than they would have other items such as a vase or a coffee pot. As a result, they are plentiful in the marketplace today. As well as the many patterns, there is also a range of forms to look out for. They also display the pattern extremely well and make an appealing visual display when arranged together on a shelf or wall. As many buyers of antiques are moving towards an increasingly decorative way of collecting, this aspect is becoming more important. 'Tennis', painted entirely freehand, is a desirable and comparatively scarce pattern.

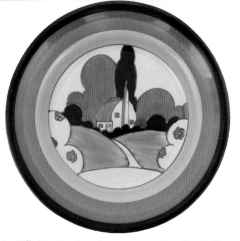

A Clarice Cliff dish, 'Sliced Fruit' pattern, with printed 'Bizarre' marks.

9in (23cm) diam

£200-300   SWO

A Clarice Cliff small side plate, 'Tennis' pattern, hand-painted with an abstract panel design within red, black, and yellow banding, with 'Bizarre' mark.

c1930   6in (15cm) diam

£300-350   FLD

A Clarice Cliff plate, 'Farmhouse' pattern, painted in colours inside yellow, orange, and black bands, with printed 'Fantasque Bizarre' factory mark.

9in (22.5cm) diam

£250-300   WW

A Clarice Cliff octagonal side plate, radially hand-painted with a star burst and triangle design in rust red, green, blue, and purple, rust-red 'Bizarre' and 'Newport Pottery' mark only.

c1928   5.75in (14.5cm) wide

£150-200   FLD

A Clarice Cliff octagonal plate, 'Whisper' pattern, hand-painted with stylised abstract leaf forms, with large 'Bizarre' mark.

c1929   8.5in (21.5cm) wide

£180-220   FLD

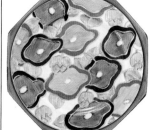

A Clarice Cliff octagonal plate, 'Blue Chintz' pattern, impressed mark for February 1932, 'Bizarre' printed marks and painted 'A'.

1932   9.5in (24cm) wide

£100-150   SWO

A Clarice Cliff plate, 'Idyll' pattern, with 'Bizarre' marks.

1935   9in (23cm) wide

£180-220   SWO

CERAMICS

Miller's Compares

This set contains both a teapot and a coffee pot, as well as a milk jug, sugar bowl and six cups & saucers (not shown), so is a truly complete set.

The desirable 'Coral Firs' pattern, produced from 1933 and also found in blue and green, is a more complex pattern that was time-consuming to create.

This shape is not as Art Deco in style as the other set, and is more traditional and so less appealing in form.

Although geometric and brightly coloured so typical of the Art Deco style, the pattern is not as instantly recognisable as 'Coral Firs' is.

A Clarice Cliff six-place tea and coffee service, 'Coral Firs' pattern, comprising six large 'Biarritz' shape tea cups with rectangular saucers, 'Bonjour' shape coffee pot, large 'Bonjour' shape teapot, large 'Bonjour' shape sugar bowl and jug, and a circular teapot stand, all hand-painted with a stylised tree-lined coastal landscape in tonal brown with matched banding, with 'Bizarre' and 'Biarritz' marks.

c1935

£2,500-3,000   **FLD**

A Clarice Cliff tankard coffee set for six, painted with triangles in purple and green, outlined in brown, comprising coffee pot and cover, six cans and saucers, with printed 'Original Bizarre' factory marks, wear, finial re-stuck.

7.5in (19cm) high

£300-400   **WW**

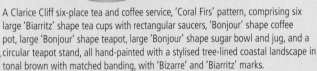

A Clarice Cliff bachelor tea service, 'Peony' pattern, 'Bonjour' shape, marked with Wilkinson, Royal Staffordshire mark.

Although popular with collectors today, the 'Bonjour' shape was produced from 1933-40 and was successful in its day, making it not too hard to find today. Early versions do not have a lip on the spout, so do not pour well!

£180-220   **ECGW**

A Clarice Cliff 'Globe' teapot and cover, 'Circle Tree' pattern, painted in colours, with printed 'Fantasque Bizarre' factory mark, minor professional restoration to spout.

The more traditional, less stylised 'Globe' shape was produced from 1927-c1936 in four sizes.

4.25in (10.5cm) high

£450-550   **WW**

A Clarice Cliff large 'Coronet' jug, 'Orange Roof Cottage' pattern, hand-painted with a stylised cottage landscape, with 'Bizarre' mark.

c1932   *8in (20cm) high*

£550-650   **FLD**

A Clarice Cliff 'Athens' jug, 'Blue Autumn' or 'Balloon Trees' pattern, with printed 'Bizarre' marks.

c1930   *8.25in (21cm) high*

£550-600   **L&T**

A Clarice Cliff 'Crown' jug, 'Delecia Oranges' pattern, painted in colours, with printed 'Bizarre' factory mark.

7in (18cm) wide

£100-150　　　　　　　　　　　WW

A Clarice Cliff 'Daffodil' breakfast cup and saucer, 'Rudyard' pattern, moulded date code for 1933, with printed 'Bizarre' marks.

1933

£200-250　　　　　　　　　　　SWO

A Clarice Cliff 'Daffodil' preserve pot and cover, 'Bridgewater' pattern, with 'Bizarre' and '4' marks.

c1933　　4.75in (12cm) high

£450-500　　　　　　　　　　　FLD

A Clarice Cliff 'Duck' egg cruet, 'Umbrellas' pattern, with printed 'Fantasque' marks, and incised 741933.

Designed by Clarice Cliff and sold in 1929, this quirky and amusing set is extremely rare, particularly together with the egg cups.

6in (15.5cm) diam

£800-1,000　　　　　　　　　　SWO

A Clarice Cliff 'Conical' two-division toast rack, 'Limberlost' pattern, with printed 'Bizarre' mark and incised '10x'.

4.75in (12cm) wide

£150-200　　　　　　　　　　　SWO

A CLOSER LOOK AT A CLARICE CLIFF CENTREPIECE

Clarice Cliff's centrepieces were expensive in their day and tended to sell in small quantities each year, making them rare today.

Like Art Deco pressed glass centrepieces comprised of bowls and figurines, many such sets were bought as wedding gifts as they were deemed more of a 'luxury' item.

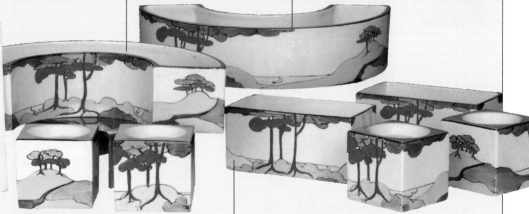

The original sales brochure is very rare and its inclusion has boosted the desirability, and the same can be said of the candleholders.

It is very rare to find a complete, intact set made up of so many pieces that have survived without damage.

A Clarice Cliff 'As you like it' table centre, 'Coral Firs' pattern, comprising two shape no.657 rectangular troughs, four shape no.658 cube candle sticks, and two shape no.659 semi-circular flower troughs, hand-painted with a stylised tree-lined coastal landscape with yellow banding, complete with the original sales brochure, with 'Bizarre' marks.

c1933

£3,000-3,500　　　　　　　　　　FLD

CERAMICS

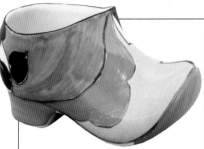

A Clarice Cliff clog, 'Feathers and Leaves' pattern, with printed 'Fantasque' marks.

5.5in (13.5cm)

£300-400 SWO

A Clarice Cliff clog, 'Crocus' pattern, with black printed marks.

Produced with some breaks from the late 1920s until 1963, 'Crocus' was the best-selling of Cliff's patterns, especially in this 'Autumn' colourway, making it easy to find today. As a result, the value of this example is less than the other example on this page. However, it makes a great focus for a collection as it was applied to so many different shapes.

6in (15cm) wide

£100-150 SWO

A pair of Clarice Cliff candlesticks, 'Solitude' pattern, shape no.310, with printed 'Bizarre' marks.

3.25in (8cm) high

£400-500 SWO

A pair of Clarice Cliff squat candlesticks, with painted geometric decoration, with 'Bizarre' marks.

4in (10.5cm) wide

£250-300 ECGW

A Clarice Cliff candlestick, 'Blue Firs' pattern, of stepped square form, with printed 'Bizarre' marks.

3.5in (8.5cm) wide

£300-400 SWO

A Clarice Cliff cigarette and match holder, 'Orange Roof Cottage' pattern, shape no.463, hand-painted with a stylised landscape with bridge, with 'Bizarre' mark.

Produced from 1931-38, this shape was adapted by Cliff from a design by Austrian architect and designer Josef Hoffman.

c1932 *1.75in (7cm) high*

£300-400 FLD

A Clarice Cliff powder puff bowl and cover, 'Bobbins' pattern, shape no.339, with 'Bizarre' mark.

5in (13cm) diam

£400-500 SWO

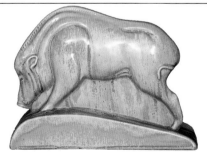

A Clarice Cliff stylised figure of a wild boar, in walking pose, raised to a domed base, picked out in tonal green glaze, with script signature.

9.5in (24cm) wide

£400-500 FLD

QUICK REFERENCE - DENNIS CHINAWORKS

- The Dennis Chinaworks was founded in Somerset, England, in 1993 by Sally and Richard Dennis.
- Sally (b.1938) studied at Walthamstow Art School and Royal College of Art and, as Sally Tuffin, launched fashion house Foale & Tuffin with Marion Foale. The company went on to epitomise the look of 1960s 'swinging' London. Foale and Tuffin closed in 1972.
- Richard trained with Sotheby's before establishing an antique glass and ceramic business and a publishing house producing books for collectors.
- In 1985 the couple started Dennis Chinaworks, but a year later Richard bought a stake in the Moorcroft pottery. Sally joined him there as a partner and design director until 1993.
- Sally left Moorcroft to concentrate on Dennis Chinaworks. There she works with a small, in-house team to throw and decorate all the wares by hand. Her designs for both companies focus on natural subjects such as plants and animals. Many are made in limited editions of varying sizes.
- Collectors will pay a premium for unique and trial pieces, limited editions of less than 50, and classic or complex patterns.
- Dennis Chinaworks has created commissions for many prestigious galleries, museums and organisations including the Royal Academy of Arts, Victoria & Albert Museum, British Museum, National Portrait Gallery and the Courtauld Gallery.

A Dennis Chinaworks 'Salmon' vase, designed by Sally Tuffin, painted in colours, impressed and painted marks.

1999   *8.5in (21.5cm) high*

£180-220   **WW**

A Dennis Chinaworks 'Pelican' vase, designed by Sally Tuffin, painted in colours on a pale-blue ground, impressed and painted marks, dated.

2000   *11.5in (29cm) high*

£250-350   **WW**

A Dennis China Works 'Eagle' 'Trial' vase, designed by Sally Tuffin, impressed 'RMc 2000d' and inscribed 'S. T. des. M Trial', dated.

2000   *15.75in (40cm) high*

£300-400   **SWO**

A Dennis Chinaworks 'Lion' vase, designed by Sally Tuffin, ovoid form, painted in colours, printed and painted marks.

2000   *8.25in (21cm) high*

£200-300   **WW**

A Dennis Chinaworks 'Heron' vase, designed by Sally Tuffin, painted in colours on a blue ground, impressed and painted marks, dated.

2001   *13in (33.5cm) high*

£350-450   **WW**

A Dennis Chinaworks 'Collector's Day' 'Grape' vase, designed by Sally Tuffin, painted in colours, printed and painted marks.

2001   *10in (25cm) high*
£80-120   **WW**

A Dennis Chinaworks stepped vase, designed by Sally Tuffin, painted with panels of stylized flowers and panels in silver lustre, numbered 2, printed and painted marks.

c2002   *10in (25cm) high*
£200-300   **WW**

A Dennis Chinaworks 'Magnolia' vase, designed by Sally Tuffin, painted in shades of blue, green, and white, impressed and painted marks, limited edition no.5/25, dated.

2004   *19in (48cm) high*
£1,000-1,500   **WW**

A Dennis Chinaworks 'Dorking Cockerel' vase, designed by Sally Tuffin, painted in colours, impressed and painted marks, dated.

2004   *14in (35.5cm) high*
£350-400   **WW**

A Dennis Chinaworks 'Koi Carp' vase, designed by Sally Tuffin, painted in colours, impressed and painted marks.

2004   *15.5in (39.5cm) high*
£250-350   **WW**

A Dennis Chinaworks 'Midnight Hare' 'Trial' vase, designed by Sally Tuffin, painted in colours on a banded pale-blue and purple ground, impressed and painted marks, dated.

2005   *5.25in (13.5cm) high*
£140-180   **WW**

A Dennis Chinaworks 'Praying Mantis' vase, designed by Sally Tuffin, impressed and painted marks, limited edition no.3/25.

2005   *12in (30cm) high*
£250-350   **WW**

A Dennis Chinaworks 'Albatross' vase, designed by Sally Tuffin, painted in colours, impressed and painted marks.

2005   *12.5in (32cm) high*
£220-280   **WW**

A Dennis Chinaworks 'Red Flower' 'Trial' stepped vase, designed by Sally Tuffin, painted with geometric foliate design in pink, red, and yellow, impressed and painted marks, dated.

2006   9.5in (24cm) high
£120-180   WW

A Dennis Chinaworks 'Penguin' candlestick, designed by Sally Tuffin, painted in colours, numbered 1, printed and painted marks to the base.

2006   10.25in (26cm) high
£350-400   WW

A Dennis Chinaworks 'Bullerswood' vase, designed by Sally Tuffin, made for the Victoria and Albert Museum, limited edition no.5/10.

16in (41cm) high
£400-600   SWO

A Dennis Chinaworks 'Polar Bear' jar and cover, designed by Sally Tuffin, painted in colours, no.5, printed and painted marks.

2003   6in (15cm) high
£250-350   WW

A Dennis Chinaworks 'Bats' charger, designed by Sally Tuffin, painted in colours, impressed and painted marks, dated.

2008   11.5in (29cm) diam
£250-350   WW

A Dennis Chinaworks 'Apple Head' 'Trial' vase designed by Sally Tuffin, impressed marks, dated.

Dennis Chinaworks introduced its innovative range of 'Head' pots in 2005. Each lidded container features a head in profile. Experimental trial pieces are sold from the studio at collectors' events or special auctions. If the range proves to be popular, examples in unusual colourways or samples showing an important aspect of the development of the design will command a premium.

2008   8in (20cm) high
£350-400   WW

A Dennis Chinaworks fashion figure, by Roger Michell, one of a series of figures based on famous fashion designers' outfits, printed mark, dated.

Roger Michell was one of the designers of Carlton Ware's legendary 'Walking Ware' range.

1985   12in (30cm) high
£100-200   SWO

A Dennis Chinaworks 'Yohji Yamamoto' figure, designed by Roger Michell, painted in colours, printed factory marks.

1985   11.5in (29cm) high
£100-200   WW

CERAMICS

QUICK REFERENCE - DOULTON

● The Doulton factory was founded in 1815 by John Doulton, Martha Jones and John Watts in Lambeth, south London. They started producing general stonewares for daily use, such as ginger beer bottles and ink wells. John Doulton's son Henry joined the firm in 1835 and expanded the business, supplying drainpipes to cities around the world. Henry's entrepreneurial success allowed the factory to focus on decorative wares, which they did from 1871.

● Students from the Lambeth School of Art designed and decorated many pieces. Some of the most successful students include siblings Arthur Tinworth (dates unknown) and George Tinworth (1843-1913), as well as Hannah Barlow (1859-1913), Florence Barlow (d.1909) and Arthur Barlow (d.1909). The designs for these 'Doulton Lambeth' pieces, which were often made in the Art Nouveau style, are characterised by their individual styles and artists' monograms. The 'faience' range was decorated with naturalistic paintings. The Doulton company received a royal warrant in 1901, after which 'Royal Doulton' marks were used on the ceramics.

A Royal Doulton creamware dish, with printed design by Cecil Aldin, of a foxhound and fox head wall trophy, printed marks 'D462?'.

11.5in (29cm) long

£150-200   SWO

A pair of early 20thC Royal Doulton vases, by Hannah Barlow, decorated with incised horses in a landscape setting, impressed and incised marks also monogrammed 'FTR', both damaged.

11.4in (29cm) high

£350-400   FLD

A Doulton Lambeth stoneware jug, by Frank Butler, with impressed mark and monogram.

5in (12.5cm) high

£150-200   SWO

A Royal Doulton Flambé vase, monogram for Frederick Moore, printed factory mark.

c1940   *7in (18cm) high*

£450-500   SK

A Doulton Lambeth stoneware vase, by Bessie Newbery, impressed marks to base.

8.3in (21cm) high

£65-75   WHP

An Art Nouveau Royal Doulton vase, by Eliza Simmance, impressed and incised marks, incised monogram, professional restoration to top rim.

8.5in (21.5cm) high

£150-200   WW

QUICK REFERENCE - DOULTON FINIALS

● British Art Nouveau artist Gilbert Bayes (1872-1953) was already well-known for his public sculptures when he was commissioned by the St. Pancras Housing Association Improvement Society to make a series of ornamental ceramic finials. The finials were placed on top of washing lines to brighten up the courtyards of housing estates in what is known today as Somers Town. This area runs roughly from Euston to Crowndale Road. Themes represented were nursery rhymes or biblical subjects. The finials were made at the Doulton factory between c1931-38. Many of them were damaged by vandalism and during the Second World War. Some were simply stolen from their original places. Making art accessible to improve people's quality of life resonated with Bayes, who was keen on making art with a social conscience. Due to their rarity and desirability, finials can sell for thousands of pounds.

A Royal Doulton stoneware brown bear, impressed marks.

3.5in (9cm) high

£300-350　　　　　　　　CHEF

An early Doulton Lambeth stoneware ewer, the body incised with donkeys, oval Doulton Lambeth mark only.

c1869-73　　　8.6in (22cm) high

£300-400　　　　　　　　DN

A Doulton Lambeth stoneware 'Tudor Rose' finial, designed by Gilbert Bayes, made for the washing line posts at St Pancras Housing Association Estates, London, modelled in relief and glazed in colours.

36cm high

£6,500-7,500　　　　　　WW

A Doulton Lambeth stoneware jug, of cycling interest, with panels entitled 'Military, Road and Path'.

c1900 8in (20.8cm) high

£160-200　　　　　　　　H&C

A Doulton Lambeth stoneware jardiniere, impressed marks to base.

8.7in (22cm) high

£90-120　　　　　　　　WHP

A Doulton Lambeth stoneware and brass-mounted oil lamp, the lamp with Hink's patent burner.

18in (46cm) high

£650-700　　　　　　　SWO

A Doulton Lambeth table lamp base, monogrammed 'EDL' on a conforming brass-mounted base incised with stylised dragons, converted to electricity.

17.7in (45cm) high

£520-600　　　　　　　WHP

A Doulton Lambeth stoneware oil lamp, probably decorated by Kate M Davis.

c1892　23in (59cm) high excluding funnel

£950-1,200　　　　　　SWO

CERAMICS

QUICK REFERENCE - FIGURES

- Under the direction of Charles Noke, a modeller at the factory, thousands of figurines were produced. Noke believed that Royal Doulton figurines could be as popular as 19thC Staffordshire pieces. Each figurine was given an 'HN' number, which stands for Harry Nixon, the then manager of the painting department.
- When Queen Mary visited the factory in 1913, she expressed her admiration for a figurine of a child in a nightgown by exclaiming 'isn't he a darling'. The very first figurine given the HN number was thus named 'Darling'.
- Collectors focus on type, colour or designer. Figurines that had a shorter run are generally worth more, as are those in unusual colourways and variations. Condition is crucial so always check for any damage, particularly with figurines that have protruding or delicately modelled parts.

A Royal Doulton 'The Parson's Daughter' figurine, designed by H. Tittensor, HN564, with printed and painted marks.

1923-49   *9.75in (24.5cm) high*

£80-120   **WW**

A Royal Doulton 'The Perfect Pair' figurine, designed by Leslie Harradine, HN581, printed and painted marks, fine hairline.

1923-38

£200-250   **WW**

A Royal Doulton 'The Bather' figurine, by Leslie Harradine, HN687.

This figurine of a bather elegantly removing her robe was the first version of its kind. Another version was issued from 1926 to 1938 and came in two colourways: blue/green and purple/black, both of which are extremely rare. This is without a doubt a very risqué piece for the time and reflects the inspiration that designers found in the female subject.

1924-49   *8in (20cm) high*

£450-500   **HAN**

A miniature Royal Doulton 'Polly Peachum' figurine, designed by Leslie Harradine, HN698, style 2, from the 'Beggar's Opera' series.

1925-49   *2.25in (5.5cm) high*

£50-70   **LOCK**

A Royal Doulton 'The Flower Seller's Children' figurine, designed by Leslie Harradine, HN1342.

1929-93

£45-55   **FLD**

A Royal Doulton 'Derrick' figurine, designed by Leslie Harradine, HN1398, with painted and printed marks.

1930-40   *8in (20cm) high*

£55-65   **FLD**

A Royal Doulton 'Pamela' figurine, designed by Leslie Harradine, HN1468, with painted and impressed marks, and 'Potted by Doulton & Co'.
1931-37   *8in (20cm) high*
£200-250   **FLD**

A Royal Doulton 'Sylvia' figurine, designed by Leslie Harradine, HN1478, with printed and painted marks.
1931-38   *10.75in (27cm) high*
£150-200   **WW**

A Royal Doulton 'Kate Hardcastle' figurine, designed by Leslie Harradine, HN1734.
1935-49   *8.25in (21cm) high*
£110-150   **LOCK**

A Royal Doulton 'Verena' figurine, designed by Leslie Harradine, HN1835.
1935-49   *8.25in (21cm) high*
£250-300   **LOCK**

A Royal Doulton 'Nell Gwyn' figurine, designed by Leslie Harradine, HN1887, with printed and painted marks.
1938-49   *7in (17.5cm) high*
£220-280   **WW**

A Royal Doulton 'Baby Bunting' figurine, designed by M. Davies, HN2108.
1953-59
£60-80   **FLD**

A Royal Doulton 'The One That Got Away' figurine, designed by M. Davies, HN2153.
£50-60   **FLD**

A Royal Doulton 'The Coachman' figurine, designed by M. Nicoll, HN2282.

1963-71 *7.7in (19.5cm) high*

£50-60 **WHP**

A limited edition Royal Doulton 'Mexican Dancer', modelled by Peggy Davies, HN2866, from the 'Dancers of the World' series, numbered 574 of 750.

1979 *9in (23cm) high*

£100-140 **FLD**

A Royal Doulton 'Lalla Rookh' figurine, designed by S. Keenan, HN2910, from the 'Ships Figurehead' series, limited edition of 950, with wooden stand and presentation box.

1981

£70-100 **PSA**

A Royal Doulton 'Chieftain', designed by S. Keenan, HN2929, from the 'Ships Figureheads' series, limited edition of 950, with wooden stand and presentation box.

1982

£200-300 **PSA**

A Royal Doulton 'Sir Winston Churchill' figurine, designed by Adrian Hughes, HN3057.

1985-present *10.25in (26cm) high*

£40-50 **H&C**

A Royal Doulton 'Henry VIII' figurine, designed by P. Parsons, HN3458, limited edition no.1253, with certificate.

Commissioned by Lawleys By Post.

1994

£200-300 **PSA**

A Royal Doulton 'Prestige' 'Jack Point' figurine, designed by C. J. Noke, HN3925, number 17 from a limited edition of 85.

1998

£700-1,000 **PSA**

Miller's Compares

The musical Old King Cole jugs come in two colourways and can be differentiated by either a yellow or a brown crown. The yellow crown is much rarer.

The 'Old King Cole' model also comes in three non-musical versions.

"Old King Cole was a Merry Old Soul" are the words of the nursery rhyme that inspired the design of this jug. The collar frill was remodelled around 1939 and Variation Two [of the non-musical variety] can be found with both deep and shallow white ruff modelings.

The tune played on the musical jugs is "Old King Cole was a Merry Old Soul."

A rare Royal Doulton 'Old King Cole' large musical character jug, no. unknown, with yellow crown.

1939   *7.5in (19cm) high*

£1,500-2,000   **PSA**

A Royal Doulton 'Old King Cole' large musical character jug, no.D6014, with slight underglazed chip to crown.

1939   *5.75in (14.5cm) high*

£250-300   **PSA**

A Royal Doulton 'Mephistopheles' character jug mug, designed by Charles Noke, D5758.

First found in 16thC German legend, Mephistopheles became best known in Goethe's drama 'Faust' of 1808. In it he is a devil who Faust sells his soul to.

1937-48   *3.5in (8.5cm) high*

£200-250   **LOCK**

A rare Royal Doulton 'Hatless Drake' character jug, designed by Harry Fenton, no.D6115, tiny glaze fault to ruff.

1940-41

£1,200-1,500   **PSA**

A rare Royal Doulton 'Winston Spencer Churchill' two-handled character jug, designed by Charles Noke, no.D6170, stamped to the base 'This loving cup was Made during the Battle of Britain as a tribute to a great leader'.

1940-41   *6.5in (16.5cm)*

£3,000-3,500   **PSA**

A Royal Doulton 'The Trapper' miniature character jug, designed by Max Henk and David B. Biggs, no.D6609.

1967-83

£600-800   **PSA**

A Royal Doulton 'Mr Quaker' large character jug, designed by Harry Sales, no.D6738, limited edition of 3500, with certificate.

1985

£100-150   **PSA**

A Royal Doulton 'Charlie Chaplin' large character jug, designed by William K. Harper, no.D6949, limited edition no.1 of 2500.

Royal Doulton always kept no.1 example of limited editions for their museum. These were sold off in 2007 in the archive auctions.

1993

£200-250   **PSA**

A Royal Doulton 'The Phantom of the Opera' character jug, modelled by David Biggs, D7017, numbered 180 of a limited edition of 2500, with a Doulton backstamp.

A stage curtain and lantern make up the handle. This jug was commissioned by Lawleys By Post to commemorate Gaston Leroux's 1910 novel 'Le Fantôme de l'Opéra'.

1995 *7in (18cm) high*

£200-300 **FLD**

A Royal Doulton 'Sir Isaac Newton' rare prototype small character jug.

£3,000-4,000 **PSA**

A rare Royal Doulton 'The Fisherman' large prototype character jug, good restoration to base.

7in (18cm) high

£2,500-3,500 **PSA**

A rare Royal Doulton 'Pearly Boy' large character jug, designed by Harry Fenton, blue colourway with pearl buttons.

1947-unknown *6.5in (16.5cm) high*

£1,500-2,000 **PSA**

A rare Royal Doulton prototype intermediate 'Clint Eastwood' character jug.

This jug was designed in 2005 as part of the celebrity film star collection but not put into production. This obvious rarity and the popularity of Clint Eastwood accounts for the high value.

£3,500-4,500 **PSA**

A rare Royal Doulton prototype 'Nelson Mandela' character jug, marked 'Pascoe & Co prototype' to base.

Several trial colourways of this jug were produced in 2005 in some of his patterned African shirts before the Nelson Mandela Foundation refused permission for the jug to be produced.

6.5in (17cm) high

£5,000-6,000 **PSA**

A rare Royal Doulton prototype intermediate 'Peter Sellers', designed in 2005 as part of the celebrity filmstar collection but not put into production.

£3,000-4,000 **PSA**

QUICK REFERENCE - DOULTON BIBELOTS

● The selection of bibelots that were produced at Lambeth are today some of the most collected items of Lambethware. Naturally their popularity and price depends on their 'artistic' value for there were countless such objects produced at Lambeth; some very plain examples, others for events, others for commercial advertising for numerous firms, and still others designed by some of Lambeth's most popular artists including Leslie Harradine, Vera Huggins, and Harry Simmeon. They date from the 1920s to 1930s but some were made for a longer period and no doubt introduced earlier, such as the Wrights Coal Tar Soap dragonfly dish. The term bibelot is a derivative from the French, meaning a trinket or small fanciful object. One only needs to look at the subjects of these fanciful ring trays, soap dishes or ashtrays to see that this name suits these imps, nymphs, comic birds and other creatures very well.

A Royal Doulton Bibelot owl, the small dish with brown owl, impressed marks 'Lambeth, England, 8667', 'MF' potter's mark.

4in (10cm) high

£350-400   LAW

A Royal Doulton Bibelot of a mouse perched on a rock, marked 'Royal Doulton, 8673'.

4in (10cm) high

£500-600   LAW

A Royal Doulton Bibelot, designed with a Kookaburra with a long yellow bill, and mounted on a small dish, impressed marks 'Royal Doulton, 8686', 'NL' potter's mark.

4in (10cm) high

£240-280   LAW

A Doulton Lambeth Bibelot, with a bird motif, impressed marks 'Doulton Lambeth, X8728, 9481'.

5.75in (15cm) across

£180-220   LAW

A Doulton Lambeth Bibelot, mounted with a seated pixie, impressed marks 'Doulton Lambeth, 8731', 'FJ' for Florrie Jones.

4in (10cm) high

£300-350   LAW

CERAMICS

A Doulton Lambeth Bibelot, of a bird with open beak, impressed marks 'Doulton Lambeth, 8740'.

3in (7.5cm) high

£600-700   **LAW**

A Royal Doulton Bibelot of a faun playing pan-pipes, impressed marks 'Royal Doulton, 8753', 'FN' potter's mark.

4in (10cm) high

£450-500   **LAW**

A Royal Doulton Bibelot, with a brown rabbit, impressed marks 'Royal Doulton, Lambeth, England, 8756', 'MB' possibly for Maud Bowden.

3.25in (8cm) high

£500-600   **LAW**

A Royal Doulton Bibelot, with a koala clinging to a branch, and leaves around the edge of the dish, marked 'Royal Doulton, X8902, 7141, Made in England', and potter's mark.

4.25in (11cm) high

£250-300   **LAW**

A Royal Doulton Bibelot dish, made for 'Silver Seal Port', modelled with a seal, impressed marks 'Royal Doulton', 'MB' potter's mark.

4.25in (11cm) diam

£500-550   **LAW**

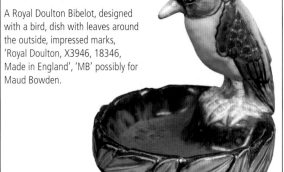

A Royal Doulton Bibelot, designed with a bird, dish with leaves around the outside, impressed marks, 'Royal Doulton, X3946, 18346, Made in England', 'MB' possibly for Maud Bowden.

4in (10cm) high

£250-300   **LAW**

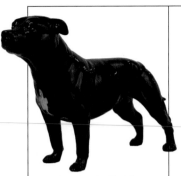

A Royal Doulton 'Staffordshire Bull Terrier', designed by Alan Maslankowski, black with white, DA101.
1990-?   *4in (10cm) high*
£20-30   **PSA**

A Royal Doulton 'Penguin', designer unknown, HN104 or HN134.

This figure exists in three colourways: black and white, flambé, and Chinese Jade.
1913-46   *4.5in (11.5cm) high*
£100-150   **FLD**

A Royal Doulton flambé 'Fox', designed by Charles Noke, seated, HN130.
1913-62   *9in (23cm) high*
£250-300   **WHP**

A Royal Doulton pair of flambé 'Cuddling Penguins', HN133, hairline crack to base.
6in (15.2cm) high
£110-150   **PSA**

A Royal Doulton flambé 'Fox', in a stalking position, possibly HN147E.
c1912-62   *9in (23cm) long*
£120-160   **WHP**

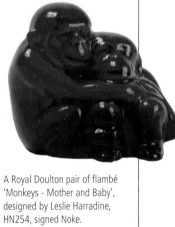

A Royal Doulton pair of flambé 'Monkeys - Mother and Baby', designed by Leslie Harradine, HN254, signed Noke.
1912-62   *3in (8cm) high*
£120-180   **PSA**

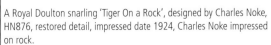

A Royal Doulton snarling 'Tiger On a Rock', designed by Charles Noke, HN876, restored detail, impressed date 1924, Charles Noke impressed on rock.
1924-46
£150-200   **PSA**

A Royal Doulton 'Fox Terrier', designer unknown, seated, HN910, restored tail.
1927-46
£40-50   **PSA**

CERAMICS

A Royal Doulton small 'Bulldog',
designed by Frederick Daws,
HN1074.
1932-85   *3.25in (8cm) long*
£60-90   **PSA**

A Royal Doulton 'Sealyham' terrier,
designer unknown, standing,
HN2509.
1938-59
£55-65   **PSA**

A mid-20thC Royal Doulton large 'Pat O'Moy' Irish Setter, designed by
Frederick Daws, HN1054, green mark, inscribed in black.
1931-60   *12in (30.5cm) long*
£350-450   **HT**

A Royal Doulton flambé 'Hare', designer unknown, seated, HN2592.
1945-96
£60-70   **PSA**

A Royal Doulton model of 'Bull Terrier', style two, designer unknown,
HN2511.
1938-59   *4in (10cm) high*
£50-60   **PSA**

A Royal Doulton large 'Prestige' series model of a 'Fighter Elephant',
designed by Charles Noke, HN2640.
                                              12in (30.5cm) high
£450-550   **PSA**

A rare Royal Doulton Sung flambé 'Cockerel', designer unknown,
crouching.
                                              3in (7.5cm) high
£2,000-2,500   **PSA**

QUICK REFERENCE - BUNNYKINS

● Bunnykins earthenware figurines were introduced in the 1930s. Only six were originally made, and the range was discontinued just before World War Two. Averaging around 4.5 to 7 inches, the original six included 'Billy', 'Mary', 'Freddie' and 'Reggie' Bunnykin, as well as a 'Farmer' and 'Mother' Bunnykin. They remain rare up until this day. Charles Noke, the Art Director who was responsible for the HN range of Royal Doulton figurines, is believed to have modelled them, as they resemble some of his character animals.

● After Royal Doulton took over the Beswick factory in 1969, a new Bunnykins range was introduced in 1972 with the DB pattern numbers. A new look was developed by Harry Sales, the Design Manager of the Beswick factory, in the 1980s. From then on, the figurines reflected children's interests. The first such figurines depicted a guitar-playing bunny called 'Mr. Bunnybeat Strumming' (DB16) and a space traveller 'Astro Bunnykins Rocket Man' (DB20).

● The words 'Made in England' were used on the base of the figurines. 'Doulton England' was sometimes used instead of the standard factory mark, which was too large to place on smaller items.

An early 1930s Royal Doulton 'Billy Bunnykin' figurine, designed by Charles Noke, red trousers, blue jacket, white bow tie with blue spots, no.D6001.
1939-c1940   *4.75in (12cm) high*
£300-400   PSA

An early 1930s Royal Doulton 'Mary Bunnykin', designed by Charles Noke, red bodice, dark-blue collar, pale-blue skirt, white apron, no.D6002, ear restored.
1939-c1940   *6in (15cm) high*
£200-300   PSA

An early 1930s Royal Doulton 'Farmer Bunnykin', designed by Charles Noke, green coat, blue and white smock, yellow bow tie, red handkerchief with white dots, no.D6003.
1939-c1940   *7.5in (19cm) high*
£300-400   PSA

An early 1930s Royal Doulton 'Mother Bunnykin' figurine, designed by Charles Noke, blue skirt, red jacket, white shawl with blue stripes, no.D6004.
1939-c1940   *7.5in (19cm) high*
£300-400   PSA

A Royal Doulton 'Tally Ho! Bunnykins', based on a design by Walter Hayward, modelled by Albert Hallam, light-blue coat and white rocking horse, yellow sweater, no.DB78, second variation, with 'BUNNYKINS' backstamp.
1988   *4in (10cm) high*
£40-50   PSA

Miller's Compares

Although the same model as DB136, this limited edition was 750.

With the yellow stripes on his arm this figure was senior to the previous figure.

But the most telling pointer to the higher value is that the limited edition was only 250.

A Royal Doulton 'Mountie Bunnykins', designed by Graham Tongue, red jacket, dark-blue trousers, and brown hat, no.DB135, limited edition, boxed.
1993
£180-220   PSA

A Royal Doulton 'Sergeant Mountie Bunnykins', designed by Graham Tongue, red jacket, dark-blue trousers, brown hat, no.DB136, limited edition, boxed.
1993
£300-400   PSA

CERAMICS

ESSENTIAL REFERENCE - VICTORIAN FAIRINGS

- Fairings were given away as prizes, or sold inexpensively at fairs for display on mantelpieces in middle-class homes. Made from a soft-paste porcelain, they usually measure around 3.5in (9cm) long. Decorated by hand in bright colours with gilt highlights, the base usually bears a caption that supports the theme of the subject shown. They date from the rise of funfairs from the mid-19thC until the early 20thC. Some were modelled as trinket boxes, with the group on the lid, or incorporated small pots to hold spills or matches.

- Themes were typically bawdy and risqué for the period, with scenes of marital life, courtship, or cheeky 'seaside' humour. Although thought of as British, most were made in Germany, with Conte & Boehme of Pössneck being one of the major manufacturers. Some of their production is marked with their logo of a shield containing an arm holding a dagger. However, a great many fairings (by whichever maker) are unmarked. From the 1870s onwards, many fairings were marked with a number that indicates the shape. These run from 2850 to 2899 and from 3300 to 3385.

- Earlier examples tend to be better quality, with more detailed and carefully applied colours. From the 1880s, quality drops with poorly applied details. Very poor quality fairings may be reproductions. These tend to have large 'air holes' in the base, and may bear model numbers in the 1800s on the base. In general, values have dropped over the past 20-30 years, primarily as they have gone out of fashion and collectors have chosen to collect the work of higher quality makers. There is still a small group of collectors who will pay good sums to own the rarest and best quality pieces. Damage reduces value considerably.

A Victorian bicycle-themed fairing, titled 'Dangerous', restored.
£200-250   H&C

A Victorian bicycle-themed fairing, titled 'To Epsom'.

Epsom was, and still is, known for its race course, meaning this couple were off to the horse races! At the height of fairings' popularity in the 1970s, an example of 'To Epsom' sold for £1,500.
£450-500   H&C

A Victorian bicycle-themed fairing, titled 'Stop thief'.

£450-500   H&C

A Victorian bicycle-themed fairing, titled 'Walk in Please'.
£280-340   H&C

A Victorian bicycle-themed fairing, titled 'Every vehicle driven by a horse, mule or ass 2d'.

This is the small version of this model.
£200-250   H&C

A CLOSER LOOK AT A FAIRING

The cycling theme means this fairing crosses collecting areas as it would appeal to collectors of cycling memorabilia as well as to collectors of fairings.

This larger audience can increase the value, as it has done here.

Bicycling themes are rarer than other themes such as marital discord or bawdy humour, and this is a very rare example, in undamaged condition.

Biycling fairings date from after the 1860s and bicycles were only more widely introduced aftert the 'bone shaker' was developed in 1865.

A Victorian love-themed fairing, titled 'A happy pair'.
£350-400   **H&C**

A Victorian love-themed fairing, titled 'Beware of a collision'.
£650-750   **H&C**

A Victorian love-themed fairing, titled 'Mal a trouver!'.
£450-500   **H&C**

A Royal Vienna love-themed fairing depicting a man kneeling beside a seated lady.
£250-300   **H&C**

A Victorian love-themed fairing, titled 'How curious it must feel to have those must aches (sic) on my lips, Charlie!'.
£550-650   **H&C**

A Victorian love-themed fairing, titled 'Love in winter'.
£550-650   **H&C**

Miller's Compares

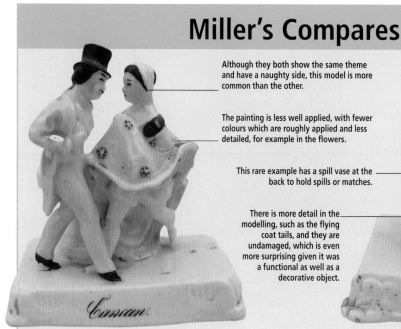

Although they both show the same theme and have a naughty side, this model is more common than the other.

The painting is less well applied, with fewer colours which are roughly applied and less detailed, for example in the flowers.

This rare example has a spill vase at the back to hold spills or matches.

There is more detail in the modelling, such as the flying coat tails, and they are undamaged, which is even more surprising given it was a functional as well as a decorative object.

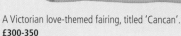

A Victorian love-themed fairing, titled 'Cancan'.
£90-120   H&C

A Victorian love-themed fairing, titled 'Cancan'.
£300-350   H&C

A Victorian love-themed fairing, titled 'Animated spirits'.

The addition of a lascivious, drunken monk is typical of the humour found in fairings. This is a rare model, perhaps as it mocked religion at a time when it was still an important part of people's lives.
£600-700   H&C

A Victorian love-themed fairing, titled 'No followers allowed', her arm restored.
£30-40   H&C

A Victorian love-themed fairing, titled 'The shoemaker in love'.
£300-400   H&C

A Victorian love-themed fairing, titled 'Marriage'.
£200-250   H&C

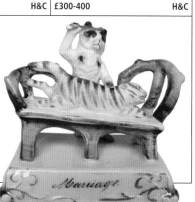

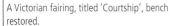

A Victorian fairing, titled 'Courtship', bench restored.

£250-300   H&C

A Victorian fairing, titled 'Cousin & Cousine'.

£60-80   H&C

A Victorian fairing, titled 'To let'.

£90-120   H&C

Judith Picks

Cross-market interest from different groups of collectors can lead to higher prices. Marble games are rarely shown in sculptures or figurines, and the marble collecting community is strong and dedicated, particularly in the US. Compared to other examples, this fairing is affordable, and the clever buyer may buy this and then offer it for sale to marble collectors. It may also appeal to collectors of juvenilia, toys, games, and other items related to childhood. It's also nicely decorated so would make an appealing addition to a collector's shelf.

A Victorian fairing, titled 'Free and independent elector'.

£100-150   H&C

A Victorian fairing, titled 'In chancery'.

£150-200   H&C

A Victorian fairing, titled 'Fair play boys'.

£70-90   H&C

A Victorian fairing, titled 'A present at night-time to an old bachelor', candle missing.

This fairing has not been found or seen by collectors before, hence the high price.
£850-950   H&C

CERAMICS

QUICK REFERENCE - HORNSEA POTTERY

● Hornsea pottery was first made in 1949 in the home of brothers Colin and Desmond Rawson in Hornsea, Yorkshire. Their miniature toby jugs proved popular and they expanded their range and production after moving to new premises in 1950. In 1954, the company moved to a new factory in Hornsea which became their primary home until the company closed in 2000.

● John Clappison (1937-2013), the son of the pottery's first investor, joined the company in 1958 and became their lead designer, producing their most collectable ranges. Desirable early examples include his 'Elegance' tableware of 1956 and the 'Summit' design of 1960. Other designers included Martin Hunt R.D.I. (b.1942) and Marion Campbell (1911-2005).

● The company became known for producing table and decorative wares that captured the look of the day in terms of form, colour and surface decoration. They also employed a number of innovative production techniques, such as direct printing. Ranges were exported internationally. All tableware designs were included in the Design Centre's influential 'Index'.

● The company became known for its kitchenware and dining ware, led by the immense success of 'Heirloom', which was mass-produced from 1966-87. A number of designs were produced in very limited numbers, and these tend to be the most sought-after and valuable today. The company also became known for its commemorative ware, and series of amusing mugs during the 1970s.

● Interest in Hornsea pottery arguably reached a peak around 10 years ago. Since then, prices have fallen but may rise again as interest is being renewed, partly due to the affordability of designs. As such, they make a great investment for the future. In all instances, examine pieces closely as these very functional pieces were often heavily used. Any damage reduces value dramatically. Many designs were also mass-produced, so look out for rare shapes and colourways, particularly from the 1950s-60s, which currently tend to be the most popular periods of production.

An early Hornsea 'Tommy Twaddle' Toby jug, modelled by Colin Rawson, full-colour version.

Modelled by Colin Rawson, this was part of a very early range of Toby jugs and character jugs. As well as being the scarce full colour version, these jugs are hard to find as they were only made in small quantities due to very limited production facilities.
1950-51   4in (10cm) high
£75-100   RHA

An early set of Hornsea 'Pink Elephants', made at the Old Hall.

Note what these cheeky elephants, even the baby one, are holding - beer bottles! There was also a story in the Bradford Telegraph and Argus in 1950 about people seeing pink elephants!
*1950   small 1.75in (4.5cm) high medium 2.5in (6.5cm) high
large 2.75in (7cm) high*
£70-90 set   RHA

An early Hornsea large 'Laced boot, with applied mouse'.

Boots can also be found with printed flowers, a moulded heart, a puppy and a tortoise - the puppy can be applied or moulded in as part of the boot.
1951   2.75in (7cm) high
£20-25   RHA

An early Hornsea 'Squirrel tree-stump' posy vase.
1952   2.75in (7cm) high
£12-15   RHA

An early Hornsea 'Large Doe'.
1952   5.75in (14.5cm) long
£40-60   RHA

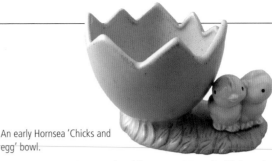

An early Hornsea 'Chicks and egg' bowl.

This very rare bowl was produced for Easter 1954 and sold through Valentine's department store in Aberdeen. The jagged eggshell held a chocolate egg. Examine the edges and peaks carefully as they are often damaged.

An early Hornsea 'Owl' match holder.

1953   *3in (7.5cm) high*

£20-25   RHA

An early Hornsea 'Scottie Dog' thistle jug.

1953   *3.2in (8cm) high*

£20-25   RHA

1954   *3in (7.5cm) high*

£100-120   RHA

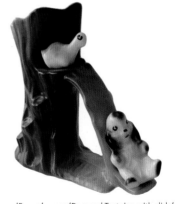

An early Hornsea 'Fauna' range 'Daisy jug with rabbits', mould no.129.

1955   *3.4in (8.5cm) high*

£15-20   RHA

An early Hornsea 'Fauna' range 'Duck' jug, mould no.A2.

This is one from the A series of six jugs.

1955   *3.2in (8cm) high*

£35-45   RHA

An early Hornsea 'Fauna' range 'Fish wave' wall vase, no mould no.

1955   *3.2in (8cm) high*

£12-15   RHA

An early Hornsea 'Fauna' range 'Dog and Tortoise with slide' tree posy, mould no.230.

This is part of a series of six different bowls and vases, each with at least one applied figurine, that made up the novelty 'Playtime' range. All were modelled by Colin Rawson.

An early Hornsea 'Fauna' range 'Dog-in-Kennel' cruet, modelled by Colin Rawson at the Old Hall, mould no.350.

1955   *2.2in (5.5cm) high*

£50-80   RHA

1959   *4.3in (11cm) high*

£15-20   RHA

CERAMICS

An early Hornsea 'Fauna' range 'Doe and Rabbit' jug, mould no.107.

1955   *7.9in (20cm) high*

£18-20   **RHA**

An early Hornsea 'Fauna' range 'Animated Tree' jug, mould no.580.

1958   *6in (15cm) high*

£15-20   **RHA**

A Hornsea 'Fauna Royal' 'Frisky Lamb' tree vase, mould no.46.

1960   *5in (13cm) high*

£15-20   **RHA**

A Hornsea 'Fauna' range 'Double Rabbit' treehouse, mould no.105.

1959   *3.5in (9cm) high*

£12-18   **RHA**

A Hornsea 'Fauna Royal' 'Fawn' bulb bowl, mould no.89.

1962   *7.3in (18.5cm) wide*

£25-35   **RHA**

A CLOSER LOOK AT A HORNSEA JUG

This is from the 'Fauna Royal' range of troughs, vases, bowls, jugs, and cruets, which was inspired by nature. Each piece was decorated with at least one charming animal.

Produced from 1960-67, it followed on from the similar Fauna range which was produced from 1954-59.

Both were hugely commercially successful, particularly the Fauna Royal range, and gave the pottery solid financial footing to develop other more avant garde designs.

This highly detailed jug was the largest piece produced in either range, and is decorated with three applied, separately moulded animal figurines.

A Hornsea 'Fauna Royal' 'Fawn and double Squirrel' tree jug, mould no.96.

1966   *11.2in (28.5cm) high*

£50-70   **RHA**

A Hornsea 'Fauna Royal' 'Butterfly-on-Flower' dish, mould no.37.

This is a rare dish, the butterfly is often damaged on examples found. The style echoes Carltonware's fruit and leaf designs of the 1930s. For an example, see page 57.

1960   *4.3in (11cm) diam*

£40-60   **RHA**

QUICK REFERENCE - DOROTHY MARION CAMPBELL

● Dorothy Marion Campbell (1911-2005) was a potter based in Yorkshire. She is best known for her animal and figural designs for Hornsea, produced from 1956 until 1957 or 1958, depending on the model. Ranging from the realistic to the highly stylised to the monochromatic, she modelled each one at home and transported the finished example to the pottery. A matte black or a (scarce) white glaze were chosen to update the company's look, something that was continued with her more stylised forms. The first animal released was the panther shown on this page. All were produced at the pottery's second production facility at Ulrome and may bear ULROME shield marks or a green Hornsea mark. After the Ulrome facility was closed in 1956 and the range was discontinued by Hornsea in 1958, it continued to be produced for a few years by Cleve Pottery. As marks often easily wear off, it is impossible to tell the difference between them. This Ibex is the rarest of this very desirable and hard to find range of black animals, and harks back to Art Deco animal figurines.

A Hornsea 'Hippopotamus', designed by Marion Campbell, mould no.561.

1956   *7.5in (19cm) long*

£80-100   RHA

A Hornsea 'Ibex', designed by Marion Campbell.

This is the rarest of the black animals.

1956   *6in (15cm) long*

£100-150   RHA

A Hornsea 'Rhinoceros', designed by Marion Campbell, mould no.562.

1956   *8.9in (22.5cm) long*

£80-100   RHA

A Hornsea 'Large Panther', designed by Marion Campbell, mould no.565.

1956   *9in (23cm) long*

£50-80   RHA

A Hornsea 'Crocodile', designed by Marion Campbell, mould no.564.

1956   *11.4in (29cm) long*

£80-100   RHA

A Hornsea large and small 'Penguin', designed by Marion Campbell, mould nos.5610 and 5611.

1956   *large 6.7in (17cm) high*

small 4.7in (12cm) high

£15-20 (small)

£25-30 (Large)   RHA

CERAMICS

A Hornsea 'Large Arctic Fox', by Marion Campbell, mould no.5616.
1956 *7in (18cm) long*
£30-40 **RHA**

A Hornsea 'Small Panther', by Marion Campbell, mould no.5618.
1956 *5.9in (15cm) long*
£40-60 **RHA**

A Hornsea set of 'Stylised Cats', by Marion Campbell, mould nos. 321, 322, 323, 324, 325.

Ceramic cat figurines with elongated, curving or straight necks were popular during the late 1950s & 60s and were produced by many potteries in the UK and across Europe.
1961-62 *largest 8.7in (22cm) high, smallest 3in (8cm) high set*
£150-180 **RHA**

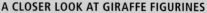

A CLOSER LOOK AT GIRAFFE FIGURINES

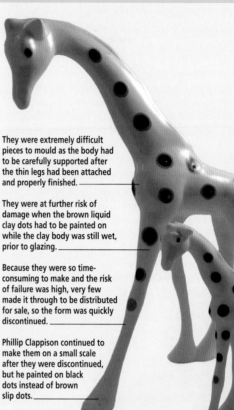

They were extremely difficult pieces to mould as the body had to be carefully supported after the thin legs had been attached and properly finished.

They were at further risk of damage when the brown liquid clay dots had to be painted on while the clay body was still wet, prior to glazing.

Because they were so time-consuming to make and the risk of failure was high, very few made it through to be distributed for sale, so the form was quickly discontinued.

Phillip Clappison continued to make them on a small scale after they were discontinued, but he painted on black dots instead of brown slip dots.

A Hornsea large and small 'Giraffe', by Marion Campbell.
1956 *11.4in (29cm) high and 5.5in (14cm) high*
large £400-500 small £300-350 **RHA**

A Hornsea 'Large Spaniel', by Marion Campbell, potted by Viggo Madsen.
1956 *7.5in (19cm) long*
£50-70 **RHA**

A Hornsea 'Large Pekinese', by Marion Campbell, potted by Viggo Madsen.
1956 *6.3in (16cm) long*
£40-60 **RHA**

A Hornsea 'Coastline' milk jug, mould no.504, designed by John Clappison in 1955.

The exterior finish and glaze is very similar to the 'Cortina' decor by West German factory Jasba, which was released in the same year. The light blue interior was soon replaced with deep carmine or yellow interiors, due to production problems.

4in (10cm) high

£8-10　　　RHA

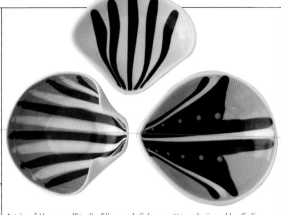

A trio of Hornsea 'Studio Slipware' dishes, pattern designed by Colin Rawson in 1955.

yellow 4.5in (11.5cm) wide

£18-20 each　　　RHA

A Hornsea 'Elegance' cream jug, mould no.504, designed by John Clappison in 1955.

5.5in (14cm) high

£15-20　　　RHA

A Hornsea 'Tricorn' sugar bowl, mould no.602, designed by John Clappison in 1957.

This range takes its name from the tricorn cross-section form of the rim. The snowflake motif is typical of the period, where inspiration was taken from something a scientist may see under a microscope to atomic designs inspired by the nuclear age.

3in (8cm) high

£20-25　　　RHA

A Hornsea 'Polka Dot' butter dish, mould no.510, designed by John Clappison in 1957.

5.5in (13.5cm) wide

£30-35　　　RHA

A Hornsea large 'Flower Holder', mould no.302, designed by John Clappison in 1957.

The design of these rare asymetric vases was based on a vase from Gustavsberg's 'Veckla' range, designed by Stig Lindberg in 1953. It was produced in two sizes. This is the large size.

6in (15cm) high

£150-200　　　RHA

A Hornsea 'Modern English Slipware' cream jug, pattern designed by Colin Rawson, mould no.409, designed by John Clappison in 1958.

4.75in (12cm) high

£15-20　　　RHA

CERAMICS

A Hornsea 'Studiocraft' vase, mould no.383, designed by John Clappison in 1960.

7.5in (19cm) high

£25-30   RHA

A Hornsea 'Lattice' vase, mould no.392, designed by John Clappison in 1961.

13.4in (34cm) high

£60-80   RHA

A Hornsea 'Tasty' dish, mould no.304, designed by John Clappison in 1960.

7.9in (20cm) long

£35-45   RHA

A Hornsea 'Impasto' fish light, mould no.701, designed by John Clappison in 1960.

Note the smaller fish swimming beside its parent, which acts as a shade covering the bulb. This scarce lamp was intended as a television lamp, and retailed for 45/- (£2.25). At the time, the subdued light from television lamps placed on top of a set was thought to help 'eye strain' from watching TV.

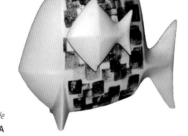

10.6in (27cm) wide

£300-400   RHA

A CLOSER LOOK AT HORNSEA LAMPS

The 'Impasto' range was designed by John Clappison and produced from 1960-63, two other items from the range are also shown on this page.

The pattern was sponged on by hand in brown and grey, where the colours overlapped or mingled, creating different effects.

Each piece bore Clappison's personal monogram, an intertwined 'JWC'.

Less popular at the time than vases, bowls or tableware, and more expensive, these lamps are very rare, especially in a pair.

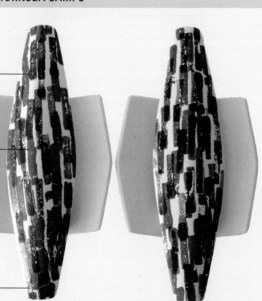

A pair of Hornsea 'Impasto' 'Athenia' wall lights, mould no.703A, designed by John Clappison in 1960.

14.6in (37cm) high

£450-550

A Hornsea 'Impasto' 'Hyphen' pattern vase, designed by John Clappison in 1960.

These elegant, tall vases were produced for shows and exhibitions. The 'Hyphen' pattern has rows of coloured short and long oblongs.

14in (35.5cm) high

£300-500   RHA

A Hornsea 'Classic Doric' jug, mould no.801, decorated by Michael Walker, designed by Alan Luckham in 1962.

8.25in (21cm) high

£30-40   RHA

A Hornsea 'Slipware' large jardiniere, mould no.871, thrown by Mr. Beadle, designed by John Clappison in 1963.

This is perhaps the most avant garde and successful shape from a range produced in many different sizes and colours. It was produced in 1963 only. The range is prone to damage, making pieces in perfect condition hard to find.

11.6in (29.5cm) wide

£70-90   RHA

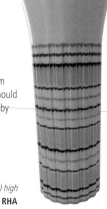

A Hornsea medium 'Rainbow' vase, mould no.548, designed by John Clappison in 1963.

9in (23cm) high

£15-25   RHA

A group of Hornsea 'Gaiety' vases, mould nos.851-855, pattern designed by Colin Rawson in 1964.

These were produced using the moulds for the vases from the 'Slipware' range, a jardiniere from which is shown on this page.

largest 13.6in (34.5cm) high
smallest 4.9in (12.5cm) high

largest £90 - smallest £35   RHA

A group of Hornsea 'Tanglewood' vases, mould nos.980-982, pattern designed by Colin Rawson, shapes designed by John Clappison in 1964.

largest 13.8in (35cm) high,
smallest 9in (23cm) high

largest £80 - smallest £35   RHA

A CLOSER LOOK AT A HORNSEA LAMP BASE

This was designed by John Clappison and modelled by Alan Luckham.

It was the result of a request from company Chairman Desmond Rawson for a 'central figure theme'.

It draws from Scandinavian ceramic design, which was fashionable and popular at the time, including designs by Bjørn Wiinblad and Stig Lindberg.

Large, highly detailed and complex to make in two pieces, it is estimated that fewer than 12 examples were made.

A Hornsea 'Bust of a young girl' lamp base.
1965   *20in (50.5cm) high*

£1,000-1,500   RHA

CERAMICS

A Hornsea 'Modern Slipware' conical-shaped cruet, pattern designed by Colin Rawson, designed by John Clappison in 1958.

4.5in (11.5cm) high

£30-35   RHA

A Hornsea 'Modern Slipware' cruet, pattern designed by Colin Rawson, designed by John Clappison in 1958.

9.5in (24cm) wide

£30-35   RHA

A Hornsea 'Medallion' cruet, pattern designed by Colin Rawson, designed by John Clappison in 1959.

vinegar 4.7in (12cm) high and sugar pot 4in (10cm) high

£40-50 for set   RHA

A Hornsea 'Coronet' cruet, mould nos.201 and 202, pattern designed by Colin Rawson, designed by John Clappison in 1960.

9.5in (24cm) wide

£30-35   RHA

Mark Picks

Hornsea Pottery is best known today for its tableware and vases, and it was these that built the company's reputation and firmed up their commercial success during the 1950s & 60s. Although a great many ranges and forms were produced, a great collection that is representative of the company's look during the period can be built by focusing on cruet sets. For me, 'Summit' is a must, and is undoubtedly my favourite. With its elegant, clean-lined form it's also typical of the mid-century modern period in terms of pattern and colour. The production technique is interesting and innovative too. After being moulded and fired at a low temperature, the bodies were dipped in coloured glaze and then placed on a motorised turntable. A sponge was then applied to the body and, as the turntable turned, it removed the glaze on the ridges, leaving it only in the grooves. Finally the body was dipped in a transparent gloss glaze and fired again. Colours comprised Charcoal, Terracotta (shown here) and Turquoise. Always examine them carefully for damage, as these practical pieces were often heavily and roughly used.

A Hornsea 'Summit' salt and pepper cruet, mould no.217, with mustard pot, mould no.219, and boat-shaped stand, mould no.218/30, modelled by Alan Luckham, designed by John Clappison in 1960.

7.9in (20cm) wide

£25-30   RHA

A Hornsea 'Spruce' salt and pepper cruet set, mould no.230, designed by John Clappison in 1960.

6.5in (16.5cm) wide

£20-25   RHA

A Hornsea 'Alpine' salt and pepper cruet, mould no.221, and a mustard pot, mould no.222, impressed triangle design, with boat-shaped stand, mould no.223, apricot colourway, designed by John Clappison in 1960.

7.75in (20cm) wide

£30-35   RHA

A Hornsea 'Imprest' plantpot, 'Fish-Eye' design, mould no.992, designed by John Clappison in 1964.

5in (13cm) diam

£20-30   RHA

A large Hornsea bird ashtray, mould no.125, designed by John Clappison in 1965.

At the time, these boxed ashtrays cost 7/11, or 25p, each. Two versions are known, one with a rounded bottom as here, and one with a flat bottom allowing it to stand upright.

9in (23cm) wide

£40-60   RHA

A Hornsea 'Gourmet 66' egg cup set, mould no.921, designed in 1966.

dish 5in (13cm) diam

£10-15   RHA

QUICK REFERENCE - HORNSEA 'HEIRLOOM'

- 'Heirloom' was Hornsea's first complete range of tableware and became, in many ways, its most famous design and product, being found in millions of homes across the UK and beyond. Highly fashionable at the time, and hugely commercially successful, it was produced for two decades from 1967-87. Colours comprised Lakeland green, Autumn brown and Midnight blue, but blue turned out to be the least popular colour by far with the public and was soon withdrawn. The instantly recognisable pattern was designed by Clappison in March 1966 and was based on the form of a calligraphic pen nib. The glaze-resist production technique was innovative, with a specially devised glaze-resistant black ink being used in the screen-printed matte-glazed areas. The shapes were derived from the 'County' range and its hallmark forms include the wooded topped storage jars, which initially had teak lids until that had to be replaced by afromosia due to cost. The straight-sided cylindrical forms were popular at the time, and were used by other makers such as Portmeirion and J&G Meakin. Hornsea's designs were intended to be stackable, to help with storage in late 20thC kitchens which were increasingly filling up with labour-saving devices and electric gadgets.

A green Hornsea 'Heirloom' teapot, designed by John Clappison in 1966.

1966-87   *5.5in (14cm) high*

£25-30   RHA

A brown Hornsea 'Heirloom' jug, butter dish, preserve pot, and spice rack.

1966-87   *the spice rack 14in (35.5cm)*

long preserve pot £8-10 spice rack £15-20   RHA

A Hornsea 'Roundalay' milk jug, mould no.924, designed by John Clappison in 1967.

4.5in (11.5cm) high

£10-15   RHA

CERAMICS

A Hornsea 'Saffron' sugar pot and milk jug.

'Saffron' used the same production process as 'Heirloom', but with a different pattern and caramel glazes. It was designed by Clappison to ride on the success of 'Heirloom', and was also hugely successful, also being produced for 20 years. Look out for examples in this pattern in Midnight blue, as these are extremely scarce.

1970-90   *the jug 4.5in (9cm) high*
sugar pot £6-8 jug £8-10   **RHA**

A pair of large Hornsea 'Geometric' cruets, 'Zig-Zag' pattern, mould no.152, designed by John Clappison in 1971.

4in (10cm) high
£12-15   **RHA**

A Hornsea 'Bronte' coffee pot, designed by John Clappison.
1972-87   *9.75in (24.5cm) high*
£12-15   **RHA**

A set of Hornsea 'Bronte' tea, coffee, sugar, and salt storage jars, designed by John Clappison.
1972-87.   *4.25in (11cm) high*
£6-10 each   **RHA**

A Hornsea 'Impact' sugar pot and egg cup, by John Clappison and Sara Vardy.
1977-81   *sugar pot 3in (7.5cm) high*
           egg cup 1.5in (4cm) high
£6-8, egg cup £3-4   **RHA**

A Hornsea 'Moonstone' cup and saucer.
1979-80   *5in (13cm) diam*
£6-8   **RHA**

A Hornsea 'Concord' cup, saucer, and plate, designed by John Clappison in 1976.
6.75in (17cm) diam trio
£10-15   **RHA**

A group of Hornsea cruets, including a pair of owl-shaped cruets, mould no.114, a pair of cat-shaped cruets, mould no.115, and a pair of bird-shaped cruets, mould no.113, designed by John Clappison in 1965.

owl 4in (10cm) high
£35-70 per set   **RHA**

QUICK REFERENCE - MUGS

● Although they were produced during the 1950s, it was the late 1960s-80s that the mug really came into its own at Hornsea. This coincided with the rise of the mug in many people's homes, and it taking over from the teacup and coffee cup. More able to withstand the rigours of modern life and better able to retain heat better, both tea and coffee could be drunk out of it, as well as other drinks such as instant hot soups. Clappison designed many from the mid-1960s-80s, mostly with amusing characters or a whimsical sense of humour, and some commemorating events. A number use the same innovative wax resist technique pioneered with Heirloom in 1967 (see page 95). Some collectors have chosen to focus on Hornsea mugs only, and some examples such as this one are challenging to find. A little like Clappison's amusing mug showing the different types of class on a train, this shows the social divisions that existed in a British pub of the period.

An early Hornsea elf-handled mug.
1950-52   3.5in (9cm) high
£15-25   RHA

An early Hornsea 'Fauna' range 'All Gone Good Boy/ Girl' series 'Dog' mug, mould no.313.

This range was to congratulate the child for having drunk all the contents.

1955   3in (7.5cm) high
£25-30   RHA

A Hornsea mug, 'Geometric' series, 'Circle', pattern no.965.
1967-70   3.5in (9cm) high
£25-35   RHA

A Hornsea 'Bar Scene' tankard, designed by John Clappison in 1970.
5in (13cm) high
£40-50   RHA

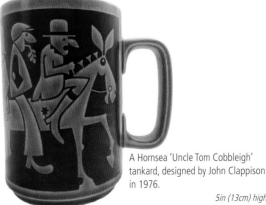

A Hornsea 'Uncle Tom Cobbleigh' tankard, designed by John Clappison in 1976.
5in (13cm) high
£40-50   RHA

CERAMICS

A 'Zoodiac' mug, created by Jack Dodd.

These were launched in July 1976 and 22,860 were sold in August alone. They were distributed in the US by Kosta Boda. They featured the name of a zodiac sign with the typical characteristics and likely personality of people born under that sign - for example; Scorpio - intense, the inspector; Aries - lively; Libra - the manager.

A Hornsea 'Playmates' mug.

1971   *3.5in (9cm) high*

£25-35   **RHA**

1975-77   *3.5in (9cm) high*

£30-40   **RHA**

A Hornsea 'January Love' mug, designed by Ken Townsend in 1976.

1976-81   *3in (8cm) high*

£10-15   **RHA**

Three Hornsea 'THE WORLDS BEST' mugs, designed by John Clappison,

'Landlady' 1978   *3.5in (9cm) high*

£35-45,

'Motorist' 1977   *3.5in (9cm) high*

£10-15,

'Motorcyclist' 1977 *3.5in (9cm) high*

£20-25   **RHA**

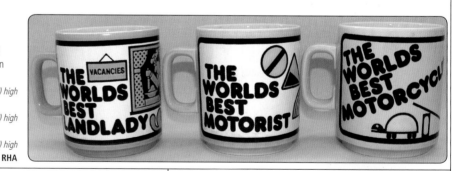

A Hornsea 'Nursery Rhyme' mug, 'Sing a Song of Sixpence', designed by John Clappison in 1978.

These mugs had large handles to make it easy for a child to hold. They were sold through larger branches of Boots retailing at £1.20 each.

1979-94   *3.7in (9.5cm) high*

£10-15   **RHA**

A Hornsea 'Phizoog' mug, 'Toothey'.

The range included 'Looney', 'Spookey', 'Moodey', 'Frootey' and 'Gloomey'.

1979-80   *3.7in (9.5cm) high*

£15-20   **RHA**

A Hornsea 'Muramic' wall-plaque, 'The Peacock', designed by John Clappison.
1971-72   *7.9in (20cm) high*
£120-170   **RHA**

A Hornsea 'Muramic' wall-plaque, 'Bird', designed by John Clappison.
1971-72   *7.9in (20cm) square*
£80-150   **RHA**

A Hornsea 'Muramic' wall-plaque, 'Fish', designed by John Clappison.
1971-72   *7.9in (20cm) square*
£80-150   **RHA**

A Hornsea 'Muramic' wall-plaque, 'Tortoise', designed by John Clappison.
1971-72   *7.9in (20cm) high*
£80-100   **RHA**

QUICK REFERENCE - MURAMICS

- 'Muramics' were wall plaques designed by John Clappison in 1970 and were produced for only six months from 1971-72 only. Each was cut from a rolled-out clay panel and decorated by hand, making each one unique. They were made by a special team of ladies in a dedicated part of the factory to avoid the delicate designs being ruined by grime or dirt from the factory. The glazes were then applied, often by screen printing, together with small discs/buttons of clay known as 'jewels'. Specialist glazes using Selenium and Cadmium were also used. Once complete, they were mounted on canvas or aformosia boards and framed. Each also bore a special silver sticker on the back. Comparatively expensive and of appeal to a more limited audience than the rest of their production, they were not produced and did not sell in great quantities. Some Muramics are rarer than others. In general, look for large examples and complex designs that involved more decorating work, as with this example. Condition is paramount. Any cracks, chips or damage at all will reduce value dramatically, hence the wider price guides given here.

A Hornsea 'Muramic' wall-plaque, 'Charioteer' designed by John Clappison.
1971-72   *7.9in (20cm) wide*
£170-250   **RHA**

A Hornsea 'Muramic' wall-plaque, 'Adam & Eve with serpent'.
1971-72   *17.5in (44.5cm) square*
£350-500   **RHA**

A Hornsea 'Muramic' wall-plaque, 'Astronaut', designed by John Clappison.
1971-72   *7.9in (20cm) high*
£80-100   **RHA**

CERAMICS

Mark Picks

I was lucky enough to attend the Hornsea Collectors Society convention last year and one range that caught my eye was the 'Strata' range of trinket boxes. The complex pattern, which almost resembles pastel rock strata (hence the name) on the lids intrigued me. The technique used to make it was both innovative and unique. Differently coloured clays were layered together into blocks and cut longitudinally into thin slivers. These were then shaped and combined into blocks, with each separate shape being deliberately misaligned. The blocks were then cut into 1mm thick slivers and laid into moulds from which the lids were cast. The lids were then polished to a non-porous finish until flush and completely flat. Lids were hexagonal, heart-shaped, circular, and oval and no two patterns are exactly alike, making each box effectively unique. The bases were impressed with a stamp bearing Clappison's signature. The blue, green, or pink pastel colours hit the style of the day perfectly, and there was nothing else on the market like it. The range won a major award and the process attracted the eye of the Chairman of Wedgwood, who was interested in buying Hornsea, but the problem was that the process was labour-intensive and thus expensive, which made the pieces expensive. As a result, it was withdrawn after only a few years. The range is somewhat ignored, so is largely afford-able, but for how long. My next challenge will be to find a very rare experimental bowl for my collection!

A Strata trinket box, designed by John Clappison, with impressed stamp.
1981-83   *2.4in (6cm) high*
£12-18   **RHA**

A Hornsea 'Midas' 15-piece coffee set.
1981-84   *coffee pot 6.9in (17.5cm) high*
£40-50   **RHA**

A Hornsea 'Cirrus' teapot.

Designed in 1980, 'Cirrus' was based on the matte 'Concept' range, produced from 1977-91. Innovative production techniques ensured that the mottled grey and white 'clouds' fused into the non-fade, oven, dishwasher and microwave proof body. Unfortunately, despite its then-fashionable almost Japanese feel, it wasn't popular and was discontinued after four years.
1981-85   *7.5in (19cm) high incl. handle*
£40-50   **RHA**

A Hornsea 'Swan Lake' pink milk jug.

This range was displayed as part of Hornsea's 'Romantic Range'.
1983-92   *3.2in (8cm) high*
£10-15   **RHA**

A Hornsea 'Cinnamon' teapot.
1980-82   *7.3in (18.5cm) high including handle*
£20-25   **RHA**

A Hornsea 'Charisma' tureen.
1979-80   *7.7in (19.5cm) diam*
£12-15   **RHA**

A Hornsea 'Bouquet' coffee pot, designed by Martin Hunt, decorated with a John Clappison design.
1982-84   *7.7in (19.5cm) high*
£10-15   **RHA**

QUICK REFERENCE - LENCI

● The Lenci factory was founded in Turin, Italy, in 1919, by Elena (Helen) Konig and Enrico Scavini to produce felt dolls and other items for children. The word 'Lenci' is an acronym from the Latin motto 'Ludus Est Nobis Constanter Industria' which means 'Play is our constant work.'

● In 1928 it introduced a range of earthenware pottery, including the figures it is renowned for today.

● Ceramics collectors look for the large-scale earthenware figures it made from 1928 until the outbreak of World War Two. The most desirable feature modern women – often unclothed or in sporting or athletic poses – decorated with bold colours.

● Elena created many of the figures, but the company also worked with designers including Sandro Vacchetti, Giovanni Grande, Essevi and Jacobi.

● The factory closed in 1964.

A Lenci Pottery figure, 'Damina Con Colombo', by Nillo Beltrami, model no.126, painted in colours, painted marks, original paper label, damages and old restoration.

12.5in (32cm) high

£750-850   **WW**

A 1930s Lenci figure, 'Angelita alla Corida', by Helen Konig Scavini, modelled as a seated lady in Spanish-style dress, hand-painted marks, restored.

14in (36cm) high

£1,000-1,500   **FLD**

A Lenci figure, a lady looking down at a dog jumping on to her dress, inscribed 'Lenci Made in Italy, Torino C M', gold 'A' with label numbered 'CF13'.

13.6in (34.5cm) high

£2,000-2,500   **SWO**

A Lenci polychrome pottery figure, 'Abissina', from a model by Sandro Vacchetti, painted in ochre, black, green and blue, signed 'Lenci MADE IN ITALY 8-8-?1', painters monogram 'Z', painted 'ESSEVI', minor chips and glaze nicks.

21in (53cm) high

£15,000-18,000   **TEN**

A Lenci model of a mother and child, 'Amore Paterno', by Sandro Vacchetti, inscribed 'Essevi', and with black painted Lenci mark and date '27-7-31'.

7in (18cm) high

£1,600-2,000   **SWO**

A Lenci bust, 'Maria Maddalena', designed by Helen Konig Scavini.

14in (36cm) high

£600-800   **ECGW**

CERAMICS

QUICK REFERENCE - LOUIS WAIN

- Louis Wain (1860-1939) made his name painting pictures of fully clothed, standing cats drinking tea, playing cards or fishing on a riverbank. After training at the West London School of Art, he worked there as an assistant teacher until becoming a freelance artist in 1882.
- To amuse his wife when she was dying of cancer, he taught their cat, Peter, to wear spectacles and pretend to read. He began to sketch the cat, which led to his obsession with all things feline.
- He went on to illustrate approximately one hundred children's books, and his work was published widely, including in the Louis Wain Annual, which ran from 1901 to 1915. His work was regularly reproduced on picture postcards. These are highly sought-after by collectors today and can fetch up to £50.
- Wain also designed several Cubist-style ceramic cats for the Austrian manufacturer, Amphora.
- Despite his popularity, Wain was a poor businessman and suffered financial difficulty throughout his life. After the death of his sister, Caroline, in 1917, he began to suffer from schizophrenia. He died in the Middlesex County Asylum, Napsbury, near St Albans.

A 'The Lucky Futurist Cat' figural vase, designed by Louis Wain, painted in colours with black 'Meow Meow' notes, facsimile signature, printed factory marks, original paper label.

5in (13cm) high

£1,300-1,800   WW

A rare 'The Lucky Bully Bulldog' figural spill vase, designed by Louis Wain, facsimile signature, printed factory marks, restored front leg.

5.75in (14.5cm) wide

£600-800   WW

A 'The Lucky Pig' figural vase, designed by Louis Wain, facsimile signature and impressed marks to base.

4.75in (12cm) high

£700-800   WW

A 'The Lucky Black Cat' figural spill vase, designed by Louis Wain, facsimile signature, impressed and painted factory marks, minor damages and overpainting to side.

5.5in (14cm) high

£1,100-1,500   WW

A 'The Lucky Knight Errant Cat' figural vase, designed by Louis Wain and the design registered in 1914, facsimile signature, repaired legs, damages.

5.7in (14.5cm) high

£600-800   WW

A rare 'The Lucky Haw Waw Cat' large figural vase, by Louis Wain, impressed facsimile signature, impressed 'The Lucky Master Cat' and '5123' to base, damages to tail and chin, oxidised colours.

8in (20.5cm) high

£1,600-2,000   WW

A rare 'The Lucky Master Cat' large figural vase, by Louis Wain, impressed facsimile signature, printed marks to base, overpainting.

11.5in (29cm) high

£3,500-4,000   WW

A Minton dessert plate, for Goode, the centre well painted in the style of Henry Mitchell with a scene of stags, and inscribed 'M 5734' in red, with the impressed Minton cypher, tiny chip to turquoise glaze.

This design is similar to the celebrated 'Sandringham Landseer' service.
1877
£150-200 H&C

A Minton plate, for Goode, with a medallion painted with a floral 'E' monogram, the crown and insignia II in gilt, the outer border with cameo-style vignettes, gilt scrolls and flowers, impressed with the Minton cypher, restored.

This is a copy of the celebrated 'Bleu Celeste' dinner service produced by Sèvres in 1778 for Catherine the Great and now displayed in the Hermitage Museum, St. Petersburg.
1883
£1,000-1,200 H&C

A Minton 'Secessionist' vase, decorated with yellow primula flowers on blue ground, printed manufacturer's mark.
c1905   9.5in (24cm) high
£150-200 MLL

A Minton 'Secessionist' vase, in turquoise and purple glazes, design no.1, printed manufacturer's mark.
9.5in (24cm) high
£200-250 MLL

A Minton 'Secessionist' vase, designed by Leon Solon and John Wadsworth, painted with Art Nouveau tree design, printed marks.
9in (22.5cm) high
£300-400 WW

A pair of Minton 'Secessionist' vases, designed by Leon Solon and John Wadsworth, painted with Art Nouveau swag design, printed marks.
13in (32cm) high
£350-450 WW

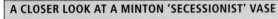

A CLOSER LOOK AT A MINTON 'SECESSIONIST' VASE

The vibrant blue, green, and yellow glazes are typical of pieces made in the Viennese Secessionist style.

The outline of the decoration was created using tube-lining. This technique uses a thin trail of slip to create the lines.

The design was created by Leon Solon and John Wadsworth. Solon was artistic director of the Minton factory from 1900-09. He created many of the pottery's 'Secessionist' pieces in collaboration with Wadsworth.

The flowing shape of the trees is typical of Secessionist and Art Nouveau decoration.

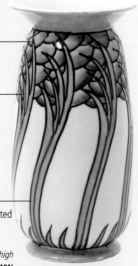

A Minton 'Secessionist' vase, painted with Art Nouveau trees, printed factory marks.
9in (22.5cm) high
£550-650 WW

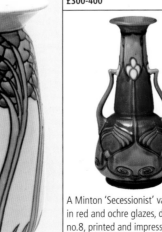

A Minton 'Secessionist' vase, in red and ochre glazes, design no.8, printed and impressed manufacturer's mark.
c1910   10in (25.5cm) high
£200-300 MLL

A Minton 'Secessionist' pottery wash jug, tube-lined with stylised motifs, printed mark 'MINTON LTD.' and 'A8', repaired hole.
12in (30.5cm) high
£100-150 SWO

CERAMICS

QUICK REFERENCE - MOORCROFT

- After studying art in Burslem, Staffordshire and Paris, and experimenting with ceramic design on his own, William Moorcroft (1872-1945) began work as a designer at the James McIntyre & Co pottery in 1897. He was promoted to manager of Ornamental Ware in 1898. 'Aurelian' and 'Florian', his first ranges, included stylised, swirling foliate and floral designs inspired by Moorish designs and the prevalent Art Nouveau style.

- Each piece was thrown and decorated by hand, with the design being applied using a technique called 'tube-lining', where the outlines of the pattern were piped onto the surface, leaving a low relief outline design. The 'cells' within the pattern were then filled with coloured, liquid glaze.

- Moorcroft left McIntyre in 1912 to found his own company in 1913 with backing from major retailer Liberty. By 1929, Moorcroft had been awarded the Royal Warrant.

- The natural world continued to be an inspiration, The Art Nouveau stylisation was left behind as tastes and fashions changed. Although many patterns were continued and developed after William's death in 1945, his son Walter (1917-2002), who took over, designed many of the company's most popular patterns.

- Early ranges from the 1900s-20s, including 'Florian', 'Claremont', and landscape-themed designs tend to be the most desirable and valuable, particularly in visually impressive or rare shapes. Some were ornamented with pewter or silver fittings when sold through Liberty. More affordable are patterns that were produced for decades into the late 20thC and beyond, and in a profusion of shapes, such as 'Pomegranate' or 'Anemone'. The marks on the base and the colours used in a design can help to date a piece.

- A growing number of collectors are beginning to focus on more contemporary pieces, produced from the 1980s onwards, by designers such as Sally Tuffin, Rachel Bishop, and Philip Gibson. Visual impact, size, and rarity are important factors. So, large pieces from strictly limited editions in good shapes that show the 'Moorcroft look' tend to fetch the best prices. Regardless of date, always examine a piece closely for any damage, which reduces value.

A Moorcroft 'Flamminian Ware' vase, designed by William Moorcroft, obscured mark, thickness of glaze obscures details of decoration, minor firing line to foot ring.

The 'Flamminian Ware' range, with its mottled monochrome and lustre glazes and impressed roundel design, was registered in April 1905. Available in red, green, or blue, it was produced until at least 1915. The design of the roundel shows Celtic or even Japanese influences.

1905-15   *8.25in (21cm) high*

£500-600   DRA

A large James Macintyre 'Florian Ware' lamp base, designed by William Moorcroft, in 'Peacock' pattern, the base with green Moorcroft signature with registration number, with several short tight lines to rim and base, some from firing, and several small chips to base.

1898-1906

£2,000-2,500

11in (28cm) high

DRA

A James Macintyre jug, designed by William Moorcroft, 'Florian' pattern, tube-lined decoration on two shades of blue, with silver-plated rim, 'Florian Ware' stamp and registered design no.326471, green signature.

8in (20cm) high

£300-400   ECGW

A James Macintyre 'Florian Ware' jardiniere, designed by William Moorcroft, 'Honesty' pattern, swollen cylindrical form with fluted rim, painted in shades of blue, printed factory mark, painted green signature.

7.25in (18.5cm) high

£650-850   WW

A mid-20thC Moorcroft Pottery tea cup and saucer, designed by William Moorcroft, 'Claremont' pattern, tube-lined and painted in dusky pink, blues, and green on a green ground, impressed, initialled in green and saucer bears paper label.

saucer 5.25in (13.5cm) diam

£400-500   HT

QUICK REFERENCE - CLAREMONT

- Instantly recognisable from the toadstool motif, 'Claremont' was introduced in October 1903 and named by Liberty. Produced for nearly forty years, early examples were produced in green and mottled blue backgrounds. By the 1920s, colouring had become darker and stronger and the drawing had become bolder. During the 1920s & 30s, it was also produced with desirable flambé glazes and in light colours on pale matte grounds. Despite being so successful, it is considered scarce, particularly when compared to ranges such as 'Pomegranate'. Always desirable, early examples in unusual and strong forms such as this example, from the mid-late 1910s, are highly sought-after and valuable.

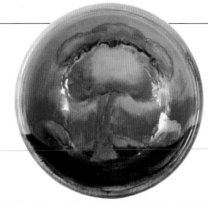

A 1920s William Moorcroft small-footed bowl, designed by William Moorcroft, 'Eventide' pattern, decorated with a tube-lined tree against a tonal ochre and red sky, impressed marks with blue flash initials.

5.5in (14cm) diam

£550-650   **FLD**

A William Moorcroft twin-handled baluster vase, designed by William Moorcroft, 'Claremont' pattern, tube-lined and painted decoration of toadstools, in bordeaux, red, and purple on a green ground, green painted signature.

5.5in (14cm) high

£2,000-2,500   **ECGW**

A Moorcroft Pottery lamp base, designed by William Moorcroft, 'Flag Iris' pattern, shouldered and footed cylindrical form, painted in colours on a blue ground, impressed marks, painted green signature.

Although less commonly found, lamp bases tend to be considerably less desirable and less valuable than vases and bowls. This is because they are harder to display effectively and many collectors who want one may only want one or two. Some are converted vase forms.

8.5in (21.5cm) high

£120-180   **WW**

A Moorcroft vase, with bearded 'Iris' on a blue ground, impressed and painted signature, marked 'Potter to the Queen'.

7in (18cm) high

£200-250   **ECGW**

A Moorcroft vase, designed by William Moorcroft, decorated in the 'Leaf and Grape' pattern, blue ground, blue painted, stamped marks.

c1930   *10in (25.5cm) high*

£300-350   **BELL**

A Moorcroft vase, designed by William Moorcroft, decorated in the 'Leaf and Grape' pattern, green ground, blue painted signature and impressed marks.

c1930   *10.25in (26cm) high*

£300-400   **BELL**

A Moorcroft Pottery vase, 'Frilled and Slipper Orchids' pattern, shouldered form, impressed marks, painted blue facsimile signature.

The successful 'Orchids' design was developed by William Moorcroft in 1937, and produced intermittently under Walter Moorcroft during the 1940s & 50s. Vases produced in 1972 commemorate the centenary of William Moorcroft's birth.

9.5in (24cm) high

£350-400   **WW**

CERAMICS

A Moorcroft Pottery bowl, 'Pansy' pattern, designed by William Moorcroft, with 'Tudric Pewter' foot, painted in colours on a blue ground, with stamped marks, 'Moorcroft Tudric 01311'.

'Tudric' was the brand name applied to Liberty's pewter table and decorative wares. 'Tudric' was produced from 1902-1930s and was made for Liberty by W.H. Haseler of Birmingham.

10.25in (26cm) diam

£400-450 — WW

A CLOSER LOOK AT A MOORCROFT COMPORT

Comports are a highly desirable and scarce form. They were time-consuming to make.

Many examples were damaged over time - always examine every part in detail.

The 'Spanish' pattern was introduced in 1910 and produced until the 1930s.

A Moorcroft Pottery twin-handled comport, designed by William Moorcroft, 'Spanish' pattern, painted in shades of pink, purple, and ochre on a mottled green ground, impressed marks.

11.75in (29.5cm) wide

£1,000-1,500 — WW

A William Moorcroft vase, designed by William Moorcroft, 'Pomegranate' pattern, with flaring neck, green painted signature, impressed Burslem factory mark.

9.25in (23.5cm)

£750-850 — TEN

A Moorcroft vase, designed by William Moorcroft, 'Pomegranate' pattern, blue signature and impressed marks to base.

6in (15cm) high

£200-250 — ECGW

A William Moorcroft vase, designed by William Moorcroft, 'Pomegranate' pattern, on a blue ground, blue painted monogram, impressed factory marks with facsimile signature and 'POTTER TO H.M.THE QUEEN'.

6.5in (16.5cm) high

£300-350 — TEN

A 1930s Moorcroft baluster vase, designed by William Moorcroft, 'Spring Flowers' pattern, on shaded green to blue ground, blue signature and 'Potter to the Queen', impressed mark, hairline crack on base then runs into the lower section of vase.

6in (15.5cm) high

£180-220 — ECGW

A Moorcroft twin-handled vase, designed by William Moorcroft, 'Wisteria' pattern, on a blue ground, green painted signature, impressed factory marks 'MOORCROFT BURSLEM'.

10.75in (27cm) across handles

£300-350 — TEN

A CLOSER LOOK AT A MOORCROFT VASE

This pattern was designed by Walter Moorcroft (1917-2002) to commemorate the centenary of William Moorcroft beginning work at Mcintyre.

The tree design harks back to his father William's popular landscape scenes, and the way the brightly coloured background landscape is depicted reflects more modern designs by those such as Rachel Bishop and Sally Tuffin.

It was released in a limited edition of 200 and proved very successful - it is still sought-after by collectors today as it is one of the last patterns Walter designed.

The form echoes the shape of the tree and shows the pattern off extremely well.

A large Moorcroft 'Trial' vase, designed by Walter Moorcroft, 'After the Storm' pattern, decorated with a tube-lined landscape against a countryside background, painted and impressed marks, signed 'W'. Moorcroft and dated '23.IV.97'.

1997   *12.5in (32cm) high*
£850-950   **FLD**

A Moorcroft Pottery plate, designed by Sally Tuffin, and decorated in the 'Cat' pattern, printed and painted marks, dated '17.9.91'.

This plate was also produced in a limited edition of 300 in 1992-93.

1991   *10in (25cm) diam*
£150-200   **FLD**

A limited edition Moorcroft vase, designed by Rachel Bishop for Liberty, 'Cymric Dream' pattern, the base with painted and printed marks and numbered 154 from an edition of 250, dated March 2000.

'Cymric' was the name given to the silver table and decorative wares sold by Liberty from 1899 onwards. Many designs were produced by Archibald Knox and this pattern uses many of his favoured design elements as inspiration.

2000   *8.25in (21cm) high*
£300-400   **ECGW**

A Moorcroft vase, by Philip Richardson, 'Fairy Rings' pattern.
c1988   *14in (36cm) high*
£300-400   **ECGW**

A Moorcroft squat vase, designed by Sally Tuffin in 1987, 'Finches' pattern, monogrammed WM, inscribed on base 'With Thanks Hugh + Maureen Edwards August 1989'.

Lawyer Hugh Edwards and his wife Maureen acquired Moorcroft in 1986, together with pottery specialist and author Richard Dennis and his wife, the designer Sally Tuffin. Together they revived the near-bankrupt company, introducing vibrant new designs and designers and founding the Moorcroft Design Studio. Dennis and Tuffin left the company in 1992 and, at the time of writing, the Edwards continue to own the company.

8in (20.5cm) high
£200-300   **ECGW**

A Moorcroft Pottery vase, designed by Nicola Slaney, decorated in the 'Fruit Garden' pattern, with tube-lined flowers, fruit, foliage, and butterflies, impressed marks.
1999   *6in (15cm) high*
£100-150   **FLD**

CERAMICS

A Moorcroft vase, designed by Rachel Bishop, 'Gypsy' pattern, dated '14/4/00'.

2000   *5.5in (14cm) high*

£120-150   **ECGW**

A Moorcroft Pottery pedestal vase, designed by Phillip Richardson, decorated in the 'Honeycomb' pattern, the body decorated with bees and honeycomb against a blue wash ground, impressed and painted marks.

This large and desirable vase is marked as a second, indicating it did not pass quality control due to a fault and was possibly sold in the factory shop. Had it been a first quality piece it may have been worth up to double this sum.

1987   *11in (28cm) high*

£200-250   **FLD**

A Moorcroft vase and cover, designed by Emma Bossons for Liberty, 'Jewel of Medina' pattern, dated.

2002   *5in (13cm) high*

£250-350   **ECGW**

A Moorcroft Pottery vase, designed by Rachel Bishop, 'Lamia' pattern, of bulbous form, decorated with bulrush and waterlilies, impressed and painted marks.

1995   *9.5in (24cm) high*

£300-350   **FLD**

A Moorcroft vase, designed by Rachel Bishop for Liberty & Co, 'Ophir' pattern, no.19 of 100.

10in (25cm) high

£300-350   **ECGW**

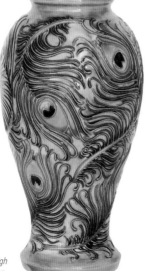

A Moorcroft Pottery vase of inverted baluster form, designed by Rachel Bishop, decorated in the 'Peacock Feathers' pattern, impressed and painted marks.

Both the pattern and form hark back to William Moorcroft's 'Florian' range produced in the early 1900s - see page 104 for examples.

10.5in (27cm) high

£350-400   **FLD**

A limited edition Moorcroft vase, designedby Philip Gibson, 'Profusion' pattern, no.32 of 100.

2001   *16.5in (42cm) high*

£900-1,200   **ECGW**

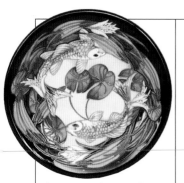

A large Moorcroft Pottery charger, designed by Phillip Gibson, decorated in the 'Quiet Water' pattern, with koi carp and water lilies, printed and impressed marks, boxed.

13.75in (35cm) diam

£200-300   FLD

A Moorcroft vase, designed by Philip Richardson, 'Reeds in Sunset' pattern.

1997/98   *7in (18cm) high*

£150-200   ECGW

A Moorcroft 'Simeon' vase, designed by Philip Gibson, on a cream shading to blue ground, impressed and printed marks, boxed.

1999   *9in (23cm) high*

£250-350   SWO

Mark Picks

Although it's an expensive piece, at 27in (69cm) high it's also enormous and makes a dramatic statement. As well as requiring great skill to pot, the pattern is extremely complex and time-consuming to produce. Rachel Bishop was only the third designer appointed by Moorcroft (following William and Walter) and was the first non-family member. Her designs are popular amongst collectors. It was also released in a limited edition of only 100 pieces as part of the top end 'Prestige' range. The size of the edition compared to the size of the market of potential buyers is of vital importance to future desirability and value. Although more modern and contemporary Moorcroft pieces are generally worth less than many classic pieces, the value of this piece looks set to rise as this example really has it all.

A limited edition Moorcroft 'Prestige' baluster vase, designed by Rachel Bishop, 'Ryden Lane' pattern, painted marks, no.55 from an edition of 100, marked 'RM3/27'.

1997   *27in (69cm) high*

£1,500-2,000   MOR

A limited edition Moorcroft vase, by Rachel Bishop, with 'Swallow' design, no.55 of 500, dated.

1997   *10in (25cm) high*

£250-350   ECGW

A Moorcroft ginger jar, by Phillip Gibson, 'Trout' pattern, dated.

1998   *6in (15cm) high*

£250-300   ECGW

A Moorcroft Pottery clock, designed by Sally Tuffin, 'Violet' pattern, painted in shades of pink, purple, and green on a dark blue ground, impressed marks.

The design of this clock was inspired by pewter- or silver-cased clocks designed by Archibald Knox for Liberty's in the early 1900s.

6.25in (16cm) high

£250-300   WW

CERAMICS

QUICK REFERENCE - POOLE POTTERY

- The company we know today as Poole Pottery began in 1921 when the Carter & Co, Pottery in Poole, England, bought a subsidiary pottery. The resulting company became known for its decorative and domestic wares. It was formally known as Carter, Stabler & Adams, but commonly referred to as Poole Pottery.
- One of the key designers of the 1920s and 30s was Truda Carter. Her work was hand-thrown and hand-decorated and featured stylized flowers and leaves and Art Deco geometric patterns. Pieces featuring animals are rarer and likely to be more desirable. Collectors will pay a premium for large, highly decorated pieces which display the pattern well.
- After WWII, the 'Contemporary' range designed by Alfred Burgess Read kept Poole Pottery at the forefront of modern design. These ceramics used simple geometric or curving linear patterns against plain backgrounds. Read worked closely with thrower Guy Sydenham and decorator Ruth Pavely.

- In 1958, Robert Jefferson became Poole's resident designer. He worked with Sydenham and designer Tony Morris to create the 'Delphis' range which gave the company a foothold in the growing Studio Pottery movement.
- Typical 'Delphis' pieces feature orange and yellow glazes and swirling patterns. The range remains popular with collectors today, although pieces do not fetch the high prices they did a few years ago.
- In 1966, Poole opened a Craft Section to produce unique Studio Pottery pieces and supply decorative ranges including 'Aegean', 'Ionian', and 'Atlantis'.
- Modern pieces are also collectable. Look for names such as Janice Tchalenko and Sir Terry Frost (1915-2003). Limited edition pieces are also sought-after.
- Early pieces were marked 'Poole England', sometimes with 'Carter, Stabler & Adams Ltd'. A dolphin was added to the mark in the 1950s and the words and dolphin logo appeared in a box after c1956. The 'Poole Studio' mark was used after c1963.

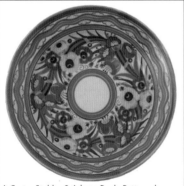

A Carter Stabler & Adams Poole Pottery charger, by Anne Hatchard, pattern 'YO', painted to the well with a band of fuchsia inside an endless wave band, impressed and painted marks.

14.5in (37cm) diam

£200-250   WW

A late 1920s Poole Stabler Adams vase, floral decorated, impressed marks to base.

9in (23cm) high

£100-150   ECGW

A Poole Pottery vase, 'TJ' pattern, decorated by Marjorie Batt.

7in (17.5cm) high

£150-200   SWO

A 1950s Poole Pottery 'Studio' bowl, by Tony Morris, decorated with an abstract block and line design, hand-painted monogram with impressed mark.

10.5in (26.5cm) diam

£600-700   FLD

A 1950s Poole Pottery 'Freeform' footed 'egg cup' vase, painted by June March, 'GBU' pattern, printed marks.

7.5in (19cm) high

£250-300   FLD

A Poole Pottery 'Atlantis' vase, by Guy Sydenham and Susan Dipple, cylindrical form with impressed decoration, impressed and incised marks.

8in (20.5cm) high

£250-300   **WW**

A Poole Pottery 'Atlantis' vase, by Guy Sydenham, with impressed decoration, glazed matte browns, impressed and incised marks.

6.75in (17cm) high

£200-250   **WW**

A Poole Pottery vase, by Guy Sydenham, with a tall neck and vertical carved base, impressed marks and monogram, incised 'A11/2'.

8.75in (22cm) high

£120-180   **SWO**

QUICK REFERENCE - POOLE ATLANTIS

- The 'Atlantis' range was the brainchild of thrower Guy Sydenham (1916-2005) and designers Alfred Read and Robert Jefferson. It was designed between 1965-66 and was still being produced in the 1970s.
- Sydenham had joined the pottery in 1931 and went on to create the modern, curving shapes that became the pottery's signature after World War Two. He became senior designer in 1966.
- Each piece was carved and glazed by hand. Sydenham produced many of the pieces. These are marked with his 'GS' seal. A simple un-glazed stoneware vase by Sydenham might be found for under £100. Other more decorative examples can fetch over £200. Rarer and highly desirable forms, such as unusual versions of the lamp base shown here, have fetched thousands of pounds.

A Poole Pottery 'Atlantis' helmet lamp, by Guy Sydenham and Beatrice Bolton, the exterior incised with chain-mail, the interior a portrait glazed orange impressed mark, incised monograms.

12in (30cm) high

£400-500   **WW**

A large Poole Pottery 'Studio' sculpture, by Tony Morris, deeply modelled as a tower of scaly fish, sold with the original Poole Pottery receipt, minor restoration.

15in (38cm) high

£1,000-1,500   **WW**

CERAMICS

A Poole Pottery 'Aegean' bowl, the dark-yellow ground decorated with brown and orange patterns.

10.5in (27cm) diam

£30-40   LOC

A pair of Poole Pottery 'Aegean' vases, of cylindrical form decorated with black swirls and hearts on a brown and yellow ground.

12.5in (32cm) high each

£30-40   LOC

A CLOSER LOOK AT AN AEGEAN WALL PLATE

The plate is decorated with three stylized 'alien' heads. These are typical of Cutler's work.

The outlines of the design are clear and strong; any mottling would reduce its desirability.

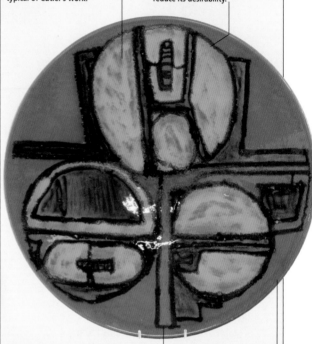

A Poole 'Delphis' charger, typically decorated on an orange ground.

10.5in (26.5cm) diam

£45-55   WHP

A Poole Pottery 'Delphis' charger, decorated with dark-blue shapes on a yellow ground.

10.5in (27cm) diam

£30-40   LOC

Cutler worked for Poole Pottery from 1969-76. Her early (from 1970) monogram was 'CC' but this changed to 'CK' in 1976 when she married.

The abstract design and green and yellow glazes are typical of the 'Aegean' range.

A Poole Pottery 'Aegean' wall plate, by Carol Cutler.

1969-76   *16in (41cm) diam*

£120-180   ECGW

A Poole Pottery 'Studio' footed shallow dish, decorated with an abstract linear pattern, against an orange ground with an orange peel effect, printed Studio mark.

8in (20.5cm) diam

£150-200   FLD

A rare Poole Pottery 'Studio' charger, by Tony Morris, with 'sheep's head' and motorbike and rider at right angle, thrown by Guy Sydenham, 'TM' monogram and Sydenham impressed triangle mark.

c1962   *14in (35.5cm) diam*

£600-700   SWO

A Poole Pottery vase, designed by Angela Wyburgh, shape no.90, printed mark.

This design is known to collectors as the 'Packet of Crisps' vase.

8in (20.5cm) diam

£150-200   SWO

A Poole Pottery 'Studio' 'Trewellard Red' charger, designed by Sir Terry Frost, with initials.

13.75in (35cm) diam

£250-300   SWO

A Poole Pottery 'Studio' charger, 'Arizona Blue', designed by Sir Terry Frost, with initials.

14in (35.5cm) diam

£100-150   SWO

A modern Poole Pottery 'Tree of Life' limited edition charger, by Jane Brewer, painted with tree of life to well and inscription to rim, in colours printed and painted marks, paper certificate.

15.75in (40cm) diam.

£150-200   WW

A Poole Pottery 'Studio' vase and cover, designed by Anita Harris, decorated with a hare, signed and dated twice.

1999   *12.75in (32.5cm) high*

£100-150   SWO

A large Poole Pottery 'Studio' modern vase, designed by Janice Tchalenko, painted with foliate columns, printed and painted marks, dated.

2000 20in (45cm) high

£300-350   WW

A modern Poole Pottery 'Studio' 'Kink' vase, by L. Whitmarsh, painted with citrus fruit, impressed and painted marks.

13.75in (35cm) high

£100-150   WW

A late 20thC or early 21stC Poole Pottery vase, typically decorated on a red ground.

9.5in (24.5cm) high

£25-30   WHP

CERAMICS

QUICK REFERENCE - ROOKWOOD

- Maria Longworth Nichols Storer established her pottery in 1880 in Cincinnati, Ohio, and named it Rookwood, after the family estate on which she grew up.
- After 1892, Rookwood developed the 'Standard Glaze', a yellow-tinted, high-gloss clear glaze often used over leaf or flower motifs. A series of portraits, often of generic American Indian characters or certain historical figures were also produced using the 'Standard Glaze'.
- A rarer aventurine 'Tiger Eye' glaze was also developed.
- Storer had a deep interest in Japanese ceramics and employed Kataro Shiriyamadani in 1887 as one of the firm's principal decorators.
- In 1894, Rookwood introduced three glazes: 'Iris', a clear, colourless glaze, 'Sea Green', which was green-tinted, and 'Aerial Blue', which was blue-tinted. The latter glaze was produced for just one year.
- In 1904, Rookwood patented a matte glaze called 'Vellum', which featured stylized flowers, landscapes and scenes, and gave a slightly hazy or frosted appearance to the decoration. Vellum was usually clear although it was also available in yellow and blue tints.
- Rookwood's 'Production' wares were developed to compete with the large number of potteries in the mass-production and cheaper end of the market. The glazes were rich and heavy and were designed to flow over the simple shapes of these lines. They did not rely on the specialist artists and decorators and they appeared without the customary artists monograms. Rookwood filed for bankruptcy in 1941.

A large Rookwood 'Standard Glaze' light vase, with lemons, decorated by Matt Daly, with 'Flame mark, 488D, MAD, L and W', with crazing, a few glaze bubbles and scratches.

1889   *13in (33cm) high*
£600-800   **DRA**

A Rookwood 'Standard Glaze' vase, with poppies, decorated by Lenore Asbury, 'Flame mark, III, 814, A, L.A.', crazed, some scratches to body, one firing line to interior.

1903   *10in (25.5cm) high*
£450-550   **DRA**

A CLOSER LOOK AT 'IRIS GLAZE'

This is decorated with the 'Iris Glaze' which was a remarkably clear, colourless glaze. It is highly refractive. 'Iris Glaze' was marked with a W for white glaze as it is white in unfired state.

There is no evidence of crazing which would detract from the value.

It was decorated by Carl Schmidt (1875-1959) - one of Rookwood's most successful decorators.

The peacock feathers decoration is particularly successful. The background colours shade from dark to light with a high sheen.

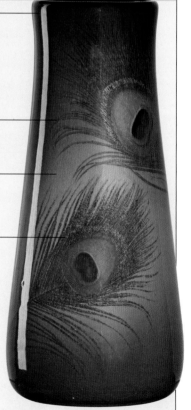

A Rookwood large 'Standard Glaze' vase, with trumpet flowers, by Kataro Shirayamadani, 'Flame mark/II/787C/artist cipher'.

1902   *11.5in (29cm) high*
£800-1,000   **DRA**

A Rookwood 'Iris Glaze' vase, with roses, by E.T. Hurley, 'Flame mark II/927D/ETH'.

1902   *8.25in (21cm) high*
£700-900   **DRA**

A Rookwood 'Iris Glaze' vase, by Carl Schmit, with peacock feathers, 'Flame mark/XI/CS/950D/W'.

1911   *8in (20.3cm) high*
£4,500-5,000   **DRA**

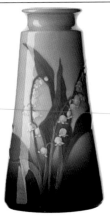

A Rookwood 'Iris Glaze' vase, with Lily of the Valley, by Lenore Asbury, 'Flame mark/X/1655E/L.A./W'.

Rookwood's new 'Iris' glaze, one of several introduced in the mid-1890s under William Watts Taylor's direction, is attributed to Rookwood garnering the Grand Prix at the Paris Exposition in 1900. In the 1910s, Rookwood embraced the Arts and Crafts movement. The company's famed 'Iris' line was discontinued in 1912, and other simplified designs and less complicated glazes were introduced.

1910　　　　　*7.75in (19.7cm) high*
£1,000-1,400　　　　　DRA

A Rookwood 'Iris Glaze' vase, with roses, by Albert Valentien, 'Flame mark/IV/940B/artist signature', overall crazing.

1904　　　　　*12.5in (32cm) high*
£2,000-2,500　　　　　DRA

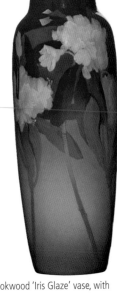

A Rookwood 'Iris Glaze' vase, with rhododendron, by John Dee Wareham, 'Flame mark/III/907C/JDW'.

In order to attain the shiny surface, the 'Iris Glaze' had an extremely high lead content that by 1912 was recognised as a health hazard.

1903　　　　　*14in (36cm) high*
£9,000-11,000　　　　　DRA

A Rookwood 'Iris Glaze' vase, with sprigs, by Sara Sax, 'Flame mark/I/196C/SX'.

1902　　　　　*7.5in (19cm) high*
£500-600　　　　　DRA

A Rookwood carved 'Black Iris' vase, with water lilies, by John Dee Wareham, 'Flame mark/903B/JDW'.

'Black Iris' is one of the most collectable glazes.

1900　　　　　*9.75in (24.8cm) high*
£10,000-13,000　　　　　DRA

A Rookwood 'Jewel Porcelain' vase, with California poppies, by Kataro Shirayamadani, 'Flame mark XXII/1065C and artist cipher'.

1922　　　　　*8.75in (22cm) high*
£3,000-3,500　　　　　DRA

CERAMICS

A Rookwood 'Sea Green' vase, with leafy branch, by Albert Valentien, Cincinnati, OH, 'Flame mark/762C/W/A.R.V./G', overall fine crazing.

1895   *5.5in (14cm) high*

£900-1,100   DRA

A Rookwood banded 'Scenic Vellum' vase, by Lenore Asbury, 'Flame mark XVIII/938D/LA'.

1918   *7in (17.8cm) high*

£950-1,100   DRA

A Rookwood 'Scenic Vellum' tile plaque, 'River Path', by Fred Rothenbusch, painted with a river landscape with tall trees, framed, impressed factory marks.

tile 9.5in (24cm) high

£1,000-1,200   WW

A Rookwood 'Green Vellum' vase, with roses, decorated by Fred Rothenbusch, 'flame mark, XIII, 295V, C and artist cipher', crazed, some minor peppering.

1913   *11in (28cm) high*

£550-650   DRA

A large Rookwood 'Matte Glaze' jardiniere, with leaves, 'Flame mark/1114DY' a few chips to high points.

1900   *11.5in (29cm) high*

£900-1,100   DRA

A Rookwood 'Wax Matte' vase, with deer, decorated by William Hentschel, 'butterfat' glaze, 'flame mark XXIX, 6112, WEH'.

1929   *8.5in (21.5cm) high*

£950-1,200   DRA

A Rookwood 'Matte' vase, with chrysanthemums, decorated by Elizabeth Neave Lincoln, 'flame mark, XIX, 112, V, LNL', crazed.

1919   *8in (20.5cm) high*

£650-750   DRA

A large Rookwood 'Production' urn, embossed with a band of quatrefoils under a fine indigo 'butterfat' glaze, and with 'Flame mark/ XVI/339B'.

1916   *14.5in (37cm) high*

£650-700   **DRA**

A Rookwood 'Production' ovoid vase, with stylized dogwood blossoms, covered in pink glaze, flame mark, dated.

1920   *9in (22.5cm) high*

£145-200   **DRA**

A Rookwood 'Production' vase, with embossed panels of fish and birds under a flowing green matte glaze, flame mark, dated.

1940   *8.5in (21cm) high*

£300-400   **DRA**

A Rookwood 'Production' vase, embossed with blossoms under a fine crystalline blue glaze, flame mark.

1930   *7.25in (18.5cm) high*

£250-350   **DRA**

A Rookwood 'Production' vase, with tulips covered in a brown glaze.

The reversed R and P logo was used on almost every piece of Rookwood pottery produced between 1886 and the end of production in 1967. Between 1886 and 1900 one additional flame was added to the logo for each year. In 1901, Rookwood stopped adding flames to the logo and started adding roman numerals below the fourteen flame mark. This continued until the end of production in 1967.

A Rookwood 'Production' squat vase, with a band of Celtic knots under plum-to-turquoise 'butterfat' glaze, horizontal lines inside rim, dated.

1915   *5.5in (14cm) wide*

£150-200   **DRA**

1914   *10.5in (26.5cm) high*

£150-200   **DRA**

CERAMICS

QUICK REFERENCE - ROSEVILLE

- The Roseville Pottery was founded in 1890 in Roseville, Ohio, USA. It initially produced utilitarian wares. The business grew, acquiring other factories, and by 1910 production was based in Zanesville, Ohio.

- The first Art Pottery range, 'Rozane', was launched in 1900. It was similar to Rookwood's popular 'Standard Glaze' range and its success led to the creation of more hand-decorated art pottery lines.

- The celebrated designer Frederick Rhead worked for Roseville from 1904–08. He created many ranges popular with collectors today, including the 'Della Robbia' and those using the squeeze-bag technique.

- By 1908 demand for such expensive wares had fallen and the company began to create successful, mass-produced, moulded ranges, which were quick and easy to produce. Artists who had been able to spend a day decorating a single piece could now decorate more than 300 in the same time.

- Many of the moulded designs were based on natural motifs. Notable designers from this time include Frank Ferrell, who created patterns and shapes from 1917–54, and George Krause who developed glazes from 1915–54. The factory closed in 1954.

- Collectors look for mass-produced pieces with clear, crisp moulding. The glazes should be correctly applied to the design. Shapes affect value, as do colours – blue is generally thought to be more desirable than brown. Common, early ranges such as 'Pine Cone' and 'Dahlrose' remain popular with collectors, as do pieces in the Art Nouveau and Art Deco style.

- Condition is paramount as cracks or chips will devalue a moulded piece by half. Fakes and reproductions are known, so check marks carefully.

A Roseville 'Aztec' vase, high-glaze finish, die-impressed mark.
1905   *9.5in (24cm) high*
£400-500   **DRA**

A Roseville 'Della Robbia' mug, unmarked.
1905   *6in (5cm) high*
£500-600   **DRA**

A Roseville 'Della Robbia' vase with daisies, 'Rozane Ware' seal and artist's initials 'AB'.
c1905   *8.25in (21cm) high*
£14,000-18,000   **DRA**

A Roseville 'Rozane Della Robbia' vase with stylized trees, with incised artist's initials to body.
c1910   *10in (25.5cm) high*
£7,000-9,000   **DRA**

A Roseville 'Della Robbia' three-handled bowl with tulips, marked with artist's initials 'HL'.
c1905   *7.5in diam*
£800-1,000   **DRA**

A Roseville 'Mat' umbrella stand, by Frederick H. Rhead, squeezebag-decorated with peacock and trees, signed 'HR' to body, incised '724' to base.

c1910   *20in (51cm) high*

£2,000-2,500   **DRA**

A Roseville 'Rozane Royal Dark' portrait vase, faint signature to body.

c1910   *9.5in (24cm) high*

£1,000-1,300   **DRA**

A Roseville 'Velmoss' two-colour flaring vase, unmarked.

12in (30cm) high

£250-350   **DRA**

A 1920s Roseville 'Vista' umbrella stand, unmarked.

20in (51cm) high

£600-700   **DRA**

A Roseville 'Futura' two-handled jardiniere, unmarked.

1924   *9in (23cm) high*

£90-120   **DRA**

A Roseville 'Futura' graduated spherical vase, unmarked.

1924   *8in (20.5cm) high*

£180-220   **DRA**

A Roseville 'Futura' spherical vase, with diamond foot, unmarked.

1924   *8in (20.5cm) high*

£300-350   **DRA**

A CLOSER LOOK AT A ROSEVILLE 'FUTURA' VASE

The angular handles and rings around the neck of the vase are typical of the architectural style of the 'Futura' range.

The 'Futura' range was made from 1924 until about 1928 and typifies the Art Deco style.

The use of a single, glossy glaze is unusual. Most 'Futura' pieces feature two or three contrasting matte glazes.

Pieces were marked with a paper label. Few of these survive.

A Roseville green 'Futura' vase, foil label.

1924   *9in (23cm) high*

£300-350   **DRA**

CERAMICS

A Roseville 'Corinthian' jardiniere and pedestal, ink-stamped mark.

1923   *30.25in (77cm) high*

£350-450   DRA

A late 1930s Roseville 'Iris' jardiniere and pedestal, glazed earthenware, die-impressed mark '647-8'.

25.75in (65.5cm)

£250-350   DRA

A 1940s Roseville 'White Rose' jardiniere and pedestal, die-impressed mark '653-8'.

25.25in (64cm) high

£220-280   DRA

A Roseville 'Pink Magnolia' jardiniere and pedestal, with raised mark.

1943   *24.75in (63cm) high*

£180-220   DRA

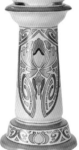

A Roseville 'Persian' jardiniere and pedestal, glazed creamware, paper label.

c1930   *32.25in (82cm) high*

£150-200   DRA

A Roseville 'Blackberry' wall pocket, unmarked.

1933   *8.25in (21cm) high*

£350-400   DRA

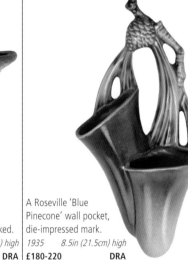

A Roseville 'Blue Pinecone' wall pocket, die-impressed mark.

1935   *8.5in (21.5cm) high*

£180-220   DRA

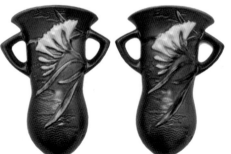

A pair of Roseville 'Freesia' wall pockets, both with die-impressed marks.

1945   *9in (23cm) high*

£130-180   DRA

A Roseville 'Sunflower' wallpocket, unmarked.

7.5in (19cm) high

£500-550   DRA

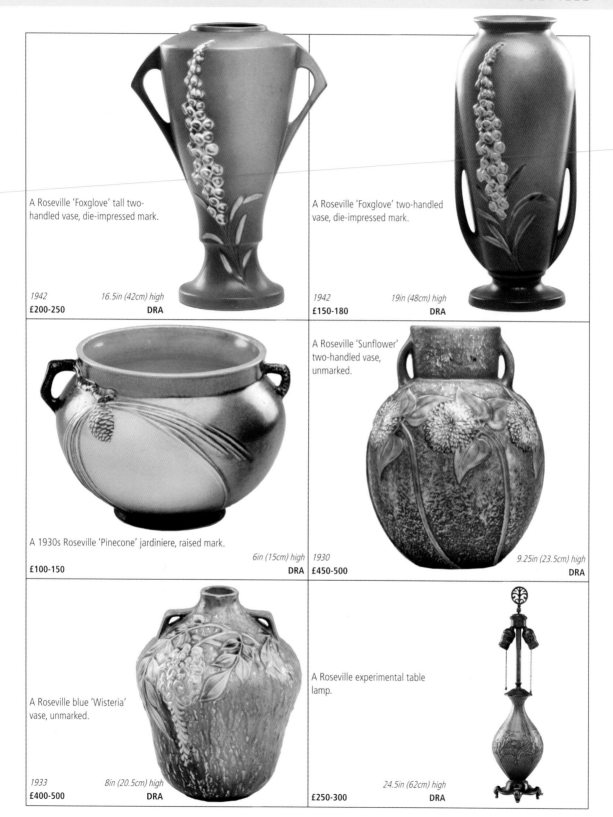

A Roseville 'Foxglove' tall two-handled vase, die-impressed mark.

1942   *16.5in (42cm) high*
£200-250   **DRA**

A Roseville 'Foxglove' two-handled vase, die-impressed mark.

1942   *19in (48cm) high*
£150-180   **DRA**

A 1930s Roseville 'Pinecone' jardiniere, raised mark.

6in (15cm) high
£100-150   **DRA**

A Roseville 'Sunflower' two-handled vase, unmarked.

1930   *9.25in (23.5cm) high*
£450-500   **DRA**

A Roseville blue 'Wisteria' vase, unmarked.

1933   *8in (20.5cm) high*
£400-500   **DRA**

A Roseville experimental table lamp.

24.5in (62cm) high
£250-300   **DRA**

CERAMICS

A limited edition Royal Crown Derby paperweight, 'The Mulberry Hall Indian Elephant', boxed with certificate.

£350-400   PSA

A limited edition Royal Crown Derby paperweight of an elephant, marked 'A signature edition of 100 for Gumps'.

8.25in (21cm) high

£500-600   PSA

A Royal Crown Derby paperweight, in the form of a seated donkey.

4.25in (11cm)

£50-60   WHP

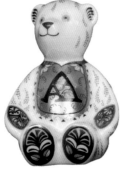

Three of a set of twenty-six Royal Crown Derby 'Alphabet' paperweights from A to Z, each with gold stopper and boxed.

£550-600 set   FLD

A limited edition Royal Crown Derby bone china Prince of Wales Investiture Commemorative, the puce and gold rearing dragon on a plinth inscribed 'The Investiture of H.R.H. Prince of Wales, Caernarvon July 1969', red printed marks and gold, no.112 of an edition of 250, fitted box and a receipt from Thomas Goode.

1969   *34.5in (13.5cm) high*

£350-400   SWO

A Royal Crown Derby bone china vessel, by Ken Eastman.

Studio potter Ken Eastman's (b.1960) innovative collaboration with Royal Crown Derby saw his characteristic forms translated into bone china, which is notoriously difficult to control during firing. The pieces were decorated with designs inspired by the factory's historic patterns, including the famous 'Imari' design in gold, red, and blue.

2009   *10in (25.5cm) high*

£200-250   SWO

A Royal Crown Derby 'Pink Glove' milk jug, attributed to Salvador Dalì, manufacturer's printed marks and Christie's paper label.

c1938-39   *4.75in (12cm) high*

£850-950   MLL

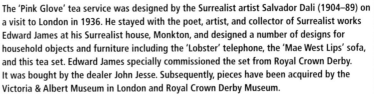

A Royal Crown Derby 'Pink Glove' plate, attributed to Salvador Dalì, manufacturer's printed and impressed marks and Christie's paper label.

The 'Pink Glove' tea service was designed by the Surrealist artist Salvador Dalì (1904–89) on a visit to London in 1936. He stayed with the poet, artist, and collector of Surrealist works Edward James at his Surrealist house, Monkton, and designed a number of designs for household objects and furniture including the 'Lobster' telephone, the 'Mae West Lips' sofa, and this tea set. Edward James specially commissioned the set from Royal Crown Derby. It was bought by the dealer John Jesse. Subsequently, pieces have been acquired by the Victoria & Albert Museum in London and Royal Crown Derby Museum.

c1938-39   *9in (23cm) diam*

£2,000-2,500   MLL

QUICK REFERENCE - ARNE BANG

● Danish potter Arne Bang (1901-83) trained as a sculptor at the Academy of Arts in Copenhagen. He founded his own studio in 1926 with Karl Halier, who had worked for Royal Copenhagen. From 1929, Bang was also associated with Holmegaard through his brother Jacob, who was lead designer there. Bang's aim was to produce high-quality handmade ceramics that were both beautiful and affordable. He was extremely successful and, during the 1930s, his studio produced many thousands of individual pieces. Shapes tend to be simple and clean-lined in a Modernist manner, but some seem to take their inspiration from Oriental ceramics. The same inspiration appears in his muted brown, green, grey, and sandy glazes, some of which also resemble Song and other early Chinese glazes. Bang's influential designs won many awards.

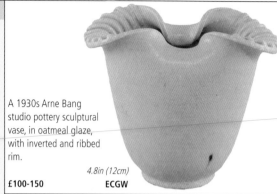

A 1930s Arne Bang studio pottery sculptural vase, in oatmeal glaze, with inverted and ribbed rim.

4.8in (12cm)

£100-150   ECGW

An Arne Bang fluted form bowl, with pale green-blue mottled glaze, painted monogram and numbered 109.

4.7in (12cm)

£200-250   ECGW

An Arne Bang studio pottery plant form vase, oatmeal glaze and dipped handles.

5.4in (14cm)

£100-150   ECGW

An Arne Bang stoneware vase, with creamy-white glaze, the base with monogram and production number.

c1940

£500-550   QU

An Arne Bang studio pottery mottled-green glaze vase, oval-flared form, incised marks and monogram, no.14.

6in (15cm)

£250-300   ECGW

A pair of Arne Bang studio pottery flower-head candle holders, green glaze, incised 'AB' marks and 'Jacob'.

3.5in (8cm)

£70-100   ECGW

CERAMICS

An Arne Bang stoneware vase, with green high-fired glaze, the base with monogram and production serial number.
c1940
£300-350   **QU**

An Arne Bang studio pottery deep bowl, with inverted rim, green pewter glaze, incised monogram, and numbered 29.
5.5in (13cm)
£150-200   **ECGW**

An Arne Bang studio pottery ribbed bowl, olive and brown, with blue centre, signed and numbered 120.

Vertically reeded decoration on the exterior is a hallmark of Bang's work.
5in (13cm)
£200-250   **ECGW**

Two Arne Bang studio pottery vertical rib pots, green on grey and green on brown glaze, incised marks.
2.3in (6cm)
£100-150   **ECGW**

Two Arne Bang studio pottery bud vases, with green-blue or green-brown glaze, both incised monogram and numbered 27.
2.75in (5cm)
£100-150   **ECGW**

A pair of Arne Bang studio pottery jugs, green on brown glaze and another blue-green and grey, unmarked.
£130-180   **ECGW**

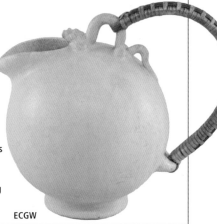

An Arne Bang studio pottery ball jug, with applied decoration and cane handle, 1930s painted monogram and numbered 151.

This organic form is characteristic of Bang's style. It is modern and clean-lined, yet is also inspired by the curving forms of nature.
£100-150   **ECGW**

A Tomas Anagrius large studio pottery 'kettle', with bird finial slab-built stoneware with light-mauve glaze, incised signature on base and inside lid 'Anagrius'.

Tomas Anagrius (b.1939) is a Swedish potter who worked for Gustavsberg and Rorstrand before setting up his own pottery. His work is featured in the Stockholm Museum collection.

12in (30cm)

£180-220   ECGW

QUICK REFERENCE - KARNEVAL

● Versatile artist and designer Stig Lindberg (1916-82) is considered a folk hero in his native Sweden. His unique hand-potted and handpainted ceramics are very sought-after across the West. The 'Karneval' range included 32 vases, dishes, and bowls. The patterns and bright colours reflect Lindberg's sense of playfulness.

● The black outlines were printed onto the body and filled in by hand by a team of decorators. The series was introduced in 1957 and proved popular with the public across Europe into the 1960s, despite being more expensive than comparative pieces by other factories. Today, large vases that display the pattern well are the most desirable. Always examine the surface closely, particularly at the rim and foot as the tin-glaze can easily chip.

A Gustavsberg Studio small stoneware footed dish, designed by Berndt Friberg in 1963, with wavy rim and streaky, micro-crystalline and mottled blue and brown glaze, the base inscribed 'BF, G Studio, F'.

5.75in (14.5cm) diam

£550-600   QU

A Gustavsberg vase or goblet, designed by Lisa Larson in 1967, moulded with a face and glazed in grey, the base with moulded marks.

9.75in (24.5cm) high

£650-700   QU

A Gustavsberg 'Karneval' tin-glazed earthenware vase, designed by Stig Lindberg, printed with numerous objects, the base inscribed 'Sweden 243', and with factory label.

14in (36cm) high

£450-500   SWO

A Gustavsberg large stoneware bulldog figurine, 'Kennel series', designed by Lisa Larson in 1972, with brown and black glazes, the base stamped 'LISA L. SWEDEN'.

These were produced in different sizes.

1972-87   *6.75in (17cm) long*

£250-300   QU

Two Gustavsberg porcelain dog figurines, 'Kennel' series, designed by Lisa Larson, comprising 'Rufus' and a bulldog, the bases painted in black 'Lisa L. Schweden'.

1972-87   *4.25in (11cm) high*

£50-70 each   PC

A Royal Copenhagen mountain goat, limited edition 7/750, printed marks and incised 'KN'.

14.75in (37.5cm) high

£220-280   SWO

CERAMICS

Mark Picks

From the 1950s onwards, Rorstrand produced a wide range of miniature vases, many designed by Gunnar Nylund or Carl Harry Stalhane. Individually potted and glazed by hand, they are incredibly accurate, well-proportioned, and perfectly formed. Glazes vary widely, from the brown or blue hare's fur-like 'ARO' to the satin matte browny-beige 'ARX'. They intrigue the eye and mind, and have a strong tactile appeal. Much of the antiques market has been moving increasingly towards decorative effects and away from connoisseur-led collections carefully displayed in cabinets. These combine the best of both worlds: not only does a small group look stunning and interesting on display, but they are also individual works of ceramic art by notable names. Also made by Gustavsberg (designed by Stig Lindberg and Berndt Friberg) is a huge variety of different vase and bowl forms decorated in any combination of glazes. Some can fetch over £250, but most cost from £25-70 each, depending on their shape, glaze, rarity, and quality. What's more, you may be lucky and hit upon a rare and desirable piece by Lindberg.

A group of ten 1950s Rorstrand stoneware and porcelain miniature vases, designed by Gunnar Nylund, the base with model numbers and artists' initials.

1.5in-5.5in (4cm-14cm) high

£355-455 for 10   QU

A 1950s Rorstrand miniature vase, designed by Carl Harry Stalhane, with mottled-brown glaze, the base with factory mark, artist's initals and number D934.

2.5in (6.5cm) high

£300-350   QU

A 1960s Rorstrand small vase, designed by Gunnar Nylund, with fine mottled and striated green and brown glaze, the base with factory mark and artist's initals.

6.25in (16cm) high

£350-450   QU

A Danish Saxbo vase, by Jais Nielsen, modelled in low relief with saints and Roman soldiers gathered around the dead Christ figure, glazed green, impressed and incised marks.

6.25in (16cm) high

£150-200   WW

A Søholm Bornholm studio vase, designed by Hølm Sorensen.

7.7in (19.5cm) high

£120-160   SWO

A Søholm 'After Thee' vase, by Gerd Hiort Petersen (b.1934), signed and numbered 3330.

c1960-61   *9.5in (24.5cm) high*

£120-160   MLL

QUICK REFERENCE - STUDIO POTTERY

● The term 'studio pottery' is used to describe pottery made by the pottery owner or by others under his or her supervision. Studio potteries are typically small in size. The pottery owner may work on their own, or with a partner or small team. Early studio pottery-type establishments were founded in the 19thC.

● As each piece can be both handmade and hand-decorated, it is effectively unique, fusing art and pottery. Although decorative, most pieces of studio pottery are functional and include vases, bowls, tableware, and teaware. Many designs hark back to traditional pottery or techniques such as slipware glazes, or Oriental designs, particularly from China and Japan and much is derived from the pioneering work of Bernard Leach (1887-1979) and Shoji Hamada (1894-1978). The Leach Pottery opened in 1920 in St Ives, Cornwall. Leach's and Hamada's influence continues to be felt today.

● The most important and often valuable work was made by a first generation of studio potters, which included Leach and his family, Hamada, Lucie Rie (1902-95), and Hans Coper (1920-81). During the 1950s-70s, studio potteries

proliferated in many places, notably Cornwall. The work of a second generation, such as Alan Caiger Smith (b.1930) and Michael Cardew (1901-83) is also highly collected. Both generations inspired later generations, whose work can often be more affordable on the secondary market (online, at traditional auctions or from specialist dealers) and who may still be potting today. In some cases, their works are already perceived as the 'antiques of the future'. Many contemporary potters, such as Grayson Perry (b.1966) use pottery to convey a message.

● Look at the base of a studio pot for an impressed, printed, painted or incised mark, which may be in the form of a motif, monogram, or signature. This will help to identify the potter, and may also help to date the pot. Investing in a reference guide showing these marks and developing a knowledge of them may pay off as many sellers do not bother to look them up, meaning that you may be able to spot a bargain. Always look for skill and quality in terms of potting, form, and overall design.

A 'Whieldon' jug, designed by Walter Keeler, of angled, faceted form, impressed seal mark to handle.

8.75in (22cm) high

£120-150   WW

An angled 'Whieldon' jug, designed by Walter Keeler, covered in a sponged glaze, impressed seal mark.

5in (13cm) high

£140-180   WW

A 'Whieldon' jug and cover, designed by Walter Keeler, with rope-twist applied handle and spout, impressed seal mark.

7in (18cm) high

£160-200   WW

A 'Whieldon' angled teapot and cover, designed by Walter Keeler, with over-slung handle and applied thorns, impressed seal mark.

'Whieldon' glazes are inspired by the brown and green mottled and 'tortoiseshell' glazes applied to pottery by the 18thC potter Thomas Whieldon (1719-95), whose pottery was based in Staffordshire.

8.5in (21.5cm) high

£500-600   WW

A 'Whieldon' jug, designed by Walter Keeler, on offset base, impressed seal mark to side.

6.75in (17cm) high

£160-200   WW

A salt-glazed teapot and cover, designed by Walter Keeler, with gun-barrel spout and over-slung handle, impressed seal mark to side.

Provenance: Purchased in 1997 directly from the artist.

9in (23cm) high

£200-300   WW

CERAMICS

A CLOSER LOOK AT A WALTER KEELER TEAPOT

Walter Keeler (b.1942) is one of Britain's most eminent living studio potters and was inspired by the refined and smooth forms of late 18thC pottery.

Forms are made by throwing and extruding clay, but any signs of the handmaking process are removed in favour of a focus on mechanical precision and strength of forms such as oil cans.

A salt-glazed teapot and cover, with gun-barrel spout, designed by Walter Keeler, on ball feet, impressed seal mark.

7in (18cm) high

£300-400   WW

He is also celebrated for his use of historic salt-glazes on un-decorated surfaces, which accentuate the smooth, mechanical feel of the piece.

Functional domestic teapots and jugs are typical forms, but Keeler modifies them, accentuating components like spouts and handles - the more exaggerated, the better.

A salt-glazed jug, designed by Walter Keeler, with angled neck and applied strap handle, impressed seal mark to body.

Modifying the basic form of a standard body is another hallmark of Keeler's work, such as here where he has split the cylindrical body of a jug into two cylinders placed at angles.

A salt-glazed teapot and cover, designed by Walter Keeler, with looping gun-barrel spout and strap handle, the conical cover with scrolling strap finial, glazed grey-blue, impressed seal mark to the side.

11.75in (30cm) wide

£750-850   WW

10.25in (26cm) high

£220-280   WW

A small salt-glazed teapot and cover, designed by Walter Keeler, impressed seal mark to side.

5.7in (14.5cm) high

£220-280   WW

A salt-glazed ovoid teapot and cover, designed by Walter Keeler, impressed seal mark to side.

8in (20cm) high

£250-300   WW

A teapot and cover, by Walter Keeler, running turquoise glaze, with yellow and brown potter's marks.

9.5in (24cm) across

£250-300   MLL

A cup form, designed by John Maltby, painted with stylised boats, exhibition paper label.

5.75in (14.5cm) high

£220-280   WW

A cup form, designed by John Maltby, painted with stylised boats, exhibition paper label.

5.75in (14.5cm) high

£220-280   WW

QUICK REFERENCE - JOHN MALTBY

● Fusing art with pottery and sculpture, John Maltby's work has been rising in interest and value over the past few years. Born in 1936, he studied pottery with David Leach from 1962-63 before founding his own pottery near Crediton, Devon, in 1964. Since 1974, he has focused on producing unique pieces that, although they are in functional forms that could be used, are perhaps better seen as artistic objects. His influences are rooted in modern, abstract art. He was inspired by abstract paintings by St Ives School artists such as Ben Nicholson, Christopher Wood, Terry Frost, and Alfred Wallis. Pablo Picasso and Paul Klee are also influences and Maltby's repeated use of certain colours and motifs, such as crosses and a collage style, are reminiscent of artworks by both these artists. As with many Cornish studio potters and artists, Cornwall's landscape is also strongly influential, from nature to harbour towns. Familiar elements such as boats, nets, buildings and the sun are reduced to geometric forms. This vase is charactertistic of Maltby's work and is highly desirable due to the typical 'modified' form, harbour subject matter, and the choice, layout and colours of the elements.

A stoneware leaning vase form, designed by John Maltby, with flat, slab rim, painted with tulip flower stem, the reverse with a bird flying past a sail motif, painted Maltby mark.

8.7in (22cm) high

£400-450   WW

A stoneware pot and cover, designed by John Maltby, with bamboo handle, painted with iron-red flowers on a buff ground, with tenmoku rim and cover, impressed seal mark, minor glaze loss.

4.7in (12cm) high

£200-250   WW

A cat stoneware box and cover, glazed in reds, impressed seal mark.

7in (18cm) high

£200-250   WW

A slab built vase, designed by John Maltby, painted with an abstract harbourscape, painted 'Maltby' signature.

9.5in (24cm) high

£3,000-3,500   WW

CERAMICS

QUICK REFERENCE - BERNARD LEACH

● Bernard Leach (1887-1979) is one of Britain's most important and influential studio potters. Together with his colleague Shoji Hamada (1892-1978) (see p.133), he revolutionised studio pottery, inspired future generations and fused together a number of critical themes and inspirations of the time. After studying and teaching in Japan from 1909-20, he allied what he had learnt there about pottery and porcelain with the ideals of William Morris and the Arts & Crafts movement. Contemplative Oriental forms and patterns were thus combined with a handmade aesthetic and traditional 17thC and 18thC English slip glazes. The pottery was also intended to be used practically in a domestic environment and be affordable to as many as possible. This porcelain plate, acquired at the St Ives Gallery near Leach's pottery, includes many of these features and inspirations. A near identical plate can be seen on page 45 in 'Bernard Leach, Hamada and Their Circle, The Wingfield Digby Collection' published by Phaidon. His family and a legion of inspired studio potters followed his teachings, the effects of which, or reactions against, are still felt in studio pottery today.

A stoneware charger, by Bernard Leach, painted with a foliate spray in shades of tenmoku and blue on an oatmeal ground, impressed Leach pottery mark, painted BL monogram, small glaze frit to underside of rim.

10.8in (27.5cm) diam

£600-700   WW

A Leach Pottery porcelain side plate, by Bernard Leach, painted with two fish to the well, in cobalt blue on a pale blue ground, the rim and back glazed olive/brown, impressed Leach pottery seal and BL monogram.

5.7in (14.5cm) diam

£1,200-1,500   WW

A large Leach Pottery vase, designed by Bernard Leach, resist decorated to the shoulder with simple scroll design, in a thick tenmoku glaze, impressed seal marks to base, small glaze nick to top rim.

10in (25cm) high

£500-600   WW

A pot and cover, by David Leach, cut-sided, tenmoku glaze, impressed potter's seal.

6in (15cm) high

£450-500   MLL

A rare Leach Pottery stoneware flagon, by David Leach, glazed to the foot with a splashed ash glaze, impressed DL and Leach Pottery seals, paper label.

In the photograph of the impressed seal mark, the mark on the left is the Leach Pottery mark and the 'DL' monogram mark indicates that it was made by David Leach. Traditional flagons such as this were made by a number of British studio potters, including Michael Cardew at Winchcombe.

11in (28cm) high

£400-450   WW

A Lowerdown Pottery stoneware ovoid vase, by David Leach, decorated in wax resist with foxglove design, under Dolomite glaze, with impressed DL seal mark.

7in (17.5cm) high

£300-350   WW

A large Lowerdown Pottery teapot and cover, designed by David Leach, with bamboo handle, painted with simple brush repeat band, tenmoku-glazed, two impressed seal marks.

8.75in (22cm) high

£250-300 **WW**

An unusual Lowerdown Pottery porcelain rice grain footed bowl, by David Leach, with flaring rim, the body pierced and glazed with celadon under tenmoku, impressed seal mark.

7.5in (19cm) high

£200-250 **WW**

A Lowerdown Pottery porcelain footed bowl, by David Leach, with cut band of decoration, impressed 'DL' seal mark.

5in (12.5cm) diam

£200-250 **WW**

QUICK REFERENCE - THE ALDERMASTON POTTERY

● **The Aldermaston Pottery operated in Berkshire, England, from 1955-2006. It was founded by Alan Caiger Smith (b.1930) and Geoffrey Eastop (1921-2014). It is known for its functional wheel-thrown earthenwares decorated with distinctive abstract patterns in tin glazes or reduction-fired lustres on tin glazes. Both glazes were reinterpreted and revived by Caiger-Smith, largely by trial and error. Caiger-Smith was also influential and many now successful studio potters studied under him.**

An Aldermaston Pottery pedestal bowl and cover, by Alan Caiger-Smith, orange lustre design, painted monogram and date cypher.

9.5in (24cm) high

£150-200 **MLL**

An Aldermaston Pottery drinks set, attributed to Alan Caiger-Smith, comprising flask and four goblets, blue, red, and black brush work, painted Aldermaston Pottery mark, stamped 'Made in England'.

the flask 10.5in (26.5cm) high

£200-250 **MLL**

An Aldermaston Pottery casserole dish and cover, by Alan Caiger-Smith, brushwork motifs, painted monogram and date cypher.

9.5in (24cm) across

£65-75 **MLL**

An Aldermaston Pottery platter, by Alan Caiger-Smith, on four feet, stylised flowerhead design, painted monogram, marked 'CA84'.

13in (33cm) high

£100-200 **WW**

CERAMICS

Mark Picks

Once said to be the 'next Troika' in terms of collectability, look, style, and rapidly rising values, most Carn Pottery (established in 1971) has remained affordable. This may be partly due to the recent economic problems, which have affected collectors' ability to spend, and partly due to the fact the pottery is still operating. As such, a good collection can still be built up affordably as most pieces cost £3-50. This may prove to be a wise investment if demand begins to exceed supply when the pottery closes. The pottery is the last surviving of the Cornish potteries producing textured, slip-moulded, and hand-decorated pottery with stylised motifs and colours inspired by the Cornish landscape. Right now, the best advice would be to focus on the larger and rare pieces, such as plaques, vases or bowls with glossy, glassy glazes in bright colours, and unusual forms. Those buying on a budget could consider characteristic cats and fan vases, which are hallmark forms. Also look out for pieces signed in pencil on the base by the pottery's founder John Beusmans.

A large Carn Pottery vase, decorated with a tubelined sunflower against a green brush wash ground, printed marks.

13.75in (35cm) high

£55-65   FLD

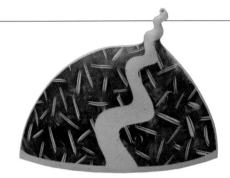

A porcelain vessel, by Gordon Cooke, with path and landscape design to each side, impressed potter's seal.

7.75in (20cm) wide

£150-200   MLL

A stoneware vase, by Waistel Cooper, covered in a pitted glaze, the interior glazed grey with brown spots, painted 'Waistel' mark.

6.25in (16cm) high

£70-100   WW

A stoneware lamp base, by Waistel Cooper.

£150-250   ECGW

An early cup form vase, by Hans Coper, resist-decorated in manganese and white, impressed seal mark.

Hans Coper (1920-81) was a highly influential German-born British studio potter who is best known for his sculptural, monumental, yet functional forms. He worked closely with Lucie Rie (see p.135) from 1946-58, whose work is similarly highly sought-after and valuable.

4.5in (11.5cm) high

£2,000-2,500   WW

A ceramic vessel, by Ken Eastman, signed 'Eastman 98'.

Born in Hertfordshire in 1860, Ken Eastman studied at Edinburgh College of Art and at the Royal College of Art, London. He exhibits widely internationally and has won many prestigious awards in the field of the ceramic arts, including the 'Premio Faenza', Italy, in 1995, and the 'Gold Medal' at the World Ceramic Exposition 2001 in Korea.

14.5in (36.5cm) high

£400-450   SWO

A teapot and cover, by Ray Finch, incised wave decoration and blue glaze, impressed potter's seal.

7.25in (18.5cm) across

£100-150   MLL

A conical form bowl, by Tessa Fuchs (1936-2012), 'The Kissing Bowl', stamped to base.

8.7in (22cm) diam

£90-130   ECGW

A sculpture, by Peter Hayes (b.1946), 'Red Bow with Gold Inset', signed and dated.

Peter Hayes (b.1946) studied at the Moseley School of Art and Birmingham College of Art before travelling extensively in Africa where he studied and made ceramics with various tribes. Inspired by his African experiences, his work is highly sculptural and is intended to work with the environment it is placed in. His distinctive surfaces and glazes, some of which are raku, are finished in an unusual manner - for example a piece is submerged in the Cornish sea for a few weeks, or washed over time in the river near his studio in Bath. They may then be waxed and polished to bring out the colours. His forms and glazes catch and hold the eye. His work has generally risen in value on the secondary market in recent years.

2007   *24in (61cm) high*

£600-700   MLL

A CLOSER LOOK AT A SHOJI HAMADA POT

Japanese potter Shoji Hamada (1894-1978) was one of the 20thC's most influential potters and is best known outside Japan for working with Bernard Leach (see p.130) from 1920-23.

He was a key member of the important 'Mingei' crafts revival and folk art movement in Japan that developed in the 1920s & 30s.

A cup used for drinking tea, the traditional unomi was a frequently used form for Hamada and fulfills many of the Mingei movement's aims of creating good quality, handmade, and functional pottery that was originally affordable.

The Oriental Tenmoku (Heaven's Eye) glaze is typical and the unomi is presented in traditional Japanese wooden box packaging.

A stoneware unomi, by Shoji Hamada, decorated in wax resist with a tenmoku glaze, in wooden box, lid signed.

3.3in (8.5cm) high

£800-900   WW

A vase, by Julian King-Salter (b.1954), in turquoise glazes and with brushwork petal design to inside of rim, impressed potter's seal and incised 'B77'.

7in (17.5cm) high

£50-60   MLL

A coil-built spiralling vase, by Julian King-Salter, glazed in colour, impressed seal mark.

10.6in (27cm) high

£70-90   WW

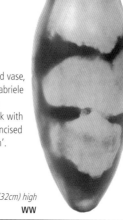

A tall burnished vase, designed by Gabriele Koch (b.1948), burnished black with pink patches, incised 'Gabrielle Koch'.

12.5in (32cm) high

£300-400   WW

A 'Garlic Bud' vase, designed by Kate Malone (b.1959), stoneware covered in a yellow crystalline glaze, etched 'Kate Malone'.

2001 *.75in (19.5cm) high*

£400-500 WW

Judith Picks

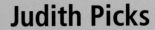

Laurence McGowan's colourful and highly detailed majolica pots are inspired by a number of different styles and movements. The decorative patterns that cover his pots are vaguely reminiscent of Moorcroft pottery, the Arts & Crafts movement, the work of William de Morgan, and Islamic ceramics. Nature is at the core of his inspiration, with highly stylised leaves, vines, flowers, and animals being commonly used. Occasionally, these patterns are embellished with bold calligraphic verses or sentences, whch adds a further dimension. Despite a life-long interest in the activity of potting and Romano-British pottery, McGowan's first career was in cartography and photogrammetry. In 1972, he took the decision to pot full-time and studied under Alan Caiger-Smith at the Aldermaston Pottery (see p.131) before founding his own pottery in Kingston, Wiltshire, in 1979. His extremely appealing and high-quality work, which is often the result of a special commission, has been growing in popularity and looks set to rise further.

A stoneware jar and cover, by Laurence McGowan, painted with a frieze of robins amongst foliage in shades of red and green on an off-white ground, the cover with stylised flower stems, painted monograms.

10.4in (26.5cm) high

£220-280 WW

A large stoneware bellied jug, by Laurence McGowan, painted with lily flowers in shades of pink, purple, and green on an off-white ground, painted monograms.

12.2in (31cm) high

£280-320 WW

A stoneware vase, by Laurence McGowan (b.1942), painted with birds amongst foliage in shades of blue, pink, and green on a white ground, painted marks.

9.6in (24.5cm) high

£300-350 WW

A stoneware charger, by Laurence McGowan, painted with lilies, in shades of pink, white, yellow, and green on a white ground, painted monograms.

14.6in (37cm) diam

£200-250 WW

A stoneware pot, by Jon Middlemiss (b.1949), resist-decorated with blue panels on a grey ground, impressed seal mark.

12.5in (32cm) wide

£120-180 WW

A Richard Parkinson Pottery owl, designed by Susan Parkinson, glazed in olive-green with scratched feathers, unsigned.

8.3in (21cm) high

£220-280 WW

A large Richard Parkinson Pottery 'Judge', designed by Susan Parkinson, model no.87, glazed in shades of blue, unsigned.

The Parkinson pottery (Richard Parkinson Ltd) operated from 1952-63, with Richard's wife Susan, who had studied at the Royal College of Art in London, producing the designs. Highly stylised figures, busts, and animals as well as functional domestic wares were produced. The slip-moulded, white-bodied pieces were decorated with green-black or brown glazes. Never inexpensive in their day, values on the secondary market rose dramatically following an exhibition and the publication of a book on the pottery in 2004. This judge bust was first introduced for the American market, and was one of a series of busts linked by the theme of wigs.

12.6in (32cm) high

£1,000-1,400   WW

A slender pottery ewer, by Amanda Popham, 'I Will Give Thanks..', painted with an acrobat performing a handstand, the reverse incised with a verse, painted signature and date to neck.

2005   *11.8in (30cm) high*

£180-220   WW

A figure and cat vase, by Amanda Popham (b.1954), signed and dated.

2007   *10.5in (26.5cm) high*

£180-220   MLL

A miniature tea set, by Mary Rich (b.1940), with banded gilt and purple decoration, impressed potter's seals.

For more information about Mary Rich, please see p.124 of the Miller's Collectables Price Guide 2012-2013.

the teapot (including handle) 6.75in (17cm) high

£150-200   MLL

A porcelain vase, by Mary Rich, impressed potter's seal.

7.5in (19cm) high

£180-220   MLL

A bowl, by Lucie Rie, of squeezed form, white glaze and bronzed rim, impressed potter's seal.

Austrian-born Dame Lucie Rie (1902-95) was one of the most famous and influential studio potters working in Britain. She studied pottery under Michael Powolny at the Vienna Kunstgewerbeschule and founded a studio in Vienna. In 1938, she fled Nazi Germany and founded another pottery in London. From 1946-58, she worked closely with a young Hans Coper, who she helped train. Her work, typified by curving forms with finely potted lips and rims and gentle glazes, is highly sought-after today. This bowl was originally purchased from Dartington Hall in June 1964.

6in (15cm) across

£1,500-2,000   MLL

A stoneware totem lamp base, by Bernard Rooke (b.1938), impressed Rooke, glazed in colours.

29.5in (75cm) high

£100-150   WW

CERAMICS

A Rye Pottery cockerel vase, printed pottery mark.

13.5in (34cm) high

£100-140   MLL

A Dartington Pottery platter, by Janice Tchalenko (b.1942), modelled in low relief and glazed in shades of blue and lavender, painted monogram, dated.

1996   16in (41cm) wide

£120-150   WW

A 'Bird Pot' sculpture, by Benny Sirota, impressed potter's seal.

Benny Sirota was one of the co-founders of Troika pottery (see p.137). This was made after Troika had closed in 1983 and was purchased from Tremayne Applied Arts in St. Ives.

18in (46cm) high

£200-250   MLL

A 1970s Tremaen slip-moulded 'Boscawen' lampbase, designed by Peter Ellery, with impressed mark.

The Tremaen pottery operated in Cornwall from 1965-88.

10.2in (26cm) high

£50-80   SWO

A stoneware vase, designed by Charles Vyse, covered to the foot in a Chun glaze, incised 'C Vyse Chelsea'.

Charles Vyse (1882-1971) founded his studio with his potter-chemist wife Nell in Chelsea, London, in 1919. His figures and pots, and the often complex glazes that decorate them, were strongly influenced by classical Chinese ceramics.

4.75in (12cm) high

£300-350   WW

A biscuit-fired vase, by Sasha Wardell (b.1956), shouldered fluted body with flaring neck, covered in a matt white glaze, impressed seal marks.

6in (15.5cm) high

£80-100   WW

A Winchcombe Pottery stoneware cider jar, by Ray Finch (1914-2012), painted with combed decoration, impressed seal mark, small glaze flake on the side of the handle.

Ray Finch (1914-2012) was one of the most prolific potters linked to Michael Cardew's Winchcombe pottery. He acquired the pottery from Cardew after WWII. This traditional form and use of slipware decoration is typical of his work.

13in (33cm) high

£120-150   WW

QUICK REFERENCE - TROIKA POTTERY

● The Troika Pottery was founded in 1962 in the Powell & Wells Pottery at the Wheal Dream in St Ives, Cornwall, England. The co-founders were potter Benny Sirota, painter Lesley Illsley, and architect Jan Thompson (who left in 1965). Success came quickly and the pottery moved to larger premises at Newlyn, Cornwall, in 1970.

● Designs evolved during the 1960s, although slip-moulded production processes remained the same to ensure consistency and allow for ease of production. Early designs tended to have glossy glazes, with the company's characteristic textured matte finishes becoming the main decorative treatment around 1974. All pieces were decorated by hand by a team of decorators.

● Influences on design included Scandinavian ceramics, the Cornish landscape around them, the work of other Cornish studio potters, and famous modern artists such as Paul Klee and Constantin Brancusi. Colours tend to be earthy and muted. Forms were clean-lined and modern. Domestic ware such as vases, dishes, bowls, lampbases,

and rare sculptural pieces were produced.

● Values vary depending on the shape and size of the piece, the decoration, the decorator, the period it was produced, and the rarity of the form. Look on the base for marks as these can help with identification and dating. A 'trident' mark was used for a few years from 1963 onwards, and the presence of 'St Ives' indicates the piece was made from 1963-70. From 1970 and the move to Newlyn until the pottery's closure in 1983, marks simply comprised 'Troika Cornwall', sometimes with the addition of 'England'.

● Initials found on the base identify the decorator, and the work of some decorators is more desirable than the work of others. In general, look for well-made, complex geometric patterns, particularly with figural or stylised pictorial designs as they tend to be the scarcest and most valuable. Always examine a piece carefully for chips and cracks as the ceramic is delicate - even a hairline crack reduces the value considerably.

A Troika 'Rectangle' vase, the base with black-painted 'Troika Cornwall' mark.

9in (22cm) high

£200-250   CHOR

A Troika 'Rectangle' vase, decorated by Ann Jones, with geometric symbols, inscribed with artist's monogram and 'Troika Cornwall' mark.

Ann Jones worked part-time at Troika from 1966-67.

8.5in (22cm) high

£160-200   SWO

An unusual mid-1960s Troika 'Rectangular' vase, probably decorated by Leslie Illsley, painted marks, trident mark, artist cipher.

Not only is this an early vase dating from the first few years of the pottery as the early trident mark indicates, but the simple, geometric, textured decoration is unusual and very successful. It also may have been decorated by Lelsey Illsley, one of the founders of the pottery. Note how the spots on the side echo the shape of the rim.

12.25in (31cm) high

£380-420   WW

A Troika large 'Cylinder' vase, black painted 'Troika St Ives England' mark, and monogram for Marilyn Pascoe.

Marilyn Pascoe worked at Troika from the 1960s until 1974.

14.5in (37cm) high

£180-220   CHOR

A Troika pottery 'Cylinder' vase, possibly by Colin Carbis, with stenciled designs, inscribed with artist's monogram and 'Troika Cornwall' mark.

14.5in (37cm) high

£180-220   SWO

A 1960s Troika cylindrical vase, decorated by Benny Sirota, painted marks.

Potter Benny Sirota was another of the three founders of Troika, hence the higher value.

7.75in (20cm) high

£400-450   FLD

CERAMICS

A Troika 'Cylinder' vase, painted by Sue Lowe, painted marks.

Sue Lowe worked at Troika from 1976-77.

7.75in (20cm) high

£160-200   **FLD**

A mid-1960s Troika 'Flask', decorated to one side with a stylised flower head and to the other an oxidised tenmoku-type green glaze with the body in a thick white glaze, the base with Trident and St Ives marks.

This is both an early 'Flask', indicated by the Trident mark on the base, and a desirable pattern that resembles a stylised lucky four-leafed clover.

6.75in (17cm) high

£450-500   **FLD**

A Troika 'Flask', the base with painted marks.

2.7in (7cm) high

£80-90   **ECGW**

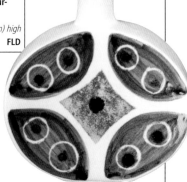

A Troika 'Flask', the base with painted marks.

2.7in (7cm) high

£60-70   **ECGW**

A Troika 'Flask', unmarked.

2.75in (7cm) high

£180-220   **FLD**

A Troika 'Wheel' vase, decorated by Louise Jinks, inscribed with artist's monogram and 'Troika Cornwall' mark.

Louise Jinks worked at Troika from 1976-81.

7.75in (19.7cm) high

£200-250   **SWO**

A Troika 'Wheel' vase, with geometric patterns to both sides, signed 'Troika, Cornwall, AB'.

Depending on the style, an AB monogram may indicate Avril Bennet (1973-79) or Alison Brigden (1977-83) as decorator. 'Wheel' vases are popular with collectors.

6.25in (16cm) high

£250-300   **MLL**

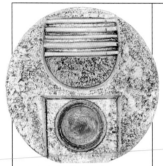

A Troika 'Wheel' vase, decorated to both sides, painted marks, monogrammed 'EW'.

The decorator who used the initials EW has not yet been identified.

6.75in (17cm) high

£150-200 FLD

A Troika 'Urn' vase, black-painted Troika mark, monogram possibly for Avril Bennett.

10in (25.5cm) high

£200-250 CHOR

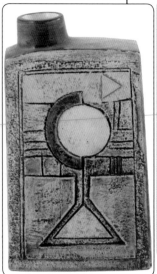

A Troika 'Chimney' vase, modelled in low relief with abstract motifs, painted marks.

7.75in (20cm) high

£300-350 WW

A CLOSER LOOK AT A TROIKA VASE

Doublebase vases were introduced in 1965.

The large and monumental form, which is reminiscent of Cornish standing stones, was also produced as a lampbase. For an example, please see the next page.

The decorator Shirley Wharf worked at Troika from 1979-80 or 81, allowing this vase to be dated.

The colours are characteristic of Troika. The geometric pattern resembles a stylised landscape with buildings and a sun, and is desirable.

A Troika 'Aztec' 'Doublebase' vase, decorated by Shirley Wharf, the base painted with initials 'SW' and Troika marks.

13.8in (35cm) high

£300-400 SWO

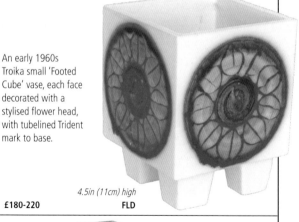

An early 1960s Troika small 'Footed Cube' vase, each face decorated with a stylised flower head, with tubelined Trident mark to base.

4.5in (11cm) high

£180-220 FLD

A 1970s Troika 'Footed Cube' vase, decorated in low relief with geometric design, painted marks.

7in (18cm) high

£220-280 WW

CERAMICS

A Troika 'Cube' vase, modelled in low relief with mask panels, painted marks, firing flaw to top rim.

5.75in (14.5cm) high

£140-180   WW

A 1970s Troika 'Cube' vase, the base with painted initials 'NR' Troika, Cornwall, England'.

6in (15cm) square

£200-250   SWO

A Troika 'Wheel' lamp base, decorated by Annette Walters, modelled in low relief with geometric panels, painted marks.

Annette Walters worked as a decorator at Troika during the late 1970s.

10.75in (27.5cm) high

£180-220   WW

A 1970s Troika 'Wheel' lamp base, the base with black-painted 'Cornwall Troika' mark.

10.5in (26.5cm) high

£300-350   CHOR

A Troika square lamp base, black-painted 'Troika Cornwall' mark to interior, and monogram 'MM'.

12.25in (31cm) high

£200-250   CHOR

A Troika lamp base, with four-sided motifs, the interior with black-painted 'Troika Cornwall' mark, and indistinct painted monogram, possibly 'AL' for Ann Lewis.

12.25in (31cm) high

£200-250   CHOR

A Troika 'Doublebase' lamp base, modelled in low relief with geometric panels, painted marks, monogram 'EW'.

14in (35.5cm) high

£280-340   WW

QUICK REFERENCE - RARITIES

● Troika produced a number of items that were sold in low quantities. Reasons for this included the fact that they were difficult or time-consuming to produce, or because they were intended for special exhibitions or events at certain retailers. Because of this rarity, prices are usually considerably higher than for more standard production shapes, such as 'Cylinder' or 'Rectangle' vases. However, after a sudden rise caused by a large number of collectors being drawn to Troika during the early 2000s, prices have fallen somewhat and have now arguably steadied. A good example are plaques, only made at St Ives from 1963-70, which have fetched over £3,000 in the past. Showing the three stages of marriage, this rather cynical 'Love' plaque is an excellent example.

A rare Troika 'Love' plaque, designed and by Benny Sirota, in shades of black, blue, and raspberry detailing, depicting the three stages of love to marriage, signed to reverse 'Troika St Ives'.

15.4in (39cm) wide

£600-700   SWO

A rare 1960s Troika 'River Thames' wall plaque, designed and probably decorated by Benny Sirota, the back with painted 'Troika St Ives' and Trident mark.

9.75in (21.5cm) high

£550-650   CHOR

A 1960s Troika 'D-plate' dish, decorated with a central flowerhead motif and radiating leaves, the back with impressed Trident mark.

7.25in (18.5cm) square

£180-220   WW

A very rare mid-1970s Troika 'Helmet' lamp base, of abstract spherical form, the base with black-painted 'Troika Cornwall England' mark.

One of the rarest, most desirable and avant garde forms produced at Troika, the 'Helmet' was designed by Lesley Illsley in 1974. It was inspired by Roman armour and the work of sculptors Constantin Brancusi and Henry Moore, who Illsley admired greatly. Also available as a lampbase, it was complex to produce, requiring a mould made of seven separate pieces.

11in (28cm) high

£800-900   CHOR

A rare Troika 'Pillar' vase, decorated by Anne Lewis, of totem form with cast and incised decoration, the base with painted marks and 'AL' monogram.

Anne Lewis worked at Troika from 1966-72.

21.75in (55cm) high

£550-650   WW

A rare 1970s Troika 'Aztec' mask, black-painted mark 'Troika' and indistinct monogram, possibly for Alison Brigden.

Alison Brigden worked at Troika from 1977 until its closure in 1983.

9.75in (25cm) high

£600-700   CHOR

CERAMICS

QUICK REFERENCE - WEDGWOOD

- The Wedgwood pottery was founded in Staffordshire by Josiah Wedgwood in 1759. Three years later he met Thomas Bentley, a Liverpool merchant who inspired in him a love of Classical decoration which would influence the factory's output. Bentley went on to be Wedgwood's business partner.
- Wedgwood's 18thC innovations included a creamware, a form of earthenware he introduced c1762. These wares became known as 'Queensware' after the firm gained the patronage of Queen Charlotte. However, it is possibly best known for its 'Jasperware', developed c1774–75. Early pieces were made from a blue, black or green base with applied white, low-relief friezes of Classical scenes. Its popularity led to other colours being introduced.
- These 18thC styles were made in the 19thC, but the 20thC saw Wedgwood employing designers to create new, modern ranges.
- Daisy Makeig-Jones (1881-1945) joined Wedgwood in 1909 and within five years was the first designer to be given her own studio. She began by designing nursery wares, but after seeing an exhibition of lustre wares she began to work with complex lustre glazes. The first range was launched in 1915 and Makeig-Jones developed elaborate patterns based on fairy tales, fables and myths.
- In 1926 Wedgwood commissioned John Skeaping (1901–80) to design a series of fourteen animals, of which it is believed only ten were produced. All the designs feature a streamlined, Art Deco style.
- New Zealand architect Keith Murray (1892–1981) joined Wedgwood in 1932. His simple, unembellished forms were decorated with matte glazes which exhibit a Modernist aesthetic. Colours include white 'Moonstone', 'Straw Yellow' and the most commonly found 'Green'.
- Artist and illustrator Eric Ravilious (1903–42) designed table and nursery wares from c1936 to 1940. Designs popular with collectors today include his coronation mug, 'Travel' and 'Garden Instruments' sets, and 'Alphabet' mug.

A Wedgwood 'Dragon lustre' bowl, designed by Daisy Makeig-Jones, with gilt dragon on streaked-blue ground, the green interior decorated with camels and cranes.

10.5in (25cm) diam

£400-500   ECGW

A Wedgwood 'Fairyland' lustre Malfrey shape pot, designed by Daisy Makeig-Jones, decorated in the 'Flame' 'Woodland Elves IV' and 'Big Eyes' pattern, printed and gilt 'Portland Vase' mark to the base with painted pattern code 'Z5360' to the base.

3.5in (9cm) high

£6,000-8,000   FLD

A Wedgwood Pottery 'Kangaroo', designed by John Skeaping, covered in a celadon glaze, impressed 'Wedgwood, J. Skeaping' marks.

8.5in (22cm) wide

£400-450   WW

A Wedgwood 'Tiger & Buck' figure, designed by John Skeaping, in a celadon glaze, impressed marks 'Wedgwood, J Skeaping'.

13in (33cm) wide

£200-300   LAW

A Wedgwood 'Fallow Deer' figure, designed by John Skeaping, in a tan glaze, impressed marks 'Wedgwood, J Skeaping'.

7.25in (18cm) high

£150-200   LAW

A Wedgwood black basalt bowl, designed by Keith Murray, impressed manufacturer's marks.

6.5in (16.5cm) diam

£250-300 **MLL**

A Wedgwood 'Globe' vase, designed by Keith Murray, in matt-green glaze, printed facsimile signature and manufacturer's mark.

1930s *6in (15.5cm) high*

£120-180 **MLL**

A Wedgwood moonstone 'Football' vase, designed by Keith Murray, printed monogram and manufacturer's mark.

7.25in (18.5cm) high

£200-250 **MLL**

A Wedgwood vase, designed by Keith Murray, with reeded decoration, printed and impressed marks.

7.75in (19.5cm)

£150-200 **SWO**

A Wedgwood 'Moonstone' bowl, designed by Keith Murray, of lobed form, printed monogram and manufacturer's mark.

8.75in (22.5cm) diam

£50-100 **MLL**

A Wedgwood side plate, decorated with the 'Alphabet' pattern by Eric Ravilious, white earthenware, underglazed transfer-printed decoration, printed and impressed mark to base.

1933 *7in (17.5cm) diam*

£100-150 **DW**

A Wedgwood 'Boat Race' punch bowl, designed by Eric Ravilious, with three transfer-printed scenes depicting various stages of a boat race and a mermaid flanked by four crossed oars, the interior with a scene of Piccadilly Circus, printed marks.

c1938 *12in (30cm) diam*

£2,500-3,000 **FLD**

A Wedgwood oval meat dish, designed by Eric Ravilious, 'Garden' pattern, date marked.

1954   *14.5in (37cm) wide*

£200-250   **ECGW**

A Wedgwood bowl, designed by Eric Ravilious, 'Garden' pattern, date marked.

1953   *9.75in (25cm) diam*

£200-250   **ECGW**

A pair of Wedgwood tureens and covers, designed by Eric Ravilious, 'Garden' pattern.

10.75in (27cm) diam

£200-250   **ECGW**

A Wedgwood bread and butter waved-edge plate, designed by Eric Ravilious, 'Travel' pattern, with a steam train emerging from a tunnel, printed marks.

10in (25.5cm) diam

£100-150   **FLD**

A Wedgwood Elizabeth II coronation mug, designed by Eric Ravilious (1903-42), printed manufacturer's mark.

c1953   *4in (10cm) high*

£300-400   **MLL**

A Wedgwood 'Ferdinand the Bull', designed by Arnold Machin, unmarked.

1941   *12in (30cm) wide*

£150-200   **ECGW**

A Wedgwood 'Variations on a Geometric Theme' plate, designed by Eduardo Paolozzi (1924-2005), limited edition of 200, printed manufacturer's mark and facsimile signature.

10.5in (26.5cm) diam

£180-220   **MLL**

QUICK REFERENCE - WEMYSS POTTERY

● The story of Wemyss starts in the 1880s. Wemyss was the brainchild of Robert Methven Heron, the owner of the Fife Pottery, who, returning from the 'Grand Tour' brought back craftsmen from Bohemia to develop a new concept in decoration. Karel Nekola became Heron's master painter. Wemyss Ware painted by Nekola was an immediate success, largely thanks to the patronage of Miss Dora Wemyss of Wemyss Castle (later to become Lady Henry Grosvenor). The pieces were aimed at wealthy middle and upper classes, and forms included plates, biscuit barrels, ink wells, tea sets and animal figures, including the large pigs and cats for which the firm is best known. They were decorated with images inspired by nature, particularly the famous cabbage roses. Thomas Goode & Company of South Audley Street, Mayfair, obtained the exclusive selling rights in London. From buttons to bedroom sets, Nekola's free style of painting was given full reign and by the turn of the century Wemyss Ware was perhaps at its peak.

● Nekola died in 1915 and was succeeded by Edwin Sandland, a painter from Staffordshire.

● In 1930, the economic depression finally closed the Fife Pottery. The rights and moulds were bought by the Bovey Pottery Company of Bovey Tracey in Devon, who employed Joseph Nekola, Karel's son, to continue the tradition. Later, the sole agency passed to a Czech, Jan Plichta. Under him, Joseph continued to paint nursery pigs and cats. He died in 1952, and Plichta later sold the rights to Royal Doulton.

● Since 1985, 'Wemyss Ware'® has been produced by the Griselda Hill Pottery Ltd® in the Fife village of Ceres.

A Wemyss pottery cat, seated, with painted cabbage roses, glass eyes, painted marks 'Wemyss Ware Made in England'.

13in (32.5cm) high

£4,000-5,000   WW

A large Wemyss cat, decorated with cabbage roses by Joseph Nekola, inset glass eyes, painted mark 'NEKOLA/ PINXT', printed mark 'PLICHTA/ LONDON/ ENGLAND', flaw to leg and torso.

post 1930   13in (33cm) high

£2,000-2,500   L&T

A Wemyss honey pot and cover, modelled as a bee skep with thatched cover, painted with flying bees, painted marks 'Wemyss, T. Goode & Co., London'.

7.25in (18.5cm) high

£2,000-2,500   L&T

A large Wemyss tabby cat, with applied glass eyes, impressed mark 'Wemyss Ware/R.H. & S.', minor restorations.

c1900   13in (32cm) high

£6,000-8,000   L&T

A large Wemyss honey pot and cover, decorated with bees and hive, painted mark 'Wemyss Ware', impressed mark 'Wemyss', minor hairline.

c1900   5.9in (15cm) high

£500-700   L&T

A Wemyss quaich, decorated with apples, the base with impressed 'Wemyss' mark, and printed 'T. Goode & Co.' retailer's mark.

10in (26.5cm) diam across handles

£400-600   L&T

CERAMICS

A Wemyss pottery pig moneybox, with a white ground, with black sponged decoration, the feet, ears, and face highlighted in pink, painted mark underneath.

5.75in (15cm) wide

£500-600   **L&T**

A small early 20thC Wemyss pig moneybox, decorated with cabbage roses by Edwin Sandland, painted and impressed mark 'WEMYSS'.

6.25in (16cm) long

£900-1,100   **L&T**

A small Wemyss pig moneybox, decorated with thistles by Joseph Nekola, painted mark 'NEKOLA/ PINXT/ PLICHTA/ LONDON/ ENGLAND'.

post 1930   *6in (16cm) long*

£300-400   **L&T**

A small Wemyss pig, impressed mark 'WEMYSS WARE/ R.H.&S'.

c1900   *6.5in (16.5cm) across*

£600-700   **L&T**

A small Wemyss pig, impressed mark 'WEMYSS WARE/ R.H.&S.', minor chip to front trotter.

c1900   *6in (16cm) long*

£200-300   **L&T**

Judith Picks

Pigs are some of the most desirable pieces of Wemyss. Who can avoid falling in love with these charming fellows!

The pigs were designed for children's nurseries and some had a slot in the back so they could be used as a moneybox. Others were personalised with a child's name and birth date. Smaller versions were designed to be used as paperweights – these are rarer still.

The sleeping piglet is probably the rarest and most desirable of all Wemyss ware - particularly coveted is the sleeping pig with a smile on his face. Large pigs like the one below are also extremely sought-after, but can't compare with the rare piglet. The naturalistic decoration stands out on the clear white background and the more colourful, rare and well-painted the design, the more desirable the piece is likely to be. A sleeping pig decorated with shamrocks sold for over £19,000. Condition is very important: to create the vibrant colours the pottery was fired at a low temperature and this means it is susceptible to chips and cracks, and restoration is expensive. As a result, pieces in perfect condition command a premium.

A particularly large Wemyss pig, painted with sprays of thistles, painted mark 'Wemyss Made In England'.

c1930   *16in (40.5cm) long*

£2,000-2,500   **DRA**

A small Wemyss pig, seated on its haunches, painted all over with shamrocks, impressed mark 'Wemyss', some restoration.

6.25in (16cm) long

£600-700   **L&T**

A Wemyss toothbrush dish, decorated with daffodils, impressed mark 'WEMYSS WARE/ R.H.&S.', printed retailer's mark.

c1900   8.25in (21cm) long
£400-600   **L&T**

A CLOSER LOOK AT A WEMYSS GARDEN SEAT

The garden seat is a very rare shape for Wemyss.

It was painted and signed by the distinguished Bohemian artist Karel Nekola.

It was almost certainly a special commision.

The decoration is also very unusual. It is painted with dog roses and briars, a pair of blue tits, a Mrs Blackcap and two Cabbage White butterflies.

A Wemyss garden seat, painted mark 'Wemyss'.

c1890   18in (46.5cm) high
£9,000-11,000   **L&T**

A large Wemyss ewer and basin, decorated with cabbage roses, ribbons and hearts in pink and green, and with cipher 'EAW', impressed marks 'WEMYSS WARE/ R.H.&S'.

These pieces formed part of an extensive set of Wemyss made as a wedding present for Lady Wolverton in 1895.

c1895   ewer 9.25in (23.5cm) high
£1,000-1,200   **L&T**

A Wemyss pin tray, decorated with buttercups by James Sharp, painted and impressed mark 'WEMYSS'.

c1900   5.75in (14.5cm) across
£500-600   **L&T**

An early 20thC Wemyss preserve jar and cover, decorated with brambles, painted and impressed marks 'WEMYSS', printed retailer's mark.

5in (13cm) high
£250-300   **L&T**

A Wemyss heart-shaped tray, decorated with narcissi, impressed mark 'WEMYSS WARE/ R.H.&S.'

c1900   11.75in (30cm) long
£600-700   **L&T**

CERAMICS

A Wemyss commemorative tankard, for 'Queen Victoria 1837-1897', retailed by Thomas Goode, painted in green and pink, with impressed and printed marks.

5.7in (14.5cm) high

£150-250   **WW**

A Wemyss commemorative goblet, for Queen Victoria's Diamond Jubilee, painted with a VRI monogram beneath a crown, pink roses, the back with a wreath, inscription and dated, impressed 'WEMYSS WARE RH&S' and printed for 'T. Goode & Co.' as retailers.

1897   *5.5in (14cm) high*

£150-200   **DN**

An early 20thC Wemyss pin tray, decorated with violets and bearing the inscription 'I looked for something sweet to send you/ And the violets asked if they would do', impressed and painted marks 'Wemyss'.

5.75in (14.5cm) wide

£400-500   **L&T**

A 1920s-30s Wemyss 'Jazzy' comb tray, decorated with cabbage roses, the base with painted 'Wemyss 213' mark.

10in (25cm) long

£150-200   **L&T**

Miller's Compares

On this example the background is pure white.

The composition of the fruit and leaves has the Wemyss free style of painting, so popular with collectors.

The shape is much more pleasing as is the addition of the green scalloped border.

It has damage to the handle.

The fruit and leaves do not exhibit the desired naturalistic feel.

This example has extensive crazing in the glaze and the background is distinctly creamy.

A small early 20thC Wemyss loving cup, decorated with apples, impressed mark 'WEMYSS WARE/ R.H.&S.'

4in (10cm) high

£500-550   **L&T**

A Wemyss tyg, painted with apples on branches, impressed 'Wemyss'.

5.75in (14.5cm) high

£150-200   **SWO**

QUICK REFERENCE - ZOOKIES

- 'Zookies' were produced by J.H. Weatherby & Son Ltd of Hanley, Staffordshire during the 1950s & 60s, and went out of production by 1970. According to records, 44 different animals were produced making this an ideal area for the 'completist' collector as the complete set can be collected. Some animals are rarer and harder to find than others and some of the later animals may in fact never have been produced.

- Averaging around 4inches (10cm) high, they are chunky and were part of a trend for such small, characterful figurines at the time, the most well-known being Wade's 'Whimsies', which were released in 1953. Decorated by hand and glazed in a glossy glaze, colours are bright and most look like characters from children's books. The largest figurine is the seal, which has unusual heart-shaped eyes. Also unusual is a zebra, which is orange and brown to fit into the range's general colour scheme, rather than black and white.

- Prices vary, but are largely affordable at around £20. Although many can be found online, they make excellent targets for car boot [flea market in the US] hunters. Look out for scarcer characters, such as a cat with a ball of wool, a fish, and a green and yellow frog, and those with cross-market appeal as they can fetch more. As they were comparatively inexpensive in their day, many were damaged when put in toy boxes, played with, or put away in lofts. Condition is always worth considering and, unless a piece is very rare or is needed to complete a collection, it's best to avoid damaged examples. As they were handpainted, look out for examples that are well-decorated, with good levels of detail.

A 1950s-60s J.H. Weatherby & Sons Ltd 'Zookie' hippo figurine.

2.75in (7cm)

£15-20   DSC

A 1950s-60s J.H. Weatherby & Sons Ltd 'Zookie' crocodile figurine.

6.5in (16.5cm) long

£15-20   DSC

A 1950s-60s J.H. Weatherby & Sons Ltd 'Zookie' giraffe figurine.

5in (13cm)

£15-20   DSC

A 1950s-60s J.H. Weatherby & Sons Ltd 'Zookie' elephant figurine.

4.25in (11cm)

£20-25   DSC

A 1950s-60s J.H. Weatherby & Sons Ltd 'Zookie' tiger figurine.

4in (10cm)

£15-20   DSC

A 1950s-60s J.H. Weatherby & Sons Ltd 'Zookie' toucan figurine.

4.25in (11cm)

£15-20   DSC

CERAMICS

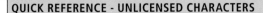

A 1950s-60s J.H. Weatherby & Sons Ltd 'Zookie' tortoise figurine.

Along with the grey and yellow pelican and a pony, the tortoise is one of the more challenging animals to find today, indicating it sold in smaller quantities at the time. This is one of the two marks found on 'Zookies'.

2.5in (6.5cm)

£20-25   DSC

A 1950s-60s J.H. Weatherby & Sons Ltd 'Zookie' Spaniel figurine.
4in (10cm)
£20-25   DSC

A pair of 1950s-60s J.H. Weatherby & Sons Ltd 'Zookie' rabbit figurines, with two colour variations.

4in (10cm)
£15-20   DSC

A 1950s-60s J.H. Weatherby & Sons Ltd 'Zookie' fawn figurine.

3in (8cm)
£15-20   DSC

QUICK REFERENCE - UNLICENSED CHARACTERS

● Although this looks like Tramp from the 1955 Disney animation film 'Lady And The Tramp', he was only marketed as a terrier figurine, and he doesn't bear any Disney copyright wording on the base or the name Tramp. The same is true of the figurines shown here that look like Lady, Bambi, and Dumbo. This was to avoid paying Disney for the right to produce an officially licensed figurine, which they would also have had to approve. At the time, the similarity would have been obvious to buyers, and they would have made an affordable option to officially licensed products by one or maybe a handful of companies. A great many companies produced such unlicensed goods, particularly in Japan and the Far East, and the names of the companies who produced them are largely unknown and, indeed, irrelevant. Although they will typically fetch less than licensed products, some are rare within their own collecting area and that factor, and the fact that most 'Lady And The Tramp' collectors would love to own an example of every Tramp produced, means that prices can be slightly higher due to cross-market interest. When buying unlicensed characters, always go for the best quality and closest similarity to the characters in the film as some look rather odd and were badly produced in cheap materials.

A 1950s-60s J.H. Weatherby & Sons Ltd 'Zookie' 'Tramp' dog figurine.
4in (10cm)
£20-25   DSC

A 1950s-60s J.H. Weatherby & Sons Ltd 'Zookie' foal figurine.

3.75in (9.5cm)
£15-20   DSC

QUICK REFERENCE - THE AMPHORA POTTERY

● The Amphora Pottery was founded by Alfred Stellmacher in 1892 in Turn-Teplitz, Bohemia, as Riessner, Stellmacher & Kessel (R.S.K.).

● It initially made porcelain figures, but is known today for its earthenware Art Nouveau vases.

● Its pieces won awards at the 1893 Chicago World's Fair and 1904 St Louis World's Fair.

● Pieces made between 1894 and 1904 often feature realistically sculptured plants and animals, prehistoric and mythical creatures, Klimt- and Mucha-style portraits, and simulated jewels.

● The factory closed during WWII.

A tall Amphora Pottery earthenware vase, painted with parrots and stylized foliage, on a textured blue ground, printed and impressed marks.

19.25in (49cm) high

£80-120   WW

An Art Deco Amphora Pottery ewer, enamelled in low-relief with a sphinx above a band of scarab motifs, impressed numbers.

15in (38cm) high

£30-50   WW

An Amphora Pottery elephant, on a green-glazed base, marked 'Amphora, Made in Czechoslovakia'.

7in (18cm) high

£50-80   LAW

An Ault Pottery earthenware ewer, designed by Christopher Dresser, with incised decoration, green glaze, design no.176, applied and impressed maker's mark.

9.5in (24cm) high

£350-400   CHEF

An Ault Pottery jardiniere, in the form of an open-mouthed fish, raised moulded mark and numbered 584.

14in (35cm) wide

£70-110   ECGW

A Belleek preserves jar and cover, in the form of a bee hive, with Belleek black stamp.

6in (15cm) high

£20-30   WHP

A 1930s Art Deco William Bennett mantel garniture, decorated by Mabel V Hodgkiss, printed marks 'S/D'.

It is believed that Mabel V Hodgkiss was a student at the Burslem School of Art and was employed at William Bennett to design and decorate in the style of the factory's 'rivals'. She took her inspiration from Clarice Cliff and Myott. The William Bennett factory in Hanley closed in 1937.

£120-180   FLD

CERAMICS

A Richard Amour for Bough Pottery, Edinburgh, wall plate, decorated with summer flowers, painted marks 'R.A./ BOUGH/', dated.

1934   9.75in (25cm) diam

£250-350   L&T

An early 20thC C.H. Brannam [Ltd?] model of a seated cat, with incised fur and white slip detailing, impressed marks.

13in (33.5cm) high

£120-180   FLD

QUICK REFERENCE - BRANNAM POTTERY

● The Brannam family worked as potters in Devon, producing slip- and sgraffito-decorated pottery. Thomas Backway Brannam started his own business in 1847 and displayed jugs at The Great Exhibition in 1851.

● In 1879, after studying art, his son Charles Hubert (1855-1937) took over the running of the Barnstaple pottery.

● As well as producing traditional wares, he introduced more up-to-date designs such as Barum Art Pottery. In 1885, Queen Victoria placed an order for four jardinieres at Brannam, which significantly raised the profile of the pottery. A year after, Charles registered the name 'Royal Barum Ware'; Barum being the Roman name for Barnstaple. It used red clay decorated with a rich, glossy blue and green glaze.

● In 1914, C.H. Brannam & Sons became a limited company. The business still exists today under the name of Candy & Co. who took over the company in 1979.

● Many marks have been used over the years. They are mostly combinations of 'C.H. Brannam', 'Barum' and 'Barnstaple'. From c1930s onwards, 'Made in England' was also used.

A pair of C.H. Brannam & Sons Ltd glazed vases, sgraffito-decorated with a deer feeding from a tree, impressed marks.

11in (28cm) high

£300-400   SWO

An Art Nouveau Brannam Barum Art Pottery [or Royal Barum Ware] oviform vase, with dragon handles, decorated with flowers and leaves, incised marks.

19.7in (50cm) high

£150-250   ECGW

A Burleigh Ware pottery charger, designed by Charlotte Rhead, with a galleon in full sail, printed and inscribed marks.

14in (35.5cm) diam

£500-600   SWO

A 1930s Art Deco Burleigh Ware water jug, decorated with a flamingo beside bullrush and water grasses, printed marks.

9.5in (24cm) high

£50-60   FLD

A Cobridge Pottery vase, of globe and shaft form, decorated with a red streaked and mottled glaze, impressed marks.

13in (32cm) high

£90-120   FLD

A Cobridge Pottery vase, decorated with a high-fired mottled blue and purple glaze, impressed marks.

10in (25cm)

£75-95   FLD

A pair of Compton Pottery bookends, cast in low relief with an archer figure, 'Bristol Guild' paper retail label.

7.25in (18.5cm) high

£300-400　　　　　　　　　　　　　　　　　　WW

QUICK REFERENCE - SUSIE COOPER

- Susie Cooper (1902-95) was a prolific ceramic designer who studied and worked in the Staffordshire potteries.
- Her stylized, innovative designs met the demand for fresh, innovative ceramics and are highly sought-after by collectors today. Among her most popular designs was the 'Kestrel' shape teaware.
- She began her career as a decorator and later as a designer for A.E. Gray & Co. Ltd, then opened her own decorating firm, Crown Works. At first she purchased blanks from local firms but later had her own pottery shapes made.
- She was named a 'Royal Designer for Industry' in 1940.
- In 1951 she bought a bone china factory in London and exhibited at the Festival of Britain. The factory merged with R.H. & S.L. Plant in the 1960s and was later taken over by the Wedgwood Group.

A 1930s Susie Cooper triangular lamp base, pattern no.E369, each facia hand-painted with stylised floral sprays, printed marks.

6in (12.5cm) high (excluding fittings)

£100-150　　　　　　　　　FLD

An 'American Bison' pottery group, by Stella Crofts, painted in colours, with incised marks, dated.

1928　　　　7.5in (19cm) wide

£400-500　　　　　　　　　WW

A 1930s Susie Cooper twin-handled soup cup and plate, 'The Homestead' pattern, decorated with a hand-painted cottage, printed script mark.

saucer 6in (15cm) diam

£120-180　　　　　　　　　FLD

A Crown Devon Fieldings musical jug 'I Love a Lassie', the front with a low-relief Scotsman dressed in Highland attire, the reverse with a printed verse, the handle formed as his walking stick, inscribed 'as ever Harry Lauder', printed marks.

9.5in (24cm) high

£70-80　　　　　　　　　FLD

A Crown Ducal pottery charger, by Charlotte Rhead, decorated with orange and brown floral bands, within a cream ground.

12.6in (32cm) diam

£50-60　　　　　　　　　LOC

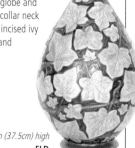

An early 20thC Della Robbia vase, designed by Liza Wilkins, of globe and shaft form, the collar neck decorated with incised ivy leaves, incised and painted marks.

14.75in (37.5cm) high

£400-500　　　　　　　　　FLD

CERAMICS

QUICK REFERENCE - DENBY MARMADUKE RABBITS

- The Denby rabbit was one of a number of novelty pieces the factory produced from the 1930s onwards.
- All Denby rabbits are known as Marmaduke. He first appeared in 1928–29 and production ceased shortly after the end of World War II.
- The rabbit was made in seven sizes – the smallest (size 00) is just under 1in (2.5cm) tall and the largest (size 4) is 10.5in (26.5cm) tall and was sturdy enough to be used as a doorstop. There was also a tail-less cotton wool container.
- Marmaduke was glazed in a variety of colours including matt and shiny green and blue, shiny brown, pastels and some rarer colours such as yellow, lime green, and pink.
- Values depend on the size, colour of the glaze, and rarity. For example, yellow is more desirable than pale brown which in turn realizes higher prices than matt cream and blue.

- Rare items such as a boxed set of menu holders will command a premium.

Four large versions of Denby's Marmaduke rabbit.

10.5in (26.5cm) high

Matt cream £150-250, Pale brown £200-300,
Canary yellow £600-800, Blue £100-200

CAN

A boxed set of six Denby Marmaduke green-glazed menu holders.

£350-450   **CHOR**

An Elton 'Sunflower' pottery vase, with a gold-crackled glaze over a deep-blue ground, with pinched shoulders, painted 'Elton' mark.

8in (20.5cm) high

£450-550   **SWO**

An Elton 'Sunflower' pottery vase, of slender form with prunts to the rim, with a gold-crackled glaze over a mustard ground, painted 'Elton' mark.

12in (30cm) high

£500-600   **SWO**

An Emile Gallé faïence cat, with a dog pendant around its neck, a lace scarf tied around its head, the body decorated with a floral design, unsigned.

c1900   13in (33.5cm)

£2,500-3,000   **TEN**

An Emile Gallé tin-glazed cat, decorated with playing cards on a sponged-yellow ground, its tail decorated with the card suites, applied glass eyes, painted 'E Gallé Nancy' to foot.

c1880   12.5in (32cm) high

£1,500-2,500   **WW**

A Goebel figure of a nude lady, impressed marks with foil sticker to the base.

10in (25cm) high

£180-240   **FLD**

A Grueby ribbed vase, circular pottery stamp to base, professional restoration to chip at rim.

c1905   *10.75in (27.5cm)*

£4,000-5,000   **DRA**

A CLOSER LOOK AT A GRUEBY VASE

The bud design is typical of Grueby. This example is crisply modelled and beautifully fired.

The yellow glaze on the buds enhances the value – less than 10% of the pottery's output used more than one colour.

The fine matter green ground is typical. The only flaws are a few flecks near the rim.

The sensuous, hand-thrown shape adds to its desirability.

A fine Grueby vase with leaves and white buds, marked circular pottery stamp, incised 'HJ 8-11' (or '17').

c1905   *7.5in (19cm)*

£8,000-10,000   **DRA**

A rare Hammersmith Bridge stoneware sculpture, 'The Bull', by Phoebe Stabler, later produced by Poole Pottery, glazed in colours, impressed Hammersmith mark, incised inscription.

13.5in (34cm) wide

£2,000-3,000   **WW**

A Theodore Haviland porcelain parrot and cover, designed by Edward Sandoz, both base and cover with facsimile signature, stamped 'Theodore Haviland, Limoges, France Copyright'.

7in (18.5cm) high

£400-500   **SWO**

A large Herend figure of a nude female attending her hair, incised and printed marks.

21.75in (55cm) high

£300-400   **BELL**

A Herend porcelain duck group, decorated in a green and gilt imari pattern, blue printed mark to base.

16.25in (41cm) wide

£350-450   **BELL**

CERAMICS

QUICK REFERENCE - CHRISTOPHER DRESSER

- Christopher Dresser (1834-1904) was an English designer, botanist, and teacher who is considered to be one of the first modern industrial designers.

- His pioneering designs combined traditional forms and motifs from many cultures, an appreciation of plants, and machine and mass production to create pieces which still appear 'modern' today.

- He was inspired by Japanese design and spent four months there in 1876–77. He visited cultural and manufacturing sites, having been commissioned by Tiffany & Co. to bring back items. He also became involved in importing Japanese artefacts.

- In 1861, he became a fellow of the Linnean Society. A year later, he published his first book, entitled 'The Art of Decorative Design'.

- As well as producing ceramic designs for Linthorpe and Ault, he worked with Elkington (silversmiths), Coalbrookdale (iron foundry), Hukin & Heath (silver and plate makers) and J.Couper & Sons (glass, notably the Clutha range), among many others.

A Hutschenreuther figure of a seated nude lady, holding a violin with a bow in hand, printed marks.

8.5in (22cm)

£100-150   FLD

A pottery vase, possibly Linthorpe, after a design by Christopher Dresser, with a spiral-twisted conical body, pinched rim, restored and chipped.

8.5in (21cm) high

£80-120   SWO

A Linthorpe Pottery vase, after a design by Christopher Dresser, impressed shape no.189, of double-gourd shape, 'Ch Dresser' facsimile signature.

6.5in (17cm) high

£150-250   SWO

A Linthorpe pottery vase, shape no.1785, with an undulating rim above a squat baluster body on circular foot, with impressed mark.

7.75in (19.5cm)

£150-250   SWO

A Madoura pottery charger, 'Service Visage Noir', designed by Pablo Picasso (1881-1973) in 1948, limited edition of 100, impressed 'Madoura Plein Feu' and Picasso Editions mark, painted edition Picasso, restored.

1948   16.5in (42cm) diam

£2,000-3,000   WW

A rare North Dakota School of Mines early drip-glaze humidor, Grand Forks, ND, signed 'U.N.D', dated.

1916   6.75in (17.5cm) high

£1,400-1,800   DRA

A North Dakota School of Mines early drip-glaze vase, Grand Forks, ND, incised illegible artist initials, signed 'U.N.D'., dated.

1912   8.25in (21cm) high

£850-1,200   DRA

A French Art Deco ceramic deer group, designed by Odette Berlot and Yvonne Mussier, after a model by Charles Lemanceau, produced under the trade name 'ODYV'.

1927-40   *18in (45.5cm) wide*

£150-250   ECGW

A 1930s Pilkingtons Royal Lancastrian vase, of swollen form with roll rim collar neck, decorated in a tonal orange crystalline glaze, impressed marks.

7in (18cm) high

£80-120   FLD

A Ruskin baluster vase, with a pink-mottled iridescent glaze, stamped marks.

1919   *7.3in (18.5cm) high*

£120-180   SWO

QUICK REFERENCE - ROZENBURG

- The Rozenburg Royal Delftware Factory was founded in 1883 by Baron Wilhelm von Gudenberg in The Hague, Netherlands, with the aim of producing traditional Delft pottery.
- However, von Gudenberg became captivated by the latest Art Nouveau designs and as a result the factory made flamboyant earthenware pieces in this style.
  - Designers included T.A.C. Colenbrander (1841-1930), who created exotic vases and dishes with whimsical, bright designs. Later 19thC pieces reflected the British Arts & Crafts style.
  - In 1899, the factory's director Jurriaan Kok (1861-1919) launched a range made from an eggshell porcelain that was so delicate it was almost unusable. The pieces were acclaimed at the 1900 World Exhibition in Paris, but success was fleeting.
  - From 1904, Rozenburg produced building materials. It closed in 1917.

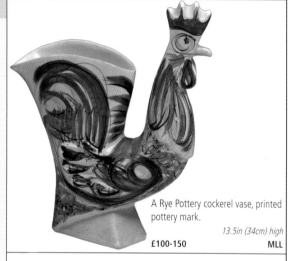

A Rye Pottery cockerel vase, printed pottery mark.

13.5in (34cm) high

£100-150   MLL

A 1930s Sadler teapot, modelled as a green racing car with silver lustre trims, OKT42 number plate, impressed marks.

9in (22.5cm) long

£60-90   FLD

A Rozenburg earthenware vase, painted in an Arts and Crafts palette, incised marks and painted 'Rozenburg', stork, K in a circle.

c1900   *16.5in (42cm) high*

£200-300   SWO

CERAMICS

A pair of 19thC porcelain cups, possibly Samson, painted with gilt-lined vignettes depicting exotic bird, butterly, insect, and flowers upon blue-scale ground, the inside with reticulated gilt border, gilt 'B' to bases.

2in (5cm) high

£200-250   ROS

A late 19thC Samson porcelain figure group, in the Meissen style, of a gentleman and two ladies playing backgammon, pseudo blue crossed swords mark, contained in a contemporary fitted case bearing a shield with three fleur-de-lis.

9.25in (23.5cm)

£300-400   WW

A 20thC porcelain figural group representing Asia, attributed to Samson, dressed with turban and colourful oriental clothing, with urn and instrument to side resting on rocky base, cupid with fez to the reverse holding shield with gilt crescent, bears gold anchor to base.

15in (38cm) high

£300-400   ROS

A CLOSER LOOK AT A VAN BRIGGLE VASE

The 'Lorelei' vase is Van Briggle's signature piece. It was first made in 1897 and is still made today. This example was made after Artus Van Briggle's death in 1904 and the departure of his wife Anne from the pottery in 1912. Pieces made during his lifetime command a premium – a superior piece by Artus might fetch £35,000 or more.

The two-colour glazing is not as subtle as that seen on earlier pieces but adds to its desirability.

The design depicts a young woman from a German legend who leaps to her death from a cliff above the river Rhine after hearing of her lover's unfaithfulness. From that day, it was said that her siren song lured unsuspecting sailors to their deaths on the jagged rocks below. Here, the moulding is soft enough to suggest the design but strong enough to be expressive.

Even though these vases were produced from a mould, they were finished by hand, which is a sign of quality.

An early 20thC Van Briggle vase, 'Lorelei', 'Persian Rose' glaze, marked 'AA VAN BRIGGLE USA'.

1922-26.   *10in (25.5cm) high*

£1,000-1,500   DRA

A 1930s French Art Deco Sèvres Vinsare polar bear, textured white 'crispée' glazes, green printed mark.

The textured pearlized glaze is typical of the Sèvres Vinsare factory. The pottery was originally the Manufacture Nouvelle de Faïence (MNF) later became Sèvres Vinsare France and existed from 1929 to about 1942.

8.75in (22cm) high

£250-350   DN

An early 20thC Van Briggle vase, 'Lady of the Lily', Persian Rose glaze, marked 'AA VAN BRIGGLE Colo. SPGS'.

c1930   *10.5in (27cm) high*

£800-1,200   DRA

An early 20thC Van Briggle vase, with stylized daisies, Mountain Crag brown glaze, marked 'AA Van Briggle Colo. Sprgs', illegible numbers, dated.

1907   *7.25in (18.5cm) high*

£600-800   DRA

A Karl Ens Volkstedt seated nude figure, modelled by P.W Goebel, incised signature, printed marks to the base.

13in (33cm) high

£100-150   **FLD**

A Wadeheath musical jug, 'The Big Bad Wolf', cast in low relief, with printed mark.

10.5in (26.5cm) high

£800-1,000   **WW**

A Wadeheath teapot, 'Donald Duck', modelled with his wings behind his back, printed marks 'Wadeheath by Permission Walt Disney'.

4in (10cm) high

£150-200   **SWO**

QUICK REFERENCE - WALRATH POTTERY

- Frederick Walrath (1871–1920) was an American studio potter who worked with a number of schools and potteries.
- He initially studied at the New York State School of Clay-working and Ceramics.
- In 1903, he taught and studied at the Arts and Crafts School of the Chautauqua Institution in Chautauqua, New York, going on to teach at the Mechanics Institute's Department of Decorative and Fine Arts in Rochester, New York, where most of the pieces found today were made.
- He briefly worked for the Grueby Pottery and was made head ceramicist at Newcomb College in 1918.
  - Walrath was famous for his use of matte glazes, which are difficult to control, using them to create sharp, detailed designs.
  - Most pieces use two colours, often in a decorative band around the top of the vase. Rarer pieces use three or four colours.

A fine and tall Walrath scenic vase, signed 'Walrath Pottery'.

c1910   *8.25in (21cm) high*

£12,000-15,000   **DRA**

A fine Walrath cylindrical scenic vase, signed 'Walrath Pottery'.

c1910   *7.5in (19cm) high*

£16,000-20,000   **DRA**

A unique Walrath table lamp, signed 'Walrath Pottery', rewired, new socket.

c1910   *12.5in (32cm) high*

£5,000-6,000   **DRA**

CERAMICS

QUICK REFERENCE - A.J. WILKINSON LTD

- The A.J. Wilkinson Ltd pottery was founded in Burslem, Staffordshire, in 1885. It produced earthenware and ironstone ornamental pieces and tablewares.
- Wilkinson's is best known as being the pottery that employed Clarice Cliff in 1916. However, hers are not the only collectable pieces.
- John Butler worked as a painter at the factory and was its art director from 1904 until 1930. Cliff was apprenticed to him as a modeller in 1919. Butler's innovations included the 'Oriflamme' range.
- Wilkinson's took over the Newport Pottery in 1920.
- It was taken over by Midwinter in 1964, and became part of the Wedgwood group in 1970.

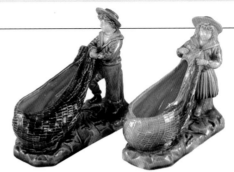

A pair of Watcombe figures, of a fisher boy and girl, each poised holding a net, high glaze over blonde terracotta, one impressed 'Watcombe Torquay'.

7in (18 cm) wide

£120-150   ECGW

A John Butler for A.J. Wilkinson large vase, 'Tahiti Regatta' pattern, of footed square baluster form, hand-painted with a stylized coastal landscape with sailing boats, silver lustre detail, hand-painted signature to the body, printed and painted marks to the base.

15in (38cm) high

£350-450   FLD

A John Butler for A.J. Wilkinson plate, hand-painted in the 'Tahiti Foam' pattern, with stylized swans in flight, hand-signed to the body, pattern name to the base, printed A.J.Wilkinson mark.

c1928   *10.25in (26cm) diam*

£200-300   FLD

A Zsolnay Pecs figural group, of two brown bears fighting, raised to a circular base, printed marks.

11.5in (29cm) high

£60-80   FLD

A large late 19thC Parian bathing figure, of a seated nude sat upon rocks drying her feet, unmarked.

16.5in (42cm)

£180-220   FLD

An Art Nouveau pottery jug and basin set, with a two-tone cream and green glaze with stylized motifs, unmarked.

12.25in (31cm) high

£50-60   SWO

An Art Deco pink-tinted glass strut clock, with a pierced brass chapter ring, on a brass stand.

9.5in (24cm) wide

£50-80   SWO

A Bulle electric mantel clock, the oak and ebonised case with a chrome front frame.

Bulle electric clocks were developed by Maurice Favre-Bulle, Marcel Andre-Moulin, and Marius Lavet just before World War One. In 1920, a patent was taken out by a company established in France. Their clocks proved to be very successful. From 1920-52, it is estimated that over 300,000 clocks were produced.

9in (23cm) high

£250-300   SWO

A CLOSER LOOK AT A VITASCOPE CLOCK

When plugged into mains power, the clock works, the marine scene is illuminated, and the ship rocks.

It was also produced with a cream or brown case. Very rare examples have a woodgrain effect.

The unusual, yet soporific, design was patented by Mr J.S. Thatcher in 1944, and amendments were made by Mr J.F. Summersgill in 1944 and 1947.

It was not produced for long. Examples are hard to find and highly desirable, particularly in working order.

A late 1940s British Vitascope Industries 'Vitascope' bakelite clock, in black with an oscillating sailing ship, with a chrome-pierced chapter ring.

12.75in (32.5cm) high

£400-600   SWO

An Art Deco rosewood-cased triple-train mantel clock, by Elliott, retailed by Garrard & Co. Ltd.

9in (23cm)

£120-160   ECGW

A large Magneta electric wall clock, grey finish with remnants of light-blue paintwork.

21.3in (54cm) diam

£400-500   SWO

A double-sided shop clock, the painted aluminium case with a square painted dial inscribed 'JAS. RAMSEY, DUNDEE', with two hoops and chain for suspension.

22in (56cm) high

£500-600   SWO

An Art Deco Smith's Leverprint clocking-in machine, with inset clock.

This was used to record and monitor workers' hours in a factory or office.

14.5in (37cm) high

£130-180   SWO

A Henry VII (1485-1509) halfgroat, York, Canterbury, profile issue, Martlet.

£150-200   DUK

A Charles I (1625-49) double crown, tower mint under the king, second bust, no inner circle, crown shield on reverse, mm, Castle, with expendant mount.

1625-42

£550-650   DUK

A Queen Anne (1702-14) half-crown, 1707E, draped bust, crowned cruciform shields on reverse.

£120-180   DUK

A Victoria (1837-1901) half-crown, with 'young head' profile, crowned shield in wreath on reverse.

1884

£250-350   DUK

QUICK REFERENCE - CONDITION

● The condition of a coin is classified in great detail with a series of two to five letter codes, from P for 'poor' condition to 'FDC', a French term implying perfect condition. There are many terms in between these, often with very narrow criteria. Although this coin looks dirty, cleaning it would be the worst thing to do. The discolouration, known as 'bloom', is desirable, as this coin is completely uncirculated (i.e. it has never been used for its intended purpose). It has gained this discolouration over years of careful storage and lack of handling. Collectors will aim to buy coins in the very best condition.

A Victoria (1837-1901) two pounds coin, with Jubilee bust, St. George and Dragon on reverse, with proof-like fields and frosting.

All the images in this section show both sides of one coin.

1887

£700-1,000   DUK

A Victoria (1837-1901) sovereign, with Jubilee bust, St. George and Dragon on reverse.

1887

£220-280   DUK

A Victoria (1837-1901) florin, with veiled bust, three shields below crown with sceptres on reverse.

1901

£50-80   DUK

A George V (1910-36) sovereign, with bare head profile, St. George and Dragon on reverse, in extremely fine condition.

1912

£200-300   DUK

A Livia (Julia Augusta, 14-29AD) mint, Rome, AE Dupondius, struck under Tiberius (22-23AD), bare-headed and draped bust of Julia Augusta as Salus Right, legend around large capital 'S.C' on reverse, with smooth chocolate toning, die-crack on obverse.

This is a scarce coin.

£250-350   DUK

A Rome Lucius Verus (161-169AD) mint, AE Sestertius, bare-headed and cuirassed bust right, Marcus Aurelius and Lucius Verus standing facing one another, clasping right hands on reverse.

£200-300   DUK

A Roman Hadrian (117-138AD) coin, AE Sestertius, laureate-draped bust facing right, Felicity on reverse holding cornucopia and caduceus.

£180-220   DUK

A Greek Bruttium Terina AR didrachm, head of the nymph Terina facing right, Nike seated left on open stool containing a single amulet, with attractive toning and a bold central strike.
c440-425BC

£220-280   DUK

A Greek Tarentum Campano-Tarentine AR didrachm, diademed head of the nymph Satyr left wearing triple-drop earrings, youth on horseback right, crowning horse with raised left foreleg, star above dolphin and TA below, with even medium-dark toning.
c280-230BC

£550-750   DUK

An Indian East India Company AV half mohur, with script between lines, twisted.

£100-150   DUK

A United States half dollar, Liberty seated above date.
1857

£120-180   DUK

A Republic of China dollar (Yuan), Yuan Shih-kai left, character marks within wreath on reverse.
1914

£50-80   DUK

QUICK REFERENCE - THE BEANO

● 'The Beano' needs no introduction, except to younger generations who may find they appreciate its anarchic sense of humour despite the lure and variety of the internet. With exceptions during World War Two, it has been published every Thursday since July 30th, 1938. The cover of this first issue showed Big Eggo getting into one of many scrapes with eggs. Around 25 copies of the first issue of The Beano are known to exist and those in 'Fine+' grade like this example can fetch up to £15,000 at auction, particularly if there are two determined bidders. Copies in lesser or poorer condition can sell for anything from £500 to £5,000. In April 1950, 'The Beano's' weekly circulation was 1,974,072 and at the time of writing it currently sells just over 30,000 copies per week. Not bad for such an 'old timer'!

'The Beano', no.17, November 19th, 1938, published by D.C. Thompson.
All issues of 'The Beano' comic from 1938, its inaugural year, are genuinely rare with only a handful of copies known to exist.
£700-1,000   PCOM

'The Beano', no.46, November 19th, 1939, published by D.C. Thompson.
£250-350   PCOM

'The Beano', no.1, July 30th, 1938, published by D.C. Thompson.
£10,000-15,000   PCOM

'The Beano', no.83, February 24th, 1940, published by D.C. Thompson.

The number of pages in comics was understandably affected by the World War Two as paper was used for the war effort. In 1938, 'The Beano' had 28 pages, by 1944 it had been reduced to 12 pages and was bi-weekly, alternating with 'The Dandy'. However, the government realised that comics were great for children's morale and they were also able to use them for propaganda purposes.
£200-300   PCOM

'The Beano', no.120, November 9th, 1940, published by D.C. Thompson.

The cover is a classic example of World War Two propaganda, with Hitler being mocked on the front cover Big Eggo strip.
£150-250   PCOM

'The Beano', no.1268, November 5th, 1966, published by D.C. Thompson.

The single panel cover artwork on this issue is strikingly desirable. The subject matter of fireworks is also collectable, and this was one of the last issues where characters were seen playing with fireworks as public perceptions of the dangers of playing with fireworks changed.
£15-20   PCOM

'The Christmas Beano', no.1275, December 24th, 1966, published by D.C. Thompson.

Christmas issues of 'The Beano' comic are widely collected due to their seasonal and attractive nature. This is a classic from 1966, with a single panel front cover.
£20-25   PCOM

'The Beano Book', 1956, published by D.C. Thompson.

This is one of several classic 'The Beano Books' with a front to rear cover story. The Beano reached its peak in readership in the 1950s with the likes of Dennis the Menace, Little Plum, Roger the Dodger and Minnie the Minx bursting onto the scene. All these key characters are seen on the front cover of this book.

£50-80   PCOM

'The Beano Book', 1941, published by D.C. Thompson.

This was the second 'The Beano Book' and is harder to find than the first one, published in 1940. In order to fetch the upper end of this value range, a copy must be in excellent condition all over.

£1,500-2,500   PCOM

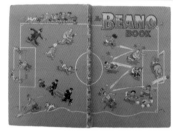

'The Beano Book', 1957, published by D.C. Thompson.

Considered by collectors to be a superb issue, this is very hard to find, especially in the immaculate condition required to fetch the upper end of this value range. This issue is unusual in that the front cover, spine and back cover form one single image - and an image including all readers' favourite characters.

£100-150   PCOM

'The Dandy Book' 1957, published by D.C. Thompson.

£30-40   PCOM

'The Dandy Summer Special', 1973, published by D.C. Thompson.

£10-15   PCOM

'The Dandy Monster Comic', 1944, published by D.C. Thompson.

Annuals from the later war years can be hard to find in the good condition this example is in, as they often suffer from loose bindings and loss of spines.

£300-500

'Dennis the Menace' book, 1958, published by D.C. Thompson.

This was the second annual and it is incredibly hard to find with its full spine. The iconic and colourful cover was by David Law (1908-71), who created and first drew Dennis and his dog Gnasher in 1951, and continued to do until 1970.

£70-100   PCOM

COMICS

'Battle Picture Weekly', 1976, published by IPC.

Published from 1975-88, this was a popular war comic for boys published by IPC in response to DC Thomson's 'Warlord' comics. Most stories were set in World War Two. It merged with 'The Eagle' in 1988.

£2-4   PCOM

The 'Beezer Summer Special', 1973, published by D.C. Thompson.

The was the first of this title's annual Summer Specials and the cover featured the hugely popular, and now classic, Raleigh Chopper bicycle.

£20-25   PCOM

'Bunty Girls Summer Special', 1973, published by DC Thompson, with artwork of Bunty on a beach.

Summer specials with appealing and bright cover artwork such as this are desirable and highly collectable.

£20-30   PCOM

'Doctor Who Weekly', no.1, October 17th, 1979, complete with free gift of pictorial transfers in original wrapper, published by Marvel Comics (UK).

£15-20   PCOM

'Knock-out' no.16, June 17th, 1939, published by Amalgamated Press.

Launched in 1939, this was intended to be a direct competitor to 'The Beano' and 'The Dandy' comics. Despite never being as popular, it lasted until 1963 and was then re-launched in 1971.

£15-20   PCOM

'Lion', 1965, published by Fleetway, a division of IPC.

'Lion' comic was a weekly boys' adventure comic which was published from 1952-74 clocking up an amazing 1,156 issues. 'Robot Archie' was an early favourite, as were anti-heroes 'The Spider' and 'The Sludge' in the 1960s.

£5-10   PCOM

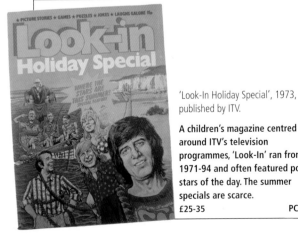

'Look-In Holiday Special', 1973, published by ITV.

A children's magazine centred around ITV's television programmes, 'Look-In' ran from 1971-94 and often featured pop stars of the day. The summer specials are scarce.

£25-35   PCOM

'Marvelman' no.195, 1957, published by L. Miller & Son.

'Marvelman' was the British comic industry's answer to America's 'Superman' - even down to his suit. 'Marvelman' ran throughout the 1950s and the youthful Young Marvelman (equivalent to Superboy) ran alongside in his own comic.

£10-20   PCOM

'Lady Penelope' no.52, January 14th, 1967, published by City Magazines.

This title ran for 204 issues, from 1966-69, and was very popular in the 1960s with Gerry Anderson's 'Supermarionation', the best known example of which was in 'Thunderbirds', and science fiction shows such as 1963's Dr Who rising in popularity on television.

£15-20   PCOM

A CLOSER LOOK AT 'STAR LORD'.

'Star Lord' was launched a year after '2000AD' and in anticipation of a sci-fi boom surrounding 'Star Wars' in 1977 - it was intended to have better production values and be for an older readership.

Despite these aims not being met, it still had a higher price which put people off - only 22 issues were published from May-October 1978.

Publisher IPC also found that having two sci-fi comics per week split the market, so its overall lack of success led it to be merged with '2000AD' in October 1978.

This was the title's only Summer Special.

'Star Lord Summer Special', 1978, published by IPC.
£20-25   PCOM

'Sally', no.1, June 14th, 1969, published by IPC.

Despite characters including 'The Cat Girl' and another 'Schoolgirl Princess', 'Sally' only ran for two years, from 1969-71. Most first issues of children's comics come with a free gift. In this case, it was cameo ring - as shown on the front cover. The presence of the free ring can increase the value to around £50, depending on condition.

£10-15   PCOM

'Spider-Man Comics Weekly', no.5, March 17th, 1973, published by Marvel Comics (UK).

This long-running British Marvel title ran from 1973-85, with 666 issues. It also starred 'The Mighty Thor'.

£3-5   PCOM

'Terrific', no.1, April 15th 1967, published by Odhams Press.

Published under Odham's 'Power Comics' imprint, 'Terrific' was quite unlike most other British comics and consisted primarily of reprinted American Marvel material such as 'The Avengers' and 'Doctor Strange'.

£5-10   PCOM

'Thundercats', no.4, April 11th, 1987, published by Marvel Comics (UK).

£2-3   PCOM

'TV Century 21 Summer Extra', 1965, complete with 'Cosmic Capers Kit' free gift.

This is one of six special spin-off comic specials from the very popular 'TV Century 21' comic, which was later named 'TV21'. It featured the likes of 'Fireball XL5', 'Stingray', 'Thunderbirds' and 'Captain Scarlet' - all of which were popular TV series. It was only published from 1965-69, making this the first Summer Extra. Without the free gift, it is worth around £80-120 in this condition.

£150-200   PCOM

COMMEMORATIVES

An early 19thC gold-lined snuff box made from 'Victory' timber, the lid, lined with unmarked gold inscribed 'This Box formed from a Splinter of THE VICTORY commanded by LORD VISCOUNT NELSON in the ever memorable engagement off Trafalgar, on the 21st Octr. 1805 in which he fell !!! But not until his superior nautical skill, & most intrepid Courage had completely overcome the combined fleets of FRANCE & SPAIN'.

3in (7.5cm) diam

£1,500-1,800   **CM**

An early 19thC silver-mounted 'Victory' timber table snuff box, the lid inset with gold-framed white glass profile of Nelson, after Tassie, mounted on bloodstone.

This box is of a type that closely matches others of similar proportions made in the immediate aftermath of Trafalgar from wood recovered in her refits initially at Gibraltar, and latterly at Portsmouth. The gold frame to the cameo and the silver base plate both with evidence of largely lost earlier engraving.

3.75in (9.5cm) wide

£1,000-1,500   **CM**

A George III silver commemorative Nelson vinaigrette, the lid inscribed 'THE.GALLANT. NELSON.DIED.OCT.21.1805.TRAFALGAR', and containing an old note reading 'Vinaigrette belonging to Lord Nelson', gilt plate added afterwards, hinged foliate-pierced grille with sponge behind, maker's marks for William Pugh, Birmingham, 1805.

1.25in (3.5cm) high

£1,400-1,800   **CM**

A commemorative silver vesta case, with applied enamel portrait of Lord Nelson, hallmarked for Howard James, Birmingham.

1885   *2.25in (5.75cm) high*

£250-350   **CM**

A ticket to Lord Nelson's funeral in St. Paul's Cathedral, signed by the Dean, black seal lower right.

4.75in (12cm) long

£2,500-3,500   **CM**

A miniature portrait medallion of Lord Nelson, in oils after Daniel Orme, within period gold pendant with unused glazed hair compartment behind.

c1810   *2in (5cm) diam*

£700-900   **CM**

A miniature portrait medallion of Lord Nelson, in oils after Daniel Orme, contained within period gold pendant with unused glazed hair compartment behind and suspension loop.

c1810   *2in (5cm) diam*

£500-800   **CM**

A late 19thC miniature portrait medallion of Lord Nelson, in watercolour and gouache, probably after Daniel Orme, contained within gilt-brass oval with decorated edges and suspension loop.

3.25in (8.5cm) high

£120-180   **CM**

A commemorative allegorical pendant, in oils and depicting a winged Victory sounding a trumpet over the action at Trafalgar holding a scroll inscribed 'NELSON victory' further inscribed around top edge 'He Conquerd when he Fell', empty glazed hair recess behind.

c1810   *1.75in (4.5cm) high*

£600-900   **CM**

An early 19thC commemorative brooch depicting Lord Nelson, after Tassie, profile possibly in black basalt, mounted on white opalescent glass, with gold-mounted border with blank cartouche to top, in a period green leather case.

1.5in (4cm) high

£400-700 CM

An early 19thC bloodstone and white glass cameo commemorative brooch depicting Lord Nelson, possibly after Tassie, white head on bloodstone edged in gold and suspended from a carved baleen floral display with gold pin behind.

2in (5cm) high

£300-500 CM

An early 19thC white glass commemorative profile of Lord Nelson, after Tassie, mounted on 3in (7.5cm) deep-blue enamel field with gilt-brass laurel wreath surround, mounted on an ebonised board with naval crown-fronted suspension loop.

6.5in (16.5cm) high

£1,600-2,000 CM

A 19thC gilt-brass profile of Lord Nelson, after Jan De Vaere, on a navy-blue cloth background, framed and glazed.

8in (20.5cm) high

£400-700 CM

A Royal Doulton Lord Nelson commemorative vase, modelled with a portrait of Lord Nelson, the reverse with inscription 'England expects every man will do his duty', impressed and incised marks.

5.7in (14.5cm) high

£150-250 WW

A Royal Doulton Lord Nelson commemorative jug, with a portrait of Lord Nelson flanked by the battle of Trafalgar, below inscription 'England expects everyman will do his duty', impressed and incised marks.

11in (27.5cm) high

£150-250 WW

A Doulton Lambeth commemorative jug for Lord Nelson, with tube-lined decoration, 'PA' mark to base.

c1902 *7.75in (20cm) high*

£80-120 LOCK

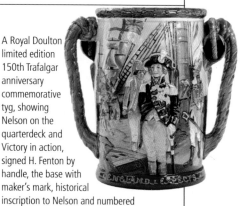

A Royal Doulton limited edition 150th Trafalgar anniversary commemorative tyg, showing Nelson on the quarterdeck and Victory in action, signed H. Fenton by handle, the base with maker's mark, historical inscription to Nelson and numbered 321/600.

10.5in (26.5cm) high

£400-600 CM

A CLOSER LOOK AT A PEARLWARE JUG

The jug is printed with a scene entitled 'John Bull Showing the Corsican Monkey'. This is based on a political cartoon by George Moutard Woodward depicting a crowd gathered around John Bull as he presents Napoleon, depicted as a small monkey, with a savage grin under an enormous bicorne, riding on the back of large bear. Imagery such as this was common during the Napoleonic wars.

On the reverse is a scroll of script signed J Harley, Lane End. This was the mark of Thomas Harley, a manufacturer at Lane End (now called Longton), who produced good earthenware services, jugs and other articles between 1805–12.

The jug is in good condition, adding to its desirability.

Some similar pieces also include a satirical verse on the reverse.

A Napoleon and John Bull pearlware jug, printed in brown and decorated in colours with an amusing scene.
c1805　　　　　　　　　　　*5.5in (14cm) high*
£500-800　　　　　　　　　　　　**H&C**

A pearlware commemorative jug, for 'PEACE of EUROPE Signed at PARIS May 30th 1814', printed in grey and decorated in colours with an inscribed tablet flanked by figures.

The Treaty of Paris marked the defeat of Napoleon following Napoleonic Wars. The treaty signed on May 30, 1814, was between France and the Allies – Austria, Great Britain, Prussia, Russia, Sweden and Portugal) on the other.

1814　　　*6.7in (17cm) high*
£200-250　　　　　　　**H&C**

A Sunderland pottery pink-lustre commemorative jug, printed with verse and dedicated to Robert Curtis and 'Success to the Coal Trade', dated.
1827　　　*8in (20.5cm) high*
£250-350　　　　　**BLEA**

A gold anchor pendant commemorating 'The Glorious 1st of June 1794', engraved on the stock 'Earl Howe' 'June 1st 1794'.

The Battle of the Glorious 1st of June was fought between the British, under the command of Admiral Earl Howe, and the French and is considered to be the first great battle between British and French fleets in the French Revolutionary War. At the end of five days of fighting, the British won a tactical victory.

1.75in (4.5cm) high
£1,200-1,800　　　　　**CM**

A Kirklands pottery character jug with top hat lid, depicting Sir Winston Churchill in morning dress.
c1941　　*10in (25.5cm) high*
£60-80　　　　　　**H&C**

A Copeland Spode white pottery figure of Sir Winston Churchill, by Eric Olson, the cigar damaged.
c1941　　*5.5in (14cm) high*
£60-80　　　　　**H&C**

A H.M.S. Mersey commemorative brass and enamel inkwell, modelled in the form of a regulation sailor's straw hat, tally inscribed 'MERSEY', the crown lifting and further inscribed 'H.M.S. MERSEY 40 CAPtn H CALDWELL CB' 'SHIPS COMPLEMENT' '600' 'TONS 3740. HORSEPOWER. 1000'.
1858　　　*6in (15cm) diam*
£180-220　　　　　**CM**

QUICK REFERENCE - ROYAL COMMEMORATIVES

- Royal commemorative items have been made since the 17thC, however it wasn't until the beginning of the 19thC that production boomed. The development of transfer printing on ceramics and the canal and railway systems meant that ceramics – which make up the majority of commemorative pieces – could be manufactured and transported economically.

- Because so much material is available to collectors, most tend to concentrate on collecting items relating to one personality or event. The current queen, and Queen Victoria, are two of the most popular collecting areas because their long reigns mean there are many different pieces to collect. However, some pieces commemorating some events are more common than others. For example, pieces celebrating Queen Victoria's marriage to Prince Albert are scarce, especially when compared to the many

pieces made to celebrate her Golden Jubilee. There is a growing interest in pieces commemorating the lives of the younger members of the current royal family.

- The work of well-known makers such as Royal Crown Derby, Royal Worcester, Copeland and Minton, who are known for producing high quality wares are generally in demand. Pieces designed by renowned 20thC designers such as Charlotte Rhead and Eric Ravilious often command a premium. However, collectors also look for brightly coloured and detailed pieces in good condition.

- Items from limited editions – particularly those from editions of less than 250 – are highly desirable but must include the box and any paper work if they are to hold their value.

- While 19thC pieces can show signs of wear, cracks and chips will lower values. Any damage to a recent piece will reduce its worth considerably.

A pottery mug, depicting the 1831 coronation of William IV, the moulded body printed in blue with portraits.

3.5in (9cm) high

£250-350   H&C

A pottery commemorative jug, the body printed in purple with named portraits centred by the Royal coat of arms inscribed 'Reform' and dated for the accession and coronation of William IV.

1831

£200-250

7in (17.6cm) high

H&C

A pottery flask, depicting the 1837 proclamation of the accession of Queen Victoria, the body printed on both sides in black with a named and dated portrait after Hayter within a blue printed border.

6in (15cm) diam

£700-1,000   H&C

A Victoria commemorative pottery mug, with purple portraits of the young Victoria with a crown (which didn't fit her) and the national emblems, the inside with a leafy scroll border, staining.

Like her uncle, William, Victoria was not expected to inherit the throne. She was crowned on 28th June 1838 in scenes of complete chaos. Nobody had rehearsed, nobody knew where to stand, and the Archbishop lost his place in the prayer book. Nevertheless, Victoria, ever the enthusiast, recorded the occasion pleasurably in her diary.

3.25in (8.5cm) high

£450-550   SWO

A named portrait bust of Victoria, in bronze, the reverse signed and dated 'Chardigny 1854', on a marble plinth.

Pierre Joseph Chardigny (1794-1866) was an accomplished sculptor in Paris receiving various awards.

6in (15.5cm) high

£200-300   H&C

A Transvaal pottery tyg, commemorating the end of the Boer War, by Copeland for Goode, in colours and gilt with portraits, flags and inscriptions, the base restored.

1900   *5.5in (14cm) high*

£300-400   H&C

COMMEMORATIVES

An Art Deco Burleigh ware plaque, celebrating the Silver Jubilee of King George and Queen Mary, designed by ET Bailey.

1935

£150-250   ECGW

A Copeland pottery commemorative tyg, decorated in colours and lined in silver, for the 1935 Silver Jubilee of George V.

6in (15cm) high

£250-350   H&C

A Hammersley loving cup, depicting the 1937 Coronation of George VI.

5.75in (14.5cm) high

£200-300   H&C

A Shelley George VI and Elizabeth coronation porcelain loving cup, printed with sepia portraits, the reverse printed with portraits of the Princesses, with gilt handles.

1937   *4in (10cm) high*

£80-120   SAS

A limited edition Royal Doulton 'H.M. Queen Elizabeth The Queen Mother' figure, HN4086, with certificate.

This figure was designed by Alan Maslankowski and produced in a limited edition of 2,000 to match the year of its release.

2000   *9in (23cm) high*

£150-200   PSA

A Paragon mug commemorating the birth of Princess Elizabeth (Queen Elizabeth II), with transfer-printed brown portrait after Marcus Adams, lined in red and gilt.

1926

£80-120   SAS

A Paragon bone china loving cup, with lion handles, made to commemorate the coronation of Queen Elizabeth II, with original certificate, a limited edition of 1,000.

c1953   *4.75in (12cm) high*

£300-400   PC

A Wedgwood Queen Elizabeth II Golden Jubilee commemorative mug, from the designs of Eric Ravilious, and gilt highlights.

c2002   *4in (10.5cm) high*

£50-80   WW

QUICK REFERENCE - DOLLS

- Mass manufacture of dolls began with moulded bisque-headed dolls, which were made primarily in Germany and France from the 1860s onwards and saw their golden age around 1900. During the 1920s & 30s, more robust materials began to be introduced, such as composition.

- The incised marks on the back of a doll's head can help to identify the maker of the doll and its date, as can facial characteristics. Look out for dolls by well-known, high quality makers such as Jumeau, Bru and better examples by larger makers such as Armand Marseille, Heubach and the French group S.F.B.J. Collectors look for clean, undamaged heads with characterful faces. Damaged bisque heads reduce values by over 50%, while original clothes generally push values upwards.

- During the 1950s, plastic replaced composition and bisque as it was more economical and versatile. Dolls became considerably more affordable and varied in terms of size and style. Over the past ten to fifteen years, these dolls have become sought-after. Look out for major names such as Pedigree, Madame Alexander, Vogue, Ideal, Roddy and Terri Lee. From the late 1950s to the early 1960s, hard, brittle plastic was replaced with softer plastics such as vinyl.

- To fetch the highest values, dolls must be in mint condition with their original clothes, all their accessories (which were often lost through play) and original boxes.

- Hair is a major consideration, as many children washed, cut or restyled hair. Character dolls can be sought-after, both those based on celebrities or story book characters.

- As with teddy bears, the 'look' and visual appeal of a doll's face and general appearance helps enormously towards desirability, as does rarity of certain models.

A Bahr & Proschild doll, with weighted blue eyes, open mouth and leather body, marked, '309, 8'.

18.5in (47cm) high

£130-160   LAW

A German Heinrich Handwerck bisque-headed doll, sleeping eyes, open mouth and teeth, pierced ears, brown mohair wig, jointed composition limbs, and body, stamped 'HW 6 1/2'.

23.75in (60cm) high

£80-100   ECGW

A German Heinrich Handwerck bisque-headed doll, with sleeping eyes and open mouth, with composite jointed body, stamped '2/12'.

22.5in (57cm) high

£90-110   ECGW

An Armand Marseille oriental 'Ellar' bisque-head doll, with open-close eyes, painted mouth and hair, jointed composition body, missing toes, crack at neck.

Despite its French name, Armand Marseille was a German company, founded in Köppelsdorf, Thüringia in 1885. They were highly prolific and produced a great many dolls of different qualities and price points.

11.5in (29cm) high

£250-300   FLD

A Heubach Koppelsdorf girl doll, with sleeping blue eyes and jointed body, impressed 'Heubach Koppelsdorf 302.1., Germany'.

11.5in (29cm) high

£65-85   ECGW

A Heubach Koppelsdorf 'Thuringia' bisque-headed doll.

18in (46cm) high

£85-95   **ECGW**

A Gebruder Heubach small character doll, with moulded hair and painted eyes and mouth, and composition limbs, also with childs' shoes etc., impressed factory mark, '7603, Germany'.

2in (23cm) high

£120-150   **LAW**

A CLOSER LOOK AT A DOLL

'Mein Liebling' generally means 'My Darling' in German. The term was a trademark used for certain dolls by Kämmer & Reinhardt of Waltershausen in Germany.

As well as the model number, 117a, the back of the head bears the incised names of two doll makers as Kämmer & Reinhardt acquired Simon & Halbig in 1920 as Simon & Halbig made most of the bisque heads for Kämmer & Reinhardt by that time.

Kämmer & Reinhardt had also acquired the Heinrich Handwerck doll factory in 1902, so many bodies on Kämmer & Reinhardt dolls were made by them.

Expensive at the time, 'Mein Liebling' dolls are rare and highly sought-after today for their delicately and realistically decorated, characterful faces with gentle expressions. At 20in (51cm) high, this is also a large example.

A 'Mein Liebling' doll, model 117a, made by Kämmer & Reinhardt for Simon & Halbig, with weighted brown eyes and closed mouth, marked, 'K & R, 117a, Simon & Halbig'.

20in (51cm) high

£1,500-2,000   **LAW**

A Kestner doll, with weighted blue eyes, and open mouth, marked, 'Made in Germany, 171, 5'.

14.25in (61cm) high

£350-450   **LAW**

A Schoenau & Hoffmeister doll, of unusually large proportions, with weighted blue eyes and open mouth, marked, 'SH, PB, 1906'.

16.5in (84cm) high

£350-450   **LAW**

A Schoenau & Hoffmeister bisque-headed doll, marked 'Porzellanfabrik Burggrub 169 7'.

22.5in (57cm) high

£60-70   **ECGW**

Judith Picks

Regardless of the maker, the way a bisque doll's head is moulded and painted is paramount to value. Some dolls are based on general characters or emotions, and some are based on specific characters. This rare doll was based on a photograph of Princess Elizabeth from c1937. Curt Schoenau, the son of company founder Arthur, commissioned the sculptor Caesar Schneider to produce the master for the head so a mould could be made. Now Queen Elizabeth II, she is the longest surviving reigning British monarch, beating Queen Victoria to the title during 2015. Memorabilia related to her is sought-after and this doll is rare. As well as making a great addition to a doll collection, it would also appeal to collectors of Royal memorabilia. A cut above the rest, this regal doll should be a good investment for the future.

A rare Schoenau & Hoffmeister doll, 'Princess Elizabeth', with weighted blue eyes and smiling open mouth, marked, 'Porzellanfabrik Burggrub, Princess Elizabeth, 5, Made in Germany'.

c1938   20in (51cm) high
£500-600   LAW

A large Simon & Halbig doll, with weighted blue eyes, open mouth and pierced ears, marked, 'S & H, 1079'.

14.5in (71cm) high
£180-220   LAW

A Simon & Halbig for Kämmer & Reinhardt large doll, with weighted blue eyes, open mouth and pierced ears, marked, 'Simon & Halbig, K & R, 62'.

24in (61cm) high
£260-300   LAW

A Simon & Halbig doll, with flirty blue eyes, open mouth with tongue, and bent limbs, stamped '126', possibly made for Kämmer & Reinhardt, marked, 'Simon & Halbig, 126'.

15in (38cm) high
£120-180   LAW

A large Simon & Halbig doll, with fixed brown eyes, open mouth and pierced ears, impressed marks, '1079, DEP, Germany'.

31in (79cm) high
£200-300   LAW

An automaton doll, with a bisque head with fixed blue eyes and open mouth, original clothing, wooden limbs and a wooden construction in the centre which when held moves the head forward and brings the hands together, marked, '179, 2/0'.

Dolls that have moving parts (known as automata) are usually sought-after, especially if operated by clockwork. Examples with no legs (and sometimes no arms) and that are mounted on a central stick are often known as marotte dolls and were held and operated by hand. Many marottes have bells, and marottes with moving parts are comparatively scarce.

15.5in (39cm) high
£220-280   LAW

A Lenci felt doll, dressed in national costume.

13.8in (35cm) high
£80-100   WW

A Chad Valley felt doll, moulded felt face with blue glass eyes and painted features, dark blonde wig, velveteen body, felt dress with hat, matching shoes with button fastening, white undergarment and socks, 'Chad Valley' label to foot.

18.5in (47cm) high

£350-450   AST

A Chad Valley 'Bambina' felt doll, designed by Mabel Lucie Attwell in the style of Peter Pan, with moulded felt face, brown glass eyes, painted features, dark blonde mohair wig. 'Chad Valley Bambina' label to foot.

21.7in (55cm) high

£400-500   AST

QUICK REFERENCE - CHAD VALLEY DOLLS

● Chad Valley's late 1920s range of dolls designed by illustrator and artist Mabel Lucie Attwell (1879-1964) are considered by many to be the best Attwell character dolls. Attwell herself was responsible for the entire doll, from the faces to the clothes. The range comprised 16 differently dressed dolls, each had a typical chubby and cheeky smiling face and the side-glancing eyes were popular during the period. They were sold in a number of sizes, dressed in fashionable clothes and sold in a 'Bed-Bye' box that could be used as a bed with a drawer in the base. As with all fabric dolls, the best prices are reserved for examples that are not faded, torn, or dirty and are complete. Attwell was so fastidious as regards design that, when Harrods held an exhibition of the dolls, she sent her maid to ensure the hairstyles were correct!

A Dean's Rag Book Co. Ltd. 'Rosemary' cloth doll, with moulded face with painted features, blonde wig, cloth body with felt arms and legs, red shoes, one with 'Dean's' label to sole, loose stitching to back, in box.

18.5in (47cm) high

£160-200   AST

A Dean's Rag Book Co. Ltd. 'Robin' cloth doll, with moulded face and painted features, blonde curly wig, cloth body with felt arms and legs, shoes, one with 'Dean's' label to sole, some marks to shirt, and three cracks to side of head, in box.

18in (45cm) high

£200-250   AST

A Chad Valley 'Bambina' felt and velvet doll, designed by Mabel Lucie Attwell, with moulded felt face with blue glass eyes and painted features, auburn curly wig, velveteen body, label to foot, with box.

18in (46cm) high

£450-550   AST

A Norah Wellings felt black doll, with side glancing brown glass eyes, painted facial features, integral velvet striped trousers with black top, neck-tie, and yellow felt hat, 'Norah Wellings' label to right foot, missing a button.

c1930s   *19.75in (50cm) high*

£50-70   AST

A 1920s-30s felt doll, with moulded face and painted features, blonde mohair wig, some holes to felt on legs, hole to back of dress, shoe lace missing.

21.75in (55cm) high

£220-280   AST

QUICK REFERENCE - PEDIGREE DOLLS

- Pedigree dolls were made by renowned British toymaker Lines Brothers Ltd., who were founded just after WWI. They later became known as Tri-ang. Although they released their first dolls made from composition in 1937, the Pedigree name wasn't registered until 1942. Plastic dolls were released after World War Two, once the factory had been released from producing armaments for the war. They soon became one of the biggest and most important makers of plastic dolls in the UK, with 'Pretty Peepers', 'Saucy Walker', and 'Beauty Skin' being as popular today as they were at the time. This doll was based on Princess Anne and released in 1953, the year of Queen Elizabeth's coronation. The clothes were designed by the Queen's couturier Norman Hartnell (1901-79). The fabric tended to disintegrate over time, making original clothes hard to find. Without them, the doll is worth up to £70. In general, boy dolls are not as popular as girl dolls.

A 1950s Pedigree 'Little Princess' doll, wearing a dress with blue spots designed by Norman Hartnell.

14in (35.5cm) high

£80-150   DSC

A 1950s Pedigree 'Bonnie Prince Charlie' doll, in replica outfit.

The replica outfit is of such high quality that it adds - rather than decreases - value.

15in (38cm) high

£60-80   DSC

A 1950s Pedigree 'Little Princess' doll, wearing a dress with red spots designed by Norman Hartnell.

14in (35.5cm) high

£100-150   DSC

A 1950s Pedigree 'Knee Bend' doll.

Pedigree first released plastic dolls with knee joints in 1955.

21in (53.5cm) high

£100-150   DSC

A 1950s Pedigree 'Saucy Walker' doll.

'Saucy Walker' dolls were introduced by Pedigree around 1952 and moved their legs as if walking when held and assisted to do so. They also turned their heads as they walked and could 'cry' as they were fitted with a 'mama' sound unit in their backs. They are popular with collectors today as they are well made and substantial with an appealing blushing face. Many collectors also remember them fondly as little girls!

21in (53.5cm) high

£75-100   DSC

A 1950s Pedigree 'Dusky Delite' doll.

10in (25.5cm) high

£20-25   DSC

DOLLS

A 1950s Pedigree plastic black toddler doll.

19.75in (50cm) high

£55-65 ECGW

A 1960s Pedigree 'Sindy Weekenders' doll, with box.

12in (30.5cm) high

£100-150 DSC

A 1970s Pedigree lilac 'Sindy Ballerina' doll, in box, in mint condition.

Sindy was created by Pedigree in 1963 to compete with Mattel's extremely popular Barbie, introduced in 1959. In 1968 and 1970, she was the best-selling toy in the UK but, by 1997, after a number of issues over her design and look, she was withdrawn from sale by owner Hasbro. In 2007, the license and name was returned to Pedigree who reissued her from 1999. Complete Sindy dolls from the 1960s & 70s in good condition and with their boxes are increasingly sought-after by collectors, but have yet to reach the high prices paid for similarly early examples of Barbie. This model, released in 1974, was a landmark doll for Pedigree. Known as 'Active Sindy', she was the most poseable doll to date as her wrists, elbows and legs could be posed but had no visible joints as they were enclosed in vinyl. Highly successful, she became the most popular doll Pedigree ever sold and a new 'Active Sindy' was sold every year from when Pedigree produced Sindy.

11in (28cm) high

£150-175 DSC

A Pedigree 'Sindy Star Dance' doll, in box, in mint condition.

1984 *11in (28cm) high*

£30-50 DSC

A 1980s Pedigree 'Ballerina Later Face' doll, in box, in mint condition. **Sindy's face was redesigned a couple of times in the 1980s, including the introduction of an 'older' Sindy.**

11in (28cm) high

£25-35 DSC

A Pedigree 'Sindy Cool Customer' outfit, in box, in mint condition.

£30-40 DSC

A Pedigree 'Sindy Boutique' outfit, on card, in mint condition.

£20-30 DSC

QUICK REFERENCE - SASHA DOLLS

- Sasha dolls were designed by Sasha Morgenthaler (1893–1975) and produced in Germany by Götz from 1965-69 and from 1995-2001 and by Trendon (originally called Frido) from 1966-86. All are collectable, but the earliest dolls are the most sought-after and valuable, with some of the rarest examples fetching several thousands of pounds. They are well detailed and can be found in a wide variety of different clothes. Although some of the dolls had names, such as Gregor, Cora and Caleb, they are known generically as Sasha dolls, after their designer. They are known for their open, almost enigmatic expressions, which are very different from the fixed smiles found on many other dolls. A play-worn example will typically fetch less than £80.

A 1980s Trendon Sasha 'Blue Gingham' doll.

16in (41cm) high

£100-200　　　DSC

A 1970s Trendon 'Gregor Denims' doll.

16in (41cm) high

£100-200　　　DSC

A 1980s Trendon 'Prince Gregor' doll.

This was one of the last dolls made by Trendon.

16in (41cm) high

£100-200　　　DSC

A 1980s Trendon Sasha 'Baby Sandy' doll, in cradle, in mint condition.

12in (30.5cm) high

£100-150　　　DSC

A 1970s Trendon Sasha 'Baby Bird' doll.

The bird is rare as it was often lost or separated from the doll through play and storage in a toy box.

12in (30.5cm) high

£100-150　　　DSC

A 1990s Gotz Sasha 'Carmen' doll.

16in (41cm) high

£250-350　　　DSC

A pair of Moni dolls.

These were manufactured by a Swiss company, Uranium, and were only sold for a short time as they were a design infringement on Sasha dolls.

1979　　　*7.5in (19cm) high*

£20-30 each　　　DSC

DOLLS

An Amanda Jane 'Jinx' doll.

Amanda Jane dolls were introduced in the late 1950s by Conrad and Elsin Rawnsley, who had founded the Amanda Jane company to produce dolls' clothes in 1952. 'Jinx' was released in 1958 and was made using moulds acquired from Nene Plastics, who produced the desirable 'Rosebud' doll (see p.184). Dolls marked with Amanda Jane brand date from the early 1960s onwards. Before then, dolls were just marked 'England'. A huge range of over 350 accessories and clothes was offered at affordable prices, allowing children to build up her wardrobe with their pocket money.

1958　　　　　　　　　　　　　　*8in (20.5cm) high*
£30-50　　　　　　　　　　　　　　　　　DSC

A 1960s Amanda Jane Crolly 'Schoolgirl' doll, made by Crolly for Amanda Jane.

12in (35.5cm) high
£30-40　　　　　　　DSC

A 1960s Amanda Jane Clodrey 'Rider' doll, made by Clodrey for Amanda Jane.

13in (33cm) high
£30-40　　　　　　　DSC

A CLOSER LOOK AT A BLYTHE DOLL

'Blythe' dolls were fashion dolls designed by Allison Katzman and produced in Hong Kong for Kenner.

Twelve different outfits were produced and there were four different versions, each with different hairstyles or wigs.

They had eyes that changed colour (using a rotating barrel inside the head) if a string was pulled, and were partly based on 'Betty Boop'.

They are very rare as they were only sold in the US, Japan and Australia and Britain for one year, in 1972. They were marketed in Britain by Palitoy. They have built up a huge cult following over the years.

The doll was reintroduced by Takara of Japan in 2001 but this rare original example from 1972 is in mint condition and still has its extremely rare box.

A 'Blythe' doll.

Doll 11in (28cm) high
£1,200-1,500　　　　　　　VEC

A 1960s Amanda Jane 'Girl' doll.

7in (18cm) high
£15-20　　　　　　　DSC

A 1980s Amanda Jane 'Girl' doll.

7in (18cm) high
£15-20　　　　　　　DSC

A Burbank 'Brownie' doll.

14in (35.5cm) high

£10-15   **DSC**

A 1970s Burbank 'Nurse Doll', in mint condition, with box.

14in (35.5cm) high

£15-25   **DSC**

A 1960s 'Chiltern Babykins' doll.

14in (35.5cm) high

£30-40   **DSC**

A 1960s Chiltern 'Babykins' doll.

19in (48.5cm) high

£30-40   **DSC**

A Chiltern 'Teen' doll, with box.

16in (41cm) high

£35-45   **DSC**

A Chiltern 'Teen' doll.

16in (41cm) high

£25-35   **DSC**

A 1970s Flair 'Daisy Long Legs' doll, designed by Mary Quant, in an 'Alibaba' costume.

Flair's 'Daisy' doll was designed by eminent fashion designer Mary Quant (b.1934) and released in 1973. She took her name from Quant's logo - a daisy flower. Flair closed in 1980, but 'Daisy' continued to be made until 1983. This 'Alibaba' costume is hard to find and increases the value.

15in (38cm) high

£50-60   **DSC**

QUICK REFERENCE - RODDY

- The company that became known as Roddy was founded in 1948. They became well-known for their moulded hard plastic dolls, some of which have an attractve highly glossy finish. Their earliest dolls had printed tin eyes, and hallmarks of many of their dolls were moulded shoes and clenched fists with raised thumbs, although other makers also used this design of hands. Their smaller dolls were popular as clothes could be knitted for them and they could be carried around in a pocket or school satchel. Faces varied from those with puffed-out cheeks to those with an open-mouthed smile or a very solemn-looking face, the latter being very popular at the time. The company moved over to soft plastic dolls in the mid-1950s and continued to make dolls until the mid-1960s when they were sold and the brand name was changed to 'Bluebell'. Roddy dolls are widely collected, but condition is vital, with any wear to the paint reducing value dramatically.

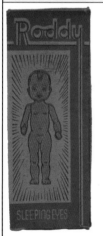

A 1950s Roddy 'Ballet Walker' doll.

13in (33cm) high

£30-50   DSC

A 1950s Roddy 'Baby Fairy' doll.

10in (25.5cm) high

£15-30   DSC

A large 1960s Roddy 'Toddler' doll.

21in (53.5cm) high

£30-50   DSC

A 1950s Roddy 'Floating Head Walker' doll.

13in (33cm) high

£20-30   DSC

A 1950s Roddy doll, with box.

£15-20   DSC

A 1960s 'Rosebud Girl' doll, in box, mint condition.

12in (30.5cm) high

£30-50   DSC

A 1960s Rosebud 'Baby First Step' doll, with box.

17in (43.5cm) high

£30-40   DSC

A 1970s Flair 'Daisy' doll, designed by Mary Quant.

9in (23cm) high

£40-50   DSC

A 1970s Flair 'Bubbles and Squeak' 'The Quant Kids', dressed by Mary Quant.

7.5in (19cm) high

£40-60   DSC

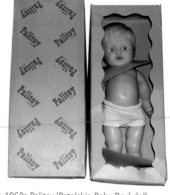

A 1960s Palitoy 'Petalskin Baby Boy' doll.

12in (30.5cm) high

£15-25   DSC

A Palitoy 'Goldilocks grow hair' doll, first issue.

1968   *15in (38cm) high*

£15-30   DSC

A 1970s Palitoy/Bradgate 'Yvonne' doll.

19in (48.5cm) high

£30-50   DSC

A 1960s Palitoy 'Petalskin Girl' doll.

Palitoy's 'Petalskin' dolls followed Pedigree's 'Beautyskin' dolls of the 1950s. Both were successful at the time. Both had bodies made from a flexible rubbery latex material stuffed with kapok, giving them a soft, skin-like appearance and feel. Heads were usually hard plastic. The latex material used for 'Beautyskin' dolls was not at all durable, and split open or dried out over a few years to the extent that most examples had to be thrown away after a few years of play. This problem was largely remedied by Palitoy for their 'Petalskin' dolls, which are much more common today.

13in (33cm) high

£20-30   DSC

A Palitoy 'Nurse' doll.

15in (38cm) high

£35-40   DSC

DOLLS

QUICK REFERENCE - ROSEBUD

● Nene Plastics, the company that produced Rosebud dolls, was founded by Eric Smith in the 1940s, after he had acquired in 1934 a company that made wooden toys. The 'Rosebud' name was registered in 1947, reputedly after a little girl who visited the factory in that year compared the lips of Smith's dolls to a rosebud! Early dolls had painted eyes, but these were replaced with glass in the late 1950s. One of Rosebud's earliest ranges had a bent right arm with a sticking-up thumb, enabling her to suck her thumb. Boy dolls had moulded hair, and girl dolls had mohair wigs in different shades. Examples from the 1960s had sightly different faces with larger eyes. The company was hugely successful, and produced over 10,000,000 dolls per year, exporting them to 72 countries. Many little girls fell in love with Rosebud dolls and they are hugely collectable today, being one of the most popular plastic dolls for collectors. 'Miss Rosebud', with her mohair wig, sleeping eyes, chubby face and charming expression, is one of the most sought-after models. Made from the early 1950s until the early 1960s, and costing 3/11d (19 pence), she was available in a variety of costumes, including this rare and desirable fairy dress.

A late 1950s Rosebud 'Knee Bend' doll, with vinyl head.

Late 1950s plastic dolls with vinyl heads are known as 'Transitionals'. The vinyl allowed the hair to be rooted into the head, rather than being glued on as a wig. It was too expensive for all the machinery to be changed as soon as vinyl was introduced, so the new heads were used on existing, hard plastic bodies and limbs.

16in (41cm) high

£50-60   **DSC**

A 'Miss Rosebud' doll.

7.5in (19cm) high

£40-60   **DSC**

A 'Miss Rosebud' 'Fairy' doll, all original.

7.5in (19cm) high

£75-100   **DSC**

A 1960s Rosebud 'Pink-haired Teen' doll, in original ball gown.

15in (38cm) high

£50-80   **DSC**

A 1960s Rosebud 'Teen' doll.

20in (51cm) high

£40-60   **DSC**

A Rosebud 'Teen' doll, with blue hair.

14.5in (37cm) high

£40-60   **DSC**

A 1960s Winfield 'Little Beauty' Teen doll, in box, in mint condition.

15in (38cm) high

£50-70   **DSC**

QUICK REFERENCE - SHEENA MACLEOD DOLLS

● After leaving art school in Aberdeen in the early 1960s, Sheena MacLeod decided to make dolls that captured the look of traditional 19thC Scottish fishwives, fishermen, island dwellers and crofters. Rather than go for inexpensive, mass-produced items, each was handmade using woven tweeds, wool tartans and other quality materials by a team of skilled part-time assistants. They grew to be very popular and, at the height of production, over 3,000 dolls were made and sold through around 40 shops in Scotland. Some were exported to the US, Japan, Australia and Sweden, and The Design Centre in London also included her dolls in its prestigious index, meaning she could attach a card tag to them. Early dolls were made from composition using plaster over a wire armature, but she moved to polyester resin in the early 1980s. Production ended shortly after. MacLeod checked the quality of every doll herself, including each of the handmade accessories.

Over 20 different dolls were made. Tags explained the doll's character and they were sold in boxes with a cellophane cover. As well as complete, mint and boxed examples, look out for tags signed by MacLeod as these are especially sought-after.

A fisherman with basket and net, designed by Sheena Macleod.

10in (25.5cm) high

£35-45   DSC

A Scottish fishwife, designed by Sheena MacLeod.

She has such high value because her tag is signed, she is boxed and comes with all her literature.

10in (25.5cm) high

£60-80   DSC

A Scottish fishwife, designed by Sheena MacLeod.

10in (25.5cm) high

£20-30   DSC

A Hebridean woman with peat and heather, designed by Sheena MacLeod.

10in (25.5cm) high

£25-35   DSC

A Skye Woman, designed by Sheena MacLeod.

10in (25.5cm) high

£30-50   DSC

An Easter Ross woman with oval 'cockles and mussels' basket, designed by Sheena MacLeod.

10in (25.5cm) high

£40-60   DSC

An Easter Ross woman with oval 'cockles and mussels' basket, designed by Sheena MacLeod.

10in (25.5cm) high

£30-40   DSC

DOLLS

A West Highland woman with spinning wheel, designed by Sheena MacLeod.

10in (25.5cm) high

£50-60   DSC

A Shetland woman, designed by Sheena MacLeod.

10in (25.5cm) high

£20-30   DSC

A fisherman with basket of herring, designed by Sheena MacLeod.

10in (25.5cm) high

£70-90   DSC

A fisherman with fish basket, designed by Sheena MacLeod.

10in (25.5cm) high

£30-50   DSC

A fisherman mending nets, designed by Sheena MacLeod.

10in (25.5cm) high

£20-30   DSC

A Shetland fisherman with lobster creel, designed by Sheena MacLeod.

10in (25.5cm) high

£35-45   DSC

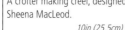

A crofter making creel, designed by Sheena MacLeod.

10in (25.5cm) high

£30-50   DSC

A crofter with cashchrom, designed by Sheena MacLeod.

10in (25.5cm) high

£70-90   DSC

A 19thC Greiner-type composition doll, with moulded hair and a stuffed body.

Greiner dolls are named after Ludwig Greiner, a German who emigrated to Philadelphia in the US in the 1830s. On 30th March 1858, he registered a patent for a shoulder-head doll made from moulded and painted papier mâché, making this one of the earliest American doll patents. After Greiner's patent expired, numerous other makers produced them.

17in (43cm) high

£85-95   POOK

A CLOSER LOOK AT A DOLL

She is made from composition, a material popular from the 1920s-30s and made from sawdust, wood glue and other ingredients such as resin or cornstarch.

She has her original clothes, a Shirley Temple book and a trunk containing clothes, which raises the value - the most valuable examples have all their accessories.

The painted composition tended to gain a fine network of cracks, known as crazing, over time and this example is crazed all over, reducing the value by over 50%.

Child film star and singer Shirley Temple (1928-2014) was popular with little girls and many dolls were made by different makers from 1934-1939, mainly in the US, when she was at the height of her fame.

A 'Shirley Temple' doll, made in the US, composition with blonde wig, flirty eyes, and open mouth with teeth, wearing polka-dot dress, with matching undergarment, white shoes and socks, crazing/cracks all over, particularly to face.

£220-280   AST

A 19thC Greiner papier mâché head and shoulder doll, with a stuffed cloth body, bearing a patent label 'No.1C' on shoulder.

30in (76cm) high

£120-160   POOK

A large wax head doll, with glass eyes and open mouth, virtually no hair left, with leather arms, one torn, and cloth feet.

27in (69cm) high

£65-85   LAW

A 1930s celluloid 'Christmas Fairy'.

5in (13cm) high

£15-20   DSC

A printed card 'Amazing Miss Britain' doll, with original packet and instructions.

These novelties were produced for the Festival of Britain in 1951. The material was fragile and not meant to last for long, making suriving examples very rare today, particularly if complete.

1951   *14in (35.5cm) high*

£10-20   DSC

DOLLS

A late 19thC box-back dolls' house and furniture, by Silber & Fleming, a two-storey dolls house with four interior rooms, with internal fittings and wallpaper. Also with a quantity of dolls house furniture and accessories, the rooms accessed from the front.

Silber & Fleming were an English manufacturer of printed paper-covered dolls' houses and associated furniture. They competed with similar houses made by German and American makers such as Bliss, Hacker or Gottschalk.

29.5in (75cm) high

£400-600 **LAW**

An early 21stC dolls' house, made in the form of a Medieval manor house, with various openings into the house and separate log store, fitted with electrics and with a quantity of dolls' house furniture, on a wooden board with a turntable.

This house and its furniture was built by Mr John S Pickard from 2000-2005.

31in (79cm) high

£100-150 **LAW**

A 1970s dolls' house, made in the style of a 1930s suburban detached house.

£50-70 **ECGW**

A late 20thC Clifton Manor dolls' house.

41.5in (105cm) high

£70-100 **ECGW**

A late 20thC large Georgian-style dolls' house, on tabletop stand.

79.5in (202cm) high

£150-200 **ECGW**

A mock-Tudor dolls' house shops.

46in (117cm) wide

£70-100 **ECGW**

A 20thC dolls' house.

47.25in (120cm) wide

£60-80 **ECGW**

An 18thC French painted paper fan, detailed with an interior court scene, the reverse with a courtly lady, the ivory sticks ornately carved with frolicking cherubs against a pierced scroll ground, boxed.

10in (25.5cm) wide

£500-600   **BELL**

A French hand-painted paper and ivory mounted fan, the leaf with figures in a landscape setting, the reverse showing a pastoral scene, with gilded ivory sticks.

c1770

£300-400   **L&T**   *10.5in (26.5cm) long*

A late 18thC French fan, gouache on vellum, three medaillons with romantic and pastoral scenes, carved, pierced, and varnished ivory sticks and articulated guards, gilt inlay.

c1780   *9.5in (24.5cm) wide*

£600-800   **RSS**

A late 18thC fan, possibly Italian, the vellum leaf painted in bodycolour, with 'The Discovery of Moses', featuring a city in the distance, having pierced and carved ivory sticks decorated with a gentleman courting a lady flanked by flowering jardinieres over Classical scalloped motifs, with similarly decorated guards having mother-of-pearl inset terminals, contained within an unmatched card fan box bearing a Duvelleroy paper label to the interior, some wear to folds.

10.75in (27cm) high

£600-800   **BON**

An early 19thC French fan 'La quiétude de la campagne', gouache on vellum, with pierced mother-of-pearl sticks and guards with metal pique.

7.in (19cm) long

£1,500-2,000   **RSS**

FANS

A French fan, the bone splines and guards with silver leaf decoration, the fan with a double-leaf hand-coloured chromolithographic medieval scene, with fitted case.

c1840   *10.75in (27cm)*

£400-450   **SWO**

A 19thC paper fan, with over-painted sections with figures in conversation and scenes of figures in landscape panels, with pierced vanes, in F. Duvelleroy case.

£120-180   **FLD**

A 19thC Continental painted silk fan, with a gallant and companion flanked by two foliate cartouche all within sequined borders, on gilt-lettered 'Duvelleroy' to the rear, stick guards.

8.5in (21.5cm) long

£120-180   **BELL**

A 19thC Continental painted silk fan, with a gallant and companions and a pastoral view with lake, with sequined foliate scrolls to the border, on carved and painted foliate ivory sticks, stick guard.

9.75in (24.5cm)

£130-200   **BELL**

An early 20thC French advertising fan 'Chemins de fer de l'Ouest', lithograph-printed paper after a work by Steinlen, printed by La Sté de Publication d'Art, with wooden sticks and guards.

11in (29.5cm) high

£400-500   **RSS**

An early 20thC Continental silk and embroidered lace fan, painted with a young lady holding a flower and signed 'Luicien' on gilt-pierced foliate mother-of-pearl sticks, stick guard.

9.5in (24cm)

£150-200   **BELL**

An early 20thC fan, the fabric leaf painted in the Art Nouveau style with figures wearing turbans, dancing with figures watching and a gentleman playing a musical instrument within a stylized woodland setting, bearing the name 'De la Bête', with mother-of-pearl sticks and guards, minor faults.

9in (23cm)

£250-350   **BON**

An 18thC Qing dynasty Canton carved ivory brisé fan, the guards carved in low relief with figures and beasts in a garden with temples, opening to twenty carved and pierced sticks with shells, insects and figures, the monogram 'GH' in the centre.

7.5in (19cm) long

£800-1,200   L&T

A 19thC Qing dynasty Chinese Canton carved ivory and painted paper fan, the guards carved in relief with figures and pavilions, with fourteen pierced and carved ivory sticks and paper panels on both sides with scenes of courtiers and attendants.

stick 11in (28cm) long

£600-800   L&T

A 19thC Qing dynasty Chinese Canton carved ivory brisé fan, the guard sticks carved in relief with figures, gardens and pavilions, opening to nineteen sticks pierced and carved with further figures and pavilions, with a black lacquer box.

10in (25.5cm) long

£800-1,200   L&T

A 19thC Qing dynasty Canton lacquer and paper fan, the black lacquer guards and fourteen sticks with figures in a garden, the paper painted panels representing scenes of court life, the figures' faces in painted ivory.

11.5in (29cm) long

£1,200-1,500   L&T

A 19thC Qing dynasty Canton '100 faces' lacquer and paper fan, the outer guards with figures in landscapes, with fourteen lacquer sticks with similar scenes and paper panels painted on both sides with scenes of courtiers and attendants, the figures' faces in painted ivory, with an associated box.

11in (28cm) long

£700-900   L&T

A CLOSER LOOK AT A FAN

The overall condition is good. The enamel is not damaged and the delicate silver filigree is intact.

The decoration features traditional Chinese subjects of figures and scholars in a mountainous landscape.

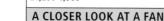

The silver guards are decorated with chased decoration which add to its decorative appeal.

The silver filigree sticks feature scrolling decoration and enamel highlights – an expensive and time-consuming technique which adds to the value.

A Chinese export silver filigree and enamel brisé fan, the guards chased with figures, the sticks with a temple and fisherman in a mountainous landscape, unmarked.

13in (33cm) wide

£3,000-4,000   L&T

A Canton ivory brisé fan, carved with Oriental figures and foliate panels, stick guard.

c1900   *8in (20.5cm)*

£500-600   BELL

FASHION

An early 1970s Ossie Clark crêpe full-length wrap dress, with long sleeves gathered to the cuffs, cut-out detail to the reverse.

labelled size 10

£250-350　　　TEN

An early 1970s Ossie Clark crêpe full-length wedding dress, buttons to both shoulders, fabric-tie waist, gathered hem, with cut-out sheer hearts and woven floral motifs.

Ossie Clark (1942-96) was one of Britain's most influential designers from the mid-1960s to mid-1970s. He studied at the Royal College of Art, graduating with first-class honours in 1965, with the collection featuring in Vogue. Clark produced under his own label, and designed for Radley and Quorum, working with Celia Birtwell (b.1941, who later became his wife), who designed fabulous prints. Ossie Clark was a 'master cutter' and by using moss crêpe he managed to make his dresses flowing and stylish. The market for vintage wedding dresses has boomed over the past few years as the ever-growing 'vintage' movement has filtered into weddings.

size 14

£400-600　　　TEN

A Balenciaga couture strapless lace dress, with a boned bodice, labelled Balenciaga, discoloration to the underarm area, minor evidence of repair with three small tears to the lace scarf, minor tear to the interior corset, light pilling to the lace surface, missing petticoat.

41in (104.5cm) long

£700-1,000　　　LHA

An 'I Was Lord Kitchener's Valet' stretch-jersey dress, with stylised print to the front, labeled 'Bon-Lon Miss Impact', together with an advertising photograph of the dress featured in Flare Magazine in April 1971.

'I Was Lord Kitchener's Valet' was a fashion shop opened by Ian Fisk and John Paul on Portobello Road in 1966. It was highly successful, partly as it attracted customers including Eric Clapton, Mick Jagger, John Lennon, and Jimi Hendrix. In 1967, they expanded and moved to Carnaby Street. They are best known for selling military jackets and clothing, such as that worn by Hendrix and The Beatles.

£70-100　　　TEN

A 1980s-90s Issey Miyake wool and silk-mix jacket, black with bronze stripes, cowl-style collar, fold-back front, frayed edging, drawstring to the back, black cotton lining.

size M

£100-150　　　TEN

A late 1960s-70s Jean Muir 'Op Art' printed silk dress, with 'Peter Pan' collar, gathered skirt with lining, not labelled.

£100-150　　　TEN

A 1980s-90s Versace leather jacket, in light tan, two front pockets, press-stud fastening.

size 40

£150-200　　　TEN

A CLOSER LOOK AT A PUNK T-SHIRT

This was owned and worn by Penny Jones, known at the time as 'Penny the Punk', who would often be spotted in Harrogate, Yorkshire, with her trademark white-dyed spiked hair.

Branded 'Clothes for Heroes', the 'Seditionaries' range was created and sold from 1976-81. The range is an important part of the punk movement, which has recently been reappraised.

The range combined all the subversive elements from the designs of Westwood and McLaren, including ripped garments, leather, chains, badges, straps, and buckles.

As the muslin is delicate, examples in good condition are hard to find.

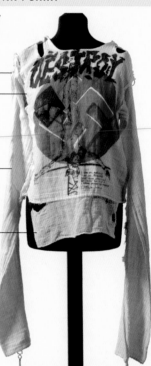

A mid-late 1970s Vivienne Westwood & Malcolm McLaren Seditionary 'Destroy' t-shirt, with printed pattern, in a cream muslin with slashed neckline, exaggerated long sleeves, black fabric label.

£500-800   TEN

A 1950s white taffeta and lace beaded dress.

Dresses such as this are popular with buyers who simply wish to wear them. Although they are typical of the 1950s, the fad for vintage that has filtered through to the High Street as well as couture, has made them almost timelessly stylish.

£50-80   SWO

A 1950s pink brocade evening dress, with matching evening coat (not shown).

£80-120   SWO

A late 1960s-70s Peter Barron floral printed sun dress, labelled.

£30-50   TEN

A late 19thC dress, with printed paisley pattern, pleated fitted bodice, gathered long skirt and blue trimming to the front.

£150-200   TEN

A 19thC white cotton Ayrshire christening gown, with central panel and bodice heavily embroidered with decorative floral motifs and garlands, lace-trimmed sleeves, together with under-dress. shoulder to hem

This is an unusually high price for a christening dress, which is due to the heavy embroidery and presence of the underdress. It is also in excellent condition. Most christening dresses have more sentimental rather than financial value.

40.5in (103cm)

£180-220   TEN

FASHION

A late 19thC hair comb, with pierced gilt-metal shaped panel, hung with chains and 'ball' drops, on a tortoiseshell hair comb.

6.25in (16cm) long

£120-180 TEN

A late 19thC carriage parasol, with a carved ivory finial and foliate-carved folding handle, with slight damage to the silk fabric shade length.

25in (64cm) long

£200-300 FLD

Two late 19thC shaped gilt-metal hair combs, mounted with twisted gilt-metal springs, with beads and hung with a 'ball' drops, on a tortoiseshell hair comb.

each 4.25in (11cm) wide

£100-150 each TEN

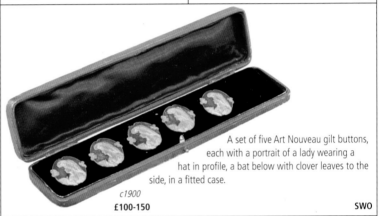

A set of five Art Nouveau gilt buttons, each with a portrait of a lady wearing a hat in profile, a bat below with clover leaves to the side, in a fitted case.

c1900

£100-150 SWO

A late 19thC Lincoln Bennett & Co. black beaver hair top hat, with a cream lining and leather inside band, embossed in gilt 'By Appointment To H.M. the King', contained in original Lincoln Bennett carrying box.

Vintage top hats in common sizes and wearable condition are sought-after as they are often better quality than many of today's examples and can be less expensive. They also add an air of 'old money' when worn to an event such as the Ascot races.

£150-200 LOCK

A late 20thC Hermès silk bow tie, autumn leaves pattern on a blue ground, in original box.

£60-80 SWO

Two similar pairs of 1970s knee-high boots, with square heel, one in silver stretch Lurex, one in gold fabric, both with side zips.

size 37

£40-60 per pair TEN

QUICK REFERENCE - HANDBAGS

- Over the past 15 years handbags have become a desirable fashion accessory. Now collectors will pay hundreds or even thousands of pounds for new or vintage examples by designers such as Chanel, Hermès, Judith Leiber, Louis Vuitton, and Gucci. Sometimes secondhand luxury bags which are still in production, change hands on the vintage market for more money than they would if they were new.

- However, many bags by less well-known makers are equally desirable and do not have such a high price tag. The 1950s are a particularly popular decade with beaded designs, novelty, woven baskets, and box-like plastic bags all available to collectors at a range of prices.

- For many women in the 1950s, leather and fabric bags remained expensive. However, the new bags made from a tough plastic, trademarked Lucite (developed in the 1930s) were affordable and their bright colours and streamlined shapes fitted with the sense of post-war optimism. If you want to buy a Lucite bag, check it carefully for cracks and other damage. With age the plastic can become brittle and make sure there is not a strong chemical smell, particularly inside the bag. The smell means that the plastic is degrading. This cannot be stopped and will affect other plastics if they are stored with the bag.

- If you want to collect designer handbags, it's important to buy them from a reputable source as there are fakes and copies on the market.

A green glass beadwork purse, the cylindrical body with gathered covering, lid with internal mirror and lined throughout with brown silk.

c1920s   *5in (12.5cm) high*

£120-180   PC

An unusual 1930s handbag with celluloid clasp in the form of a pagoda roof, with monkey finial.

£120-180   ECGW

An early 1950s rigid red leather bag, with two handles, polka-dot lining, and a mirror on the interior of the lid.

8.75in (22cm) wide

£80-120   PC

A CLOSER LOOK AT A LUCITE HANDBAG

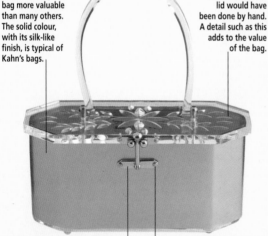

Blue lucite is a rare colour, making this bag more valuable than many others. The solid colour, with its silk-like finish, is typical of Kahn's bags.

The carved decoration on the lid would have been done by hand. A detail such as this adds to the value of the bag.

The distinctive clasp, which features three metal balls, is typical of a Charles S. Kahn bag and highly desirable.

Most Kahn bags included a paper label inside the bag below the hinge of the lid. These may have become detached and lost over the years.

A 1950s turquoise Lucite handbag, by Charles S. Kahn, Miami, Florida, with clear lid and handles.

c1953   *8in (20.5cm) wide*

£800-1,200   PC

A 1950s Lucite wedding handbag, unsigned, the clear lid can be removed and flowers, a scarf, or other decoration placed inside.

c1950   *7.5in (19cm) wide*

£300-500   PC

A 1950s red Lucite purse with entwined handles and decorative clasp.

8.5in (21.5cm) wide

£1,000-1,500   PC

A 1950s hand-decorated bag, by Souré NY, with a Bakelite handle.

13.75in (35cm) wide

£80-120   FAN

FASHION

A white woven basket handbag, decorated with felt fruit baskets.

1950s   *8.5in (22cm) wide*

£80-120   **PC**

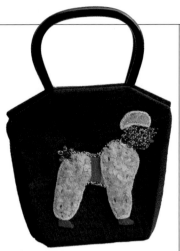

A 1950s bag, by Jolles Original, decorated with an applied poodle.

                                          11in (28cm) high

£80-120   **PC**

A 1950s Chinese Mr Jonas woven wicker handbag, with cut-felt Scottie dog decoration, with label to the coloured fabric interior.

                                       12.25in (31cm) wide

£80-120   **PC**

A very rare Walborg beaded poodle purse, American.

Poodles became an important fashion statement in the 1950s, inspired by chic Parisian fashion. Walborg's beaded bags are highly sought-after, thanks to the originality of the designs and quality of the workmanship. This entire bag is made of tiny pearlescent beads on threads which were hand-woven onto the base. A 1940s version of this bag, made from black beads, is even more desirable.

c1955   *13.5in (34cm) high*

£1,200-1,500   **PC**

A silver-plated clutch bag, by Christian Dior, of rectangular form, with gadroon decoration, marked 'Made in Italy', signed 'Christian Dior'.

£120-180   **SWO**

A Judith Leiber black satin and polychrome embroidery clutch evening bag, set with Swarovski crystals, in the original box, with brass tag.

                                          9in (23cm) wide

£500-800   **DRA**

A Gucci black suede and leather 'Masterpiece' shoulder bag, with zip top, gilt fittings, and chain, with dust cover.

c1970

£150-250   SWO

A Gucci 'Sukey' tote handbag, in beige and khaki, with dust cover.

£200-300   SWO

A Louis Vuitton canvas and leather 'Alma' bag.

£120-180   ECGW

A Louis Vuitton golden-yellow patent leather vernis 'Houston' tote bag, serial no.LW0030, with dust bag and care card.

£200-300   SWO

QUICK REFERENCE - HERMÈS 'BIRKIN' BAG

- For many collectors, the Hermès 'Birkin' bag is the ultimate piece to add to their collection. A new example is said to cost at least £5,600, with specialist leathers and customised clasps adding thousands more. Hermès no longer takes orders for them, but customers can request one and hope it becomes available. As a result, vintage and secondhand models are in great demand.
- The 'Birkin' bag was created in 1984 after the actress Jane Birkin – after whom it is named – described her ideal bag to Hermès' then chief executive Jean-Louis Dumas. Demand grew in the 1990s with the rise of the 'it bag' and its appearance on the television show Sex and the City.
- In June 2015, a pink, diamond-encrusted crocodile skin 2014 'Birkin' became the most expensive handbag ever sold. An anonymous bidder paid HK$1.72m (£146,000) including commission for the bag at Christie's international handbags and accessories auction in Hong Kong.
- Hermès other celebrity-named bag, the Sac à Dépêches, better known as the 'Kelly' bag after the actress Grace Kelly was photographed holding one to strategically hide her pregnancy, is also in demand.
- Copies, fakes, and bags based on both designs abound (see the 'Kelly'-style bag by Baronessa Franchetti on this page) but are worth significantly less, so always buy from a reputable dealer or auction house.

A Chanel black quilted lambskin '2.55' double-flap bag purse, serial number visible.

Coco Chanel believed that modern women should not be inconvenienced by having to use a hand-held handbag. Her solution was the 2.55, designed to be like a French soldier's shoulder bag. This classic example features the typical diagonal hand-stitching, which replicates quilting. It is desirable, despite its worn appearance. This is an original, but many modern copies exist. Study the quality of the real thing.

£800-1,200   SWO

A Baronessa Franchetti red leather handbag, in the Hermès 'Kelly' style, with padlock and key.

£120-180   SWO

A Ralph Lauren alligator skin metallic gold 'Ricky' bag, in original box with dust bag and authentication card.

Provenance: This bag was gifted to the vendor during a special show to launch the opening of the Ralph Lauren store in Asia. It comes with a personal handwritten note from the Ralph Lauren Asia team.

A Hermès 'Birkin' tan leather handbag, with gilt-metal mounts, white stitching, lacking protector bag, padlock and keys, with original card box.

2000   *13.75in (35cm)*

£4,000-5,000   TEN

£7,000-8,000   SWO

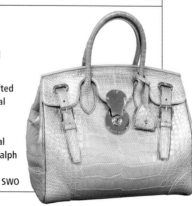

QUICK REFERENCE - FORNASETTI

● Piero Fornasetti (1913-88) was an Italian designer of furniture, interiors, ceramics, glass, and other homewares. The antithesis of the prevailing Modernist and Mid-Century Modern movements, his designs were inspired by the Classical world and have heavily decorated surfaces. Designs are usually in gilt and monochrome. Some have a hint of humour or Surrealist appeal. His design aesthetic set him apart from his contemporaries and many of his products sold well at the time. Over the past 20 years, his work has been reappraised and is attracting attention from collectors and interior designers. As such, prices have been rising, especially for furniture and rare homewares.

A 1950s Piero Fornasetti brass 'Giraffa' (Giraffe) tray, the brass body finished in black and decorated with a coloured lithograph, marked with a label reading 'FORNASETTI MILANO MADE IN ITALY'.

23.5in (60cm) high

£450-550   QU

A 1950s Piero Fornasetti brass 'Braccio' (Arm) tray, the brass body finished in black and decorated with a monochrome lithograph, marked with a label reading 'FORNASETTI MILANO MADE IN ITALY'.

23.25in (59cm) high

£800-1,200   QU

A mid-late 20thC pair of Piero Fornasetti steel bookends, finished in black with gilt lithographed double Grecian head motifs, with 'Fornasetti Milano, Made in Italy' labels.

These Fornasetti designs were some of the brand's most economical objects to produce. They are still in production today.

7.75in (20cm) high

£350-550 the pair   MLL

A mid-late 20thC Piero Fornasetti enamelled steel matchbox cover, made for Vespa motorbikes, with printed gilt marks.

6in (15cm) long

£150-250   WW

A 1950s Piero Fornasetti 'Cammei con Greca' (Cameos with Greek frets) umbrella stand, the brass cylinder decorated with brown, gold, and black lithographed cameos, marked 'FORNASETTI MILANO MADE IN ITALY'.

This item was re-issued in this colourway in the 1990s and 2000s.

22.5in (56cm) high

£600-800   QU

An early 1960s Piero Fornasetti 'Piede Romano' (Roman Foot) ceramic umbrella stand, highlighted in gilt, the base with printed Fornasetti mark, minor professional restoration to the top rim.

This item was also produced in black and was re-issued in the late 1990s and 2000s.

22in (57cm) high

£350-450   WW

A mid-20thC set of six Piero Fornasetti ceramic appetizer dishes, with internal gilt rims and applied monochrome transfers of Classical patterns, the base of each marked 'FORNASETTI MILANO MADE IN ITALY'.

Sold in sets of six, there were 28 different sets to choose from.

3in (8cm) high

£400-600 for six   QU

FOSSILS

QUICK REFERENCE - FOSSILS

- Fossils are without a doubt the oldest 'antiques' one can collect. They have seen a resurgence of popularity in recent years. The majority of new buyers use them to add impact or a quirky curiosity to a room interior. As such, they often appreciate their visual appeal more than their academic importance. The 'look' of the fossil and the way it has been 'prepared' - the term for revealing the fossil(s) and displaying them - is therefore extremely important. Even common fossils such as ammonites can appeal to these new buyers, who might display them like sculptures.
- Always consider size, rarity, where it was collected from, and the precise species of the animal's remains. Condition is also important, with scuffs, chips, and other damage reducing value both to collectors and those who appreciate how they look.

A large Middle Jurassic period ammonite (Perisphinctes) fossil, collected in Madagascar, well-ribbed and defined.
150 million years old   *12in (30cm) diam*
£300-500   **DW**

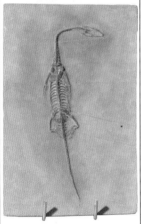

A display of Upper Jurassic period ammonites and belemnites, collected from the Volga River, Russia.
140 million years old   *8.25in (21cm) high*
£500-600   **DW**

A large pair of cut-through ammonites (Cleoniceras), polished to reveal the intricate chambers, which have been preserved in calcite and limestone.
5in (13cm) wide
£150-250   **DW**

A well-preserved Triassic period fossil of a marine reptile (Keichousaurus hui), set in a rectangular matrix.
c225 million years old   *7.5in (19cm) wide*
£180-220   **DW**

A large fossil of a seal baculum (a seal's penis bone), collected on St Lawrence Island, Alaska, USA. approx.
10,000 years old   *7in (18cm) long*
£180-220   **DW**

A large fossil of a Megalodon tooth (Carcharocles Megalodon), collected on the East Coast of Florida.

The Megalodon's scientific name translates from Latin as 'big tooth', which is evident in the size of this tooth. The Megalodon was one of the largest animals to have ever lived and reached a length of around 60 feet.
4.75in (12cm) long
£100-150   **DW**

A fossil of an egg from a giant elephant bird (Aepyornis Maximus), comprised of a composite of the broken shell, collected on Madagascar.

The giant elephant bird was the largest bird that ever lived. The species became extinct as a result of human activity during the 17thC.
1,000 years old   *13in (33cm) high*
£300-500   **DW**

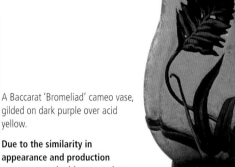

A Baccarat 'Bromeliad' cameo vase, gilded on dark purple over acid yellow.

Due to the similarity in appearance and production processes to the blue vase shown on this page, this vase was probably designed for the 1909 'Exposition International de l'Est de la France'. The esteemed Baccarat factory was founded in 1765 and continues today, even though the precise company name has changed over time.

c1909   *11in (28cm) high*
£1,200-1,500   **M&DM**

A Baccarat 'Vase aux Nepenthes' (pitcher plant) cameo vase, gilded on dark purple over pale blue.

This vase was designed for the 1909 'Exposition International de l'Est de la France' - both the vase and design drawings are shown and identified as such in 'Baccarat: La Légende du Cristal', by Michaela Lerch, published by Paris Musées, 2015.

11in (28cm) high
£1,200-1,500   **M&DM**

A late 19thC Baccarat vase, with unusual Chinoiserie style polychrome enamelling and metal applications.

c1889   *6in (15.5cm) high*
£600-750   **M&DM**

A pair of Baccarat 'Datura' lead crystal cameo vases, gilded with red highlights and on classic early Art Deco Baccarat metal bases.

This bright tone of green is a very distinctive Baccarat colourway.

c1920   *10in (25.5cm) high*
£800-1,000   **M&DM**

A Baccarat vase, cut with swags in an Edmund Enot bronze/ormolu 'cage', with elephant heads and birds, signed 'E Enot' on the bronze and 'E. Enot/6.R. Chauveau-Lagarde/Paris' on the glass.

Edmond Enot had a showroom in the prestigious Avenue de L'Opera and sold bronze and metal sculptures and objects, and metal-mounted glass and ceramics.

c1898   *6in (15.5cm) high*
£1,200-1,500   **M&DM**

A small Baccarat finger bowl, with applied 'bleeding heart' flower and stalk bronze rim.

c1895   *4in (10cm) wide*
£150-180   **M&DM**

A pair of Baccarat cameo perfume bottles, gilded on dark purple over pale blue depicting lilies.

c1910   *6in (15.5cm) high*
£400-500   **M&DM**

A Harrach cameo vase, with translucent white opal over green depicting flowers, designed by Josef Petricek, with Harrach shape code on the base.

This is 'in the English style' as it is very similar to designs produced by English glass factories based in Stourbridge, such as Thomas Webb & Sons.

c1890   *8in (20.5cm) high*

£1,000 -1,500   **M&DM**

A Harrach cameo vase, with orange-red over colourless, the foliate design also iridised and gilded.

c1900   *9in (23cm) high*

£1,000-1,200   **M&DM**

A small Harrach cameo vase, gilded with green over opal white with the sun in clouds over a pond.

This vase is often wrongly attributed to Daum. This style of solid sun is a commonly found motif on Harrach's cameo glass. Some have radiating rays.

c1900   *3in (8cm) high*

£1,000-1,200   **M&DM**

An Aesthetic period Harrach gilded and silvered 'Oxblood' vase, in dark red over opal white, designed in the Japanese 'moriage' fashion, signed with the Harrach three feather or 'propeller blade' mark and gilding codes.

Oxblood refers to the deep red colour that is similar to glazes used on Chinese porcelain. Here it is created by casing opaque white glass in transparent dark red glass. 'Moriage' is a type of raised decoration used on some Japanese pottery that is similar to the spriging used on Wedgwood's world-famous Jasperware.

c1875   *7in (17.75cm) high*

£350-400   **M&DM**

A pair of large mottled finish vases, with thin silver overlay depicting flowers, by Karl Goldberg,

Goldberg won a Bronze medal at the Paris 1900 Worlds Fair for his innovative metallic-look finishes on glass, created by applying chemicals to the surface.

c1900   *9in (23cm) high*

£1,000-1,200   **M&DM**

A pair of Karl Goldberg silver overlay vases on deep blue, depicting oak branches with acorns.

c1900   *8in (20.5cm) high*

£300-400   **M&DM**

A Rindskopf blue 'pulled and feathered' iridised vase, with applied and melted-in tulip floral and foliate decoration and frilled rim.

c1900   *14in (35.5cm) high*

£400-500   **M&DM**

GLASS

A 1930s Moser 'Organica' vase, model no.6935, amethyst glass form, the base with acid-etched signature, designed by Heinrich Hussmann in 1929.

Despite certain shapes (including this one) going back into production after the war in 1945, this is a rare range. Although they look moulded, the dynamic curving and swirling grooves are all cut and polished by hand on a grinding wheel, which requires great skill and care.

8in (20.5cm) high

£180-220   WW

A 1930s Art Deco Haida Fachschule enamelled footed vase, with silvered rim and foot and yellow, white, blue and black chevron and squiggly line enamelled design, unsigned.

12in (30.5cm) high

£220-280   MHC

QUICK REFERENCE - SKRDLOVICE 'ANTIQUE GLASS'

● **In the early days of the Skrdlovice factory (founded in 1941) resources were basic meaning very little colourless, clear glass could be made. So founder Emanuel Berànek produced a type of glass which hid imperfections which was used for nearly all production from 1942-c1950. Similar to 'pulegoso' glass produced on Murano for centuries, his 'Antique Glass' range was translucent, full of bubbles and had an uneven surface. It is usually found in a creamy white, but may also be tinted in light blue, pink, amber or brown. It was produced by adding salts such as sodium carbonate to the molten batch. Although it was successful and sold across the world, examples can be very hard to find today, particularly in large sizes.**

A late 1940s Skrdlovice 'Antique Glass' vase, in bubbly light blue glass with applied brown powder trail and applied lime green spot and handles, pattern no.4633, designed by Emanuel Berànek in 1946.

10.75in (27cm) high

£300-350   MHC

A purple flaring bowl, cut and etched with biplanes, clouds, moon and other sky related images, with original foil label from the Železný Brod glass school, signed 'JL 1937'.

This is almost certainly a student piece, produced as part of a student's course. A large number of cut and/or enamelled pieces can be found on the market from this and other glass schools, such as the one at Novy Bor. Values depend on the size, skill and appeal of the designs.

1937   *8in (20.5cm) wide*

£600-800   M&DM

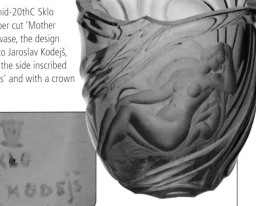

A unique mid-20thC Sklo Kodejs amber cut 'Mother and Child' vase, the design attributed to Jaroslav Kodejš, a panel on the side inscribed 'Sklo Kodejs' and with a crown motif.

Jaroslav Kodejš (b.1938) is best known for his jewellery designs produced at Železný Brod. This is a very high quality piece, and may have been produced as part of his education and training in glass design, or else in addition to his jewellery designs at the Zelezny Brod factory.

7in (17.5cm) high

£500-600   MHC

A very rare mid-late 1940s Skrdlovice 'Little Scarf' vase, from the 'Antique Glass' range, in bubbly light blue glass with applied maroon-brown powder rim, pattern no.4512, designed by Milena Velísková in 1945.

Designed as World War Two ended by one of the earliest designers brought into work at the factory, these tiny vases are extremely rare.

3in (7cm) high

£80-120   MHC

A very rare early 1960s Skrdlovice cased vase, pattern no.6070, the dark burgundy core overlaid with light blue glass and with an outer opaque yellow sprial, with triform rim, designed by Marie Stáhlíková and Milena Velísková in1960.

With its different layers, attenuated form and applied outer spiral, this very tall vase was time-consuming and complex to make. As such, it was expensive and it was only produced in small quantities for a short period of time.

£350-450   MHC

A 1970s Exbor vase, the colourless square-section tapering body body flashed in green, the corners cut with columns of undulating curves, unmarked, designed by Oldrich Lipsky in c1964.

8.75in (22cm) high

£250-350   FLD

An Exbor 'Monolith' vase, with tapering triangular-section body, the green core cased in colourless glass, a red ribbon swirl and an amber outer layer, the polished concave pontil mark with an acid-etched 'Exbor' mark, designed by Pavel Hlava c1957.

With its internal spiralling ribbon and unusual form, the is rarer than most of Hlava's 'Monolith' vases for Exbor.

8.75in (22.5cm) high

£350-450   MHC

A Moser ovoid vase, no.54303, the colourless body decorated with a stylised opaque green flower and stem and cased in yellow-amber, with factory acid stamp to base, designed by Jiri Suhajek in 1976.

8in (20cm) high

£400-600   QU

A scarce late 1960s Moser (Karlovarské Sklo) ovoid vase, the blue body with join inside the aperture and cased with orange and colourless glass layers, designed by Vladimir Mika in 1967.

£320-380   MHC

A 1970s Prachen glassworks 'Applied Vase', no.47691, the amber glass body with with applied blue stylised leaves and prunts moulded with dots, designed by Josef Hospodka in 1969.

Although the applied parts are blue, they appear green due to the amber yellow body.

10.25in (26cm) high

£320-380   MHC

A late 1960s Chribskà 'Mica Diamond' large cylinder vase, the blue body with moulded diamonds containing mica powder, cased in orange glass, with polished base, designed by Josef Hospodka in 1965.

These are often mistaken for having been produced on Murano.

10.5in (26.5cm) high

£250-350   MHC

GLASS

An early 20thC D'Argental cameo glass vase, cased in magenta over a graduated red-to-orange ground and cut with a tree-lined lake scene, cameo signature to the body.

6.75in (17cm) high

£600-650   FLD

A purple on orange D'Argental cameo vase, depicting lilies, signed 'D'Argental' with a Cross of Lorraine, made by Paul Nicolas.

c1920   *11in (28cm) high*

£1,800-2,000   M&DM

A dark brown on orange D'Argental cameo vase, depicting trailing grape vines, signed 'D'Argental' with a Cross of Lorraine, made by Paul Nicolas.

c1920   *14in (35.5cm) high*

£2,200-2,600   M&DM

QUICK REFERENCE - D'ARGENTAL

- The St Louis glassworks created the D'Argental brand name around 1918, predominantly for its cameo glass inspired by the successful work of Gallé and Daum. It was relatively unsuccessful until the arrival in 1919 of Paul Nicolas, a protegée of Émile Gallé and his chief designer, and a group of ex-employees from Gallé's factory.
- Cameo pieces signed 'D'Argental' and with a small 'SL' monogram are generally not connected to Nicolas and his colleagues. Early pieces designed by Nicolas were signed 'St Louis Nancy', but this was soon changed to 'D'Argental' with Nicolas adding a small Cross of Lorraine to the pieces he made himself. Pieces signed 'Paul Nicolas' (often with 'Nancy') were made for him to sell.
- Nicolas worked for St Louis through the 1920s and into the 1930s on a diminishing basis, and then worked on one-off commissions until his death in 1952. The glass was usually lead crystal, which allowed for a high level of detail to be wheel-cut into the surface. Dark, reddish brown, and caramel colours are typical.
- Although not currently as well-known as their competitors, D'Argental and Nicolas produced very high-quality pieces. Interest in them is rising, and as a result, prices have gone up. They could be a good investment for the future as more research is undertaken.

A red on orange D'Argental cameo vase, depicting a tiger orchid, signed 'D'Argental' with a Cross of Lorraine, made by Paul Nicolas.

c1920   *10in (25.5cm) high*

£1,800-2,000   M&DM

A brown on orange D'Argental cameo vase, depicting trailing hops, signed 'D'Argental' with a Cross of Lorraine, made by Paul Nicolas.

c1920   *13in (33cm) high*

£2,200-2,600   M&DM

A brown on orange D'Argental cameo vase, depicting irises, signed 'D'Argental' with a Cross of Lorraine, made by Paul Nicolas.

c1920   *16in (40.5cm) high*

£1,200-1,500   M&DM

A brown on red-orange D'Argental landscape cameo vase, depicting the château de Tournoël and surrounding trees, signed 'D'Argental' with a Cross of Lorraine and 'château de Tournoël', made by Paul Nicolas.

A gift from Paul Nicolas to his brother Émile (founding secretary of the École De Nancy).

c1920   *13in (33cm) high*
£2,200-2,500   **M&DM**

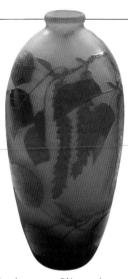

A red on orange D'Argental cameo vase, depicting catkins, signed 'D'Argental' with a Cross of Lorraine, made by Paul Nicolas.

c1920   *8in (20.5cm) high*
£1,500-1,800   **M&DM**

A monumental brown on orange D'Argental cameo vase, depicting finely detailed orchids, signed 'D'Argental' with a Cross of Lorraine, made by Paul Nicolas.

c1920   *14in (35.5cm) high*
£3,200-3,600   **M&DM**

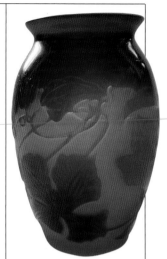

A small brown, red, and orange D'Argental cameo vase, depicting trailing clematis, signed 'D'Argental', made by Paul Nicolas.

c1921   *5in (12.75cm) high*
£500-600   **M&DM**

A small brown, red and orange D'Argental cameo vase, depicting trailing honeysuckle, signed 'D'Argental' with a Cross of Lorraine, made by Paul Nicolas.

c1920   *7in (17.75cm) high*
£1,100-1,300   **M&DM**

A CLOSER LOOK AT AN ART DECO CAMEO VASE

Most of the other companies producing Art Deco cameo glass had moved on to machine production by this stage, meaning D'Argental was one of the last companies making it by hand.

The design is in the earlier Art Deco style, rather than the more geometric, later Art Moderne style that most associate with the term Art Deco.

The design, motifs, and the form echo those found in the Far East. Exotic Oriental designs were influential at the birth of the Art Deco style.

Very different from much asymmetric, naturally inspired Art Nouveau cameo patterns, this design includes repeated motifs and is structured.

A large Art Deco red and brown on orange D'Argental cameo vase, signed D'Argental with a Cross of Lorraine, made by Paul Nicolas.

c1925   *10in (25.5cm) high*
£2,500-3,000   **M&DM**

A tall brown on orange D'Argental cameo vase, depicting an orchid, signed 'D'Argental' with a Cross of Lorraine, made by Paul Nicolas.

c1920   *12in (30.5cm) high*
£2,000-2,500   **M&DM**

GLASS

A tall green on pink D'Argental cameo vase, depicting trailing catkins, signed 'D'Argental' with a Cross of Lorraine, made by Paul Nicolas.

c1920   12in (30.5cm) high
£2,000-2,500   M&DM

A tall red on orange D'Argental cameo vase, depicting trailing wisteria, signed 'D'Argental' with a Cross of Lorraine, made by Paul Nicolas.

c1920   14in (35.5cm) high
£2,000-2,500   M&DM

A small botanical red on orange D'Argental cameo vase, depicting crocuses, signed 'D'Argental', made by Paul Nicolas.

c1920   5in (12.75cm) high
£700-800   M&DM

A red on orange D'Argental cameo vase, depicting trailing wisteria, signed 'D'Argental' with a Cross of Lorraine, made by Paul Nicolas.

c1920   9in (23cm) high
£1,200-1,500   M&DM

A very rare purple on blue D'Argental Berger lamp, depicting nasturtiums, signed 'D'Argental', and Berger on the metalwork, glass made by Paul Nicolas.

This piece was displayed in the 2010 École De Nancy exhibition on Paul Nicolas and was included in the exhibition book.

c1925   8in (20.5cm) high
£3,000-3,500   M&DM

A blue on pale-green D'Argental cameo vase, depicting trailing leaves, signed 'D'Argental' with a Cross of Lorraine, made by Paul Nicolas.

c1920   7in (17.75cm) high
£800-1,200   M&DM

A monumental purple on clear D'Argental cameo bowl, depicting grape vines, signed 'D'Argental' with a Cross of Lorraine, made by Paul Nicolas.

c1920   13in (33cm) diam
£2,500-3,000   M&DM

QUICK REFERENCE - DAUM

● Jean Daum (1825-85) purchased a glassworks in Nancy, France in 1875 but it was his sons who produced the Art Nouveau glass for which the name is celebrated. They were inspired to do so after visiting an exhibition of glass by Émile Gallé. As with Gallé, nature and Far Eastern images were influential. A variety of production techniques were used, such as handcarved and acid-etched cameo, enamelling and iridising. In 1899, they patented a technique for embellishing the inner surface of a vase, adding one or more layers of colour. A number of notable glass artists worked for them including Amalric Walter, Charles Schneider, and Henri Bergé. In 1925, they began producing colourless crystal glass as well as cased and acid-etched cameo glass in the Art Deco style. Fakes are known - always look for quality in terms of carving and also in the finishing of the body itself. Uncomfortably bright and vivid colours, particularly in combination with one of those factors, should also be regarded with suspicion.

A rare Daum Nancy miniature enamelled glass vase, painted with a tropical scene of houses before palm trees, painted 'Daum Nancy' mark.

2in (5cm) wide

£600-700   WW

A Daum Nancy enamelled glass Winter Landscape vase, acid-etched in low relief, enamelled 'Daum Nancy' mark.

Detailed and atmospheric winter scenes on miniatures such as this are scarce and highly desirable. Delicately painted by hand, this is effectively art on a vase. Take note of the size of these vases, they are shown at around half life size on this page!

4.75in (12cm) high

£3,000-4,000   WW

A Daum Nancy enamelled glass vase, enamelled with violets, in purple and green on a mottled ground, cameo 'Daum Nancy France' signature.

3.5in (8.5cm) high

£1,500-2,000   WW

A rare Daum Nancy miniature enamelled vase, painted with silver birch trees before a sunset sky, painted 'Daum Nancy' mark.

2in (5.5cm) wide

£800-1,000   WW

A Daum cameo water lily quatrefoil bowl, acid-etched and enamelled in pink and greens, signed in relief 'Daum Nancy' and with Cross of Lorraine mark.

5in (13cm) diam

£750-850   MLL

A Daum salt, with cameo and enameled winter scene with barren trees rising from a snow-covered ground, on a mottled yellow and orange background, signed on the underside in black enamel 'Daum Nancy' with the Cross of Lorraine.

2in (5cm) diam

£900-1,100   JDJ

A Daum cameo glass vase, mottled red glass cased in bright yellow, decorated with stylised chrysanthemum flowers, etched 'Daum & Nancy' to foot.

10.25in (26cm) high

£1,800-2,200   WW

A Daum fire-polished vase, the brownish-red cameo floral decoration against a clear-glass background with cased-yellow interior, with patches of wheel-carved martelé around the body and on the foot, with etched signature 'Daum Nancy' with the Cross of Lorraine.

5.75in (14.5cm) high

£1,000-1,500   JDJ

A rare Daum Nancy enamelled cameo glass vase, enamelled with Rowan berry fronds, cameo signature.

3.5in (8.5cm) high

£1,400-1,600   WW

A 'Monnaie du Pape' Daum Nancy cameo glass vase, decorated with honesty stems, cameo signature.

4.75in (12cm) high

£1,000-1,300   WW

A Daum mahogany jade glass vase, wheel-cut 'Daum & Nancy' mark.

15in (38.5cm) high

£500-600   WW

A Daum blue glass mascot or paperweight, in the Art Deco style, designed by Alexandre Fassianos, engraved signature, signed.

3.7in (9.5cm) high

£55-65   FLD

QUICK REFERENCE - LALIQUE

● René Lalique (1860-1945) is one of the Art Deco movement's most important and influential designers. His high-quality pieces were primarily mould-blown or pressed, rather than hand-blown. He was commercially highly successful and his designs inspired the work of other companies such as Sabino, Etling, and a host of smaller factories. Opalescent glass was a hallmark of his designs. Other glass was produced in colours such as blue, green, or red, or were stained to accentuate details of the design. Many of his designs have been produced for decades and marks can help to date them. Before Lalique's death in 1945, signatures include the 'R' for René, as with this example. After 1945, his son Marc changed the company name and removed the 'R' from signatures. An 'R' in a circle - the 'registered trademark' symbol - indicates a later piece, as does the inclusion or use of the word 'Cristal'. Marks can be complex, so consult a specialist guide.

A late 1920s-30s René Lalique opalescent 'Domremy' pattern vase, frosted and finished with a light-blue patination, signed on the underside in etched block letters 'R. Lalique France', designed in 1926.

8.5in (21.5cm) high

£1,000-1,500   JDJ

A late 1920s-30s René Lalique opalescent 'Druide' pattern vase, with moulded decoration of vines and berries, light-blue patination and engraved script signature 'R. Lalique France 937', designed in 1924.

6.5in (16.5cm) high

£700-1,000   JDJ

A late 1920s-30s Lalique 'Bacchantes' pattern vase, moulded with a band of ladies pouring water from urns, the base with wheel-cut 'R. Lalique, France' signature, two chips to the base rim, designed in 1927.

With its elegant ladies pouring water from vessels, 'Bacchantes' is one of Lalique's most-loved Art Deco patterns.

7in (18.2cm) high

£1,500-2,000   SWO

A 1930s Lalique clear, frosted, and black enamelled 'Dahlia' pattern vase, the base with moulded 'R. Lalique' mark, designed in 1931.

This pattern is more commonly found in perfume bottle, powder jar, and bowl forms.

5.25in (13cm) high

£1,800-2,200   WW

A 1930s Lalique 'Muguet' pattern bowl, with blue-stained highlights, the base with etched 'R. Lalique France' mark, designed in 1931.

9.5in (24cm) diam

£1,200-1,800   SWO

A 1930s Lalique 'Epins' pattern clear and frosted bottle and stopper, with blue staining, cast 'R Lalique' to base.

4.5in (11cm) high

£250-350   WW

A late 20thC Lalique 'Sanglier' car mascot, the base etched 'Lalique, France', with 'Lalique Cristal' label, designed in 1929.

3.5in (9cm) long

£60-90   MLL

A set of six late 20thC Cristal Lalique 'Treves' pattern hock glasses, each with an olive-green glass bowl, on a scroll-engraved faceted tapering stem and circular foot, engraved 'Lalique France'.

7.5in (19cm) high

£180-220 for six   DN

GLASS

A Monart glass vase, probably shape EF, light-blue graduated to mottled green and yellow with whorls, paper label.

11in (27.5cm) high

£450-550   MLL

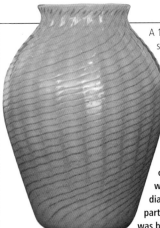

A 1930s Monart glass vase, shape F, with vertical fluted and wrythen spiral body below an everted neck, enamel decorated with rows of blue spots over a jade-green ground.

This pattern requires more skilled work to create, in addition to the application of the blue spots. The threads were trailed over the body diagonally while rotating the partially blown body, before it was blown into a vertically ribbed mould to give the fluting. Finally, the vase was blown and finished using hand tools.

9.5in (24cm) high

£850-950   FLD

A 1930s Monart glass vase, shape N, cased in clear crystal over a tonal brown to orange ground with vertical pull-up pattern over an opal interior.

After the brown mottles were applied, the molten glass was literally 'pulled' using the points of a glassmaking tool - a little like the icing on a Bakewell tart!

8in (20cm) high

£300-350   FLD

A 1930s Monart glass ginger jar, shape Z, decorated with a turquoise-green paisley swirl over the jade-green ground.

Ginger jars are scarce and desirable, and lids are often lost or broken. Always check around the neck and rim of the lid for damage.

8in (20cm) high

£800-900   FLD

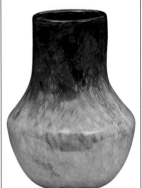

A late 1920s-30s Monart glass vase, shape GA or FB, red graduating to mottled orange with splashes of green and blue.

12in (30cm) high

£130-180   MLL

A late 1920s-30s Monart stoneware glass vase, shape GA, decorated with green and blue pulls on a mottled green ground, unsigned.

8.25in (21cm) high

£350-400   WW

QUICK REFERENCE - MONART

- Monart glass was produced from 1924-61 by John Moncrieff Ltd, in Perth, Scotland. It was the result of a collaboration between the Spanish glassmaker Salvador Ysart and his sons and the wife of the factory's owner, Isobel Moncrieff. The Ysarts led design and manufacture.
- The range is typified by its vibrant and often mottled patterns found on over 300 shapes comprising vases, bowls, dishes and lamps. Many shapes were inspired by Chinese ceramics. Such mottled or 'cloudy' art glass was popular during the 1920s & 30s.
- The mottled patterning was made by rolling a colourless or coloured body in differently coloured powdered enamel, or enamel chips, which were melted into the body in the furnace. Sometimes copper particles, known as aventurine, were added and the mottled surface was manipulated into patterns using glassmaker's tools. One of the most desirable patterns made with tools this way is 'Paisley Shawl', with its tight swirls.
- Values vary depending on the shape, size, colouring, and pattern, but have fallen since the high point of the market in the early 2000s, with the exception of rare pieces.

A large 1930s Monart glass vase, shape B, enamel decorated in a 'Paisley Shawl' design of tonal blue and white scrolls over a deep-red ground.

8in (20cm) high

£1,300-1,800   FLD

A late 1920s-30s Monart glass vase, possibly shape OE, turquoise graduating to orange.

9in (23cm) high

£75-95   **MLL**

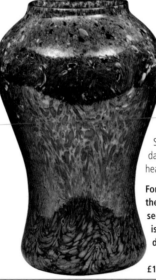

A late 1920s-30s Monart glass vase, with 'Paisley Shawl' decoration, shape C, dark-blue with all-over lustred heavy whorls.

For more information about the 'Paisley Shawl' pattern, see the previous page. This is a desirable colour and a desirable and large form.

9in (23cm) high

£1,300-1,800   **MLL**

A late 1920s-30s Monart glass bowl, mottled blue graduating to green with pin-wheel streaks, partial paper label.

c1936   *10.5in (26.5cm) diam*

£200-250   **MLL**

A late 1920s-30s Monart glass bowl, clear graduating to light-blue, gold aventurine.

10in (25.5cm) diam

£100-150   **MLL**

A late 1920s-30s Monart glass bowl, black graduating to turquoise with whorls, gold aventurine.

8in (20cm) diam

£100-150   **MLL**

A CLOSER LOOK AT A MONART VASE

As the name suggests, this rare range was inspired by Far Eastern cloisonné enamels, which were a source of inspiration to the factory owner's wife, Isobel Moncrieff.

The opal body was coated in green and blue powdered enamels, which were melted into the body in the heat of the furnace.

Unique to each piece, the slightly textured and fissured pattern was created by plunging the still hot vase into cold water, which caused the surface to fracture. The body was then blown into form, pulling the blue and green fragments apart.

Blue is scarce, but it would have fetched more if it had been a vase. The range was also available with a 'fumed' iridescent finish.

A large 1930s Monart glass bowl, shape X, decorated in a tonal-blue and jade-green 'Cloisonné' finish with fissured decoration over an opal interior, retains original paper label.

9.5in (24cm) wide

£600-800   **FLD**

A Monart glass bowl, probably shape FH, mottled blue graduating to green with whorls, gold aventurine.

11.75in (30cm) diam

£120-160   **MLL**

GLASS

QUICK REFERENCE - MURANO

- The many glass factories on the island of Murano, near Venice in Italy, saw an explosion of experimentation, innovation and creativity after World War Two. Traditional techniques practised for centuries were refreshed and brought into the 20thC by new designers intent on creating a riot of colour and modern forms. By the late 1950s, the movement was in full swing, having enjoyed commercial and critical success, and Murano glass was once again at the forefront of glass design.

- Designs by certain influential designers at the island's major factories tend to be the most desirable and valuable. These include Venini (founded 1921), Barovier & Toso (founded 1878, renamed in 1942), and Seguso Vetri D'Arte (1933-92). Designers include Paolo Venini, Fulvio Bianconi, Dino Martens, Flavio Poli, and Ercole Barovier.

- The best starting point is to study a collection of reliable reference books and auction catalogues to build up a knowledge of forms, colours, and the story behind the designs. This will enable you to identify the work of these designers and factories as much of it is unsigned. Copies and even fakes made during the period and more recently, abound. Also look and try to handle as many authenticated pieces as possible as this will help you build up a feel for what is right and what is wrong.

- Also consider the technique - the more complex and time-consuming it is, the more a piece is likely to be worth. Some designs were produced in very small quantities or are considered landmarks in the development of mid-century modern Murano glass, so are highly prized and valuable.

- Away from the work of leading designers and factories, the market is much wider and more affordable. Vases, bowls, animals, and figurines can be found for anything from £20-400. Ashtrays can make an affordable way to own a piece from many designs as smoking is now unfashionable and few wish to own and display them. One of the most common types of glass is the multi-coloured, multi-layered 'sommerso' glass. Look out for well-balanced forms in bright colours with well-executed, clearly demarcated layers.

A Venini & C. large 'fazzoletto' handkerchief vase, designed by Fulvio Bianconi and Paolo Venini from 1948-49, the white interior cased with transparent red, the base with 'venini italia' acid stamp.

11in (27.7cm) high

£600-650   QU

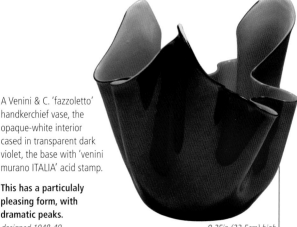

A Venini & C. 'fazzoletto' handkerchief vase, the opaque-white interior cased in transparent dark violet, the base with 'venini murano ITALIA' acid stamp.

This has a particularly pleasing form, with dramatic peaks.

designed 1948-49   *9.25in (23.5cm) high*

£1,000-1,400   QU

A Venini & C. large 'fazzoletto' handkerchief vase, in azure and milky-blue glass, the base inscribed 'venini 94'.

1994   *12in (30cm) high*

£450-500   QU

A Venini & C. miniature 'fazzoletto' handkerchief vase, the white interior cased with iridescent black, the base with 'venini murano MADE IN ITALY' acid stamp.

designed 1948-49   *3.5in (9cm) high*

£450-500   QU

A Venini & C. 'fazzoletto' handkerchief vase, with alternating pink and white spiral 'zanfirico' canes, the base with 'venini murano ITALIA' acid stamp.

designed 1948-49   *6.25in (16cm) high*

£600-700   QU

A Venini & C. 'fazzoletto' handkerchief vase, with alternating violet and white spiral 'zanfirico' canes, the base with 'venini murano ITALIA' acid stamp.

designed 1948-49   *4.5in (11cm) high*

£250-300   QU

A Venini & C. colourless cased orange ovoid 'Inciso' vase, designed by Paolo Venini in 1956, the base with circular 'venini murano ITALIA' acid stamp.

14in (36cm) high

£950-1,200   **QU**

A Venini & C. colourless cased azure blue and green ovoid 'Inciso' vase, the base with 'venini murano ITALIA' acid stamp.

'Inciso' is one of three techniques applied to the exterior surface of glass that are united by use of a cutting machine or grinding wheel. Known as 'cold working' because the piece is cold rather than hot and ductile, all give the glass a matte appearance and look almost cloudy. 'Inciso' (incised) is made by cutting very fine shallow lines all over the body of the piece, and 'battuto' is made by cutting wider, shallow slices into the surface to give an almost hammered effect. 'Velato' (veiled) is perhaps the most delicate and makes the surface look like it has been abraded with a stiff wire brush.

designed 1956   *14in (36cm) high*

£1,500-2,000   **QU**

A Venini & C. colourless cased azure-blue and green tapering 'Inciso' vase, the base with 'venini murano ITALIA' acid stamp.

designed 1956   8in (20.5cm) high

£1,000-1,400   **QU**

A Venini & C. pink and white 'zanfirico' vase, with diagonal application of canes, designed by Paolo Venini in 1954, the base with 'venini murano ITALIA' acid stamp.

This vase was acquired from the Venini company archive and is accompanied by a certificate stating as such from Venini.

8.25in (21.2cm) high

£1,100-1,400   **QU**

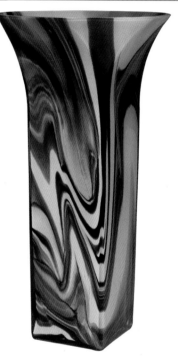

A Venini & C. large opaque white square section vase with flared rim, with randomly applied violet swirls, designed by Sergio Asti in 1970, the base inscribed 'Asti Venini Murano'.

Sergio Asti (b.1926) is a notable Italian architect, industrial designer and interior designer who founded his own design studio in Milan in 1953. He has worked for many notable companies including Fiat, Knoll (during the 1970s), Fontana Arte and Venini. His work for Venini can be hard to find and is sought-after.

15.75in (40.2cm) high

£2,300-2,800   **QU**

A Venini & C. colourless cased rose pink 'Corroso' vase, with a wavy rim, designed by Carlo Scarpa in 1936, the base with 'venini murano ITALIA' acid stamp.

This vase was acquired from the Venini company archive and is accompanied by a certificate from Venini stating this. This provenance, particularly on a piece of this period, is highly desirable and contributes considerably to the value. 'Corroso' is a cold-working technique where the surface of the glass is attacked using acid to create a matte 'corroded' appearance.

6.5in (16.6cm) high

£1,600-2,000   **QU**

A Venini & C. colourless, yellow and green cased 'Inciso' cylindrical vase, designed by Paolo Venini in 1955, the base with 'venini murano ITALIA' acid stamp and factory paper label.

4.75in (12.2cm) high

£200-250   **QU**

GLASS

A CLOSER LOOK AT AN 'INCALMO' VASE

Fulvio Bianconi (1915-96) is a celebrated graphic designer, artist, and glass designer whose work for Venini is varied, idiosyncratic and highly sought-after.

This colour combination of azure blue and red was frequently used by Bianconi in designs from his 'Forato' and 'A Fasce' ranges to his landmark 'Pezzato' range.

'Incalmo' is a challenging technique where separate bubbles of differently coloured glass are blown to identically matching sizes so that they can be joined together to make the piece when the glass is still hot.

This 'Doppio Incalmo' (double incalmo) vase takes this technique one stage further as three carefully sized pieces of glass must be blown, rather than two.

A Venini & C. 'A Doppio Incalmo' vase, with violet, rose, and azure-blue sections, designed by Fulvio Bianconi in 1950, the base with 'venini murano ITALIA' acid stamp.

11.75in (30cm) high

£2,000-2,500   QU

A Venini & C. cylindrical green-cased colourless vase, with applied and melted in opaque violet wavy trails, designed by Gianni Versace in 1995, unsigned.

This vase was a trial piece or prototype and was acquired from the Venini archive. It is accompanied by a certificate of provenance from the company. Although typically rare, or even unique, by their very nature, trial pieces can be difficult to sell. Although Versace is a well-known and hotly collected name, it is a dark and murky design unlike his other designs for interiors and couture.

9in (23.2cm) high

£900-1,000   QU

A Venini & C. 'Kelo' black, opaque white and red-cased vase, with a wavy cross-section and angular rim, designed by Timo Sarpaneva in 1990, the base inscribed 'venini 90 Sarpaneva'.

This is an unusual vase for Sarpaneva, who is best known for his 'incalmo' 'Tuuli' range of vases, decanters, dishes, and bowls, which was designed for Venini at around the same time as this piece.

18.5in (47cm) high

£1,300-1,600   QU

A Venini & C. colourless, violet and cobalt-blue-cased 'Forato' vase, with two holes creating handles, designed by Fulvio Bianconi in 1951, the base inscribed 'venini italia'.

The use of the two-line inscribed 'venini italia' mark indicates this piece was made from 1966-70. For more information about the 'Forato' range, please see p210 of the Miller's Collectables Price Guide 2014-2015.

16.75in (42.5cm) high

£500-600   QU

A Venini & C. colourless and green-cased tapering conical 'Inciso' vase, designed by Paolo Venini in 1956, the base with 'venini murano ITALIA' acid stamp.

17.25in (44cm) high

£1,000-1,300   QU

A Venini & C. 'A Fasce' vase or tea light wind lamp, the colourless body with applied columns of yellow, grey, purple, and blue glass panels, designed by Fulvio Bianconi in 1952, unsigned.

10.5in (27cm) high

£450-500   QU

A Venini & C. 'Folto' vase, the opaque blue body with opaque light violet rim and applied horizontal green threads, designed by Mary Ann 'Toots' Zynsky in 1984, the base inscribed 'Zynksy x venini 89'.

Mary Ann 'Toots' Zynsky (b.1951) is a notable American studio glass designer best known for her vibrantly coloured asymmetric and organically formed bowls made up of many differently coloured opaque glass threads.

1989   *10.5in (26.5cm) high*

£1,100-1,300   QU

A Venini & C. colourless, opaque, and moss-green cased ribbed ball vase, designed by Napoleone Martinuzzi in 1930, the base inscribed 'venini 95 Carlo Scarpa'.

The incorrectly engraved designer name on the base shows that even large and prestigious companies such as Venini get it wrong sometimes! This is an excellent Art Deco design and is usually popular with collectors as it works well in many different styles of interior.

1995   *11.75in (30cm) high*
£600-700   QU

A Venini & C. tonal green bottle vase, designed by Vittorio Zecchin in 1922, the base with three-line 'venini murano ITALIA' acid stamp.

£500-600   QU

A Venini & C. colourless and light amber 'Veronese' baluster vase, designed by Vittorio Zecchin in 1921, the base with inscribed 'venini 2007' mark.

This series of designs by Zecchin is typical of the delicate yet Classically-inspired forms produced by the company in the early 20thC. This was one of the first designs produced at Venini, which was founded in the same year.

2007   *12in (30.5cm) high*
£700-800   QU

A Venini & C. tonal cobalt-blue 'Veronese' baluster vase, designed by Vittorio Zecchin in 1921, the base with three-line 'venini murano ITALY' mark.

11.5in (29.5cm) high
£1,100-1,300   QU

QUICK REFERENCE - LATER RE-ISSUES

● Many of the designs produced for Venini by notable designers were produced for some time after the year they were designed. Some may have been in constant production since they were first introduced, some may be re-issues to commemorate an anniversary or due to demand or the entire product range being refreshed. In general, such later examples tend to be less highly valued by collectors, even though they can be almost identical to the initial production. Sometimes, however, colour tones are very slightly different. They can be brighter and more vibrant, and the finishing can be better. Always pay close attention to the marks on the base as they can help to date a piece. Three line or circular acid-stamp marks reading 'venini murano ITALIA' date from before 1966. An inscribed 'venini italia' mark on two lines indicates a date from 1966-70. After 1970, two-digit numbers together with a vibropen inscribed 'venini italia' or similar indicate the year of production. Hence, '89' is 1989. Two-letter initials indicate the designer. Here, 'tw' stands for Tapio Wirkkala. This item was produced in three examples. Ultimately, value depends on the desirability of the design and the quantity of examples produced. Those **in constant production since they were first introduced will be much more common.**

A Venini & C. colourless and red glass 'Bolle' bottle vase, made using the 'incalmo' technique, designed by Tapio Wirkkala in 1966, the base inscribed 'venini tw 89'.

1989   *7in (17.8cm) high*
£700-800   QU

A Venini & C. blue and violet 'A Doppio Incalmo' cylindrical stoppered bottle, designed by Fulvio Bianconi and Paolo Venini in 1953, the base with circular 'venini murano ITALY' mark.

15in (38cm) high
£1,000-1,300   QU

A Venini & C. blue and yellow 'A Fasce' cylindrical stoppered bottle, designed by Fulvio Bianconi and Paolo Venini in 1953, the base with three-line 'venini murano ITALY' mark.

12.5in (31.5cm) high
£400-500   QU

GLASS

A Venini & C. blue, red, and yellow cased and banded 'A Fasce' bottle, designed by Fulvio Bianconi and Paolo Venini in 1953, the base with circular 'venini murano ITALY' mark.

This is an unusual and desirable colour combination.

16.5in (42.3cm) high

£1,100-1,300   QU

A Venini & C. light amber, opaque white, and opaque yellow cased and banded 'A Fasce' bottle, designed by Fulvio Bianconi und Paolo Venini in 1953, the base with etched 'venini 88' mark.

1988   *5.5in (39.5cm) high*

£700-800   QU

A Venini & C. tonal blue 'Inciso' stoppered bottle, designed by Paolo Venini in 1956, the base with inscribed 'venini 90' mark and factory label.

1990   *8.25in (21.3cm) high*

£260-300   QU

A Venini & C. blue and yellow 'A Canne' bottle, with red and green vertical applied canes, the design attributed to Gio Ponti c1948, the base with acid-stamped 'venini murano ITALY' mark.

20in (50.3cm) high

£1,400-1,800   QU

A Venini & C. tapered table obelisk, with white and light-green spiralling internal 'zanfirico' column, designed by Paolo Venini in 1950, the base with acid-stamped 'venini murano MADE IN ITALY' mark.

5in (12.8cm) high

£600-700   QU

A Venini & C. deep-red 'Inciso' tall triangular section bottle, designed by Paolo Venini in 1956, the base with inscribed 'venini 90' mark and factory label.

1990   *16.25in (41.2cm) high*

£300-350   QU

A Venini & C. 'A Spirale' dish, with multi-coloured radiating curved canes emanating from the centre, designed by Fulvio Bianconi in 1950, the base with acid-stamped 'venini murano ITALIA' mark.

Dishes can be challenging to make, especially in large sizes, as they have to be 'spun' out by the glassmaker who had to pay close attention to gravity to avoid one side being thicker than another, or the piece losing its oval or circular form.

6.5in (16.5cm) diam

£350-400   QU

A Venini & C. 'A Spirale' dish, with alternating dark violet and rose pink curved spiralling panels, designed by Fulvio Bianconi in 1950, the base with acid-stamped 'venini murano ITALIA' mark.

6.75in (17cm) diam

£300-350 QU

A Venini & C. square vase, with an applied orange trail, designed by Ludovico Diaz De Santillana for Pierre Cardin from 1968-70, the base inscribed 'venini Pierre Cardin'.

c1970 *4.75in (12cm) high*

£300-350 QU

A Venini & C. paperweight, with applied and melted-in opaque white and light blue trails, designed by Ludovico Diaz De Santillana for Pierre Cardin from 1968-70, the base inscribed 'venini Pierre Cardin'.

This is part of a series of square or rectangular vase, bowl and paperweight forms. These are decorated with broad trails in different colours applied almost like paint, that were designed by and with Pierre Cardin in the late 1960s and early 1970s. They are yet to fetch high prices, perhaps as Cardin's name was arguably diluted during the 1980s & 90s when it was applied to many things from wallets to frying pans.

c1970 *5in (12.5cm) high*

£250-300 QU

A Barovier & Toso cobalt-blue 'Efeso' bulbous vase, with random and randomly sized internal air bubbles, designed by Ercole Barovier in 1964, the base inscribed 'barovier e toso murano' and with factory label.

13.5in (34.5cm) high

£850-950 QU

A Barovier & Toso cobalt-blue 'Efeso' vase, with C-shaped handle, with random and randomly sized internal air bubbles, designed by Ercole Barovier in 1964, the base inscribed 'barovier e toso murano' and with factory label.

This angular form is much more typical of Scandinavian mid-century glass, but the inspiration for this range and its forms was taken from excavated ancient Roman glass and ceramics.

11.5in (29cm) high

£600-650 QU

A Barovier & Toso 'Cordonato Oro' flat bottle-shaped vase, with vertical spiralling reeding and internal gold 'aventurine' flakes, designed by Ercole Barovier.

c1950 *11.5in (29.5cm) high*

£500-550 QU

A Barovier & Toso yellow-gold and azure-blue 'Intarsio' dish, designed by Ercole Barovier in 1962.

The 'Intarsio' technique involves rolling the hot colourless or coloured glass body over (usually triangular) fragments of differently coloured glass. The heat of the body melts the fragments and they adhere to the surface, before being fused seamlessly in the heat of the furnace. The piece is then blown and manipulated into its final form.

9.5in (24.5cm) long

£250-300 QU

GLASS

A CLOSER LOOK AT A BAROVIER & TOSO VASE

The base is inscribed with an inscription 'to the dear friend Zino da Ercole', presumably by Barovier himself, which is an exceptionally rare and personal feature.

Ercole Barovier (1889-1974), artistic director of Barovier & Toso from 1926, was renowned for his wide variety of inventive and often complex techniques.

This design is extremely rare. The shape would have required great skill to make as it is very challenging to keep the 'murrines' in the correct shape without being stretched or distorted.

The colourless body is covered with blue, green, purple and white opal 'murrines' which are complex to make and were made separately before being applied.

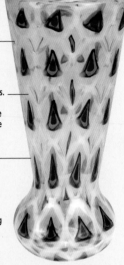

A very rare Barovier & Toso 'Tessere Policrome' vase, designed by Ercole Barovier in 1963, the base inscribed 'a il amico carissimo Zino da Ercole'.

11.5in (29.2cm) high

£17,000-20,000　　　　QU

A Barovier & Toso 'Diamanti' vase, the colourless body covered with dark-purple edged square 'murrines' in yellow, blue, red and green, with dark-violet and white zanfirico threads, designed by Ercole Barovier in 1968, the base inscribed 'barovier e toso murano' and with factory paper label.

12.5in (32cm) high

£3,000-4,000　　　　QU

A Barovier & Toso 'Graffito' baluster vase, with white and blue oxidised streaks, random bubbles and golf leaf 'aventurine' flakes, designed by Ercole Barovier in 1969, with factory paper label.

13.25in (33.8cm) high

£800-900　　　　QU

A Barovier & Toso 'Neomurrino' conical footed vase, the colourless body covered with black bordered white 'murrines' and with an applied black foot, designed by Ercole Barovier in 1972, the base inscribed 'barovier & toso murano' and with retailer's label.

6.75in (17cm) high

£600-650　　　　QU

Judith Picks

The work of Toni Zuccheri (1936-2008) was acclaimed during the 1960s & 70s, but has been less popular than that of other designers until recently. Collectors and connoisseurs are now beginning to re-appraise his work, partly as some of the work of other, currently better-known designers (such as Fulvio Bianconi) is becoming harder to find, more expensive and more frequently faked. Zuccheri also produced designs that combine great visual impact with often complex techniques and a strong feeling for period design. His star looks set to rise further as more of his designs are uncovered and re-appraised. Look out in particular for his range of birds produced in the early 1960s at Venini that won a prize at the 1964 Venice Biennale - these can fetch over £12,000.

A Barovier & Toso 'Incalmo' vase, the body formed of black and white segments and with an applied black rim, designed by Toni Zuccheri in 1986, the base inscribed 'barovier & toso murano tz 86' and with factory label.

1986　　　*8.75in (22.5cm) high*

£850-950　　　　QU

An Archimede Seguso glass vase, ribbed, shouldered pale-pink glass with gold 'aventurine' inclusions, on applied foot, the base etched 'Archimede Seguso Murano'.

This design was shown on the back cover of 'I Quadernio di Archimede Seguso' issue no.2, published in 1994.

17in (43cm) high

£500-600　　　　WW

A Vetreria Archimede Seguso green ovoid vase, with internal gold leaf 'aventurine' flakes and vertical reeding, designed by Archimede Seguso from 1950-55.

11.5in (29cm) high

£350-400   QU

A Vetreria Archimede Seguso colouress, red and blue cased bottle 'sommerso' vase, designed by Archimede Seguso from 1956-61.

Archimede Seguso (1909-99) became artistic director at the factory that became known as Seguso Vetri D'Arte in 1934. In 1942, he left to set up his own glassworks, Vetreria Archimede Seguso. Both factories, but particularly Seguso Vetri D'Arte, excelled at producing high-quality 'sommerso' designs, usually incorporating a number of colours.

19in (48.2cm) high

£700-800   QU

A Vetreria Archimede Seguso cylindrical stoppered bottle, with internal gold leaf 'aventurine' flakes, designed by Archimede Seguso in 1980, the base inscribed 'Archimede Seguso Murano'.

13.75in (35cm) high

£400-500   QU

An Aureliano Toso 'Mezza Filigrana' vase, with conical body and spherical foot, the colourless body overlaid with spiralling white and dark-violet threads with internal gold leaf 'aventurine' flakes, designed by Dino Martens in 1954.

13.5in (34.2cm) high

£400-500   QU

QUICK REFERENCE - ORIENTE

● **Although this dish may look like a rather haphazardly produced trial piece, the 'painterly' designs of the artist Dino Martens (1894-1970) were a critical part of the Mid-Century Modern revival of glass design on Murano. Combining modern abstract art with complex techniques and 'new' vibrant colours, the 'Oriente' range typifies the explosion of colour and creativity that occurred on Murano after World War Two. Introduced at the 1952 Venice Biennale, it came in a variety of extravagant and curving forms. It would have shocked an audience used to traditional Muranese designs produced since the 19thC. His larger vases and ewers can fetch anything from £2,000-15,000, making this comparatively simple bowl an excellent and affordable way to own an example of this landmark design.**

An Aureliano Toso 'Oriente' dish, with light blue, red, white, dark violet and copper 'aventurine' patches, designed by Dino Martens in 1955.

6in (15.7cm) diam

£500-600   QU

A large Barbini Glassworks Murano glass vase, streaked yellow and white glass cased in clear, the base with etched signature and date to base.

1958   *23.5in (60cm) high*

£350-400   WW

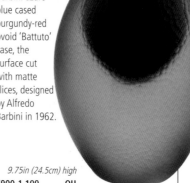

An Alfredo Barbini azure-blue cased burgundy-red ovoid 'Battuto' vase, the surface cut with matte slices, designed by Alfredo Barbini in 1962.

9.75in (24.5cm) high

£900-1,100   QU

GLASS

An M.V.M. Capellin bottle vase, in toned violet glass, with two small handles, designed by Vittorio Zecchin.

This form is shown in the exhibition catalogue for the Vittorio Zecchin exhibition held at the Museu Corer in Venice in 2002.

7.5in (19cm) high

£400-450   QU

A Cenedese sculptural tazza, designed by Antonio da Ros, in uranium tint green glass with an internal blue tear drop to the stem, unmarked.

c1960   *10.25in (26cm) high*

£300-500   FLD

An I.V.R Mazzega 'A Fasce' large dish, the colourless glass body with blue, green, and red concentric circles, designed by Gino Mazzega in 1960.

16in (40.5cm) diam

£300-350   QU

An I.V.R Mazzega 'A Fasce' stoppered jar, the colourless glass body with blue, green, and red concentric circles, designed by Gino Mazzega in 1960.

Jars are comparatively complex to make as the stopper or lid has to be made to a specific size to work with the body.

7in (18cm) high

£350-400   QU

QUICK REFERENCE - CARLO MORETTI

● Carlo Moretti was founded in 1958 and is best known for its 1960s-70s ranges of single-colour vases, bowls, and drinking goblets with a satin-matte finish, as well as its range of different forms with white bodies decorated with differently coloured swirls. Less well known are the company's later designs, some of which were produced in comparatively small quantities. Typically of very high quality with superb finishing and strong colours and forms, these may prove to be a good investment for the future. They are currently affordable on the secondary market, especially when compared to retail prices and similar examples by other companies. Giovanni Moretti (b.1940) is Carlo's brother and co-founded the factory with him. Initially dealing with marketing, corporate image, and PR, he took over the reins of the factory after Carlo died in 2008.

A Carlo Moretti vase, the colourless ovoid body overlaid with black and a wide band of black and red 'murrines', designed by Giovanni Moretti, signed 'Giovanni Moretti' and with factory label.

10.25in (26cm) high

£200-250   QU

A La Murrina 'Saturno' cylindrical bottle vase, the toned light-blue body with an applied yellow, white, and light-blue 'murrine', designed by Lino Tagliapietra in 1968.

The oval form is an applied murrine. It is enlarged and stretched into random long, oval shapes as the body is blown and worked. The name 'Saturno' applies to the rings of the murrine which echo the rings of the planet Saturn. Tagliapietra (b.1934) is one of the world's most respected glass artists and designers.

16.75in (42.7cm) high

£400-450   QU

A La Murrina 'Saturno' bottle vase, the toned violet body with an applied yellow, white, and red 'murrine', designed by Lino Tagliapietra in 1968.

8.25in (21cm) high

£400-450   QU

An early 21stC Salviati & C. colourless, yellow, and red-cased heart-shaped vase, the base with 'SALVIATI' acid-stamp and with factory label.

10.25in (26cm) high

£300-350   QU

A Seguso Vetri D'Arte colourless, red-brown and green-cased 'sommerso' teardrop-shaped vase, model no.11993, designed by Flavio Poli in 1958.

Flavio Poli (1900-84) is celebrated for his multi-coloured cased 'sommerso' designs, which are typically monumental in feel and have strong, curving forms. He began working at Seguso in 1934 and produced the majority of them from the 1940s-60s. Their immense success meant that they have been (and continue to be) widely copied and imitated by a myriad of factories, making identification hard. It is best to refer to company catalogues and reference books to ensure that shape and colour tones are correct for Seguso, but also always consider the quality of the piece, which should be very high.

12.25in (31.4cm) high

£1,000-1,400   QU

A Seguso Vetri D'Arte ball vase, the toned opaque turquoise-green body with gold leaf 'aventurine' flakes, by an unknown designer.

2.5in (6.5cm) high

£100-140   QU

A Fratelli Toso 'murrine' miniature double-handled bottle vase, the colourless body overlaid with violet, white, green, and rose pink 'murrines'.

c1910   *3in (7.8cm) high*

£140-160   QU

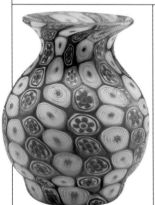

A Fratelli Toso 'Murrine' small vase, the colourless body overlaid with vertical bands of white, green, and light brown 'murrines'.

c1910 5.25in (13.5cm) high

£300-350   QU

A 1960s-70s Murano glass colourless, yellow, and green-cased teardrop form 'sommerso' vase, by an unknown maker.

15.75in (40cm) high

£300-350   WW

A 1960s-80s Murano glass violet and azure-blue 'sommerso' vase, by an unknown maker.

11.5in (29cm) high

£400-450   QU

A Murano Glass 'millefiori' large goblet vase, the body overlaid with green and multi-coloured 'murrines', the spreading circular foot with gold leaf 'aventurine' inclusions.

'Millefiori' means 'thousand flowers', and refers to the mass of small, detailed 'murrines', which almost resemble a field filled with flowers.

14in (37cm) high

£750-850   CHEF

GLASS

A pair of Murano glass figural candlesticks, each modelled as a figure supporting a column candlestick, white and 'latticino' glass with 'aventurine' inclusions, unsigned.

13.75in (35cm) high

£500-600   WW

A pair of Murano glass figural candlesticks, possibly by Seguso, each modelled as a kneeling figure in elaborate costume offering up two sconce, in white and black glass with 'aventurine' inclusions, unsigned.

9in (23cm) high

£300-400   WW

A Murano glass Blackamoor candlestick, possible by Seguso, in red and clear glass with 'aventurine' inclusions, unsigned.

The value of these widely produced figurines is largely down to the size and complexity. Other things to consider are: the level and quality of detail, the different types and colours of glass used, and the subject matter.

A Murano glass figural lamp base, possibly by Seguso, modelled as a young couple in medieval dress wearing tricorn hats, unsigned.

2.75in (55.5cm) high

£300-400   WW

14.5in (37cm) high

£400-500   WW

A Vetreria Vistosi 'Pulcino' bird sculpture, the green body with applied blue and red 'murrines', mounted on metal feet, designed by Alessandro Pianon in 1962.

This is one of the less commonly seen forms from Pianon's highly sought-after and amusing range of sculptural, stylised birds.

13in (33cm) high

£2,500-3,000   QU

A Vetreria Vistosi 'Pulcino' bird sculpture, the spherical orange body with crushed orange chips and applied 'murrine' eyes, mounted on metal feet, designed by Alessandro Pianon in 1962.

8.5in (21.5cm) high

£2,500-3,000   QU

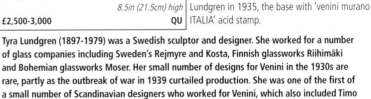

A rare Venini & C. blue bird, designed by Tyra Lundgren in 1935, the base with 'venini murano ITALIA' acid stamp.

Tyra Lundgren (1897-1979) was a Swedish sculptor and designer. She worked for a number of glass companies including Sweden's Rejmyre and Kosta, Finnish glassworks Riihimäki and Bohemian glassworks Moser. Her small number of designs for Venini in the 1930s are rare, partly as the outbreak of war in 1939 curtailed production. She was one of the first of a small number of Scandinavian designers who worked for Venini, which also included Timo Sarpaneva and Tapio Wirkkala in the 1960s.

10.25in (26cm) long

£1,200-1,400   QU

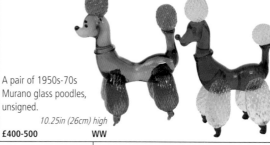

A Murano glass bird sculpture, modelled as four birds resting on a branch, black glass cased in clear with silver 'aventurine' inclusions, applied paper label 'Vetri Artistici Arte 80 Murano'.

13in (33cm) wide

£65-75   **WW**

A 1960s-70s Murano Glass figure of a stylised pelican, decorated with fine internal black and blue 'zanfirico' canes, and applied black glass beak and feet, with indistinct signature.

6.75in (17cm) high

£60-80   **FLD**

A mid 20thC Italian Murano 'sommerso' art glass figure of a stylised bird, with elongated tail, the body cased in clear crystal over tonal red with gold 'aventurine'.

15.25in (39cm) long

£55-75   **FLD**

A pair of 1950s-70s Murano glass poodles, unsigned.

10.25in (26cm) high

£400-500   **WW**

An extremely rare Cristalleria Murano-Milano (Barovier & Toso) fox, the colourless body with violet canes, designed by Ercole Barovier in 1929.

Pay close attention to form and design as not all animals made on Murano were inexpensive novelties or souvenirs. This large fox is from a very early and rare series of amusing and animated animals designed by Barovier from 1927-29 that also included a sleek tiger.

c1930

£3,000-4,000   **QU**

A Venini & C. stylised fish sculpture, the colourless body with dark violet, yellow, and red canes on a light ochre ground, designed by Kenneth George Scott in 1951.

17in (43.5cm) long

£1,000-1,400   **QU**

A 1960s Gino Cenedese 'Aquarium' block, containing weed, the pond floor and two multicoloured fish.

9in (23cm) long

£450-500   **QU**

A 1950s-60s Gino Cenedese 'Aquarium' block, containing weed, the pond floor and three multicoloured fish.

12.5in (31.5cm) long

£500-600   **QU**

QUICK REFERENCE - SCANDINAVIAN GLASS

- Glass designed and produced in Scandinavia shortly before and after World War Two has risen dramatically in desirability and popularity over the past ten years. Although many say the height of the market was five years ago, prices have plateaued. Some may peak again. Names that were previously largely unknown outside Scandinavia are now well-known by collectors across the world, and the almost global influence of the designs and their designers is now better understood.

- The work of major designers and factories is generally the most desirable and highest valued. Factories include Orrefors, Kosta Boda, Holmegaard, and Nuutajärvi Notsjö, and designers include Vicke Lindstrand, Sven Palmqvist, Per Lütken, Timo Sarpaneva, and Tapio Wirkkala. Many designers moved from factory to factory. Although much glass is unmarked, some have inscribed marks which can help identify the factory, designer, and even the date of manufacture.

- There were also a large number of smaller, arguably secondary factories such as Lindshammar, Flygfors, and Ekenas. It may well be worth researching and collecting the best designs by their most notable designers as many pieces are still comparatively affordable as they are not yet on the radar of most collectors. Often, the very best and the biggest pieces would have been the most expensive in their day, so fewer would have been made and sold. Aim to buy these.

- In general, the 1950s saw an asymmetric style, with curving forms and cool colours inspired by natural forms such as buds and leaves. Scandinavian glass from the 1960s was inspired by nature's textures, from rock to tree bark. Colours also changed, becoming stronger and brighter, with vivid oranges, green, blues, and reds becoming a part of the palette. Techniques were also developed and widened, the most complex of which were 'Graal' and 'Ariel'.

An Orrefors 'Ariel' crystal glass bowl, designed by Edvin Öhrström, decorated with vertical air trap with pale-green tint, the base with engraved signature.

3.7in (9.5cm)

£120-150   FLD

A late 20thC Orrefors 'Ariel' bowl, of shallow circular form, decorated with a random linear design with air bubble detail, the base with engraved signature, designed by Jan Johansson in c1974.

Jan Johansson began working at Orrefors in 1969. His designs are indicated with the letter 'J', or, after 1980, 'JJ', before the shape or model number engraved on the base.

6.75in (17cm) diam

£400-600   FLD

An Orrefors slip 'Graal' vase, designed by Edvard Hald, the base with inscribed mark with engraved Hald signature.

The 'Slip Graal' technique was developed by Edvard Hald in the late 1930s and involves grinding the lines into the body while it is being rotated. Those made before 1953 were marked with an 'S'.

c1954   *4.75in (12cm) high*

£300-400   FLD

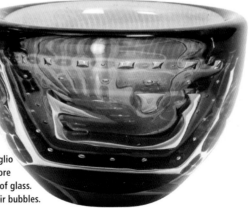

An Orrefors 'Ariel' glass vase, by Edwin Öhrström, thick-cased glass, internally decorated, in blue cased in clear, the base with incised marks and signature.

The 'Ariel' technique was developed after the 'Graal' technique by Vicke Lindstrand in 1937. Like 'Graal', the design is cut intaglio into the underlying body before being cased in another layer of glass. Unlike 'Graal', it focuses on air bubbles.

4.75in (12cm) high

£600-700   WW

An Orrefors 'Fiskegraal' glass vase, by Edward Hald, clear glass with green and brown overlay, acid-etched fishes and water plants, signed.

The reflections and refractions in the glass mean there appear to be more fish.

1944   *7.5in (18.5cm) high*

£800-900   FIS

A large late 20thC Orrefors 'Graal' vase, cased in clear crystal over tonal blue, decorated with abstract nude figures wrestling, designed by Hermann Wintersteller, the base with engraved marks.

11.5in (29cm) high

£200-300   FLD

A late 20thC Orrefors 'Graal' vase, designed by Olle Alberius, internally decorated with stylised sailing boats in dark blue over clear-crystal ground, engraved marks.

Alberius has used colourless glass and a band of different sailing boats all around the body of the piece to give the sense of a busy regatta. The effect is reminiscent of the 'Fiskegraal' bowls and vases designed by Edvard Hald in 1937 and produced for decades after, due to their commercial success. For an example of a 'Fiskegraal' bowl, see the previous page, bottom right.

9.5in (24cm) high

£350-450   FLD

A CLOSER LOOK AT ORREFORS

This dramatically coloured piece has a yellow cobra coiled around the body and lid. It was created with the cameo technique, where the black outer layer was cut away to reveal an underlying yellow layer.

The form cleverly echoes a snake charmer's basket, and the finial is modelled as a cobra about to strike.

Hermann Wintersteller founded the Orrefors GlasAtelje (Orrefors Glass Studio) in 1989 after working with Ingwald Westholm at Vrigstad Kristall Glashytta which opened in 1982 and closed in 1987.

Most of his designs are bold, striking, and sculptural, with clear lines, and he frequently used complicated techniques such as 'Graal', 'Ariel', and cameo.

In November 2012 there was an auction of many of his pieces signed Orrefors Glasateljé HW

A later 20thC Orrefors glass jar, designed by Hermann Wintersteller, of footed ovoid form with a domed cover, the base with engraved signature.

15in (38cm) high

£300-500   FLD

An Orrefors glass vase, designed by Vicke Lindstrand, flaring clear glass on black glass foot, cut with a stylised female figure.

7.25in (18.5cm) high

£70-100   WW

An Orrefors glass vase, designed by Edward Hald, faceted tapering clear glass internally decorated with aubergine web design, etched 'Orrefors Edward Hald', minor nicks.

13in (33.5cm) high

£350-400   WW

An Orrefors 'Popglas' goblet, designed by Gunnar Cyren in 1966, with multi-coloured cylindrical stem, the rim of the foot engraved 'Orrefors Expo 596-67 Gunnar Cyrén'.

Gunnar Cyren (1931-2013) joined Orrefors as a designer in 1959 having trained as a goldsmith. In 1966, he introduced opaque colours to Orrefors to critical acclaim. His 'Pop' glasses, with their pared down forms and coloured stems, are deemed a landmark in Scandinavian glass and can be hard to find. The marks indicate this is an early example, dating from 1967.

8.5in (22cm) high

£400-450   QU

GLASS

A 1960s Swedish Flygsfors mould-blown glass vase, designed by Wiktor Berndt, the base with etched signature and '61'.

8in (20cm) high

£100-150   SWO

An Iittala colourless-cased purple glass vase, designed by Tapio Wirrkala in 1960, the base engraved 'Tapio Wirrkala, 3386'.

1960-65   7in (18cm) high

£130-180   SWO

A 1930s-50s Kosta blue glass footed vase, designed by Elis Bergh in 1930, with internal optical ribbing, the base etched 'OFLA409/4A'.

7.25in (18.5cm) high

£50-70   WW

A late 20thC Kosta Boda 'Artists Collection' vase, designed by Ulrica Hydman Vallien, hand-enamelled with stylised birds over a mottled grey ground, the base with hand-painted and engraved marks.

6.25in (16cm) high

£130-180   FLD

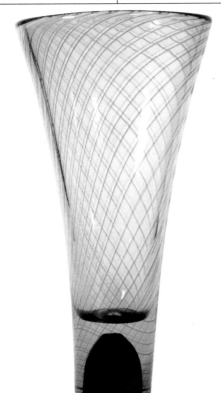

A Kosta Boda tapering vase, designed by Ann Wahlström in 1990, the thickly blown body with internal air bubbles and applied horn-like prunts, limited edition 2/10, the base inscribed 'Ann Wahlströhm, 8 AW/ED 934001/10 Kosta Boda A WAHLSTRÖHM EDITION 2/10'.

15in (40.5cm) high

£350-400   QU

A late 20thC Kosta Boda glass vase, designed by Goran Warff, decorated with fine spiral lines and bullicante bubbles, the base with engraved signature, limited edition 2/100.

15.25in (43.5cm) high

£750-850   FLD

A Lindshammar moulded green glass lemonade set, designed by Gunnar Ander c1960.

the jug 11.25in (28.5cm) high

£150-200   QU

A CLOSER LOOK AT A GLASS BIRD

Artist Oiva Toikka produced his first glass bird in 1972 and a range of four was released in 1981, over 400 different designs have been produced since then.

At least one new design is released each year, which has encouraged collectors to build collections. New releases are eagerly anticipated.

The decoration is complex to make, particularly the trailed and pulled patterns that imitate feathers. Many also have an iridised finish.

Although some designs were produced for years, with some still in production, those that have been discontinued have steadily risen in price as demand exceeds supply.

A Nuutajärvi Notsjö glass bird, designed by Oiva Toikka, limited edition 1867/3000, etched signatures, label attached.

£400-450

5.5in (14cm) high
SWO

A Nuutajärvi Notsjö figure, designed by Oiva Toikka, modelled as an abstract owl with applied face decoration, over a tonal blue and green lattice pattern body, with original label, engraved marks.

5.5in (14cm) high

£500-600

FLD

A scarce Nuutajärvi Notsjö blue moulded 'Light Tower' candle or tea light holder, designed by Oiva Toikka in 1964, the base inscribed 'Nuutajärvi Notsjö' and with factory label.

Similar examples were designed by Nanny Still for Riihimäen Lasi Oy in the late 1960s, but these are smaller and considerably less detailed as well as being more commonly found.

1964-73   27.5in (69.5cm) high
£300-350   QU

A scarce Nuutajärvi Notsjö 'Pantteri' vase, designed by Saara Hopea in 1954, the thickly blown ovoid colourless body with blistered violet spots, the base inscribed 'S. Hopea Nuutajärvi Notsjö 55'.

4.5in (11.5cm) high
£600-700   QU

A post-war Nuutajärvi Notsjö small 'Ariel' crystal glass bowl, designed by Kaj Franck, internally decorated with wrythen spiral air trap lines to the pale golden-amber ground, acid signature to the base.

4in (10cm) wide
£130-180   FLD

A 1970s Riihimaki Kumela Oy glass vase, designed by Pentti Sarpaneva, of stepped square section with relief-moulded panels decorated with an applied pierced-brass rim over the graduated amber to clear ground, engraved signature.

5.5in (14cm) high
£60-80   FLD

GLASS

QUICK REFERENCE - STEUBEN

- The Steuben Glass Works was founded in 1903 by Thomas G. Hawkes and Frederick Carder in Steuben County, New York. In 1904, Carder, who was manager, patented an iridescent glass which he called 'Aurene', (from 'aurum', the Latin word for gold) which resembled Tiffany's desirable 'Favrile' glass.
- The range was produced until 1933 in blue, brown, green and red, including plain and patterned pieces and pieces with combined colours. As well as the colour of the base glass, the size and shape, the level of iridescence is important to value - this example is pleasingly even across the body with very strong red and blue highlights near the neck, which are appealing features.
- In 1918, the company was acquired by The Corning Glass Works and new ranges were added which expanded colour, pattern and form. These included 'Calcite', 'Verre de Soie' and 'Cluthra'. Cameo glass was also made at this time, often using shaped decals and acid to eat through the upper layer to reveal the layer beneath in the intended design.
- In 1933, the factory was reorganised due to repeated annual financial losses. Carder was replaced and coloured glass was phased out and replaced by designs produced solely in a brilliant new '10-M' colourless glass made with a new formula developed by production manager Robert J. Leavy in 1932.

A Steuben gold 'Aurene' vase, with red highlights at the neck, platinum iridescence at the lip and pink interior highlights, signed on the underside 'Steuben Aurene 2683'.

10.5in (26.7cm) high

£600-700   JDJ

A Steuben blue 'Aurene' vase, with gold iridescence at the neck, signed on the underside 'Steuben Aurene' and numbered, some surface scratches.

6.75in (17cm) high

£550-650   JDJ

A Steuben blue 'Aurene' 'tree trunk' vase, with purple highlights, signed on the underside 'Aurene 2744'.

6in (15.2cm)high

£650-750   JDJ

A large Steuben gold 'Aurene' vase, signed on the underside 'Steuben Aurene' and numbered, with some very minor roughness to edge of foot.

12in (30.5cm) high

£1,000-1,400   JDJ

A Steuben gold 'Aurene' footed bowl, with three applied feet and subtle pink highlights, signed on the underside 'Aurene 2536'.

6in (15.2cm) diam

£400-500   JDJ

A Steuben green 'Cluthra' vase, with light to emerald green colouring, unsigned, with a large filled bubble and shell-shaped flake on the underside of the foot. **Steuben's 'Cluthra' range is not to be confused with James Couper's earlier 'Clutha' range, produced in collaboration with Dr Christopher Dresser. 'Cluthra' was devised by Frederick Carder and produced during the 1920s and is characterised by a mottled surface effect comprised of large, random air bubbles combined with large, non-uniform particles. Green and purple are typical colours. See p.239 for an example of a 'Clutha' vase.**

7.75in (19.7cm) high

£400-500   JDJ

An Art Deco Steuben vase, with a rosaline overlay over an acid-textured alabaster background, on an alabaster foot, unsigned.

The 'sharp' square stylised roses contrast well with the gentle curves of the form, which are echoed in the curving leaves and stems.

6in (15.2cm) high

£550-600   JDJ

A Steuben vase, with rosaline overlay over alabaster glass, with acid cut-back flowers and vines.

8.25in (21cm) high

£400-450   JDJ

A Steuben bowl, with green jade overlay on a textured alabaster body, acid cut back in the 'Fircone' design, unsigned.

8in (20.3cm) diam

£350-400   JDJ

A Steuben 'Silverina' amethyst bowl, unsigned.

'Silverina' was devised by Frederick Carder in the 1920s and was made by rolling the partially formed body in mica flakes and covering them and the body in a layer of coloured glass. This decorative effect was then combined with controlled air bubbles to complete the 'Silverina' look.

10in (25.4cm) diam

£250-300   JDJ

A Steuben iridescent green 'Jade' vase, with a band of platinum iridescent threading around the rim.

6in (15.2cm) high

£400-450   JDJ

A Steuben 'Oriental Poppy' scent bottle, with vertical opalescent ribbons and flower-shaped stopper, unsigned.

5in (12.7cm) high

£1,300-1,600   JDJ

A Steuben yellow 'Jade' scent bottle, with matching stopper numbered '10', unsigned, some roughness from production to the lip, stopper ground to fit.

4.5in (11.5cm) high

£500-550   JDJ

GLASS

QUICK REFERENCE - HERMAN & STUDIO GLASS

- Studio glass is the name given to glass made from the mid-1960s onwards by individual glass artists mainly working on their own or assisted by a small team working outside of a factory environment. Each piece is unique. Although functional pieces were made, much of the work is artistic in nature.
- In the early 1960s, Americans Dominick Labino (1910-87) and Harvey Littleton (1922-2013) developed a small furnace (and associated glass formula) that could be built and operated outside a factory.
- Sam Herman (b.1936) was a student of Littleton and Labino and brought the techniques to the UK in 1966. He began working at the Royal College of Art, London, where he taught a pioneering group of British studio glassmakers. He helped found The Glasshouse in 1969, a glass studio and shop in the centre of London, which supported new studio glassmakers. He also produced designs for Val St Lambert in Belgium and Rosenthal in Germany.
  - His work has increased in value over recent years as collectors have re-appraised his position within the studio glass movement. Early and large works tend to to be the most sought-after, particularly from his days at the Royal College of Art. Many pieces are signed, and some are dated. Forms can indicate a period but rarely can an exact date be pinpointed, as some recur across Herman's lengthy career.

A Sam Herman studio glass bottle, of flattened form with pulled neck with irregular rim, the colourless cased tonal orange-red body with applied blue and white enamel surface decoration, the base inscribed 'Samuel J Herman'.

15.25in (38.5cm) high

£1,000-1,500   WW

A Sam Herman tall bottle-form vase, the colourless cased tonal aubergine body with iridescent finish, powdered and chipped enamel decoration and green and red trails, the base inscribed 'Samuel J Herman'.

13.75in (35cm) high

£1,200-1,800   WW

A Sam Herman studio glass vase, of irregular form, the tonal brown, red, and orange body with red and blue applied enamel chips and powder and iridescent areas, the base inscribed 'Samuel J Herman'.

These deep brown-red-orange tones are commonly used in Herman's work.

10in (25cm) high

£1,000-1,500   WW

A Sam Herman irregular solifleur bottle, the colourless glass body surface decorated with purple striations and iridescent areas, the side inscribed 'Samuel J Herman'.

8.75in (22cm) high

£700-1,000   WW

A 1970s Sam Herman studio glass vase, of irregular form with random applied coloured straps, silver chloride and powdered enamel applications and iridescent areas, unmarked.

Iridescent patches on Herman's work are often created by using silver chloride in the glassmaking process. Sometimes it is intentionally applied to an area, sometimes it appears random when it has escaped from the moil - the area where the gob of molten glass joins the blowing iron while the piece is being formed.

11.5in (29cm) high

£400-600   FLD

A 1980s Sam Herman flaring square section studio glass vase, the opalescent and colourless glass body with yellow and aubergine internal stripes, the base inscribed 'Samuel J Herman'.

9.25in (23.5cm) high

£250-350   WW

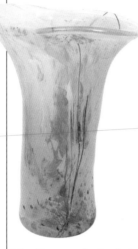

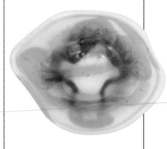

A Sam Herman studio glass vase, with slightly waisted body and flaring asymmetric rim, with applied polychome swirls and trails and enamel power and chips, the base inscribed 'Samuel J Herman 1977'.

1977   *17.5in (44.5cm) high*
£350-450   **QU**

A Sam Herman studio glass flaring cylindrical vase, with irregular top rim, surface decorated with blue, turquoise, and lustrous powdered and chipped enamel, the base inscribed 'Samuel J Herman 1981'.

1981   *10.75in (27cm) high*
£700-1,000   **WW**

A Val St Lambert vase, designed by Sam Herman, the opaque white body decorated with applied and melted iridescent trails and matched upper rim, the base inscribed 'SJH' and numbered and with original factory label.

Herman produced designs for Val St Lambert twice. The range this vase is from was known as 'Eldorado'.

8.25in (21cm) high
£700-1,000   **FLD**

A Sam Herman studio glass large irregular platter, the colourless glass streaked with applied opaque and lime-green enamels and trails, the base etched 'Samuel J Herman 1971'.

1971   *18in (46cm) wide*
£550-750   **WW**

QUICK REFERENCE - PÂTE DE VERRE

● **Pâte de verre is a technique where coloured or colourless glass is ground down into small chips, mixed with a binding paste such as gum arabic and water, then applied to the inside of a mould. When the mould interior is covered, it is inserted into a kiln. The binding material is burnt off and the chips melt and fuse together. When cool, the piece can be removed as one piece from the mould. A granular, typically translucent or opaque effect is given. The technique has been used since ancient times and reached a golden age with Daum and Art Nouveau glass designer Amalric Walter.**

A large flat charger, of irregular form, with a yellow and red swirl, cased in clear, the base inscribed 'Samuel J Herman 1976 SA1198'.

This was made at the 'Jam Factory' in Adelaide, South Australia. Herman was invited by the South Australian Government to found a glass studio in this building that housed a collective of artists. He arrived in 1974 and returned to the UK in 1979.

1976   *19.75in (50cm) wide*
£1,500-2,000   **WW**

A Tessa Clegg pâte de verre light-green and light-pink bowl, the base inscribed 'TESSA CLEGG 1986'.

1986   *6.25in (16.5cm) diam*
£300-500   **QU**

A contemporary Bob Crooks 'Spirale Incalmo' studio glass decanter, of footed ovoid form with a slender stopper and fine golden amber and ruby spiralling threads, the base with engraved signature.

15in (38cm) high
£100-150   **FLD**

GLASS

A contemporary Bob Crooks studio glass 'Spirale Incalmo' compressed conical vase, with oval section, the body comprised of a green body below a blue threaded collar rim, the base with engraved signature.

Bob Crooks (b.1968) is one of Britain's most accomplished studio glass artists. In many instances, he takes traditional Venetian techniques and updates them with modern, curving forms. This vase combines 'zanfirico' and 'incalmo' techniques.

15in (37cm) high

£100-150   FLD

A Iestyn Davies for Blowzone large hand-blown studio glass 'Virtu' bowl, cased in purple over white and pink, cut through with wrythen oval lozenge panels, the base signed and dated.

The combination of finely and perfectly applied layers in contrasting colours with cuts that reveal them is typical of Davies' exceptional work.

1999   *9.5in (24cm) diam*

£350-450   FLD

A contemporary Stephen Foster studio glass flared and footed bowl, internally decorated with a blue-threaded lattice pattern over a graduated green to colourless ground, the base with engraved signature.

14in (36cm) diam

£100-150   FLD

A Kyohei Fujita studio glass lidded box, the colourless body with blue, violet, white flecks, and gold leaf fragments on a blue ground, the base incribed 'K. Fujita', with original wooden box.

Kyohei Fujita (1921-2004) was a Japanese studio glass artist. He is best known for boxes that are often very small in size and recall traditional Japanese lacquered boxes in their mottled and gilt decoration.

3in (8cm) high

£1,800-2,200   QU

A Jack Ink studio glass lidded box, with six sides, the opaque-brown ground decorated with multi-coloured enamel chips, oxides and metal foil, signed 'Jack Ink 1575'.

10.25in (26cm) long

£600-800   QU

A Peter Layton for London Glassblowing 'Landscape' range vase, of compressed spherical form, decorated with an abstract landscape with multi-coloured chips, trails, and canes, the base with engraved signature.

10.25in (26cm) high

£400-600   FLD

An Annette Meech for Glasshouse de Sivignon glass charger, of smoky-grey glass with coloured rings to rim, signed and dated.

The Glasshouse de Sivignon was founded in France in 1999 by pioneer studio glass artists Annette Meech and Christopher Williams.

1984   *20in (52cm) diam*

£120-180   CHOR

A Whitefriars Art Deco 'Sapphire Blue' cut vase, pattern no.9032, rising from a square base and with each corner cut with a mitre-cut line, canted corner and slice-cut edge, designed by William Wilson in 1935.

Also known as Powell & Sons, Whitefriars was founded in London in the 17thC and closed in 1980. Although its Victorian glass is sought-after, the most desirable and widely collected designs are from the 20thC. At the top are designs from designer Geoffrey Baxter's 'Textured' range of the late 1960s and early 1970s. Whitefriars produced only a small number of cut designs.

1935-37 8in (20cm) high

£300-400 FLD

A Whitefriars Art Deco 'Golden Amber' 'Comets' pattern-cut vase, pattern no.8988, the body with lens-cut discs with horizontal mitre-cut lines with lens-cut discs above and stars below, designed by William Wilson in 1934.

1934-37 8in (20cm) high

£700-1,000 FLD

A 1930s Whitefriars 'Sea Green' 'Moon' bowl, pattern no.8737, decorated with frosted lens-cut discs, designed by Barnaby Powell and Albert Tubby in 1932.

10.5in (27cm) diam

£150-200 FLD

An early 1960s Whitefriars flared glass vase, cased in clear crystal over deep blue with internal white cane thread decoration, designed by Geoffrey Baxter in 1961.

8.5in (22cm) high

£150-200 FLD

A Whitefriars 'Kingfisher Blue' 'Banjo' vase, pattern no.9861, 'Textured' range, designed by Geoffrey Baxter in 1966.

One of Baxter's best-known shapes, the 'Banjo' was available in 'Kingfisher Blue' from 1969-c73. It is one of the more desirable and rarer colours, along with 'Meadow Green'.

1969-c73 *12.5in (32cm) high*

£1,000-1,500 FLD

A Whitefriars 'Meadow Green' large 'Drunken Bricklayer' vase, pattern no.9672, 'Textured' range, designed by Geoffrey Baxter in 1966.

Pay close attention to the colour tone and colourless casing when buying the smaller 8.25in (21cm) high version as those with a more vibrant mid-green, heavy colourless casing at the base and no polished concave pontil mark are likely to be fakes. For more information, see p260 of the Miller's Collectables Price Guide 2010-2011.

1970-72 *13in (33.5cm) high*

£600-800 SWO

A Whitefriars 'Willow Grey' 'Nuts & Bolts' or 'Hobnail' vase, pattern no.9668, 'Textured' range, designed by Geoffrey Baxter in 1966.

This is easily confused with the smaller 'Mobile Phone' vase, which is 6.5in (16.5cm) high and has round moulded prunts, not square indentations as here.

1967-70 *10.5in (27cm) high*

£200-300 FLD

GLASS

A Whitefriars 'Amethyst' 'Hoop' vase, pattern no.9860, 'Textured' range, designed by Geoffrey Baxter in 1966.

1967-c73   *11.5in (29cm) high*

£280-380   **FLD**

A Whitefriars 'Kingfisher Blue' 'Cucumber' vase, pattern no.9679, 'Textured' range, designed by Geoffrey Baxter in 1967. **This was produced in 'Kingfisher Blue' from 1969 until c1973.**

1969-c73   *12in (30cm) high*

£200-300   **FLD**

A late 1960s-70s Whitefriars 'Meadow Green' 'Totem' vase, pattern no.9671, 'Textured' range, designed by Geoffrey Baxter in 1966.

1967-c77   *10.25in (26cm) high*

£200-300   **FLD**

A late 1960s-70s Whitefriars 'Willow Grey' 'Sunburst' vase, pattern no.9671, 'Textured' range, designed by Geoffrey Baxter in 1966, with original label.

1967-c73   *6in (15cm) high*

£250-350   **FLD**

A Whitefriars orange 'Studio Range' vase, pattern no.S11, with silver chloride stripes, designed by Peter Wheeler in 1969.

1969-c70   *6in (15cm) high*

£250-350   **FLD**

A CLOSER LOOK AT A WHITEFRIARS VASE

'Lichen' is a very rare combination of green swirls on a pewter body.

It was only produced in 1970, making examples very rare today.

It was part of a series of 'Streaky' vases designed by Geoffrey Baxter in the early 1970s. They recall the Streaky vases in brighter colours of the 1930s designed by Marriott Powell.

This is a hitherto unrecorded shape, so may have been a trial piece for the range or an experiment.

A late 20thC Whitefriars 'Lichen' vase, the colourless cased cylindrical body with shouldered neck, decorated with green swirls over a pewter coloured ground.

1970   *5.75in (14.5cm) high*

£200-300   **FLD**

A Dartington colourless cased blue 'Extra Large Marguerite Vase' floor vase, no.FT35, modelled in low relief with a flower stem, designed by Frank Thrower in 1967.

This was released in 'Kingfisher Blue', 'Midnight Grey' and colourless glass in 1967 and withdrawn in 1970 due to its high price of 76/-. In 1993, it was re-released in this blue as well as in a dark green and colourless glass, all cased in colourless glass, at a cost of £29.95.

15.25in (39cm) high
£250-350   WW

An André Delatte small orange bowl, with black and white enamelling, signed 'A Delatte Nancy'.
c1920   *3in (8cm) high*
£250-350   M&DM

A miniature André Delatte orange vase, with polychrome enamelling, signed 'A Delatte Nancy'.
c1920   *3in (8cm) high*
£250-350   M&DM

An André Delatte cameo glass vase, footed, flaring form, mottled white and purple glaze cased in purple, decorated with daisy flowers cameo, signature 'De Latte Nancy'.

Much Delatte cameo glass was cut using acid rather than by hand on a wheel.
9.75in (24.5cm) high
£350-450   WW

A CLOSER LOOK AT A FIGURINE

Istvan Andras Komáromy (1910-75) studied medical science but found he had a talent for making medical glassware. Soon, he started making glass sculptures.

He became successful quickly and travelled all over Europe, settling in England where he taught glassmaking and produced handmade glass sculptures and tableware for the Royal Family, retailer Thomas Goode & Son, and Harrods, to name but a few.

Elegant dancers with outstretched limbs and leaping animals such as stags are typical of his work. He favoured opaque white glass, often contrasted with black.

Using a bunsen burner to heat the glass rods until they were ductile, each piece was delicately manipulated, formed, and joined by hand.

An Emile Gallé cameo glass 'Paysage' vase, overlaid and acid-etched with a lakeside view, signed in cameo with star preceding.
1904-06   *11.75in (29.5cm) high*
£600-800   BELL

A 1930s Gray-Stan large vase, designed by Elizabeth Graydon-Stannus, decorated with applied black side stripes over a mottled tonal blue and white ground, the base with engraved signature.
14.5in (37cm) high
£600-800   FLD

A 1930s-60s figurine of a leaping stag and lady, designed and made by Istvan Komáromy, mounted on a black ebonised wood base.
9in (23cm) high
£200-300   SWO

GLASS

A Mdina Glass 'Cut Ice' vase, designed by Michael Harris, the core with turquoise, brown, and yellow mottles and overlaid with thick colourless glass, one side cut with two large polished panels, the base signed 'Michael Harris, Mdina Glass, Malta'.

c1971   *8.25in (21cm) high*

£500-700   PC

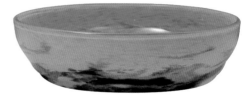

A mid-1970s-80s Mdina Glass 'Fish' vase, after a design by Michael Harris, the green mottled and striated blue core overlaid with colourless glass, the base unsigned.

8.9in (22.5cm) high

£120-180   LOC

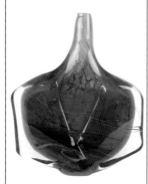

A Mdina Glass 'Fish' vase, based on a design by Michael Harris, the brown, blue, and green mottled core overlaid with thick colourless glass, the base inscribed 'Mdina Glass 1976' and with signature for Eric Dobson.

Eric Dobson founded Mdina Glass with Michael Harris in 1968. He was largely responsible for running the business and marketing, rather than design.

1976   *8.5in (21.5cm) high*

£150-200   SWO

A late 1970s-80s Mdina Glass 'Tiger' vase, the base inscribed 'Mdina'.

The green, blue, sandy, and brown mottled 'Tiger' range was introduced by Eric Dobson in the mid-1970s.

4.75in (11.8cm) high

£20-30   SWO

A Muller Frères glass bowl, the colourless body with yellow, orange, and blue mottles, the base marked 'Muller Frères, Luneville'.

11.75in (30cm) diam

£80-120   MLL

A CLOSER LOOK AT A PAUL NICOLAS VASE

Paul Nicolas was the chief designer at St Louis Glassworks, producing designs for their D'Argental range. See p.204 for examples.

Nicolas designed for St Louis on a diminishing basis during the 1930s, and until his death in 1952, Nicolas only produced unique pieces himself, such as this enamelled piece and cameo glass.

Daum was in financial trouble after WW2 and was forced to sell blanks inexpensively. It was cheaper to buy one of their blanks than commission one to be made.

As the decoration is painted all around the colourless body, there is a superb sense of perspective, making the small group of cyclamen appear as it would in nature.

A rare Paul Nicolas vase, decorated with enamelled cyclamen on a Daum blank, signed and decorated by Paul Nicolas.

c1950   *6in (15.5cm) high*

£700-£800   M&DM

An early Pantin large cameo glass vase, green on clear cameo with enamelled flowers, signed.

Pantin was established near Paris in 1851, and moved to Pantin in 1855. After WW1, it merged with DeGras & Cie.

c1889   *14in (35.5cm) high*

£1,600-£1,800   M&DM

A Quezal gold iridescent 'Jack in the Pulpit' vase, with vertically ribbed foot and stem, strong pink and purple highlights, the lightly ruffled rim shading to orange, signed in the polished pontil 'Quezal'.

9in (23cm) high

£600-800   JDJ

A CLOSER LOOK AT A GLASS VASE

The presence of the Eiffel Tower probably indicates that this was made for the 1889 International Exposition in Paris. Alexandre Gustave Eiffel's famous iron tower was opened then, acting as the gateway to the exhibition.

It is made from a derivation of Lithyalin glass - an opaque, often marbled glass that resembles stone. It was developed by Frederick Egermann in Bohemia in 1828.

A high-quality piece, it would have been a comparatively expensive souvenir, bought by wealthy visitors to the exhibition, rather than a piece made only for display at the exhibition.

Sèvres also made similar glass but the form, style of decoration, and the fact that this is cut and polished all around rather than moulded, indicates that it is by Reidel.

A Reidel art glass vase, the tapering mottled orange angular body decorated in gilt with the Eiffel Tower and a balloon to the opposite side.

9.25in (23.5cm) high

£400-600   SWO

A Scailmont mould-blown vase, designed by Henri Heemskerk, with geometric floral panels, signed in the cast 'Scailmont HH'.

Scailmont was founded in 1901 in Manage, Belgium. It specialised in non-crystal decorative pieces, and much of its production is mould-blown with a satin finish. Henri Heemskerk was their designer from 1924-51 and produced a large number of Art Deco designs.

11.5in (29cm) high

£100-150   WW

A Schneider glass vase, with a bubbly and mottled body in red and orange, on a wrought-iron stand.

26in (66cm) high

£300-500   SWO

A 1930s Schneider trumpet-form vase, the mottled translucent white body with applied red foot and matching rim.

£500-700   ECGW

A Schneider 'Le Verre Français' Charder cameo glass vase, flaring cylindrical form, amber glass cased in brown, etched 'Le Verre Français', signed in cameo 'Charder'.

Charder was a trade name used by Schneider, formed by using the first and last letters of the full name of one of the founders, Charles Schneider. It was used on a subdivision of the 'Le Verre Français' range of cameo glass. it is characterised by thick, often mottled glass with a thin, highly polished glossy top layer in a contrasting colour.

11.25in (28.5cm) high

£500-700   WW

A Schneider 'Le Verre Français' vase, attributed to Charles Schneider, stencilled 'FRANCE' to base.

10.5in (27cm) high

£40-70   MLL

A Stevens & Williams 'Silveria' glass toothpick holder, with silver foil inclusions and random green glass threading, unsigned.

'Silveria' glass is extremely rare. It uses a process developed around 1900 by John Northwood, where a bulb of colourless glass was rolled over silver leaf before being cased in another layer of colourless glass. The metallic silvery body was also sometimes decorated with powdered enamels or randomly applied trails, as here. It was initially made at Stevens & Williams in Stourbridge, England, but a couple of other similar techniques were developed by other glass companies. This tiny toothpick holder is extremely rare - a small luxurious piece using a complex and expensive technique.

2in (5cm) high

£2,000-3,000   JDJ

Mark Picks

This brightly coloured, visually appealing range was produced from 1938 onwards by Stevens & Williams, one of Britain's best-known high-quality glass companies. Compared to other ranges, it is rare as production ceased a few years later due to the onset of WW2. It can be found in a variety of clean-lined, modern shapes and looks as modern as it did over 70 years ago. Some forms have optical ribbing, which adds a further visual dimension. For some reason, it is largely ignored by collectors and tends to fetch under £70. Cut examples are rare and tend to be the most valuable, but even those can sell for less than £200-300. The cutting on this example is similar to designs by Keith Murray, who worked for the company and for Wedgwood around the same time this vase was made.

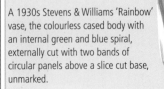

A 1930s Stevens & Williams 'Rainbow' vase, the colourless cased body with an internal green and blue spiral, externally cut with two bands of circular panels above a slice cut base, unmarked.

9.75in (25cm) high

£120-180   FLD

An early 20thC Stuart & Sons pedestal glass bowl, with wavy rim, and wrythen spiralled lines over the green ground, unmarked.

6in (15cm) high

£150-200   FLD

A Tiffany iridescent brown 'Favrile' vase, with flashes of pink and purple to the iridescence, signed on the underside 'L.C. Tiffany-Inc. Favrile 6463N'.

8in (20.5cm) high

£450-550   JDJ

A Tiffany turquoise-cased opaque-white 'Favrile' vase, with a bulbous body and gourd-shaped neck, with a very light iridescence, signed on the underside 'L.C. Tiffany-Favrile', two raised blemishes on the side.

10.75in (27.5cm) high

£600-800   JDJ

A pair of Tiffany light-green salts, with subtle gold iridescence, both unsigned, numbered 'X3041' and 'X3044'.

2.5in (6.5cm) diam

£200-300 the pair   JDJ

A pair of Val St Lambert candlesticks, with applied colourless glass trails on mottled green bases.

6in (15cm) long

£200-300   SWO

A Sabino 'Verart' clear and frosted emerald-green glass vase, decorated with a flock of flying birds over a stylised wavy sea, etched 'Verart Paris'.

8.25in (21cm) high

£200-300   WW

A pair of Hannah Moore Walton bowls, each painted with dragonflies and flowering water plants, painted monogram 'HW'.

Hannah Moore Walton (1863-1940) was an artist who set up a studio in Glasgow with her sister Helen. Both decorated ceramics and glass, often with motifs associated with water, although Hannah is best known for flowers. They were sisters of George Walton (1867-1933), the Scottish architect and designer, and can be considered part of the influential Glasgow movement.

c1900   *4.25in (11cm) diam*

£400-600   L&T

A very rare James Couper & Sons large 'Clutha' vase, designed by George Walton, of cylindrical tapering form with broad rim, the green glass body with milky trailing inclusions.

'Clutha' glass was patented in the 1890s by James Couper & Sons. It is typically greenish, but examples in turquoise, yellow, browny-green, or smokey-black are also known. Besides Walton, pioneering and notable industrial designer Christopher Dresser also produced designs for the range. See p.228 for an example of a 'Cluthra' vase.

c1900   *15.75in (40cm) high*

£1,800-2,200   L&T

A 1930s W.M.F. large 'Ikora' vase, the upper section in jade-green and the lower in ruby-red, both with applied and melted-in powdered and chipped enamel decoration.

16in (41cm) high

£200-300   FLD

An early 20thC colourless mould-blown vase, with applied green vertical columns and silver-mounted rim, hallmarks rubbed.

4.7in (12cm) high

£50-70   LOC

A set of three 19thC Newcastle dump weights, of domed form, each internally decorated with stylised flowers.

tallest 4.75in (12cm) high

£180-220   FLD

JEWELLERY

QUICK REFERENCE - JEWELLERY

- Jewellery is one of the oldest forms of decorative art and has been worn by men and women since prehistoric times. Designs are varied and are produced in a wide array of techniques and materials. Rings, brooches, necklaces, earrings, and bracelets are some of the most popular forms of jewellery.
- Brooches are sometimes thought of as less fashionable, but they were considered the height of elegance in the 19th and early 20th centuries. A tight bodice or a décolleté neckline for evening wear would not have been complete without a large brooch or a necklace. The hair was often worn in elaborate hairstyles that showcased the ears, which provided a further canvas for the display of earrings.
- At the end of the 19thC, technical progress made it possible for jewellery to be mass-produced and more affordable. However, this new type of jewellery was usually lower quality, which provoked craftsmen to react against the machine-made. Craftsmen's guilds encouraged craftsmen to design and make jewellery from start to finish.
- The Art Deco period brought about a new appreciation for the machine-made aesthetic, characterized by geometric forms.

A Charles Horner silver and enamel pendant necklace, pierced and cast Secessionist panel and drop, stamped marks, Chester.

1.5in (4cm) long

£150-200   **WW**

A Charles Horner silver and enamel pendant necklace, pierced whiplash foliate form, with enamelled silver drop stamped marks, Chester.

1912   *1.25in (3cm) wide*

£350-450   **WW**

A Charles Horner silver and enamel pendant necklace, modelled as a butterfly, enamelled in shades of blue and green, stamped marks, Chester.

1in (2.5cm) wide

£150-200   **WW**

A Charles Horner Arts and Crafts silver brooch, in the form of a Celtic knot, Chester marks, maker's mark 'CH' for Charles Horner, obscured date letter.

1.25in (3cm) wide

£200-250   **WW**

A Charles Horner silver bar brooch, in the form of a swallow in flight, entwined 'CH' mark.

These brooches were similar in style to those made by Liberty & Co., whose highly detailed jewellery items became iconic of the Art Nouveau period, but tend to be less detailed.

2in (5cm) wide

£30-40   **WHP**

A Charles Horner silver and enamel bar brooch, pierced and cast in low-relief with Art Nouveau foliate design, stamped marks, Chester.

1.2in (3cm) wide

£130-180   **WW**

QUICK REFERENCE - CHARLES HORNER

- Charles Horner was a British jewellery maker who established his business in Halifax, England. It is believed that he also offered watches, clocks, silverware, tableware and spectacles throughout his career. After he passed away in the 1890s, his sons further developed the business and produced pieces that have become very collectable today.

- Charles Horner jewellery is best-known for its Art Nouveau, Arts and Crafts or Art Deco aesthetic. Pieces were made in a relatively inexpensive, mass-produced manner, which made them more affordable to the middle classes. The company's output was extensive and included hatpins, pendants, brooches, bangles, bracelets, and rings, amongst other things. Designs are characterised by simple figural motifs and decorative interlacing inspired by Celtic Art.

- Items were largely decorated with semi-precious stones such as opal and amber, or with simple techniques like enamelling. The Charles Horner company had its own enamelling department.

- Much of Charles Horner silver was hallmarked in Chester.

A Charles Horner silver brooch, of oval form set with a turquoise glazed ceramic plaque, presumably by Ruskin, Chester.

1918   *1.5in (3.7cm) wide*

£50-60   WHP

A Charles Horner silver brooch, set with three heart-shaped purple-coloured stones in the form of a three-leaf clover, Chester.

1908   *0.8in (2cm) wide*

£150-200   WHP

A Charles Horner silver brooch, set with three heart-shaped green-coloured stones in the form of a three-leaf clover, Chester.

1904   *0.8in (2cm) wide*

£90-130   WHP

A Charles Horner silver brooch, in the form of a crescent moon, Chester.

1900   *1.2in (3cm) wide*

£35-40   WHP

A Charles Horner silver brooch, with set cabochon purple coloured quartz, Chester.

1914   *0.75in (2.2cm) diam*

£40-50   WHP

A Charles Horner silver bar brooch, of openwork design set centrally with a single purple-coloured stone, entwined 'CH' mark.

1.6in (4cm) wide

£30-40   WHP

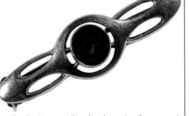

A Charles Horner silver bar brooch, of openwork design centrally set with a red-coloured stone, stamped 'CH, Sterling'.

1.5in (2.9cm) wide

£45-55   WHP

JEWELLERY

A Charles Horner 9ct yellow-gold brooch, of openwork design, set with oval opal, Chester.
1905 *1in (2.5cm) wide*
£85-95 **WHP**

A Charles Horner silver brooch, of openwork design set centrally with a heart-shaped amber-coloured stone, flanked by two further stones, Chester.
1907 *1.8in (3.5cm) wide*
£75-85 **WHP**

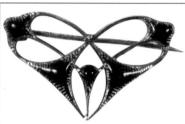

A Charles Horner silver brooch, of openwork design decorated in green and peacock blue enamel, Chester.
1903 *1.3in (3.2cm) wide*
£75-85 **WHP**

A Charles Horner silver brooch, of openwork design, set with three thistle-cut purple coloured stones, Chester.
1911 *1in (2.4cm) diam*
£30-35 **WHP**

A Charles Horner silver brooch, of openwork design, set with thistle-cut amber coloured stone, Chester.
1911 *1in (2.6cm) wide*
£45-50 **WHP**

A silver and enamel decorated brooch, of circular form centrally depicting a thistle, stamped 'CH, Sterling'.
0.9in (2cm) diam
£35-40 **WHP**

A silver brooch, of openwork design set, thistle-shaped purple coloured stone, stamped 'CH, Sterling'.
1in (2.4cm) wide
£60-70 **WHP**

A Charles Horner silver brooch, of openwork design, set amber coloured stone and pale-blue enamel, Chester.

1908   *1.2in (3.1cm) wide*
£20-30   **WHP**

A Charles Horner silver pendant, of openwork design and centrally decorated in coloured enamels with a pink rose, Chester.

1914   *0.7in (1.8cm) wide*
£50-60   **WHP**

A Charles Horner silver novelty pin, depicting 'Felix the Cat' and decorated in black enamel, entwined 'CH' mark.

Felix the Cat is believed to have been conceived by New Jersey cartoonist Otto Messmer in the 1920s. So successful were Felix cartoons that they attracted audiences as large as the ones at silent movies. One might wonder what the connection between Charles Horner and Felix was, but due to his immense popularity, he was featured on a variety of merchandise - this unusual novelty pin being only one example of the Felix the Cat franchising efforts.

0.9in (2.2cm) long
£25-30   **WHP**

A Charles Horner silver and enamel decorated brooch, in the form of a butterfly, stamped 'CH, Sterling'.

1in (2.5cm) wide
£35-40   **WHP**

A pair of Charles Horner silver cufflinks, decorated in blue enamel, Chester.

1930   *0.5in (1.2cm) wide*
£70-80   **WHP**

A pair of Charles Horner silver cufflinks, decorated with a geometric pattern in pale-blue and silver enamel, entwined 'CH' mark.

0.7in (1.7cm) wide
£140-180   **WHP**

A pair of Charles Horner florally engraved silver cufflinks, entwined 'CH' mark.

0.5in (l.2cm) wide
£40-50   **WHP**

A Georg Jensen silver brooch, model no.251, pierced rectangular form cast with twin leaping dolphins, stamped marks.

1.5in (4cm) wide

£250-300   WW

A Georg Jensen sterling silver brooch, designed by Arno Malinowski , design no.256.

1930s   *(4.5cm) long*

£200-300   SF

A Georg Jensen sterling silver brooch, design no.187.

c1915   *(4cm) wide*

£300-400   SF

QUICK REFERENCE - GEORG JENSEN

- Georg Jensen was born in 1866 in Raadvad, Denmark, and was a son of a knife grinder. At the age of 14, he apprenticed at a goldsmith's in Copenhagen. Later on, he would remain in the Danish capital to set up his silversmith workshop. Thanks to a grant, Jensen had the opportunity to tour Europe at the age of 26. The Arts and Crafts and Art Nouveau movements that he witnessed influenced his work, which was highly praised by critics. His pieces featured detailed and sculptural decoration of fruit and flowers and tendril forms for feet, handles, and finials. The Georg Jensen company employed very talented designers such as Johan Rohde (1865-1935), Harald Nielsen (1892-1977), Henning Koppel (1918-81), and Vivianna Torun Bülow-Hübe (1927-2004). Many designs by Johan Rohde, for example, are still manufactured by the company today. So successful was Georg Jensen during his time that his distinctive style is used as a benchmark reference.

A Georg Jensen silver brooch, designed as two birds with a spray of corn at the centre, detailed 'Georg Jensen, Sterling Denmark 250', import mark London.

1960

£300-400   BELL

A Georg Jensen silver 'Moonlight Grapes' brooch, designed by Harald Nielsen, no.217A, stamped with a maker's mark used from 1945 onwards.

£250-300   SWO

A Georg Jensen sterling silver hollow brooch, no.189, a flower head with a cabochon lapis lazuli centre, stamped with a maker's mark used from 1945 onwards, with import hallmark for London 1899, signed, with Georg Jensen outer box.

£300-400   SWO

A Georg Jensen silver moonstone set brooch, no.159, of circular open foliate form, with curling tendrils to the centre, marked 'Denmark 9259', stamped with a maker's mark used from 1945 onwards.

£350-450   SWO

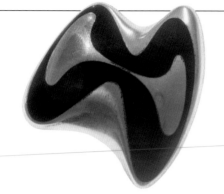

A Georg Jensen silver and green enameled brooch, designed by Henning Koppel, in an abstract curved design, detailed 'Georg Jensen 925 S Denmark 315', import mark London 1969, later engraved 'R.E.P 1982', with a Georg Jensen case.

£500-600   BELL

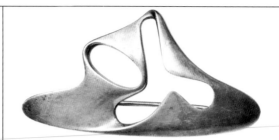

A Georg Jensen silver 'Amoeba' brooch, designed by Henning Koppel, model no.325, manufacturer's mark, numbered and stamped 'Sterling, Denmark'.

Henning's first piece created for Georg Jensen was the Amoeba bracelet with each link its own shape and design, both abstract yet incredibly organic, defining his style. He later created this brooch.

2.25in (5.5cm) wide

£180-220   MLL

Judith Picks

Henning Koppel (1918-81) was educated as a painter and a sculptor but his international fame came as a silversmith. He was employed by Georg Jensen in 1946, and his artistic expression is shown both in large pitchers, sculptural bowls, jewellery, and cutlery. He considered himself an anti-functionalist. His mission in life was to make everyday products beautiful as well as practical. His early designs were for jewellery and the forms were flowing and organic looking, closer to the work of other artists of his time like Aalto, Calder, and Dali than anything ever produced at the Georg Jensen silversmithy. He was a leader in the Scandinavian modern design movement. At the first glance, Koppel's silver might look uncomplicated and simple, but it demanded the highest skilled craftsmen to execute it. Henning Koppel was totally uninterested in the demands of mass production, he focused on the art of pure beauty. To him functionalism was not possible to applicate on silver as a material. He used an organic expression with soft, fluid lines. Some of my favourite pieces of jewellery were designed by Henning Koppel!

A Georg Jensen silver brooch, designed by Henning Koppel, model no.316, abstract form stamped marks.

3in (7cm) wide

£300-350   WW

An abstract silver pin, with blue enamel decoration, back stamped 'HK', designed by Henning Koppel for Georg Jensen.

c1945   *2in (5cm) wide*

£700-800   PC

A silver bracelet, designed by Flemming Eskildsen for Georg Jensen, design no.171, formed of seven plain oval concave panels, one concealing the box clasp, stamped marks, import marked for London 1977, light scratches, clear marks.

7in (18cm) long

£180-220   DN

A Georg Jensen silver 'Puzzle' bangle, of modernist design.

£450-550   TEN

JEWELLERY

A Van Cleef & Arpels gold terrier brooch, with a sapphire-set collar and with a sapphire-set eye, marked 'VCA 1V183 1'.

0.71oz

£4,000-5,000   **BELL**

A Danish silver 'Skønvirke' amber brooch, designed by Holger Fischer, set with four graduated amber cabochons, with an amber pendant drop, marked '830S', stamped with maker's mark.

c1950

£80-120   **SWO**

A two-colour gold, sapphire, and ruby wheatsheaf spray brooch, a spray of wheat in yellow and rose gold, with five scattered circular mixed-cut rubies and sapphires, marked '9ct'.

c1950

£100-150   **SWO**

A silver-gilt Britannia lion head brooch, designed by David Thomas, hallmarked London, revolving clasp broken.

1986

£80-120   **SWO**

A Murrle Bennett silver and enamel brooch, with a lion rampant in blue, stamped marks.

1.25in (3cm) wide

£150-200   **WW**

A French enamelled butterfly brooch, set with rose-cut and old-cut diamonds, in white collet settings, one diamond deficient.

c1900   *1.25in (3cm)*

£1,300-1,800   **LAW**

A platinum, diamond, and onyx insect brooch, attributed to Chaumet, the bug with head and body inset with round brilliant-cut diamonds, and the wings with onyx.

1.5in (3.6cm)

£900-1,100   **LAW**

An enamel and silver brooch, designed by Bernard Instone, stamped with a maker's mark and 'Silver'.
1.25in (3cm) diam
£160-200   MLL

A Continental yellow metal, split-pearl and quartz-mounted swallow brooch, stamped '15'.
£120-150   LOC

QUICK REFERENCE - THE CARTIER PANTHER

● Cartier is without a doubt one of the most prestigious jewel companies in the world. It was founded in 1847 by Louis-François Cartier and was established in Paris. It was his grandson, Louis Cartier, who developed the brand and made it what it is today. Branches can be found in the world's capitals New York, London, and high fashion and luxury jewellery's spiritual birthplace, Paris. In 1914, the Cartier 'panthère' made its debut. Louis Cartier commissioned a French artist called George Barbier to draw a lady with jewels and a panther. What exactly led to this idea is unknown, but the artwork was used in advertising and the feline became the brand's iconic mascot. The first Cartier product to feature the panther was a wristwatch with a spotted design that was inspired by its fur. Apart from being a beautiful animal, it reflects people's fascination with the exotic. Since then, it has been incorporated into numerous other pieces such as pendants and brooches. In 2014, Cartier celebrated the 100th anniversary of the panther's introduction with a special 56-piece 'Panthère de Cartier' collection.

A German Jugendstil 900-standard silver and enamel brooch, marked 'Dépose 900', with unidentified 'GS' maker's mark.
£300-400   SWO

A Skønvirke Danish silver brooch, with an oval amber cabochon set to the centre, with a repoussé surround of scrolls, marked '826S'.
c1910
£150-200   SWO

A David-Andersen sterling silver enamelled brooch/pendant, designed by Uni David-Andersen, with a checked/tartan pattern of guilloché enamel, a concealed wire bale and brooch pin, signed 1925-present, Norway-sterling, with import hallmark for London.
1964
£180-220   SWO

A Cartier 'Panthère' brooch, modelled as a prowling panther with emerald eyes and a cabochon onyx nose.
2in (5.5cm) long
£2,500-3,000   LAW

A Cartier 'Panthère' brooch, the gold head set with an emerald eye.
1.5in (3.5cm) long
£2,200-2,800   LAW

A Cartier 'Panthère' pendant on chain, the hanging panther in a doubled-over position, with marquise diamond-cut eyes, on a pendant bale set with round brilliant-cut diamonds, hung on an anchor-link two-colour chain.
chain 18in (46cm) long
£4,000-5,000   LAW

JEWELLERY

An Arts and Crafts silver, enamel, and blister pearl pendant, on a baby belcher chain.

£300-400   SWO

A German Art Deco necklace, attributed to Jakob Bengel, a fringe centrepiece of green Galalith plaques between chrome plated beads, curved chrome plated decorated tube to a chrome plated back chain.

c1930

£200-250   SWO

A CLOSER LOOK AT MURRLE BENNETT

This pendant by the collectable jewellery firm Murrle Bennett has fashionable silver and enamel Arts and Crafts decoration.

It is further enhanced by being designed by Archibald Knox, who famously worked for Liberty & Co.

The pierced triangular frame has Celtic knot decoration, which was much copied by other firms.

It is fully marked with the stamped 'MB' roundel and '850'.

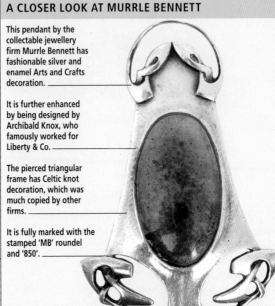

A Murrle Bennett silver and enamel pendant.

1.5in (4cm) high

£800-900   WW

A German Art Deco necklace, attributed to Jakob Bengel, a centrepiece composed of a mottled brown Galalith bead between chrome-plated beads and tapering brown Galalith sections, to chrome-plated tube and curved bars to the back.

c1930

£100-150   SWO

An Edwardian gold garnet pendant, by Murrle Bennett & Co., marked '9ct' and with maker's monogram.

£50-60   SWO

A moonstone and turquoise pendant, in 15ct. gold.

3in (7.5cm) high

£650-750   LAW

A peridot and diamond pendant.

1.25in (3cm) diam

£1,200-1,500   LAW

An Art Nouveau pendant on chain, designed by Archibald Knox, enamelled in blue and green, inset with split pearls and faceted lime-green stones, to a fine trace link chain.

chain 16.5in (41.5cm) long

£5,500-6,000   LAW

A pair of 9ct-gold oval cufflinks, by Spencer & Co., Birmingham, one side with four coats-of-arms, inscribed 'Motor Cycle Club' and 'Founded 1901', one of the plain sides engraved 'London-Land's End 1928 W A Le Brun. Solo.', with chain links, in a case.

From its inception in 1901, the Motor Cycling Club (MCC) staged a series of social runs and race meetings and members regularly participated in the national 1000 miles trial. Soon though it was running three long-distance reliability trials of its own: the London/ Edinburgh; the London/Exeter and the London/Lands End, all of which are still held today with record entries from competitors on two, three and four wheels. This may explain why the club has survived when other once great clubs have fallen by the wayside.

c1927   *0.6oz*

£140-180   **DN**

A pair of 15ct-gold turquoise and gold cufflinks, each set with an oval turquoise cabochon.

£200-250   **LAW**

A pair of ruby and gold cufflinks, each gold link of swirl form and set with an oval cabochon ruby.

£1,400-1,800   **LAW**

A pair of gold, malachite, and diamond cufflinks, each malachite disc is centred with a fox mask set with rose-cut diamonds and ruby eyes.

£500-600   **LAW**

A pair of 19thC gold reverse-carved crystal intaglio hunting cufflinks, designed by Boucheron, each depicting a huntsman jumping a fence, signed to the reverse, with click fittings, French marks, with Boucheron case.

£750-850   **LAW**

QUICK REFERENCE - CUFFLINKS

- What do the Duke of Windsor and Cary Grant have in common? They both loved wearing cufflinks. Louis XIV, however, did not. He preferred to use coloured string to fasten his sleeves.
- Researchers found that the history of cufflinks is closely connected to that of the shirt. The idea of the cufflink started in 18thC Europe, when men often used pairs of identical buttons, joined by chains, to fasten their sleeves.
- The modern shirt-sleeve cuff, which evolved in the mid-19thC, was stiffened with starch. This made it more difficult to use a simple button mechanism. Cufflinks thus came in handy.
- During the 19thC, cufflinks became more commonplace. This was largely due to advances in technology, which allowed them to be mass-produced.
- Even women wore them. The Gibson Girls, suffragettes, and Marlene Dietrich were fans.
- Cufflinks are both functional and decorative objects. Over the centuries, they have been treated as miniature canvases.

A pair of 9ct-gold cufflinks, sunburst design, initialled, hallmarked.

0.18oz

£50-60   **LOC**

A pair of gold, enamel, pearl, and diamond cufflinks, designed by The Goldsmiths and Silversmiths Co. Ltd, each oval link set with rose-cut diamonds and graduated pearls, with blue enamel decoration, in fitted case.

£750-850   **LAW**

A pair of gold, coral, and black onyx stud earrings, each set with a circular coral cabochon within a surround of black onyx.

£200-300   **LAW**

A pair of 18ct-gold, ruby, and diamond target stud earrings, each set with circular-cut diamonds and calibre-cut rubies.

£800-900   **LAW**

JEWELLERY

An Arts and Crafts silver bracelet, with enamel decoration, by James Fenton, Birmingham hallmarks.

1908   *7in (18cm)*
£300-400   **WW**

A sterling silver enamel 'ORCADES' bracelet, by Mappin and Webb, with plaques decorated with mint-green enamel letters to spell out the name 'ORCADES', a matching plaque link charm with blue and white enamel decorated flag of the 'Orient Line', Birmingham. 1953

'ORCADES' was a ship of the 'Orient Line' that was built at Barrow by Vickers Armstrong. It was launched on 14 December 1948. It was the first purpose-built vessel for migrant trade and sailed the Australia-New Zealand route. It took part in the June 1953 'Coronation Review' off Spithead and provided accommodation for two weeks during the 1956 Melbourne Olympics.

A 15ct-gold nautical pennant bracelet, formed with seven hexagonal gold links, each centred with a pennant with enamel decoration, within a blue enamel border.

7.25in (18.5cm) long
£450-550   **LAW**

£80-120   **SWO**

An enamel wide 'Houses' bangle, designed by Frey Wille, with polychrome enamel houses in two rows.

£180-220   **SWO**

An 18ct-gold pin, with a fox mask and inset stones, in a fitted leather case.

2.5in (6cm) long
£200-250   **LAW**

A Victorian diamond stick pin, set with rose-cut diamonds, in gold.

£200-250   **LAW**

A fox pin, the fox mask set with cabochon ruby eyes, and old-cut and rose-cut diamonds pavé set throughout.

This was purchased from Leighton, of Burlington Arcade on 10th January 1962, by Guy Wayte, infamous owner of Tatler, and eccentric gentleman. It is accompanied by the purchase receipt.

2.5in (5.8cm) long
£450-500   **LAW**

A diamond-set bombé form modernist dress ring, graduated old European cut, old Swiss cut, cushion-shaped old Swiss-cut and brilliant-cut diamonds, marked '18CT'.

c1960   *size R*
£180-220   **SWO**

A Marcel Boucher brooch, gold-plated rhinestones and faux sapphires, signed 'Boucher'.
1950s 2in (5cm) long
£60-100 PC

A 1960s Alice Caviness raspberry leaf pin, of textured gold tone metal with pavé-set faux ruby cabochons.
2.75in (7cm) long
£50-70 PC

A pair of vintage gold-plated Chanel simulated pearl and twisted rope clip-on earrings.
£160-200 SWO

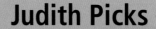

A silver and resin brooch, by Nichola Fletcher, of parachute form, in shades of orange and green.

This was included in an exhibition at the Peter Potter Gallery, Haddington, in 1977.
1977 1.5in (4cm) long
£60-80 TEN

A Maison Gripoix flower pin, with green poured glass petals and leaves set in gilt wire, and with a ruby glass centre.
c2001 2.75in (7cm) diam
£400-500 PC

Judith Picks

I have owned this wonderful Joseff of Hollywood pin for 15 years. My husband John Wainwright bought it from friends at Cristobal who have a wonderful shop in Church Street Marylebone, London. Eugène Joseff was born in 1905 in Chicago. He moved to California in the late 1920s to exploit his great passion – jewellery design – in one of the few booming industries of the period: Hollywood. He soon met with incredible success, both as a designer and a supplier of jewellery to the major film studios. He specifically developed a coppery-gold coloured matte finish (known as Russian gold), which minimized the cameraman's problem of over-reflectivity when filming gold jewellery under powerful studio lights. He leased his pieces to the studios and was able to accumulate an archive of nearly 3 million pieces available for re-hire. From 1937, he then developed a retail line of jewellery, sold via some 500 'exclusive' stores throughout the United States and abroad. It is these pieces that are now so much in demand.

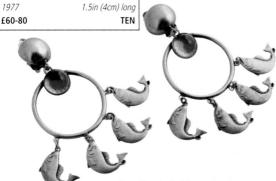

A pair of Joseff multiple fish pendant-hoop earrings, Russian-gold-plated with topaz crystal cabochons.
1940s 3.5in (9cm) long
£120-150 Cris

A 1940s rare Joseff 'Moon God with Ruff' pin, Russian-gold with clear rhinestone eye tremblers.

Moon God pins without a ruff are generally worth around a quarter of the price.
2.5in (6.25cm) diam
£800-1,000 PC

JEWELLERY

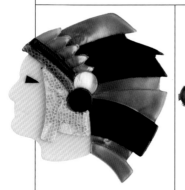

A 1950s Kramer New York bracelet, comprising four strands of twisted gilt-mesh and beads, marked 'KRAMER OF NEW YORK'.

6.75in (17.5cm) long

£40-50   **PC**

A 1950s pair of earrings, attributed to Rousselet, comprised of multicoloured glass drops set on gold-tone chains.

2.75in (7cm) long

£50-80   **PC**

A Schiaparelli pin and earrings, with textured amethyst cabochons and crystal.

£200-250   **PC**

An early 1980s Lea Stein 'Indian Chief' pin, made of blue, black, grey; and white laminated Rhodoid with lace inclusions.

2in (5.5cm) high

£80-95   **PC**

A 1950s Trifari 'Maltese Cross' pin, gold-plated with blue cabochons, textured blue enamel and clear rhinestones.

2.5in (6.25cm) diam

£100-140   **PC**

A late 19thC Continental yellow metal, cabochon stone, and split-pearl-mounted necklace, nine flower heads suspended from a rope twist chain, in a fitted case.

£850-950   **LOC**

An early 20thC paste set pendant, centred on an open-backed oval emerald-coloured stone, facet-cut, within a border of twelve old cut clear stones and surrounded by four stone-set closed-backed fleur-de-lis.

£110-140   **FLD**

A pair of unsigned 1960s 'Pop Art' large papier mâché hoop earrings, painted in simulation of traditional stone, bone or leather Native- or Mesoamerican earrings.

3.75in (9.5cm) long

£35-45   **PC**

QUICK REFERENCE - ART DECO LAMPS

● Lamps incorporating elegantly posed naked or barely clothed athletic ladies were typical of the Art Deco period. Their poses were largely based on earlier Modernist ideals about health, exercise, and athletics. Some were however based on dance movements, or the expensive highly fashionable bronze and ivory figurines designed by sculptors such as Ferdinand Preiss. The use of figural forms for lamps (or candlesticks) was not a new idea, from Blackamoors of the Georgian period to all manner of forms from warriors to shepherds during the Victorian period. Most Victorian and later examples are made from spelter alloy, which was less expensive than bronze, lighter in weight, but more brittle. Always look for good proportions and quality in terms of pose, finishing and details such as the face and hands. Avoid examples that are split, broken, or dented, as the alloy can be very hard to repair and doing so may cause more damage.

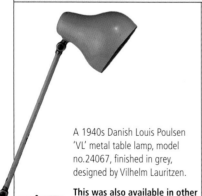

An Art Deco patinated spelter table lamp, of a lady holding a globe shade, on a marble plinth.

25.6in (65cm) high

£300-350   SWO

A patinated-metal figural lamp base, modelled as a topless woman balancing on a flaring, square plinth, holding up a green-striped glass ball shade, stamped 'REGISTERED'.

18.5in (47cm) high

£150-200   WW

An Art Deco spelter lamp, the Alsatian seated next to a pink-coloured globe shade.

10in (25cm) wide

£100-150   SWO

A 1930s table globe lamp, by Joseph Lucas Ltd, with a glass sphere with a printed map of the world, on a chrome-plated ring and domed black base, some damage.

Joseph Lucas is best known for manufacturing vehicle lighting such as car headlights, bicycle lamps, and lenses for other lighting. Lamps incorporating globes showing the Earth were popular from the 1930s onwards, particularly in the US. Just like the many table globes produced at the time by companies such as Philips, many were intended for children, igniting their imaginations about travel and foreign cultures. Higher quality examples were desirable decorative items, with some being connected to events such as world's fairs. They continued to be popular into the 1950s & 60s as sci-fi movies gained popularity and as the 'space race' gathered momentum.

14.6in (37cm) high

£150-200   FLD

A 1940s Danish Louis Poulsen 'VL' metal table lamp, model no.24067, finished in grey, designed by Vilhelm Lauritzen.

This was also available in other colours, including white.

18.7in (47.5cm) high

£400-600   QU

A 1950s Swedish aluminium, brass, and red-finished metal table or wall lamp, with conical shade.

This lamp can also be hung on a wall and positioned to light a room.

£250-350   QU

A 1960s Swedish Luxus small table lamp, the teak body varnished and painted black, designed by Uno Kristiansson and Östen Kristiansson in 1958, with a rose pink fabric shade.

12.6in (32cm) high

£200-300   QU

A 1960s Spanish Lupela red and silver finished desk lamp.

The disc-like shade, the curving, and the straight arm that connects seamlessly to the base are features that were originated and used by larger Spanish competitor Fase.

15.7in (40cm) high

£100-150   ECGW

A 1960s Danish Fog & Mörup cast-iron and copper-covered metal 'Studio' table lamp, designed by Jo Hammerborg, the base marked 'OMI Typ 299'.

22in (56cm) high

£800-1,200   QU

A late 1960s-70s Danish Louise Poulsen 'PH5' table lamp, designed by Poul Henningsen in 1964, brass and painted sheet metal, the base with maker's label.

£800-1,200   QU

One of a pair of 1960s Danish Louis Poulsen 'PH5' hanging light pendants, designed by Poul Henningsen in 1958.

15.75in (40cm) diam

£300-400 pair   SWO

A CLOSER LOOK AT A TABLE LAMP

Robert Welch (1929-2000) was a leading British industrial designer best-known for his designs for stainless steel tableware such as cutlery and tea sets.

In 1966 he was approached by architectural lighting company Lumitron to design a light. The result was inspired by Scandinavian examples and is quintessentially mid-century modern in form and its use of clean lines, acrylic, and silvery metal.

The range also included a spherical form ceiling lamp and a taller floor lamp.

Many examples were retailed through Habitat (founded by design leader Sir Terence Conran in 1964). The lamp was used for many years on the set of hit comedy show Morecambe & Wise.

A perspex and polished-aluminium Lumitron table lamp, designed by Robert Welch in 1966.

21.25in (54cm) high

£200-300   WW

A late 1960s Italian Ferrari 'Old Timer' plastic lamp, designed by Design Verona, modelled as a toucan with big red beak, cast marks.

Produced in a variety of colour combinations, this amusing lamp almost fits into the Postmodern design movement. The large beak is the shade. If you're lucky enough to find one of these hard-to-find lamps, be aware of condition as the plastic is brittle and easily cracked and chipped.

9in (23cm) high

£140-180   WW

QUICK REFERENCE - LOUIS VUITTON

● The name Louis Vuitton has become synonymous with luxury luggage. The company was founded in Paris in 1854 and became enormously successful very quickly when it introduced its waterproof, canvas-covered, and airtight grey 'Trianon' trunk in 1858. The trunk's innovation was a flat top, which allowed it to stack when being transported. Previously, trunks had domed tops, to allow water to run off, but Vuitton's trunk was waterproof. In 1876, the company began to use a beige and brown striped fabric to differentiate their products from their many imitators. Their chequerboard 'Damier' fabric was introduced in 1888. The internationally recognised 'Monogram Canvas' was launched in 1896. The design, that includes quatrefoils and flowers and the LV monogram, was based on the Victorian trend for Japanese and Chinese designs. The company diversified early on and has since produced a wide range of luggage, including special commissions. Today, these commissions (especially if for notable clients or for a special purpose), along with its trunks are generally the most desirable and valuable items. Trunks are often used decoratively, stacked in a corner of a room or used as a coffee table. They vary in size and come in large, almost walk-in type wardrobe trunks. Although this very early and rare Vuitton trunk has a domed top, it may date from after 1858 as fashions and demands didn't change overnight. Domed trunks continued to be made by many makers for decades. Even though it is an early and rare example of a Vuitton trunk, it isn't as valuable as one may think as it doesn't have the all-important cachet and snob factor: the Vuitton monogram or 'Damier' fabric. Condition is important, especially for late 20thC luggage. The addition of travel labels to romantic destinations can enhance desirability.

A Louis Vuitton 'Steamer' leather and wood trunk, original Louis Vuitton label no.736327, with brass locks and an internal lift-out tray, stamped on each end with the initials 'St G' for the St George family, the brass lock stamped 'Louis Vuitton, New Bond St London, Paris, 07551', the brass clasps stamped 'LV'.

This trunk was commissioned by the St George family, and has remained in the family since the 1930s.

c1930s   *23in (58cm) high*

£3,000-4,000   **LAW**

A vintage Louis Vuitton cabin trunk, label no.189013, in tan leather, with quilted lid, lacking tray.

Leather-covered trunks by Vuitton are uncommon.

£2,400-2,800   **ECGW**

A vintage Louis Vuitton cabin trunk, label no.730270, with monogrammed decoration, silk-lined interior, with tray.

£3,000-4,000   **ECGW**

A Louis Vuitton dome-top travelling trunk, with metal bracings, the interior with a blue printed design, no tray, labelled 'Louis Vuitton, 4 rue Neuve des Capucines, Paris'.

43.75in (111cm) wide

£500-600   **SWO**

A vintage Louis Vuitton suitcase, label no.812122, with monogrammed decoration, silk interior, lacking tray.

£800-900   **ECGW**

A Louis Vuitton monogram canvas hard-sided suitcase, leather trim, attached leather travel tag, and brass hardware, stamped 'Louis Vuitton'.

32in (81.5cm) long

£1,000-1,200   **LHA**

LUGGAGE

A Louis Vuitton hard-sided suitcase, serial no.957895, of monogrammed canvas, brass-mounted corners, locks and latches, interior-webbed straps, with two keys and luggage label, 'LV' stamped trim reinforced with rivets.

28in (71cm)

£1,000-1,200   SWO

An early 20thC Louis Vuitton gentleman's pigskin dressing case, fully fitted leather and silk-lined interior, with glass and silver bottles and many other accessories, the brass case clasps stamped 'L.V', the lock stamped 'LOUIS VUITTON, PARIS and LONDON', the interior also stamped 'LOUIS VUITTON, no. 561833'.

Each piece of Louis Vuitton luggage usually features a combination of impressed numbers and letters. Vuitton hold records for all these numbers and can give information such as when the piece was made and who it may have been made for, if applicable.

20in (51cm) wide

£1,300-1,600   BLO

A Louis Vuitton vanity case, serial no.962954, of monogrammed canvas with soft leather handle, brass-mounted corners, locks and latches, interior with tan leather straps, two keys and luggage label, 'LV' stamped trim reinforced with rivets, lift-out tray deficient.

15.75in (40cm)

£1,000-1,200   SWO

An early 20thC Asprey crocodile-skin suitcase, with brass mounts and locks, the interior stamped in gilt 'ASPREY LONDON'.

23.5in (60cm) long

£400-500   WW

An early 20thC Army & Navy crocodile-skin suitcase, the brown silk-lined interior previously fitted, with gilt-metal locks, the lid with gilt initals 'M.L.G.', stamped '81 ARMY & NAVY C.S.L. MAKER LONDON'.

20.75in (53cm) long

£400-500   WW

A leather suitcase, part fitted with a vanity compartment with ivory-backed brushes, and boxes, the lid with initials 'R.C.S.'., with a smaller vanity case, with glass bottles, brushes, and various utensils.

the larger 24in (61cm) long

£200-300   WW

A Holland & Holland leather and brass-mounted cartridge case, the lid with initial 'J' with the remains of a Cunard White Star label, the interior with five divisions and a printed trade label 'BY SPECIAL APPOINTMENT TO H.M. THE KING, HOLLAND & HOLLAND, Gun & Rifle Manufacturers, 98, NEW BOND STREET, LONDON. ESTABLISHED 1835'.

Holland & Holland are a prestigious country pursuits store in the centre of London. This is a very high quality case and is still useable and very desirable.

15.75in (40cm) long

£400-500   WW

A Hammond Bros. leather and brass-mounted cartridge case, the lid with a brass plaque with intials 'H.B.', the interior with seven divisions and with a paper trade label 'HAMMOND BROS. Gun Manufacturers 40 JEWRY STREET, WINCHESTER, ESTABLISHED 1928', and a card for 'Capt. H. N. Berry'.

21.5in (54.5cm) long

£200-300 WW

A Wilkinson & Son leather and brass-mounted case for a pair of shot guns, the lid inscribed 'Douglas Pennant', the baize-lined interior with a lift-out tray and with a paper trade label inscribed 'WILKINSON AND SON, Gun & Sword Manufacturers TO HER MAJESTY, The War Department and the Council of India, NO. 27 PALL MALL, LONDON.'.

34in (86cm) long

£200-300 WW

An Asprey & Co travelling case, with three silver-topped glass bottles, two jars, two brushes and comb, each engine-turned and engraved with a crest, three leather boxes and easel mirror, a steel button, scissors and nail file, the other side with straps for clothing, the case stamped and with protective outer case stamped 'R.S.G.C-S', with the coronation hallmark.

1953 *13.5in (34.5cm) long*

£500-600 BLO

An Art Deco dressing case, with silver and pale-green enamelled bottles and brushes.

£80-120 ECGW

An early 20thC brown leather dressing case, with chrome and glass bottles, brushes, mirror, and further fittings, in its original cloth cover, initialled 'J.R.W.'.

23.25in (59cm) high

£140-180 SWO

A suite of 1960s-70s Samsonite 'Fashionaire' white vinyl luggage, with an orange fabric lining, with three graduated suitcases, vanity case and holdall.

the largest suitcase 25.5in (65cm) wide

£200-250 TEN

MECHANICAL BANKS

An American painted cast-iron 'Jolly' mechanical money box.

c1900   8in (20.5cm) high
£80-120   **WW**

A painted cast-iron 'Trick Dog' mechanical money box, by Shepard Hardware Co., titled, with key, the underside marked 'PAT. JULY 31 1888'.

c1900   8.5in (22cm) wide
£450-500   **WW**

A cast-iron 'Bad Accident' mechanical bank, manufactured by J. & E. Stevens Co.

                              10in (25.5cm) long
£400-450   **POOK**

A cast-iron mule entering barn mechanical bank, manufactured by J. & E. Stevens Co.

£250-350   **POOK**

A cast-iron 'I Always Did 'Spise A Mule' mechanical bank, manufactured by J. & E. Stevens Co.

£180-220   **POOK**

A cast-iron 'Independence Hall Tower Centennial' mechanical bank, manufactured by Enterprise.

£200-300   **POOK**

A cast-iron 'Frog on Lattice' mechanical bank, manufactured by J. & E. Stevens Co.

£350-400   **POOK**

MECHANICAL MUSIC

A Symphonion musical box, playing 10 1/8-inch discs, with mechanical lever operation in figured walnut case, together with fifteen metal discs.

13in (33cm) wide

£500-700   **FLD**

An Edison GEM Phonograph, serial no.326884D, playing four and two minute repeat, with a model K reproducer, in an oak case with painted tin trumpet horn, together with assorted cylinders.

£250-350   **FLD**

A Regal horn gramophone, with an oak case, Regal soundbox and tin horn, in working order with winding handle.

c1910   *8.75in (22cm) high*

£300-400   **LAW**

A 1920s German Nier & Ehmer Metallwarenfabrik 'Nirona' portable gramophone, finished in maroon, together with a tin case.

£150-200   **FLD**

A Wurlitzer 1015 jukebox 'One More Time Vinyl', one hundred selection playing 45rpm records, push-button operation within fluorescent arch bubble and wooden case mounted with chrome fittings.

Introduced in November 1945, this is one of the most well-known, visually appealing, and globally successful jukeboxes of all time. Made during the 'golden age' of the jukebox after WW2, over 56,000 units were sold in less than 2 years. Designed by Paul Fuller and sometimes known as the '1015-Bubble', it has featured in many films and TV series, including 'Cheers', 'Friends', and 'Back To The Future'.

1945-47   *59.75in (152cm) high*

£3,500-4,500   **FLD**

A 1920s Swiss Thorens 'Excelda' portable gramophone, together with original carrying case.

10.75in (27cm) wide

£80-120   **FLD**

A mid-1960s Garrard Pye Type 1005 'Stereophonic Projector System' record player, in a fitted case with the original Decca LP, together with a mahogany table with sabre legs.

This curved record player, with its speaker concealed behind the dial panel, was designed to project the sound around the entire room. Its wooden case was intended to allow it to match other furniture and blend in.

£50-80   **LOC**

An early 20thC Lachenal & Co. thirty-nine key rosewood concertina, with pierced sides, mahogany case.

£300-500   **FLD**

METALWARE

A Tiffany Studios bronze pen rack, acid-etched pine needle pattern with green slag glass backing, marked 'Tiffany Studios New York 1003'.

5.25in (13.5cm) wide

£500-550   JDJ

A small Tiffany Studios '9th Century' pattern picture frame or calendar frame, set with green and blue glass cabochons, signed 'Tiffany Studios New York 1618'.

6in (15.5cm) wide

£850-950   JDJ

A pair of Tiffany Studios 'Zodiac' bookends, in a rich brown patina with green highlights, each bookend has felt glued to the underside so no markings are visible, with some minor wear to patina.

5in (13cm) wide

£600-650   JDJ

A Tiffany Studios bronze 'Bookmark' inkwell, finished in gold and gold dore and has clear glass insert, marked 'Tiffany Studios New York 864'.

This exact piece is pictured in Bill Holland's book Tiffany Desk Sets, pg. 155, fig 11-4.

4.25in (11cm) wide

£350-400   JDJ

QUICK REFERENCE - TIFFANY STUDIOS

● Tiffany Studios was founded by Louis Comfort Tiffany (1848-1933), son of the famous jeweller Charles Lewis Tiffany (1812-1902). Although best known by that name, his company used many different names from when it was founded in 1878, only being called Tiffany Studios from 1902 until it went bankrupt and closed in 1932. Best known for his glass, architectural decoration and lamps, the company gained a metal (bronze) foundry at its Corona, Queens factory in 1897. Two different surface effects were applied to its metal desk accessories, this gilt effect and a darker bronze. It is not known when desk accessories were introduced, but they became immensely successful amongst a wealthy clientelle from c1905 onwards. Over 20 patterns were produced, all of which were richly embellished with complex cast pattern and many of which were combined with his celebrated glass or less expensive 'slag glass', made up of different colours of glass mixed together. Some patterns, such as 'Miniature' and 'Etched Crozier', are rarer than others. Desk sets comprised at least six different items, always with an inkwell and letter rack, and vases, bowls and other items were also produced with metal bases or frames. Look out for scarcer items such as letter scales, as these can be highly sought-after by collectors looking to complete sets.

A Tiffany Studios '9th Century' pattern double letter rack, with blue and green glass cabochons, signed 'Tiffany Studios New York 1620'.

6in (15.5cm) wide

£1,200-1,500   JDJ

A Tiffany Studios 'American Indian' letter opener, marked 'Tiffany Studios New York 1189', minor nicks to edges of blade and some wear to patina.

10.5in (26.5cm) long

£300-350   JDJ

A Tiffany Furnaces Art Deco paper knife, hammered surface of the handle and lower blade has silver patina while the blade has a brown patina, signed 'Louis C. Tiffany Furnaces', blade has several small bends.

11in (28cm) long

£550-600   JDJ

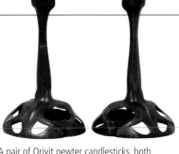

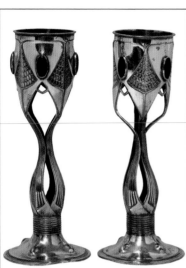

A pair of Orivit pewter candlesticks, both stamped 'Orivit 2284'.

Orivit A.G. was founded in 1894 in Germany by Wilhelm Schmitz (1863-1939). Production began in 1896, using a special metal alloy comprised of 89.85% pewter, 7.9 % antimony, 1.9 % copper and 0.12 % silver, giving a richer and brighter pewter effect. Although sales were good and they won a number of prestigious prizes, the company collapsed financially in 1905 and was acquired by WMF.

A pair of Art Nouveau silver-plated candlesticks, with blue cabochons, stamped '3312A EP'.

7.75in (19.5cm) high

£100-150   SWO

7in (18cm) high

£300-500   SWO

A WMF twin handled silverplated syphon stand, with decoration of flowing tendrils.

£150-200   ECGW

A WMF plated tray, with a lady in a sinuous dress, the handle an iris, stamped mark.

Ladies with long flowing hair and diaphanous dresses, that often merge into each other and any surrounding pattern, are typical motifs on WMFs art metal wares.

An Art Nouveau copper jug by J.S & S.

7.5in (19cm) high

£50-60   WHP

12.4in (31.5cm) wide

£200-250   SWO

A WMF Art Nouveau pewter stamp box, cast in low relief with clover on long sinuous stems, stamped mark.

5in (13cm) wide

£180-220   WW

A Liberty & Co. 'Tudric' pewter desk stand, centred with an inkwell, with enamelled cabochons, with clear glass liner, stamped 'English Pewter 0404'.

Although most of Liberty's pewter 'Tudric' wares are thought of of Arts & Crafts in style, many verge on the curving, naturally inspired Art Nouveau style, such as this inkwell.

9in (23cm) wide

£600-650   SWO

A pair of pewter candlesticks, by James Dixon & Sons, with strap and stud decoration, stamped marks.

James Dixon & Sons, founded in Sheffield, England in 1806, were one of the 19thC's most prolific and celebrated makers of high quality pewter and electro-plated metalwares.

8.75in (22cm) high

£500-600   SWO

A pair of Arts and Crafts candlesticks, stamped 'DRYAD'.

8in (20cm) high

£200-250   SWO

A pair of Liberty & Co. 'Tudric' pewter candlesticks, with removable drip pans, stamped '0871'.

6.5in (16.5cm) high

£250-300   SWO

A pair of Liberty & Co. Tudric pewter vases, with hammered finish, stamped 'Tudric Pewter 01431'.

7.5in (19cm) high

£400-500   SWO

A Liberty & Co. pewter 'Tudric' bomb vase, designed by Archibald Knox, decorated in low relief in 'Honesty' design.

Archibald Knox (1864-1933) was the most celebrated and prolific designer of Liberty & Co's pewter 'Tudric' and silver 'Cymric' wares. He was heavily influenced by Celtic art and frequently used traditional Celtic motifs and lines in his designs. His range of clocks are amongst his most sought-after and valuable designs, and often fetch many thousands of pounds.

7.25in (18.5cm) high

£250-300   MLL

A Liberty & Co. 'Tudric' pewter biscuit box and cover, designed by Archibald Knox, with stylised flower head panels, stamped 'Made in England', 'English Pewter 0194'.

4.5in (11.5cm) high

£350-400   SWO

A Liberty & Co. 'Tudric' pewter four-piece tea set, designed by Archibald Knox, stamped 'English Pewter RD420290/0231', and a matching tray, stamped 'Tudric Pewter 043'.

Although this seems like a low price for five pieces of pewter designed by Arts & Crafts design champion Knox, tea sets such as this are less desirable as they cannot be used. They also look less good on display than vases, bowls or clocks, which can arguably be used as well.

19.25in (49cm) wide

£250-300   SWO

A Walker & Hall 'Pride' stainless steel four piece tea set, designed by David Mellor, with black nylon handles and finials, stamped marks.

Pay attention when looking at this landmark set and look out for silver hallmarks. It was also produced in solid silver by the same company and these sets can fetch over £2,000 at auction!

6.3in (16cm) high

£450-550   WW

A Robert Welch for Old Hall 'Alveston' tea and coffee set with stainless steel tray.

£80-120   ECGW

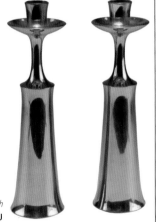

A pair of 1950s Danish Dansk Designs brass candlesticks, designed by Jens Quistgaard, the bases stamped 'DANSK' and 'IHQ'.

The 'IHQ' mark on the base of Dansk Design items indicates that they were designed by their notable lead designer, Jens Quistgaard (1919-2008).

9.4in (23.8cm) high

£250-300   QU

Mark Picks

Mid-century domestic designer metalware produced in the UK is largely ignored by many collectors, particularly when compared to Scandinavian examples. Robert Welch's work in stainless steel for Old Hall has been well explored, as have the precious metal designs by those such as Gerald Benney (see p.319) and Stuart Devlin, but the stainless steel work of these latter two, and other period designers, is still under-rated and as such, probably under-priced. Eric Clements (b.1925) is a good example. He studied at the Birmingham College of Arts and Crafts and the Royal College of Art in London. He then became a teacher, Head of Industrial Design at the Birmingham College of Art, and a consultant designer at London's prestigious and historic jeweller and silversmith Mappin & Webb. He was influenced by Scandinavian metal designs, after travelling there in the late 1940s, which can be seen clearly in his many designs. Identifying his designs now, while they are largely affordable, may prove to be a wise investment.

A Mappin and Webb electroplated four-piece tea service, designed by Eric Clements, stamped manufacturer's mark and facsimile signature.

the hot water jug 7.5in (19cm) high

£60-80   MLL

A pair of 1960s Swedish Ystad Metall vases, made from painted orange tubing, stamped 'Ystad Metall MADE IN SWEDEN'.

12in (30.5cm) high

£300-350   QU

A pair of Danish Tinos lacquered bronze vases, stamped 'TINOS BRONCE MADE IN DENMARK'.

6.2in (15.8cm) high

£1,000-1,400   QU

A pair of bronze Wiener Werkstätte bookends, of stirrup form, with stamped marks.

4in (10.5cm) high

£150-200   SWO

METALWARE

A Georg Jensen pewter sugar sifter, designed by Henning Koppel, the base marked 'GEORG JENSEN PEWTER, HK DENMARK, 036'.

designed 1960   *4in (10.6cm) high*

£150-200   **QU**

A Georg Jensen silver tea caddy or canister, with blue enamel detailing, designed by Henning Koppel, the base marked 'DESSIN HK, GEORG JENSEN im Perlenkranz, DENMARK STIRLING'.

designed in 1968   *3.25in (8.5cm) high*

£1,000-1,200   **QU**

A rare 1960s Torben Örskov & Co black lacquered sheet metal wastepaper bin, with bamboo-covered handles, designed by Finn Juhl and Goethe Bang in 1955.

Finn Juhl (1912-89) was Danish architect and designer, who was one of the leading lights of mid-century Danish design. He is best known today for his furniture designs and he is widely credited with being a major force behind introducing Danish design to the US.

13in (33.5cm) high

£1,000-1,300   **QU**

A CLOSER LOOK AT A GROUP OF BOWLS

These bowls won a gold medal at the Milan Triennale in 1954 and were discontinued in 1996.

They have recently been re-released by Danish company Normann.

Named after a combination of the designer's surname Krenchel and Eternit (a fibre cement), the exteriors are matte black and the interiors are shiny coloured enamel.

Krenschel pays attention to shapes surfaces to make the design as appealing as possible - very simple, they are perfectly balanced and eye-catching.

A group of 1950s-60s Danish Torben Örskov & Co. enamelled 'Krenit' bowls, comprising eight small and two large bowls, designed by Herbert Krenchel in 1953.

biggest 9.8in (25cm) diam

£850-950   **QU**

A 1940s Danish Just Andersen large bronze dish, with a dark-green and black patina, with mirrored design of a mermaid and seahorses, the base marked 'JUST, B 2169, DENMARK'.

13.5in (34.5cm) high

£1,300-1,600   **QU**

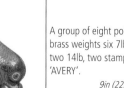

A late Victorian cast bronze door knocker, modelled as a scaly dolphin-like fish with trident tail, hinged on a bracket with bolt and circular base plate.

11.8in (30cm) long

£80-120   **MOR**

A group of eight polished brass weights six 7lb and two 14lb, two stamped 'AVERY'.

9in (22.5cm) high

£200-300 for eight   **WW**

A collection of medals awarded to Second Lieutenant John Henry Strode Batten, the King's Regiment, Liverpool, comprising Queen's and King's South Africa medals with clasps for Cape Colony, Defence of Ladysmith, Orange Free State, Trans Vaal, South Africa, 1901 and 1902, together with dress uniform, a court sword and an engraved cigar box, and a letter written by Batten during the defence of Ladysmith, on December 1st 1899.

The letter to Batten's grandfather details life inside the besieged South African town of Ladysmith. Personal letters give insight into the human side of war and are popular with collectors.

£700-1,000   DUK

A George V-issue military cross, contained in its case of issue, with original ribbon and top suspender, together with a 1914 star awarded to Lieutenant Bertram Maurice Kenny of The Queen's Regiment.

Bertram Maurice Kenny, a member of the Irish gentry, was a serving officer at the start of WWI. He embarked for Flanders and France on 13th August 1914. After surviving the war and reaching the rank of Major, Kenny retired in October 1925 due to ill health caused by his war wounds. He died the following year, aged only 41.

£700-1,000   LAW

A group of three medals awarded and named to Private Charles Buchanan of the 9th London Regiment, comprising a George V Military Medal named to '395453 Pte C Buchanan 9/ Lond R.' and British War & Victory Medals named to '395453 Pte C Buchanan 9-Lond.R.', together with photographs taken by Buchanan.

After serving as a stretcher bearer in France and Flanders with the 9th London Regiment, Buchanan served in the RAF as a carpenter and died of pneomonia aged 37 in 1936 while serving in the Sudan. He was only 18 years old when he was put forward for a gallantry medal in 1919.

£450-550   LAW

A group of WWII gallantry medals, with miniatures, awarded to Flight Lieutenant Stanley Paige, 135079, including a Distinguished Flying Cross, 1945, a 1939/45 Star, a Burma Star, an Italy Star, and Defence and Service medals, together with associated paperwork, log books, silk maps, and newspaper cuttings .

Flight Lieutenant Stanley Paige was awarded the DFC for his courage and devotion to duty involving his dangerous but vital recovery of an early version of a German V1 flying bomb in 1944. He successfully completed other highly dangerous missions, such as dropping supplies to the 14th Army during the Campaign of Burma. On the 4th of June 1946, the London Gazette wrote, 'At all times he [Paige] has set an inspiring example by his courage and devotion to duty'.

£3,500-4,500   DUK

A group of WWII gallantry medals, comprising a George medal, a 1939/45 star, a France and Germany star, a Defence medal, a Service medal, a George VI coronation medal, 1937, and a long service and good conduct medal, awarded to Regiment Sergeant Major Ernest Joseph Legg, 5719780, with a collection of related ephemera including photographs, letters, newspaper cuttings, release book, certificate of service and related items.

Sergeant Major Ernest Joseph Legg enlisted in the Queen's Royal Regiment, Dorchester, in 1920. He went on to serve throughout the Second World War and was discharged in 1951 after displaying great courage and a fine example to his men. He was awarded the George Medal in 1941 for his selfless courage in recovering bodies from, and helping wounded men leave, a hidden minefield.

£4,500-5,500   DUK

A group of four medals, comprising a George VI service medal with Malaya clasp, Korea medal, United Nations Korea medal, and an Elizabeth II service medal with clasp, South Arabia, Cpl. C.K. Young. K.O.Y.L.I. 22204742.

£400-600   DUK

MILITARIA

A cased Gentleman's Companion of Honour medal, with partial ribbon and hook mounts, with GRI reverse with nicely toned finish, enamel appears to have very little damage or deterioration.

This award was created by George V in June 1917 as a reward for outstanding achievements in the arts, literature, music, science, politics, industry, and religion. Until 1943, the Order comprised only 50 people and the reigning monarch, but this was expanded to 65 members plus the monarch, with provisions for some Commonwealth realms. As a result, examples rarely come up for sale and are highly prized when they do.

£2,800-3,800   LAW

A Waterloo medal, awarded to William Taylor of the Royal Artillery Drivers, with large suspension loop and blue/crimson ribbon, dated June 18 1815.
1815
£1,000-1,500   LOC

A miniature naval general service medal, with bar inscribed 'Boadecia', awarded for the action that took place in the Indian Ocean between British and French ships.

It was the arrival of the flagship HMS Boadecia, commanded by Admiral Josias Rowley, that rescued Gordon and HMS Ceylon from their captivity, having struck his colours after a hard-fought action. The French then surrendered to Rowley, not attempting after that to defend the Ile de France.
1810
£350-450   LAW

A WWII gilt-brass submariner's brooch, modeled as a pair of dolphins flanking an enamelled crown and anchor, inscription to reverse.
1.7in (4.3cm)
£50-70   LOC

A yellow-metal and enamelled RAF sweetheart brooch, stamped '9 CARAT'.

These were bought by servicemen and given to their wives or girlfriends as a memento while they were away.
£100-150   LOC

A German WWI gold-plated sweetheart brooch, in the form of a Rumpler Taube aircraft, with a Union Jack silk handkerchief and leather pouch.
£120-180   DUK

A 9ct-gold curved rectangular cigarette case, the cover engraved with the badge of Canadian Army Service Corps, with inscription inside for Captain T. Telford, with Birmingham hallmarks.

Although nearly all of the value of this case comes from the quantity of gold, it would be interesting to research Captain Telford's career.
1917   *108 gms*
£800-1,200   BELL

A 'Victory in Europe' commemorative copper cigar box, engraved with the battle fields of Europe in WWII, with stamped marks to base.

6.3in (16cm) wide

£180-220　　BELL

A WWI leather and chain-mail tank mask, belonging to Major Geoffrey Hampson, DSO, Royal Tank Corps, with a photograph of Major Hampson in uniform.

According to the Tank Corps Book of Honour, Hampson was awarded the Distinguished Service Order 'for most conspicuous gallantry and devotion to duty and leadership during the three days operations on August 8th, 9th and 10th, 1918 in the vicinity of Beaucourt-en-Santerre'.

£1,200-1,800　　DUK

A WWII German Luftwaffe wrist compass, with a black Bakelite case and original leather straps.

£100-150　　DUK

An Imperial German hunting knife, with a silver-plated pommel and silver-plated cross guard in the form of deer hooves, the blade etched with hunting scenes, with original leather and silver-plated mounted scabbard, by Eickhorr Solingen, with maker's stamp.

17.5in (44.5cm)

£700-1,000　　DUK

A post-WWII Commando knife with an alloy grip, by William Rodgers, Sheffield, England, with a leather scabbard.

William Rodgers is closely and proudly associated with the British Commando Regiment and the iconic Fairbairn-Sykes Commando knife.

£150-200　　DUK

QUICK REFERENCE - TANK MODEL

● Models such as this were probably made by factories during and after the war as 'souvenirs' and are often classified as 'Trench Art', even though they weren't made in trenches. Tanks were introduced at the little-known Battle of Flers-Courcelette in September 1916 during WWI and played a pivotal role. Although the tank was often unreliable, it helped break the stalemate of trench warfare by making frontline troops mobile. Although the cavalry had proven decisive to success in battles such as at Mons near the start of the war, trench warfare had rendered the cavalry useless. The idea for this armoured, weaponised vehicle was taken from farm machinery with moving tracks that could cope with rough terrain, and was pushed by Lieutenant-Colonel Ernest Swinton. Although unsuccessful at the Somme, the tank endured to play a crucial role in subsequent conflicts.

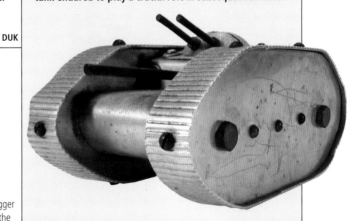

An early 19thC four-barrel percussion pistol, by Horton Salop, the trigger guard and barrel engraved with floral scroll decoration, the cocks in the form of dolphins, with a leather pouch stamped 'J. Moore, Salop'.

8.25in (21cm) long

£2,200-2,800　　DUK

A Trench Art aluminium model of a WWI tank.

6.7in (17cm) wide

£60-100　　WHP

OIL LAMPS

A Victorian oil lamp, having an etched cranberry glass shade over a moulded pink glass reservoir, and a black fluted column with a brass Corinthian capital and a square stepped base.

29.1in (74cm) high excluding funnel

£500-600   **SWO**

A Victorian oil lamp, with a cranberry and clear etched glass shade, over a pink moulded glass reservoir and column with enamelled highlights, on a stepped circular black glazed pottery plinth.

27in (68.5cm) high excluding funnel

£550-650   **SWO**

A Victorian oil lamp, with an etched cranberry and clear glass, crimped edge shade, a similar moulded reservoir, an embossed brass column and a black glazed pottery plinth.

20in (50.5cm) high excluding funnel

£600-700   **SWO**

A Victorian oil lamp, having an etched green glass shade and a cut-glass reservoir, on a silver-plated stop fluted column with a Corinthian capital and a square-stepped base, stamped 'Brock & Son, 276 George St., Edinburgh'.

The Classical Corinthian column, cut-glass reservoir and general level of quality and detail on this example help to make it as valuable as it is.

31in (78cm) high excluding funnel

£650-750   **SW**

A Victorian oil lamp, having an etched green and clear glass shade with a crimped edge, a moulded green glass reservoir and a spreading brass base.

20in (51cm) high excluding funnel

£300-350   **SWO**

A Victorian oil lamp, having a domed etched yellow and clear glass shade over a moulded yellow glass reservoir and a silverplated Corinthian column on a stepped square base.

27in (69cm) high excluding funnel

£500-600   **SWO**

A Doulton Lambeth stoneware oil lamp, having an etched glass shade over a stoneware mounted reservoir and body, in blue, green, and brown on a brass base, probably decorated by Kate M Davis.

c1892   *23in (59cm) high excluding funnel*

£800-1,200   **SWO**

A pair of Chinese Qianlong famille rose baluster vases and covers, painted with baskets of flowers with moulded and applied squirrel and vine decoration, the cover with a Buddhist lion finial, one with damage.

12.5in (32cm) high

£650-850   **BELL**

A pair of 19thC Chinese Canton famille rose vases, converted to table lamps, with gilt dog handles, the shoulders draped with gilt lizards, painted with courtly figures in interiors and mixed flora and fauna to square panels against a dense ground of foliage and insects.

Although they make great pieces for decorators, vases or jars that have been drilled and convered to lamps are usually of little interest to collectors unless they are extremely rare or important. In all instances, the value is generally reduced by well over 50%.

24in (61cm) high

£300-400   **MOR**

A late 19thC Cantonese famille rose porcelain vase and cover, the cover with a seated figure knop, painted with figures at their daily business on a scrolling foliate and insect ground.

c1800   *25in (63.5cm) high*

£1,200-1,500   **AH**

Miller's Compares

The handles formed as fu dogs on this example are much better moulded and painted, and are undamaged.

The coloured glazes are brighter, the symbols, beasts and protagonists are more numerous and the additional moulded areas are crisp and highly detailed.

The main scene is smaller, with fewer people, and they and their faces are less well-painted and have fewer details.

The white glazed porcelain is pitted and less crisp and overall the painting is more smudgy and shows signs of having been much more quickly executed, with less care and attention.

A late 19thC Chinese Canton Qing Dynasty famille rose vase, the scalloped flared mouth over a neck with fu lion handles and scalloped edge to the shoulder above moulded crawling dragons, with courtly ladies having tea, against a ground filled with butterflies, flowers and precious objects.

24.5in (62cm) high

£2,000-3,000   **L&T**

A late 19thC famille rose Cantonese vase, the neck with frilled rim and gilded mythological beasts, painted with figures in interiors, court scenes and birds, insects and flowers, on a foliate and scroll ground.

24.5in (62cm) high

£350-450   **DA&H**

A 19thC Chinese famille rose 'millefleurs' vase, with coral-coloured shaped handles, decorated with blooms, the interior and base glazed turquoise, a four character mark which reads 'qian mu de tang'.

15in (38cm) high

£2,000-3,000   **WW**

A 20thC Chinese famille rose rouleau-shaped vase, painted with two horses beneath a large pine tree, with two lines of calligraphy to the reverse, the base with a four character mark which reads 'yi tao zhai'.

14in (35cm)

£1,700-2,000   **WW**

ORIENTAL

A pair of early 19thC Chinese export famille rose platters, with a serpentine rim, decorated in underglaze blue and polychrome enamels depicting a pair of Ho Ho birds, chrysanthemum, peonies and bamboo shoots.

17.5in (44cm) wide

£400-600   **L&T**

A late 19thC Cantonese famille rose dish, with pierced and clobbered border, painted with exotic birds and flowering shrubs.

10in (25.5cm) diam

£650-850   **TRI**

QUICK REFERENCE - FAMILLE ROSE

● Some antique Chinese porcelain is described by the predominant palette of colours used for the decoration. Using French words, these are known as the 'famille' (family) and include famille rose (pink), jaune (yellow), noire (black) and verte (green). Famille rose is mainly pink or purple and was introduced around 1720, replacing the earlier famille verte palette. Typically featuring foliage, flowers, symbols and panels often showing people, it was popular and continued to be fashionable during the 18th and 19th centuries. By quantity, it is the most common type of Chinese porcelain produced for export to the West from the 19thC into the early 20thC. Quality, and so values, vary widely - for more information, see the 'Miller's Compares' feature on the previous page.

A Chinese Qianlong porcelain wine cooler, with mask handles, painted in famille rose enamels with a basket of flowers below a fluted border.

7.5in (19cm)

£2,000-3,000   **TEN**

An 18thC Chinese famille rose model of a lady, a lotus leaf sceptre in her left hand.

10in (25.5cm) high

£800-1,000   **WW**

A 19thC Chinese famille rose model of a Buddhist monk, with a scroll in his left hand, his throne with the inscription 'Xi Tian Da Shan Zi Zai Fo', and reticulated cash design.

12.5in (32cm) high

£1,000-1,500   **WW**

An 18thC Chinese famille rose ewer, cover and basin, painted with flower sprays and phoenix feathers, the cover moulded with shells and flowers, the ewer and cover with painted marks.

The form is based on a German Meissen model. A similar ewer and cover are shown in 'China For The West' by CD Howard and J Ayers, Vol.II, p.561.

13.25in (33.5cm)

£1,200-1,800   **WW**

A late 19thC Chinese porcelain plaque, painted in famille rose enamels with an extensive landscape with a river, figures, pavillions, a bridge, and a horse, with hardwood frame and stand.

14.5in (37cm) high

£2,500-3,000   **BELL**

A near pair of Chinese Kangxi blue and white baluster vases, painted with river landscapes with figures and boats.

8.75in (22cm) high

£1,500-2,000   BELL

A 19thC Chinese blue decorated porcelain vase, with a period celadon glaze ground, handles shaped as kylin.

Kylin, or Qilin, are mythical hooved beasts, similar to a chimera, that are said to be associated with serenity or prosperity. They are said to appear before a sage or illustrious ruler.

17in (43cm) high

£80-100   LOCK

An 18thC Chinese provincial ginger jar, decorated with a river scene in underglaze blue.

6.25in (16cm) high

£30-50   LOCK

A mid-20thC Chinese porcelain bowl, with a handpainted 'millefleurs' pattern, and gilt edges.

Ceramics decorated with all-over flowers have been produced for centuries - millefleurs means 'a thousand flowers'. They are similar to and, together with Indian textiles, may have helped inspire fashionable Western chintzware ceramics produced from the late 19thC onwards.

9.5in (24.5cm) diam

£20-30   LOCK

A Tang Dynasty male tomb attendant figurine, the characteristically elongated body form wearing a traditional long robe, repair to arm and neck.

During the Tang dynasty, sculptural representations of humans and animals were frequently placed in burial chambers to honour the deceased. The naturalistic modelling of this mould-made figure's facial features is quite striking. The high cheekbones may suggest that this gentleman had Turkish origins as China was quite cosmopolitan during this period. The lustrous glaze that enriches the surface is typical of the innovations in glazes made by artists of the Tang period.

c700 CE   *12.75in (32.5cm) high*

£800-1,200   ARTM

A 19thC Chinese terracotta Yi-Xing tea pot, decorated with bamboo leaves and text to the side, character marks to the base and underside of lid.

Yixing teapots are made from clay excavated in and around Yixing in the eastern Chinese province of Jiangsu. They date back to the 10thC and are used to brew teas. They became popular with scholars and, due to this, their desirability grew. Today, examples are still made in Dingshan (also known as Dingshu). The clay teapot absorbs a tiny amount of tea and is only washed out in water every time it is used so that, after time, the flavour and colour of the tea are preserved and accentuated.

2.5in (8.5cm) high

£45-55   LOCK

A Chinese Tang dynasty model of a fat lady's head, taken from a larger figure and mounted on a modern stand.

During the stability of the innovative Tang Dynasty (approx. 618-907 AD), fat women were deemed beautiful. Their size was representative of health, wealth, self-indulgence and of the increased social freedom of women.

618-907AD   *8in (20cm) high*

£300-400   WW

ORIENTAL

A pair of early 18thC Japanese Edo period Imari vases and covers, with raised and moulded flowers, with a woman amongst flowering peony and chrysanthemum.

8.75in (22cm) high

£400-500

BELL

An early 20thC Japanese Noritake vase, with a pattern of reserves and dragons in iron red, blue, green and yellow and highlighted in gilt, marked 'noritake' to the base.

Nortiake was founded in 1876, by Ichizaemon Morimura VI and his brother Toyo. Then named Morimura Gumi, it became known as Morimura Brothers in 1881. Following huge success exporting their ceramics, particularly to the US, a new factory was built at Noritake, near Nagoya, in 1904. The company only officially changed its name to Noritake in 1981.

£40-60

LOCK

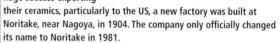

An early 20thC Japanese Satsuma vase, with a geisha against a pale ground with blue and gilt decoration, with a six-character mark to the base.

£20-30

LOCK

A 19thC Japanese vase, with flowers and a figure in a garden, the base with three-character mark.

11.5in (29cm) high

£30-40

LOCK

A 19thC Japanese bottle vase, with birds and foliage, original stopper and marks to base.

13.75in (35cm) high

£40-50

LOCK

An early 19thC Japanese Imari charger, with a bonsai tree in a jardiniere, with extensive gilding.

Bonsai trees are a less commonly found motif on ceramics, particularly on their own rather than as part of a garden scene.

14in (35.7cm) across

£40-50

LOCK

An early 19thC Japanese Imari dish, with crimped rim and extensive gilt detail.

12.25in (31cm) diam

£30-40

LOCK

A pair of 19thC Chinese carved ivory figures, of a Mandarin and his wife, with blackened carved details.

11.8in (30cm) high

£350-450   **WHP**

A Japanese Meiji period (1868-1912) ivory okimono of a peasant, beside a portable cabinet, holding a broom and a gourd vase, signed on red lacquer reserve, chipped.

8.75in (22cm) high

£250-300   **BELL**

A late 19thC Chinese export ivory carving of two dragons, entwined and chasing the (tama) sacred pearl, amidst clouds with birds and flowers.

6in (15cm) long

£300-400   **MOR**

QUICK REFERENCE - PUZZLE BALLS

- Also known as 'mystery' or 'puzzle' balls, these balls contain anything from three or more concentric smaller, freely moving balls. Each ball is typically highly carved, and incorporates holes. Although the 'puzzle' could be to align the holes through all the balls, the name applies more to the fact that one can muse over the mystery or puzzle of how these intricate pieces were carved from a single solid piece of ivory. The most complex example known has over 40 layers! Examples carved with auspicious beasts or symbols are meant to bring good fortune, and the form indicates the 'eternal' circle. The number of layers can also have meaning, with four often indicating the four points of the compass.

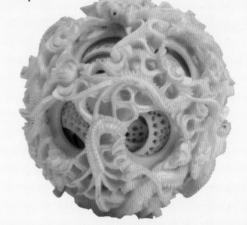

An early 20thC Cantonese export ivory pierced concentric ball, the inner balls pierced with geometric designs, the outer layer carved with dragons amongst cloud scrolls.

3.25in (8cm) high

£200-300   **BELL**

A late 19thC to early 20thC Japanese ivory belt buckle, in the form of a monkey's head, with carved inset signature to the reverse.

2.5in (6.5cm) wide

£150-200   **FLD**

A 19thC Chinese carved bamboo brushpot, carved in deep relief with a continuous lotus, with a dragonfly and a frog.

7.5in (19cm) high

£300-400   **BELL**

A late 18thC or early 19thC Chinese red cinnabar lacquer cover, on a later stand, profusely carved with three dragons chasing a flaming pearl against breaking waves inside key pattern borders, the stand with four scroll supports, some damage.

12in (30cm) wide

£400-500   **BELL**

ORIENTAL

A late 19thC Chinese cloisonné charger, with two pheasants amongst flowering branches inside a reddish-brown border filled with flowers, the underside with spaced flowers against a turquoise and key pattern ground.

25in (64cm) diam

£350-450   **BELL**

A late 19thC or early 20thC Japanese cloisonné charger, depicting a bird amongst foliage.

£20-30   **LOCK**

A late 19th to early 20thC Chinese cloisonné vase, decorated with butterflies and blossom.

7in (18cm) high

£80-120   **LOCK**

A 19thC Chinese black lacquered and tooled gilt-decorated table cabinet, the doors enclosing a single shelf interior, the decoration of figures and pagodas, on boats and in gardens.

21in (53cm) wide

£550-650   **LOC**

A late 19thC Cantonese export black lacquer chinoiserie decorated sewing box, with fitted interior.

15in (38cm) wide

£200-300   **BELL**

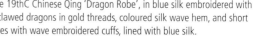

A late 19thC Chinese Qing 'Winter Dragon' robe, in blue silk embroidered with five clawed dragons in gold threads, with coloured silk wave hem, long sleeves, brown fur cuffs, and lined to the inside with white rabbit fur.

The date, fine condition, and the high quality and level of detail of this robe make it so desirable. Today, robes such as these are popularly displayed by running a length of dowelling through the arms and hanging them from a wall.

£5,000-7,000   **TEN**

A late 19thC Chinese Qing 'Dragon Robe', in blue silk embroidered with five clawed dragons in gold threads, coloured silk wave hem, and short sleeves with wave embroidered cuffs, lined with blue silk.

£2,000-3,000   **TEN**

A Fred Aubrit red, white, and blue crown paperweight, signed on base.

2.5in (6.5cm) diam

£45-55   POOK

A Rick Ayotte plum paperweight, signed and inscribed limited edition 50/90.

3.5in (8.75cm) diam

£600-650   POOK

A Rick Ayotte red and white poinsettia paperweight, signed and inscribed 'AP/2' '87'.

3.75in (9.4cm) diam

£600-650   POOK

A Rick Ayotte red Christmas cactus with berries paperweight, signed and inscribed 'Ed/50' '88'.

3.5in (8.75cm) diam

£500-550   POOK

A Bob Banford pink primrose paperweight with a star-cut base, signed in cane.

3in (7.5cm) diam

£300-350   POOK

A Bob Banford paperweight with two orange chrysanthemums and a waffle-cut base, with 'B' monogram signature cane.

3in (7.5cm) diam

£250-300   POOK

A Chris Buzzini floral paperweight, signed and inscribed '90 DA 7/40'.

3in (7.5cm) diam

£450-500   POOK

PAPERWEIGHTS

A Jim D'Onofrio frog paperweight, signed and inscribed '92 0174'.

3.25in (8.12cm) diam

£500-550   **POOK**

A Cathy Richardson yellow cactus paperweight, signed.

c2008   3in (7.5cm) diam

£180-220   **POOK**

A Ken Rosenfeld paperweight, with a sunflower and daffodils on a blue ground, initialed in cane and inscribed 'KR '96'.

2.5in (6.25cm) diam

£150-200   **POOK**

A Jim D'Onofrio paperweight, with a giraffe's neck and head within a spray of tree limbs, leaves, and flowers, signed on the side with etched signature 'Jim D'Onofrio 950540 Artist Proof'.

3.5in (9cm) diam

£520-600   **JDJ**

A Harold Hacker floral paperweight, on a snow ground.

2.75in (6.87cm) diam

£180-220   **POOK**

A Cathy Richardson octopus paperweight, signed.

Lampworking master Cathy Richardson is also known for her similar glass 'spheres' and has won many awards for her work, which can be found in a number of private and public collections. The seabed is a recurring inspiration in her work.

c2008   3in (7.5cm) diam

£350-400   **POOK**

A Daniel Salazar limited edition snow-white paperweight, with a dragonfly and purple flowers, signed and inscribed '3-85'.

3in 7.5cm) diam

£130-180   **POOK**

A Paul Stankard limited edition yellow cactus paperweight, signed in cane and inscribed '16/25' 'A672'.

c1979   *3in (7.5cm) diam*

£400-450   **POOK**

A CLOSER LOOK AT A PAPERWEIGHT

Taking the art of the paperweight to new levels, American Paul Stankard (b.1943) is one of the most influential, highly skilled and important paperweight artists in the world.

He uses a technique known as 'lampworking', where tiny segments of coloured glass are extruded, bent, manipulated, and joined together to create tiny three-dimensional 'sculptures' which are then cased in colourless glass as paperweights, spheres, or obelisks.

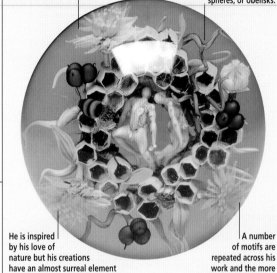

He is inspired by his love of nature but his creations have an almost surreal element to them, as if a tiny part of a fantasy forest floor has been taken and frozen in glass.

A number of motifs are repeated across his work and the more there are, the higher the value of the weight in general.

A Paul Stankard 'Root People' paperweight, decorated with a honeycomb, honeybee, two red ants, a band of flowers, and berries, extending root labelled 'Seeds', 'Moist' or 'Fertile', signed near the foot 'Paul Stankard RH002 1998'.

1998   *3in (8cm) diam*

£3,000-3,500   **JDJ**

A Paul Stankard cymbidium orchid paperweight, signed in cane and inscribed 'A432'.

c1985   3in (7.5cm) diam

£1,000-1,400   POOK

A Joshua Steindler floral paperweight, signed and dated.

2007   *3in (7.5cm) diam*

£90-120   **POOK**

A Mayauel Ward paperweight, with a butterfly and wisteria on a sky ground, signed.

2.75in (6.8cm) diam

£90-120   **POOK**

A Mayauel Ward paperweight, with a moon and an oak tree, signed.

2.75in (6.8cm) diam

£90-120   **POOK**

QUICK REFERENCE - MONTBLANC

- The golden age of the fountain pen was during the 1910s–30s, even though they were produced a few decades earlier. They began to be collected during the 1970s and interest peaked, together with values, during the 1990s.

- Most collectors still choose to collect one brand, such as Parker, Montblanc, or Waterman, a particular period or type of material (such as plastic or metal filigree) or filling system. Larger companies attract the most buyers. Rarity and quality count as much towards value as brand, as does a pen's visual impact. Look out for unusual celluloids or pens with complex metal overlays. Classic models, such as the Parker 51 or 75, can also be more popular.

- As the supply of the best vintage pens made before the 1970s has begun to dry up and prices rise, 'modern' and contemporary pens have risen in desirability - particulaly if they are from limited editions. During the 1990s, the market for such pens mushroomed, led by Montblanc. Their 'Lorenzo de Medici' of 1992 is seen by many as the first significant limited edition pen that appealed to collectors.

- The manufacturer, the size of the edition, the materials used and the reason behind the release of the pen are all factors that affect value. Many are made to commemorate great creative minds, important events, or anniversaries. Edition sizes are sometimes rather cynically tailored to 888 pieces as 8 is an auspicious number in the Far East, where there are many collectors. As such, any edition number with 8 in it, such as 008 or 088, will be the most sought-after and valuable.

- Unused, un-inked pens in mint condition fetch a premium, but the highest prices are reserved for pens that are still sealed in their cellophane. It is vital that a pen is complete with all its packaging and associated literature, and typically includes a lavish box. Often costing thousands of pounds to buy new, their values on the secondary market remain largely consistent, but as demand outstrips supply, prices can rise dramatically.

A Montblanc limited edition ballpoint pen, 'Ernest Hemingway', from the 'Writers Edition' series, with a red resin barrel and dark brown resin cap, and engraved with Hemingway's facsimile signature.

30,000 Hemingway ballpens were produced, but they were not individually numbered within that edition.
issued 1993
£450-550   DN

A Montblanc limited edition fountain pen, 'Ernest Hemingway', from the 'Writers Edition' series, from a limited edition of 20,000, engraved with Hemingway's facsimile signature, the nib stamped '18K', in a Montblanc box with paperwork and outer card sleeve, uninked.

Aptly, the box is in the shape of a book.
issued 1992
£1,400-1,800   BLO

A Montblanc limited edition fountain pen, 'Imperial Dragon', no.4625/4810, with a silver dragon clip set stone eyes, the medium nib stamped '750', uninked, in original box, with service certificate, card and slip cover and outer packaging.

A variant with an 18ct. solid gold clip in a limited edition of 888 examples was also offered. 8 is considered an auspicious number in China, hence the choice of edition size for this very Chinese-inspired pen.
issued 1994
£1,300-1,600   DN

A Montblanc limited edition fountain pen, 'Meisterstück' 'Agatha Christie', no.0126/4810, from the 'Writers Edition' series, with silver cap band and vermeil silver clip in the form of a snake, with sapphires to the eyes, the two-colour nib stamped '18K', in a Montblanc box, printed outer card sleeve, paperwork and white outer card sleeve, uninked, in excellent condition.

The form and design of this pen is based on Montblanc pens from the 1920s. Examples with a vermeil (gold-washed silver) clip with sapphire eyes were limited to 4,810 examples, and those with silver clips with ruby eyes were limited to 30,000 examples.
issued 1993
£1,200-1,500   BLO

A Montblanc limited edition mechanical pencil, 'Oscar Wilde', no.09278/12000, from the 'Writers Edition' series, with pearl and black marbled resin body, with gilt trim and clip, the body with Oscar Wilde's facsimile signature, in a Montblanc box with outer printed sleeve and International Service Certificate.
issued 1994
£150-200   BLO

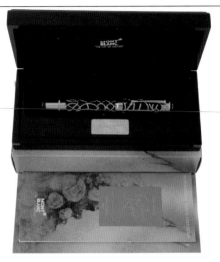

A Montblanc limited edition fountain pen, 'Alexandre Dumas', no.09682/20000, from the 'Writers Edition' series, with gold-plated mounts, the medium nib stamped '750', uninked, in original box, with service certificate, slip cover and outer packaging.
issued 1996
£450-550   BLO

A Montblanc limited edition fountain pen, 'Prince Regent', no.4566/4810, from the 'Patron of the Arts' series, with blue resin cap and barrel and silver gilt filigree overlay, the medium nib stamped '18K' with crown motif, in a Montblanc lacquer box with printed outer card sleeve, white card sleeve and paperwork.
issued 1995
£1,200-1,600   DN

A Montblanc limited edition fountain pen, 'Semiramis', no.2554/4810, from the 'Patron of the Arts' series, the black resin body encased in a cage of gold-plated fretwork, the clip set with an enamel motif of the heraldic animal, 'Ishtar', with 18-carat gold nib, in a Montblanc lacquer display box, with all documentation.
issued 1996
£1,000-1,400   BLO

A Montblanc limited edition fountain pen, 'Catherine the Great', no.2323/4810, from the 'Patron of the Arts' series, the aubergine resin cap and barrel, with gold-plated overlay, in a Montblanc lacquer box with documentation, uninked.
issued 1997
£1,000-1,400   BLO

A Montblanc limited edition fountain pen, 'Peter the Great', no.2323/4810, from the 'Patron of the Arts' series, the green resin cap and barrel with gold-plated overlay, the nib stamped '750', uninked, in original box with documentation.
issued 1997
£1,200-1,600   BLO

A Montblanc limited edition fountain pen, 'Alexander the Great', no.2661/4810, from the 'Patron of the Arts' series, with a marbled lacquer barrel and reeded plated cap, in a Montblanc box with documentation, fountain pen is sealed.
issued 1998
£1,000-1,400   BLO

A Montblanc limited edition fountain pen, 'Year of the Golden Dragon', no.0079/2000, the 18ct.-gold clip modelled as a dragon with a freshwater cultured pearl in its mouth, the medium nib stamped '18K', with a piston filling system, uninked, in a Montblanc lacquer display box, with documentation.

Please see the white porcelain example of this pen, shown over the page, for more information. This is a desirable low number.
issued 2000
£2,500-3,000   DN

A CLOSER LOOK AT A MONTBLANC PEN

This variation has a Meissen porcelain barrel and cap that has been handpainted with a dragon - founded in 1710, Meissen is a highly prestigious and historically important porcelain factory based in Dresden, Germany.

This pen was also made in black resin in an edition of 2,000 examples (see previous page), unusually it can fetch as much as this version due to the popularity of the pen's theme and because the pen's black design is preferred by some users and collectors.

This design was released in 2000, the Chinese year of the Dragon.

Only 888 examples of this version of this pen were made, and this example is complete with all its packaging.

A Montblanc limited edition fountain pen, 'Year of The Golden Dragon', no.528/888, with gold plated trim, the nib stamped '18K', uninked, in a Montblanc lacquer display box.

issued 2000

£2,500-3,000   DN

A Montblanc limited edition fountain pen, 'Andrew Carnegie', no.2458/4810, from the 'Patron of the Arts' series, the clip in the form of a nude woman, the nib stamped '18K', in a Montblanc lacquer display box with documentation, uninked, light scratches and scuffs.

issued 2002

£1,200-1,500   BLO

A Montblanc silver fountain pen, 'Meisterstuck' 'Solitaire', no.146, the nib stamped '18K', the body stamped '925', in a Montblanc box with outer card packaging, uninked.

£350-450   BLO

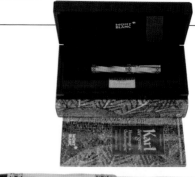

A Montblanc limited edition fountain pen, 'Karl der Grosse/Hommage a Charlemagne', no.1188/4810, from the 'Patron of the Arts' series, with a spiralling silver barrel and cap, and gold plated pierced decoration at each end and to the cap band, the two colour medium nib stamped '18K', uninked, in its original green lacquer box, with documentation.

issued 2000

£1,000-1,400   DN

A Montblanc limited edition fountain pen, 'Qing Dynasty', no.1562/2002, the cap made from carved jade depicting a dragon, the nib stamped '18K' and engraved with a dragon, uninked, in its original green lacquer box with paperwork and outer card sleeve.

issued 2002

£2,500-3,000   DN

A Montblanc limited edition platinum '144' fountain pen and '164' ballpoint pen, 'Meisterstuck', with yellow gold plated bands to cap and body, with a yellow 18ct-gold nib, pen no.KP0114, ballpoint pen no.KP0150, both stamped 'Pt 950', uninked, in a Montblanc black lacquer box, and outer card sleeve.

As the bodies are made from platinum, rather than being platinum plated, they had a very high retail price. As such, very few examples have sold, certainly compared to Montblanc's other pens.

£3,000-4,000   DN

An Ancora 88 limited edition resin fountain pen, 'Graal', no.23/88, the hand painted body depicting a Knight Templar on horseback, with the motto 'NON NOBIS, DOMINE, NON NOBIS, SED NOMINI TUO DA GLORIAM', and the clip with a red enamel Templar's cross, the medium nib stamped 'uO', uninked, in an Ancora box with paperwork.

£300-400   DN

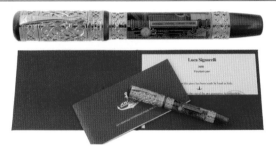

An Ancora 88 limited edition fountain pen, 'Luca Signorelli', no.04/88, the broad nib stamped 'uO', with a cartridge/converter filling system, uninked, with a certificate, warranty booklet and card.

Inspired by the work of the Italian renaissance artist Luca Signorelli (1445-1523), the body is handpainted with a depiction of the Annunciation.

£400-500   DN

An Ancora limited edition red resin fountain pen, 'Demonstrator', no.06/88, the translucent red marbled resin cap and barrel, with engraved gilt trim, and medium nib stamped 'uO', with a spring loaded pump action filling system, uninked, with a certificate, warranty booklet and card.

Demonstrators are pens with transparent or (less commonly) translucent bodies that allow you to see the internal working of the filling system, feed and nib, as well as the level of ink inside. Initially made for salesmen to take to retailers, they became popular and were produced for sale from around the 1970s onwards. However, only certain models were made as demonstrators and they are extremely rare compared to standard production line pens.

£180-220   DN

A CLOSER LOOK AT A DUNHILL PEN

Goldfish and natural scenes are typical, but some motifs relate to or tell stories - this refers to a well-known 11thC haiku, the Genji Monogatari (Tale of Genji) by Lady Murasaki Shikibu.

The torpedo shape indicates this pen was made in the 1930s, even though the alliance between Dunhill, a British luxury gentlemen's retailer, and Namiki, a Japanese pen maker, dates back to 1927.

Dunhill Namiki pens are decorated with traditional Japanese maki-e lacquer, which can take many months to apply, especially if the pattern is complex.

Most Dunhill Namiki pens are signed by the lacquer artist that decorated them, and some artists are more desirable and famous than others - Shotensai Mitsunaka is unknown.

A Dunhill Namiki lacquer fountain pen, the lacquered cap and barrel with black hira-maki-e background, the barrel with a taka maki-e cuckoo in flight with raden abalone shell eye, with a gold lacquer signature with a red kakihan after it, believed to read 'Shotensai Mitsunaka', lever filling system, original Namiki nib.

c1930

£4,500-5,500   DN

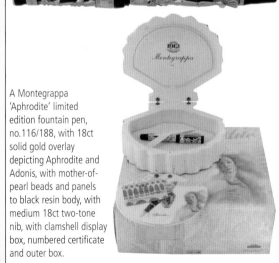

A Montegrappa 'Aphrodite' limited edition fountain pen, no.116/188, with 18ct solid gold overlay depicting Aphrodite and Adonis, with mother-of-pearl beads and panels to black resin body, with medium 18ct two-tone nib, with clamshell display box, numbered certificate and outer box.

A version with a solid silver overlay was also produced in an edition of 1,912 pieces. 1912 was the year Montegrappa was founded. It is usually less valuable, fetching around a third of the value of this example.

issued 1997

£4,500-5,500   DN

A Montegrappa limited edition fountain pen, 'Silver Dragon', no.1213/1912, designed by Federico Mont, the marbled grey body mounted with two high-relief Chinese dragons with ruby eyes, the medium two colour nib stamped '18K', uninked, with a lacquered wood box, and documentation.

Although they are dragons, the curling design harks back to the highly desirable and rare 'snake pens' produced by eminent makers Parker and Waterman during the early 20thC.

£1,000-1,400   DN

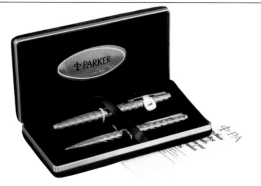

A cased set of two Parker '180' gold-plated pens, comprising a fountain pen and matching ball pen.

c1980

£150-200   SWO

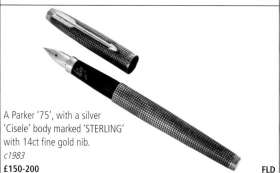

A Parker '75', with a silver 'Cisele' body marked 'STERLING' with 14ct fine gold nib.

c1983

£150-200   FLD

Mark Picks

Onoto pens were made by eminent printer De La Rue from 1905 until 1958, although the company made other pens and stylographs as early as the 1880s. The unusual name was chosen as the pronunciation was the same in every language and didn't mean anything in another language - £50,000 was allocated to promote it. Produced from the 1930s-40s, the Magna was one of the company's largest and highest quality pens and is considered to be its most handsome by knowledgable collectors. This plastic is also one of the more desirable colour variations. All of this is important - most pen collectors are men and the large size, story, visual appearance and style appeals greatly. Not only that, but the Magna is a great writing pen. All of this should make the value of this classic pen remain at least constant, and it'll be much admired when it's being used too!

An Onoto-Magna fountain pen, the nib marked 'De La Rue Onoto 14ct London 6', in speckled amber celluloid body, black end caps.

£400-500   FLD

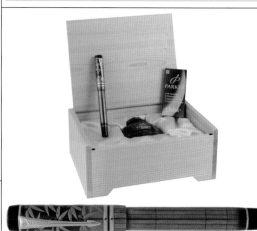

A Parker 'Chikurin' 'Duofold' limited edition maki-e lacquer fountain pen, the cap with a chikurin in raised taka maki-e, on a togidashi maki-e background, the blind cap signed by Tatuya Todo, uninked, limited to 150 pieces, in a Parker wooden box with ink, cartridges and outer card sleeve.

The plain wood box is similar to those used to contain Japanese art pottery.

issued 2001

£750-850   DN

Miller's Compares

The capstan inkwell form is based on the capstan found on ship decks - the wide base provides stability when the pen is dipped in.

This example is smaller in size - size matters when it's displayed on a gentleman's desk.

This example has an inset watch by Waltham, a well known and good quality American watchmaker.

The maker's marks are rubbed on this example, so the maker cannot be identified, the other is by Deakin & Francis, a well known maker.

An inkwell with watch, by Deakin & Francis, Birmingham, of capstan style, the hinged lid lifting to reveal a white faced watch, Waltham and Co. English Lever, and glass insert inkwell.

1912   *6.25in (15.5cm) diam*

£900-1,200   **L&T**

A table inkwell with watch, Birmingham, of capstan style, the hinged lid lifting to reveal a white faced pocket watch, plain lever movement and glass insert inkwell.

1908   *4.5in (11.5cm) diam*

£650-750   **L&T**

Port and starboard inkwells, by Samuel Jacob, London, in the form of red and green glass ships lanterns.

Novelty forms are desirable and rare - especially if they cross into another market such as marine and nautical memorabilia as here.

1905   *4.5in (11cm) high*

£1,300-1,800   **L&T**

A late 19thC travelling inkwell, in the form of a globe, some damage.

2.56in (6.5cm) diam

£100-150   **FLD**

A late Victorian brass owl inkwell, with glass eyes, the head hinged to a vacant interior, the foliage as a pen rest.

3.75in (9cm) wide

£250-300   **WW**

A 1930s Carvacraft butterscotch cast phenolic double inkwell, with sliding covers to reveal a black and red inkwell, impressed marks.

Look out for green Carvacraft as it is both rarer and more valuable, often fetching over 1.5 times the value of the amber/butterscotch version.

11.4in (29cm) long

£200-250   **FLD**

An Art Deco ivory and ebony desk stand, with carving of tribal heads, with matching blotters and pen holder.

stand 9.8in (25cm) wide

£200-250   **ECGW**

PENS & WRITING

A CLOSER LOOK AT AN INKWELL

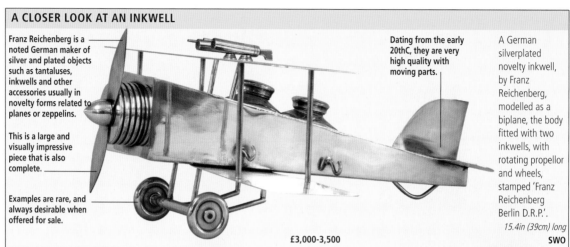

Franz Reichenberg is a noted German maker of silver and plated objects such as tantaluses, inkwells and other accessories usually in novelty forms related to planes or zeppelins.

This is a large and visually impressive piece that is also complete.

Examples are rare, and always desirable when offered for sale.

Dating from the early 20thC, they are very high quality with moving parts.

A German silverplated novelty inkwell, by Franz Reichenberg, modelled as a biplane, the body fitted with two inkwells, with rotating propellor and wheels, stamped 'Franz Reichenberg Berlin D.R.P.'.

15.4in (39cm) long

£3,000-3,500   **SWO**

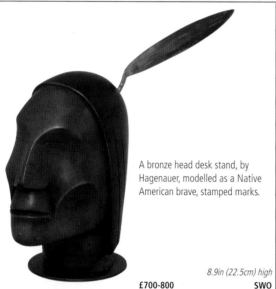

A bronze head desk stand, by Hagenauer, modelled as a Native American brave, stamped marks.

8.9in (22.5cm) high

£700-800   **SWO**

A Victorian bloodstone desk seal, engraved with a coat of arms and with a faceted bloodstone handle, with the original fitted case, detailed 'WYON 287 REGENT STREET. W.'.

£750-850   **BELL**

A Victorian ivory desk seal, with carved top over a hand clasping a hardstone mounted-metal matrix.

3in (8cm) long

£180-220   **BELL**

A late Victorian novelty telescopic propelling pencil, by S. Mordan & Co., in the shape of a duck, with suspensory ring and registered design lozenge.

Mordan's ingenious novelty shaped propelling pencils are usually the most sought-after and valuable of the company's products.

c1890   1.5in (3.5cm) long (unextended)

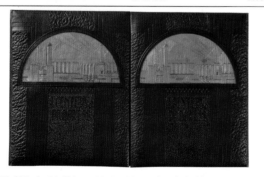

A World Trade Fair Chicago 1934 writing pad, with double-opening leather outer with Art Deco decoration and legend 'A Century Of Progress' to each door.

18in (46cm) long

£80-120   **TEN**

£650-750   **LAW**

QUICK REFERENCE - PICTORIAL ADVERTISING

- The late 19thC saw the birth of the pictorial advertising poster, with the high point being the 1900s-30s when influential and prolific designers pushed the boundaries of what could be printed in fashionable styles of the day. The trend for advertising posters slowly declined after World War II, when other forms of advertising such as television took over.
- One of the most important factors to consider is the brand and the product depicted. 'Household names' such as Heinz and Guinness are usually desirable and are often valuable as they have large followings of collectors. Look for striking images with bold, bright colours, and designs that are typical of the period.
- A representative design by a notable designer, such as Alphonse Mucha or Bernard Villemot, will also help. However, the most important factor is visual appeal.
- Smoking, biscuits, and more niche areas such as bicycling, can prove very popular. Although the market may be smaller in size, the dedication of collectors ensures buoyant prices. Always look for posters in the best condition. Even though restoration can improve the appearance of a damaged example, it can be expensive.

'CYCLES ROCHET', a French bicycle advertising poster, designed by Charles Tichon, printed by Kossuth, Paris, horizontal fold, repaired tear through top margin, minor restoration in bottom corners, framed.

61.25in (156cm) high

£700-800   SWA

'PARFUMS DES FEMMES DE FRANCE' 'VIVILLE', a French perfume advertising poster, designed by Jean de Paleologue (1860-1942), printed by Atelier de l'Affiche, Paris, overpainting and restoration along vertical and horizontal folds, minor tears and wrinkling in margins, creases in image.

Paleologue used the acronym 'PAL' on his posters.

1896   51in (130cm) high

£650-750   SWA

'BIÈRES DE LA MEUSE', a beer advertising poster, designed by Alphonse Mucha (1860-1939), printed by Chaix, Paris, published in 'Maitres de l'Affiche' plate 182, matted and framed.

Czech artist and designer Alphonse Mucha is considered by many to be a founding father of the visual poster. Mucha's much-reproduced work, primarily executed in the Art Nouveau style, is highly desirable. His style incorporates sinuous patterns and women with flowing locks. The lady here is similar to the figure shown for 'Summer' in Mucha's 'Season' series published the year before.

1899   15in (39cm) high

£2,500-3,000   SWA

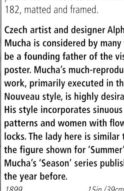

'CYCLES DECAUVILLE', a French Art Nouveau bicycle advertising poster, designed by E. Clouet, printed by J. Kossuth, Paris, with some tears and repaired tears, creases and abrasions, folded.

1894   51.5in (131cm) high

£350-450   SWA

'PEINTURE ÉMAIL LE PACIFIC', an enamel paint advertising poster, designer unknown, printed by Charles Verneau, Paris, trimmed to image, framed.

51.5in (131cm) high

£350-450   SWA

'ST. RAPHAËL QUINQUINA', a French wine advertising poster, designed by Jean de Paleologue 'PAL' (1860-1942), printed by Chardin, Paris, creases, abrasions, repaired tears, and wrinkles in margins and image, tears and minor losses at edges, restoration and minor losses along vertical and horizontal folds.

63in (160cm) wide

£250-300   SWA

'The Centlivre Tonic', an American medicinal tonic advertising poster, designer unknown, a tear through the upper edge into the image, matted and framed.

c1895   *19.75in (50cm)*
£400-500   SWA

'GUIGNOLET' 'COINTREAU', designed by Gustave-Henri Jossot (1886-1951), printed by Camis, Paris, repaired tears and overpainting along vertical and horizontal folds, minor repaired tears at edges, punch holes in left margin.

1898   *51.5in (131cm) high*
£1,500-2,000   SWA

A CLOSER LOOK AT A POSTER

This poster was a landmark image that changed advertising poster design and revolutionised Cappiello's career.

The success of this design allowed Cappiello to fully realise his now highly recognisable and individual design style.

The lady in a green dress was loosely based on those seen at the Folies Bergère, and became a hallmark character for Cappiello.

The red horse caught people's attention the most and people at the time began asking for 'red horse chocolate'.

'CHOCOLAT KLAUS', a French chocolate advertising poster, designed by Leonetto Cappiello (1875-1942), printed by P. Vercasson, Paris, extensive expert overpainting in image, vertical and horizontal folds, creases and abrasions in image, restoration in margins, framed.

1903   *62in (157.5cm) high*
£2,000-2,500   SWA

'A PERFECT .RELISH.' 'HEINZ TOMATO KETCHUP', designer unknown, creases and abrasions in image, skinning in top margin, staining in bottom margin.

This is a very rare, early poster for a much-loved, globally recognised brand. Heinz released its tomato ketchup in 1897, and by the date of this poster in around 1907, the company was producing 13 million bottles per year!

c1907   *31in (79cm) high*
£2,500-3,000   SWA

'CITROËN QUINZAINE', a French car advertising poster, printed or published by H.M. Boutin, Paris, abrasions in image, framed.

1920   *46.25in (117.5cm) high*
£450-500   SWA

'DETMER WOOLEN CO.', an American clothing fabric advertising poster, designer unknown, Tailoring Arts Publishing Co., New York, tears and creases at edges, staining, abrasions and foxing in margins and image, printed on thick paper.

1920

'Baumann', a Swiss hat advertising poster, designed by Otto Baumberger (1889-1961), published by Bollmann, Zurich, creases and abrasions in margins and image, overpainting in upper left edge.

28in (71.5cm) wide
£300-350   SWA

c1930   49.75in (126.5cm) high
£750-850   SWA

Mark Picks

Posters for popular, long-established household brands known across the world will always be popular and desirable. The more stylised and appealing the design, the more it is likely to fetch, particularly if it's early in date. Those showing any iconic logo or image associated with the brand, like this or Kellogg's rooster, are particularly desirable. Sandeman's silhouette of a Spanish 'Don' with his cloak and wide-brimmed hat was designed in 1928 by Massiot, who was taken on that year to revive advertising for the brand of sherry introduced in 1790. As the first poster to feature this now globally recognised, striking symbol, this has the best chance of always being desirable and valuable.

'SANDEMAN', designed by George Massiot, repaired tears, restoration, and abrasions in image, mounted to board.
1928   *61in (155cm) high*
£1,500-2,000   **SWA**

'SÖHNLEIN RHEINGOLD', designer unknown, light offsetting in image.
45.5in (115.5cm) long
£650-750   **SWA**

'My Goodness MY GUINNESS', designed by John Gilroy (1898-1985), minor tears at edges, creases, abrasions, and scratches in margins and image.

1935   *21.25in (54cm) high*
£500-550   **SWA**

'BONS CÉPAGES' 'LE VIN DE L'ÉPARGNE', designed by Jacques Auriac (1922-2003), printed by De la Vasselais, Paris, tears, repaired tears, and minor losses at edges, creases and abrasions in margins and image.
61in (155cm) high
£200-250   **SWA**

'BALLY', designed by Bernard Villemot (1911-89).
1982   *23.5in (59.5cm) high*
£300-350   **SWA**

'GUINNESS for Strength', designed by John Gilroy and Stevens, printed by Mills & Rockleys Ltd., Ipswich, creases and abrasions along vertical and horizontal folds, paper.

Artist John Gilroy's 'Guinness For Strength' campaign dates from the early 1930s, and plays on the idea that the vitamins Guinness is said to contain make you stronger. It was an iconic campaign, with the best-known image being a workman effortlessly carrying a huge iron girder. Animals are another hallmark feature of Guinness' advertising, and derive from the early campaign involving a hapless zoo keeper whose pint of Guinness keeps being stolen by the animals he is looking after.
60in (152.5cm) high
£1,000-1,500   **SWA**

'EVIAN', designed by Hervé Morvan (1917-80), printed by De la Vasselais, Paris, creases, minor restoration and abrasions in image, vertical folds.
24.5in (62cm) long
£150-200   **SWA**

POSTERS

QUICK REFERENCE - TRAVEL POSTERS

- Evoking senses of romance, glamour, and of the relaxation of holidays, the striking, stylish, and picturesque images on travel posters were aimed at tempting people away from their everyday lives. As more people could afford to take holidays and travel, and as modes of transport grew in variety across the 20thC, the genre of advertising or promotional posters grew.

- The golden age was the 1910s-30s, led by cruise lines and railways. Posters continued to be released after WWII, but they slowly declined in importance due to the rise of other forms of advertising. The introduction of increasingly affordable air travel in the 1950s saw another boom in poster design. This has become a burgeoning area; prices should rise as the supply of pre-war posters declines.

- Posters with bright, saturated or sun-soaked colours that show romanticised holidays always have appeal. Modern or Art Deco stylisation, the brand the poster is for, the designer or artist, and condition are also important.

- Folds and tears can be removed professionally, but any damage to the image itself is sometimes impossible to repair satisfactorily and reduces the value. Many collectors choose to back posters onto linen to preserve and strengthen them, but this should only be done by a professional.

'CORNWALL', designed by Ronald Lampitt for GWR, printed by J. Weiner, London, water stain along bottom edge, loss in lower left corner, restored losses, repaired tears, and overpainting in margins and image.

This poster was part of a series of three that all share the same unusual technique of using groups of coloured shapes to make up the design. In 1936, The Railway Gazette said 'The richness of colour and design obtained by the Romans in their tesselated pavements have inspired a new style of Great Western Railway poster'.

1936　　　　　*49.25in (125cm) wide*
£1,200-1,800　　　　　**SWA**

'FILEY - FOR THE FAMILY', a London and North Eastern Railway poster, designed by Reginald Edward Higgins (1877-1933), printed by Vincent Brooks, Day & Son, Ltd., London, minor creases, abrasions, and restoration along vertical and horizontal folds and in margins and image, minor repaired tears at edges.

Higgins only designed a handful of railway posters. This Art Deco example is perhaps his most successful.

1925　　　　　*39.5in (100.5cm) high*
£1,500-2,000　　　　　**SWA**

'BLACKPOOL', a British Railways poster, designed by Septimus Edwin Scott (1879-1965), printed by London Lithographic Co., London, minor restoration and chipping along vertical and horizontal folds, overpainting in image.

1949　　*49.75in (126.5cm) long*
£1,500-2,000　　　　　**SWA**

'Peterborough', a London and North Eastern Railway poster, designed by Fred Taylor (1875-1963), printed by The Dangerfield Printing Co. Ltd., London, creases in margins and image, restoration along vertical and horizontal folds.

c1935　　　*50in (127cm) long*
£500-600　　　　　**SWA**

'SOMERSET', a Great Western Railway (GWR) poster, designed by Frank Sherwin, printed by Stafford & Co Ltd, Netherfield, Nottingham, and London, depicting the Pack Horse Bridge, Allerford.

40in (102cm) high
£600-700　　　　　**LAW**

'GREAT YARMOUTH AND GORLESTON ON SEA', a London, Midland and Scottish Railway or London and North Eastern Railway poster, designed by Septimus Edwin Scott (1879-1965), printed by Jarrold & Sons, London, vertical and horizontal folds.

c1935　　　*49.5in (126cm) long*
£2,500-3,000　　　　　**SWA**

'SOUTHERN ARIZONA' 'Southern Pacific', designed by Ray Bethers (1902-73).

c1935 23in (58.5cm) high

£400-450 SWA

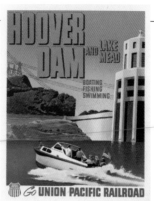

'HOOVER DAM AND LAKE MEAD' 'Go UNION PACIFIC RAILROAD', designer unknown, creases at edges, minor abrasion in image, skinning on verso.

This is the small format version of this poster. The Hoover Dam was built from 1931-36 and was named after President Herbert Hoover (1874-1964).

15.75in (40cm) high

£200-250 SWA

'NEW YORK' 'PENNSYLVANIA RAILROAD', designer unknown, repaired tears, overpainting, minor restored losses, and restoration in margins and image.

Posters such as this, which offer a view of major cities at a certain point in time, and thus are almost cartographic, are always of interest.

c1955 40.24in (102.5cm) high

£800-900 SWA

'LE SUD ALGÉRIEN' 'Nuit Saharienne', an Algerian national railways poster, designed by S. Besse, printed by Bacconnier, Algeria, repaired tears at edges, creases, and abrasions in image.

c1930 39.5in (100.5cm) high

£1,500-2,000 SWA

A CLOSER LOOK AT A RAILROAD POSTER

Along with Maynard Dixon and Maurice Logan, who also designed posters for the Southern Pacific, San Franciscan commercial artist Hall was an active member of 'The Thirteen Watercolorists', which became the Society of Western Artists.

The Southern Pacific Railroad began advertising their streamlined trains via posters in 1936, making this an early example.

The strong diagonal line and exaggerated sense of perspective of the railway emphasises the direct, yet long nation-crossing nature of the railway.

This geometric line is accentuated by the rectangles created by the strong horizon and the clearly demarked colours.

'Crossing GREAT SALT LAKE on Southern Pacific', designed by William Haines Hall (1903-77), repaired tears at edges into image, creases in margins and image, restored loss in lower left corner.

1940 23in (58.5cm)

£700-900 SWA

'CHEMINS DE FER ALGÉRIENS DE L'ÉTAT' 'LE SUD ALGÉRIEN TEMACINE - TOUGGOURT', an Algerian national railways poster, designed by Eugene Deshayes (1865-1954), printed by Bacconnier, Algeria, extensive restoration, some damage in image.

This is Deshayes' only poster.

1925 40.75in (103.5cm) high

£650-750 SWA

'GO BY TRAIN TO CÉVENNES', lithographic poster, designed by Saindré (?), printed by Editions Paul-Martial, Paris, linen-backed, unframed.

39in (99cm) high

£250-300 SWO

'LE MONT ST. MICHEL', a French state railways poster, designed by Leon Constant-Duval (1877-?), printed by Lucien Serre & Sie Paris, repaired tear and restoration at bottom edge into text, minor restored losses, repaired tears and overpainting in margins, creases, abrasions, and minor restoration in margins and image.

c1925   *39.5in (100.5cm) high*

£550-600   **SWA**

'VISITEZ LA CÔTE D'AZUR', a French national railways trains and coaches poster, printed by Perceval Paris, lithographic poster, linen-backed, unframed.

The primary colours and angular, collage style of this poster recall the work of artist Henri Matisse (1869-1964), who lived and worked in Vence, near Nice (the second largest city of the Cote d'Azur) during his later years.

39in (99cm) high

£350-450   **SWO**

'VISIT GARHMUKHTESHWAR', designer unknown, printed by East Indian Railway Press, Calcutta, minor repaired tears in margins, light creases in margins and image, ink stamp on verso showing through upper margin and image.

Even though it is unsigned, it is likely that this poster of the Ganga Temple was designed by Dorothy Newsome, who designed a number of travel posters promoting India. As the language shows, this is the Hindi version.

c1935   *39.5in (100.5cm) high*

£650-750   **SWA**

'JAPAN' 'JAPANESE GOVERNMENT RAILWAYS', designed by Peter Irwin Brown (1903-?), printed by Toppan Printing Co., Tokyo, minor restored losses and restoration in margins and corners, horizontal fold, minor restoration in image.

c1935   *39.75in (101cm) high*

£600-700   **SWA**

A CLOSER LOOK AT A TRAVEL POSTER

Estonian designer Gert Sellheim (1901-70) moved to Sydney in 1947 and is most famous for designing the kangaroo logo used by Australian national airline Qantas in the same year.

The inclusion of the word KODAK also makes this appealing to camera collectors.

Despite this, the biggest appeal comes from the instantly likeable artwork of a healthily tanned man and lady running down a beach, having fun together.

It was designed in 1935 during the most desirable period for travel posters and is typical of the genre at the time.

'To the SEASIDE BY TRAIN' 'TAKE A KODAK', designed by Gert Sellheim (1901-70) and Phelan (dates unknown), repaired tears at edges, minor abrasions in margins and image.

c1935   *40in (101.5cm) high*

£900-1,000   **SWA**

'SEE MEXICO THIS YEAR' 'Southern Pacific', designed by Maurice Logan (1886-1977), replaced right margin, expert overpainting in top and right margins into image, minor repaired tear at left edge.

In 1917, Logan and five other Californian painters joined together to form the 'Society of Six', a group of artists whose work was typified by fields of bold colours. Although they were considered unusual at the time their work is now seen as an important part of American art.

1932   *23in (58.5cm) high*

£800-900   **SWA**

'SEE THE PRIDE OF SCOTLAND' 'CANADIAN PACIFIC', designed by W.G. Finch, overpainting and restoration in margins, repaired tears and restoration in image.

c1929   *35.75in (91cm) high*

£700-800   **SWA**

'CHICAGO' 'UNITED AIR LINES', designer unknown, minor restoration in corners, colours attenuated, framed.

As well as being iconic of the city metropolis, the steel and plate glass skyscrapers shown are representative of the influential International Modernist style of architecture championed by architect Mies van der Rohe (1886-1969) and exemplified in his Seagram Building in New York, opened in 1958.

40in (107cm) high

£600-700   SWA

'fly TWA to CHICAGO', designer unknown, minor restored loss in lower right corner, minor restoration at edges.

1957   *39.5in (100.5cm) high*

£450-550   SWA

'GLASGOW by CLIPPER' 'PAN AMERICAN WORLD AIRWAYS', designer unknown, Pan American World Airways, Inc., overpainting in margins.

1951   *42.5in (108cm) high*

£200-250   SWA

'FLY TO INDIA BY B•O•A•C', designer unknown, minor repaired tears, restored losses, and creases at edges, framed.

c1950s   *30in (76.5cm) high*

£450-500   SWA

'NEW YORK' 'FLY THERE BY QANTAS', designed by Harry Rogers (1929-2012), printed by Posters Pty. Ltd., Australia, restored losses and skinning in top margin, light staining in margins.

One in a series of posters designed to promote the major destinations along Qantas' routes. Others include Hawaii, Rome, Hong Kong, and London.

c1960   *37.75in (96cm) high*

£1,000-1,500   SWA

'San Francisco via TWA', designer unknown, repaired tears, creases, abrasions, and restoration in margins and image, airbrushing in upper image.

c1950s   *40in (101cm) high*

£800-900   SWA

'UNITED AIR LINES' 'SAN FRANCISCO', designed by Joseph Binder (1898-1972), minor creases and abrasions at edges, paper.

This desirable poster is one of a series of six posters that Binder designed for United Airlines in 1957.

1957   *40in (101cm) high*

£1,800-2,200   SWA

'707 JET FLAGSHIPS' 'AMERICAN AIRLINES', designed by Herbert Danska (1932-), minor tears at edges, creases and time-staining in margins and image, paper.

The Boeing 707 was the first mass-produced civilian jet aircraft in the United States. Its maiden flight was on December 20, 1957, and it was put into transatlantic service by Pan American in 1958. American Airlines began using the aircraft for transcontinental flights in 1959. The 707 ushered in the Jet Age and brought about many fundamental changes in the airline industry.

c1959   *40in (101.5cm) high*

£500-600   SWA

POSTERS

'S.S. AMERICA' 'UNITED STATES
LINES', designed by Lester Beall
(1903-69), minor creases in
margins and image, metal strips
affixed to top and bottom and
hook on verso for hanging, paper.
c1952   *30in (76cm) high*
£1,000-1,500   **SWA**

'"SIERRA" Dampfer I. Klasse'
'Nach SÜD- AMERIKA', designed
by Bernd Steiner (1884-1933),
printed by Heilig & Bartels,
Bremen, repaired tears and
restoration at edges, some
affecting image, minor abrasions
in image, recreated bottom
margin.

**From 1922, Norddeutscher
Lloyd put the first of four
Sierra-class ships into service,
primarily running on the
South American routes, but
occasionally between Europe and America. Here, Steiner pays so much
attention to the fashionable clothes that it is hard to tell whether the
poster is advertising a shipping company or a fashion store.**
c1925   *39in (99cm) high*
£1,200-1,800   **SWA**

'Lido all the way' 'Italian Line',
designed by Paolo Federico
Garretto (1903-89), repaired tears
and creases in margins and image,
silkscreen.
1937   *36in (91.5cm) high*
£800-900   **SWA**

Judith Picks

Originally displayed in the Paris Metro,
this striking poster promotes the
French Railway's car ferry service to
England and Ireland. The image is an
unabashed, updated version of a poster advertising the
famous cruise liner, the Normandie, designed by Adolphe
Mouron (Cassandre) in 1935. As well as the strong graphic
suggestion of the ship's massive size, Conseil has even
replicated smaller details such as the flock of birds flying
around the hull. Although the Sealink brand hardly had
the glamour and luxury that was associated with the
Normandie, the graphic appeal and historical reference of
the poster should ensure that it has a following - partiularly
as an original 1935 poster for the Normandie could cost
well over £10,000.
Furthermore,
modern posters
from underground
networks can be
rare as they were not
kept and were often
destroyed through
use.

'Sealink', designed by
Perceval Conseil, printed
by Lalande-Courbet, Paris,
minor creasing in image.
1982   *66.75in (170cm) high*
£300-400   **SWA**

'SCOTLAND IT'S HIGHLANDS AND
ISLANDS', designed by Tom Gilfillan (1932-
53), printed by John Horn Ltd, Glasgow,
with restoration.

**Although it looks like a British railway
poster from the 1920s-30s, it actually
advertises the Caledonian MacBrayne
ferry service. Gilfillan designed about
half a dozen posters for the LMS Railway.**

                                      38.5in (97cm) long
£2,000-3,000   **SWA**

'BY TRAM FROM HAMMERSMITH
WIMBLEDON OR SHEPHERDS
BUSH', an Underground Electric
Railways Company Ltd original
poster, designed by Fred Taylor
(1875-1963), printed by Vincent
Brooks Day & Son, no.17.
1922   *40in (102cm) high*
£900-1,200   **SWO**

'LONDON'S
TRAMWAYS'
'THE ZOO BY
TRAMWAY
TO CAMDEN
TOWN',
designed by
Van Jones
(dates
unknown),
repaired tears
at edges,
some affecting
image,
overpainting
and minor
creases in
image, skinning in upper margin,
repaired pin holes in corners.
**This is a rare and desirable
poster and the colourful
Modernist image of parrots is
hugely appealing.**
1927   *29in (75cm) high*
£2,000-2,500   **SWA**

'SPRING IS GAY' 'Travel by Greyhound', designed by Rod Ruth (dates unknown), tears at edges, some affecting image, paper.

38in (96cm) high

£300-350 SWA

'Voyages en Algérie et Tunisie', designed by Henri Polart (dates unknown), printed by D. Daude, Paris, repaired tears, restored losses, creases, and restoration in margins and image and along vertical and horizontal folds, repaired pin holes in corners.

1910 *41in (104cm) high*

£500-600 SWA

'SURFING AUSTRALIA', designer unknown, printed by Troedel & Cooper Pty. Ltd., Melbourne, repaired tears and minor creases at edges.

This very rare poster shows that the beach was already a recognisable part of Australian culture by the 1930s. Bathing at the sea for health and fitness had become popular during the 1880s and, by the 1930s, surfing was enjoyed by many. The fact that a lady is shown at this date is also interesting and although women were shown participating more in sports during the early 20thC, surfing is very unusual. An important poster to the history of surfing, this is the larger of two sizes and is thought to be the only one known in this size.

c1935 *40in (101cm) high*

£2,500-3,000 SWA

'OFF TO THE NORTH FOR WARMTH' 'TO QUEENSLAND', designed by Percival Albert (Percy) Trompf (1902-64), printed by David Whyte, Brisbane, some tears and creases affecting image, some staining.

Trompff is known for his posters for the Australian National Travel Association and the Victorian Government Railway.

1938 39in (99cm) high

£2,200-2,800 SWA

A CLOSER LOOK AT A COLONIAL POSTER

This poster was printed in Hanoi during the height of French colonialism.

It is one of an exceptional and highly desirable series of Art Deco travel posters designed by Ponchin for Indochina.

The French took control of Indochina (Cambodia, Laos, and Vietnam) in 1863 and effectively stayed in power for nearly a century until 1953.

It depicts the wonders of the ancient Angkor Wat temples in the jungles of Cambodia, capturing the lush tropical setting perfectly.

'CAMBODGE ANGKOR' 'L'INDOCHINE FRANÇAISE', designed by Joseph-Henri Ponchin (1897-1962), printed by D'Extreme-Orient, Hanoi, restored losses at edges, some affecting text, expertly recreated left margin, restoration along vertical and horizontal folds, colours attenuated, matted and framed.

1931 *42.75in (108cm) high*

£2,000-2,500 SWA

'EGYPTE RAU', designer unknown, printed by A.O.P., Cairo, repaired tears, restoration and overpainting in margins and image.

The United Arab Republic (Republique Arabe Unie, in French, hence 'RAU') was a name taken by Syria and Egypt in 1958, when they entered into a short-lived political union. Syria withdrew in 1961, but Egypt continued to be referred to as the United Arab Republic until 1971.

c1960 *38.25in (97.5cm) high*

£300-350 SWA

'EGYPT', designed by M. Azmy, printed by Institut Graphique Egyptien, repaired tear in bottom margin, pin holes in bottom corners, minor abrasions in image.

c1938 *38in (97.5cm) high*

£1,200-1,800 SWA

POSTERS

'WÖRTHSEE', designed by Richard Knab and Hans Heinrich Koch, printed by Oscar Consee, Munich, expert extensive overpainting in margins and image, minor creases and abrasions in image.

1928   *46.75in (111cm) high*

£600-700   **SWA**

'SCHEVENINGEN', designed by Louis C. Kalff (1897-1976), printed by Mouton & Co., The Hague, repaired tears and creases in margins.

The majority of Kalff's posters were designed for Philips, for whom he worked for nearly 40 years. He only designed a few travel posters, and this is considered to be his best. The stylisation, colour, and design evokes the Art Deco style perfectly. Dutch Art Deco and Mid-century Modern style is an emerging market.

c1930   *39.25in (100cm)*

£2,000-2,500   **SWA**

'ACQUI' 'LA GRANDE PISCINA TERMALE', designer unknown, printed by Barabino & Graeve, Genova, repaired tears at edges, some into image and text, overpainting in upper right image, light creases and abrasions along vertical and horizontal folds.

Advertising an Italian thermal pool, this is a very colourful, very rare poster in a highly desirable Modernist style. The sense of perspective is dramatic and accentuated by the angle of the title and the curves of the bather's bodies.

1933   *55in (140cm) high*

£3,500-4,000   **SWA**

'DO YOU KNOW THE LAND?' 'ITALY', designed by Ruggero Alfredo Michahelles (1898-1976), printed by Gros-Monti & Co., Turin, loss in left margin, tear in lower right corner, creases and abrasions in image, paper.

This is one from a series of photomontage travel posters designed by the brother of Futurist artist Ernesto Michahelles (Thayaht).

c1935   *39in (99cm) high*

£600-700   **SWA**

'le lac de Côme Italie', designer unknown, printed by Grafische Ripamonte, Orsenigo, repaired tears at edges, abrasions in margins and image.

Locations make a major difference to value. Lake Como is known as a resort favoured by a great many wealthy people and celebrities. As such, they can afford to pay large sums of money for great-looking posters like this one. Many are displayed in their other homes, reminding them of their lakeside retreat or holiday destination.

1933   *38in (96.5cm) high*

£3,000-3,500   **SWA**

'SAN FRANCISCO', designed by Howard Koslow (1924-), printed by Penn Prints, New York, restored loss in lower left corner, slightly affecting image, minor creases, abrasions and restoration in margins and image.

1964   *36.75in (100cm) high*

£800-900   **SWA**

'LAS ARENAS', designed by Josep Renau-Montoro, (1907-82), printed by Graficas Valencia, Sevilla, minor abrasions and restoration at edges.

c1932   *39.25in (100cm) high*

£2,000-2,500   **SWA**

QUICK REFERENCE - SKIING POSTERS

● Skiing is seen as a glamorous and romantic sport, favoured by the rich and famous. Many skiers choose to commemorate their passion by displaying skiing posters in their homes. Prices have risen faster than for many other posters because of wealthy buyers.

● A number of factors are important when considering value. Stylised and striking images will always be desirable, particularly if they date from the 1930s-50s. Vibrant colours are also good features, as is a modern stylisation. A combination of drama, humour, or speed will also add desirability.

● Condition is also important, as these posters are primarily bought by people who are generally not collectors. One of the most important factors, however, is the resort or country shown. Although exclusive resorts can often fetch the highest prices, the increased demand from more widely visited resorts can push up prices for more common posters. Some resorts will always be more sought-after than others, prices can vary widely as fashions change, or small groups of buyers aim to own a particular poster.

● Posters lacking skiers and dynamism tend to be more affordable, as are those from the 1970s-80s, which are possibly currently under-valued.

'U.S. SKI TEAM' 'WORLD CHAMPIONSHIPS', designer unknown, minor restoration in margins and image.
1966   29.75in (75.5cm) high
£550-650   SWA

'NEW HAMPSHIRE', designed by Ted Hunter, trimmed left margin, light creasing in margins and image, paper.
          35in (89cm) high
£950-1,100   SWA

'NATIONAL and STATE PARKS', designed by Dorothy Waugh (1896-1996), printed by U.S. Government Printing Office, Washington D.C., minor repaired tears, creases, and overpainting at edges, minor abrasions in lower image.

Unlike the other posters in Waugh's series for the National Parks, this bold, Modernist poster differs in the manner in which it was printed. The grey areas on the geometrically rendered skier and in the image have been created using a photo-offset process. Her other posters were all created by letterpress.
c1934   40in (101cm) high
£750-850   SWA

'III Olympic Winter Games' 'Lake Placid, USA', designed by Witold Gordon (1885-1968), tears at edges, some affecting image, creases and abrasions in margins and image, tape on verso, paper.

This early, rare poster is important as 1932 was the first year that both the Summer and Winter Olympic Games were held in the US, rather than in Europe. The landmark nature of these Games also means that collectors of Olympic memorabilia would vie to own this poster, which contributes to the high value.
1932   40in (102cm) high
£5,500-6,500   SWA

'Austria', printed by Christoph Reisser's Söhne, Vienna, minor creases in margins and image.
c1935   37.5in (95.5cm) high
£800-900   SWA

'Join the sun on a ski-run in FRANCE', designed by Dubois, printed by S.A. Courbet, Paris, minor tears and creases at edges, paper.
1950s   39in (99cm) high
£250-300   SWA

'WINTER IN GERMANY', designed by Ludwig Hohlwein (1874-1949), printed by Herm. Sonntag & Co., Munich, tears and creases at edges, some affecting image, paper, framed.
c1935   39.5in (100.5cm) high
£400-500   SWA

POSTERS

'ALLARD DE MEGÈVE', designed by Gaston Gorde (1908-95), printed by Editions Gaston Gorde, Paris.
c1935   39.5in (100.5cm)
£250-300   SWA

'Flexible Flyer' 'SPLITKEIN', designed by Sascha Maurer (1897-1961), minor restoration at edges.
c1935   37.25in (95cm)
£1,500-2,000   SWA

'St. Moritz', designed by Werner Weiskonig (1907-82), printed by Orell Fussli, Zurich, overpainting, creases, and restoration in margins and image, repaired tears and restored losses at edges, water stains in left margin, repaired pin holes in corners.
1946   39.5in (100.5cm) high
£800-900   SWA

'Winter Sport in USSR', photo by L. Skurikhin, horizontal crease through central image, creases in margins and image, paper.
                        24.5in (63cm) high
£500-600   SWA

A CLOSER LOOK AT A SKIING POSTER

This is the German version.

Alex Diggelmann was a Swiss artist who won three awards for his poster designs, one in 1936 and two in 1948.

The skier flying through the air at speed is dramatic and desirable, and this image and format was used at other times.

The design is clever, although minimal and not varied and vibrant, the blue suggests the Alpine sky as well as mountains and snow.

Many of Diggelmann's designs use similarly minimal design elements, often based around one key figure or motif, yet these are powerful enough to hold the viewer's attention.

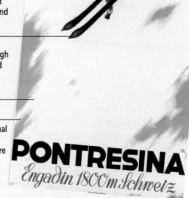

'PONTRESINA', designed by Alex Walter Diggelman (1902-87), printed by Gebr. Fretz, Zurich, minor repaired tears at edges, light creases and abrasions in image.
c1930   39.5in (100.5cm) high
£4,500-5,500   SWA

'BILGERI - SKI = AUSTRÜSTUNG', designed by Carl Kunst (1884-1912), printed by Reichhold & Lang, Munich, light staining in top margin, minor repaired tear at bottom edge.
c1910   30in (76.5cm) long
£650-750   SWA

'...those heavenly carpets by LEES' 'BEAUTY UNDERFOOT', designer unknown, overpainting in corners.

                        29.75in (76cm) high
£200-250   SWA

'POLISH PAVILION' 'NEW YORK WORLD'S FAIR 1939', designed by JHR, minor repaired tears at edges, creases and abrasions in margins and image.

1938   *39in (99cm) high*

£650-750   **SWA**

A CLOSER LOOK AT AN OLYMPIC POSTER

The inclusion of the Houses of Parliament, a recognisable symbol of London and Great Britain, makes a strong political statement and emphasises their survival during the war, which ended only three years before.

The discus thrower is an icon of the Olympic Games and juxtaposing this with the Houses of Parliament equates the Games with London.

This is the medium format of the poster. All have risen in value recently as London hosted the Games again in 2012.

The hands of Big Ben's clock face are set at four o'clock, the time the Games were officially declared open by George VI.

'OLYMPIC GAMES' 'LONDON', designed by Walter Herz (1909-65), printed by McCorquodale & Co., London, repaired tears, creases, abrasions and restoration in image and along sharp vertical and horizontal folds, scratch in image.

1948   *29.75in (75.5cm) high*

£2,500-3,000   **SWA**

'visit the New York World's Fair 1964-1965' 'See the fair from the air' 'Ride the AMF MONORAIL', unknown designer, minor creases and abrasions in margins and image.

                    52in (132cm) long

£650-750   **SWA**

'FOIRE INTERNATIONALE DE PRAGUE', designed by Cardos, printed by Neubert, Prague, minor restoration in image, repaired tears and creases in margins and image, matted and framed.

1935   *40in (101cm) high*

£350-400   **SWA**

'SEE THE GAS EXHIBIT' 'DAILY MAIL IDEAL HOME EXHIBITION', coloured lithographic poster.

          30in (76cm) high

£60-80   **SWO**

'PARKER AND WATTS CIRCUS' 'KIT CARSON JR.', designer unknown, losses in margins, creases at edges, some affecting image, paper.

          41in (104.5cm) high

£150-200   **SWA**

'L'ODEON', a Clarice Cliff poster, advertising the exhibition, printed in colours.

          23.25in (59cm)

£60-80   **WW**

'LE SOCIALISME CONTRE LE BOLCHEVISME' 'POUR UNE EUROPE LIBRE', designer unknown, printed by Editions C.E.A., Paris., repaired tears at edges, light foxing in margins and image, repaired pin holes in corners.

c1942   47in (119cm) high

£650-700   **SWA**

'WE STAND FOR PEACE AND WE ASSERT THE CAUSE OF PEACE', designed by B. Belopolsky (1909-78), printed by Iskustvo, Moscow, minor restoration along vertical and horizontal folds, creases and restoration in margins.

1950   34in (87cm) high

£750-850   **SWA**

'SIBERIE', designer unknown, printed by Paix et Liberte, Paris, vertical and horizontal folds, minor chipping at edges, paper.

c1952   23.75in (60.5cm) high

£300-350   **SWA**

'FREEDOM AMERICAN-STYLE', designed by Boris Prorokov (1911-72), printed by Fine Arts, Moscow, minor creases in image, paper.

1971   34.25in (87cm) high

£350-400   **SWA**

A CLOSER LOOK AT A RUSSIAN POSTER

Ukrainian Viktor Koretsky was one of the Soviet Union's greatest propaganda artists.

He was heavily influenced from c1931 until his death by the photo montages of German John Heartfield (born Helmut Herzfeld, 1891-1968) who was a pioneer in using art for political purposes.

He specialised in combining gouache and staged photographs to create direct and emotionally powerful images, representing the (intended) Soviet way of life.

Almost following Modernist principles, fitness and strength were desired attributes for Soviet people, be they soldiers, workers or, as here, young adults.

'YOU WANT TO BE LIKE THAT - TRAIN!', designed by Viktor Koretsky (1909-98), printed by Soviet Artist, Moscow, repaired tear and creases at edges, abrasions in image.

1966   23.25in (60cm) wide

£700-800   **SWA**

'Leningrad', designer unknown, repaired tears and abrasions at edges, staining and creases in margins and image, minor loss and sticker in lower right corner, ink stamp in upper left corner, faded.

This poster was produced by the Soviet tourist agency Intourist, and shows that Lenin towers above and leads the Soviet people, even when they are at their leisure.

c1930s   38.5in (98cm) high

£500-550   **SWA**

'PALAIS DE GLACE' 'Champs-Elysées', designed by Jules Cheret (1836-1932), printed by Chaix, Paris, minor restoration and overpainting in margins and image.

Between 1893 and 1900, the influential French Art Nouveau artist Cheret designed seven posters for the Palais de Glace, an ice-skating rink located on the Champs-Elysées. Here, the elongated format which he used for three of the designs, allowed him to more fully render the gracefully controlled movement of his beautifully dressed central figure.

1894 *95in (241.5cm) high*
£3,000-3,500 **SWA**

'MADISON SQUARE THEATRE SUCCESS' 'YOUNG MRS. WINTHROP', a theatre poster, designer unknown, loss in right margin, text banner affixed to bottom.

1882 *36.25in (92cm) high*
£250-300 **SWA**

'THE CHAP BOOK' 'THANKSGIVING NO.', designed by William H. Bradley (1868-1932), horizontal fold, tears and creases at edges, some affecting image, paper, framed.

Bradley's style combined a strong sense of the Arts & Crafts and Art Nouveau movements with the work of Aubrey Beardsley. This poster was deemed so important to the Art Nouveau movement at the time that it was included in the show that opened Siegfried Bing's influential Salon de l'Art Nouveau on December 26, 1895. It became so popular with collectors that it went out of print in two months! The 'Chap Book' was the first in a run of late 19thC literary and art magazines.

1895 *21in (53.5cm)*
£1,500-2,000 **SWA**

'NEWMANN'S WONDERFUL SPIRIT MYSTERIES', designer unknown, printed by Donaldson Litho Co., Kentucky.

28in (71cm) high
£400-500 **SWA**

'Good Posture and proper diet promote health', designer unknown, light creasing in margins, skinning on verso, paper.

18in (45cm) high
£200-250 **SWA**

'Mighty Small but Mighty!', a work incentive poster, printed by Mather & Company, Chicago.

1929 *44.5in (113cm) high*
£350-400 **SWO**

'WEAPONS FOR THE IDF' 'THE DEFENSE FUND', designed by Paul Kor (Kornowski) (1926-2001) and Samuel Grundman, tear in upper image, vertical and horizontal folds, tape on verso in upper corners, paper.

1956 *27.25in (69cm) high*
£750-800 **SWA**

A 1950s British Railways Midland Region enamelled station totem sign for 'Kenilworth'.

36.6in (93cm) wide

£450-550   **LOC**

A 'HONITON' enamel railway sign, from Honiton station platform.

96in (244cm) wide

£450-550   **LAW**

A Great Northern Railway cast-iron 'BEWARE OF TRAINS' sign, repainted.

Collectors prefer signs with their original paint, even if it is damaged. Although repainting will brighten up a battered sign, it will usually reduce the value.

£50-80   **TEN**

A London Chatham and Dover Railway 'private property' cast-iron sign.

22in (56cm) long

£500-700   **FLD**

A Great Western Railway '6144' locomotive cast-iron number plate, from Prairie Tank, from a 6144 61XX Class 2-6-2T Prairie Tank locomotive.

1931   *25.5in (65cm) wide*

£600-800   **LAW**

A South Eastern & Chatham Railway 'Incorporated by Act of 1899' panel, with various crests at the centre, the wooden panel with two metal strips on the back and an old label which reads, 'The property of H R Newman, 43 Russell Rd London W14'.

21.25in (54cm) square

£300-400   **LAW**

A GWR railway clocking-in clock, made by the National Time Recorder Co Ltd, GWR 3943, with an oak case and glass front, with a plaque inside, with its key, in working order.

Reputably from the goods yard at Taunton Station.

38.5in (98cm) high

£400-500   **LAW**

A scrapbook autographed by all four Beatles in 1963, with a circular photograph of the band in 1963.

Sold together with various black and white photographs of the group, this set was obtained by a lady who was taken backstage at a TV recording of 'Thank Your Lucky Stars' in 1963 by her father who worked on the programme. The signatures are well placed, well-signed and above a visually appealing photograph of the group looking as many love to remember them.

£3,500-4,500   COT

A 1960s autograph album page signed by the Beatles when they played at the Plaza Old Hill Halesowen, West Midlands, England, signed in blue and black ballpoint ink with date and the venue on the opposite buff colour page, together with a further signature by George Martin, 'Good luck', cut out from white paper and laid down with a note in blue pen 'George Martin 5th Beatle ATV Studios', together with other television character signatures.

The brother of the person who collected these signatures worked as electrician and lighting engineer at the Plaza during the 1960s. From the way it is signed, it appears that George Harrison may have been signed by one of the other Beatles, possibly Paul. This was not unusual, and any or all of The Beatles' signatures could be written by other band members, or even roadies or secretaries. However, their signatures at this period were often underdeveloped and can have slight differences in style. For more information about Beatles' signatures, please see p303 of the Miller's Collectables Handbook 2012-2013.
1963
£500-800   FLD

A 1960s Margo of Mayfair 'With The Beatles Talc' powder tin, with portraits of The Fab Four, complete with contents.
8in (20cm) high
£150-200   FLD

A 1960s Boots compact for cream powder featuring The Beatles, boxed.
3.25in (8cm) diam
£250-350   FLD

A presentation photograph and paper slip signed 'Elvis Presley', with PSA/DNA authentication slip.
£450-550   WHP

A Gibson Flying V Centennial 100th Anniversary series electric guitar, limited edition, only 100 made, made in USA, ser.no.1970 9, with certificate, warranty card, sash, strap, banner and hard case.
c1994
£3,000-4,000   GHOU

A rare Fender Stratocaster Chris Rea Signature electric guitar, limited edition, made in Mexico, ser.no.MN9124064, with Fender hard case.

These guitars were made as a limited run of five hundred. This is one of the first batch of fifty that were sold with the proceeds donated to Children in Need UK. The guitar comes with all the original hang tags, the Fender Artist Signature Series video about the guitar, two guitar slides.
c1999
£850-950   GHOU

A Fender Stratocaster electric guitar, made in USA, ser.no.56818, black finish, with usual wear to the body including scratches and chips to finish, some corrosion and rusting to metal parts, original Fender hard case, strap and inspection tag.
c1975
£1,500-2,000   GHOU

A Victorian mounted 'Annagelb' glass scent bottle, with a twist-open, hinged cover, embossed with a whippet, unmarked.

Annagelb (Anna yellow) is glass that is coloured yellow by adding uranium to the molten batch. It was developed in 1834 by factory owner Josef Reidel (1816-94) and named after his wife Anna.

3.4in (8.5cm) long

£200-300   **LAW**

A Victorian mounted aquamarine-coloured cut-glass scent bottle, with embossed, hinged cover, unmarked.

4in (10cm) long

£200-300   **LAW**

A late Victorian silver scent bottle, by J.M. Banks, in the form of a small curly ram's horn, suspensory chain and screwcap, with Birmingham hallmarks.

1890   *2.5in (6.5cm) long*

£100-150   **LAW**

A Victorian silver Aesthetic Movement scent bottle, by Sampson Mordan, London, engraved with a humming bird, the interior with a stopper.

c1880   *2in (5.4cm) long*

£250-350   **WW**

A Victorian silver-mounted ceramic egg scent bottle, probably by Sampson Mordan, London, with screw-off cover, maker's marks partially worn, also marked with a registration number.

1887   *1.5in (3.5cm) long*

£80-120   **WW**

A French Argy Rousseau enamel perfume bottle and stopper, depicting a parrot in a cage, signed in full.

French glassmaker and designer Joseph-Gabriel Rousseau, who used the name Argy Rousseau, is best-known for his pâte de verre works. For more information on this technique, see p231. This delicately enamelled perfume bottle is of very high quality.

c1921   *6in (15.5cm) high*

£800-£1,000   **M&DM**

QUICK REFERENCE - BOURJOIS BAKELITE PERFUME

● **This desirable 'Evening in Paris' range from Bourjois also includes a grandfather clock and a front door and doorstep, both made in a similar mottled blue Bakelite. A tortoise and a shell can be found in a darker mottled blue Bakelite. Examine the ears, hinge, and corners closely, as they are often broken, which reduces value by over half. This is also a more serious problem than the lack of the (easily replaced) perfume bottle inside.**

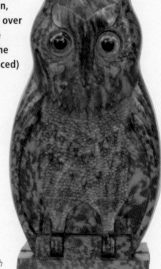

A 1930s Bourjois mottled blue Bakelite perfume bottle holder, containing original blue glass 'Soir de Paris' labelled perfume bottle.

3.75in (9.5cm) high

£100-150   **FLD**

QUICK REFERENCE - SCIENTIFIC INSTRUMENTS

- Scientific instruments from the Italian Renaissance are extremely rare and are largely the preserve of museums, but there is plenty of scope to build a collection of instruments produced from the 17thC to the late 19thC. Perhaps surprisingly, values for most instruments apart from the very best and rarest, have fallen in general terms over the past decade as they have become unfashionable.

- Most collectors choose to focus on one type of instrument, such as the microscope, or on one area, such as optical instruments or navigational instruments. Materials vary from ivory to lacquered brass, with the majority being made from the latter material due to its properties of durability. As precision was critical, they were usually finely engineered and of very high quality.

- Apart from the type of instrument and how well it was made, consider the date, the maker, the precise function and way it achieves that, and any other wording or markings found. The work of certain makers such as Benjamin Martin, J.B. Dancer, Dollond, and George Adams is typically more desirable than unmarked instruments or those by lesser known makers.

- Always look for accessories and an original case, as these will add to desirability and, usually, value. Totally complete and original instruments will always fetch a premium, particularly those that are traditionally accompanied by a plethora of accessories such as microscopes. Look at address details under a name or on a label as these can help to date a piece to a specific period. Makers based in central city locations were usually highly skilled and important and may have had connections to royalty, key figures in history or naval or similar services.

- Beware of 20thC and contemporary reproductions. These are usually made from a brighter yellow brass and the engineering of the mechanical movements such as the rack and pinion focusing is not usually precise or of high quality. Skilfully made reproductions can be sought-after if the originals are no longer available or because they are too expensive. Although scientific and other instruments are not hard to find on the market, always aim to buy from a specialist auction house or dealer, particularly if you are new to the area.

A late 19thC to early 20thC brass monocular microscope, by J Swift and Son London, no.1342, triple-lens holder on folding legs and stand in a fitted leather case with accessories.

£250-300   FLD

A late 19thC brass monocular adjustable microscope, by J Swift & Son London, no.575, in fitted leather case with accessories.

£200-250   FLD

A monocular brass and metal microscope, by R & J Beck, with lenses and accessories, and with part of its original box, marked, 'R & J Beck, 6206, London'.

£60-100   LAW

An R & J Beck Compound star model monocular microscope, no. 15931, on a cast-iron foot, contained in the original oak case but lacking its accessories.
c1890
£60-90   TEN

An Ernst Leitz Wetzlar microscope, no. 286372, with brass barrel, black lacquered stage and stand, dual rack and pinion focussing, slide positioner and condenser, in original wooden case with Magnification Table inside door, with nine prepared slides.

£160-200   TEN

SCIENTIFIC INSTRUMENTS

An early 20thC Ernst Leitz student's magnifying stage, brass with black base and stage, having single 10x magnifying lens and single-sided planar mirror, engraved 'Birkbeck College Zool Dept 10', in case stamped 'BCBD 11'.

£40-60   **TEN**

A small mid-18thC simple microscope, probably English, with folding handle and lens, specimen pin with securing nut, within cardboard box with marbled paper cuff.

closed 2.25in (5.5cm) high

£180-220   **CM**

A CLOSER LOOK AT A MICROSCOPE

The wooden base is a box that contains the microscope and its accessories once they have been unscrewed and folded flat.

From the late 18thC onwards, the study of botany and natural history became popular and these small microscopes could be carried around for use in the field.

Robert Banks (active 1796-1834) was a high-quality maker in The Strand, London. Charles Darwin took a very similar microscope to this on his travels on board the Beagle.

A number of other slightly different forms and types are known, including Gould and Cary, but it is always vital that all the accessories and parts are there, as here.

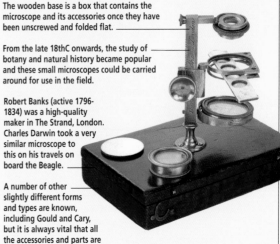

An early 19thC simple pocket microscope, by Banks, London, rack and pinion focus, single-sided mirror, platform, live box, white/ebonised disc, threaded eyepiece and single four-specimen slide, in a fitted box with thread securing to lid, signed 'Banks Invt. 441 Strand London'.

4in (10cm) diam

£750-850   **CM**

An early 19thC pocket microscope, attributed to Thomas Rubergall, London, with ebonised wooden base supporting mirror, socket for square section shaft with spring slide stage, specimen clamp and three swivel lenses, in a fish-skin covered case.

This example comes with a card box containing ten 4-specimen slides, numbered 1,2,3,6,7,8 and 10, plus three unnumbered associated examples.

4.25in (11cm) diam

£650-750   **CM**

A 19thC microscope preparation cabinet, by Angus & Co London, with medical bottles, microscope slides and preparatory equipment, and other accessories including clamps etc.

cabinet 8in (20cm) high

£500-600   **LAW**

A late 20thC reproduction of a mid-19thC lacquered brass Culpeper-type microscope, together with extra lenses and accessories, in a case, the interior fitted with drawer.

The Culpeper-type, named after the instrument maker Edmund Culpeper (c1670–1738), is typified by a tripod stand and sliding tube. They were typically sold inside pyramidal cases containing accessories. Those sold by him bear a trade label in the case. He developed the type from 1725-30 and they continued to be made into the mid-19thC. Although unsigned examples were made during this period, a quantity of unsigned brass examples have surfaced in the past twenty years which appear to be late 20thC reproductions. Overly heavy wear to the brass or damage that appears to have been caused by fire are typical signs of a reproduction. Also consider the screws and areas around them.

case 13.5in (34cm) high

£200-300   **PC**

An English 1.25in (3cm) monocular, the shagreen tube with gilt-embossed Morocco-covered single draw, with contemporary card storage case with faux fish-skin covering, unsigned.
c1760   *3in (7.5cm) high*
£350-400   **CM**

A CLOSER LOOK AT A MAGIC LANTERN

They were developed by the Dutch scientist Christiaan Huygens in the late 1650s and saw their golden age in the late 18thC and early 19thC as part of scary shows known as 'phantasmagoria'.

Originally illuminated by magnified sunlight, candle or oil lamp, the invention of the Argand lamp (1790s), Limelight (1820s) and then the electric arc lamp (1860s) made them brighter and safer.

Mahogany and brass framed examples such as this are usually high quality, and Watson (active 1837-1948) was a renowned maker based in Holborn, London. They became known as W.Watson & Son in 1868.

Magic lanterns are an early form of slide projector, using painted and later printed glass slides, that were used as a form of entertainment or for educational purposes.

A late Victorian mahogany and brass magic lantern, by W Watson & Sons, London, the 8in (20.3cm) lens with rack and pinion focusing and mahogany sliding plate holder, the body hinged to allow adjustment of inclination, sliding doors revealing the now electrified light source, and blued metal chimney.
                    19in (48.5cm) long
£300-400   **AH**

A pair of 7x50 Kriegsmarine U-boat binoculars, stamped for maker 'beh' (Leitz), no.'369422', Kriegsmarine mark and issue number '29778', with leather neck strap.
                    8.5in (21.5cm) high
£1,000-1,300   **CM**

An Ernst Plank metal magic lantern, single-fixed lens with three circular discs, with original paper-overlaid pine carrying case.
£120-150   **FLD**

A French 'Le Taxiphote' mahogany stereo slide viewer, with glass slides illustrating waterways, with 12 additional sets of slides stored beneath the viewer, slides dated.
1923
£450-550   **TEN**

A Monarch hand-held stereo viewer, with a mahogany box containing various views.
£100-150   **TEN**

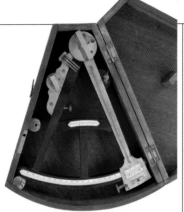

A 19thC vernier octant, by Walker & Son, Liverpool, the wooden 'T' frame with inset scale divided to 105°, lacquered brass index arm and fittings including pinhole sights, three shades and pin feet, with box, signed.

radius 13in (33cm)

£550-650   CM

A 19thC vernier sextant, by Crichton, London, silvered scale divided to 150°, index arm with magnifier, seven shades, ebonised handle and feet, in case with accessories, and trade label for Francis M. Moore, Belfast, the arc signed and inscribed for retailers Norie & Wilson.

radius 7.5in (19cm)

£450-550   CM

A Kaisermarine Vernier sextant, by H. Haecke, Neukölln, with silvered scale divided to 130°, no.'7252', sighting tube, seven shades, pin feet and wooden handle inset with Kaisermarine emblem and no.'1816'.

radius 7.25in (18.5cm)

£450-550   CM

A modern brass planispheric astrolabe, after Jean Fusoris (15thC) with single plate engraved for latitude of London, the reverse for Paris, rete for nineteen stars, the back engraved with shadow square, degree scale, zodiac calendar, and unequal hour scale.

Originating in pre-Christian Greece, this complex and sophisticated navigational instrument was made until the mid-17thC in Europe and until the 20thC in some Islamic countries. This example was made in 1985 using the reprinted treatise by Jean Fusoris found in E. Poules 'Un Constructeur d'Instruments Astronomiques au XV Siècle', 1963, from the Science Museum, London. An original, similar example can be seen at the History of Science Museum, Oxford. Original examples, particularly from Europe, are scarce and very valuable.

8.25in (21cm) diam

£200-300   CM

A drum sextant, in lacquered brass signed E.R. Watts, Old Kent Rd., London, detachable sighting tube, threaded cover inscribed 'F. Livsey', contained in leather case dated '1866'.

c1866   *4in (10cm) diam*

£120-160   CM

A 6in (15.2cm) star globe, by Ernst Schotte & Co., paper gores laid over metal shell, set within brass horizon and meridian rings on metal frame support, lacking Kriegsmarine marks, probably issued to the Kriegsmarine c1944-45.

8in (20.5cm) high

£250-350   CM

A brass theodolite, with silvered scale with vernier, needle clamp and spirit level, the sighting tube with cross wires and spirit tube over, mounted on arc with silvered scale and rack-and-pinion adjustment, signed and inscribed 'Thomas Rubergall' 'Optn. to H.R.H. the Duke of Clarence' '24 Coventry St. London'.

Most theodolites would fetch well under half this value. This example is of high quality and was made by the important maker Thomas Rubergall (active 1802-54) and bears wording relating to Royal patronage.

c1840   *10.5in (26.5cm)*

£1,200-1,500   CM

A rare pocket compass sundial, by John Fowler, in engraved brass with black wax filling, folding gnomon, blued-steel needle, signed 'J Fowler' fecit between 'III' and 'VIII'.

John Fowler worked between 1721 and 1750 from The Globe, Sweeting's Alley by the Royal Exchange, London, and specialised in sundials and compasses.

c1730   2.75in (6.5cm) diam
£400-600   CM

An English pocket compass sundial, the 3in (7.5cm) paper-covered mica card with sealing wax balancing, suspended in brass bowl with removable pierced dial and folding gnomon and threaded brass lid with compass rose glued within.

c1740   3.5in (9cm) diam
£150-200   CM

An early 19thC ivory pocket compass, by Gilbert & Sons, London, sealing wax balancing, removable brass pin, supporting inner ivory card damping ring and turned, threaded lid, the 1.75in (4.5cm) mica-backed card with jewelled pivot signed 'Gilbert & Sons, near Ye India House, Londoni'.

2.5in (6.5cm)
£600-800   CM

An early 19thC Dutch dry card compass, by Gebroeders Polak, Vlissingen, in exotic hardwood, the 3.75in (9.5cm) printed card signed and sealed within white-lined oak bowl.

6in (15cm) high
£300-400   CM

A French surveying compass, by Jacques Canivet, half blued-steel needle on jewelled pivot with retainer under, silvered circumference scale, glazed with retaining spring, sliding lid, pivoted side sight and inset table attachments underneath, contained in wooden case counter signed on inset brass plate 'Canivet à la Sphére à Paris', with 4in (10cm) printed compass rose signed 'Canivet A Paris' by South.

c1760   7in (18cm) high
£400-600   CM

A 19thC miner's dial, signed J. Casartelli, Manchester, with 5in (13cm) silvered dial, brass dial cover, bubble levels, folding sights, in a fitted box with accessories.

12.5in (31.5cm)
£600-700   CM

QUICK REFERENCE - DIPTYCH DIAL

- Often known as diptych dials, these dials comprise two plates hinged together. Opening the plates up stretches a string which acts as the gnomon to place a shadow on the horizontal sundial plate. They usually also contain a magnetic compass and may also give the latitudes for major cities, allowing them to be set correctly to enable an accurate time reading to be taken. Incised words and marks are typically stained in colours, from black to green or red. Others feature a wind rose with pointer and lunar disc with calendar. They were most popular from the late 16thC until the early 17thC, with Nuremburg being a major centre of manufacture. They were, however, made into the mid-19thC as this example demonstrates. Ivory was typical, but fruitwoods and other woods were also used. Look out for earlier examples by makers such as Georg Hartmann, Hans Tucher, and Hans Trochel, as these are rare and valuable.

A mid-19thC ivory pocket compass sundial dial, by Smith, Beck & Beck, with 0.75in (2cm) printed paper compass dial, the base marked for solar hours, string gnomon to lid with instructions, gilt-brass support and securing hooks, signed.

2.25in (6cm) wide
£400-500   CM

SCIENTIFIC INSTRUMENTS

A 19thC sand glass, with hand-blown bulbs joined at middle with twine, with turned bone end plates with three bone 'bamboo form' supports.

5.75in (14.5cm) high

£400-600   CM

A rare early 19thC French hourglass, the reservoir bulb with sand joined to four 15-minute bulbs with cloth and wire binding, in brass frame with six wire supports.

8in (20cm) high

£1,500-2,000   CM

QUICK REFERENCE - SANDGLASSES

● Sandglasses were developed in the Mediterranean during the 12thC and are closely associated with navigation at sea. In association with other intruments, they were used for plotting magnetic bearings and distance on charts, measuring a course and ascertaining speed. They were also used in monasteries, at courts and at school to provide a distinct period of time. Early examples were made of two flasks joined with wax and bound with cord, as here. Double flasks blown in one piece were developed by the end of the 18thC. Very few were marked with a maker's name and it can be hard to date examples unless they are marked with decoration in the style of a particular country or period.

An 18thC mariner's portable ½-hour watch glass, with hand-blown bulbs joined with twine and wire binding, filled with volcanic sand, in a leather case lined with marbled paper, the ends decorated with rudimentary eight-point compass roses.

4.75in (12cm) high

£1,800-2,200   CM

A 20thC reproduction of an 18thC-style sandglass, with bulbs blown as a single unit, in wooden holder, covered with morocco leather.

8.75in (22cm) high

£40-50   CM

An early 19thC French engraved brass pocket rule, inscribed to top 'TABLE POUR MESURER TOUTTE SORIE DES PAYS' with list of European cities and towns with distances, the reverse with linear scales divided '0-400' entitled 'POULS DU RHIN', maker's mark (?) '4'.

5.75in (14.5cm) high

£450-550   CM

An early 19thC brass rule, engraved with a set of scales inscribed 'Linia Planorum Poligeni in Circulo Poligani Aequalia Corpora in Scriptibilia Corpora Aequalia Subtenfe Solide Metalle', the reverse inscribed with a 60° arc and a linear scale.

5.75in (14.5cm) long

£600-700   CM

A scissor-type combination parallel rule and protractor, signed 'J. Search London'.

c1780   *6in (15.5cm) wide*

£500-600   CM

A drawing set etui, signed on the ivory rule 'Is Search Crown Court Soho London', the silver compasses with steel points and pen, in shagreen-covered case with silver cap engraved 'J Rofe 1754'.

James Search worked between 1771-1881 and specialised in drawing instruments, circumferentors and telescopes.

c1754   *4.75in (12cm) high*

£500-600   CM

A Fuller-type calculating slide rule, by W.F. Stanley, in fitted box with maker's label, with an instruction pamphlet published by W.F. Stanley dated 1879, model no.1.

c1880   *18in (45.5cm) diam*
£220-280   **CM**

A Curta Calculator Type II, no.'517106', marked 'Made in Liechtenstein (Custom Union with Switzerland) by Contina Ltd, Mauren', system designed by Curt Herzstark, with metal canister, with instructions.

£400-450   FLD

An early 20thC wood-cased 'Comptometer', by Felt & Tarrant Mfg. Co.

The comptometer was the first commercially successful key-driven mechanical calculator, and was patented in 1887 by American inventor and industrialist Dorr Eugene Felt (1862–1930). His company was founded in 1889 and continued into the 1970s.

£30-50   WHP

A type-I Curta calculator, with fitted plastic tube, serial no.'63444', stamped to base.

c1965   *4.75in (12cm) high*
£350-400   CM

An early 20thC oak-cased barograph.

Used for measuring and recording changes in atmospheric pressure over a period of time, many standard oak-cased barographs have fallen in value by 50% or more over the past decade. This is probably due to a dramatic drop in interest in vintage instruments, and the fact that most barographs are actually very similar making building a varied collection difficult.

14.5in (37cm) wide
£250-300   BELL

A Campbell-Stokes Early Sunshine recorder, in brass with vertical sphere holder, the sphere is unclamped, and 4in (10cm) glass sphere, mounted on wooden base.

When placed in the sun, the glass ball magnified the sunlight and created a beam of light that burnt a line onto or a hole into a piece of paper or card marked with gradations and held on the brass curving support. It was used to record the amount of sunlight across a period of time in one location. This version was invented by John Francis Campbell in 1853 and modified in 1879 by Sir George Gabriel Stokes.

£400-500   TEN

A set of six concentrically stored bronze cup weights: 4oz (stamped 'IIII'), 2oz ('II') 1oz ('I') 1/2oz, 1/4oz and solid 1/4oz, the latter three unmarked.

largest 1.75in (43cm) diam
£120-150   TEN

SCULPTURE

A pair of Art Deco chrome-plated metal alloy nude female figures, after Limousin, holding baskets of posies, mounted on onyx plinths.

13.6in (34.5cm) high

£100-150   **SWO**

An Art Deco bronze fawn sculpture, indistinctly signed, on a marble base.

6.8in (17.2cm) high

£70-100   **SWO**

A Georges Omerth French gilt-bronze and ivory figure of a young boy dressed as a clown his costume moulded with comedy and tragedy masks, signed 'Omerth' and numbered '5746', on an onyx base.

Little is known about Omerth, but he was active from c1895-1925 and produced a number of figurines of theatrical characters and dancers.

c1920   *7.2in (18.2cm) high*

£700-1,000   **SWO**

Mark Picks

As any Art Deco fan who watches the BBC Antiques Roadshow knows, the stunning bronze and ivory sculptures of elegant ladies and dancers by the likes of Demétre Chiparus, Ferdinand Preiss, and Bruno Zach are scarce and highly valuable. Quintessentially Art Deco, they were also prized and expensive in their day, as well as being the height of style and fashion. As a result, they were widely copied, typically in less expensive spelter and an early veined ivory-like plastic called Ivorine. Quality of these copies vary widely, and some of the best were produced by Menneville. It's possible that these elegant figurines, often incuding borzoi dogs, were designed by notable Italian sculptor Ugo Cipriani (1897-1960), but only further research can confirm this. All in all, in terms of price, quality, look, and period authenticity, this represents great value. And it may prove to be a good investment if the link to Cipriani is proved.

An Art Deco patinated spelter and Ivorine table centre sculpture, modelled as a lady wearing a long flowing dress and holding a fan, mounted on a raised marble and onyx plinth, signed 'Menneville'.

17in (43cm) high

£600-800   **SWO**

A 1920s-30s gilt-patinated bronze model of a naked dancer, cast from a model by Daniel-Joseph Bacqué, the dancer wearing a cap, her right leg raised, and mounted on circular marble base, cast 'Bacqué' to underside of foot.

15.75in (40cm) high

£500-800   **WW**

A 1920s-30s patinated bronze model of a nude dancer, cast from a model by Josef Lorenzl, mounted on a veined green onyx base, signed in the cast 'Lorenzl'.

10.75in (27cm) high

£1,200-1,800   **WW**

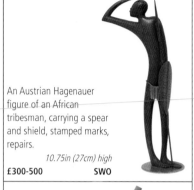

An Austrian Hagenauer figure of an African tribesman, carrying a spear and shield, stamped marks, repairs.

10.75in (27cm) high

£300-500   SWO

A Brian Wilsher mahogany sculpture, with two interlocking sections to a recessed centre, unsigned.

For more information about Wilsher and his sculptures, please see p324 of the Miller's Collectables Price Guide 2012-2013.

26in (66cm) high

£500-700   SWO

A Bernard Reynolds carved walnut 'Maquette for a 40' Monument'.

Bernard Reynolds (1915-97) studied at Norwich and Westminster Schools of Art. During 1937-8 he was associated with Henry Moore and contributed to the Surrealist Object Exhibition at the London Gallery. He was a lecturer at Ipswich School of Art until 1981 and contributed to a number of East Anglian sculpture exhibitions. He was also a Fellow of the British Society of Sculptors.

28.3in (72cm) high

£200-300   SWO

A patinated bronze figure of a Bachanalian woman, cast from a model by Bruno Kruse, on black marble base with red marble panels, signed in the cast 'B Kruse'.

15.75in (40cm) high

£700-1,000   WW

A late 20thC T. Gorerino green marble sculptural study of a female nude.

23.75in (60cm) high

£100-150   WHP

A mid-late 20thC Modernist patinated metal sculpture, with applied cast roundel of musical instruments, on a stepped ebonised wood base.

16in (41cm) high

£100-150   WW

A late 20thC Peter Wright sculpture of interlocking figures, limited edition 78/200, signed and numbered.

7in (18cm) across

£200-300   MLL

SEWING

QUICK REFERENCE - SEWING

- Sewing accessories are still collected today, even though the art has declined dramatically since the introduction of affordable sewing machines in the early 20thC and the rise of consumerism and inexpensive clothes produced in the Far East. What was once seen as a genteel and virtuous activity is now seen as time-consuming and redundant. Nevertheless, the nostalgia and craftsmanship of the objects behind the craft drives many collectors.

- Most sewing objects found today date from the 19thC onwards, when mass-production began to boom. 18thC and earlier examples are highly prized due to their rarity. Victorian sewing accessories and tools were made from a variety of materials, including silver, gold, ivory, bone, mother-of-pearl, tortoiseshell and, most commonly, wood. Silver was also frequently used as the price of silver dropped during the Edwardian period.

- Collectors tend to focus on one type of item, such as thimbles, pin cushions, needlecases or etuis. Variety abounds for pin cushions and many different types of thimble can also be found. Early examples tend to fetch high prices. Many homemade pieces can be found, and these are often more charming than factory-made pieces. In general, look out for finely hand-crafted pieces in precious metals, or ones that display high levels of detail. These are likely to be the most valuable.

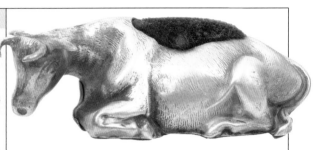

A 19thC silver pincushion in the form of a recumbent cow, lightly engraved coat, blue velvet infill, marked with lion passant, crown and maker's mark 'H. W. & Co.'.

This is an unusual form which is both well and realistically detailed.

2.5in (6cm) long

£1,200-1,500   **BLEA**

An Edwardian silver novelty donkey pin cushion, by Sydney & Co., Birmingham.

c1909   *3in (7.5cm) long*

£450-550   **DN**

An Edwardian novelty pin cushion, by Adie & Lovekin, Birmingham, in the form of a pig, lined and loaded.

Pigs are very popular animals for pin cushions, probably as they have a large surface area on their backs that can be used as the cushion. Values depend on the maker. Adie & Lovekin, for example, are a good quality, desirable maker. This example is described as 'loaded', meaning that the interior cavity has been filled with an inexpensive heavy metal to give it weight and solidity. Silver is a lightweight material and it would have been too expensive to cast out of solid silver so, to make it practical, it was weighed down internally.

1906   *2.5in (6.5cm) long*

£200-250   **LAW**

An Edwardian silver novelty porcupine pin cushion or toothpick holder, by Levi & Salaman, Birmingham.

c1904   *2.75in (7cm) long*

£250-350   **DN**

An Edwardian silver novelty swan pin cushion, by Adie & Lovekin Ltd, Birmingham.

c1906   *2.5in (6cm) long*

£170-200   **DN**

An Edwardian novelty silver chick pin cushion, by S. Mordan and Co, Chester, modelled as a chick emerging from an egg.

1906   *1.5in (4cm) high*

£150-200   **WW**

An Edwardian novelty pin cushion, by Crisford & Norris, Birmingham, in the form of a crocodile or alligator, with glass eyes.

1907   *4.25in (10.8cm)*

£400-500   **LAW**

A silver novelty pin cushion, modelled as a roller skate, by Crisford and Norris, Birmingham, some damage.

1910   *2.5in (6.5cm) long*

£150-200   **WW**

A novelty silver shoe pin cushion, by S. Blanckensee and Sons Limited, Chester, with ribbon laces and a wooden under-sole.

1911   *5in (12.5cm) long*

£100-150   **WW**

QUICK REFERENCE - AKSEL HOLMSEN

- Aksel Holmsen (1873-1972) trained with renowned Norwegian silversmith and jeweller David Andersen from 1889-92. He completed his journeyman's piece in 1901 and worked for Andersen until 1904.
- He then set up his own enamelling workshop in Oslo, became officially licensed in 1906, moved to Sandjeford in 1932 and finally closed the company in 1971.
- The company is known for its very high quality enamelled jewellery from floral pins to bangles - thimbles are comparatively rare.
- Calm dusk scenes featuring people or animals such as a stag are one of his most loved designs and required a considerable amount of skill and time to execute successfully.

A Norwegian silver and enamel thimble, by Aksel Holmsen, enamelled with a moose and forest scene with birds, below a moonstone top, marked to the interior apex 'pliers and compass mark/925S/2'.

£1,000-1,400   **BLEA**

A Norwegian silver and enamel thimble, by Aksel Holmsen, enamelled with an elegantly dressed woman gazing at a sailing boat on a lake, with trees and mountains, moonstone top, marked to the interior apex '925/ pliers and compass mark/Norway/I'.

£1,000-1,400   **BLEA**

A Norwegian silver and enamel thimble, by Aksel Holmsen, enamelled in vertical guilloche with additional enamelled flowers to the rim, below a waffle top, marked to the interior apex 'pliers and compass mark/Norway/ Sterling/925S/2'.

£650-750   **BLEA**

A rare 19thC English pictorial silver thimble, depicting a bridge with a buoy or tower with two figures in a rowing boat, a three-masted sailing ship nearby.

Scenic thimbles, showing a scene on a band around the base, are more commonly associated with American thimbles.

£650-750   **BLEA**

A 14ct-gold sewing thimble, with engine-turned decoration.

0.75in (2cm) high 0.1oz

£110-150   **LOCK**

A rare Tunbridge ware silk ribbon box, of house type, the cottage with a thatched roof, a devil painted to one window, cracks in the roof.
c1840   4.75in (12cm) high
£400-500   DN

A rare early Tunbridge ware house-type tape measure, painted with a thatched cottage, marks, scratches, and abrasions to surface consistent with age and use, chip to lower corner, tape with damage.
c1830   1.5in (3.5cm) high
£400-500   DN

A rare early Tunbridge ware beehive-type tape measure, formed as a straw skep, minor wear to decoration, surface marks.
c1820   1.5in (4.2cm) high
£300-350   BLEA

A 19thC Tunbridge ware tape measure, having decorated body with label 'A Tunbridge Wells Gift'.
                           2.75in (6cm) high
£110-150   LOCK

Miller's Compares

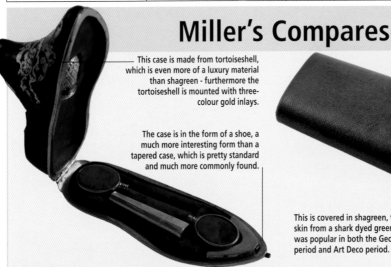

This case is made from tortoiseshell, which is even more of a luxury material than shagreen - furthermore the tortoiseshell is mounted with three-colour gold inlays.

The case is in the form of a shoe, a much more interesting form than a tapered case, which is pretty standard and much more commonly found.

This is covered in shagreen, the skin from a shark dyed green - it was popular in both the Georgian period and Art Deco period.

Even though the contents of this example are complete and those in the other are not, it would be worth finding replacements, difficult as it would be, as the value would be raised greatly.

A late 18thC continental gold-mounted tortoiseshell novelty sewing etui, in the form of a shoe with a trodden-down heel, a hinged sole and three-colour-inlaid work, the interior now only containing the handles from a pair of scissors, a thimble and a needle case, unmarked.
                           4.5in (11cm) long
£1,200-1,500   LAW

A George III mounted shagreen etui, fitted with a pair of mounted steel scissors, a mounted steel penknife, a bodkin, and a folding bone tablet, unmarked.
                           4in (10cm) long
£220-280   LAW

A Victorian silver-gilt sewing etui, the penknife by William Jones, London, the pencil by Sampson Mordan, with a penknife, a needle case, a pencil, a pair of tweezers/ear cleaner, a bodkin, a spike and two pairs of steel scissors, plus an unmarked gold thimble set with pearls, in a fitted ivory case, initialled.
1873
£400-500   WW

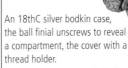

An 18thC silver bodkin case, the ball finial unscrews to reveal a compartment, the cover with a thread holder.
                        3.5in (9cm) long 1oz
£300-400   WW

QUICK REFERENCE - SILVER

- The price of an ounce of silver has fallen dramatically since it reached a high point of £30.66 in April 2011. Nevertheless, it fluctuates widely and the fate of many silver objects depends on it. The higher the price, the more 'average' silver such as uninteresting teasets and plain vesta cases, card cases, cutlery or boxes was melted down as its scrap value was higher than its value to a collector.

- Despite this, small silver novelty items produced from the late 18thC onward have performed well over the past decade, largely due to their consistent appeal amongst collectors and, where applicable, their rarity. Even items that have no practical use today, such as vinaigrettes, or those that can be incorporated within a home and are still desirable, buck the current trend for decorative antiques.

- In the first instance, learn how to read hallmarks and invest in a good guide. Then learn how to recognise the makers' marks of notable makers such as Nathaniel Mills, Walker & Hall, Joseph Willmore or Sampson Mordan. Also look out for the names of notable retailers such as

Thornhill or Leuchars. Certain makers also specialised in and are known for certain objects, such as Mills and card cases, boxes and vinaigrettes. Some types of items are also more desirable than others. Whilst photograph frames are eternally popular due to their practical use, vinaigrettes, pepperettes and menu card holders all have their groups of dedicated collectors.

- Quality and fine detailing will add value to a piece. Items with cross-market appeal, such as a vesta case showing a horse race, will also push the price higher. Silver is a comparatively soft metal and, as these pieces were typically made to be used, they can be worn or damaged with dents or splits. Damage on silver pieces can be repaired, but this can be expensive. The 'ghostly' remains of damage can often still be visible.

- As silver is handled and exposed to the environment, the outer surface oxidises and becomes grey and dull. When silver is cleaned, a thin layer is removed, and when done too often will reduce the level of detail on a piece.

A matched set of four silver-mounted Wedgwood menu card holders, by Cohen and Charles, Chester, with two green and two blue Jasperware panels of classical figures, within plain silver mounts, on raised circular bases.

1905   *1.5in (3.5cm) high*

£200-300   **WW**

A set of four silver menu card holders, by Mappin and Webb, Sheffield, pierced and engraved with game birds and a hare.

1912   *1.5in (3.5cm) diam 2.8oz*

£300-400   **WW**

A set of four silver heart-shaped menu card holders, by S. Mordan and Co, Chester, on heart-shaped bases, in a fitted case.

1905 and 1906   *2.9oz*

£300-400   **WW**

A silver-mounted Worcester porcelain toothpick holder, by Sanders and Mackenzie, Birmingham, set with a central panel of two highland cattle, with a partially obscured panel.

As the panel shows a delicately and realistically depicted cattle produced at Royal Worcester, it may have been painted by the renowned decorator John Stinton Jnr (1854–1956), who was celebrated for his cattle scenes. As it is set into a frame, if a signature is present it has been covered up.

1929   *3.5in (8.5cm) high*

£200-300   **WW**

A set of four silver and abalone shell menu card holders, by Cohen and Charles, London, modelled as Dutch boys and girls, with bone faces and traditional dress.

1911   *2.5in (6.5cm) high*

£200-300   **WW**

A pair of novelty silver menu card holders, by F.J. Ross, Sheffield, modelled as a standing 'Trusty Servant'.

The 'Trusty Servant' character features on a 1579 wall painting by John Hoskins (1566-1638). It is meant to embody various domestic virtues.

1897   *2.25in (5.5cm) high 0.8oz*

£250-300   **WW**

A matched set of four menu card holders, in the form of the Royal Naval Crown on canted oblong bases, maker's mark 'JWB', Birmingham, in fitted case.

1927/1935   *1.2in (3cm) high 3oz*

£350-400   **LAW**

A modern silver pepper mill, by R. Comyns, London, barrel-form, reeded banding.

1970   *2.5in (6.5cm) high*

£100-150   **WW**

A Victorian novelty silver dumb-bell pepper pot, by Johnson and White, London, screw-off pierced cover.

Dumb-bell-shaped items are not uncommon. Cocktail shakers can also be found in this form. The shape is also practical, with the waisted central stem allowing for a good grip for fingers or hands, depending on the size.

1887   *2.75in (7cm) high 1.1oz*

£100-150   **WW**

A novelty silver owl pepper pot, by H. Atkins, Sheffield, the body apparently unmarked, with green glass eyes.

Owls are popular animals for collectors of novelty silver pieces, and can be found on a variety of objects from inkwells to stamp boxes, and bookmarks to letter openers.

1913   *2.5in (6cm) high 1.9oz*

£300-400   **WW**

A CLOSER LOOK AT A SET OF MENU CARD HOLDERS

Although much royal memorabilia is of lower quality and has fallen in desirability over the past few decades, these were superbly made with great attention to detail.

They were made by Garrard & Co. Ltd (established 1735), one of the world's most prestigious silver and goldsmiths. On top of this, they are the oldest jewellery house in the world and a holder of numerous Royal Warrants.

The fleur-de-lys is a popular and widely appealing motif - these could be used to great effect on a contemporary dining table.

It is a set of ten examples, which is more useful than a pair or set of four, as is more commonly seen.

A set of ten silver menu or place card holders, by Garrard & Co Ltd, London, made to commemorate the wedding of HRH Prince Charles and Lady Diana Spencer, the knopped baluster bases surmounted with the feathers of the Prince of Wales rising through a gold coronet of alternate crosses and fleur-de-lis and the motto 'Ich Dien', the bases engraved 'The Royal Wedding July 1981', in a fitted case.

1981   *each 1.5in (4cm) 110oz*

£1,000-1,500   **TEN**

A pair of modern novelty silver chauffeur salt and pepper pots, maker's mark WW, London.

1993   *3.5in (9cm) high 3.5oz*

£400-500   **WW**

A cast-silver novelty three-piece cruet set, by William Comyns & Sons Ltd (Richard Comyns), London, modelled as penguins with black bead eyes.

c1966   *the tallest 3in (7cm) high 277g 8.9oz*

£550-600   **DN**

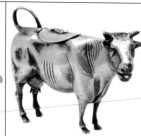

An early Victorian nutmeg grater, by Joseph Wilmore, Birmingham, oval tubular in section, with a hinged cover and a hinged side revealing a tinned steel rasp.

From the late 17thC into the early 19thC, nutmeg was added to punch, toddies, ales or wine. As well as being an exotic and fashionable spice, it was reputed to have health benefits. In order to be able to add freshly grated nutmeg, the seed pod was carried around in a container with an integral steel grater. Silver is typical, but examples were also made in enamelled metal, ivory, brass and woods. Although many were small rectangular or rounded boxes, variety abounds. Nutmeg graters with high levels of detail or workmanship, or novelty forms or by renowned makers, fetch more.

1841   2.5in (6.4 cm) long 1.2oz
£450-500   LAW

A pair of silver sauceboats, each with a shaped rim, scrolled handle and raised on three hoof-shaped feet, Sheffield.
1917   12.3oz
£100-150   BELL

A European cow creamer, the hinged cover to the back with a fly motif, the tail looped over to form the handle, probably Dutch.
1875-1900   3.5oz
£600-700   BELL

Mark Picks

Gerald Benney (1930-2008) was one of the most influential British silver and goldsmiths of the 20thC. He was also the first British craftsman to hold four Royal Warrants simultaneously. From the 1960s-90s, along with his colleagues Stuart Devlin, David Mellor, Louis Osman and Christopher Lawrence, his work helped to define British metalware and ensured the continuation of British silversmithing. Benney's work is known for its simple, yet monumental forms, and has an aura of elegant splendour. Although influenced by the purity of Scandinavian Modernism, he is best known for his textured surfaces. These came about by accident during the 1960s, when Benney was beating a piece of silver into shape by accidentally using a hammer with a damaged head. The damaged head added texture to the previous flat silver, which intrigued Benney. He accentuated the damage, producing even more interesting textures that he would go on to use throughout his career. This fine candelabrum, made for Bramshill House Police Training College, has all the features one would hope to see in a piece by Benney: a simple monumental form, superb levels of texture and a large size. To top it off, it is an early date for textured work.

A set of six Art Deco silver napkin rings, Birmingham.

The geometric form, minimal machined detail and gilt-washed interior make these extremely smart and as appealingly modern today as they were over 80 years go.

1921   7oz
£200-250   WHP

A set of six George VI silver and multi-coloured enamelled coffee spoons, by Turner & Simpson Ltd., Birmingham, in fitted case.

Coffee spoons such as these tend to fetch under a third of the value of this set, even when they are made of solid silver and boxed as here. This set fetched what it did because of the brightly coloured 'harlequin' enamelling, which is also undamaged.

1921
£100-150   ECGW

A silver candelabrum by Gerald Benney, London, with a central tapered conical base, heavily textured, beneath a slender tapered spire engraved with the 'Police College' badge and with a textured cup candle holder to each side, the base rim inscribed with presentation engraving.

1963   32oz
£4,500-5,000   BELL

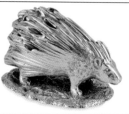

A Victorian novelty silver toothpick holder, J Barclay Hennell, London, modelled as a porcupine on a rockwork base.

1883   2.5in (6cm) 4oz
£1,200-1,500   L&T

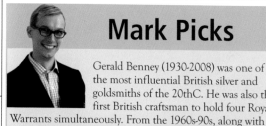

QUICK REFERENCE - VINAIGRETTES

● Vinaigrettes are small boxes that contain a perforated internal hinged surface, under which a sponge soaked in smelling salts, pleasant smelling oils or vinegar was stored. As a fashionable Georgian or Victorian lady (or gentleman) moved through major cities such as London, they would open the box and inhale the pleasing or cleansing smell in order to combat the revolting stench of the sewers and waste that permeated the dirty streets. The interiors were typically washed in gold to prevent damage or staining from the liquid. The outer lid, and sometimes the entire box, was typically decorated with motifs ranging from the monogram of the owner within an engine-turned panel, to repoussé scenes of notable, or even obscure, buildings. The most sought-after vinaigrettes are typically decorated with the latter, and many of them were made by the Birmingham silversmiths run by Nathaniel Mills (1746-1840) and his sons. At the time, they were sold as upmarket tourist souvenirs and it is thought around 200 different scenes were made. Pay close attention to the building itself as some obscure buildings, and even some scenes of popular buildings, are very rare and desirability and values can climb steeply. This example of Chichester Cathedral is a very good example, being worth over five times the value of a similar vinaigrette with a common scene, and over twelve times the value of a good, yet plainer example.

A George III plain canted oblong vinaigrette, by Samuel Pemberton, Birmingham, with domed cover and base, the gilt interior with a filigree grille.
1802   *1.7in (4.2cm) long 0.7oz*
£300-350   **LAW**

A George III engraved vinaigrette, by Matthew Linwood, Birmingham, the cover with a shepherdess and sheep by a field gate, the gilt interior with simulated filigree grille.
1809   *1.2in (3cm) long 0.6oz*
£550-650   **LAW**

A William IV engine-turned vinaigrette, by Nathaniels Mills, Birmingham, with plain wire borders and a vacant oblong cartouche on the cover, gilt interior.
1834   *1.5in (4cm) long 0.75oz*
£250-350   **LAW**

A rare early Victorian engraved 'castletop' vinaigrette, by Nathaniel Mills, Birmingham, with a view of Chichester Cathedral and its bell tower in the right foreground, the base with a vacant cartouche, gilt interior.
1843   *1.25in (3.cm) long 0.4oz*
£6,000-8,000   **LAW**

A Victorian engraved 'castletop' vinaigrette, by Nathaniel Mills, Birmingham, with a view of the Houses of Parliament, gilt interior, replacement grille.

1844   *1.8in (4.5cm) long 1.1oz*
£550-600   **LAW**

A rare Victorian engraved 'castletop' vinaigrette, by Nathaniel Mills, Birmingham, with the old castle at Balmoral, gilt interior.

Queen Victoria and Prince Albert bought the lease of the old castle at Balmoral in 1848 and purchased the property in 1852. Finding the residence too small, a new palace (the current Balmoral) was built. Construction began in 1853 and was completed in 1856. The old castle was formerly in the possession of the Farquharson family of Balmoral.

A small engraved 'castletop' vinaigrette, by Nathaniel Mills, Birmingham, with engine-turned sides and base, a view of St. Paul's Cathedral, gilt interior.

1851   *1.25in (3.2cm) long 0.35oz*
£900-1,000   **LAW**

1851   *1.8in (4.8cm) long 0.6oz*
£1,500-2,000   **LAW**

A Victorian engraved 'castletop' vinaigrette, with a view of the Brighton Pavillion, gilt interior, the base cartouche initialled, maker's mark 'JF', Birmingham.

1861   *1.2in (3cm) long 0.25oz*

£650-750   **LAW**

A Victorian embossed 'castletop' card case, by Nathaniel Mills, Birmingham, with a view of York Minster in relief, flanked by floral scrolls, the reverse centred by a cartouche, initialled.

Silversmith Nathaniel Mills (see Quick Reference on previous page) was also renowned for producing 'castletop' card cases which are also highly collectable.

1844   *3.3in (8.5cm) high 1.6oz*

£1,200-1,500   **LAW**

A Victorian calling card case, chased with a monogram and crest within a cartouche on an engine-turned ground within floral chased border, Birmingham, maker's mark 'G U'.

1877   *3.75in (9.5cm) high 1.92oz*

£180-220   **DA&H**

A George III silver barrel-shaped box, by Thomas Morley, London, reeded border, pierced cover.

1798   *1.5in (4cm) long 0.5oz*

£100-150   **WW**

An Art Deco dressing table box, by Adie Brothers, Birmingham, the cover enamelled in light-blue over an engine-turned ground, loaded base.

1929   *4.25in (10.9cm) diam*

£220-280   **LAW**

A Continental blue and white enamelled box, gilt interior, with English import marks for London, retailed by 'ASPREY'.

Always examine the enamel all over the box as any damage reduces the value considerably. Restoration is extremely expensive and generally always visible, unless the entire piece is stripped and re-enamelled which also costs a sum usually well in excess of the value of the finished box. As well as being washed in gold inside, the cobalt blue of this box is very attractive. It was also retailed by Asprey.

1920   *2.3in (6cm) diam 2.4oz*

£250-300   **LAW**

A late Victorian silver vesta case, by Sampson Mordan, London, enamelled with a horse and rider in a 'point-to-point' race.

Always examine the quality of the scene when looking at pictorial enamelled boxes. Sampson Mordan were a notable and renowned maker of small silver and gold objects and propelling pencils, and quality is typically high. Had this been horse racing rather than point-to-point, the value may have more than doubled!

1888   *2.25in (5.7cm) long 1oz*

£350-400   **LAW**

A small 20thC Continental box, enamelled on the cover with gold and powder blue, gilt interior.

1920-30   *1.6in (4cm) diam 0.9oz*

£180-220   **LAW**

SILVER

An Art Deco silver and mother-of-pearl dressing table set, comprising candlesticks, bottles, mirror, and brushes.

Despite their charm, workmanship, quality and beauty, dressing table sets such as these are typically very hard to sell unless they are by a very notable maker or made from highly valuable materials. The main reason for this is the inclusion of brushes, be they for hair or clothes. Put simply, for hygiene and other reasons, nobody wishes to brush their hair or use a brush that brushed the hair or clothes of someone who is now dead. The amount of silver used is often very low and, as they were practical items, there is usually some damage from where something was dropped or dented. This is rarely worth restoring given the value of such sets, unless it has sentimental value. Despite this, this is a good price for a set with a number of more desirable and commercial items, such as the candlesticks, the bottles and even the mirror. As such, it is likely to be split up.

£150-200   ECGW

QUICK REFERENCE - POSYHOLDERS

● These small conical holders were filled with tiny flowers, known as 'nosegays', to chase away the foul smells and views of Victorian streets, just like a vinaigrette (see page 320). Some also believed that the pleasant, natural smell warded off ill health caused by smelling something bad, although this is obviously not medically accurate. They were also said to have been used by fashionable young ladies to show their acceptance of a gentleman courting her. If a gentleman sent her flowers, a lady would fill her posy holder with them and wear it to a ball or event, with the ring attached to her finger, to show she approved. In the US, these posy holders were often known as 'tussie mussies', with 'tussie' being an old English word for nosegay and 'mussie' referring to the damp moss that was used inside to give the flowers water. Less expensive versions were made from thin pressed brass or pinchbeck, an alloy of copper and zinc.

A Victorian gilt-metal and silver posy holder, pierced and embossed foliate scroll decoration, with a clip and pin, mother-of-pearl handle, with a finger ring.
c1880   *5.75in (14.5cm) long*
£180-220   WW

A Danish Georg Jensen sterling silver bookmark, no.60, with a leaf-shaped page holder with raised vine and berry decoration, a pierced handle with raised flower head and bead decoration, marked '925S Denmark GJLd', import hallmark, London.
1977
£120-150   SWO

Victorian silver miniature postal scales, by Collins & Cook, Birmingham.
1899
£100-150   ECGW

An Edwardian novelty silver coal scuttle stamp box, by Clark and Sewell, Birmingham, the hinged front embossed with cherubs.
1909   *1.5in (3.5cm) high 0.5oz*
£200-250   WW

A silver revolving desk calendar, by Padgett and Braham, London.
1928   *5.5in (13.5cm) long*
£220-280   WW

An Elizabeth II silver pheasant table ornament, by C J Vander Ltd, Sheffield.
2002   *4in (10cm) high 16oz*
£650-750   LAW

An Elizabeth II silver pheasant table ornament, by C J Vander Ltd, Sheffield.
2003   *5.5in (14cm) high 32oz*
£1,000-1,500   LAW

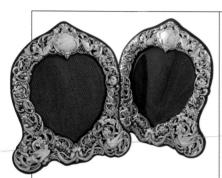

A matched pair of large late-Victorian and Edwardian silver photograph frames, one by William Comyns, London, the other by Mappin and Webb, London, replacement easel backs.

1900/1909   *11.25in (28.5cm) high*

£1,500-2,500   **WW**

An Edwardian silver photograph frame, by Synyer and Beddoes, Birmingham, leather-covered wooden back with an easel support.

1902   *8.75in (22.5cm) high*

£250-300   **WW**

An Edwardian silver photograph frame, by S. Blanckensee Limited, Chester, with a bull dog and 'Pallatine & Counties Bulldog Club', and three lions in a shield, wooden easel back.

1907   *9in (23cm) high*

£200-250   **WW**

Judith Picks

Murrle Bennett & Co. were a high-end retailer based in Regent St. in London, from 1896-1914. They sold Art Nouveau and Seccessionist jewellery primarily made in Pforzheim, Germany, and they probably collaborated with Liberty & Co. Their look was very Central European in style and was characterised by bold, Modernist forms and the use of cabochon stones such as turquoise. This is a representative example of their designs that is also in excellent condition and highly wearable. It was designed by the sadly shortlived designer Patriz Huber (1878-1902), a member of the infuential Darmstadt colony of artists. A comparable example of this buckle can be seen in 'Patriz Huber 15th May -28th June 1992, Ateliers im Museum Künstlerkolonie, Darmstadt', page 77.

A pair of silver photograph frames, by W. I. Broadway and Co, Birmingham, wooden easel backs with strut supports.

1911   *15.25in (38.5cm) high*

£1,500-2,500   **WW**

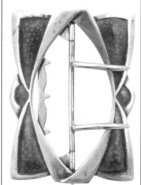

An Art Nouveau silver hair slide, the pierced body set with green stone roundel, unsigned.

       3.54in (9.5cm) wide

£150-200   **WW**

A Secessionist silver and lapis lazuli belt buckle, designed by Patriz Huber, retailed by Murrle Bennett & Co, stamped import marks for Murrle Bennett & Co London.

1901   *1.75in (4cm) wide*

£600-700   **WW**

A silver and enamel waist clasp, pierced and cast in low-relief with Art Nouveau mistletoe design.

       5in (12.5cm) wide

£200-250   **WW**

A silver and enamel buckle, stamped 'JW' marks, Birmingham.

1911   *2.25in (5.5cm) high*

£100-150   **WW**

SILVER

A George III silver baby's rattle and whistle, possibly by Daniel Hockley, London, with coral teether, with three bells, and with a ring attachment, some bells missing.

Values for these still desirable childrens' toys drop when bells are missing or there is damage to the red or orange coral teether. Large sized examples with many bells and extravagant levels of decoration are worth considerably more.

possibly 1798   *4.25in (10.5cm) long*

£150-200   WW

A George III silver baby's rattle, with a ring attachment and four bells, with a coral teether, maker's mark of Hester Bateman, London, repair to teether.

c1770   *6in (15.5cm) long*

£450-550   WW

An Edwardian novelty silver owl whistle, with glass eyes, with import marks for Birmingham, importer's mark of Spurrier and Co.

1903   *1.5in (4cm) long 0.1oz*

£300-400   WW

A George IV 'Gibson patent' silver medicine spoon, by Charles Gibson, London, hinged cover, inscribed 'C. Gibson Inventor, 71 Bishopsgate Street'.

This spoon is designed closed with a small spout so that medicine could be carefully poured into the mouth of the sick person without spillage when they were lying in bed, or too weak to open their mouth.

1828   *5.5in (13.5cm) long 1.1oz*

£400-500   WW

An Edward VII silver gaming butt marker, maker Sampson Mordan & Co., London, with engraved lion crest one side, and monogram on the other, the hinged lid with ten numbered gilt butt markers.

1901   *2in (5cm) high*

£950-1,200   LOCK

A Victorian novelty silver tot cup, by Alfred Fuller, London, modelled as the head of an oriental man, the handle modelled as a pig tail, gilded interior.

1892   *1.75in (4.5cm) high 1.1oz*

£300-400   WW

An Edwardian silver novelty hunting horn candle douser, by S. Mordan and Co, London.

Hunting, shooting and fishing themes were very popular during the late Victorian and Edwardian period.

1901   *12in (30.5cm) long 1.3oz*

£150-200   WW

A 1950s Dunhill 'Aquarium' lighter, the Lucite panels carved and painted internally with fish amongst waterweed, the base with cast marks.

3.9in (10cm) wide

£1,000-1,400   WW

A 1950s Dunhill 'Aquarium' lighter, the body with intaglio decorated Lucite panels of exotic fish amongst sea plants.

3.9in (10cm) wide

£550-600   LOCK

A late 20thC Dunhill gold-plated 'Rollagas' lighter, with engine turned decorated body, with its original box.

2.6in (6.5cm) long

£75-85   LOCK

Mark Picks

Although their colourful plastic nature makes them appear kitsch and of low quality to many people, 'Aquarium' lighters are both hard to find and highly sought-after. Introduced in 1949, each one was handcrafted, with the design being carved and painted internally to give the visual effect of an aquarium. Dunhill is also arguably the 'Rolls Royce' of lighters and smoking memorabilia. Always examine them under a magnifying glass as the paint can flake and bubble. As the name suggests, fish are the most common motif, but also look out for birds (these scarce lighters are known as 'Aviary' lighters) or other, even rarer motifs such as ships, cars or hunting and shooting themes and scenes. When I began my career in the mid-1990s, these would struggle to fetch more than a couple of hundred pounds - how times have changed now that they have been reappraised and reached new levels of appreciation from collectors!

A 1950s Dunhill 'Aquarium' desk lighter, with plated metal mounts and internally carved and painted Lucite penels, decorated with fish, marked to base.

3.9in (10cm) wide

£1,400-1,800   ROS

A Dunhill gold-plated 'Tallboy' table lighter, with a fine hammered finish, no box.

4.5in (11cm) high

£90-120   SWO

A late 20thC Bulgari solid 18ct-gold lighter, retailed by Dunhill, with two colour gold vertical ribs to the oval body, impressed 750.

The high value is largely due to the material used, but also the alliance between two great names - one in very high quality jewellery and one in superb smoking accessories.

3in (7.5cm) high 2.8oz

£1,000-1,400   DN

A late 20thC Dupont gold-plated lighter, with an engine turned body.

2.4in (6cm) high

£50-60   LOCK

SMOKING

A CLOSER LOOK AT A TABLE LIGHTER

Ronson's 'Rondelight', in the shape of a billiard ball, was introduced in 1929 and discontinued in 1939.

The sphere contains a pocket lighter, which is removeable.

As well as being sold alone, a number of different stands were produced for it - this is a very rare form.

Introduced in the mid-1930s, the Egypytian lady reflects the Egyptomania that resulted from the 1922 discovery of Tutankhamun's tomb and propelled Egyptian designs to contribute to the Art Deco movement and style.

A Ronson 'Rondelight' plated table lighter, modelled as an Egyptian lady holding the detachable globe lighter in a dish, with presentation label 'Presented to F J Miller Esq./ By his colleagues/ Boston. Feb. 22nd 1938'.

c1935   *6.75in (17cm) wide*

£1,000-1,200   SWO

A novelty lighter in the form of a gorilla, lights when head is pulled back, signed `Masaï`.

2.4in (6cm) high

£55-65   LOCK

A novelty silver lighthouse candle holder or table cigar lighter, simulated brick decoration, detachable base, maker's mark worn, with hallmarks for London.

1912   4.5in (11.5cm) high 2.6oz

£120-160   WW

A 9ct-gold cigarette case, with engine-turned decoration, presentation inscription to the interior, with hallmarks for Chester.

1923   2.4oz

£600-700   BELL

A 9ct-gold cigarette case, by Cartier, London, with calibre-cut sapphire thumb piece, numbered 9814 and 960, engraved inside the cover 'To F. Armstrong From H.H. The Maharaja of Baroda', signed, maker's mark J C, in a fitted gilt-tooled pink leather-bound Cartier case.

Fred Armstrong was a Newmarket race horse trainer who trained a number of racehorses belonging to to the Maharajah of Baroda in the 1940s. Pratapsinha Gaekwad (1908-68) succeeded his grandfather, Maharajah Sayajirao Gaekwad III, as the Maharaja of Baroda in 1939. In 1911 Sayajirao III commissioned Jacques Cartier to reset his entire jewellery collection in modern platinum settings. Although nothing came of this initial project, Jacques Cartier's visit to India in 1911 laid the foundations of extremely fruitful and enduring relationships between Cartier and Indian Royal families, culminating in the re- setting of Indian Royal jewellery collections into modern European styles during the 1920s.

1943   5in (13cm) long

£3,000-3,500   BLO

A 9ct-gold-mounted crocodile leather cigar case, with a 9ct gold band with two heraldic crests.

6in (15cm) high

£250-300   LOCK

A 9ct-gold vesta case, by Joseph Walton and Co, London, initialled.

1913   0.9oz

£200-250   WW

A pair of French celluloid cigarette cases, one marbled cream, with yellow-sleeved ivorine hand holding a green pebble forming the clasp, the other in a deep-chocolate and blue marble, the blue checked sleeve hand curving over the edge as the clasp, stamped 'Foreign'.

£250-300   WW

A rare Art Deco silver patent mechanical cigarette dispenser, by Asprey & Co., London, with a rounded twist finial revealing the upper vesta section with some original matches, the body opening at each corner section, cedar-lined, pat. no.40928, no date letter.

c1935   *23cm (9in) high*

£2,500-3,000   BLO

A Robj pottery pipe holder, modelled as a seated Chinaman, printed marks, professional restoration to base.

The restoration has reduced the value of this piece considerably,. Had it been in perfect condition it may have fetched over 5 times more.

5.3in (13.5cm) high

£25-30   WW

A late 20thC Hermès Paris ashtray, with painting of a Mongolian horseman.

Many such items by luxury goods retailers are worth a small fraction of their original retail cost, but these ashtrays buck the general trend. Made from Limoges porcelain and costing over twice the amount this fetched when bought new, these are sought-after by both people who smoke and, more recently, collectors - sometimes the two are one person!

7.7in (19.5cm) wide

£150-200   ECGW

An American Art Deco silver and green enamel smoking compendium, by Udall and Ballou, comprising five graduated ashtrays and a matchbox holder, initialled, pierced handle.

4.25in (11cm) diam 16oz

£400-500   WW

A silvered-metal cigar cutter, modelled as the head and neck of a racehorse, mechanism working freely.

£100-120   GBA

A Victorian silver table vesta box, by Walter Thornhill & Co. (Hubert Thornhill), London, the cover with 'Matches' in blue enamel, the hinged front lowering to release the cover, light scratches.

1887   *2.75in (7cm) long*

£220-280   BLO

QUICK REFERENCE - SPORTING MEMORABILIA

- Sporting memorabilia is collected across the world, with most collectors focusing on one sport. They may focus on one type of object, such as golf clubs or signed football jerseys. Football (soccer in the US), golf, baseball, cricket and tennis are perhaps the most popular sports. The sheer quantity of collectors vying to own pieces from that sport and build a collection means that values can be very high. Date, the fame of any player or team connected to the piece, and the importance of the game the piece is related to, are amongst the most important factors that govern value.

- Items worn by a player in the event, or that are directly related to him, her, or it, are typically the most valuable objects. If an item is connected to a major sporting event, it should be accompanied by authoritative documentation.

- This is important with items dating from the late 20thC onwards, when increasing amounts of signed memorabilia was produced for a collectors' market. A football jersey signed by David Beckham may not have been used by him in a game, or even owned by him - it is simply signed by him

and may be one of a large quantity that he was asked or paid to sign.

- More general sporting memorabilia like paper ephemera, particularly football programmes and tickets for important matches, can be extremely valuable, especially if the game was cancelled, ended early, or was deemed important. Photographs or posters add variety and visual appeal to a collection.

- Always pay attention to the form and the materials a piece is made from, and any name it may bear. It's worth learning the history of the sport, as early memorabilia can be very rare and highly desirable. A good example is the tennis racquet, which changed shape over time, or golf balls and clubs which changed in similar ways over time. Also look out for pieces related to female players, as this growing and important area can yield some suprisingly high values. Condition is always important as collectors enjoy displaying what they own. Those pieces in the best condition will always usually find a ready market of buyers.

A red Hamburg no.7 jersey, worn by Kevin Keegan, season 1979-80, with a pennant presented at the Hamburg v Hajduk Split European Cup quarter-final first leg in Hamburg and a cased Hamburg souvenir coin.

This jersey was given by the Hamburg team general manager Gunther Netzer, along with a pennant and souvenir coin, to Jim Rowan, the linesman who officiated this match. There were also photographs and newspaper articles that illustrate and complete the provenance.

£1,200-1,600   GBA

A signed Paul Gascoigne replica England 1990 World Cup jersey, signed in blue marker pen below the no.19, with a 'Tears of Gazza' colour photograph, title plaque, mounted, framed and glazed.

32.75in (73cm)

£300-350   GBA

A signed Stan Collymore Liverpool no.8 away jersey, season 1995-96, Premier League badges, signed in black marker pen with personalised inscription, the reverse lettered COLLYMORE.

This jersey was signed by Stan Collymore after the match v Aston Villa at Villa Park 31st January 1996.

£300-400   GBA

A black Aston Villa away jersey, worn by David Ginola, season 2000-01, Premier League badges, the reverse lettered 'GINOLA', with a COA from Aston Villa FC merchandising department.

£200-300   GBA

A signed Bobby Charlton Manchester United tribute shirt, signed in black marker pen on the no.9, with title plaque stating Sir Bobby's appearances and goals record for United, mounted, framed and glazed, with a COA that incorporates a photograph of the signing.

31.25in (79.5cm)

£250-350   GBA

A signed Alan Shearer Newcastle United all-time leading goal scorer tribute shirt, signed in black marker pen on the no.9, mounted above goal scoring record plaque and two colour photos, mounted, framed and glazed.

33in (84cm) high

£220-280   GBA

A signed David Beckham England 2002 World Cup red replica jersey, signed in black marker pen on the no.7, mounted with a colour photograph of Beckham celebrating his penalty goal v Argentina, title plaque, mounted, framed and glazed.

33in (84cm) high

£300-350   **GBA**

A CLOSER LOOK AT A PAIR OF FOOTBALL

These boots were worn by Shay Brennan (1937-2000), who played for Manchester United for most of his sporting life.

They were worn during the 1968 European Cup Final at Wembley Stadium where Manchester United won, with Brennan playing right back.

Manchester United are a widely collected and highly popular team and this was the first time an English team had won the European cup.

They are accompanied by a letter of authenticity signed by Brennan's widow.

A pair of football boots, worn by Shay Brennan.

£1,000-1,500   **GBA**

A signed Patrick Vieira red and white Arsenal Champions League jersey, signed in black marker pen, mounted, framed and glazed.

35in (89cm) high

£300-400   **GBA**

A pair of signed Wayne Rooney football boots, salmon pink Nike T90, both signed in black marker pen to the toes.

£220-280   **GBA**

A pair of silver Nike boots, signed Marco Materazzi 2006 World Cup, both signed in black marker pen and inscribed 'WC06', the boots personalised 'DAVIDE, ANNA, GIANMARCO, MM23, WC06'.

During the 2006-07 season, the controversial player Materazzi (b.1973) was voted Serie A Defender of the Year. This was a yearly award organized by the Italian Footballers' Association (AIC) since 2000 to 2010 as part of the 'Oscar del Calcio' awards event, given to the defender who has been considered to have performed the best over the previous Serie A season.

£500-600   **GBA**

A pair of child's vintage leather football boots, in virtually unused condition, English child's size 11.

£120-150   **GBA**

A late 19thC leather football, made up of eight panels with leather lacing.

Football memorabilia or kit from before the 1920s is very rare. By their very nature, footballs were treated roughly and most were discarded when they became battered and scruffy, others dried out and became brittle and misshapen over time. This survivor is extremely rare.

£2,000-2,500   GBA

A brown leather football, signed by the Tottenham Hotspur 1960-61 double-winning team, with stencilled inscription 'TOTTENHAM HOTSPUR F.C., 1960/61', the signatures now quite faded, including Danny Blanchflower, Les Allen, Ron Henry, Peter Baker, Tony Marchi, Maurice Norman, and Terry Dyson.

The 1960-61 season marked the club's 43rd year of competitive football and was their most successful up to that point. They won the Football League's First Division for the second time and the F.A. Cup for the third time.

£500-600   GBA

A football signed by Pelé.

This football was signed at the World Travel Market in London in 1985 when Pelé was an ambassador for Air Portugal.

£150-200   GBA

A football signed by the England 1990 World Cup squad, fully signed by the 22-man squad, and additionally by physio Norman Medhurst, sold with a COA from Hamleys Toy Store in London where the ball was won in a prize draw.

£350-400   GBA

A football signed by the England team, includes signatures from Shearer, Sheringham, Seaman, Southgate, and Ince.

c1996

£150-200   GBA

A match ball from the UEFA Champions League final Bayer Leverkusen v Real Madrid played at Hampden Park, Glasgow, 15th May 2002, bearing 7 autographs from finalists, including Michael Ballack.

This ball was kept by a steward on duty at Hampden Park, and was accompanied by a certificate of authenticity stating this. The signatures are somewhat faded - had they not been, it could have fetched up to 50% more.

£500-600   GBA

QUICK REFERENCE - THE VALUE OF SUCCESS

● On the Antiques Roadshow, we see a lot of sporting medals similar to this. Although they have sentimental value to their owner, their financial value is usually very low, sometimes being little more than the weight of the material itself. Only growing interest in a player or team can add value, which is created when they achieved success. Values only start to rise if interest does in either the player or the team. Some teams, such as Manchester United, are collectable but there may also be a historian or collector interested in some of the smaller teams too. The reason the medal was awarded also comes into play. Stanley Matthews' (1915-2000) 9ct gold 1953 F.A. Cup Final winner's medal combined all the very best factors one should look for - an internationally famous player, a key and well-known match, a collectable team and a desirable period in footballing history. As a result, it sold for over £250,000 at auction in 2014! The medal shown here is less illustrious, but still highly desirable. The 1920 FA Cup Final between Aston Villa and Huddersfield was played at Stamford Bridge. Aston Villa, who its original owner Sam Hardy played for, won 1-0 with a goal scored in extra time by Billy Kirton to clinch the trophy for a record sixth time.

A 15ct-gold F.A. Cup winner's medal, awarded to Sam Hardy of Aston Villa, inscribed '1920, ENGLISH CUP, ASTON VILLA FC., WINNERS, S. HARDY'.
1920

£6,500-7,000   GBA

A 9ct-gold 1921-22 Football League Division Two Championship medal, awarded to Sam Hardy of Nottingham Forest, inscribed 'THE FOOTBALL LEAGUE, CHAMPIONS, DIVISION 2, WINNERS, 1921-22, NOTTm. FOREST F.C., S. HARDY'.

The Football League Division 2 for 1921/22 was won by Nottingham Forest with 56 points, 4 points ahead of Stoke. Both teams were promoted to Division 1.

£1,100-1,500   GBA

A silver medal awarded by the Uruguayan Football Association to the 1930 World Cup winning footballer Ernesto Mascheroni, the obverse struck with a goalkeeper making a flying save, the reverse inscribed 'E.MASCHERONI, 1930, A.U. DE F.'.

£2,500-3,000   GBA

A silver-gilt London Football Association Challenge Cup winner's medal, won by a Chelsea footballer in season 1949-50, inscribed 'LONDON FOOTBALL ASSOCIATION CHALLENGE CUP COMPETITION, WINNERS, 1949-50', in original paper box.

The 1949-50 London Challenge Cup Final was won by Chelsea who defeated Brentford 3-0 in a replay at Fulham, after a 4-4 draw at Arsenal.

£500-600   GBA

A 9ct-gold Football Association England v Wales 1919 Victory International medal, inscribed 'THE FOOTBALL ASSOCIATION, ENGLAND v WALES, 1919, VICTORY INTERNATIONAL'.

There were two England Victory Internationals versus Wales in 1919. The first was at Ninian Park on 11th October, with Wales winning 2-1. This medal was awarded for the second match on 19th October at the Victoria Ground, Stoke, with England winning 2-0.

£1,500-2,000   GBA

A cased 14ct-gold and blue enamel Football Association of Wales Amateur Cup runner-up medal 1935-36, by Usher of Birmingham, with a Chester Assay Office hallmark, inscribed 'Football Association of Wales, Amateur Cup, winners, 1935-36, Llay Welfare F.C.'.

Llay Welfare beat Treharris Athletic 3-1 in a replay. The final tie had ended as a 1-1 draw.

£400-450   GBA

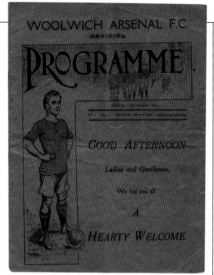

A Woolwich Arsenal 1913 programme.

This programme was produced for the first game ever played at Highbury after the team's owner Sir Henry Morris made the team's base there in that year.

£3,500-4,000   LOCK

A Manchester United v Blackpool programme, 13th January 1917.

£2,500-3,000   GBA

A F.A. Cup final Bolton Wanderers v West Ham United programme, 28th April 1923.

£700-800   GBA

A 1927 F.A. Cup final Arsenal v Cardiff City programme, with facsimile colour replacement covers.

£300-400   GBA

A CLOSER LOOK AT A FOOTBALL PROGRAMME

England-Germany football rivalry is legendary. Many British football fans consider Germany to be their main sporting rivals. Interestingly, German fans see the Netherlands as their main sporting rivals!

Although rivalry dates back to early matches in 1899, this is the programme for the first full international match played between the nations.

Despite this it was a friendly match. England led for much of the match, but it ended with a draw of 3-3.

It has good graphics and appeals to a wide range of age groups - particularly those that remember the controversial English win in the 1966 World Cup, as well as semi-finals in the 1990s!

A Germany v England international programme, played at the Deutsches Stadion, Berlin, 10th May 1930.

£2,500-3,000   GBA

A Brentford v Manchester United programme, 10th October 1936.

£250-300   GBA

A Manchester United v Huddersfield Town programme, 26th November 1938.

£300-400   GBA

A 1950 World Cup Final Brazil v Uruguay programme, the game played at the Maracana, Rio de Janeiro, 16th June 1950.

This match was played before a world record attendance of 200,000 spectators. Although the format was different in 1950, with a 4-team final round group, due to previous results this match was effectively the final tie. Uruguay won 2-1. The bookmakers had priced Brazil at odds of 1 to 10 on to lift the Jules Rimet Trophy.

£550-650   GBA

An Argentina v England programme, the game played at the River Plate Stadium in Buenos Aires, 17th May 1953.

This is a combined programme that also covers the Argentinian F.A. XI v The Football Association XI on 14th May 1953. The England game was suspended after 23 minutes and then abandoned due to heavy rain waterlogging the pitch.

£600-700   GBA

A Norwich City v Manchester United programme, 5th May 1954.

This was the Norfolk and Norwich Charities Cup played at Carrow Road.

£500-600   GBA

A 1966 World Cup final programme, signed on the front cover by the England goalscorers Geoff Hurst and Martin Peters.

£400-500   GBA

A Manchester City season ticket, season 1901-02, issued to a Mr Boswell, the word 'Groundsman' corrected by hand to read 'Ground Committee', black leather-covered boards, gilt, numbered 22.

£300-400   GBA

A Gordon Clayton's Wolverhampton Wanderers player's ticket, season 1937-38, booklet with old gold cloth-covered boards bearing Wolves monogram, named to Clayton on inside front board, then four pages of printed player's instructions.

Centre-forward Gordon Clayton joined Wolves from Shotton Colliery in October 1932 and made a total of 47 League appearances, scoring 34 goals. This ticket was issued for his final season at the club. In fact he left in October 1937 to join Aston Villa, before finishing his career at Burnley although he did 'guest' for Swansea during World War II.

£200-300   GBA

A Fulham FC player's ticket, season 1934-35, named to Sharman.

£100-150   GBA

A CLOSER LOOK AT A FOOTBALL TICKET

This ticket is rare because it had to be surrendered in its entirety at the ground's turnstiles to gain admission.

Significantly, this was the last occasion that Newcastle United won a major trophy, winning with six goals against two.

NEWCASTLE UNITED № 5483
FOOTBALL CO. LTD

Inter-Cities Fairs Cup
FINAL — 1st Leg

(Valid only for First Match at St. James' Park)
For Details see Public Announcements

ADMIT TO

GALLOWGATE ENCLOSURE

(See reverse side for Plan)

Entrance by Turnstiles: STRAWBERRY PLACE
ADJACENT "A" STAND

Secretary

To avoid delays and congestion, it is advisable that Ticket Holders are in position half an hour before Kick-off

St James' Park is Newcastle United's home ground and has been their home since 1892, although football has been played there since 1880.

Gallowgate is an interesting stand - named after the location of the city's gallows, the contruction of the first stand there kicked off the long-standing controversy and battles over expansion between the ground and local residents.

A rare ticket for the Newcastle United v Ujpesti Dozsa Inter-Cities Fairs Cup final home leg, played at St James Park, 29th May 1969, for the Gallowgate Enclosure, vertical and horizontal folds.

£600-800   GBA

A monochrome version of the official Uruguay 1930 World Cup poster.

21in (53cm) high

£200-300   GBA

An official 1966 World Cup poster, the design featuring the tournament insignia, an orange leather football, a globe and the Jules Rimet trophy, mounted, framed and glazed.

This poster is as valuable as it is due to the large size and because it is a scarcer version of this popular poster that shows the World Cup, the Earth and a football.

27in (69cm) high

£650-750   GBA

A rare 1934 World Cup special edition magazine 'Storia Del Calcio Azzurro', published by Cosmos, Milano, June 1934.

£500-600   GBA

A Manchester United 1956-57 Football League Championship dinner & dance menu, for an event held at the Midland Hotel, Manchester, 16th December 1957.

£600-650   GBA

A signed colour photograph of David Beckham, 9 by 6in, portraying Beckham in action captaining Manchester United, signed in black marker pen and inscribed '7', mounted, framed and glazed.

17in (43cm) high

£150-200   GBA

A Spanish football pennant listing an international squad, below a map of Spain.

c1960 14.5in (37cm) long

£80-120 GBA

A 1962 World Cup pennant, the margin formed by the national flags of the competing nations, inscribed 'CAMPEONATO MUNDIAL DE FUTBOL, COPA JULES RIMET, CHILE, 1962'.

A pennant for the FC Inter v Bayern Munich Champions League tie, played in Munich, 15th March 2011.

This has an interesting provenance, having come from a former FC Inter Team Director.

17in (43cm) high

£200-300 GBA

24in (61cm) long

£450-550 GBA

A shield made to commemorate Arsenal's first appearance in an F.A. Cup final in 1927, inscribed gilt 'ARSENAL FOOTBALL CLUB', set with a shelf-mounted gunmetal miniature replica of a cannon and inscribed 'The Gunners', all on a rectangular wooden backboard with wall fittings, the reverse dated, signed and inscribed '1927, J. HARRIS, WOOLWICH'.

33in (84cm) high

£250-300 GBA

A replica of the World Cup trophy, manufactured at the time of the 2002 World Cup, a gilt plaster cast, being a realistic replica of the original trophy.

15in (38cm) high

£250-350 GBA

A French painted-chrome cigarette dispenser, modelled as a brown leather football, believed to have been made as a souvenir for the 1936 Olympic Games, with top-mounted ring-pull to lift upper hemisphere revealing numerous gilt-metal cigarette holders, titled 'Olympia', mechanism in need of attention.

5in (13cm) diam

£50-80 GBA

A tobacco jar and cover, by Longchamp of France, in the form of a leather-covered ceramic model of a football, the ball lacing used to lift the cover.

6.5in (17cm)

£100-150 GBA

SPORTING

A 1960s-70s continental ceramic liqueur set with football design, the main vessel shaped as a football with a player as a handle, wooden tap and stand for hanging six drinking cups.

7.75in (20cm) high

£50-100   GBA

A 1969-70 Football League Cup runners-up tankard, electroplated, engraved 'THE FOOTBALL LEAGUE CUP, 1969-70, RUNNERS UP'.

Manchester City defeated West Bromwich Albion 2-1.

4in (10cm) high

£550-650   GBA

QUICK REFERENCE - CROSS-MARKET APPEAL

● This combines a number of desirable features that appeal to a number of different groups of collectors. Although it's a fairly standard vesta case form, it could easily appeal to vesta case collectors as an advertising piece. It would also appeal to collectors of Wolverhampton Wanderers memorabilia, particularly as the team won the F.A. Cup this year. There's also a strong, if small, dedicated group of collectors who collect Colman's Mustard advertising, and this would appeal to them too as this is a rare piece. Most Colman's memorabilia comprises posters, other paper ephemera, ceramics, tins and jars. Without the branding or commemorative oval, this piece would be worth around £15-20. Due to their presence and the demand they create from three different markets, the value rises by twenty times.

A 'Sharp Shooter' money box, by Chad Valley, designed as a boy's book with Wembley football scene.

Chad Valley were a prolific maker of good quality toys, jigsaws, puzzles, and teddy bears.

£300-350   GBA

A Colman's Mustard vesta case, commemorating the victory of Wolverhampton Wanderers in the 1908 F.A. Cup final, in white metal and blue enamel, inscribed 'TO COMMEMORATE WOLVERHAMPTON WANDERERS VICTORY, ENGLISH CUP, CRYSTAL PALACE, APRIL 25th 1908'.

2in (5cm) long

£350-450   GBA

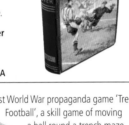

A First World War propaganda game 'Trench Football', a skill game of moving a ball round a trench maze to the goal guarded by 'The Kaiser', the German outfield players printed on the playing area comprising Count Zeppelin, Von Sanders, Von Der Goltz, Von Moltke, Enver Pasha, Von Hindenburg, Von Bulow, Little Willie, Von Terpitz and Von Kluck, printed instructions on a paper label to the reverse.

c1915

£400-500   GBA

A cased set of six Edwardian gentlemen's waistcoat buttons, set with coloured prints of football and rugby scenes, four football, and two rugby.

As well as being early memorabilia dating from the 1910s, these could have actually been worn by a football fan, adding practical appeal and thus raising desirability.

£550-600   GBA

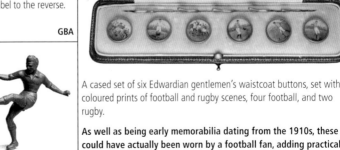

A small spelter figure of a footballer, bronze patina, set on a marble plinth.

7.5in (19cm) high

£50-100   GBA

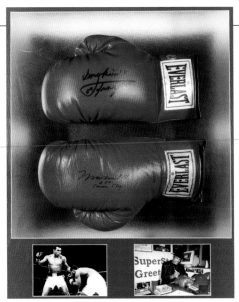

A pair of Everlast boxing gloves, the left hand signed 'Muhammad Ali aka Cassius Clay', the right hand signed 'Smokin' Joe Frazier', mounted in a glass-fronted wooden display case, with photographs of both fighters and title legend, sold together with separate certificates of authenticity.

Just because these gloves are signed by Ali and Frazier, it does not mean that they wore them, or even owned them. It is most likely that they were simply asked to sign them by a fan. Always look for a provenance, and read it carefully. These are appealing as they are professionally framed, which is an expensive activity, and are ready for display on a collector's wall. They are also attractively mounted with great photographs of each boxer.

27.5in (70cm) long

£2,500-3,000   GBA

A pair of dark-red Davega boxing gloves, with the left hand double-signed by Tony DeMarco and Carmen Basilio, signatures in gold marker pen, somewhat faded, mounted in a display case (not glass-fronted) with title plaque.

22.5in (57cm) high

£200-300   GBA

A left-hand boxing glove signed by Evander Holyfield, title plaque, mounted, framed, and glazed.

17.75in (45cm) long

£100-150   GBA

A left-hand Lonsdale boxing glove, signed by Frank Bruno, inscribed 'Best Wishes'.

£50-80   GBA

A pair of boxing trunks and a glove, both signed 'Leon Spinks', both items with a certificate of authenticity.

£200-250   GBA

A pair of Title boots, worn by John H. Stacey in his last professional fight versus Georges Warusfel in Islington, 23rd May 1978, autographed by various fighters and personalities who were there on the night.

£400-500   GBA

A pair of Everlast boxing gloves, signed by Muhammad Ali and Ken Norton, the left-hand signed by Ali, the right signed by Norton, sold with a COA for each glove signed by Jerry Haack.

£500-700   GBA

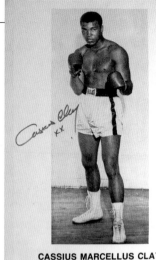

CASSIUS MARCELLUS CLAY
First Professional Promotional Photo (1960)
Heavy Wt. World Champion - Muhammad Ali

Borgen's Boxing Promotions and Collectables
BUY · SELL · TRADE   (216) 856-7047

A photograph of Cassius Clay, aka Muhammad Ali, signed 'Cassius Clay', depicting Cassius Clay full length standing in boxing pose with raised gloves.

Cassius Clay Jr was born in Kentucky, USA, in 1942 and became one of the most famous boxers in the history of the sport. He began training in 1954, aged 12, and won 100 bouts with only five losses as an amateur. In 1960, around when this photograph was taken, he turned professional, and also won the Light Heavyweight gold medal at the Summer Olympics in Rome. As well as being a superb image, this is a rare, early promotional image from the very start of his professional career. The signature is also full, clear and well-placed on the image.

c1960   8.5in (21.5cm)

£1,800-2,200   **GBA**

A pair of Everlast boxing trunks, signed by Sugar Ray Leonard.

£100-150   **GBA**

An official programme for the 'Theatre Network Television' screening of the Sonny Liston v Cassius Clay World Heavyweight Championship fight in Miami Beach, 25th February 1964.

£300-400   **GBA**

A Chris Eubank signed caricature print, inscribed 'To All at Babe Ruth's, Best Wishes', mounted, framed and glazed.

21.25in (54cm) long

£40-60   **GBA**

A boxing silk commemorating the Pedlar Palmer v Billy Plimmer World Championship fight, inscribed 'PEDLAR PALMER, BEAT BILLY PLIMMER AT THE NATIONAL SPORTING CLUB, FOR THE BANTAM WEIGHT CHAMPIONSHIP OF THE WORLD AND £800, DECR. 12th 1898'.

30in (76cm) long

£150-200   **GBA**

A French pottery jug, depicting a boxing match, decorated in colour on both sides, cracked, marked 'F.B. boxe' to base.

7.25in (18.5cm) high

£50-80   **GBA**

A cast-bronze sculpture of a boxer, rich-brown patina, mounted on a marble base, fitting of figure to base in need of attention.

8.5in (21.5cm) high

£100-150   **GBA**

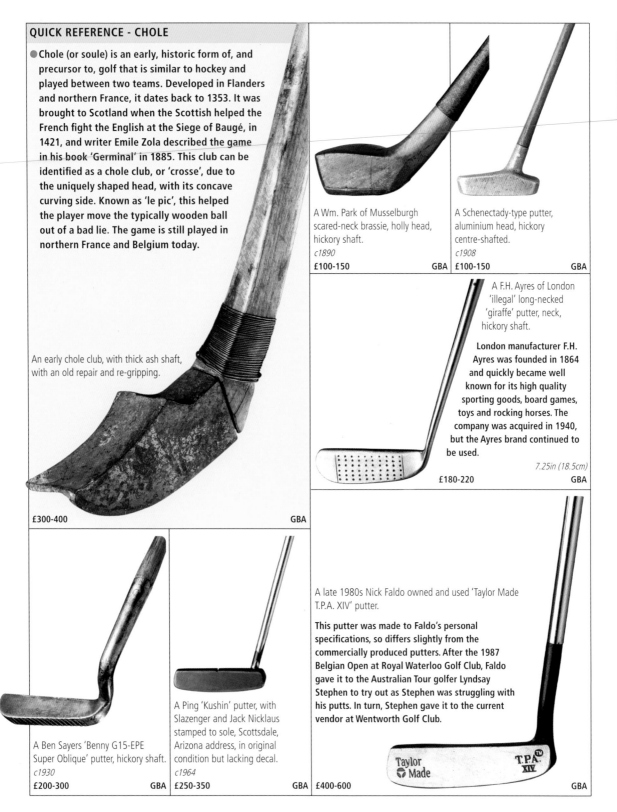

QUICK REFERENCE - CHOLE

- Chole (or soule) is an early, historic form of, and precursor to, golf that is similar to hockey and played between two teams. Developed in Flanders and northern France, it dates back to 1353. It was brought to Scotland when the Scottish helped the French fight the English at the Siege of Baugé, in 1421, and writer Emile Zola described the game in his book 'Germinal' in 1885. This club can be identified as a chole club, or 'crosse', due to the uniquely shaped head, with its concave curving side. Known as 'le pic', this helped the player move the typically wooden ball out of a bad lie. The game is still played in northern France and Belgium today.

An early chole club, with thick ash shaft, with an old repair and re-gripping.

£300-400   GBA

A Wm. Park of Musselburgh scared-neck brassie, holly head, hickory shaft.
c1890
£100-150   GBA

A Schenectady-type putter, aluminium head, hickory centre-shafted.
c1908
£100-150   GBA

A F.H. Ayres of London 'illegal' long-necked 'giraffe' putter, neck, hickory shaft.

London manufacturer F.H. Ayres was founded in 1864 and quickly became well known for its high quality sporting goods, board games, toys and rocking horses. The company was acquired in 1940, but the Ayres brand continued to be used.

7.25in (18.5cm)
£180-220   GBA

A Ben Sayers 'Benny G15-EPE Super Oblique' putter, hickory shaft.
c1930
£200-300   GBA

A Ping 'Kushin' putter, with Slazenger and Jack Nicklaus stamped to sole, Scottsdale, Arizona address, in original condition but lacking decal.
c1964
£250-350   GBA

A late 1980s Nick Faldo owned and used 'Taylor Made T.P.A. XIV' putter.

This putter was made to Faldo's personal specifications, so differs slightly from the commercially produced putters. After the 1987 Belgian Open at Royal Waterloo Golf Club, Faldo gave it to the Australian Tour golfer Lyndsay Stephen to try out as Stephen was struggling with his putts. In turn, Stephen gave it to the current vendor at Wentworth Golf Club.

£400-600   GBA

SPORTING

A hand-hammered gutty golf ball, in reasonable condition.

The term 'gutty' refers to gutta percha, the material used to make this ball. A form of rubber, it was cheaper and so replaced balls made of leather and feathers around 1848, and was used until the turn of the 20thC. Pay attention to the surface as smooth gutty balls are often early examples and are highly sought-after, as are those with interesting moulded patterns such as a map of the world.

c1865

£300-400   GBA

An original artwork for a 'Booth's Gin' advertisement poster, featuring a Walker Cup golfer using a gin bottle as a tee, mixed media, pen and ink, watercolour heightened with bodycolour and coloured pastels, indistinctly signed lower right.

24in (61cm)

£250-300   GBA

A fully signed photograph of Bernard Langer's 2004 Ryder Cup European Team, signed in marker pen.

This European team won the Ryder Cup in this year, a margin of 18½ to 9½ points - the largest margin ever achieved by a European team in the Cup's history. It was also the largest margin of defeat for the US team on home soil, as well as their worst ever defeat since the competition began in 1927.

10in (25.5cm) wide

£300-400   GBA

'The Rules of Golf', as adopted by the Royal and Ancient Golf Club of St. Andrews, green cloth covers, gilt, printed 'W C Henderson & Son, St Andrews'.

September 1899

£700-1,000   GBA

A 13th hole pin flag, used at the 1989 US Open Championship at Oak Hill Country Club, sold with a signed letter of provenance.

£300-500   GBA

A Victorian silver-plated golfing stand, set with a figure of a golfer at the top of his backswing, pair of glass inkpots, pen rest.

8in (20cm) wide

£300-400   GBA

A late Victorian rectangular silver vesta case, embossed with golfing motifs, including clubs, flags, and balls, Birmingham.

1896

£400-500   BELL

A Williams-Renault Formula 1 pitlane mechanics overalls, a Nomex suit with body length zip, by OMP of Italy, the team logos including full sponsorship branding, also featuring Elf, Goodyear, Magneti Marelli, Renault and Williams logos, a stitched FIA accreditation on the back of the collar.

This suit is similar to the Williams racesuit that Ayrton Senna wore before his death in 1994, except that the main sponsors logo appears on the back of this pitlane garment, rather than its front.
1994
£1,000-1,500   GBA

A Michael Schumacher Italian Grand Prix worn Ferrari racesuit, the waistband bearing his initial, surname and German flag, a Nomex suit by OMP featuring the Ferrari escutcheon and logo patches for sponsors, the back of the collar with stitched 2002 FIA accreditation.

The year 2002 marked Michael Schumacher's record-equalling fifth F1 World Championship, but in the race this suit was worn for, Schumacher finished second behind his team-mate Rubens Barrichello, whose two-stop pitstop strategy proved faster than Schumacher's one-stop.
2002
£10,000-12,000   GBA

A Michael Schumacher 2006 British Grand Prix worn Ferrari racesuit, the waistband bearing his initial, surname, and German flag, a Nomex suit by OMP, featuring logo patches for the Ferrari escutcheon and major sponsors.

Purchased from a private collector, this suit was worn at the British GP where reigning World Champion Michael Schumacher managed to beat his eventual Ferrari successor, Kimi Raikkonen, to 2nd place, albeit 13 seconds behind the Renault of Fernando Alonso.
£13,000-15,000   GBA

A Fernando Alonso 2006 San Marino Grand Prix worn Renault racesuit, with main sponsors, a stitched 2006 FIA accreditation on the back of the collar, marked in ink 'Driver: F.Alonso, Date/Nr: 06-06' above the barcode and ref no.

A Fernando Alonso 2008 Japanese Grand Prix worn Renault racesuit, with sponsors logos, a stitched 2008 FIA accreditation on the back of the collar, the zip marked in ballpoint pen 'Driver: Alonso, Date/Nr: 12 10 08' above the barcode and ref no.

Purchased from Formula Sport in Luxembourg, this suit is from Alonso's final GP victory for Renault. This followed a controversial win in Singapore and deservedly marked his 21st success for the team.
£6,000-7,000   GBA

In the process of becoming the eighth driver to win back-to-back F1 World Championships, Fernando Alonso had to give his best at Imola to beat Michael Schumacher, who was enjoying his final season at Ferrari.
£6,000-8,000   GBA

An Ayrton Senna signed 1990 Monaco Grand Prix framed photograph, his marker pen signature on a 7-by-5in black and white photograph, mounted and glazed in a larger frame.

£450-550   GBA

A group of Ayrton Senna signed Formula 1 ephemera, with his ink pen signature on two black and white Toleman prints, dated '93', undated on a Monaco 1987 sticker, dated '92' on World Champion sticker and dated '93' on a Monaco 1993 sticker, with a rare set of dayglow McLaren car decals.
10in (17.5cm)
£500-600   GBA

SPORTING

A CLOSER LOOK AT A GRAND PRIX POSTER

Ayrton Senna (1960-94) is widely considered to be the best and most influential Formula One driver.

Even though his signature is not rare, this poster for the 1994 Italian Grand Prix in San Marino was signed by Senna at the race itself and comes with a sales receipt and a letter of provenance.

Senna was tragically killed in an accident at this race, making this one of his last ever signatures.

It is also signed by his teammate, the driver Damon Hill - both signatures are good and well-placed on the poster.

A rare Ayrton Senna signed 1994 San Marino Grand Prix poster, the official Formula 1 Imola event design with the marker pen signature of Williams-Renault teammate Damon Hill, both dated '94'.

39in (99cm) high

£3,000-3,500   GBA

A double-signed photograph of Nigel Mansell giving Ayrton Senna a lift post-1991 British GP, their ink signatures both dated '91'.

Right from the start, Mansell and Senna were both way ahead of their rivals in this race but, on the last lap, Senna ran out of fuel. As a result, British driver Mansell took the top spot on the podium to huge applause from his countrymen. Mansell gave Senna, who was classed fourth in the end, a lift as he completed his lap of honour.

10in (25.5cm) long

£300-400   GBA

A Michael Schumacher signed 1994 Benetton large colour photograph, his marker pen signature dated '94', a British photographer's stamp on the reverse.

It is often overlooked that Schumacher's first two F1 World titles were won with Benetton in 1994 and 1995.

10in (25.5cm) long

£100-150   GBA

A Champion novelty wall clock in the form of a full-face race helmet, quartz digital movement, by Spedia of Paris.

12in (30cm) high

£120-180   GBA

A Jordan-Mugen Honda 198 Formula 1 diecast 1:8 scale model by Amalgam, the 1998 no.9 Damon Hill car with full branding, the base with two brass plaques, one bearing a facsimile Eddie Jordan signature, the other Amalgam contact details, with a fitted plexi-glass cover.

This is an Amalgam Premium model with a difference in that it lacks the usual edition number on its brass plaque and a certificate. This is because it is reputed to have belonged to Eddie Jordan, which is why it bears his signature. Originally acquired by an employee at Silverstone circuit who personally knew the F1 team boss.

25in (65cm) long

£1,000-1,500   GBA

An Ayrton Senna 1986 Australian Grand Prix JPS Lotus-Renault 98T rear-wing endplate, a left-hand side plate in fibreglass, with letter of authenticity.

This part came from 98T chassis no.4, which was the last ever JPS Lotus to be driven by Ayrton Senna in F1.

1986   *(56cm) 22in*

£1,500-2,000   GBA

A St Louis Olympic Games athlete's participation medal, by Dieges & Clust, New York, the obverse with a naked athlete, the reverse with an eleven line legend, and the shields of St Louis, France, and USA on a background of ivy leaves.

A version of this medal was presented to officials, but had a loop at the top allowing it to be hung from a ribbon, and a bar so it could be worn as a badge. This medal has no loop, nor traces of where one may have been removed. As such, it was the version presented to participating athletes.

1904

£15,000-18,000   GBA

QUICK REFERENCE - OLYMPIC MEDALS

● The Olympics are renowned for their gold, silver, and bronze medals, a convention that was introduced at the 1904 games. These medals, awarded to athletes for winning a competitive event are perhaps the most sought-after and rarest of all Olympic memorabilia - partly as few athletes or the families of athletes part with them. Values vary depending on desirability, which is governed by a number of factors including the age and rarity of the medal, the fame of the athlete and the importance of the sport or event. Away from these, Olympic Participation Medals (known as OPMs) are awarded to all athletes, judges, and officials who take part in each Olympic Games and act as a souvenir of the event. As such, they are much more common than event medals and make a more affordable entry point into Olympic medal collecting, ranging from a couple of hundred pounds up. Even though the original recipient of this medal is unknown, this is the largest Olympic winner's medal ever awarded, and one of only 36 awarded at the 1936 Games. As such it is very rare.

A Garmisch-Partenkirchen 1936 Winter Olympic Games gold winner's medal, designed by Richard Klein, struck by Deschler, München, with legend 'IV OLYMPISCHE WINTERSPIELE', in red leatherette case, scuffed, original recipient unknown, gold-plated silver, .990 hallmark on the edge.

1936

£35,000-40,000   *4in (10cm) diam*
                                                           GBA

A St Louis 1904 Olympic Games bronze prize medal, won by Robert Stangland, by Dieges & Clust, New York, inscribed 'OLYMPIAD, 1904', and 'UNIVERSAL EXPOSITION, ST LOUIS, U.S.A., RUNNING BROAD JUMP', the case inscribed in gilt 'MEDAL FOR OLYMPIC GAMES UNIVERSAL EXPOSITION, ST. LOUIS U.S.A., F.J.V. SKIFF, DIR. OF EXHIBITS, JAS. E. SULLIVAN, CHIEF'.

This bronze medal was awarded to the American long-jumper Robert Stangland (1881-1953) for his 6.88 metre 'running broad jump', as the sport was known then. Stangland also won an Olympic bronze in the Triple Jump that year. It retains its original case, even though it is slightly battered.

£20,000-25,000   GBA

A 1908 London Olympic Games silver participation medal, by Vaughton, designed by Bertram Mackennal, with a winged figure of victory, and a quadriga winning a chariot race.

£500-600   GBA

An Antwerp Olympic Games silver medal, designed by Josue Dupon, minted by Cossemans of Brussels, awarded to the British tennis player Winifred Geraldine Beamish in the women's doubles lawn tennis event, inscribed 'VII OLYMPIADE, ANVERS, MCMXX', the edge inscribed 'RUNNERS-UP, LADIES' DOUBLES, MRS. A.E. BEAMISH (AND MISS E.D. HOLMAN)'.

In an all-British final, Mrs Beamish and Miss Holman were defeated by Winifred McNair and 'Kitty' McKane Godfree 8-6, 6-4. Winifred Geraldine Ramsey was born at Forest Gate, London, 23rd July 1883. She married the tennis player Alfred Beamish with whom she competed in mixed doubles events including the 1920 Olympic Games where they were eliminated in the Second Round.

1920

£5,500-6,000   GBA

A boxed gold-plated 1936 Berlin Olympic Games participant's medal, designed by O. Placzek, in original red circular paper box.

£250-300   GBA

A London 1908 Olympic Games competitor's badge, silvered metal and blue enamel, inscribed 'COMPETITOR'.

£400-500   GBA

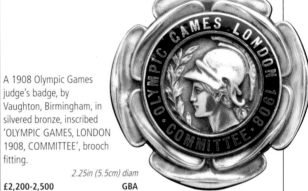

A 1908 Olympic Games judge's badge, by Vaughton, Birmingham, in silvered bronze, inscribed 'OLYMPIC GAMES, LONDON 1908, COMMITTEE', brooch fitting.

2.25in (5.5cm) diam

A Melbourne 1956 Olympic Games Team Official's badge, enamelled metal, inscribed 'OLYMPIC GAMES, MELBOURNE 1956', with red ribbon stamped 'TEAM OFFICIAL'.

£400-600   GBA

A rare Melbourne 1956 Olympic Games official medic's badge, enamelled metal, inscribed 'OLYMPIC GAMES, MELBOURNE 1956', with pink ribbon stamped 'MEDICAL'.

£1,500-2,000   GBA

£2,200-2,500   GBA

An official Swedish National Olympic Committee badge, for the London 1908 Olympic Games, gilt-metal, enamel Swedish national flag, inscribed 'LONDON 1908'.

£500-700   GBA

A linen official banner that hung at the Blyth Arena during the figure skating competitions at the 1960 Squaw Valley Winter Olympic Games, inscribed 'WELCOME, VIII OLYMPIC GAMES'.

102in (260cm) long

£1,000-1,200   GBA

A 1936 Berlin Olympic Games steel bearer's torch, designed by Carl Diem, made by Krupp factory.

This torch was carried during the first Olympic torch relay in 1936 from Olympia, Greece, to Berlin - a distance of 3,075 km that was completed in 12 days.

£2,500-3,500   GBA

A CLOSER LOOK AT AN OLYMPIC TORCH

These torches were made to carry the flame and be carried by numerous athletes along a route from Olympia in Greece to the venue of the Games. As such, a number of identical examples exist.

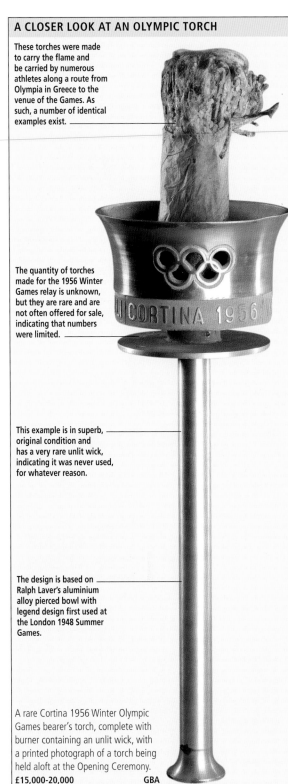

The quantity of torches made for the 1956 Winter Games relay is unknown, but they are rare and are not often offered for sale, indicating that numbers were limited.

This example is in superb, original condition and has a very rare unlit wick, indicating it was never used, for whatever reason.

The design is based on Ralph Laver's aluminium alloy pierced bowl with legend design first used at the London 1948 Summer Games.

A rare Cortina 1956 Winter Olympic Games bearer's torch, complete with burner containing an unlit wick, with a printed photograph of a torch being held aloft at the Opening Ceremony.

£15,000-20,000   **GBA**

A Sarajevo 1984 Winter Olympic Games official stainless steel bearer's torch, with gold-coloured bowl, Sarajevo '84 legend, set on a plastic base with a plaque reading 'OFFICIAL SUPPLIERS OF XIV OLYMPIC WINTER GAMES SARAJEVO '84 - MIZUNO CORPORATION - MITSUBISHI MOTORS CORPORATION', with original certification and literature.

This excellent example has no darkening from the Olympic flame as is usually the case.

22.5in (57.5cm) high

£5,500-6,000   **GBA**

A Vancouver 2010 Winter Olympics stainless steel and aluminium torch, designed by Leo Obstbaum, Canadian symbols, Olympic Rings and 'With Glowing Hearts' also translated in French, in original carrying pouch.

37.25in (94.5cm) long

£5,000-5,500   **GBA**

A Torino 2006 Winter Olympic Games blue-coated metal torch, designed by Pininfarina of Torino.

A sleek and modern design reminiscent of Philippe Starck's favoured forms, this torch is also unusually (and almost impractically) heavy, weighing just under 2kg.

30in (77cm) long

£4,000-4,500   **GBA**

A 1908 Franco-British Exhibition/ Olympic Games London souvenir leather money purse, inscribed gilt 'LONDON EXHIBITION, 1908'.

£100-150   **GBA**

A Dutch Société Céramique Maastricht colour-printed beaker, commemorating the football competition at the 1928 Amsterdam Olympic Games, front and reverse shown.

1928   *5in (12.5cm) high*

£150-200   **GBA**

SPORTING

A Derby scarf commemorating the victory of Pretender.

Silk scarves, typically covered with equestrian motifs such as these, are popular purchases or gifts at race meets. This is an exceptionally rare and early survivor, but is in very poor condition. Had it been in better condition, it could have fetched well over twice this amount.

1869

£150-200   GBA

A silk scarf commemorating the victory of Papyrus, damaged.

1923

£80-120   GBA

A rare silk scarf, published by Galeries Lafayette, commemorating the Grand Prix de Paris in 1935, with printed details of the race since its inception in 1863.

This race was won by Baron Edouard de Rothschild's 'Crudité'. This scarf is typical of traditional Epsom Derby scarves.

34in (86cm) square

£100-150   GBA

A Derby scarf commemorating the victory of Nimbus.

1949

£100-150   GBA

A silk Festival of Britain Derby scarf, commemorating the victory of Arctic Prince.

1951

£60-90   GBA

A silk Derby scarf, commemorating the victory of Tulyar.

1952

£100-150   GBA

A ladies' silk scarf, published by Wetherall, Bond Street, London, commemorating the victory of Nicolaus Silver in the Grand National.

1961

£100-150   GBA

A ladies' silk scarf, commemorating the victory of Mr H.J. Joel's Royal Palace in the 1967 Derby, in unused condition.

£120-150   GBA

A signed pair of Frankie Dettori jockey breeches, by Ornella Prosperi of Milan, embroidered inscription to both legs reading 'L. DETTORI', signed to the right leg in black marker pen.

£150-250   GBA

A pair of exercise plates, for the Grand National winners Red Rum and Aldaniti, identified by slips of paper with each shoe.

Red Rum (1965-95) was a legendary thoroughbred steeple chaser who achieved an unmatched historic treble when he won the Grand National in 1973, 1974, and 1977. Aldaniti (1970-97) was a racehorse who won the Grand National on 4 April 1981. He also starred in the 1983 film 'Champions' alongside the actor John Hurt.
£500-600   GBA

A go-to-bed white metal candlestick, decorated with a steeplechaser and jockey, the handle thumbpiece with a horse's head, the base designed to hold a box of matches.
4.25in (11cm) long
£85-95   GBA

A CLOSER LOOK AT A HOOF INKWELL

Although they may seem gruesome to our eyes today, horse hooves converted into ashtrays, inkwells, or other desk equipment were popular during the Victorian and Edwardian periods.

Frederick James 'Fred' Archer (1857-86) was an English flat race jockey, described as 'the best all-round jockey that the turf has ever seen'. He committed suicide in 1886 due to the loss of his wife in childbirth.

Ormonde won the Triple Crown in 1886 providing Archer with the final major success of his career.

It is possible that Dick could be Richard Chapman, the Duke of Westminster's long-time Eaton Stud groom where Ormonde had been foaled in 1883.

A commemorative silver-plated metal-mounted horse's hoof inkwell, commemorating the jockey Fred Archer, the cover inscribed 'MEMOIR OF FRED ARCHER'S MOUNT ORMONDE, 1886, FROM SYD TO DICK'.
£300-500   GBA

A set of 'Eclipse' gentlemen's plastic and metal vest buttons, all set with a print of a thoroughbred's head, on the original maker's paper card, bearing a date in pencil of 1907.
£220-280   GBA

SPORTING

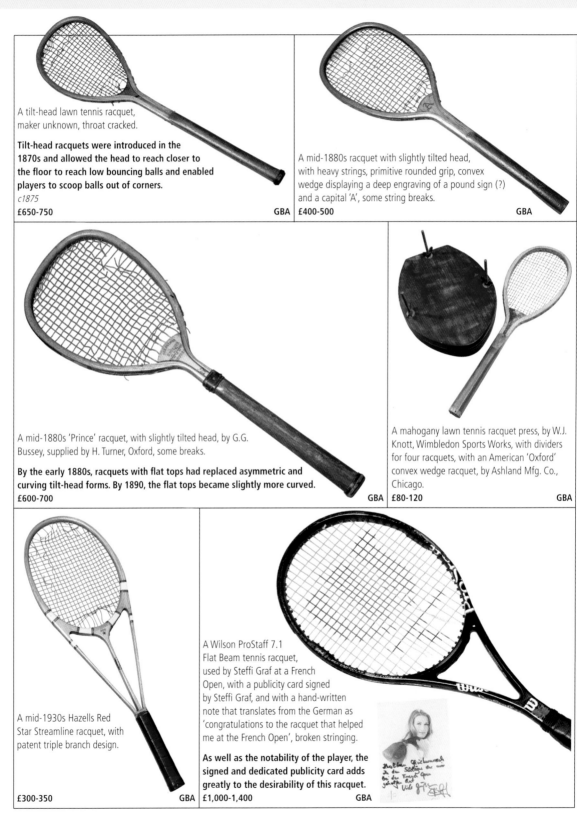

A tilt-head lawn tennis racquet, maker unknown, throat cracked.

Tilt-head racquets were introduced in the 1870s and allowed the head to reach closer to the floor to reach low bouncing balls and enabled players to scoop balls out of corners.
c1875
£650-750   GBA

A mid-1880s racquet with slightly tilted head, with heavy strings, primitive rounded grip, convex wedge displaying a deep engraving of a pound sign (?) and a capital 'A', some string breaks.
£400-500   GBA

A mid-1880s 'Prince' racquet, with slightly tilted head, by G.G. Bussey, supplied by H. Turner, Oxford, some breaks.

By the early 1880s, racquets with flat tops had replaced asymmetric and curving tilt-head forms. By 1890, the flat tops became slightly more curved.
£600-700   GBA

A mahogany lawn tennis racquet press, by W.J. Knott, Wimbledon Sports Works, with dividers for four racquets, with an American 'Oxford' convex wedge racquet, by Ashland Mfg. Co., Chicago.
£80-120   GBA

A mid-1930s Hazells Red Star Streamline racquet, with patent triple branch design.

£300-350   GBA

A Wilson ProStaff 7.1 Flat Beam tennis racquet, used by Steffi Graf at a French Open, with a publicity card signed by Steffi Graf, and with a hand-written note that translates from the German as 'congratulations to the racquet that helped me at the French Open', broken stringing.

As well as the notability of the player, the signed and dedicated publicity card adds greatly to the desirability of this racquet.
£1,000-1,400   GBA

A CLOSER LOOK AT A TENNIS TROPHY

William Tatem Tilden II (1893-1953), nicknamed 'Big Bill', was an American male tennis player who is considered one of the greatest tennis players in the history of the sport.

It is both an early tennis trophy and one awarded to a legendary player.

It dates from very early in his career and may even be the first surviving trophy that he won. It's remarkable that he was only 11 years old at the time.

The Onteora Club was in the Catskill mountains of New York and had been visited by Tilden since he was 7 years old.

An early tennis trophy, won by William T. Tilden, the glass-bottomed pewter trophy engraved, 'Tennis Tournament, Onteora 1904, Boys Doubles, won by W. T. Tilden & John Forbes'.

4.5in (11cm) high

£900-1,100 GBA

A Wimbledon Lawn Tennis Championships bronze semi-finalists medal, the original recipient and year unknown, the reverse inscribed 'THE LAWN TENNIS CHAMPIONSHIPS'.

£200-250 GBA

A brass and wooden shield, commemorating the winners and runners-up at the 1952 Lawn Tennis Championships at Wimbledon, mens and ladies singles and doubles and mixed doubles.

The singles champions at this sporting event were Mo Connelly and Frank Sedgeman.

7.5in (19cm)

£75-85 GBA

A silver Rackets trophy, in the form of a bowl with gilded interior, supported by three rackets tied together with rope, unmarked.

8.75in (22cm) high 15.3oz

£100-150 GBA

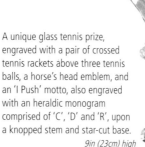

A unique glass tennis prize, engraved with a pair of crossed tennis rackets above three tennis balls, a horse's head emblem, and an 'I Push' motto, also engraved with an heraldic monogram comprised of 'C', 'D' and 'R', upon a knopped stem and star-cut base.

9in (23cm) high

£850-950 GBA

An 1889 Amersham lawn tennis tankard trophy, wooden-lined, silver plate-banded, engraved 'Amersham Lawn Tennis Tournament 1889'.

5.5in (14cm) high

£85-95 GBA

A pair of silver-plated tennis candlesticks, the candle holders supported on a tripod of racquets, each with a ball in between.

7.5in (19cm) high

£250-300 GBA

SPORTING

A pair of French 19thC spelter figures, with the unusual sporting subject of 'jeu de balle au tambourin', each signed 'Lauergne' and set on an ebonised base.

14.5in (37cm) high

£300-400   GBA

A bronze of a lady tennis player, modelled playing a backhand stroke, on a marble base.

c1880s   *5.5in (14cm) high*

£150-200   GBA

A Hagenauer-style gold-patinated bronze figurine, of a male tennis player in a serving pose, unmarked.

4.5in (11.5cm) high

£150-200   GBA

A silver-patinated Hagenauer figurine, of a male lawn tennis player making an overhead shot, stamped 'Austria'.

The Hagenauer workshop was established by Carl Hagenauer in Vienna, Austria, in 1898. It became known for Art Nouveau style metalware. In 1925, his son Franz (1906-86) joined the company. He was a member of the influential Wiener Werkstätte and introduced highly stylised metal sculptures in clean-lined, modern forms. His work was successful and widely imitated.

3.5in (9cm) high

£100-150   GBA

A Victorian silver cigar cutter, designed as a tennis racquet, two 'tennis balls' to draw out cutter, hallmarked Birmingham.

c1890

£200-250   GBA

An 1890s American sterling silver letter opener, designed with a tilt-head tennis racquet handle.

10in (25.5cm) long

£150-250   GBA

A CLOSER LOOK AT A TENNIS RACQUET PENCIL

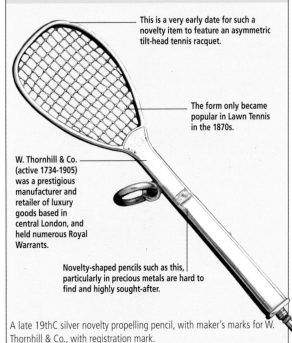

This is a very early date for such a novelty item to feature an asymmetric tilt-head tennis racquet.

The form only became popular in Lawn Tennis in the 1870s.

W. Thornhill & Co. (active 1734-1905) was a prestigious manufacturer and retailer of luxury goods based in central London, and held numerous Royal Warrants.

Novelty-shaped pencils such as this, particularly in precious metals are hard to find and highly sought-after.

A late 19thC silver novelty propelling pencil, with maker's marks for W. Thornhill & Co., with registration mark.

1878

£300-500   GBA

QUICK REFERENCE - SILVER KNIFE RESTS

● In addition to equipment and kit used to play tennis, small, well-made items like these knife rests appeal greatly. Although not of much practical use today, their high level of detail, and the fact that they are made from silver, make them sought-after.

A silver-plated toast rack with dividers, designed as flat-topped tennis racquets, with tennis ball feet.
c1890s
£200-300   **GBA**

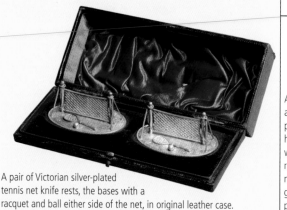

A pair of Victorian silver-plated tennis net knife rests, the bases with a racquet and ball either side of the net, in original leather case.
c1885
£200-300   **GBA**

A large pottery jug and wash-bowl, probably American, hand-painted in gold with images of tennis rackets, balls and a net, on a turquoise ground, gold-painted pattern number.
c1895   the bowl 15in (38cm) diam
£200-250   **GBA**

'LOVE AND TENNIS SUITE 1974', after 'Erte' (Romaine de Tirtoff), signed in pencil by the artist, limited edition lithograph numbered 45/260, mounted, framed and glazed, with the original certificate of authenticity.
34in (86cm) long
£300-400   **GBA**

A copy of 'Racquet & Tennis Club', by St Jorre (John), privately published for members only in 2007, a history of the famed New York club, bound in leather with gilt detailing, in similar slip case.
£300-400   **GBA**

One of a group of 9 official posters for the Stella Artois tennis championship, at Queen's Club, including 7 autographed examples by McEnroe, Connors or Becker, all uniformly mounted, framed and glazed, with a larger version of the championship poster signed by Boris Becker.
12.5in (44cm) long
£200-250   **GBA**

A pair of Venus Williams signed 'EleVen' ladies' tennis shoes, her own design exclusively for Steve & Barry's, size 7, both signed to the heel in black marker pen.
£180-220   **GBA**

An autographed cricket bat, inscribed 'WIMBLEDON CHARITY CRICKET MATCH, MR J.B. HOBBS XII v WIMBLEDON & DISTRICT XVIII, SEPTEMBER 16th 1933, CHAMPION COUNTY, THE REST OF ENGLAND', signed by Hobbs to the shoulder, and by the Yorkshire (Champion County) and rest of England teams, the other side of the bat, inscribed 'TEST MATCH, WEST INDIES v ENGLAND, PLAYED AT KENNINGTON OVAL, AUGUST 12th 1933', signed by the West Indies and England teams.

1933

£500-550　　　　　　　　　GBA

A Victorian cricket buckle, portraying a wicket keeper up to the stumps, with a registered design mark for 1863.

£80-120　　　　　　　　　GBA

A character jug of the cricketer W.G. Grace, by Manor, Staffordshire, with another from the series titled 'Golfer'.

6.75in (17cm) high

£300-350　　　　　　　　　GBA

A CLOSER LOOK AT A FISHING REEL

The Hardy 'Bouglé' reel was introduced in 1903 and is a variation of the highly successful company's 'Perfect' reel.

It was commissioned by notable French fisherman and tournament caster Louis Bouglé (1864-1924) who wanted a lighter weight, smaller diameter reel without losing any capacity.

A silver-plated cricket inkstand, with presentation inscription, with a batsman between two cut-glass inkpots, inscribed for a 21st birthday present to 'J.S. Downham from Exchange Cricket Club, June 23rd 1886'.

10in (26cm) long

£150-200　　　　　　　　　GBA

As Hardy brought in its castings until 1937, rather than make them themselves, they had to file down the cage on each reel by hand, making it the 'ultimate' handmade production reel.

Unlike many special commissions from individuals, the Bouglé was both practical and successful. It sold for nearly four decades, but never in great numbers as it cost around 50% more than a standard 'Perfect' reel.

A wooden cricket bat letter opener, with an ash blade and a holly handle.

10in (26cm) long

£40-50　　　　　　　　　GBA

A Hardy 'Perfect' reel, with the owner's initials marked on the surface.

3.75in (9.5cm)

£350-400　　　　　　　　　LAW

A Hardy 'Bouglé' patent fishing reel, alloy fly reel with ivory winder and tension adjuster, also with a Hardy fly tin, Hardy hook etc.

2.5in (6.5cm)

£2,000-2,500　　　　　　　　　LAW

A Westley Richards fly fishing trout reel.
c1910   *3in (7.6cm) wide*
£60-80   **BELL**

A Victorian silver vesta case, by Samuel Levi, Birmingham, with a fisherman, marked with a registration number.
1884   *1.5in (4cm) long*
£300-350   **WW**

A green and black Jahangir Khan 1 Unsquashable racquet, used by Jahangir Khan when winning the 1983 British Open Championship, with a newspaper cutting noting that this racquet was won in a raffle by British squash player Dave Sanders in 1983.

This was the second of Jahangir Khan's sequence of ten consecutive victories in the British Open Championship between 1982 and 1991.
£500-600   **GBA**

A John F. Marshall Racquets Trophy, a further 'House' trophy acquired by Marshall while at Rugby School, engraved 'J. F. Marshall, 1st. House, Racquets, Rugby, 1892', unmarked.
5.75in (14.5cm) high
£120-180   **GBA**

QUICK REFERENCE - RARITY & VALUE

● **Eton Fives is a game similar to squash played in a three-sided court, but hands are used instead of racquets. Developed in the late 19thC at Eton College, Berkshire, it is not played widely. Most Fives courts are found in British public schools - they number less than 20. Memorabilia related to Fives is very rare. But rarity doesn't always indicate high values. Fives is a niche sport and even those who played it as children are rarely interested in collecting memorabilia related to it. As a result, demand is low, especially compared to most other sports. Furthermore, memorabilia is extremely limited in quality and variety. Balls are unremarkable and often worn, and pictorial representations and other memorabilia were not produced in large numbers. This means that it's challenging to build up a good collection. Although those that do collect are usually dedicated, the lack of wider competition keeps prices low (or affordable, depending on your opinion). Having said all of this, co-author Mark Hill did play Fives once or twice in a Fives court when he was a pupil at the Royal Grammar School in Guildford, England. His attempts were hardly worth a trophy like this, however, and are best forgotten!**

An Eton School silverplated trophy, awarded for the game of Eton Fives in 1890, inscribed 'R.E. RICHARDSON, WINNER OF, HOUSE FIVES, WITH, G. LYSLEY, ETON 1890'.

6.25in (16cm) high
£60-100   **GBA**

A baseball, signed by the Yomiuri Giants including Sadaharu Oh, in case and mounted on a woden plinth.

The retired Japanese-Taiwanese baseball player Sadaharu Oh holds the world lifetime home run record, having hit 868 home runs during his professional career.
£100-150   **GBA**

A Continental leather money purse, with an enamelled metal lid portraying a competitive cyclist.
c1900
£100-140   **GBA**

SPORTING

A rare cased set of six Edwardian waistcoat buttons set with coloured prints of lawn bowls.

£100-150   GBA

A Nadia Comaneci Romanian international competition gymnastics leotard, with the tricolours of the Romanian national flag, with a Nadia-signed copy of Ioan Chirila's book 'Nadia' and a group of photographs of the gymnast.

Nadia Comaneci (b.1961) won three gold medals at the Montreal 1976 Olympic Games and famously was the first gymnast to record a perfect score of 10 for her performance on the uneven bars. The Omega scoreboard was only designed to display three digits and therefore displayed a score of 1.00 which caused a momentary delay before spectators at the Montreal Forum gave her a standing ovation. Comaneci won two further gold medals at Moscow in 1980 taking her career tally of medals of all colours to nine. She received the Olympic Order, the highest award given by the IOC, in 1984 and 2004 and is the only person to have achieved this. Nadia was also inducted into the International Gymnastics Hall of Fame.

£8,000-12,000   GBA

A pair of vintage leather running spikes, with suede lining, size 10.

£300-400   GBA

The match ball, by Gilbert, from the Scotland v England rugby union international at Murrayfield, 15th February 1986.

This ball was given to the current vendor by the Scottish international lock Alister Campbell who was a neighbour in the Scottish border town of Hawick. The ball was originally signed by the Scottish team, including Campbell, that defeated England 33-6 in the match, but the signatures are now virtually illegible.

£100-200   GBA

An Edwardian pottery Rugby jug, with comic rugby scene to one side, crazing, some rim chopping.

9in (23cm) high

£50-80   SAS

An Art Deco silver greyhound trophy, inscribed 'PRESENTED TO MR C C KEEN'S "ATAXY" BY THE DIRECTORS OF THE WOLVERHAMPTON GREYHOUND RACECOURSE ON THE OCCASION OF THEIR 10th ANNIVERSARY MEETING, 13th JANUARY 1938', on composition base.

Ataxy was a St Leger and Cesarewitch winner, and broke the track record when winning the Leger.

8in (20cm) high

£200-250   GBA

An Abendroth Bros. 'Uncle Sam Jr.' cast-iron toy stove, inscribed '1876'.

23in (58.5cm) wide

£450-500   POOK

A Belleville Stove Works 'Midget' cast-iron, nickel, and tin toy stove.

27.5in (70cm) high

£800-900   POOK

A Dent 'The Queen' cast-iron and nickel toy stove.

20in (51cm) wide

£180-220   POOK

QUICK REFERENCE - MINIATURE STOVES

● Cast-iron stoves became popular in American kitchens during the 1840s, and could be found in many homes by the 1880s. American toymakers were keen to capitalise on this and produce miniature versions for children to play with. A number of makers produced them, some specialising in them and some such as Kenton, Hubley and Stevens also producing other toys. Values vary widely, depending on the maker, the size, style, and level of detailing. The presence of original accessories such as metal frying pans and saucepans will also add to desirability, as can enamelling. As electric ovens began to take over in real homes from the 1920s onwards, the manufacture of cast-iron toy stoves declined. Other, cheaper materials such as plastic introduced around the same time also led to their demise during the 1940s. Some of these miniature stoves were not toys, but were rather samples for salesmen of real stoves, or display models. Furthermore, some stove makers also made miniature toy stoves. Both toys and samples are highly collectable, but it's likely the majority of examples found are from the former category.

A Detroit Stove Works 'Jewel Range Jr.' cast-iron, nickel, and tin toy stove.

18.25in (46.5cm) wide

£950-1,100   POOK

A Drake MFG. Co. 'Empire State' cast-iron, nickel, and tin toy stove, with a miniature griddle.

19.5in (49.4cm) high

£450-550   POOK

An Engman-Matthews 'The Range Eternal' cast-iron, nickel, and tin toy stove.

30in (76cm) high

£800-900   POOK

An Ideal cast-iron, tin, and nickel toy cook stove, no. 5, with provenance linking it to Franklin and Eleanor Roosevelt.

23.5in (59.5cm) wide

£500-600   POOK

STOVES MINIATURE

A Karr Range Co. enamelled, iron, and tin toy cook stove, with a blue mottled surface and nickel trim.

21in (53.5cm) high

£700-800   **POOK**

A Kenton 'Globe Range' cast-iron and tin toy stove, with a copper flashed surface.

22in (56cm) wide

£450-550   **POOK**

A Lionel electric toy stove, no. 455.

33.5in (85cm) wide

£2,000-2,500   **POOK**

A J. & E. Stevens Co. 'Rival' cast-iron and nickel toy stove, with a cast-iron tea kettle.

Stevens is also known for its range of cast-iron money banks, see pp258-9 for examples.

18in (46cm) wide

£200-300   **POOK**

A J. & E. Stevens Co. 'Rival' cast-iron, nickel, and tin toy stove, with a miniature cast-iron frying pan.

stove 3.25in (8.5cm) high

£200-250   **POOK**

A Wetter 'Gothic' cast-iron and nickel toy stove.

17.75in (45cm) wide

£850-950   **POOK**

An 'Ideal' cast-iron, nickel, and tin toy stove, no. 5.

19.5in (49.5cm) wide

£300-350   **POOK**

A cast-iron, nickel, and brass toy stove, with original copper cookware.

23in (58.5cm) wide

£150-200   **POOK**

QUICK REFERENCE - TAXIDERMY

- Taxidermy was popular from the mid-Victorian to Edwardian eras. It began to go out of fashion in the 1930s and by the 1970s the art had practically died out. Over the past 50 years, taxidermy has been seen as 'bad taste' and associated with cruelty.
- Over the past decade, there has been a resurgence of interest in taxidermy, with interior decorators, collectors, and those looking for something quirky. Part of this has been driven by a rise in 'eclectic' interests and styles in interior design.
- Traditionally, animals were stuffed and mounted in glazed wooden cases. These would often be decorated with naturalistic grounds. More common wild animals such as pheasants or geese can often be found for under £80. More exotic animals such as polar bears, tigers, or giraffes are rarer and considerably more expensive.
- When approaching value, consider the type and species of animal, its size, and how well it is stuffed and mounted. Ideally, it should be very realistic. Also consider the taxidermist as well as labels bearing the name of the maker, which can often be found on the case or mount. The work of skilled and well-known exponents such as Peter Spicer, John Cooper, and Rowland Ward tends to be of most interest and value.
- Always examine condition carefully as it can be very expensive, and sometimes impossible, to restore damaged examples. We do not condone the creation of modern examples. The sale and movement of many stuffed animals is strictly controlled, particularly those made after 1947 and are exotic or endangered species.

A contemporary stuffed and mounted fox (Vulpes vulpes), by Mike Gadd, with a partridge in its jaw, on a figured wood oval plateau applied with moss.

40.5in (103cm) long

£200-250   TEN

A stuffed and mounted fox, by Hutchings of Aberystwyth, with a bird at its feet and feathers in its mouth, in a wooden and glazed case, unmarked.

Hutchings operated in Aberystwyth, Wales, from the 1860s until 1942. Highly prolific, they are regarded as one of the best provincial taxidermists. Although known primarily for their stuffed birds, their stuffed and mounted foxes and badgers, which were produced in vast quantity, are also noteworthy.

case 32.75in (83cm) high

£220-280   LAW

A pair of early 20thC stuffed and mounted red squirrels, by G. White of Salisbury, in a naturalistic setting with painted backboard, in a glazed cabinet, Salisbury taxidermist label.

Stylised groundwork and delicately painted clouds are a hallmark of White's work, together with taped, rather than beaded, cases.

16in (40.5cm) wide

£100-150   DW

A stuffed and mounted perch, by John Cooper & Sons, Radnor Street, London, within a naturalistic setting, with a J. Cooper label and a further label reading 'LARGE PERCH - a fine perch of 3lbs 5ozs was taken in the lower waters of Mr Tiel's preserves at Rye House, Hoddesden, by Mr H.M. Clive a few days since. Mr Cooper, of St Luke's, has it to preserve. This makes the second perch of about the same weight taken recently by Mr Clive in Hertfordshire - Greville F', inscribed 'February 1873', in a bow-front glass case.

Stuffed fish tend to be more 'palatable' and attract fans from the legions of fishermen across the world, particularly if they are prized specimens. This is also dated, includes details about its provenance, and was preserved by Cooper, a desirable and skilled taxidermist.

1873   *22.5in (57cm) long*

£1,200-1,600   HT

An early 20thC stuffed and mounted pike, in a naturalistic setting, bow-fronted glazed case, lacking one side panel.

37.5in (95cms) wide

£150-200   DW

A late Victorian set of three stuffed and mounted small owls, against a naturalistic background, in a scumbled effect wooden and glazed case.

case 17.5in (44cm) high

£80-120   LAW

A cased stuffed and mounted tawny owl feeding a younger tawny owl, in a glazed and wooden case, with a plaque, 'Tawny Owl Strix Aluco'.

Although owls are protected under the Wildlife & Countryside Act 1981, this example can be sold without restriction as it was made before 1947.

case 16in (41cm) high

£100-140   LAW

Judith Picks

As well as interior design, events in popular culture, such as films, can have an effect on desirability and prices for many antiques and collectables. Although this owl is not exceptional in the eyes of taxidermy collectors, the price indicates that it may appeal to other groups of people. The Harry Potter phenomenon appealed to both children and adults. Although a child may find a real stuffed owl a little scary or upsetting, it may appeal to an adult fan who wants to include something related to their passion at home. A clever dealer selling to the right audience may even add a small, suitably styled plaque to the case reading 'Pigwidgeon', 'Hermes' or even 'Hedwig Snr'…!

A mid-19thC stuffed and mounted long-eared owl, in a naturalistic setting, in a glazed case, painted backboard.

18in (46cm) high

£65-75   DW

A late 20thC stuffed and mounted buzzard, set on a felt base, in a glass case, taxidermist's label and Department of the Environment license number on base.

25in (64cm) high

£150-200   DW

An early 20thC stuffed and mounted red kite, with two contemporary collector's labels, one manuscript label reading 'The Red Kite', the second 'Species Red Kite, Number 512 from the Peter Farrington Collection, Wilmslow Cheshire'.

26.25in (66.5cm) high

£130-180   DW

A mid-20thC stuffed and mounted barnacle goose, in a naturalistic setting, in a glazed case, one panel with short crack, damp-stained backboard.

22.75in (58cm) wide

£65-75   DW

An early 20thC stuffed and mounted pinkfoot goose, in a naturalistic setting, in a glazed case, painted backboard, splits to painted canvas base.

23in (58cm) wide

£65-75   DW

A group of late 19thC or early 20thC stuffed and mounted birds, including two kestrels (Falco tinnuculus) and a magpie, wooden and glazed case.

case 19.5in (49cm) high

£90-120   LAW

A mid-20thC stuffed and mounted cock pheasant, in flight, on a stained wooden board for wall hanging, with original taxidermist label for Philip Leggett.

36in (92cm) long

£40-50   DW

A pair of late 20thC stuffed and mounted stone curlews, in a naturalistic setting with egg, in a glazed wooden case, taxidermist's label to backboard.

2.75in (70cm) wide

£90-120   DW

A CLOSER LOOK AT A GOOSANDER

Based on Pilgrim Street, Newcastle, Robert Duncan was a skilled and talented second generation taxidermist and his work is collected today.

Instead of using a trade label, he typically signed and dated his work in pencil, usually in the top left corner of the case.

His groundwork is typically bare and minimal, lacking in any vegetation - this partly forces the eye to examine the specimen itself.

Cases have been found so far with dates ranging from 1862-1909, which potentially indicates his working life.

A stuffed and mounted goosander, by Robert Duncan of Newcastle upon Tyne, in a naturalistic setting in glazed case, signed and dated in pencil.

1900   *22in (56cm) high*

£300-400   HT

A taxidermy case containing a group of stuffed and mounted game birds, including corncrake, snipe, duck, partridge, pheasant, etc., in a naturalistic setting.

Once the preserve of cold, echoing staircases in Victorian or Edwardian country houses or museums, these large cases containing multiple birds are always worth examining. Not only are they visually impactful and display the complex art of the taxidermist at its best, but there's a possibility a rare bird or two may be contained within. In some cases (no pun intended), this can raise the value considerably more than the desirability of the taxidermist and the complexity and appeal of the arrangement. It can pay to develop your ornithological knowledge!

44in (112cm) wide

£850-1,000   CHOR

TAXIDERMY

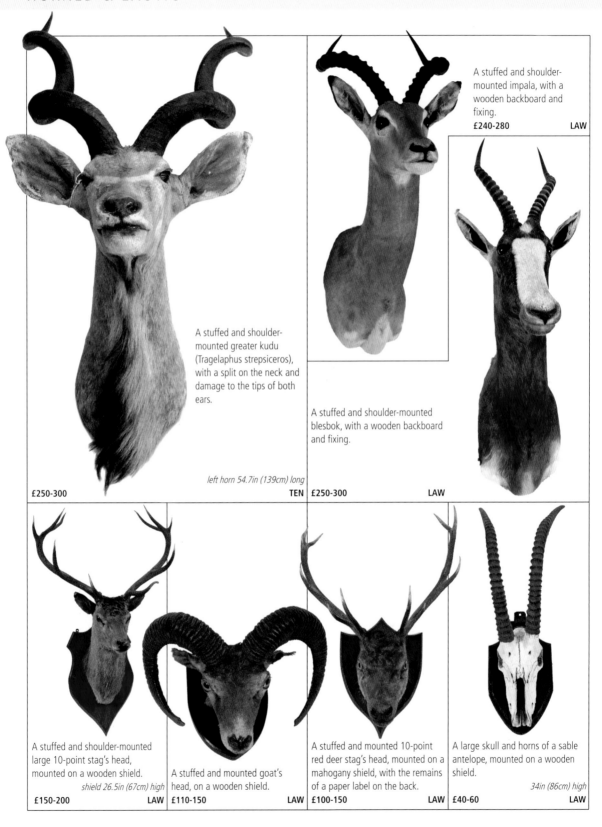

A stuffed and shoulder-mounted greater kudu (Tragelaphus strepsiceros), with a split on the neck and damage to the tips of both ears.

left horn 54.7in (139cm) long

£250-300   **TEN**

A stuffed and shoulder-mounted impala, with a wooden backboard and fixing.

£240-280   **LAW**

A stuffed and shoulder-mounted blesbok, with a wooden backboard and fixing.

£250-300   **LAW**

A stuffed and shoulder-mounted large 10-point stag's head, mounted on a wooden shield.

shield 26.5in (67cm) high

£150-200   **LAW**

A stuffed and mounted goat's head, on a wooden shield.

£110-150   **LAW**

A stuffed and mounted 10-point red deer stag's head, mounted on a mahogany shield, with the remains of a paper label on the back.

£100-150   **LAW**

A large skull and horns of a sable antelope, mounted on a wooden shield.

34in (86cm) high

£40-60   **LAW**

A stuffed and head-mounted black wildebeest (Connochaetes gnou), shot in 1978.

29.5in (75cm) from the wall

£180-220 TEN

A stuffed and head-mounted lion (Panthera Leo).

c1900

£400-600 PC

A stuffed large boar's head, mounted on a carved wooden shield in the Black Forest style, the shield carved with foliage.

£230-280 LAW

A modern stuffed serval (Leptailurus serval), in pouncing pose, with damaged fur, with original export tag.

This comes with proof of legal import.

25in (64cm) long

£300-350 TEN

A stuffed fruit bat, with metal loops for suspension, some rubbed and lost fur, splits to skin, and re-glued tears in the wings.

Large bats such as this have enormous appeal in today's market. They are primarily bought by those looking for a quirky Victorian, Gothic style, or 'steampunk' interior. The fact that this bat has its arms outstretched makes it even more appealing. Dating from the 1930s, it's also a rare survivor - bats are very delicate.

c1930   *wing span 27.6in (70cm)*

£210-250 TEN

A 19thC carapace of a giant South American river turtle (Podocnemis expansa), silver-painted interior, the polished outer surface lacking scutes.

Carapace is the technical term for the upper part of the exoskeleton of an animal, often a shell. As well as having been used as decoration for centuries on items such as tea caddies or boxes, turtle or tortoise shells tend to be more widely acceptable forms of taxidermy. They are often polished to show the colour variations and natural patterning and then hung on walls. In some instances, treated and cut-up parts of shells are used to repair items such as tea caddies and boxes. As such, they are of value to restorers as well as interior decorators.

A stuffed large crocodile head, with mouth partially agape.

Note that this is much larger than, and a different species to, the many thousands of (usually small), inexpensively and rapidly treated alligator heads sold as souvenirs in places such as the Everglades in Florida.

c1920   *25in (64cm) long*

£750-850 DW

26.75in (68cm) long

£1,800-2,200 AH

TECHNOLOGY

An Ekco 'RS3' brown Bakelite radio, with a circular speaker and fret-cut panel of stylised trees.

1931   *18in (46cm) high*

£400-600   SWO

A Philco '444' Bakelite radio, with controls from medium and long wave.

This curving set was known as the 'People's Set'. It cost six guineas or six pounds and six shillings.

1936   *15.5in (39cm) high*

£150-200   LAW

A 1950s Bush Bakelite cased 'TV22' television receiver.

Released in 1950, this classic vintage TV has a 9in (23cm) screen. Costing £35 and 10 shillings, it was one of the least expensive TV sets on the market at the time and sold in comparatively large quantities. It could be tuned by its owner to either one of the two BBC transmitters available at the time, as well as the proposed three channels.

1950-52

£120-180   SWO

An Ericsson 'GPO' skeleton telephone, hand-crank operation, with ebonite ear and mouthpiece on a cradle stand over two bells, with an early flex attached, no.16.

11.5in (29cm) high

Est £350-550   FLD

An early 20thC American The National Cash Register Company cash register, the bronzed case embossed with Art Nouveau motifs, with marble shelf, on ebonised wooden base, bears labels, model/size no. 357, serial no. 669679.

21.5in (55cm) wide

£350-450   DA&H

A rare jade-green plastic 'GPO 200 Series' telephone.

This telephone is known to collectors as the 'Pyramid'. Green is the most valuable colour, followed by red. Replicas and copies have been made and are worth a fraction of the value of authentic vintage examples. Look under the arm of the handset; on authentic examples, the moulded numbers should be in a recessed panel, not raised above the rest of the surface.

£1,000-1,500   RW

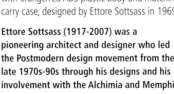

A 1970s Olivetti 'Valentine' portable typewriter, with orange/red ABS plastic body and matching carry case, designed by Ettore Sottsass in 1969.

Ettore Sottsass (1917-2007) was a pioneering architect and designer who led the Postmodern design movement from the late 1970s-90s through his designs and his involvement with the Alchimia and Memphis groups.

£300-400   SWO

QUICK REFERENCE - TEDDY BEARS

- German company Steiff (1877-) is perhaps the most well-known and prestigious bear maker. Margarete Steiff (1847-1909), who lived in Giengen, south Germany, made jointed bears from 1902-03 onwards based on her nephew Richard's designs (active 1902-c34). Confined to a wheelchair, she occasionally made stuffed toys with left-over material from her uncle's fabric factory. The first jointed bear was exhibited in 1903 at the Spring Fair in Leipzig. It was only after Richard further tweaked the design in 1904 that it became successful.

- According to trade legend, American president Theodore Roosevelt refused to shoot a bear cub tied to a tree while out hunting in Mississippi in 1902. Shortly after, the Washington Post published a cartoon, illustrating that particular hunting escapade. Spotting a marketing opportunity, Morris Michtom (who later founded The Ideal Novelty and Toy Co.) is believed to have produced one of the first American 'teddy' bears. Other companies soon followed suit.

- The Merrythought teddy bear factory was established in 1930 in Coalbrookdale, Shropshire. It was set up by W.G. Holmes and H.G. Laxton. Merrythought is famous for its 'Cheeky' bear, introduced in 1957 and characterised by its floppy ears with bells inside.

- Materials, colour, form and labels can be used to identify and date bears. Before WWII, bears had longer limbs, pronounced snouts and humped backs. They feel solid because they were usually made from mohair and stuffed with wood shavings or kapok (wool). Post-war bears have shorter limbs, less pronounced snouts and rounder heads. Synthetic materials were used from the 1960s onwards. Damaged bears can usually be restored by professionals, but be aware that tears, stains, replaced pads and worn fur will reduce value.

- Large bears or bears in unusual colours are desirable, as are those that have an endearing expression. Limited edition bears, especially from well-known brands such as Steiff, tend to fetch good prices on the secondary market. Be aware of replicas. If ever in doubt, remember that an original bear's smell cannot be replicated!

An early original Steiff 'blank button' teddy bear, fully jointed arms and legs, with swivel head, light golden mohair, original boot button eyes, with straw/woodwool stuffing, heavy pronounced snout with hump to rear.
c1905   *16in (40.5cm) high*
£1,000-1,200   **EBA**

A CLOSER LOOK AT A STEIFF BEAR

This bear is both kapok and excelsior stuffed, making him very light in weight.

He is 5-ways jointed and made from mohair which has aged to a delightful apricot colour.

The bear has a prominent back hump and classic early Steiff proportions.

His face is detailed with black shoebutton eyes and a black hand-embroidered nose and mouth.

He retains his blank button and traces of his white ear tag as his Steiff IDs.

A fine and early Steiff mohair bear with blank button, slight wear to felt pads, otherwise very good condition.
c1906   *12in (30cm) high*
£1,800-2,200   **JDJ**

An early large Steiff bear with button, felt pads with holes and essential repairs, light overall mohair thinning.

Bear collectors are very discerning about the facial expression of a bear. This bear has a soulful, pensive face detailed with black shoebutton eyes, trimmed muzzle area, and a black hand-embroidered nose and mouth.
c1907   *30in (75cm) high overall*
£3,000-4,000   **JDJ**

An early Steiff centre seam beige mohair teddy bear with button, 5-ways jointed, right paw pad professionally restored, non-working growler, very light playwear.
1907   *24in (60cm) high*
£4,500-5,000   **JDJ**

An early apricot Steiff teddy bear, general mohair thinning and loss, some excelsior separation in limbs, very small open seam on shoulder, both hand paws with numerous holes, feet paws with very minor holes and splitting at cardboard edges, retains his tiny trailing F Steiff button and traces of his white ear tag as his Steiff IDs.
c1907   *19in (49cm) high*
£1,800-2,200   **JDJ**

TEDDY BEARS

An early Steiff teddy bear, with 'STEIFF' period button to right ear, original boot button eyes, blonde mohair, fully jointed limbs, good pronounced snout and woodwool stuffing, the snout having black stitching to end, with black stitching also to ends of arms and legs.

c1908   13in (33cm) high

£700-800   **EBA**

A large and early blonde Steiff bear with button, pads replaced, possible nose restitching and minor and professional repair to tip of muzzle.

c1910   24in (62cm) high

£1,800-2,200   **JDJ**

A rare early white Steiff centre-seam bear with button, paw pads generally good with a few small repairs, pinholes, and light dust, bear has slight mohair thinning in muzzle area.

This bear is a combination of so many features Steiff bear collectors love. At 20in (50cm) high, he's large in size and his white mohair is hard to find and highly desirable. Importantly, the line of vertical stitching down his forehead indicates he's a 'centre seam' bear. This allowed Steiff to make the most economical use of the mohair fabric. Only one in seven bears had this feature and, as well as being rare, it somehow gives these bears' expressions more character. Finally, he's also in great condition with all his original features.

20in (50cm) high

£6,000-7,000   **JDJ**

An early Steiff teddy bear, with 'STEIFF' button to ear, jointed limbs with boot button eyes and woodwool stuffing, pronounced snout with defined hump to rear.

This teddy comes with his lifelong 'bed' - an Edwardian small cloth bound child's trunk, a photograph of the original owner (pictured with a toy), a collection of counting blocks and various other 'bedding' for the bear.

c1910

£850-950   **EBA**

An early original Steiff 'Rubin' teddy bear, glass eyes, white mohair fur, elongated limbs, pronounced snout and defined hump to rear, stitching in black to snout and end of limbs, fully jointed, ear button not present.

c1912   10in (25.5cm) high

£450-600   **EBA**

A Steiff almond buff bear on wheels, with shoe button eyes and stitched nose, rotating head, metal axles with cast-iron wheels, leather collar, with extended 'S' on original ear button.

c1910-27   15in (38cm) wide

£1,300-1,600   **JDJ**

An early 20thC white Steiff bear, with original button in his ear and original felt pads.

10in (25.5cm) high

£900-1,200   JDJ

An early Steiff centre seam bear, with button, all pads replaced, nose and mouth stitching replaced, repairs to muzzle area, general mohair loss.

The bear has Steiff's distinctive early look and proportions, including long arms, big feet, and a pronounced back hump.

c1915   *20in (50cm) high*

£1,800-2,400   JDJ

An early 1920s white mohair Steiff bear, 5-ways jointed, with black glass eyes, with 'F' button.

18in (44cm) high

£3,500-4,000   JDJ

A CLOSER LOOK AT A STEIFF BEAR

At 28in (72cm) high when standing, he is unusually large and may even have been as big as the child he was given to and loved by!

His limbs as well as his body are chubby, and he has over-sized eyes, giving him an almost toddler-like appearance.

He was obviously loved with care, or from a distance, as his fur is still overall shaggy. White is also a highly desirable colour.

He is in superb condition, with his original, correctly coloured paw pads and claw and nose stitching.

A mid-1920s Steiff bear with button, with very minor spotting on foot pads, non-working growler.

28in (72cm) high overall

£4,000-5,000   JDJ

An early 1920s brown and blonde-tipped large mohair Steiff bear, 5-ways jointed, with chubbier appearance and oversized eyes and smaller back hump, with 'F' Steiff button, with working growler.

28in (70cm) high

£5,000-6,000   JDJ

A 1920s white shaggy mohair Steiff teddy bear with button, 5-ways jointed, foot pad possibly replaced, seam stitching on back of one arm, otherwise very good condition.

27in (66cm) overall

£2,000-2,500   JDJ

A late 1940s Steiff blonde mohair bear, with glass eyes, original pads and stitching and ear button, lacking tag.

This bear was one of the last produced before the introduction of the new, plumper and rounder 'Original Teddy' form in 1951.

13.5in (34cm) high

£350-400   PC

A 1920s brown Steiff teddy bear, with button, 5-ways jointed, solidly stuffed, cardboard lining can be seen in the soles of the paw pads, possible partial nose restitching, the right paw pad and one ankle has been professionally restored.

27in (69cm) high

£1,300-1,600   JDJ

A 1950s Steiff white mohair teddy bear, with pronounced snout, jointed limbs and definition to claws and limbs, blue waistcoat and ear button missing.

£150-200   EBA

A Steiff 'Millennium 2000' bear, in blonde mohair, with original box.

£70-90   ECGW

A replica Steiff 'Margaret Strong' cream-coloured teddy bear, No.'157/32'.

18.5in (47cm) high

£90-120   FLD

A replica Steiff 'Margaret Strong' teddy bear, in cream mohair, with certificate.

28.5in (72cm) high

£150-200   FLD

A white and blue mohair 'Uncle Sam' bear, arm-jointed only, with harlequin-style red, white, and blue colouring, felt paw pads, back seam restitched.

This teddy was most likely produced by the boutique and little-known toy firm Art Novelty Company of New York.

c1908   15in (39cm) high
£800-900   **JDJ**

An early Bing bear, with early silver mark, 5-ways jointed, with small ears, black shoebutton eyes, shaved muzzle and a black hand-embroidered nose and mouth, light overall mohair loss, paw pads with wear and restoration, non-working growler.
c1910
£1,000-1,400
21in (54cm) high
JDJ

A rare 1950s shop window display Chad Valley 'Hygenic Toys' bear, with original glass eyes and blue neck ribbon, with the standard-sized small Chad Valley label.
48in (122cm) high
£170-200   **EBA**

A Dean's Rag Book stuffed teddy bear, golden mohair, moulded black nose and original eyes, label attached to pad on leg, in original condition.

£110-160   **EBA**

Judith Picks

What's not to love about this one-of-a-kind display-sized 'Cheeky' bear? Here is a 5-ways jointed 'Cheeky' who measures a whopping 36 inches tall. This particular bear is 1 of 1 ever made, and is called 'Love and Understanding Cheeky.' It is estimated that this gentle giant was manufactured 15-20 years ago. He is made from long and lovely thick blonde mohair. His paw pads are made from tan felt, and his traditional shaped muzzle is made from orange-tan velvet. His face is detailed with oversized black button eyes and a black embroidered nose and mouth. He is decorated with a huge blue and gold ribbon. Of course, he has bells in his side-facing ears. He has a Tide-Rider Merrythought tag stitched onto one footpad, and 'Cheeky Love and Understanding 1 of 1' embroidered on the other one. He comes with an official Merrythought Certificate, which is signed by the late Oliver Holmes, Managing Director, and Jacqueline Revitt, Merrythought's long time Design Director. The condition is like new.

An early Merrythought Cheeky bear, with bells sewn into his large ears, light playwear, pawpads on feet possibly replaced.

c1960   15in (38cm)
£85-95   **JDJ**

A Merrythought 'Cheeky' bear, with signed testimonial certificate.
36in (91.5cm) high
£400-500   **JDJ**

CERAMICS

QUICK REFERENCE - TOBY JUGS

- Toby jugs generally depict historical, fictional or popular characters wearing period attire and tri-corn hats.
- The introduction of Toby jugs can be attributed to Ralph Wood I and II of Burslem, Enoch Wood, Thomas Hollins and William Pratt who worked in various parts of England like Staffordshire, Leeds and Portobello.
- The exact origin of the name 'Toby jug' is uncertain. Some suggest that it was named after an 18thC Yorkshire drinker called Henry Elwes, whose nickname was Toby Fillpot (or Philpot), whilst others think that it has connections to Shakespeare's character Sir Toby Belch.
- Figures appear disproportionate because their heads are modelled much larger than the bodies and their facial features are exaggerated, much like caricatures.
- Translucent, coloured lead glazes are used to highlight the different parts of the figures and give them a slightly unfinished look. They have been popular since they were first made in the 1760s and are very sought-after by collectors.
- They often portray ale drinkers in sitting positions, but from the 19thC onwards, many variations were produced including standing figures holding pipes, sporting squires, sailors, female characters, and military personalities.

A Yorkshire Prattware standing Toby jug, a bottle and cup clutched against his broad stomach, the inside hat rim and base sponged with broad stripes, the handle modelled as a figurehead, minor damages.
c1810-20   *7.75in (19.5cm) high*
£400-500   **WW**

A 19thC Staffordshire Toby jug, seated wearing a mustard, blue, and brown sponged frock coat with matched breeches, unmarked.
9.5in (24cm) high
£600-700   **FLD**

An early 19thC Walton pearlware Toby jug, of traditional form, wearing a brown coat and checked waistcoat, with warty and ruddy complexion, his foaming jug of ale painted with a blue foliate design, applied scroll mark to the base.
10in (25.5cm) high
£300-400   **WW**

A 19thC pearlware 'Hearty Good Fellow' Toby jug, standing with body turned slightly to the left, holding a jug of ale in his right hand, a clay pipe in his left, wearing a bold checked waistcoat.

A 'Hearty Good Fellow' Toby jug, originated in the late 18thC, but mostly produced in the Victorian era. Shows a standing man, pipe in left hand, jug of ale in right hand, both held tightly to his chest. Many later Victorian examples have the annotation 'Hearty Good Fellow' on the base.
10.5in (27cm) high
£300-400   **WW**

A 19thC pearlware Toby jug, of 'Ordinary' type, his foaming ale spilling over the side of his floral-decorated jug, his coat decorated in a bright turquoise green.

Most Toby jugs can be described as 'Ordinary' type which is an elderly man, with tricorn hat, sitting on a chair, wearing a frock coat, with a large jug of ale on his left knee, with his right hand in front of the jug. The handle is formed as part of the back of the chair.
9in (23cm) high
£300-400   **WW**

A Yorkshire pearlware Toby jug, of 'Ordinary' type, holding a patterned jug of ale and a hexagonal cup, the base and his hat sponged in green, black, and yellow, with a caryatid handle.
c1820-30   *9.75in (24.5cm) high*
£250-300   **WW**

An early 19thC pearlware Toby jug, typically moulded in frock coat and breeches, the foaming jug on his knee unusually modelled as a grotesque bird-type creature with large beak, the handle with a scroll terminal, some retouching or restoration to his hat.

10in (25.5cm) high

£450-550 WW

An early 19thC Davenport pearlware Toby jug, of conventional form, seated holding a foaming jug of beer upon a sponge-decorated base, dressed in brightly coloured attire, impressed marks.

9.75in (25cm) high

£120-180 FLD

A large 19thC Toby jug, seated wearing brightly coloured attire holding a foaming jug of ale, all raised to a green step base, his face with warts and blue eyes, unmarked.

13.5in (34cm) high

£400-500 FLD

A 19thC Toby jug, seated in a corner armchair smoking a long clay pipe and holding a lidded tankard, dressed in a long blue frock coat, burnt red breeches and a polka dot cravat, with long grey hair, unmarked.

11in (28cm) high

£250-300 WW

A 19thC Toby jug, modelled as a standing figure wearing a red frock coat and pink polka dot waistcoat holding a foaming jug of ale and a clay pipe stood upon a naturalistic pedestal base, the handle formed as a tree stump, unmarked.

11.5in (29cm) high

£250-350 FLD

A mid-19thC Staffordshire 'Gin Woman' Toby jug, standing and holding a bottle in her left hand, a cup or glass in her right, brightly enamelled with striped collar and skirt.

8in (20.5cm) high

£150-200 WW

A mid-19thC female 'Snuff Taker' Toby jug, of 'Portobello' type, standing and taking a pinch of snuff, wearing a striped skirt and blue jacket, the base sponged in green.

9.75in (24.5cm) high

£200-250 WW

A 19thC unusual Staffordshire Toby jug, of 'Ordinary' type, with pink lustre coat and further lustre decoration to his jug of ale.

9.5in (24cm) high

£300-400 WW

Judith Picks

These jugs were retailed by Soane & Smith of Oxford Street, London over the duration of the Great War. Certificates produced to accompany the jugs indicated production numbers varying between 250 and several hundred of each with the rarest being Botha. Full sets, such as the one designed by Sir F Carruthers Gould for Wilkinson, are very rare. This set comprises jugs that depict Lord Kitchiner, General Botha, King George V, and President Wilson, amongst others. The centenary of the First World War, which took place in 2014, increased interest in this type of Toby jug. Prices paid at auction have gone up as a result.

This is the rare Botha Toby jug.

This is the King Toby jug.

A complete set of eleven Toby jugs, designed by Carruthers Gould for Wilkinson, each depicting the Allied commanders in World War 1, well decorated in colours and gilt, the undersides each printed with marks and facsimile signature, the King 310mm, Foch with restoration to hat rim, Joffre with repair to hat rim and flaking enamel to base, Haigh repaired hat rim.

the king 12in (31cm) high

£8,000-9,000   H&C

A 19thC Toby jug and cover, formed as a seated lady wearing a pattern apron and shawl, her bonnet forming the cover, unmarked.

11in (28cm) high

£60-70   FLD

A massive Devonmoor advertising Toby jug, seated and holding a tankard and a pipe, wearing a blue coat and happy expression.

Only a handful of these out-sized jugs are believed to have been made at Devonmoor, probably during the factory's second period of manufacture after 1922.

c1930   *24in (61cm) high*

£400-500   WW

A Copeland Spode Toby jug, 'Winston Churchill' decorated in colours, printed mark.

c1941   *8.4in (21.3cm) high*

£200-250   H&C

QUICK REFERENCE - CORGI TOYS

● The success of Dinky Toys, and particularly their Supertoys range launched in 1947, inspired Mettoy (founded in 1933) to release their own range of diecast models. The result was Corgi Toys, launched in 1956. To differentiate them from their competitors, they were more detailed, being the first to have clear plastic windows. They also had other features such as opening doors and boots, as well as sprung 'Glidamatic' suspension from 1959.

● During the 1960s & 70s, a range of models was produced to tie in with popular television programmes and films, such as James Bond, Chitty-Chitty Bang Bang, and Batman. They were extremely popular at the time and continue to be so today, particularly the James Bond models. Along with gift sets, these tend to be the most sought-after subject areas.

● Variation is very important when considering value and desirability. Consider features such as the body colour, the colour of seats and the model's interior, the wheels, decals and stickers. Some features or combinations of them are rare or highly desirable.

● Condition is also extremely important, with most collectors aiming to buy a model or gift set that is as close to the condition it was in when it left the shop or, preferably, the factory. These 'mint' examples will always command a premium. The condition of the box is almost as important as the condition of the model. Never be tempted to repaint a playworn model as that won't increase its value.

A Corgi Toys 'Citroën D.S.19', no.210, finished in metallic green, with original box.

The earlier variation - with a yellow body and red roof - is usually slightly more valuable.

1957-60

£70-100   ECGW

A Corgi Toys 'Hillman Imp Monte Carlo 1966', no.328, in metallic blue with white flash to sides, cream interior, racing number 107, with Monte Carlo plaques front and rear, boxed with paperwork.

If a yellow and red advertising card for this model is included, the price can rise by over 20%.

1966-67

£80-120   W&W

A Corgi Toys 'Lotus Elan S2 Open Top', no.318, in metallic blue with 'I'VE GOT A TIGER IN MY TANK' decal to boot lid, black interior, complete with driver, boxed, one wheel inverted.

1965-67

£50-70   W&W

A Corgi Toys 'Aston Martin D.B.4', no.218, wheels with applied Corgi wire stickers, spares included, boxed, minor wear, minor chips to vehicle.

1960-62

£60-80   W&W

A Corgi Toys 'Mercedes-Benz 300SL Hardtop', no.304S, in a pale anodised gold-coloured plated finish with a red roof, RN3 to bonnet, boxed with Corgi leaflet, minor mottling to finish.

The variation with a white body and red roof can fetch over twice the value of this colourway.

1962-63

£70-100   W&W

A Corgi Toys 'Mini Cooper S Monte Carlo 1967' Competition Model, no.339, with Monte Carlo Rally plaques front and rear and racing number 177, in a standard Morris Mini-Cooper box for model no.227, with paperwork and factory applied label for 339.

1967-71

£150-200   W&W

A Corgi Toys 'Mini Cooper S SUN - RAC Rally', no.333, racing number 21, in a standard Austin Seven box no.225, with factory applied label for 333, one end flap detached but present.

Apart from being a desirable and collectable Mini, this special issue was sold in 1966 only, making it comparatively hard to find.

1966

£120-180   W&W

TOYS & GAMES

A Corgi Toys 'Morris Cowley Saloon', no.202M, with flywheel motor and orginal box.

This model was also offered without the flywheel motor as no.202 from 1956-61. That model is generally worth around a third less than this version.

1956-59

£70-100   ECGW

A Corgi Toys 'Riley Pathfinder Saloon', no.205M, with flywheel motor and original box.

1956-59

£80-120   ECGW

A Corgi Toys 'Studebaker Golden Hawk', no.211, with original box.

The white version is worth around the same as the blue version.

1958-60

£45-55   ECGW

A Corgi Toys 'Vanwall Racing Car', no.150, with original box.

This model was released with a number of variations in terms of body and seat colour and 'VANWALL' and racing number '1' decals, but they are all worth roughly the same amount, with condition affecting value the most.

1957-61

£50-80   ECGW

A Corgi Toys 'Commer Refrigerated Van', no.453, with 'WALLS ICE CREAM' decals, with original box.

1956-60

£40-60   ECGW

A Corgi Major Toys 'Ecurie Ecosse Racing Car Transporter', no.1126, in metallic blue with yellow wording to sides, boxed, with paperwork, some damp damage to lid.

Available in dark and light metallic blue, this model was also included in gift set no.16 - see p.374 for an example. This colourway is the most valuable. Others are usually worth about 25-30% less.

1961-65

£80-120   W&W

A Corgi Toys 'Bedford Utilecon Fire Tender', no.405M, with friction motor, with original box.

An example of this model without the friction motor (no.405) is finished in bright or dark green. It tends to be around a third less than this variation.

1956-59

£40-60   ECGW

A Corgi Toys 'Massey-Ferguson 65 Tractor With Shovel', no.53, with original box.
1960-66
£50-80   ECGW

A Corgi 'Thunderbird Missile', no.350, guided missile with the navy-blue assembly trolley, the pale-green rocket with red plastic nose, boxed.
1958-62
£60-80   LOCK

A Corgi 'James Bond's Aston Martin', model no.261, DB5 finished in gold with metal roof, complete with internal display mount and 'Top Secret' letter, boxed.

This eternally popular model was released with the film 'Goldfinger', starring Sean Connery as Bond.
1965-69
£180-220   LOCK

A Corgi Toys original 1967 issue 'Chitty Chitty Bang Bang', no.266, complete with all four original figures, wings front and rear, boxed, minor wear but window requires replacing.
1968-72
£120-180   W&W

A CLOSER LOOK AT A CORGI CAR

One of James Bond's iconic cars, this Lotus submarine car was taken from the film 'The Spy Who Loved Me', released in July 1977.

The missiles are still attached to the sprue. The model is in truly mint condition.

The packaging is in overall good to very good condition and comes with its ultra rare original red, black, and white outer card sleeve (not shown).

It is in the same condition it left the toy shop, which makes it highly desirable. Had the box been in better condition, it could have fetched more.

A Corgi 'James Bond Lotus Esprit', no.269, with '007' red bonnet label, comes with missiles attached to sprue, in film strip box, with 'hammer and sickle' logo, some small splits to cellophane, complete with outer carded sleeve finished in red, black, and white, with 'The New James Bond Corgi' to header.
1977-83
£1,200-1,800   VEC

A Corgi Toys 'The Green Hornet's Black Beauty', no.268, with opened bag containing three missiles and three spinners, boxed.
1967-72
£120-180   TEN

A Corgi Toys 'Land-Rover and Pony Trailer Gift Set No.2', painted green, with beige back cover, pony, and red horse trailer, with original box and packaging.

The variation with the all-red Land Rover is usually slightly more valuable.

1958-68

£100-150   ECGW

A Corgi Toys 'Lions of Longleat Gift Set No.8', comprising a Land Rover, zebra-striped livery, a hunter with rifle, a yellow plastic cage, a red barrel, meat, and two lions with den, boxed, some wear, plastic window replaced.

1968-74

£100-150   W&W

A Corgi Major Toys 'Chipperfield's Circus Gift Set No.12', with crane truck and cage in red, blue, and yellow livery, jib complete with hook, animal cage complete with two polar bears, minor wear, boxed with packing pieces.

1961-64

£120-180   W&W

A CLOSER LOOK AT A GIFT SET

This very large set is one of the rarest gift sets. It is extremely difficult to find in truly complete and excellent condition - especially with all the boxes.

It would have been very expensive in its day. It was only sold from 1963-66.

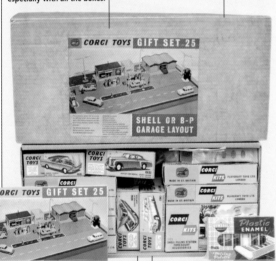

It includes a playmat and small items of street furniture, so it was usually opened and played with. Pieces were worn or lost during play.

Released in time for Christmas 1963, it was the culmination of a series of individual accessories released from 1960 onwards.

A Corgi 'Shell/BP Garage Gift Set No.GS25', comprising a 'Bentley Continental Sports Saloon', no.224, an 'Austin 7 Mini', no.225, a 'Chevrolet Corvair', no.229, a 'Ford Consul Classic', no.234, a 'Ford Zephyr Motorway Patrol Car - Police', no.419, all with correct collector's club folded leaflets, plus 'Corgi Kits' 3 x 'Batley Garage', no.601, 'AA and RAC' Telephone Boxes, no.602, 2 x 'Lamp Standards', no.606, 'Shell Filling Station', no.608, 'Shell Forecourt Accessories', no.609, scale figures, Humbrol paints, Aurora Glue and play mat with roads, with a general assembly instruction colour leaflet.

1963-66

£3,500-4,500   VEC

A Corgi Major Toys 'Ecurie Ecosse Racing Car Transporter And Three Racing Cars Gift Set No.16', comprising a transporter in metallic dark blue with yellow wording to sides, a 'Vanwall Formula 1 Grand Prix Car 150S' in red with racing number 25, a 'Lotus Mark II Le Mans Racing Car 151A' in blue, with racing number 7 and a 'BRM Formula 1 Racing Car 152S' in light green, with racing number 3, all three in their individual boxes, contained within the gift set box, complete with packing and some paperwork, very minor wear, driver of Vanwall missing.

1961-65

£500-700   W&W

A Corgi Toys '1965 Monte Carlo Rally Gift Set No.38', comprising 'B.M.C. Mini Cooper S' in red with white roof, with racing number 52, a 'Rover 2000' in metallic maroon with white roof, with racing number 136, and a 'Citroën D.S.19' in light blue with a white roof, with racing number 75, contained in their original display box, some wear to outer box.

1965-67

£600-800   W&W

QUICK REFERENCE - DINKY SUPERTOYS

●Dinky Toys began life as 'Model Miniatures' to accompany Hornby railway sets in 1931. By 1934, their popularity had ensured that they had gained their own brand and identity as a range. After World War Two, the company built on its prewar success by expanding its ranges. In 1947, they introduced 'Supertoys', a range of lorries modelled to the standard Dinky scale of 1:48. In 1950, a number of Guy vans was included in the range, followed by the Bedford 'S' cab in 1955 and the 'Guy Warrior' cab in 1960. Supertoys were typically sold in blue and white horizontally striped boxes. They were marketed as separate to Hornby's railways. To many diecast collectors, especially those who grew up playing with them, these are the most desirable Dinkys. Rare variations and models fetch high prices. The name was used until 1965.

A Dinky Supertoys 'B.B.C. T.V. Roving Eye Vehicle' diecast model, no.968, with original box and cover.
1959-64
£90-120   ECGW

A Dinky Supertoys 'B.B.C. T.V. Extending Mast Vehicle' diecast model, no.969, with windows, with cover.
1959-64
£100-150   ECGW

A Dinky Supertoys 'B.B.C. T.V. Mobile Control Room' diecast model, no.967, with original box and cover.
1959-64
£100-150   ECGW

A Dinky Supertoys Foden 14-Ton 'Mobilgas' Tanker, no.941, with 'Mobilgas' decals, boxed.
1956
£80-120   LAW

A Dinky Supertoys 'A.E.C. Tanker', no.991, with 'SHELL CHEMICALS' decal, original box and cover.
1955-58
£100-150   ECGW

A Dinky Supertoys 'Slumberland Guy Van', no.514, complete with both red doors, boxed with applied label, with minor wear.
1950-52
£80-120   W&W

A Dinky Supertoys 'Big Bedford Heinz' van, no.923, with 'Heinz 57 Varieties' decal, boxed.

Look out for the rare variation featuring a 'Tomato Ketchup' bottle and advertising decal, as that can fetch over five times more.
1955-58
£120-180   FLD

A Dinky Supertoys 'Car Carrier with Trailer' diecast model, no.983, with original box and cover, together with 'Loading Ramp for Pullmore Car Transporter', no.994, with original box.

1958-63

£150-200

ECGW

A Dinky Supertoys 'Recovery Tractor', no.661, military vehicle, with original box and cover.

1957-65

£70-100

ECGW

A Dinky Supertoys 'R.A.F. Pressure Refueller', no.642, finished in R.A.F. blue, with original box and cover.

1957-62

£60-80

ECGW

A Dinky Supertoys 'Medium Artillery Tractor', no.689, military vehicle, boxed.

1957-65

£50-80

BELL

A French Dinky Supertoys Brockway Bridge Truck, no.884, military vehicle, complete with bridge load, boxed, minor wear.

1962-64

£70-90

W&W

A set of six 1930s Dinky Toys 'Austin Covered Trade Box' wagons, containing three blue and three maroon-fawn models, box a little faded, with original dividers.

£300-500

TEN

A CLOSER LOOK AT AT A DINKY TOY

Branded delivery vans are popular subjects for collections, particularly pre-war examples.

As with all diecast toys, variations are important - the all-red bodied version of this model is usually worth around half of the value of this one, depending on condition.

This model was produced in this black and red colourway from 1934-35.

It has a Type 1 cab design and plain solid wheels. Look out for painted wheels as these fetch a premium.

A Dinky pre-war 'Sharp's Toffee' delivery van, type-1 'Dinky Toys', no.28h, cast to underside of cab roof, black body, chassis, red rear body, 'Sharp's Toffee Maidstone' to sides, tinplate radiator surround, bare-metal solid wheels.
1934-35
£2,200-2,800 VEC

A Dinky Toys 'Mayo Composite Aircraft', no.63, in original blue cardboard box.

Beware of metal fatigue with Dinky's planes. They were made with a metal alloy that degrades and crumbles over time.
1939-41
£180-220 ECGW

A Dinky Toys 'Austin A40 NESTLÉ'S' van, no.471, finished in red with decal, with original box.
1955-60
£70-100 ECGW

A Dinky Toys 'Aston Martin DB3 Sports' car, no.110, finished in light green with red-ridged hubs, with racing number '22', boxed.
1956-59
£180-220 DN

A Dinky Toys 'Lady Penelope's Fab 1' car, no.100, with original card box.

Look out for the luminous pink version, which can fetch up to double the price of the standard pink version.
1967-75
£100-150 LOC

A mid-late 1930s Dinky Toys trade box, for six '33c Open Wagons', dirty, lacks inserts.

This rare trade box fetched this price because it will increase the value of the wagons that will be put inside it.
£150-200 TEN

A 19thC Cantonese carved ivory chess set, including a full set stained red and the remainder in white, figures carved to resemble Chinese officials, horsemen, elephants, and soldiers, one white knight lacking.

Had this set been complete, it could have fetched over twice this amount. Although it is not impossible to find a replacement, the colour and condition of the piece may not match the rest of the set.

largest 4in (10cm) high

£150-250   DW

A mid-late 19thC Jaques ivory 'The Staunton Chessmen' chess set, comprising white and stained red pieces, the king stamped 'Jaques' London, the knight and rook stamped with a crown, in original sarcophagus-shaped box with gilt-tooled decoration and lettering.

Considered a landmark in chess, the 'Staunton' set - named after a famous player and released in 1849 - is a must-have for every collection. This fine and early luxury example carved in ivory comes with an unusual and high-quality box.

the king 4.5in (11cm) high

£4,500-5,500   CHOR

An early 20thC Jaques Staunton 'Chessmen' weighted wooden chess set, with paper label to lid and brass plaque 'Presented to Rev. T J Johnson by the 2nd Rossendale Company Boys Brigade', in mahogany box, one black pawn damaged.

King stand 3.25in (8cm) high

£400-600   TEN

An Art Deco Asprey Ltd banded wood gaming chip stand, with a chrome handle, with five dice, labelled 'Asprey London Made in England'.

10.2in (26cm) wide

£550-750   SWO

A hand-coloured engraved game, 'Wallis's Elegant and Instructive Game Exhibiting the Wonders of Nature in each Quarter of the World', with central title cartouche and 26 numbered vignette scenes, sectionalised on linen, with original instruction booklet and original card slipcase, some soiling and wear.

18thC and early 19thC board games were the preserve of the very wealthy. Like pocket globes, they represented the expansion of the British empire and trade and also had an educational use for children.

1824   *25in (64cm)*

£1,000-1,500   DW

A 1930s British 'Mickey Mouse Table Tennis' set, consisting of a net with a card Mickey & Minnie figure 'pulling' at the ends, two bats depicting Mickey and Minnie, contained in a card box with illustrated lid, in fair to good condition.

£180-220   TEN

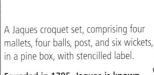

A Jaques croquet set, comprising four mallets, four balls, post, and six wickets, in a pine box, with stencilled label.

Founded in 1795, Jaques is known for its high-quality games as much as it is for its chess sets. The company is still in existence today.

£200-300   L&T

QUICK REFERENCE - TINPLATE

● In an age before plastic, tin-plated steel known as 'tinplate' replaced wood as the material of choice for toys from the mid-19thC onwards. The versatile metal sheets could be bent, embossed, stamped, painted and, later, printed with designs. Most examples found on the market today date from the early 20thC, with late 19thC and earlier examples generally being rare.

● Germany became the centre of tinplate toy production, with a few other factories in other countries such as France and the US being founded later in the 19thC. Major makers included companies such as Märklin (founded 1856), Bing (1863-1933), and Schreyer & Co (Schuco) (1912-78). Often fitted with mechanical or clockwork mechanisms allowing them to move, their production is typically of high quality and sought-after.

● After World War Two, production shifted to Japan, although some surviving German companies still continued to produce toys. The subjects of the toys also changed. Although cars, planes, and amusing novelties such as those produced by Lehmann (founded 1881) were still produced, robots, UFOs and space age-inspired toys began to be made. Many of these were battery-powered and had flashing lights or sound as well as moving parts.

An early 20thC English tinplate clockwork model racing car, with painted detail.

11in (28cm) long

£300-500   ECGW

A 1920s German TippCo racing car, lithographed in red with cream-black lining, pressed radiator with TCO monogram, tin driver figure, adjustable steering and registration TC9590, the model is fitted with a later battery mounting on the base but has no lamps or obvious lamp mountings, a little dirty and wear from use.

This is a large and detailed model in a desirable form by a notable maker.

19in (49cm) long

£1,800-2,200   TEN

An early 20thC Lehmann tinplate clockwork 'OHO' car, with lithographed decoration and driver.

In the style of an early 'horseless carriage' automobile, this can also be found with other lettering, such as 'ALSO'.

4in (10.5cm) long

£180-220   POOK

A late 1960s-70s Japanese Asahi battery-operated 'Lotus 49 Ford F1', the tinplate body lithographed in red, gold, and white, with plastic engine block and driver, in original box.

The Lotus 49 was a Formula One racing car designed by Colin Chapman and Maurice Philippe for the 1967 Formula One racing season. Driven by Jim Clark, it sped to victory that season.

16in (41cm) long

£70-100   TEN

A 1950s Japanese tinplate and steel 1951 Cadillac, finished in light green, with some scratches and wear.

This classic and highly detailed car is very similar to Marusan's highly sought-after 1951 Cadillac, designed by Matsuzou Kosuge. Due to the car's widespread popularity, Cadillac toys sold very well at the time.

9in (23cm) long

£250-350   POOK

A Gunthermann tinplate double-decker trolley bus, with driver figure and wire for electric light to the front, battery compartment below.

This is a large and well-detailed model by a desirable maker.

19.75in (50cm) long

£1,000-1,500   FLD

TOYS & GAMES

A 1950s Brimtoy tinplate clockwork model trolley bus, with lithographed details.

6.75in (17cm) long

£50-80   ECGW

A Karl Bub clockwork tinplate fire engine, with four tin figures, two part ladder and electric lamp holder to front of cab, registration 'KB788'.

19in (48cm) long

£450-550   TEN

A 1950s Tipp Co friction-powered motorcycle, with driver, plastic windshield with 'Tippco' metal logo and saddle bags to rear, defective mechanism and slight fading to one side.

This is marked 'WESTERN GERMANY', which helps to date it to the period after the division of Germany. Tipp & Co was founded in 1912 and closed in 1917 and is known for its series of motorbikes, often with sidecars. Always play close attention to the condition of the tires, both metal and plastic, as they become worn with play.

11in (28cm)

£250-350   TEN

A Lehmann 'New Century Cycle', no.345, with plain-blue side, driver with Union Jack in hand and red-striped parasol, in original box with monochrome label.

£1,000-1,500   TEN

A CLOSER LOOK AT A TINPLATE CAROUSEL

Active from 1844-80, Althof, Bergmann and Co. were a toy importer, distributor, and maker based in New York City, who exhibited their wares at the 1878 Philadelphia Centennial Exhibition.

Today their rare and very high-quality toys are highly sought-after. Their tinplate Santa on a sleigh pulled by goats holds the record for the most expensive tinplate toy. In 2010, it sold at auction for $161,000.

As well as being one of the largest tinplate carousels made, it is the only known early tin clockwork carousel made by an American toy manufacturer.

Even though the blue finish on the base is worn this example is in otherwise good condition and retains its orginal fabric umbrella. Had it been in better condition, it could have fetched up to $10,000.

An Althof, Bergmann & Co. tinplate and wood clockwork carousel, with six painted gondolas and horses with riders, and fabric umbrella.

18.5in (47cm) high

£2,500-3,500   POOK

A 1920s Lehmann 'Balky Mule', no.425, with clown lithography to wheels, clown's body is loose.

This was one of Lehmann's most popular and successful toys. Consequently, it is not too hard to find today.

4.25in (11cm) high

£80-120   TEN

A 1930s Marx lithographed tinplate wind-up 'Moon Mullins and Kayo' hand car.

Like many of Marx's toys, this can be found in different colourways, with at least three known for this model.

6in (15cm) long

£150-250   POOK

An unusual Hausser lithographed tinplate greenhouse, with glass windows and rising roof panels, six earthenware flower pots and saucers and a tin watering can, stamped 'Hausser' to base.

11in (27cm) long

£400-600   TEN

QUICK REFERENCE - TRI-ANG 'SPOT-ON' RANGE

● Spot-On diecast models were introduced in 1959 by leading British toy factory Tri-ang, who began life as G&J Lines Ltd, and then Lines Bros Ltd after WWI. They were aiming to gain some of the booming diecast market dominated by Dinky and the recently founded Corgi Toys. To differentiate their models from those of their competitors, Tri-ang made every vehicle, from cars to lorries, to the same scale - 1:42. That way, they would look correctly sized when placed together and act more as 'models' than toys. They were produced in a newly built factory in Dublin, Ireland, until 1967, when Tri-ang acquired Dinky Toys. After that, some dies were sold to a New Zealand company that produced some interesting variations. With these diecast toys, condition and variation can impact value.

A Tri-ang Spot-On 'Morris 1100', model no.262, in bright-red with white interior, 'GTM 110' number plates, boxed with minor wear.
1963
£80-120 W&W

A Tri-ang Spot-On 'NSU Prinz 4', model no.193, in bright Red with white interior, 'PJL 113' number plates, boxed with paperwork.
1963
£70-100 W&W

A Tri-ang Spot-On 'Austin Healey 100-Six', model no.105, in light metallic-blue with pale-yellow interior, boxed with paperwork, some damage to one flap, number plates missing.
1959
£150-200 W&W

A Tri-ang Spot-On 'Triumph TR3a Sports', model no.108, in metallic light-green with lemon interior, 'PZL108' number plates, complete with original screen, boxed, with paperwork, one outer end flap damaged.

Light blue with dark blue seats or cream with dark brown seats tend to be the most valuable variations of this desirable car, and can fetch over 25% more.
1960
£200-300 W&W

A Tri-ang Spot-On 'Volkswagen Beetle', model no.195, in bright-red with crossed flags to bonnet, racing decal '6', spare wheel and light to roof, 'RFS 186' number plate and white interior, boxed, minor wear.

This appears to be an unusual variation - racing number 6 should be on a light blue car. Red bodies are usually numbered 11.
1963
£150-200 W&W

A Tri-ang Spot-On 'Ford Thames Trader with Three Log Load', model no.111/aOt, in light-blue with black chassis to cab, 'LXG111' to trailer, boxed, no packing, some tears to box plus split to one end, some chipping to vehicle.

Dark blue, red, or yellow versions of this model are usually worth around 25% more.
1961
£120-180 W&W

A Tri-ang Spot-On 'ERF 68G Flatbed Lorry With Planks', model no.109/2P, in mint-green with a black cab roof and a grey chassis, with plank load, 'PLM109' number plate to rear only, boxed with packing, some splitting/tape marking.

The yellow bodied variation can fetch around a third more.
1960
£120-180   W&W

A Tri-ang Spot-On 'Austin Prime Mover', with articulated flat float with sides, model no.106A/1, in shades of light blue with black chassis to cab, 'TPO106' number plate to trailer, boxed, packing with some age wear.
1960
£80-120   W&W

A Tri-ang Spot-On 'Bedford 'S' Type 2000 gallon Shell-BP tanker', model no.158A/2, in red and green livery, cab with black chassis 'BTW115' number plate to front of cab, boxed, with packing, surface tearing to both ends.

A variation with a yellow cab and white tank can fetch up to twice as much as this version.
1961
£250-350   W&W

A Tri-ang Spot-On 'Jones Mobile Crane', model no.117, in red and white, complete with original box with packing.
1963
£180-220   ECGW

A Tri-ang Spot-On 'Royal Occasion Set, 'Tommy Spot Gift Set', model no.806, consisting of a model no.260 Royal Rolls Royce, six guard figures and Tommy Spot, in original pictorial window box with sign to front 'Royal Occasion' with Tommy Spot - box.

The internal pictorial stand could be used almost like a theatre backdrop. This is one of the most valuable and sought-after of the eight 'Tommy Spot' gift sets.
£600-800   TEN

A large Tri-ang red-painted 'A5 No. 93 London Transport Bus', model no.3060, for 'Wimbledon, Morden, Putney BDG. STN.'.
These were often sat on and ridden by children, so examples in great condition like this can be scarce. Buses are popular vehicles for collectors and form an area known as 'busiana'.
12.25in (31cm) high
£250-350   ECGW

A rare 1930s Tri-ang Minic clockwork Searchlight, model no.49ME, in original box.
£150-200   LOCK

Mark Picks

I own this figure. But not the packaging. I was born in 1975 and quickly became an avid Star Wars fan. Like many children, my parents indulged me with these comparatively inexpensive toys from time to time, and the mysterious Boba Fett was a character I longed to own. When I did receive him, I tore him out of the plastic and threw away the packaging. In retrospect, my child-self lost my adult-self the price of a deposit on a house. But that's what all of us did, hence the great rarity of these 'carded' figures - especially on unopened cards that are in great condition. The nostalgic appeal is clear. But, would I spend over £20,000 on a mint and carded figure of one of my favourite characters? No, I wouldn't. At the end of the day, this is a mass-produced item. I'd much rather spend that sum of money on a unique, skilfully made antique. I still have my Boba Fett in the way I remember playing with him and, if I didn't, a few pounds would buy me an identical replacement. But that's just me and, being a diehard collector myself, I can totally understand those that seek out the very best of what they love.

An early 1980s Palitoy 'Star Wars, The Empire Strikes Back' Boba Fett figure, in near mint to mint condition, within a near mint to mint bubble, with the slightest of scuffs to edges, upon a near mint unpunched '30B' card, with slight creasing below the right hand edge of the Palitoy logo, rear of card with surface "pull" where a price sticker was removed.

figure 3.75in (9.5cm) high

£22,000-28,000   VEC

A Palitoy 'Star Wars, The Empire Strikes Back' FX-7 3 ¾" figure, in mint condition, within an unopened near mint bubble, with extremely slight scuffs, upon a near mint '30A' un-punched card back, with slight creasing to the centre of card and across the bottom right hand corner and top right hand edge and with very minor scuff to top right hand card edge.

FX-7 was a Rebel Alliance medical droid that attended to Luke Skywalker after he was rescued from the clutches of the Wampa on the ice planet of Hoth.

figure 3.75in (9.5cm) high

£3,000-5,000   VEC

A 1980s Palitoy 'Star Wars, The Empire Strikes Back' FX-7 Medical Droid figure, in near-mint-to-mint condition, unopened within an excellent-plus bubble upon an excellent-plus un-punched 30-figure back card.

This figure is nearly identical, even in terms of condition, to the example above, which sold for a third of the value of this one. The reason for this is that these unopened, 'carded' figures in mint condition on mint cards are extremely rare. Every tiny bit of wear counts. When more than one collector has a gap in their collection, or collects a particular character, prices escalate rapidly.

figure 3.75in (9.5cm) high

£7,000-8,000   VEC

A 1980s Palitoy 'Star Wars, The Empire Strikes Back' IG-88 (Bounty Hunter) figure, unopened bubble, 30B un-punched card back, original price sticker, minor wear. **One of the most accurate figures produced by Kenner/Palitoy.**

figure 3.75in (9.5cm) high

£6,000-8,000   VEC

A late 1970s Palitoy Star Wars 'Jawa' figure, with vinyl cape, the bubble in excellent condition, base of bubble stem is crushed and slightly coming away from card, upon un-punched 12-back card. **When parents saw this very small figure, they begrudged paying the same price as for a larger, standard-sized figure. It bore little resemblance to the Jawas in the film and to the photograph on the card back. In order to make the figure look more accurate, the plastic cape was replaced with a fabric poncho. Loose Jawa figures are often redressed in a cape made from the larger cape of the more common Obi Wan Kenobi.**

figure 3.75in (9.5cm)

£8,500-9,500   VEC

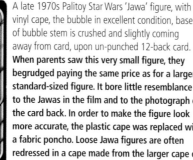

A mid-late 1980s Palitoy/General Mills 'Star Wars, Return of the Jedi' Yak Face figure, no weapon within an indented bubble, 70D un-punched Tri-logo card back.

YakFace wasn't sold domestically in the US and has become one of the 'legendary rare' Star Wars figures, along with the vinyl-caped Jawa, despite online auctions being a good source of affordable loose examples.

£1,000-1,500   VEC

TOYS & GAMES

An American Buddy L pressed steel International ride-on hydraulic dump truck.

26in (66cm) long

£280-320   POOK

An American Buddy L pressed-steel hook and ladder truck.

25.5in (65cm) long

£350-450   POOK

A CLOSER LOOK AT A SOAP BOX RACER

This is one of the rarest Lesney diecast toys and was considered the company's only flop by founders Jack Smith and Jack Odell.

Although some have quoted 10,000 were made and then scrapped, Jack Odell is reported to have said ten gross were made (1,440) and then sold to wholesalers.

Despite this, collectors believe that less that 30 examples have survived, although it very difficult to track quantity as some sales may be the same example changing hands between collectors.

Some are moulded 'A Lesney Product Made in England' on the base and some are not - beware of the limited edition of 500 made by Perfect Toys in the 1990s.

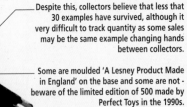

A Lesney 'Soap Box Racer' with bronze cart with 'Soap' in proud lettering on one side and 'Soda' on the other, with seated boy figure dressed in brown with blue scarf, the cart in good-to-excellent condition, some wear mainly to highlights, the boy in good conditon with general chipping.

1947

£800-1,200   TEN

An American Arcade cast iron double-decker bus, with the original box,

7.75in (19.5cm) long

£600-800   POOK

A late 1940s American Toledo Casting Corp. 'Al-Toy' cast-aluminum Jeepster.

This company became famous in the late 1940s for its realistic CJ-2A jeep.

15.5in (40cm) long

£500-700   POOK

An English 1950s 'Austin J 40' roadster pedal car, constructed in heavy grade steel, with adjustable pedals and pneumatic rubber tyres, with a white steering wheel, imitation engine details, leather upholstery and dashboard.

62in (160cm) long

£1,200-1,800   ROS

A mid-20thC British Austin J 40 pedal car, constructed in heavy grade steel, with adjustable pedals and pneumatic rubber tyres, in near original condition.

£1,500-2,000   ECGW

A 1920s-30s Wells 'Mickey Mouse Handcart', with composition figures of Mickey and Minnie on a clockwork handcart, with card tunnel and track, generally in good to excellent condition, figures have surface crazing and one of Minnie's arms is broken off at the shoulder, in original box with full colour label, box in good to fair condition.

£400-600   TEN

A 1950's Meccano Set 'No 9' in original box, with paperwork, some pieces unused.

£350-450   ECGW

A 19thC child's rocking horse, with painted coat, hair mane and tail and saddle, in good condition but frame appears to have been rebuilt.

29.5in (75cm) high approx.

£400-600   AST

A Danish beechwood rocking horse, marked 'Kay Bojesen', designed by Kaj Bojesen in 1936.

28.7in (73cm) long

£500-800   QU

A 1960s Danish painted wood soldier, marked with a Kringle motif on a plaque.

This is roughly the same size as a child and was probably used as part of a display in a toy shop. A Kringle is a Scandinavian version of a pretzel and looks similar, but is usually more solid.

45in (115cm) high

£500-800   QU

QUICK REFERENCE - TRAINS

● The mid-19thC saw the arrival of the first model (or toy) trains although they were stylised, bulky and unrealistic. Many were made from wood or cast iron. More realistic trains made from painted and then printed tinplate were developed by the 1890s. Primarily made by German makers including Märklin (est.1759), and Gebrüder Bing (1863-1933) they were fitted with clockwork or live steam mechanisms. Many were exported across Europe and to the US, although production and export dropped during the two World Wars.

A Bing gauge I clockwork 0-4-0 locomotive and 4-wheel tender, with bell-operated from cab, lacks con-rods.

£350-400   TEN

A late 1920s Bing 0-gauge LMS ex LNWR precurser 4-4-2T locomotive, RN no.6820, fitted with Leeds 8-volt DC electrics, for 3-rail operation, with vacuum pipes and coal rails to bunker, minor chips.

£120-150   W&W

A Carette gauge 1 live steam 2-2-0 'Stork Leg' locomotive and L&NWR tender, boiler in plain metal with chimney, steam dome and whistle, marked with 'GC & Co.' logo to cabside, boiler has some scorch damage.

£450-500   TEN

A Carette gauge I 2-2-0 live steam 'Stork Leg' locomotive, with GCN roundel to cabside, with four-wheel tender, with reproduction headlamp, tender lacks one buffer.

£600-700   TEN

A Marklin gauge I live steam 0-4-0 Midland Railway locomotive and 4-wheel tender, no.281, locomotive faded, with burner.

£400-450   TEN

A Marklin gauge I baggage car, no.18891, with lifting observation roof, fitted with internal electric lamp.

2in (31cm) long

£90-120   TEN

A CLOSER LOOK AT A HORNBY TRAIN

This set is very rare, but is particularly so when in such excellent condition. It may have fetched more if it only had one goods van as when sold and if the missing card insert for one of the wagons was still present.

It was one of two sets launched just before the war in 1938 as part of Hornby's legendary Dublo range.

A Hornby Dublo 'Cardiff Castle' 2-rail WR 4-6-0 tender locomotive, no.2221, RN no.4075, in Brunswick green livery, boxed, with packing.
£90-120 W&W

This GWR livery and 6699 numbering is the same as the example shown on the Dublo launch artwork in 1938, making it highly desirable to collectors.

The leaflets are complete. The box, pictorial label and leaflets are in very good condition overall, although one corner of the label is torn and taped.

A rare pre-war Hornby Dublo clockwork DG7 tank goods set, consisting of 0-6-2T GWR locomotive, no.6699, in original corrugated card wrap with correct 'G.W.' diamond sticker, GW open, 2xGW goods and GW Park Royal brake van, eight curved and two straight 2-rail track pieces with brass rails, with key, 'Guarantee', 'Tested & Guaranteed' and 'Instructions' leaflets, in original blue card box with correct label to lid end (D102), torn at one corner and some taping.
£1,800-2,200 TEN

A Hornby Special L.M.S. 4-4-0 tender locomotive, no.2, RN no.1185, clockwork motor, restored lined maroon livery, unboxed.
£120-180 DN

A Hornby Dublo 2-rail 2019 2-6-4 tank goods train set, comprising BR standard class 4 2-6-4T locomotive, RN no.80033, with a flat wagon with 'Insul Meat' container, a flat wagon with a Dublo Dinky tractor load, a bolster wagon with timber load and a 20-ton brake van, with some track, boxed, minor wear.
£90-120 W&W

A Hornby Special 0-gauge 6-volt 3-rail electric 4-4-2 tank locomotive, no.2, RN no.5154, some light wear.
£140-180 W&W

A Hornby 'Flying Scotsman' 0-gauge 4-4-2 LNER locomotive and tender, no.4472, finished in green livery.
£180-220 FLD

A Hornby 0-gauge 4-4-2 tender locomotive, no.3, 'Lord Nelson' clockwork example, repainted by Bill Bellenie and equipped with no.2 special tender, some scratching.
£140-180 W&W

TRAINS

A Hornby 0-gauge livery locomotive and tender, no.50153, together with 'L N E R' livery locomotive, no. 460, knocks, dents and paint losses.

£50-90   ECGW

A Hornby 'Flying Scotsman' 00-gauge live steam locomotive, with transformer and control unit, boxed, as new.

£350-450   ECGW

A CLOSER LOOK AT A HORNBY TRAIN

Released in 1937, a few years after the real locomotive was introduced, the Princess Elizabeth was the flagship of Hornby's range at the time. It featured on the front of the catalogue for that year.

It was sold as a scale model. Incredible attention to detail was paid to it, right down to the tapered boiler and buffers.

It was also the only 0-gauge 4-6-2 locomotive and the only 0-gauge locomotive with six drive wheels that Hornby ever produced.

This example is in very good condition but the box is worn although sound. Had it been in better condition, the value could have been 50% higher.

War broke out only a few years after it was introduced, and the company's focus moved to Dublo (introduced in 1938) after, meaning this was one of the most impressive 0-gauge ever built.

A Hornby 'Princess Elisabeth' 0-gauge LMS class 3-rail 20-volt electric 4-6-2 tender locomotive, RN no.6201, in lined 'Crimson Lake' livery, with vacuum pipes, safety valves, LMS hooter, in an original wooden presentation case, the case is worn but sound, minor chips to locomotive.

£1,300-1,600   W&W

A Hornby 0-gauge 'Pullman' passenger set, no.2, a c/w 4-4-0 MLL locomotive, part nut and bolt construction, lacks cab roof, two 'Pullman' saloon coaches, very minimal damage, in leather-style box with proud lettering, lacks all four sides of lid.

£400-500   TEN

A Hornby Series 'Metropolitan' 0-gauge 2-six volt electric locomotive, boxed.

£350-450   FLD

A Hornby Series 'Coal Wagon', with 'Hornby Railway Company' coal load, one coupling lacks loop, with box.

£150-200   TEN

A Hornby Dublo 2-rail 'Restaurant' BR, no.4071, with box.

£100-150   TEN

A CLOSER LOOK AT AN AMERICAN FLYER

American Flyer was founded in 1907 to compete with Lionel and Ives, and was sold to Lionel in 1966.

In 1925 they released a high-quality, premium range of electric trains that could run on Lionel tracks. They cost around $100 at the time, which was equivalent to a full month's wages for an average person.

Marketed as 'Wonder Trains', they had patriotic names such as 'American Legion' and 'Mayflower'. This set was considered a flagship model of the range.

The high price tag and the Wall Street Crash in 1929 meant that few sets were sold. As a result, they are rare today - especially complete and with their boxes (not shown).

An American Flyer wide gauge four-piece 1927 'President's Edition' train set, to include a no.4687 engine, an 'Annapolis' observation car, a 'West Point' passenger car, and a 'United States Mail' car, with the original boxes, five sections of track, and a 1927 catalog.

£2,200-2,600   **POOK**

A rare issue Bassett-Lowke 0-gauge 3-rail electric standard tank 0-6-0T (freelance) locomotive, in green lined black Southern livery, unusually no.90, normally 947, boxed, with packing.

£400-450   **W&W**

A Bassett-Lowke 0-gauge Stanier class 4P 2-cylinder 2-6-4T locomotive, an 8-volt DC 3-rail electric example, RN no.2603, with vacuum pipes, drop link couplings, tank vents, hand-rails, sprung buffers.

Bassett-Lowke were founded in 1901 in Northampton, and closed in 1965. They commissioned fine-quality sets from other makers in Germany and England and marketed and distributed them, rather than making the trains themselves. The brand was later acquired by Hornby, who continue to sell trains under this prestige name.

£1,000-1,200   **W&W**

A Bassett-Lowke 0-gauge 3302 C/w 4-4-0 LMS compound locomotive, no.1082, tender heavily weighted with lead shot, with box.

£200-300   **TEN**

An Exley 0-gauge GWR 1st/2nd corridor coach, no.2663.

£150-200   **TEN**

An Exley 0-gauge 'Midland' railway 1st/3rd compartment coach with clerestory roof, no.2720.

£350-400   **TEN**

A Fleischmann HO-gauge livery locomotive, no.4370, boxed.

£30-50   **ECGW**

TRAINS

A Mettoy Railways battery-operated tin-plate and plastic O-gauge 'Express Train Set', a 'Bulleid' locomotive and tender, with 2-4-0 wheel arrangement and 4-wheel tender/'Mettoy', RN no.393, with 2 4-wheel Pullman cars and a quantity of track, including a 'stop' rail, boxed with inserts, some splitting to lid, with instruction and accessory booklet.

£80-100   W&W

A Roco HO-gauge locomotive, no.43427, boxed.

£30-40   ECGW

A Roco HO-gauge 'Krokodil OBB Elektrolokomotive' locomotive, BR no.1189, no.1449A, boxed.

£55-65   ECGW

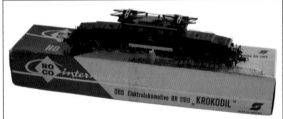

A Roco HO-gauge 'Krokodil OBB Elektrolokomotive' locomotive, BR no.1189, no.1449A, boxed.

£45-50   ECGW

A Roco HO-gauge locomotive, no.43698, boxed.

£25-35   ECGW

A Tri-ang class EM2 co-co electric locomotive 'Electra' R.351, RN no.27000, with plastic roof, with both pantographs, boxed, with a loose Steeple Cab.

£110-140   W&W

A Wrenn Railways city class 4-6-2 tender 'City of Stoke-on-Trent' locomotive, RN no.6254, boxed with instruction sheet and packing pieces, minor wear.

£90-120   W&W

A Wrenn W2241 'Duchess of Hamilton' locomotive, no.6229, with instructions, stamped 'Packer No.3', boxed.

£120-150   TEN

A Fleischmann HO-gauge livery locomotive, no.4340, boxed.
£30-40   ECGW

A HAG 'Bodensee Toggenburg' HO-gauge rolling stock, nos.425 and 455, boxed.
£30-40   ECGW

A Lawrence Scale Models constructed 'Blacksmiths Models' 00-gauge kit 'GWR' newspaper van 868, with maker's plaque to base dated 12/4/87.
1987
£120-150   TEN

A Lawrence Scale Models 00-gauge 'GWR' brake/3rd corridor coach 5294, with maker's plaque to base dated 23/1/89.
£120-150   TEN

A Lionel standard gauge train set, a no.408E engine, a parlour car, an observation car, and a dining car.
£950-1,200
                    POOK

A Lionel Lines 3-rail electric 2-4-2 tender locomotive, an outside cylinder locomotive of North American outline, copper finish to unpainted parts, RN no.262E, with an eight-wheel bogie tender, with three bogie cars equipped with lighting, an observation car, a 'Pullman' car and a baggage car with four sliding doors.
£100-150
                    W&W

A Lionheart Trains 0-gauge 'G W R' pannier tank steam 0-6-0 locomotive, no.7400, rail to surround needs fixing.
£400-450   ECGW

TREEN & CARVINGS

QUICK REFERENCE - TREEN

- The term 'treen' refers mainly to small pieces made from turned wood. They are usually small, made from woods such as beech, elm or chestnut, and were designed to be used around the home, on a farm or in a workshop. Some of the most common items are snuff and spice boxes, drinking vessels, spoons, measures, salts, bowls and utensils.
- The earliest pieces available to the collector today date from the 17thC and the most desirable pieces date from c1720 to c1800. Many of the pieces on the market now date from the 19thC. As there are many of them, and they are often ignored by collectors, values tend to be lower. It is also worth noting that as the 19thC progressed fewer items were made from wood as advances in technology meant they could be made morn quickly and economically from pottery or metal.
- When buying treen, look carefully at the quality of the carving, the wood used and the age of the item. It is worth remembering that the more decorative the piece, the more desirable it is likely to be. A warm, rich patina, built up over years of use, will also add to the value.

A George III mahogany novelty snuff box, carved as a ram's head with curved horns and a hinged cover, crown of head professionally restored.

c1780   *2.5in (6cm) high*

£500-600   **DN**

A rare 18thC box wood partridge snuff box.

c1790   *3.75in (9.5cm) long*

£800-1,000   **PC**

A coquilla nut snuff box, with fine carving of Napoleon with his marshals on the lid, the reverse depicts the widow and her son.

A coquilla is a Brazilian palm tree nut. It has a thick, hard shell, which is often used for carving.

c1790   *3.25in (8.3cm) wide*

£400-500   **PC**

Judith Picks

I have been collecting treen for many years and was immediately drawn to this particularly grumpy man in a cape, hand in a pocket, with bone buttons. Snuff boxes have always fascinated me - perhaps his grumpiness was due to excessive use! Snuff is fermented, dried, ground and flavoured tobacco, and was 'discovered' some 500 years ago in America by Christopher Columbus, who encountered the Native Americans inhaling a mysterious powder during his second voyage of discovery (1494-6). Initially used by aristocracy, by the 19thC, thanks to increased production and reduced cost, the habit spread much more rapidly to the middle and lower classes. In London alone there were 400 snuff shops. Collecting treen snuff boxes can be rewarding. On the next few pages there are fine examples made at the end of the 18thC and beginning of the 19thC in England, with humorous figures and shoes. What is interesting is that snuff is making an early 21st century come back, particularly with the hip 20's and 30's. Where smoking is now considered at best anti-social and at worst a criminal offence – a delicate pinch of snuff is once again considered rather refined.

A French coquilla nut novelty snuff box, engraved 'R.M', old repair on foot has detached.

c1790   *2.5in (6.5cm) high*

£700-800   **DN**

A French coquilla nut novelty snuff box, carved as a man in a cap and cape putting his hand in a pocket, with two-colour glass eyes and bone buttons, splits, hinge doesn't shut totally, later glued repair on foot.

c1790   *3.5in (9cm) high*

£700-900   **DN**

A George III horn novelty snuff box, in the form of a cat, with bone teeth and a brass collar, probably later cork stopper, brass colour listing away slightly.

c1790   *2.5in (6.2cm) high*

£400-500   **DN**

A George III mahogany novelty snuff box, in the form of a great ape's or gorilla's head, with glass eyes and bone teeth, surface marks consistent with age and use, minor scuff to nose.

c1800   2.5in (6.5cm) long

£600-700   DN

Three views of an early 19thC carved coquilla nut snuff flask, with stopper, the body with an angel and musical trophies, to a bugbear type base.

3.5in (8.5cm) long

£350-450   WW

A 19thC silver-mounted mahogany novelty snuff box, carved as a horse's head, with an engine-turned oval cover and mount.

c1820   3.5in (9cm) high

£650-750   BLEA

A late 19thC carved treen 'hunting' snuff box, in the form of a wild boar head, with glass eyes, the hinged cover with a fox head.

4in (10cm) long

£300-350   WW

A large 19thC treen snuff shoe, with a sliding cover and brass tack inlay.

7in (17.5cm) long

£800-1,200   WW

A 19thC treen and brass inlaid snuff shoe, with a hinged cover and decorated with flowers.

3in (7.5cm) long

£120-180   WW

A 19thC treen snuff shoe, with a sliding cover and brass tack inlay.

5.5in (14cm) long

£150-200   WW

TREEN & CARVINGS

A mid-Victorian laburnum shoe snuff box, with a turned-up toe, steel, and brass stud decoration, surface marks consistent with age and use, a few chips to the sole.

3.5in (8.5cm) long

£220-280 DN

A 19thC treen snuff sandal, the lid with a ring handle and inset with a bone plaque, the carved foot with bone toenails.

4.25in (11cm) long

£300-400 WW

A treen single-handled scoop, with incised stylised tree decoration.

4.75in (12cm) high

£200-250 WW

An 18thC treen bowl, of oval form.

18in (46cm) wide

£300-400 WW

A lignum vitae mortar and pestle, each turned from single sections and polished.

Lignum vitae (Guaiacum officinale) is a dark brown, black-veined wood exported from South America and the West Indies to Europe from the 17thC. It was used for oyster veneers and parquetry and was particularly useful for turned bowls and other treen.

c1770 *the pestle 11.5in (29cm) high*

£300-400 CM

An 18thC turned and stained walnut mortar and pestle, the former of waisted cylindrical form and with shallow horizontal mouldings, the latter with bulbous end and handle.

12in (30cm) high

£300-350 DN

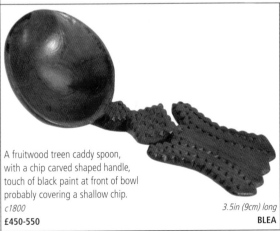

A fruitwood treen caddy spoon, with a chip carved shaped handle, touch of black paint at front of bowl probably covering a shallow chip.

c1800

3.5in (9cm) long

£450-550 BLEA

A rare 19thC hand-painted wooden carving of a snarling poodle, with damage and restoration.

£2,000-3,000 T&F

An early Victorian railway truncheon by William Parker of Holborn, painted with a crown and city armorial's above 'London and Birmingham Railway'.

18in (46cm) long

£250-350   WHP

A pair of matching 19thC carved and turned coquilla nut and treen ornaments, the basket bases with screw-off covers having a screw-off acorn shaped finial.

7in (17.5cm) high

£700-900   WW

A Black Forest carved wooden novely coat hook, in the form of a gentleman in breeches, doffing his hat and clutching a walking stick, with two buckhorn hooks.

12.25in (31cm) long

£200-300   LAW

A Swiss Black Forest carved and stained Lindenwood bear, probably Brienz, with growling expression, painted mouth, nose leather detail.

c1890   *17in (43cm) long*

£2,000-2,500   TEN

An early 20thC Black Forest carved bear, with characterful face, glass eyes, painted teeth and tongue, modelled on all fours in the standing position with an integral woven basket bound to his back, some old cracking.

48.5in (123cm) long

£2,000-3,000   DW

QUICK REFERENCE - KAY BOJESEN

- Kay Bojesen (1886–1958) trained as a silversmith, was apprenticed to Georg Jensen and worked in Germany, France and Copenhagen. He created more than 2,000 items and was one of Denmark's most prolific 20thC designers. He is best known for wooden toys, including this monkey which was designed in 1951 and has become a design classic. He also created jewellery, cutlery, teapots and silver goblets. The toys were inspired by the birth of Kay's son Otto. His aim was to create imaginative toys which were simple, solid and would inspire children to play. This monkey is made from limba wood and teak and it is so popular that an example of it is now in the Victoria & Albert Museum in London. This example dates from the early 1960s.

An oak 'Mouseman' bookend of curved form.

6in (15cm) high

£80-120   WHP

A pair of 'Mouseman' oak napkin rings.

Robert Thompson (1876-1955) was a furniture-maker from Kilburn, Yorkshire. He became known as the 'Mouseman' because his work is signed with the carved figure of a mouse. He used oak to make well-crafted pieces with a distinctive adzed finish that gives a subtle rippled effect to the surface. The firm he founded still exists today.

£60-80   WHP

A Wooden Monkey, designed by Kay Bojesen, stamped 'KAY BOJESEN DENMARK COPYRIGHT'.

c1960

£700-1,000   SWO

TRIBAL ART

QUICK REFERENCE - TRIBAL ART

- Tribal art is the term used to describe the cultural, ritual and functional items produced by the indigenous peoples of Africa, Oceania, South East Asia, Australia and the Americas. As such, it was primarily and initially made for actual use rather than for use as decoration or for aesthetic appreciation. Pieces are collected not only for their deep historic and ethnographic significance, but also for their great visual impact when displayed in today's eclectic interiors. Social and ethnographic interest has grown since Africa was opened up by explorers from the 18thC onwards, and due to increasing levels of trade across the world. Artists and designers came to appreciate the qualities of tribal art from the late 19thC onwards, but this was particularly strong during the early 20thC due to the influence of artists such as Pablo Picasso. Since the 1980s, tribal pieces have featured heavily in fashionable interiors.
- Many items deal with core human themes such as life and death, fertility and spiritual beliefs. Not all tribes made the same items and some tribes are better known for one type of item, such as masks. Most collectors choose to focus on one type of item, such as masks from the Dan tribe, or one tribe.

- Age and provenance are key indicators to value. Older pieces from the 19thC with a verifiable history are generally the most valuable - particularly if they were collected from the area they originated from before the early 20thC. Use adds wear and patination, which are other good signs to look for, but examine and ideally handle as many authentic, original pieces as possible at dealers or auction houses, as patina can be skilfully faked. Patina and wear, as well as style, can help to indicate a period of manufacture, but it is generally very hard without a provenance.
- Values have risen dramatically in the past twenty years, particularly at the upper end of the market for older pieces with provenances, which have become the preserve of wealthy collectors and museums. From the early 20thC onwards, pieces were made purely for export or to be purchased by tourists as souvenirs or representative pieces from the tribes they visited. These were made in profusion. Quality varies greatly.
- For ease of identification, the pieces shown in this section are ordered by type and then by general visual appearance, rather than by tribe.

A Dan mask, with ribbed coiffure outline and white pigment.

15in (38cm) high

£450-550   WW

An Angolan mask, with light engraving to forehead and below the eyes.

8in (20.5cm) high

£300-400   WW

An Igbo mask, with narrow forehead and carved circles around the eyes, polychrome decorated.

9in (23cm) high

£400-500   WW

A Marka mask, with red cloth and stamped sheet brass mounts.

The Marka tribe of Mali are neighbours of the Bamana (or Bambara) people and their masks are often very similar. Elongated, thin forms are typical, with long noses and protruding lips at the base of the mask and downward-facing eyes that show respect. The main difference between Bamana and Marka masks is the Marka's use of applied metal (or shell) details, or as here shaped brass panels. These masks were used in ceremonies for successful harvests, hunts or to commemorate circumcision, an important part of a young man's journey through life into acceptance as part of the tribe.

15in (38cm) high

£450-500   WW

A Punu mask, with ebonised, white, and red pigment.

12.25in (31cm) high

£250-300   WW

A Yaure mask, with pointed coiffure and white pigment decoration.

15.5in (39.5cm) high

£650-750　　　　　　　　WW

A CLOSER LOOK AT A YAURE MASK

The Yaure tribe of the Côte D'Ivoire are located between the Baule and Guro and Gban tribes, and share similarities with them.

They are known for their high quality, artistic masks, many of which have animal attributes as here where a bird stands on top.

High foreheads with elaborate or neatly coiffured hair above pierced almond-shaped eyes are typical features.

The masks are considered to hold dangerous ju spirits and dances may occur after a tribesman has died to establish equilibrium to the tribe. Those with black pigment are worn in dances to help the dead tribesman's spirit move to the other world.

Edges of their masks are often serrated.

A Yaure mask, with a bird crest.

15.5in (39.5cm) high

£500-600　　　　　　　　WW

A Fang-style mask, ebonised, red pigment.

15.5in (39.5cm) high

£450-500　　　　　　　　WW

A Kuba mask, with a woven headdress, applied cowrie shells and feathers, on a later stand.

The Kuba use over twenty different types of mask, which are known for their rich decoration that may include cowrie shells, animal hair, fur, beads, hide, and feathers.

13in (33cm) high

£500-600　　　　　　　　WW

A Nigerian mask, with protruding coiffure and flat nose, with red ebonised and white decoration, with fibre attachment.

12in (30.5cm) high

£250-350　　　　　　　　WW

An Eket-style mask, with black, white, and blue pigment.

11.5in (29cm) high

£200-250　　　　　　　　WW

TRIBAL ART

A Dan mask, surrounded by cloth, applied cowrie shells, bells, and fibre.

12.5in (32cm) high

£350-400   WW

A Cameroon mask, with applied beads and copper discs.

15.5in (40cm) high

£400-450   WW

A Cameroon helmet mask, with horns and an animal crest.

15.5in (39.5cm) high

£400-450   WW

A Marka mask, with sheet metal and fabric tassels.

18.25in (36.5cm) high

£200-300   WW

A Mossi bird mask, with an open diamond cresting, ebonised red and white pigment, with old repairs.

Mossi masks are typically highly decorated in colours and are often emblematic of animals, representing an animal or god that appears in times of need. They are often long with pointed chins. Some may have horns or carved human figures.

33.5in (85cm) high

£450-550   WW

A Burkino Faso bird mask, polychrome decorated.

25in (63.5cm) high

£400-450   WW

A Mambila mask, with protruding eyes, open muzzle, ears and horns, orange, ebonised and white pigment.

Mambila masks are often of highly stylised animals, as with this example. Along with their statues, masks were kept hidden from the eyes of women in a net hung inside a hut built up on stilts and guarded by the head of the family. They were worn in rituals and masquerades to celebrate the start and end of the agricultural cycle.

24in (61cm) high

£400-450   WW

A Bamileke buffalo head helmet mask, with white ebonised and red pigment.

16.75in (42.5cm) high

£450-500   WW

A Bwa plank mask.

42.25in (107.5cm) high

£350-400   WW

A CLOSER LOOK AT AN AFRICAN MASK

The Bembe people of central Africa mainly produce masks, which are kept in sacred caves when not in use.

The Echawokaba mask is one of the best known and resembles a stylised owl, an animal the dancer is said to come into contact with when wearing it.

It has two faces representing balance in society and nature, the most recognisable of which is this, with its concave round or oval eye sockets with diamond or star-shaped eyes and tiny holes in the middle.

It represents a bush spirit and is used for the worship of ancestors, the initiation of new, often young, tribesmen and the ceremonies preceding a hunt.

A Bembe Echawokaba helmet mask, with red and white pigment.

18in (46cm) high

£500-600   WW

A Baga mask, polychrome-decorated, on a stand.

27.75in (70.5cm) high

£200-250   WW

A Bambara antelope headdress, with incised decoration, on a later wood stand.

15.25in (38.6cm) high

£500-600   WW

A Bambara antelope headdress, with a later stand.

These traditional masks are known as 'Tji Wara' masks, with 'tji' meaning work and 'wara' meaning animal. They represent the antelope, a mythical being who taught man how to farm. When worn, the mask encourages the tribespeople to work together for a good harvest or represents a good farmer. Both a male and female version always dance together, perhaps further representing fertility and abundance in harvest.

31in (79cm) high

£550-600   WW

A Hemba warrior figure, with cross back coiffure.

25.5in (65cm) high

£400-450   WW

A Congo standing female figure, with body scarifications.

12.75in (32.5cm) high

£250-350   WW

A Chokwe standing figure, with ridged coiffure, coffee bean eyes, left arm missing.

12.25in (31cm) high

£300-350   WW

QUICK REFERENCE - YORUBA IBEJI

● In Yoruba culture, twins are believed to be sacred. If one dies, the family will commission a Babalawo (a father of the mysteries) to carve a small figure to 'replace' the lost twin as the loss is bad fortune for both the family and village. The parents will then dress and care for the wooden figure as if it was a real child, decorating it with cowrie shells and other accessories as befits their status. Despite this rather unsettling story, they are popular with collectors although many were carved purely for sale rather than representation of a dead child and associated 'use'.

A Yoruba Ibeji female figure, with a four-point coiffure with blue pigment, with beads, brass necklace, and bangle.

9.75in (25cm) high

£400-500   WW

A Yoruba Ibeji female figure, the remains of blue pigment to coiffure, with bead and iron bangles.

9.75in (25cm) high

£200-300   WW

A Yoruba female offering figure, holding a vessel with a child on her back and a pot on her head, polychrome decorated.

18in (46cm) high

£400-450   WW

QUICK REFERENCE - BAULE FIGURES

● The large Baule tribe of the Côte D'Ivoire is particularly known for its wooden sculptures. Representing spirits and closely connected to the supernatural world, the figures fulfill a number of functions. The Baule believe that before they were born into this world, they existed as spirits, with each one having a mate. Each man also owns his wife, the blolo bian, and each wife owns her husband, the blolo bla. If the spirit version of one spouse becomes upset due to jealousy, a figure representing that spirit may be carved and lavished with attention to placate and appease them, perhaps also to fix the marital discord. Baule figures are typically carved on a stand or pedestal and have their hands resting on their abdomen as a gesture of peace. Necks are elongated, and faces are typically scarified and have bulging, oval eyes. Hair is usually very detailed and often divided into plaits. This example is well-carved, with a good level of detail and an elegant, curved form. Compare this and the equally good example to the right to the other three on this page to see this.

The presence of an inventory number is also a good sign, but it would have been better to have known which collection this came from so the full story behind its date could be found.

A Baule standing female figure, with a crested coiffure and scarifications, with ebonised highlights, the base with inventory no.5149, on a later wood stand.

14.25in (36cm) high

£1,000-1,400   WW

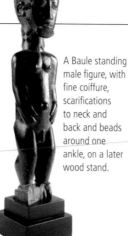

A Baule standing male figure, with fine coiffure, scarifications to neck and back and beads around one ankle, on a later wood stand.

11.5in (29cm) high

£1,000-1,400   WW

A Baule seated female, with an offset coiffure and white pigment to eyes and mouth.

Comparing the level of detail and the form and quality of this figure to the example in the Quick Reference explains why this one is worth around a quarter of the value of the finer example.

17.5in (44.5cm) high

£300-350   WW

A Baule standing female figure, with coiffure and scarifications to back of neck, the girdle strap with polychrome decoration.

15.25in (39cm) high

£400-450   WW

A Baule style carved ivory standing figure, with elaborate coiffure, face and body scarifications with hands gripping beard.

7.5in (19cm) high

£450-550   WW

A Luba standing female figure, with body scarifications.

33in (84cm) high

£500-600   WW

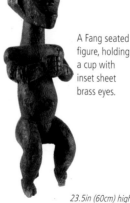

A Fang seated figure, holding a cup with inset sheet brass eyes.

23.5in (60cm) high

£300-350   WW

TRIBAL ART

A Yoruba staff for Shango, with a kneeling female with thunderaxe and holding two clubs, with beads, on a later stand.

Shango is an Orisha, a spirit that represents one of the manifestations of god, and is a royal ancestor of the Yoruba tribe. Thought to control thunder and the great powers of nature, staffs carved with Shango's symbol, a double-headed axe (seen on top of the figure), are carried in front of processions held in his honour. Consumed by his powers, it was hoped that he would be appeased so it will rain thunder and lightning down upon the Yoruba's enemies and those who do not respect him, rather than on them.

15in (38cm) high

£450-500   WW

A Kongo maternity figure, seated with back scarifications, filed teeth, a metal bead to her forehead, cradling a child, on a later stand.

10.25in (26cm) high

£350-400   WW

An Anyi or Attye standing female figure, with plumed coiffure, ring neck, scarifications and beads, on a later wood stand.

17in (43cm) high

£750-850   WW

A CLOSER LOOK AT AN ASHANTI DOLL

With its instantly recognisable disc-shaped head, the Ghanaian Ashanti tribe's Akuba doll has become an iconic piece of tribal art, partly as its highly stylised, almost Modernist, form has great decorative appeal.

It is a fertility doll, and was supplied by the tribe's herbalist to a woman who feared infertility - she wore it tied to her back until she became pregnant. They were also given to children to encourage fertility later in life.

Amongst the Ashanti tribe, the line of descent passes through the female line, so it is particularly important that women conceive - those that do many times over are highly respected.

A vast number have been produced to satisfy demand, particularly during the 20thC for tourists - older, decorated pieces and particularly those that show wear from use and a strong provenance are highly sought-after.

An Ashanti akuba female doll, the back of the head incised decoration, with beads, on a later stand.

14.5in (37cm) high

£500-600   WW

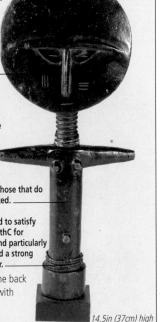

A Dogon kneeling female, with raised arms.

25.5in (65cm) high

£400-450   WW

A Gabon fertility figure, with red and white pigment to the face and a dug-out back.

19in (48.2cm) high

£500-700   WW

A Senufo heddle pulley, with a bird head finial and incised line decoration, on a later stand.

6.5in (16.5cm) high

£200-250   **WW**

A Baule heddle pulley.

This heddle pulley was used for weaving on a narrow-band loom. Many were carved with sculptural or figural representations.

7.75in (20cm) high

£400-450   **WW**

A Somalia wood headrest, the open twin supports with carved interlaced basket weave design.

6.25in (16cm) high

£150-250   **WW**

A South African zoomorphic headrest, depicting a buffalo, some aged cracks and glossy surface.

Headrests are a popular collecting area, and were used by tribespeople when sleeping, sometimes to preserve a hairstyle. The cracks and glossy surface indicates that this example may have seen some use and wear. The colour and patina are also appealing, as is the buffalo. Many are simple geometric forms, often carved with abstract, geometric symbols.

6.25in (16cm) high

£1,200-1,600   **WW**

A Nigerian Tiv axe, the blade issuing from a round head with a coiled metal bound stem and a cast-brass handle.

13.75in (35cm) long

£250-350   **WW**

An African tribal shield, Oromo from Ethiopia.

29.5in (74.5cm) diam

£400-450   **DN**

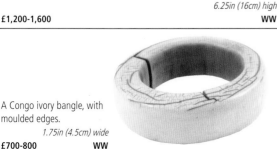

A Congo ivory bangle, with moulded edges.

1.75in (4.5cm) wide

£700-800   **WW**

An Ashanti carved wood panel, depicting Oba with attendants and two soldiers, a priest and a mounted male.

41in (104cm) wide

£250-350   **WW**

TRIBAL ART

QUICK REFERENCE - INUIT SCULPTURE

- Much of what is deemed 'Inuit Art' today has been made since the 1950s, when the work of Alaskan and North Canadian sculptors and artists was discovered by a young Canadian artist called James Houston. Over the past twenty years, the market has been researched and has mushroomed in size. Most of the sculptures are carved in a local soapstone that varies in tone from grey to green. Some are embellished with whalebone and other found materials.
- The primary indicator to value is the artist, with the work of some fetching tens of thouands of pounds. Following that is the appeal, abstraction and dynamism (and even the implied humour) of the piece, and how closely it follows the style of that artist.
- Sculptures are usually signed on the base, sometimes in Roman letters or syllabics, but often with a combination of numbers and letters given to the artist as an identifier as the Inuit did not have a tradition of a written language.

A carved stone 'Mother and Child' sculpture, by Thomas Sivuraq (b.1941), number E2- 236, from Baker Lake, signed in syllabics.

17in (43.2cm) high

£500-800   WAD

A carved stone, wood and antler 'Hunter with Harpoon', by Davidee Kavik (1915-?), from Sanikiluaq, number E9-130.

9in (23cm) high

£150-200   WAD

A carved stone and antler 'Drum Dancer' sculpture, by Pudlalik Shaa (b.1965), number E7- 1906, from Cape Dorset, signed in syllabics.

7.5in (19cm) high

£180-220   WAD

A carved stone and antler 'Annagali' sculpture, by Judas Ullulaq (1937-1999), number E4-342, from Gjoa Haven, signed in syllabics.

Judas Ullulaq (1937-99) is one of the most sought-after Inuit artists of the 20thC and is considered to have founded the influential Netsilik school which is known for its asymmetry and influence from traditional mysticism and supernatural stories. He began by carving ivory miniatures, moving on to soapstone later. He is celebrated for his bizarre, contorted figures that typically have grotesque and highly expressive features. Some are embellished with inset ivory, antler or whalebone details to accentuate that feature. He was heavily influenced by his nephew Karoo Ashevak, whose work is similarly highly sought-after.

10.5in (27cm) high

£1,500-2,000   WAD

A carved stone and antler 'Dancing Walrus' sculpture, by Alariaq Shaa (b.1978), from Cape Dorset, signed in Roman with syllabics.

9.5in (24cm) high

£300-500   WAD

A carved stone 'Alighting Bird' sculpture, by Adla Ashevak, from Cape Dorset, signed in Roman.

12in (30.5cm) long

£500-800   WAD

A carved stone 'Scenting Polar Bear' sculpture, by an unidentified artist, probably from Cape Dorset or Lake Harbour.

Polar bears in various poses are highly popular and commonly found. Those by Pauta Saila, which are typically caught mid-dance, are valuable and sought-after.

8in (20.3cm) long

£120-180   WAD

QUICK REFERENCE - WATCHES

● Interest in vintage wristwatches, and wristwatches in general, has grown rapidly over the past two decades and they are now held as status symbols, investment pieces and sometimes almost as commodities. The trend was led by men's magazines, and a smarter, more formal look combined with an eye for retro fashions returning to menswear. A large injection of wealth into the market came from new buyers and collectors working at financial institutions and living in the Middle and Far East.

● Value is affected by a number of factors, including the maker, the complexity of the movement, the date of manufacture, and the material used in the watch. High end, high quality brands with a global reputation such as Rolex, Omega and Patek Philippe will always be sought-after due to their quality. Iconic models tend to be the most collectable, with many collectors focusing on one type, such as Omega's Constellation range.

● The more complex a watch is, the more it is likely to be worth. Chronographs and watches with extra features such as sun and moon phases, alarms or perpetual calendars will usually be valuable. Such features are known as 'complications'. Although damaged or broken watches can be repaired, this can be expensive particularly if the watch is complex - any repairs should always be done by a professional and it is best not to open, or try to open, a watch's back yourself.

● Many watches can be dated by the style of the case, and sometimes other details such as the dial, hands and markers. Small, round 'pill-like' watches that look like pocket watches with wire lugs usually date to the early 20thC. Rectangular watches and glitzy, sparkling ladies' cocktail watches are generally from the late 1920s-30s. From the late 1940s onwards, watches became more stylised as forms and designs fused with jewellery. During the 1950s, simple, circular styles with pared down dials were popular. During the late 1960s & 70s, watches often were increasingly influenced by fashion, becoming bulkier, more sculptural and sometimes futuristic in look.

A stainless steel Rolex 'Oyster' wristwatch, no.143391 2280, the dial signed 'Rolex Oyster Royal'.

1.25in (3cm) diam

£400-500   **LAW**

A Rolex 'Oyster Precision' stainless steel centre seconds wristwatch, screw-down winding crown, screw back with engraved inscription, ref:6422, 1958, lever movement no.N38774, case no.6422 and dated, case serial no.333320.

c1958   13in (3.5cm) wide

£500-600   **LAW**

A 1950s-60s Rolex gentleman's stainless steel wristwatch, with sweep seconds dial.

1.5in (3.8cm)

£2,500-3,000   **LAW**

A Rolex 'Oyster Precision' stainless steel bracelet watch, 17 jewels, Alpha hands, centre seconds, screw-down crown and back, case, with a stainless steel Rolex Oyster bracelet, ref.6422, no.273161, cal.121.0, signed.

c1943   1.5in (3.5cm) diam

£900-1,100   **BLO**

A Rolex 'Oyster Perpetual Datejust Superlative Chronometer' stainless steel automatic calendar centre seconds wristwatch, ref:1603, calibre1570, 26-jewel lever movement no.D555885, case serial no.2438629, Rolex stainless Steel jubilee bracelet, signed.

1970   1.5in (3.5cm) wide

£1,300-1,600   **LAW**

WATCHES

A CLOSER LOOK AT AN OMEGA WATCH

The Seamaster was introduced in 1948 and became one of the company's most important and prestigious postwar watch types together with the Constellation.

Combining accuracy, consistencey and strength, it was fitted with an automatic movement that had a 'bumper' rotor that rotated only part of a circle and bounced off small springs at each end of the section.

The two-colour, quartered dial with centre second hands, and baton and dagger markers and hands are appealing and desirable features.

They are commonly found with stainless steel, or gold-plated cases under the 'De Ville' brand, solid 18ct gold is rare - solid pink gold is even rarer and more collectable.

An Omega Seamaster 18ct-gold automatic centre seconds wristwatch, calibre501, lever movement no.16675236, signed.

1960   *1.5in (3.5cm) wide*

£1,000-1,500   LAW

An Omega 'Ladymatic' 18ct-gold cushion-form bracelet watch, 24 jewels, on an integral 18ct. gold Omega woven bracelet, with box.

The Ladymatic was launched in 1955 and was the first automatic wristwatch for ladies. After being discontinued for some time, the brand was revived around 2005.

c1967   *1in (2.2cm)*

£950-1,150   BLO

An Omega De Ville gold-plated and stainless steel automatic wristwatch, with date aperture and sweep seconds hand.

The De Ville brand was applied to dress watches.

£200-250   LAW

A gentlemen's gold-plated Omega Automatic Genève strap watch, centre second sweep and date, polished bezel to a satin finish gold-plated case, stainless steel screw back.

c1970

£150-200   SWO

An Omega gentleman's stainless steel 'Constellation' chronometer electronic f.300 Hz wristwatch, with box.

The high-end Constellation range was introduced in 1952 and the back of their cases are moulded with a motif of the dome of an observatory surrounded by a curve of stars of different sizes to indicate they are Observatory-certified chronometers. Many consider the movements amongst the best made for a mass-produced watch, and Constellations from the 1950s-70s have become increasingly collectable.

the dial 1.5in (3.5cm)

£350-450   LAW

An Omega Constellation Chronometer D-shaped electronic calendar centre seconds wristwatch, f300Hz, electronic movement, signed.

c1970   *1.5in (4cm) wide*

£400-450   LAW

An Omega Speedmaster Professional stainless steel chronograph wristwatch, Mark II, calibre no.861, lever movement no.'32635194', screw back with Speedmaster monogram, no.145.014, stainless steel bracelet, with boxes and paperwork.

1970   *1.5in (4cm) wide*

£1,000-1,300   LAW

An unusual Cartier 18ct-gold 'Tank Chinoise' quartz wristwatch, 4 jewels, red enamel borders, screwed-down back, case, with 18ct. gold Cartier buckle, cal.057, ref.2305, no.CC81436, signed.

c1975   *0.75in (2cm) wide*
£1,300-1,600   **BLO**

A Chopard gentleman's 'Gran Turismo XL' stainless steel automatic wristwatch, 25 jewels, screwed-down glazed back, case, with stainless steel Chopard clasp, ref.8997, no.1558262, signed.

c2005   *1.75in (4.5cm) diam*
£1,200-1,500   **BLO**

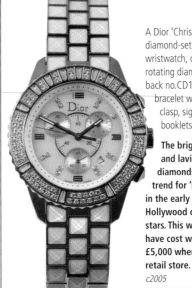

A Dior 'Christal' stainless steel and diamond-set calendar chronograph wristwatch, quartz movement, rotating diamond-set bezel, case back no.CD11431K FK8492, Dior bracelet with double deployant clasp, signed, with boxes and booklets.

The bright, reflective steel and lavish use of sparkling diamonds is typical of the trend for 'bling' that developed in the early 2000s, led by some Hollywood celebrities and rap stars. This watch would probably have cost well in excess of £5,000 when bought new from a retail store.

c2005   *1.5in (4cm) wide*
£1,600-2,000   **LAW**

A CLOSER LOOK AT A FAVRE LEUBA WATCH

Favre-Leuba was one of the first watch companies in Switzerland, being founded in 1718 by watch enthusiast Abraham Favre, and being officially registered as a manufactory in 1737.

Now owned by Indian luxury goods company Titan Industries, the brand will be relaunched sometime from 2016-17.

This style of chunky and heavy metal-cased early 1970s watch has become fashionable recently, with many contemporary fashion brands such as Nixon copying or being inspired by them.

An Eberhard Chrono 4 Temerario stainless steel tonneau-shaped automatic calendar chronograph wristwatch, with 24-hour Indication, back no.31047 5825 3ATM, Eberhard strap, signed.

c2005   *2.25in (5.5cm)*
£1,000-1,300   **LAW**

A gentleman's gold-plated Girard-Perregaux mechanical strap watch, case no.9517 MF.

£100-150   **SWO**

Although now forgotten by most people, the revival of the brand may increase interest in vintage watches by the company, especially as many pre-Quartz era models were very high quality.

A gentlemen's gold-plated Favre Leuba Sea Raider Compressor 36000 bracelet watch, case no.36002A, with box.

c1973
£200-300   **SWO**

An International Watch Company 18ct-gold watch, tonneau form nickel lever movement, case, no.1086106, calibre C.87, signed.

Rectangular Art Deco style watches are popular, especially if the Art Deco stylisation continues to the markers or numbers, hands and face.

c1930   *overall 1.5in (4cm)*
£1,200-1,600   **BLO**

WATCHES

A Longines gentleman's stainless steel and gold-plated wristwatch.

1.5in (3.5cm) diam

£200-250 LAW

A Longines gentleman's stainless steel wristwatch, with inscription to the back case.

1.5in (3.5cm) diam

£250-300 LAW

A small Movado 14ct-gold chronograph wristwatch, 17 jewels, with a stainless steel bracelet, cal.90, no.100T51, ref.49013, signed.

Movado has always been a strong brand in the US, and the use of a 14ct case indicates this was made for the American market. Solid gold Movado chronographs are very rare, and their movements are good quality. From 1969 onwards, most Movado chronographs were rebadged Zenith chronographs - Zenith was unable to use its brand in the US, so they acquired Movado to gain a foothold in this important market for their watches.

c1950 *1.5in (3.5cm) diam*

£3,500-4,000 BLO

A Piaget 18ct-gold slim wristwatch, 18 jewels, adjusted to 5 positions and temperature, case, ref.9613, no.108367, cal. 9P, no. 651144, with a presentation inscription, signed, the case back engraved 'In appreciation Jim 1966'.

c1966 *1.25in (3.2cm) diam*

£900-1,200 BLO

Mark Picks

Tudor watches were developed in 1926 out of the founder of Rolex, Hans Wildorf's, desire to produce high quality watches that were less expensive than a Rolex. The Montres Tudor S.A. company was officially founded in 1946 and the name became widely known as a sub-brand of Rolex, particularly due to the fact that most watches closely resemble their more expensive brothers and sisters. Quality is still high, even though they don't use Rolex's in-house manufactured precision movements, the bought-in Valjoux movements are very good. The brand is still in existence today but is building its own design identity, moving away from being a less costly imitator of Rolex, so it will be intertesting to see where this goes and how it may affect interest in vintage examples. Buying Tudor is a considerably less expensive way of buying the desirable Rolex look, and perhaps even shows you know a little something about wristwatches!

A Tudor 'Oyster Prince Date Day' gentleman's two-colour bracelet watch, 25 jewels, case, ref.94613, no.986134, cal. ETA 2834-1, signed.

c1983 *1.5in (3.5cm) diam*

£850-950 BLO

A gentleman's bi-colour Seiko automatic bracelet watch, bicolour bracelet with original swing ticket, in unworn condition, swing ticket ref.CW0022-P CAL7009, case no.781027.

c1970

£160-200 SWO

A Tag Heuer Gents Formula 1 wrist watch, boxed with paperwork, serial no.XE4661.

£300-400 LOC

A Vacheron & Constantin 18ct-gold wristwatch, 15 jewels, 5 adjustments, 18ct. gold buckle, no.247222, no.397266, signed, erased engraving on the case back.

c1925 *1in (2.5cm) wide*

£1,000-1,300 BLO

A military WWI silver wristwatch.

Note how similar the style of this early wristwatch is to small pocket watches, simply with the addition of wire lugs to attach it to the strap.

c1916   *1.5in (3.5cm)*

£400-500   **LAW**

An Art Deco 9ct-gold wristwatch, no.345745, with a Glasgow import mark and no.348019, lever movement signed Peerless, S&Co, under a crown in an oval cartouche.

In 1894 Stauffer & Co imported IWC (International Watch Company) movements from Switzerland and ,when they had the monopoly of this market, they started stamping their movements S&Co. Peerless was a trademark registered by Stauffer & Co in 1896.

1937   *1.5in (3.5cm)*

£1,400-1,600   **LAW**

A French lady's platinum-cased, diamond and black onyx-set dress wristwatch, on an associated white gold woven-mesh link bracelet, with a foldover clasp.

c1920

£1,000-1,500   **BELL**

A lady's diamond cocktail wristwatch, on a chain bracelet with ladder clasp.

£200-250   **LAW**

An 18ct-gold open-faced pocket watch, three quarter plate movement, with watch key and case.

1.5in (4cm) diam

£400-500   **LAW**

An 18ct-gold open-faced pocket watch, no.8538 to the inner case.

1.5in (3.8cm) diam

£220-280   **LAW**

An 18ct-gold open-faced pocket watch, with subsidiary seconds dial, with engine-turned decoration to the back case.

1.5in (4cm) diam

£300-350   **LAW**

A Henry Capt 18ct-gold open-face chronometer pocket watch, 15 jewel Henry Capt bar movement, bi-metallic split balance, with subsidiary seconds dial, no.34867.

Founded by Henry Daniel Capt, who had worked with Isaac Piguet, Henry Capt was based in Geneva, Switzerland and had offices in London and Paris. In 1887, they were the first Swiss company to enter a watch into the Kew Watch Trials. In 1880, the company was sold to Gallopin.

c1900   *the case 2.25in (5.5cm) diam*

£700-800   **BLO**

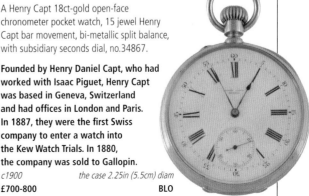

A Movado slim 18ct-gold keyless lever watch, with Art Deco motifs, fine nickel lever movement, 15 jewels, case, no.378044 3724, signed.

c1920　　　　　*1.75in (4.5cm) diam*

£600-650　　　　　　　**BLO**

An 18ct-gold full hunting cased pocket watch, glass missing.

1.5in (4cm)

£650-700　　　　　　　**LAW**

A CLOSER LOOK AT A POCKET WATCH

Solid gold half or full hunters are worth more than standard pocket watches because there is more gold in the body due to the extra hinged lid.

This watch was made by Dent & Co of London, founded in 1814 by Edward Dent, which gained a reputation for building high quality precision watches and other timepieces.

They made the Standard Clock that kept Greenwich Meantime, Sir Winston Churchill's first watch was by Dent, and they made the movement of London's world famous Big Ben clock.

In 1846, Dent also patented 'The Keyless' pocket watch that could be wound and set by twisting the crown rather than using a key - this is an example.

An 18ct-gold half hunting cased pocket watch, by Dent, engraved with initials and crest to the back case, with fitted case by Dent.

2in (5cm) diam

£1,300-1,800　　　　　　　**LAW**

A gentleman's 9ct-gold-cased, keyless wind, half hunting cased pocket watch, retailed J.W. Benson, London, with a gilt-metal watch chain.

Half-hunters have a small aperture in the protective hinged lid through which the time can be told. Full hunters, often just called Hunters, have a solid lid which needs to be flipped open for the time to be read.

£450-500　　　　　　　**BELL**

A 9ct-gold open-faced pocket watch, the dial signed Cyma.

1.75in (4.5cm)

£180-220　　　　　　　**LAW**

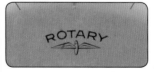

An Art Deco-style 9ct-gold Rotary mechanical pocket watch, the case with engraved inscription, hallmarked London 1962, case no.51424, suspended on a gold chain, with case.

Although seen by many as a 'modern' high street brand, Rotary was founded in 1895 by Moise Dreyfuss in the Swiss town of La Chaux de Fonds. The family still own the company, making it the oldest family run and owned Swiss watchmaker. Their now famous 'winged wheel' logo was introduced in 1925.

c1960

£150-200　　　　　　　**SWO**

A Reuge musical pocket watch, the gold-plated case engraved with a cartouche.

Reuge are most widely known for their musical mechanisms such as cylinder music boxes, some of which were placed inside jewellery boxes or the bases of novelty 'singing' bird cages. The company was founded in Sainte-Croix, Switzerland in 1865 by Charles Reuge and its first products were musical pocket watches.

£500-600   FLD

A Georgian gold fob watch, the movement signed 'Viger, Paris' and no.786.

1.25in (2.8cm) diam

£150-200   LAW

A Georgian silver cased pocket watch, the dial painted with a scene of figures and buildings by a lake, hallmarked for London.

1784   *1.5in (4cm) diam*

£180-220   LAW

An Omega silver open-face chronograph watch, keyless lever, bi-metallic compensation balance, blued steel overcoil balance spring, inside lid signed.

c1910   *2.25in (5.5cm) diam*

£350-450   BLO

A silver full hunting cased pocket watch, the movement signed 'J. R. Arnold Charles Frodsham', no.19173, hallmarked for London.

1855   *2in (5cm) diam*

£220-280   LAW

A Victorian lady's fob watch, dial within a surround of small pearls, with red guilloche enamel and diamond set flowerhead decoration to the back case, suspended from an anchor and diamond crescent surmount, in gold, with box.

2.5in (6.5cm)

£900-1,200   LAW

A lady's diamond-set and enamel fob watch, lever movement, inside back cover stamped '14k' and no.15492.

c1900   *1.25in (3cm) wide*

£650-750   LAW

WINE & DRINKING

QUICK REFERENCE - FOLKE ARSTRÖM

- Folke Arström (1907-97) began his career as an artist and moved into Industrial Design in the 1930s. He was artistic director for AB Gense for 20 years after designing for Guldsmeds Aktiebolaget from 1936-40.
- As well as being a pioneering Scandinavian industrial designer, he had a keen sense of what would be commercially successful, and designed many other items including the award-winning 'Focus' cutlery.
- This cocktail shaker was sold with small 'matching' goblets with conical metal bowls and black plastic stems.
- Along with corkscrews, cocktail shakers are amongst the most valuable of drinking collectables, particularly if they date from the 'golden age' of the Art Deco period and have strong period styling or novely forms.

A Swedish silver-plated cocktail shaker, by Guldsmeds Aktiebolaget, designed by Folke Arström in 1935, with black plastic top, the base with 'G.A.B.' maker's mark and 'NS ALP' marks.

21.5cm high

£400-600   **QU**

A 1930s electroplated nickel cocktail shaker, by Mappin & Webb, designed by Keith Murray, with stepped cover and strainer to interior, the foot and shoulder with turned-band decoration, the base with stamped marks.

Keith Murray (1892-1981) was an influential New Zealand-born architect and designer. Although he worked during the Art Deco period and his designs echo that style, much of his work can also be termed Modernist. He produced designs in glass for Stevens & Williams, but is best-known today for his clean-lined designs for Wedgwood executed from 1932. His work is being re-appraised by collectors and prices may yet rise further as more is understood about it.

5in (13cm) high

£300-400   **WW**

An Art Deco 'The Master Incolor' cocktail shaker, with a stepped-plastic body and a dial on the plated cover turning to reveal seven cocktail recipes individually.

Typical of the colours of the 'Age of Jazz', this cocktail shaker was available in other colours including cream and red. This green is scarce and desirable. Always examine the body closely as splits appear as dark fine lines and reduce the value dramatically.

11.2in (28.5cm) high

£800-1,200   **SWO**

A 1930s-50s chrome and frosted-glass cocktail shaker, the body printed with two rows of recipes, with plated top.

Although some were produced in the 1930s, many of these glass-bodied shakers printed with recipes were made in the 1950s and 60s. After the war, quality varies widely. Cheaply chrome-plated, light-weight examples are usually worth under £100, often even under £50.

11in (28cm) high

£140-180   **SWO**

A silver cocktail shaker, by The Goldsmiths & Silversmiths Co. Ltd, of typical plain three-part form, with retailer's marks and London hallmarks.

1947   *8in (20cm) high*

£650-850   **BLO**

A late Victorian silver-mounted cut-glass claret jug, by Atkin Brothers, the collar engraved with two vacant cartouches, flowers and foliage, the body with three registers of differing cutting, clear marks and bright engraving, with Sheffield hallmarks.

1899   *9.5in (24cm) high*

£400-600   **BLO**

A set of three glass decanters, in a tan leather travelling case by Homa.

8.7in (22cm) wide

£50-70   **WHP**

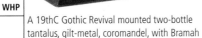

A 19thC Gothic Revival mounted two-bottle tantalus, gilt-metal, coromandel, with Bramah lock.

11in (28cm) wide

£80-100   **BELL**

A Victorian silver spirit flask, with engraved decoration, with screw-off top, Birmingham.

1852   *4.8oz*

£300-350   **BELL**

A Victorian silver spirit flask, by Alfred Taylor, Birmingham, with screw-off top, with a monogram.

1868   *4.25in (10.7cm) high 2.7oz*

£220-280   **WW**

A Victorian silver-mounted glass spirit flask, by J. Vickery, London, the pull-off drinking cup with a monogram, with screw-off top.

1868   *5.5in (13.5cm) long 2oz*

£100-140   **WW**

A silver and crocodile skin spirit flask, with a silver screw cap and detachable cup, marked 'M & W' for Mappin & Webb, Sheffield.

5in (13cm) high

£150-200   **LAW**

A late 18thC English glass 'sealed' wine bottle, the seal moulded 'I WATSON Esq BILTON PARK'.

c1760   *9.5in (24cm) high*

£250-350   **BELL**

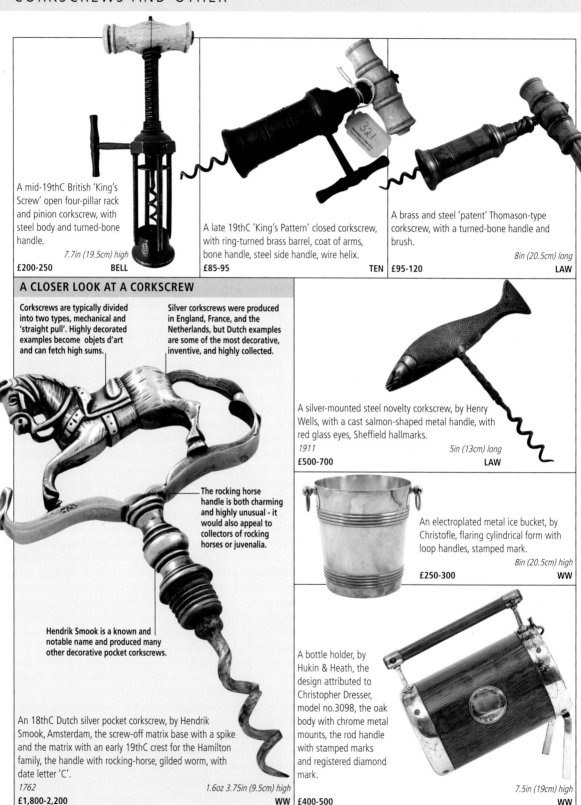

A mid-19thC British 'King's Screw' open four-pillar rack and pinion corkscrew, with steel body and turned-bone handle.

7.7in (19.5cm) high

£200-250   **BELL**

A late 19thC 'King's Pattern' closed corkscrew, with ring-turned brass barrel, coat of arms, bone handle, steel side handle, wire helix.

£85-95   **TEN**

A brass and steel 'patent' Thomason-type corkscrew, with a turned-bone handle and brush.

8in (20.5cm) long

£95-120   **LAW**

A CLOSER LOOK AT A CORKSCREW

Corkscrews are typically divided into two types, mechanical and 'straight pull'. Highly decorated examples become objets d'art and can fetch high sums.

Silver corkscrews were produced in England, France, and the Netherlands, but Dutch examples are some of the most decorative, inventive, and highly collected.

The rocking horse handle is both charming and highly unusual - it would also appeal to collectors of rocking horses or juvenalia.

Hendrik Smook is a known and notable name and produced many other decorative pocket corkscrews.

An 18thC Dutch silver pocket corkscrew, by Hendrik Smook, Amsterdam, the screw-off matrix base with a spike and the matrix with an early 19thC crest for the Hamilton family, the handle with rocking-horse, gilded worm, with date letter 'C'.

1762   *1.6oz 3.75in (9.5cm) high*

£1,800-2,200   **WW**

A silver-mounted steel novelty corkscrew, by Henry Wells, with a cast salmon-shaped metal handle, with red glass eyes, Sheffield hallmarks.

1911   *5in (13cm) long*

£500-700   **LAW**

An electroplated metal ice bucket, by Christofle, flaring cylindrical form with loop handles, stamped mark.

8in (20.5cm) high

£250-300   **WW**

A bottle holder, by Hukin & Heath, the design attributed to Christopher Dresser, model no.3098, the oak body with chrome metal mounts, the rod handle with stamped marks and registered diamond mark.

7.5in (19cm) high

£400-500   **WW**

Every item illustrated has a letter code that identifies the dealer, auction house or private collector that owns or sold it.

AH
HARTLEY'S
www.andrewhartleyfinearts.co.uk

ARTM
ARTEMIS GALLERY
www.artemisgallerylive.com

AST
ASTON'S AUCTIONEERS & VALUERS
www.astonsauctioneers.co.uk

BELL
BELLMANS
www.bellmans.co.uk

BLEA
BLEASDALE'S
www.bleasdalesltd.co.uk

BLO
DREWEATTS & BLOOMSBURY
www.bloomsburyauctions.com

BON
BONHAMS
www.bonhams.com

C
COTTEES AUCTION HOUSE
www.cottees.co.uk

CAN
CANTERBURY AUCTION GALLERIES
www.thecanterburyauctiongalleries.com

CHEF
CHEFFINS
www.cheffins.co.uk

CHOR
CHORLEY'S
www.simonchorley.com

CHT
CHARTERHOUSE
www.charterhouse-auction.com

CM
CHARLES MILLER
www.charlesmillerltd.com

CRIS
CRISTOBAL
www.cristobal.co.uk

DA&H
DEE, ATKINSON & HARRISON
www.dahauctions.com

DN
DREWEATTS & BLOOMSBURY
www.dnfa.com

DRA
RAGO ARTS & AUCTION CENTER
www.ragoarts.com

DSC
BRITISH DOLL SHOWCASE
www.britishdollshowcase.co.uk

DUK
DUKE'S
www.dukes-auctions.com

DW
DOMINIC WINTER
www.dominicwinter.co.uk

EBA
EAST BRISTOL AUCTIONS
www.eastbristol.co.uk

ECGW
EWBANK'S
www.ewbankauctions.co.uk

FAN
FANTIQUES
London, UK

FIS
DR. FISCHER KUNSTAUKTIONEN
www.auctions-fischer.de

FLD
FIELDINGS
www.fieldingsauctioneers.co.uk

GAZE
T W GAZE
www.twgaze.com

GBA
GRAHAM BUDD AUCTIONS
www.grahambuddauctions.co.uk

GHOU
GARDINER HOULGATE
www.gardinerhoulgate.co.uk

GORL
GORRINGES
www.gorringes.co.uk

GYM
GOLDING YOUNG & CO
www.goldingyoung.com

H&C
HISTORICAL & COLLECTABLE
www.historicalandcollectable.com

HALL
HALLS
www.hallsgb.com/fine-art

HAN
HANSONS AUCTIONEERS
www.hansonsauctioneers.co.uk

HT
HARTLEY'S
www.andrewhartleyfinearts.co.uk

JDJ
JAMES D JULIA
www.jamesdjulia.com

L&T
LYON & TURNBULL
www.lyonandturnbull.com

LAW
LAWRENCES
www.lawrences.co.uk

LHA
LESLIE HINDMAN
www.lesliehindman.com

LOC
LOCKE & ENGLAND
www.leauction.co.uk

LOCK
LOCKDALES
www.lockdales.com

M&DM
M&D MOIR
www.manddmoir.co.uk

MHC
MARK HILL COLLECTION

MLL
MALLAMS
www.mallams.co.uk

MOR
MORPHETS
www.morphets.co.uk

PC
PRIVATE COLLECTION

PCOM
PHIL-COMICS AUCTIONS
www.phil-comics.com

POOK
POOK & POOK
www.pookandpook.com

PSA
POTTERIES AUCTIONS
www.potteriesauctions.com

QU QUITTENBAUM
KUNSTAUKTIONEN
www.quittenbaum.de

RHA
RITA HASDELL
rita.hasdell@btinternet.com

ROS
ROSEBERY'S
www.roseberys.co.uk

RSS
ROSSINI SA
www.rossini.fr

RW
RICHARD WINTERTON
AUCTIONEERS
www.richardwinterton.co.uk

SAS
SPECIAL AUCTION SERVICES
www.specialauctionservices.com

SK
SKINNER AUCTIONEERS
www.skinnerinc.com

SWA
SWANN AUCTION GALLERIES
www.swanngalleries.com

SWO
SWORDERS
www.sworder.co.uk

T&F
TAYLER & FLETCHER
www.taylerandfletcher.co.uk

TEN
TENNANTS
www.tennants.co.uk

TOV
TOOVEY'S
www.rupert-toovey.com

TRI
TRING MARKET AUCTIONS
tringmarketauctions.co.uk

VEC
VECTIS
vectis.co.uk

W&W
WALLIS & WALLIS
wallisandwallis.co.uk

WAD
WADDINGTON'S
waddingtons.ca

WHP
W & H PEACOCK
peacockauction.co.uk

WW
WOOLLEY & WALLIS
woolleyandwallis.co.uk

If you wish to have any item valued, it is advisable to contact the dealer or specialist in advance to check that they will carry out this service and whether there is a charge. While most dealers will be happy to help you with an enquiry, do remember that they are busy people with businesses to run. Telephone valuations are not possible. Please mention the Miller's Collectables Handbook & Price Guide by Judith Miller and Mark Hill when making an enquiry.

ADVERTISING
Junktion Antiques Ltd.
www.junktionantiques.co.uk

Dan Tinman
Focus on the Past
www.dantinman.com

ANIMATION ART
Art You GREW Up With
www.artyougrewupwith.com

ART DECO
Scarab Antiques
www.scarabantiques.com

The Design Gallery
www.designgallery.co.uk

AUTOGRAPHS
The Autograph Collectors Gallery
www.autograph-gallery.co.uk

AUTOMOBILIA
Automobilia Planet
www.automobiliaplanet.com

Finesse Fine Art
www.finesse-fine-art.com

Junktion Antiques Ltd.
www.junktionantiques.co.uk

The Lalique Mascot Collectors' Club
www.brmmbrmm.com

BANKNOTES, BONDS & SHARES
Colin Narbeth & Sons Ltd.,
www.colin-narbeth.com

Intercol London
www.intercol.co.uk

BOOKS
Dominic Winter
www.dominicwinter.co.uk

Dreweatts & Bloomsbury
www.bloomsburyauctions.com

Zardoz Books
www.zardozbooks.co.uk

BREWERIANA
Junktion Antiques Ltd.
www.junktionantiques.co.uk

CERAMICS
Beth Adams
Alfies Antique Market
www.alfiesantiques.com

AD Antiques
www.adantiques.com

Central Collectables
www.centralcollectables.com

China Search
www.chinasearch.co.uk

Cornishware.biz
Vintage-Kitsch
www.cornishware.biz

Gallery 1930
18 Church St, London NW8 8EP
Tel: 020 7723 1555

Tony Horsley
www.tonyhorsley.co.uk

KCS Ceramics
www.kcsceramics.co.uk

Andrew Muir
www.andrew-muir.com

Sue Norman
www.suenormanblueand
whitechina.co.uk

Retroselect
www.retroselect.com

Geoffrey Robinson
www.robinsonantiques.co.uk

Vintage Living & Lifestyle Ltd
www.vintagelifestyle.co.uk

CIGARETTE CARDS
Pat O'Connell
www.cardstocollect.com

COINS & BANK NOTES
British Notes
www.britishnotes.co.uk

Coincraft
www.coincraft.com

Intercol London
www.intercol.co.uk

Colin Narbeth & Sons Ltd
www.colin-narbeth.com

COMICS
The Book Palace
www.bookpalace.com

Comic Book Auctions
www.compalcomics.com

Phil's Comics
www.phil-comics.com

COMMEMORATIVE WARE
Commemorabilia
www.commemorabilia.co.uk

Historical & Collectable
www.historicalandcollectable.
com

Royal Commemorative China
royalcommemoratives@hotmail.
com

Susan & Peter Rees
www.commemorativeceramics.
co.uk

COSTUME & ACCESSORIES
Ashman's Antiques & Old Lace
www.ashmansvintage.com

Linda Bee
www.graysantiques.com

Beyond Retro
www.beyondretro.com

Decades
www.decadesemporium.co.uk

Rokit
www.rokit.co.uk

David Saxby
www.davidsaxby.co.uk

Steptoe's Dog Vintage Wares
www.steptoesantiques.store.
bugle.com

Kerry Taylor Auctions
www.kerrytaylorauctions.com

Vintage Modes
Grays Antiques Market
www.vintagemodes.co.uk

Vintage to Vogue
www.vintagetovoguebath.co.uk

COSTUME JEWELLERY
Cristobal
www.cristobal.co.uk

Eclectica
www.eclectica.biz

Scarab Antiques
www.scarabantiques.com

William Wain
www.williamwain.com

DOLLS
British Doll Showcase
www.britishdollshowcase.co.uk

Glenda O'Connor
www.glenda-antiquedolls.co.uk

Victoriana Dolls
www.heatherbond.co.uk

FIFTIES, SIXTIES & SEVENTIES
20th Century Marks
www.20thcenturymarks.co.uk

Discover Vintage
www.discovervintage.co.uk

Fragile Design
www.fragiledesign.com

The Modern Warehouse
www.themodernwarehouse.com

Modo Italia
www.modo-italia.com

Nanadobbie
www.nanadobbie.com

Planet Bazaar
www.planetbazaar.co.uk

FILM & TV
Prop Store
www.propstore.com

GLASS
**Antique Glass at
Frank Dux Antiques**
www.antique-glass.co.uk

Artius Glass
www.artiusglass.co.uk

Cloud Glass
www.cloudglass.com

Glass Etc
www.decanterman.com

Grimes House Gallery
www.cranberryglass.co.uk

**Jeanette Hayhurst
Fine Glass**
http://www.cotswolds-antiques-
art.com/antiques-dealers/d/
jeanette-hayhurst/154

Andrew Lineham Fine Glass
www.antiquecolouredglass.com

Francesca Martire
www.francescamartire.com

M&D Moir
www.manddmoir.co.uk

Newsum Antiques
www.newsumantiques.co.uk

KITCHENALIA
Appleby Antiques
www.applebyantiques.net

Below Stairs of Hungerford
www.belowstairs.co.uk

Jennifer's Cutlery
www.jenniferscutlery.co.uk

Jane Wicks Kitchenalia
www.antiques-atlas.com/
janewickskitchenalia

MILITARIA & MEDALS
Jim Bullock Militaria
www.jimbullockmilitaria.com

The Old Brigade
www.theoldbrigade.co.uk

Garth Vincent
www.garthvincent.com

West Street Antiques
www.antiquearmsand
armour.com

MODERN TECHNOLOGY
Junktion Antiques Ltd.
www.junktionantiques.co.uk

PAPERWEIGHTS
Alan and Helen Thornton
www.pwts.co.uk

Weights-n-things
www.weights-n-things.com

PENS & WRITING
Battersea Pen Home
www.penhome.co.uk

Hans's Vintage Pens
www.hanspens.com

The Pen & Pencil Gallery
www.penpencilgallery.com

PLASTICS & BAKELITE
Paola & Iaia
www.alfiesantiques.com

POSTCARDS
PC Postcards
www.pcpostcards.co.uk

POSTERS
At The Movies
www.atthemovies.co.uk

DODO
www.dodoposters.com

Limelight Movie Art
www.limelightmovieart.com

The Reelposter Gallery
www.reelposter.com

Rennies Seaside Modern
www.rennart.co.uk

Barclay Samson
www.barclaysamson.com

POWDER COMPACTS
Mary & Geoff Turvil
www.glitzguru.com

RADIOS & MECHANICAL MUSIC
On the Air Ltd.
www.vintageradio.co.uk

Junktion Antiques Ltd.
www.junktionantiques.co.uk

Stephen T P Kember
www.antique-musicboxes.co.uk

The Talking Machine
www.thetalkingmachine.co.uk

RAILWAYANA
GW Railwayana Auctions
www.gwra.co.uk

ROCK & POP
**Briggs Rock & Pop
Memorabilia**
www.usebriggs.com

Sweet Memories
Vinyl Records
www.vinylrecords.co.uk

Tracks
www.tracks.co.uk

SCIENTIFIC, TECHNICAL, OPTICAL & PRECISION INSTRUMENTS
Charles Miller
www.charlesmillerltd.com

Flea Glass Ltd
www.fleaglass.com

SMOKING
Richard Ball
www.lighter.co.uk

SPORTING MEMORABILIA
Graham Budd
www.grahambuddauctions.co.uk

Bob Gowland
www.foliozine.co.uk/bob_
gowland

Rhod McEwan Golf
www.rhodmcewangolf.com

Manfred Schotten
www.sportantiques.co.uk

Sporting Antiques
www.sportingantiques.co.uk

TELEPHONES
Candlestick & Bakelite
www.candlestickand
bakelite.co.uk

Telephone Lines
www.telephonelines.net

TOOLS
Tony Murland Antique Tools
www.antiquetools.co.uk

TOYS & GAMES
Collectors Old Toy Shop
(John & Simon Haley)
www.collectorsoldtoyshop.com

Garrick Coleman
www.antiquechess.co.uk

Dave's Classic Toys
www.ukmodelshops.co.uk/
shops/1724-DavesClassicToys

Mike Delaney
www.vintagehornby.net

Donay Games
www.donaygames.com

The House of Automata
www.automatomania.com

Intercol London
www.intercol.co.uk

The Magic Toybox
www.magictoybox.co.uk

Metropolis Toys
www.metropolistoys.co.uk

Special Auction Services
www.specialauctionservices.com

Sue Pearson Dolls & Teddy Bears
www.suepearson.co.uk

Teddy Bears of Witney
www.teddybears.co.uk

Toydreams
www.toydreams.co.uk

Vectis Auctioneers
www.vectis.co.uk

Wallis & Wallis
www.wallisandwallis.co.uk

Wheels of Steel (Trains)
www.graysantiques.com

WATCHES
70s Watches
www.70s-watches.com

Kleanthous Antiques
www.kleanthous.com

The Watch Gallery
www.thewatchgallery.co.uk

WEIRD & WONDERFUL
Doe & Hope
www.doeandh.ope.com

The following list of general antiques and collectables centres, markets and shops has been organised by region. Any owner who would like to be listed in our next edition, space permitting, or who wishes to update their contact information, should email info@millers.uk.com.

LONDON
Alfie's Antiques Market
www.alfiesantiques.com

Camden Passage Antiques Market
www.camdenpassage
islington.co.uk
(Monday, Wednesday, Friday, Saturday
and Sunday mornings)

Covent Garden Antiques Market
www.jubileemarket.co.uk/antiques
(Mondays from 5am–5pm)

Grays Antiques Market
www.graysantiques.com

Kensington Church Street Antiques Centre
58-60 Kensington Church Street, W8 4DB

Northcote Road Antiques Market
www.northcoteroadantiques.co.uk

Portobello Road Market
www.portobelloroad.co.uk
(Every Saturday from 6am)

Spitalfields Antiques Market
www.oldspitalfieldsmarket.com
(Thursdays 10am-4pm)

BEDFORDSHIRE
Ampthill Antiques Emporium
www.ampthillantiques
emporium.co.uk

BERKSHIRE
The Collectors Centre
www.collectorscentrereading.co.uk

Great Grooms at Hungerford
www.greatgrooms.co.uk

BUCKINGHAMSHIRE
Antiques at... Wendover
www.antiquesat
wendover.co.uk

CAMBRIDGESHIRE
Cambridge Antiques Centre
www.cambsantiques.com

Waterside Antiques Centre
www.watersideantiques.co.uk

DERBYSHIRE
Alfreton Antique Centre
www.alfretonantiquescentre.com

Bakewell Antiques & Works of Art
http://bakewellonline.
co.uk/place/93/
BakewellAntiquesWorksofArt.html

Heanor Antiques Centre
www.alscar.co.uk/heanor

Matlock Antiques & Collectables
www.matlockantiques.co.uk

DEVON
The Quay Antiques Centre
www.quayantiques.com

ESSEX
Debden Barns
www.debdenbarns.co.uk

GLOUCESTERSHIRE
Durham House Antiques
www.durhamhousegb.com

Long Street Antiques
wwww.longstreetantiques.com

Lorfords
www.lorfordsantiques.com

Top Banana Antiques Mall
www.topbananaantiques.com

HEREFORDSHIRE
The Secondhand Warehouse & Antique Centre
www.secondhandwarehouse
leominster.co.uk

HERTFORDSHIRE
By George Antique Centre
Tel: 01279 600 985

KENT
Bagham Barn Antiques
www.baghambarnantiques.com

Burgate Antiques Centre
vkreeves@burgate1.fsnet.co.uk

Fontaine
www.fontainedecorative.com

Junk Deluxe
www.junkdeluxe.co.uk

Otford Antiques and Collectors Centre
www.otfordshopping.co.uk/shops/
otford-antiques-and-collectors-
centre

LANCASHIRE
GB Antiques Centre
www.gbantiquescentre.com

Heskin Hall Antiques
www.heskinhallantiques.co.uk

Karlen Antiques Centre
www.antiquesshipper.co.uk

LINCOLNSHIRE
Hemswell Antique Centres
www.hemswell-antiques.com

St Martins Antiques Centre
www.st-martins-antiques.co.uk

NORTHAMPTONSHIRE
Brackley Antique Cellar
www.facebook.com/
brackleyantiquecellar

NOTTINGHAMSHIRE
Newark Antiques Centre
www.newarkantiquescentre.com

OXFORDSHIRE
Deddington Antiques Centre
www.deddingtonantique
centre.co.uk

The Lamb Arcade Antiques & Lifestyle Centre
www.thelambarcade.co.uk

The Quiet Woman Antiques Centre
www.quietwomanantiques.co.uk

The Swan at Tetsworth Antiques Centre
www.theswan.co.uk

SOMERSET
Old Bank Antiques Centre
www.oldbankantiques
centre.com

STAFFORDSHIRE
Compton Mill Antique Emporium
http://www.leekonline.co.uk/
shopping/antiques/compton/
antique-emporium.htm

Potteries Antique Centre
www.potteriesantiquecentre.com

SURREY
Christique
www.christique.com

Kingston Antiques Centre
www.kingstonantiques
centre.co.uk

The Packhouse
www.packhouse.com

Talbot House Antique Centre
www.talbothouseantiques.com

EAST SUSSEX
The Brighton Lanes Antique Centre
www.brightonlanes
antiques.co.uk

Brighton Flea Market
www.flea-markets.co.uk

Church Hill Antiques Centre
churchhilllewes@aol.com

In My Room
www.inmyroom.co.uk

Lewes Flea Market
www.flea-markets.co.uk

Snooper's Paradise
www.northlaine.co.uk/visit/profile/
snoopers-paradise

WEST SUSSEX
Arundel Bridge Antiques
www.arundelantiques.co.uk

WARWICKSHIRE
Stratford-upon-Avon Antique Centre
www.stratfordshops.webs.com/
antiquescentre.htm

WEST MIDLANDS
Yoxall Antiques and Fine Arts
www.yoxallantiques.co.uk

CENTRES, MARKETS & SHOPS

WORCESTERSHIRE
Foley House Antiques
www.facebook.com/Foley-house-antiques-1552686074947329/

YORKSHIRE
The Antiques Centre York
www.theantiquescentreyork.co.uk

The Ginnel Antiques Centre
http://www.harrogate.co.uk/the-ginnel-antique-centre/

SCOTLAND
Georgian Antiques
www.georgianantiques.net

Now and Then
www.oldtoysandantiques.co.uk

Rait Village Antiques Centre
www.rait-antiques.webnode.com

**Scottish Antiques
& Arts Centre**
www.scottish-antiques.com

WALES
Afonwen Antiques
www.afonwen.co.uk/antiques

IRELAND
Powerscourt Centre
www.powerscourtcentre.ie

MAJOR FAIR & SHOW ORGANISERS

Antiques for Everyone
Birmingham
www.antiquesforeveryone.co.uk

Cooper Antiques Fairs
Tatton Park (Cheshire), Antiques (Yorkshire), The Cotswolds (Gloucestershire) and Buxton (Derbyshire).
www.cooperevents.com

The Decorative Antiques & Textiles Fair
Battersea, London
www.decorativefair.com

IACF (International Antique & Collectors Fair)
Newark (Nottinghamshire), Ardingly (Sussex), North Weald (Essex), Newbury (Berkshire), Redbourn (Hertfordshire), Swinderby (Nr. Lincoln) and Shepton Mallet (Somerset)
www.iacf.co.uk

LAPADA
London
www.lapada.org

Olympia International Art & Antiques Fair
London
www.olympia-antiques.co.uk

Penman Fairs
Petersfield (Hampshire), Chester (Cheshire), Chelsea (London), Firle Place (East Sussex), Burford (Oxfordshire).
www.penman-fairs.co.uk

Arthur Swallow Fairs
Donington Park (Derbyshire), Lincoln (Lincolnshire).
www.arthurswallowfairs.co.uk

The following list of auctioneers who conduct regular sales by auction is organised by region. Any auctioneer who would like to be listed in the our next edition, space permitting, or to update their contact information, should email info@millers.uk.com.

LONDON
Bonhams
www.bonhams.com

Graham Budd Auctions
www.grahambuddauctions.co.uk

Christie's
www.christies.com

Chiswick Auctions
www.chiswickauctions.co.uk

Criterion Auctioneers
www.criterionauctioneers.co.uk

Dreweatts & Bloomsbury
www.bloomsburyauctions.com

Charles Miller
www.charlesmillerltd.com

Lots Road Auctions
www.lotsroad.com

Rosebery's
www.roseberys.co.uk

Sotheby's
www.sothebys.com

Kerry Taylor Auctions
www.kerrytaylorauctions.com

BEDFORDSHIRE
W & H Peacock
www.peacockauction.co.uk

BERKSHIRE
Dreweatts & Bloomsbury
www.dreweatts.com

Historical & Collectable
www.historicalandcollectable.com

Special Auction Services
www.specialauctionservices.com

BUCKINGHAMSHIRE
Amersham Auction Rooms
www.amershamauctionrooms.co.uk

CAMBRIDGESHIRE
Cheffins
www.cheffins.co.uk

CHANNEL ISLANDS
Martel Maides Auctions
www.martelmaidesauctions.co.uk

CHESHIRE
Wright Marshall
www.wrightmarshall.co.uk

CLEVELAND
Vectis Auctioneers
(Toys & Dolls)
www.vectis.co.uk

CORNWALL
W H Lane & Son
www.whlane.co.uk

David Lay FRICS
www.davidlay.co.uk

CUMBRIA
Mitchells Antiques & Fine Art Auctioneers & Valuers
www.mitchellsantiques.co.uk

Penrith Farmers' & Kidds
www.pfkauctions.co.uk

DERBYSHIRE
Bamfords Ltd.
www.bamfords-auctions.co.uk

Hansons Auctioneers
www.hansonsauctioneers.co.uk

DEVON
Bearnes Hampton & Littlewood
www.bhandl.co.uk

Chilcotts
www.chilcottsauctioneers.co.uk

S J Hales
www.sjhales.com

DORSET
Charterhouse
www.charterhouse-auction.com

Duke's
www.dukes-auctions.com

Onslows
www.onslows.co.uk

Semley Auctioneers
www.semleyauctioneers.com

ESSEX
Reeman Dansie
www.reemandansie.com

Sworders Fine Art Auctioneers
www.sworder.co.uk

GLOUCESTERSHIRE
Chorley's
www.simonchorley.com

The Cotswold Auction Company
www.cotswoldauction.co.uk

Mallams Fine Art Auctioneers & Valuers
www.mallams.co.uk

Moore, Allen & Innocent
www.mooreallen.co.uk

Dominic Winter
www.dominicwinter.co.uk

HAMPSHIRE
Andrew Smith & Son
www.andrewsmithandson.com

Hannam's
www.hannamsauctioneers.com

Jacobs & Hunt
www.jacobsandhunt.com

HEREFORDSHIRE
Brightwells
www.brightwells.com

HERTFORDSHIRE
Tring Market Auctions
www.tringmarketauctions.co.uk

ISLE OF WIGHT
Island Auction Rooms
www.islandauctionrooms.co.uk

KENT
The Canterbury Auction Galleries
www.thecanterburyauctiongalleries.com

Gorringes
www.gorringes.co.uk

LANCASHIRE
Capes Dunn
www.capesdunn.com

LEICESTERSHIRE
Gilding's
www.gildings.co.uk

LINCOLNSHIRE
Batemans
www.batemans.com

Golding Young & Mawer
www.goldingyoung.com

MERSEYSIDE
Cato, Crane & Company
www.cato-crane.co.uk

NORFOLK
T W Gaze
www.twgaze.com

Keys Fine Art Auctioneers
www.keysauctions.co.uk

Knights Sporting Auctions
www.knights.co.uk

NOTTINGHAMSHIRE
Mellors & Kirk
www.mellorsandkirk.com

OXFORDSHIRE
Bonhams
www.bonhams.com

Holloway's Auctioneers
www.hollowaysauctioneers.co.uk

Mallams
www.mallams.co.uk

SHROPSHIRE
Halls Fine Art
www.hallsgb.com/fine-art

Mullock's
www.mullocksauctions.co.uk

SOMERSET
Clevedon Salerooms
www.clevedon-salerooms.com

Lawrences Auctioneers
www.lawrences.co.uk

STAFFORDSHIRE
Potteries Specialist Auctions
www.potteriesauctions.com

Louis Taylor
www.louis-taylor.co.uk

Richard Winterton Auctioneers
www.richardwinterton.co.uk

SUFFOLK
Durrants
www.durrants.com

AUCTIONEERS

Lacy Scott & Knight
www.lskauctioncentre.co.uk

Lockdales
www.lockdales.com

Tony Murland Antique Tools
www.antiquetools.co.uk

Neals
www.nsf.co.uk

SURREY
Ewbank's
www.ewbankauctions.co.uk

Fryer & Brown Auctioneers
www.fryerandbrown.com

Wellers
www.wellersauctions.com

EAST SUSSEX
Burstow & Hewett
www.burstowandhewett.co.uk

Eastbourne Auctions
www.eastbourneauction.com

Gorringes
www.gorringes.co.uk

Inmans
www.inmansauctions.co.uk

Wallis & Wallis
www.wallisandwallis.co.uk

WEST SUSSEX
Bellmans
www.bellmans.co.uk

Denhams
www.denhams.com

Summers Place Auctions
www.summersplaceauctions.com

Toovey's
www. tooveys.com

TYNE & WEAR
Anderson & Garland
www.andersonandgarland.com

Corbitts (Stamps)
www.corbitts.com

WARWICKSHIRE
Locke & England
www.leauction.co.uk

WEST MIDLANDS
Fellows Auctioneers
www.fellows.co.uk

Fieldings
www.fieldingsauctioneers.co.uk

WILTSHIRE
Robert Finan
www.robertfinan.co.uk

Gardiner Houlgate
www.gardinerhoulgate.co.uk

Henry Aldridge & Son
www.henry-aldridge.co.uk

Woolley & Wallis
www.woolleyandwallis.co.uk

WORCESTERSHIRE
GW Railwayana Auctions
www.gwra.co.uk

Phillip Serrell
www.serrell.com

EAST YORKSHIRE
Dee Atkinson & Harrison
www.dahauctions.com/fine-art-saleroom

NORTH YORKSHIRE
David Duggleby
www.davidduggleby.com

Tennants
www.tennants.co.uk

SOUTH YORKSHIRE
BBR Auctions
www.onlinebbr.com

Sheffield Auction Gallery
www.sheffieldauctiongallery.com

Sheffield Railwayana
Auctions
www.sheffieldrailwayana.co.uk

WEST YORKSHIRE
Hartleys
www.andrewhartleyfinearts.co.uk

Thomson Roddick & Medcalf
www.thomsonroddick.com

SCOTLAND
Bonhams
www.bonhams.com

Lyon & Turnbull
www.lyonandturnbull.com

McTear's
www.mctears.co.uk

WALES
Peter Francis
www.peterfrancis.co.uk

Welsh Country Auctions
www.welshcountryauctions.co.uk

IRELAND
Adam's
www.adams.ie

Mealy's
www.mealys.com

Ross's Auctioneers & Valuers
www.rosss.com

Whyte's
www.whytes.ie

The following list is organised by the type of collectable. If you would like your club, society or organisation to appear in our next edition, or would like to update your details, please contact us at info@millers.uk.com.

The National Association of Decorative & Fine Arts Societies (NADFAS)
www.nadfas.org.uk
An arts charity with a network of local societies and national events.

ADVERTISING
Antique Advertising Signs
The Street Jewellery Society
www.streetjewellery.org

AUTOGRAPHS
Autographica
www.autographica.co.uk

AUTOMOBILIA
Brmmm Brmm Classic Network
www.brmmbrmm.com

BAXTER PRINTS
The New Baxter Society
c/o Reading Museum
& Art Gallery
www.newbaxtersociety.org

BOOKS
The Enid Blyton Society
www.enidblytonsociety.co.uk

The Followers of Rupert
www.rupertbear.co.uk

BOTTLES
British Bottle Review
www.onlinebbr.com

BREWERIANA
The Association for British Brewery Collectables
www.breweriana.org.uk

CERAMICS
Carlton Ware World
www.carltonwareworld.com

Clarice Cliff Collectors Club
www.claricecliff.com

Collecting Doulton & Beswick
www.collectingdoulton.com

Fieldings Crown Devon Collectors Club
www.fieldingscrowndevonclub.com

Friends of Blue
www.fob.org.uk

Goss Collectors' Club
www.gosscollectorsclub.org

Hornsea Pottery Collectors' & Research Society
www.hornseapottery.co.uk

M I Hummel Club
www.hummelgifts.com

Mabel Lucie Attwell Club
www.mabellucieattwellclub.com

Moorcroft Collectors' Club
www.moorcroft.com/Site/Collectors

Myott Collectors Club
www.myottcollectorsclub.com

Poole Pottery Collectors' Club
www.poolepotterycollectorsclub.net

Potteries of Rye Collectors' Society
www.potteries-of-rye-society.co.uk

The Shelley Group
www.shelley.co.uk

SylvaC Collectors Circle
www.sylvacclub.com

Official International Wade Collectors Club
www.wadecollectorsclub.co.uk

CIGARETTE CARDS
Cartophilic Society of Great Britain
www.card-world.co.uk

COINS & BANK NOTES
British Numismatic Society
www.britnumsoc.org

Royal Numismatic Society
www.numismatics.org.uk

International Bank Note Society
www.theibns.org

The Scripophily Society
www.scripophily.org

COMMEMORATIVE WARE
Commemorative Collectors Society & Commemoratives Museum
www.commemoratives
collecting.co.uk

COMICS
The Beano & Dandy Collectors' Club
www.phil-comics.com/collectors_club.php

COSTUME & ACCESSORIES
The British Compact Collectors' Society
www.compactcollectors.co.uk

The Costume Society
www.costumesociety.org.uk

DISNEYANA
Walt Disney Collectors' Society
www.wdccduckman.com

DOLLS
The Doll Club of Great Britain
www.dollclubgb.com

The Fashion Doll Collectors Club of Great Britain
www.fashiondollcollectorsclubgb.co.uk

EPHEMERA
The Ephemera Society
www.ephemera-society.org.uk

FILM & TV
The James Bond International Fan Club
www.007.info

Fanderson – The Official Gerry Anderson Appreciation Society
www.fanderson.org.uk

GLASS
The Carnival Glass Society (No valuations)
www.thecgs.co.uk

The Glass Association
www.glassassociation.org.uk

Isle of Wight Studio Glass Collectors' Club
www.isleofwightstudioglass.co.uk/collectors-club

Jonathan Harris Studio Glass Collectors Club
www.jhstudioglass.com/Collectors-Club

KITCHENALIA
National Horse Brass Society
www.nationalhorsebrasssociety.org.uk

The Old Hall Club,
www.oldhallclub.co.uk

MECHANICAL MUSIC
Musical Box Society of Great Britain
www.mbsgb.org.uk

The City of London Phonograph & Gramophone Society
www.clpgs.org.uk

METALWARE
Antique Metalware Society
www.antiquemetalwaresociety.org.uk

MILITARIA
Military Historical Society
www.themilitaryhistoricalsociety.co.uk

The Orders & Medals Research Society
www.omrs.org

PAPERWEIGHTS
Paperweight Collectors Circle
www.paperweightcollectorscircle.org.uk

Caithness Glass Paperweight Collectors Members Society
www.caithnessglass.co.uk/collectors

PENS & WRITING
The Writing Equipment Society
www.wesonline.org.uk

PERFUME BOTTLES
International Perfume Bottle Association
www.ipba-uk.co.uk

CLUBS & SOCIETIES

PLASTICS
The Plastics Historical Society
www.plastiquarian.com

POSTCARDS
Postcard Pages
www.postcard.co.uk

POTLIDS
The Pot Lid Circle
www.thepotlidcircle.co.uk

QUILTS
The Quilters' Guild
of the British Isles
www.quiltersguild.org.uk

RADIOS
The British Vintage Wireless Society
www.bvws.org.uk

RAILWAYANA
Railwayana Collectors Journal
www.prorail.co.uk

SCIENTIFIC & OPTICAL INSTRUMENTS
Scientific Instrument Society
www.scientificinstrumentsociety.org

SEWING
International Sewing Machine Collectors' Society
www.ismacs.net

The Thimble Society
www.thimblesociety.com

SMOKING
The Lighter Club
of Great Britain
www.lighterclub.co.uk

SPORTING
International Football Hall of Fame
www.ifhof.com
Programme Monthly & Football Collectable
www.pmfc.co.uk

British Golf Collectors Society
www.golfcollectors.co.uk

Rugby Memorabilia Society
www.rugby-memorabilia.co.uk

STAMPS
Postal History Society
www.postalhistory.org.uk

Royal Mail Stamps & Collecting
www.rmspecialstamps.com

STANHOPES
The Stanhope Collectors' Club
www.stanhopes.info

STAINLESS STEEL
The Old Hall Club
www.oldhallclub.co.uk

TEDDY BEARS & SOFT TOYS
Dean's Collectors Club
www.deansbears.com

Merrythought International Collectors Club
www.merrythought.co.uk

Steiff Club
www.steiff.com

TOYS
The British Model Soldier Society
www.bmssonline.com

Corgi Collector Club
www.corgi.co.uk/club

Hornby Collectors Club
www.hornby.com/uk-en/clubs

The Matchbox Club
www.matchboxclub.com

Collectables are particularly suited to online trading. When compared with many antiques, most collectables are easily defined, described and photographed, whilst shipping is relatively easy, due to average sizes and weights. Collectables are also generally more affordable and accessible, and the internet has provided a cost-effective way of buying and selling without the overheads of shops and auction rooms. A huge number of collectables are offered for sale and traded daily over the internet, with websites varying from global online marketplaces, such as eBay, to specialist dealers' sites.

• There are a number of things to be aware of when searching for collectables online. Some items being sold may not be described accurately, meaning that general category searches, and even purposefully misspelling a name, can yield results. If something looks or sounds too good to be true, it probably is. Using this book should give you a head start in getting to know your market, and also enable you to tell the difference between a real bargain and something that sounds like one. Good colour photography is absolutely vital. Try to find online listings that include as many images as possible, including detail shots, and check them carefully. Be aware that colours can appear differently between websites, and even between computer screens.

• Always ask the vendor questions about the object, particularly regarding condition. If no image is supplied, or you want to see another aspect of the object, ask for more information. A good seller should be happy to cooperate if approached politely and sensibly.

• As well as the 'e-hammer' price, you will very likely have to pay additional transactional fees such as packing, shipping and possibly regional or national taxes. Ask the seller for an estimate of these additional costs before leaving a bid, as this will give you a better idea of the overall amount you will end up paying.

• In addition to large online auction sites such as eBay, there are a host of other online resources for buying and selling. The internet can also be an invaluable research tool for collectors, with many sites devoted to providing detailed information on a number of different collectables.

INTERNET RESOURCES

Miller's Antiques & Collectables
www.millersonline.com
Miller's website is the ultimate one-stop destination for collectors, dealers or anyone interested in antiques and collectables. Join the Miller's Club to search through a catalogue containing many thousands of authenticated antiques and collectables, each illustrated in full colour and accompanied by a full descriptive caption and price range. Browse through practical articles written by Judith Miller, Mark Hill and a team of experts to learn tips and tricks of the trade, as well as learning more about important companies, designs and the designers behind them. Read Judith's blog and order the full range of Miller's books. You can also search the best fully illustrated A-Z of specialist terms on the internet; a dealer, appraiser and auctioneer database; a guide to silver hallmarks; and learn about care and repair of your antiques and collectables. The site is continually updated, so check back regularly to see what's new.

1stdibs
www.1stdibs.com
A website which allows international dealers and galleries to sell high-end antiques, art, jewellery, watches and fashion online.

The Antiques Trade Gazette
www.antiquestradegazette.com
The online edition of the UK trade newspaper, including British auction and fair listings, news and events.

The Association of Art & Antiques Dealers (LAPADA)
http://lapada.org
The largest association of professional art and antiques dealers in the UK with over 550 members (some are from overseas). Members must have a high level of experience, quality of stock and knowledge of their subject. They can list items for sale on the association's website.

Auction.fr
www.auction.fr
An online database of auctions at French auction houses. A subscription allows users to search past catalogues and prices realised.

Barnebys
www.barnebys.co.uk
A search engine for arts, antiques and rarities listed by auction houses and art dealers from around the world. As well as allowing users to search current auctions for items for sale, they can look at millions of realized prices from completed auctions.

eBay
www.ebay.com
Undoubtedly the largest and most diverse of the online auction sites, allowing users to buy and sell in an online marketplace with over 52 million registered users from across the world.

La Gazette du Drouot
www.drouot.com
The online home of the magazine listing all auctions to be held in France at the Hotel de Drouot in Paris. An online subscription enables you to download the magazine online.

Invaluable
www.invaluable.co.uk
Provides a database of worldwide auction listings from over 4,000 art, antiques and collectables auction houses. User can search details of both upcoming and past sales and also find information on a number of collectors' fields. Basic information is available free, access to more in depth information requires a subscription. Online bidding live into auctions as they happen is also offered.

Live Auctioneers
www.liveauctioneers.com
An online service which allows users to search catalogues from selected auction houses in Europe, the USA and the United Kingdom. Visitors to the site can bid live via the Internet into salerooms as auctions happen. Registered users can also search through an archive of past catalogues and receive a free email newsletter.

Maine Antique Digest
www.maineantiquedigeSt.com
Online version of America's trade newspaper including news, articles, fair and auction listings and more.

Rubylane
www.rubylane.com
An international e-commerce website allowing dealers to sell antiques, art, vintage collectables and jewellery.

Rubylux
www.rubylux.com
An international luxury e-commerce website selling antique and modern design and through specialist catalogues, online auctions and themed sales.

The Saleroom.com
www.the-saleroom.com
An online service that allows users to search catalogues from selected auction houses in Europe, the USA and the United Kingdom. Visitors to the site can bid live via the internet into salerooms as auctions happen. Registered users can also search through an archive of past catalogues and receive a free email newsletter.

WorthPoint
www.worthpoint.com
An online database which allows users to identify, research and value antiques, art and vintage collectables.

INDEX